CHRISTIANITY AND MYTHOLOGY

CHRISTIANITY AND MYTHOLOGY

JOHN M. ROBERTSON

GYAN

Published by

GYAN

Gyan Publishing House
5, Ansari Road
Daryaganj, New Delhi-110002
Phone: 011-47034999, 9811692060
E-mail: books@gyanbooks.com

Distribution Network
gyanbooks.com
India, USA, Canada, UK, Australia, France

ISBN: 978-81-212-9308-2 (PB)
First Published, 1900

2nd Impression 2023

Printed at: Gyan Press, Delhi.

CHRISTIANITY AND MYTHOLOGY

AUTHOR: JOHN M. ROBERTSON

CHRISTIANITY AND MYTHOLOGY

BY

JOHN M. ROBERTSON

ISSUED FOR

THE RATIONALIST PRESS ASSOCIATION, LIMITED

LONDON

WATTS & CO., 17 JOHNSON'S COURT, FLEET STREET

1900

CORRIGENDA.

P. 37, Note 2. *Read*, See hereinafter, Part III., p. 417.
P. 110, Note 4. *For* miraculous *read* miraculously.
P. 124, Note 1. *For* Mithraism, § 6, *read* Part III., p. 417.
P. 187, Note 8. For *Hierosolyma* read *Hierozoicon*.
P. 190, Note 6. *Read*, See hereinafter, Part III., pp. 329–330.
P. 208, Note 1. *After* See, *read* hereinafter, Part III., pp. 330–1.
P. 208, Note 2. *Read*, See hereinafter, Part III., passim.
P. 215, Note 1. *Read*, See hereinafter, Part III., p. 417.

CONTENTS.

PART I.

THE PROGRESS OF MYTHOLOGY.

PAGE

CHAP. I.—THE SCIENCE AND ITS HISTORY.

§ 1. The Problem 1
§ 2. The Scientific Beginnings 3
§ 3. The Relation to Christianity 12

CHAP. II.—MODERN SYSTEMS.

§ 1. The Etymological and Solar Schools . . . 19
§ 2. The Movement of Anthropology: Tylor . . . 25
§ 3. *A priori* Evolutionism: Spencer 28
§ 4. The Biological Correction 30
§ 5. Fresh Constructions, Reversions, Omissions, Evasions . 34
§ 6. Mr. Lang and Anthropology 40

CHAP. III.—THE SEPARATIST FALLACY.

§ 1. The Theistic Presupposition 52
§ 2. The Metaphysic of Religion 65
§ 3. Mr. Grant Allen's Theorem 71

CHAP. IV.—THE STAND FOR THE BIBLE.

§ 1. Hebrew Mythology 79
§ 2. Christianity and "Degeneration" 95
§ 3. The Psychological Resistance to Evidence . . . 101
§ 4. The Problem of Non-Miraculous Myth . . . 111
§ 5. The Problem of Priority 117

PART II.

CHRIST AND KRISHNA.

I. THE NATURE OF THE PROBLEM.

Standpoint of the Investigation. Current Presuppositions. Vice of Christian Method. Rationalism committed to no Historical Presupposition 129

II. The Question of Priority. PAGE

Old Date of Orthodox Hypothesis. Theories of Giorgi. Hyde. Missionaries. Jones. Maurice. Jones's Presuppositions. Polier. Paulinus. Kleuker. Moor. Creuzer. Reactionary Spirit of English Religious Archæology. Suppression of Evidence . 131

III. Age of Indian Documents.

Ritter's Criticism. Extravagance of Indian Chronology. Oldest Inscriptions. Origin of Writing. Müller and Tiele. Oral Preservation of Lore. Brahman Method of Study. The Druids 135

IV. The Special Documents.

Age of Vedas. Developments of Indian Religion. Vogue of Krishnaism. Its Documentary Bases. Phases of Krishna . 138

V. The Krishna Legend.

Barth's Synopsis. Solar Significance. Krishna Black, Hiding, or Night Sun. Black Deities in other Systems. The Vegetal Spirit Theory. Krishna and Arjuna. Osiris and Typhon. Krishna originally a "Demon." Supersedes Indra. Contrary Christian View. Note on the Black Osiris . . 141

VI. The Christian Argument.

Wheeler's *History*. Thesis of its *Athenæum* Critic. His Presuppositions. Professor Müller's Apologetics. Superior Candour of Continental Scholarship. Weber's Attitude. General View of Sanskritists. Wheeler on Question of Imitation . 148

VII. The Central Disproof.

Antiquity of Kansa Myth. Bhandarkar on Patanjali. Weber's Admissions. The Main Question Settled 154

VIII. Antiquity of Krishnaism.

Further Proofs. Bhitâri Pillar Inscription. Bayley's Inscriptions. Khandogya Upanishad. Müller and Weber . . 156

IX. Invalid Evidence.

Lassen on the Hercules of Megasthenes. Criticism of Tiele. Wilson's Position. Upheld by Weber and Senart. Bala Râma's Characteristics. His Close Correspondence with the Hercules of Megasthenes. Râma Chandra 160

X. Weber's Theory.

His General Attitude; Theory of Early Greek Influence and Imitation of Christianity; Doctrine of Faith; Festival Details. § 1. Criticism of his Positions; The Kansa Myth; Problem of Christian Origins; Virgin and Child derived from Isis and Horos; De Rossi on the Catacomb Madonnas; Pre-Christian Child-carrying Goddesses; Juno; Dêmêtêr; Venus; Alitta; Aphroditê; British Museum Nomenclature; India and Egypt; Tiele's Criticism of Weber; Buddha Virgin-born; Jerome's Testimony;

PAGE

Krishnaite Name-giving; Early Christian Placing of Nativity on Epiphany; Christmas a Pre-Christian Festival; Name-day in Hercules Worship; Name-day in Mazdeism; Baptizing on Epiphany; Abyssinian Usage. § 2. The Birth-Festival and the Purânas; Weber's Explanation Accepted; Purâna Legends not necessarily Late; Birthdays of Gods Astrological; Krishna and Star Rohini; Krishna Nativity in July; Significance of this; Birthday of Horus in July; Hindu Festivals; Mattu Pongal and St. Anthony's Day; Myth Derived from Ritual; Krishnaite and Roman Festivals; The "Swinging" Festival 163

XI. The Solar-Child Myth.

Connection of Kansa Legend with Legend of Cyrus. Parallel Legends. The Coat of Many Colours. Dangers Run by the Divine Child. The Myths of Sargon, Horos, and Moses. Confucius Miraculously Born. The Messianic Cyrus and Jesus. The Massacre of the Innocents. The Child Speaking at Birth. The Birth in a Cave. The Child Born on a Journey. Maya and Mary. The Mythological River. The "Taxing" Journey. The Myth of the Seven Gates 188

XII. The Stable and Manger.

Weber and Senart on the Krishna Ritual. The Manger-basket of Dionysos, Hermes, Zeus, and Ion. Bas-reliefs in the Catacombs. Ox and Ass. Cows and Stable. Isis and the Virgin Cow. Horus Born on Christmas Eve. Virgin, Child, and Manger Myth pre-Christian in Egypt. Cow Myth in Mithraism. Ox and Ass Symbolic. The Christian Legend. The Text in Habbakkuk. The Cave Motive. Agni the Babe God in the Veda. Myths concerning Him. Agni and Dionysos twice Born. The Cow-shed in the Krishna Ritual and in Catacomb Sculpture. The Symbolic Ass. Images in Christism and Krishnaism. Joseph and the Ass. Virgin-Myth Ritualized in Egypt. The Magi. Antiquity of the Babe-Sun-God. Dramatic Ritual in Krishnaism and Christism 197

XIII. The Myth of St. Christopher.

The name *Christophoroi*. Cognate Terms. The *Pastophoroi*. The Charge of Child-eating. The Christian Mysteries Secret. Testimonies of Clarkson, Palmer, Trollope, and Hatch. Child-carrying in Pagan Cults. The Sacramental Eating of Baked Images. General Use of such Images. The Principle of *Eating the God*. The Krishna Myth and the Christian. St. Christopher's Day 215

XIV. Indian and Christian Religious Drama.

Weber's View. Wilson's. Buddhist Testimony. "The Toy-Cart." Devakî and Vasudeva. Dramatic Ritual in Early Christism. Evidence of St. Proclus. Dramatic Origin of the Eucharist and the Mass. Early Christian Religious Drama.

PAGE

The Liturgies. The Greek Mysteries. Persistence of the Pagan Drama 227

XV. THE SEVEN MYTH.

§ 1. The Seven Brother Martyrs; The Seven Sleepers; The Seven Priests; Contact of Mithraism and Christism; The Banquet of Seven; Cox on the Seven Myth; The Sleepers and Martyrs = the Seasons and Pleiads. § 2. The Seventh Month; Devakî's Children; Vedic Myth of the Eighth Child; The Younger Brother; The Seven Planetary Spirits; Eight Egyptian Cosmic Powers; The Week Myth; Semitic Usage; Saturn; Possible Myth Connections; Alteration in Order of Months. Birthday Festival Dates 235

XVI. THE DESCENT INTO HELL.

Introduction of the Dogma. Pagan Precedents. Osiris. Hermes, Dionysos, Adonis, Orpheus, Zamolus, Mithra, Apollo. Balder and Arthur. Krishna's Descent. Cerberus. The "Two" rescued "Sons" in both Legends. Also in Legend of Buddha. The Dragon. Christian Borrowings from Buddhism . . 249

XVII. SPURIOUS AND REMOTE MYTH-PARALLELS.

The Address to the Fig-tree. Doctrine of Immortality. Transfiguration. Feet-washing. Raising the Widow's Son. Anointing the God. Judas and his Bag 258

XVIII. EXPLANATION OF THE KRISHNA MYTH.

§ 1. Its Obviously Solar Character; Repetitions in Solar Mythology; Krishna and Agni; Cox's Analysis; Krishnaite Syncretism; The Three Râmas = One; The Cult of Bala Râma. § 2. Weber's Chronological Scheme; Senart's Refutation; Weber's Answer; Its Insufficiency. § 3. Buddhist and Other Parallels . 261

XIX. KRISHNAITE AND CHRISTIST DOCTRINE.

§ 1. Weber's Misconception of Wilson; Wilson's Real Opinion. § 2. Lorenser on the Bhagavat Gitâ; His Error as to "India"; Vague Early Use of the Name; Chrysostom's Evidence; No Early Hindu Translation of Gospels. § 3. Date of the Gitâ; Telang's Suggestion; Lorinser's Parallels; Their Futility; Pagan and New Testament Parallels; Universal Theology and Ethics; Brahman and Christian Pantheism. § 4. *Bhakti* and *Sraddhâ*; Christian Doctrine of Faith from Judaism; Its Universality; Muir, Telang, and Tiele, on the Indian Doctrine; Position of Senart and Barth 274

XX. THE "WHITE ISLAND."

Weber's Thesis. Lassen's Argument. Telang's Refutation. Tiele's Endorsement. Senart and Barth Take Same Ground. Christian Tritheism and Monotheism 290

XXI. The Crucifixion Myth. PAGE

The Error of Moor and Higgins. Was there an Asiatic Crucifixion Myth? Andrade and Giorgi on the Crucifixion Myth in Tibet. Indra Crucified. Dr. Oldfield's Corroboration. Krishna on the Tree. The "Two Thieves." Frauds on Wilford. Wilson on Gnostic Borrowings from India. Epiphanius' Testimony. Difficulty of the Question. Orthodox Criticism. Jacolliot . 294

XXII. Summary.

Results Positive and Negative. The Christian Hypothesis Found Untenable and Absurd. All the Evidence Against It. Presumption of Some Christian Borrowing from Krishnaism as well as from Buddhism 299

Part III.

THE GOSPEL MYTHS.

Preamble.

First Division. Myths of Action.

§ 1. The Virgin Birth 317
§ 2. The Mythic Maries 319
§ 3. The Myth of Joseph 326
§ 4. The Annunciation 328
§ 5. The Cave and Stable Birth 329
§ 6. The Birthday 331
§ 7. The Massacre of the Innocents 332
Note on the Moses Myth 333
§ 8. The Boy Jesus in the Temple 334
§ 9. The Upbringing at Nazareth 335
§ 10. The Temptation 343
§ 11. The Water-Wine Miracle 356
§ 12. The Scourging of the Money-Changers . . . 358
§ 13. The Walking on the Water 358
§ 14. The Healing of Two Blind Men 359
§ 15. Other Myths of Healing and Resurrection . . 360
§ 16. The Feeding of the Five Thousand . . . 362
§ 17. The Anointing 363
§ 18. The Riding on the Ass and Foal 366
§ 19. The Myth of the Twelve Apostles 370
§ 20. The Characteristics of Peter 378
§ 21. The Myth of Judas Iscariot 384
§ 22. The Last Supper 386
§ 23. The Transfiguration and the Passion . . . 392
§ 24. The Crucifixion 394
§ 25. The Seamless Robe 414

		PAGE
§ 26.	The Burial and Resurrection	416
§ 27.	The Banquet of Seven	418
§ 28.	The Ascension	420

SECOND DIVISION. MYTHS OF DOCTRINE.

§ 1.	The Jesuine Discourses in General	423
§ 2.	The Preaching of John the Baptist	432
§ 3.	Jesus as a Preacher of Universalism	433
§ 4.	Jesus as Messiah	434
§ 5.	Jesus as Preparing the Kingdom of God	437
§ 6.	The Sermon on the Mount	440
§ 7.	The "Lord's Prayer"	450
§ 8.	The Woman Taken in Adultery	457
§ 9.	Gnostic and Cryptic Parables	460
§ 10.	The Late Ethical Parables in Luke	462
§ 11.	The Discourses of the Fourth Gospel	463
	Epilogue	470

PREAMBLE.

The three treatises making up this volume stand for a process of inquiry which began to take written form nearly fifteen years ago. It set out with a certain scientific principle and a certain historical purpose: the principle being that Christian Origins should be studied with constant precaution against the common assumption that all myths of action and doctrine *must* be mere accretions round the biography of a great teacher, broadly figured by "the" Gospel Jesus; while the practical purpose was to exhibit "The Rise of Christianity, Sociologically Considered." To that end I was prepared to assume a primitive cult, arising in memory not of a great teacher but (perhaps) of an obscure thaumaturg, concerning whom there is preserved, in the Epistles of Paul, only the tradition of his crucifixion. But the first independent explorations, the first rigorous attempts to identify the first Jesuists, led to a series of fresh exposures of myth. "Jesus of Nazareth" turned out to be a compound of an already composite Gospel Jesus, an interposed Jesus the Nazarite, and a superimposed Jesus born at Nazareth. And none of the three aspects equated with the primary Jesus of Paul. Each in turn was, in Paul's words, "another Jesus whom we have not preached." And the Twelve Apostles were demonstrably mythical.

While, therefore, a sociological foundation was in a measure reached, it was plain that the ground had not yet been cleared of mythology; and at that stage I even surmised that, in view of the known frequency alike of Messiahs and Jesuses in Jewry, an actual succession of Jesuses might be the historical solution. Such a theorem represented a still imperfect appreciation of the scope and dominion of the principle of Myth; and it fitly chanced that the sociological inquiry was arrested for the time as a literary task, though continued as a study.

Soon after, at the request of the late Mr. Bradlaugh, I undertook the research concerning "Christ and Krishna" by way of solving scientifically and objectively a simpler general problem in mythology and hierology; and about the same time the undertaking of an independent research into Mithraism further enabled me to see the Christian problem in a fuller scientific light. Thus the original inquiry, never discontinued as a subject of thought, led gradually to a conception of Mythology as a more catholic science, or a more scientific classification of certain knowledge, than it has yet been shown to be in the hands of its cultivators, admirable as much of their work is. That view I have now tried to set forth critically and historically in the opening treatise on "The Progress of Mythology." The study on "Christ and Krishna," which first appeared serially in Mr. Bradlaugh's journal and was reprinted (1889) with additions and corrections, is now again a good deal expanded, and in parts rewritten. It seeks on one hand to illustrate, in detail, what seems to me the right method of dealing with certain problems glanced at in the opening treatise; and on the other hand to lead organically into the general problem of Christian mythology. Finally, the survey of "The Gospel Myths," portions of which were also published serially, is recast and greatly enlarged, by way of finally clearing the mythological ground for sociology "proper."

As regards the theoretic problem, I cannot better

prepare a reader to catch my point of view than by indicating it critically as against the diverging doctrine of the recently-published work of Dr. Percy Gardner entitled "Exploratio Evangelica," a treatise in many respects wise and stimulating, which came into my hands only when the bulk of this volume was in type. As I regard it, Dr. Gardner's treatise relies unduly on the old, untested, metaphysical conception of mythology. Consider, for instance, the proposition that "probably at that time [early Christian age] in all the Levant *the true myth-making age was over. But the faculties which had been employed in the construction of myth were still at work.* And they found their natural field in the adaptation of history to national and ethical purpose."[1] Such language seems to me to confute itself: in any case, the whole drift of the present work is a gainsaying of such divisions as the one thus sought to be drawn. Dr. Gardner speaks again[2] of "the vague and childish character of *the true myth.*" I submit that there are all degrees of vagueness and childishness in myth, from the grossest to the slightest, and that though there may be classification there can be no scientific sunderance. A myth commonly so-called, when all is said, is simply a false hypothesis (whether framed in bad faith or in good faith) which once found easy credence; and when inadequate or illusory hypotheses find acceptance in our own time, we see exemplified at once the play of the myth-making faculty and that of the normal credulity on which it lives.

Any "explanation" which is but an *a priori* formula to account for an uncomprehended and unanalyzed process of phenomena is a "true myth" in so far as it finds utterance and acceptance. Some myths are less fortuitous, more purposive, than others; and a question

[1] Work cited, p. 149. [2] *Id.* p. 108.

might fairly be raised as to whether there is not here a true psychological distinction. My answer is that we can never demonstrate the entire absence of purpose: it is always a question of degree; and it makes little scientific difference in our elucidation whether we impute more or less of ignorant good faith, provided we recognize variation. A quite primitive myth may have been a conscious fiction on the part of its first framer; but the credulity of its acceptors assimilated it in exactly the same way as others framed in better faith.

Even if, however, we restricted ourselves to false hypotheses framed in absolute good faith, the old conception of myth remains a stumbling-block to be got rid of. It obscures our comprehension of the psychological process even of myths commonly so-called. Dr. Gardner, for instance, writes that "the Phœnician kinsmen of the Jews retained down to quite late times the terrible custom of human sacrifice. Its abolition very early among the Hebrews was a mark of their unique religious consciousness, and a sign of their lofty destiny."[1] This proposition I should describe as the quasi-explanation of an uncomprehended process in terms of the phenomena themselves; as in the propositions that opium has a dormitive virtue, and that nature abhors a vacuum. And such explanations, I submit, so far as they are accepted, are myths, made in just the old way, though with far higher intellectual faculties. Even as the movement of the sun and planets was not scientifically accounted for by supposing them to be tenanted by Gods or guiding spirits, so the evolution of a community and its culture is not accounted for by crediting the community with "unique consciousness" and "lofty destiny." The old explanation was a myth; the other is only myth on a different plane of instruction.

[1] Work cited, p. 105.

The effect of this change of theoretic standpoint must needs be considerable, at least as regards phraseology. I will merely say that, conceiving myth thus comprehensively, I have sought to track and elucidate it by lines of evidence not usually made to co-operate. Myth in the Gospels, on the view here taken, is to be detected not merely by means of the data of comparative mythology, but also by means of analysis of the texts. As Baur argued long ago, from criticism of the history we must come to criticism of the documents. But the later criticism of the documents, prepossessed by old conceptions of myth, has often made little account of concrete mythology, and has so fallen back on Hegelian formulas—that is, on philosophical myths—where real solutions were quite feasible. At the same time, students of mythology have often taken myth for biography, for lack of analysis of the texts. As illustrating my idea of what is to be gained by the concurrent use of both procedures, I may point to the subsections of "Gospel Myths" dealing with (*a*) the Myth of the Temptation, and (*b*) the Myth of the Upbringing at Nazareth. The first undertakes to trace an ostensibly fortuitous myth by various methods of comparative mythology, in particular by colligating clues in art and in literature; the second undertakes to trace a relatively purposive myth by analysis of the texts which gradually construct it, leaving part of the problem of the motives, in the latter case, for a wider historical inquiry. And here we have cases which test the old theory of myth—Baur's and Dr. Gardner's conception of "the true myth." The first myth, we say, is ostensibly fortuitous, the second ostensibly purposive. But neither assumption is susceptible of proof. The first myth, in its Christian aspect, *may* have originated in a deliberate fiction by a priest who gave what he knew to be a false explanation of a picture or sculpture; the second *may* have originated in good faith, with a theorist who did not believe that the first Christian Nazarenes were so called in the sense of Nazarites. In fine, what makes a myth "truly" so is not the state of mind of the man who first framed it, but the state of mind of those who adopted it. And that state of mind is simply uncritical credulity.

It may be that in some process of textual criticism in the treatise on "The Gospel Myths" I have unknowingly put forward theses already advanced by other critics. The German literature in that department is so immense that I have not sought to compass even the bulk of it, having read a good deal with little decisive gain. Much of it is a mere prolongation of dispute over the more problematical, leaving the less problematical line of demonstration unoccupied. It seems in every way more profitable to put the case afresh from my own standpoint, on the lines of my own chosen approach, which is the result or sequel of a survey of previous methods; and to do this without even criticising a whole series of such methods which strike me as finally fallacious. Not that they were not meritorious in their circumstances; on the contrary, they frequently convey a melancholy impression of a great expenditure of intellectual power to no effectual end. In comparing Bruno Bauer, for instance, with "safe" modern practitioners like Bernhard Weiss, one cannot but be struck by the greater originality and acuteness of the free-lance. But the bulk of the work of Bruno Bauer is practically thrown away by reason of his false Hegelian or quasi-Hegelian method; for he is more Hegelian than Strauss, and constantly frames his solutions in terms of the more problematical rather than in terms of the less. Every phenomenon in the text is by him accounted for through an *a priori* abstraction of the constructive consciousness of the early Christian community, acting as it theoretically needs must; so that we get psychological and sociological myth in place of theological. The negation is right; the affirmation is wrong.

Broadly speaking, such work as Bruno Bauer's, and much of that of Strauss, answers to Comte's conception of the normal rise of a metaphysical mode of thought as the first departure from a theological; this though Bauer thought that he and Weiss and Wilke and others had reached the true "positive" standpoint. The truth is that none of us—certainly not Comte—could make the transition so promptly as he supposed himself to have done; at best we grow less and less metaphysical (or, as I should prefer to put it, less *a priori*), more and more "positive." This appears even in the weighty performance of F. C. Baur, a much more "positive" thinker and investigator than Bruno Bauer, whose error of method he exposed with perfect precision. Common prudence, therefore, dictates the admission that the method of the following treatises is likely to suffer in some degree from survivals of the "metaphysical" method. I claim only that, so far as it goes, it is in general more "positive," more inductive, less *a priori*, more obedient to scientific canons, than that of the previous critics known to me who have reached similar anti-traditional results. It substitutes an anthropological basis, in terms of the concrete phenomena of mythology, for a pseudo-philosophical presupposition.

That this will give it any advantage as against the ecclesiastical defence would be too much to look for. I have suggested that that defence represents, however unconsciously, the organization of an economic interest; that the ostensible course of criticism is not a matter of the logical evolution of discovery, as in a disinterested science; but of the social selection of types of teacher. No stronger brain than Baur has dealt with historical theology in

Germany since his day: either through their own choice of other careers or the official selection of other candidates, the stronger German brains have mostly wrought in other fields. So, in the Church of England, we see no continuous advance in the application of clerical ability, from Milman onwards, to the problems of Christian Origins. If the capable men are there, they are mostly gagged or obstructed. The late Dr. Edwin Hatch, the one Churchman who in our time has done original and at the same time valid and important service in that field, appears to have been in a measure positively ostracised in his profession, though the sale of his works shows their wide acceptability even within its limits. The corporate interest and organization avail to override unorganized liberalism, there as elsewhere.

When then Dr. Percy Gardner, writing as a layman, avows that he cannot hope "to escape the opposition and anger which have always greeted any attempt to apply to the Christian creed the principles which are applied freely to other forms of faith,"[1] I may well count on a worse if more cursory reception for a book which in places represents him as unwarrantably conservative of tradition. Such treatises properly appeal to serious and open-minded laymen. Unfortunately the open-minded laity are in large part satisfied to think that traditionalism is discredited, and so take up an attitude of indifference to works which any longer join issue with it. None the less, those who realize the precariousness of modern gains in the battle against the tyranny of the past must continue the campaign, so doing what they can to save the optimists from, it may be, a rude awakening.

J. M. R.

June, 1900.

[1] Work cited, p. 118.

CHRISTIANITY AND MYTHOLOGY.

PART I.

THE PROGRESS OF MYTHOLOGY.

Chapter I.—The Science and its History.

§ 1. *The Problem.*

There are stages in the history of every science when its progress can be seen to consist in applying to its subject-matter a wider conception of relations. Scientific progress, indeed, mainly consists in such resorts to larger syntheses. In geology, as Mr. Spencer points out, "when the igneous and aqueous hypotheses were united, a rapid advance took place"; in Biology progress came through "the fusion of the doctrine of types with the doctrine of adaptations"; and in Psychology, similarly, an evolutionary conception partly harmonized the doctrines of the Lockian and Kantian schools.[1] It is true that Mr. Spencer proceeds to turn the generalization to the account of his theorem of a "Reconciliation" between "Religion" and "Science," on a ground which he declares to be outside both—that is, to belong to no science whatever. Nevertheless, the general proposition as above illustrated is just; and there is an obvious presumption that it will hold good of any science in particular.

It is proposed in the present inquiry to try whether the renewed application of the principle may not give light and

[1] *First Principles*, p. 22.

leading in the science—if we can agree so to call it—of mythology. By some the title may be positively withheld, on the ground that mythology so-called is seen in recent discussions to be only a collection of certain lore, to which are applied conflicting theories; and it is not to be denied that there is enough of conflict and confusion to give colour to such an account of the matter. But inasmuch as there has been progress in course of centuries towards scientific agreement as to certain classifications of the phenomena; and as this progress can be shown to consist in successive extensions of the relations under which they are contemplated, there is reason to conclude that mythology is a science like another, though latterly retarded more than others by the persistence of pre-scientific assumptions.

Myth, broadly speaking, is a form of traditionary error; and while the definition of mythology turns upon the recognition of the special form, the bane of the science has been the more or less complete isolation of it in thought from all the other forms. The best analogy for our purpose is perhaps not any of those cited from Mr. Spencer, but rather the case of Astronomy, where Newton's great hypothesis was by way of seeing planetary motions as cases of motion in general. Any form of traditionary error, it seems clear, must occur in terms of the general conditions of traditionary error; and such error in general must be conceived in terms of men's efforts at explanation or classification of things in general, at successive stages of thought. Yet in our own time, under the ostensible reign of Naturalism, after ages in which men looked at myth from a point of view that made almost invisible the psychological continuity between myth-makers' mental processes and their own, we find accomplished students of the science still much occupied in setting up walls of utter division between the mythopoeic and all other mental processes; between the different aspects of early classification; between the aspects of myth; between myth and "religion," religion and magic, myth and early morals, myth and legend, myth and allegory, myth and tradition, myth and supernaturalist biography. If past scientific experience can yield us any guidance, it would seem that such a tendency is frustrative of scientific progress.

§ 2. *The Scientific Beginnings.*

Gains there have certainly been, in the past half century. When we compare its results with those of the previous ten or even four centuries, as sketched in the *Introduction à l'Etude de la Mythologie* of Eméric-David,[1] we must admit a considerable progress; though if we should chronicle as he did the backward treatises as well as the others we could make a rather chequered narrative. The definite gain is that the naturalist method, often broached but not accepted before our time, is now nearly though not quite as generally employed in this as in the other sciences, whereas in past times there was an overpowering tendency to handle it from the point of view of that belief in "revelation" which so completely vitiated the study of Greek mythology in the hands of Mr. Gladstone, the last eminent practitioner on the old basis. How effectively that belief has retarded this science in particular may be partly gathered from Eméric-David's historical sketch.

Beginning with Albric in the eighth century, Maimonides in the twelfth, and Boccaccio in the fourteenth, the learned academician makes out a list of between seventy and eighty scholarly writers on mythology down to Benjamin Constant. He might have extended the list to a hundred; but it is duly representative, save in that it oddly omits all mention of Fontenelle, whose essay *De l'origine des fables*, as Mr. Lang points out, substantially anticipated the modern anthropological and evolutionary point of view.[2] This was of all previous treatises the one which could best have enlarged and rectified the French historian's own method,-and he either overlooks or wilfully ignores it, taking note only of the very one-sided view of the anthropological principle presented later by De Brosses and his disciple Benjamin Constant. It may be helpful at this point, however, to note the manner of the progression, as very fairly

[1] Paris, 1833. [2] As does his *Histoire des Oracles*, 1686.

set forth in the main by Eméric-David, and in part by Karl Ottfried Müller, in his earlier *Prolegomena*.[1]

The movements of advance and reaction in the history of mythological science, then, may be thus summarily and formally stated.

1. In rationalistic antiquity, the principle of evolution was barely glimpsed; and on the one hand the professed mythologists aimed at multiplying symbolical or allegorical meanings rather than tracing development, while on the other the school of Evemeros framed a set of false "naturalistic" explanations, being equally devoid of the requisite historical knowledge. The mythologists sank the fabulous personalities of the Gods in symbols; the sceptics sank them in actual human personages.

2. A substantially scientific beginning was made by the late school which reduced the symbolism of the older schools to a recognition of the large part played by sun and moon in most systems. In the hands of Macrobius (4th c.) this key is applied very much on the lines of the modern solar theory, with results which are still in large part valid. But that step of science, like nearly every other, was lost under Christianity and the resurgence of barbarism.

3. The Christian Fathers, when not disposing of Pagan Gods as demons, had no thought save to ridicule the old mythologies, failing to realize the character of their own.

4. The scholars of the Renaissance recognized the principle of Nature-symbolism, as set forth by Macrobius; but when, in the sixteenth century, scholarship began to classify the details of the pagan systems, it had no general guiding principle, and only accumulated data.

5. Bacon, who made symbolism his general principle of interpretation, applied it fancifully, slightly, and without method. Selden and others, with much wider knowledge, applied the old principle that the pagan deities were personalized nature-forces, as sun and moon. But others, as

[1] Neither supplies a complete survey; and the present sketch is of course only a bird's-eye view. For others, see Preller, *Griechische Mythologie*, Einleitung, § 7; Decharme, *Mythologie de la Grèce Antique*, Introd., pp. vi.–xx.; and Father Cara, *Esame critico del sistema filologico e linguistico, applicata alla mitologia e alla scienza delle religione*, Prato, 1884.

Leibnitz, Vossius, Bochart, and Mosheim, confused all by the theological presupposition (adopted from the ancient atheists) that the pagan deities were deified men, and by assuming further that the early life of antiquity was truly set forth only in the Bible.

6. Other earlier and later theologians, as Huet, though opposed by critical scholars such as Selden, Basnage, and Vico, went still further astray on the theory that pagan Gods were perversions of Biblical personages; and that all pagan theologies were perversions of an earlier monotheism. Such an application of comparative method as was made by Spencer of Cambridge (*De Legibus Hebræorum*, 1685) was far in advance of the powers of assimilation of the time.

7. Sceptics like Bayle derided all explanations alike, and ridiculed the hope of reaching any better.

8. New attempts were in large part *a priori*, and some went back to Evemerism, as that of Banier, who saw myth origins in perversions both of historical fact and of Biblical narratives. The sound theorem of personalized forces was reiterated by Vico and others, and that of savage origins was thrown out by Fontenelle, but the theological method and premisses overrode scientific views. Other rationalists failed to apply the clue of evolution from savagery, and wrongly staked all on purposive allegorizing.

9. The Naturalism of De Brosses (*Du Culte des Fétiches*, 1760), while rightly pointing towards savage life, ignored the many grades between fetichism and the higher paganism, and thus failed in the main to win even rationalistic students. On the other hand, the great astronomical and symbolical system of Dupuis (chief work, 1795), a development from the ancient positions of Macrobius, carefully applied to the Gospels and to the Apocalypse, did not account for the obscurer primitive elements of myth, though it rightly carried the mythological principle into the surviving religions. This was effectively done also in the slighter but more brilliant work of Volney, *Les Ruines* (1791), which proceeds on an earlier research by Dupuis. In England and Germany the deistic movement of last

century also led to the recognition of myths in the Old Testament.[1]

10. In the same period, Heyne developed a view that was in large part scientific, recognizing that myth is "the infant language of the race," lacking "the morality and delicacy of a later age," and that in later periods early myths were embellished, altered, and poeticized. He radically erred, however, in assuming that the early myth-makers only provisionally albeit "necessarily" personified natural forces, and always knew that what they said had not really happened. On the other hand, while teaching that their myths came to be literally believed by posterity, he erred in ascribing to the Homeric bards a conception of these myths as pure symbol; this conception having originated with the theosophic priests of Asia and Egypt, whence it reached the post-Homeric Greek rationalists. Voss,[2] opposing Heyne as he later did Creuzer, did not improve on Heyne's positions, leaning unduly to the belief that primeval man allegorized reflectively, and making too much of the theory of deified ancestors, later insisted on by Mr. Herbert Spencer.

11. A distinct advance in breadth of view was made by Buttmann,[3] who purified Heyne's doctrine as to the essential primitiveness or aboriginality of typical myth, and freshly laid the foundations of Comparative Mythology, recognizing that the same primitive mode of thinking could give rise to similar myths in different nations independently of intercourse, and calling for a comprehensive collocation. He thus naturally made too little of the special local significance of many myths.

12. Creuzer,[4] on the other hand, while rightly recognizing

[1] Preller (*Griech. Mythol.* ed. 1860, i. 20) finds a predilection to particular points of view in the different nations--the Italians arguing for allegory, the Dutch for perversion of the Bible, the French for Evemerism and other pragmatic principles, and the Germans standing for an original monotheism. But this classification, as Preller implicitly admits, is only loosely true; and it no longer holds good in any degree.

[2] *Mythologische Briefe*, 1794.

[3] Treatises between 1794 and 1828, collected in *Mythologus*, 2 Bde. 1828-9.

[4] *Symbolik und Mythologie der alten Völker, besonders der Griechen*, 4 Bde. 1810-12.

that personification was a fundamental law of early thought, nevertheless founded on the false assumption of a "pure monotheistic primitive religion," and so stressed the idea of reflective allegory as to obscure his own doctrine that primeval man personified forces quite spontaneously. Yet he introduced real clues—as that of the derivation of some myths from ritual, and that of verbal misconception, a theory later carried to excess by F. G. Welcker, and still later by Max Müller. He also noted the fact—fallaciously stressed by Mr. Lang in our own day—that the primitive mind made no such distinction between spirits and bodies as is made in later theology. Hermann, proceeding on similar fundamental lines, likewise conceived myth too much in terms of the constructive allegorizing of priesthoods, overlooking the spontaneous and relatively fantastic beginnings of savagery.

Alongside of these later German writers, whom he does not mention, Eméric-David does not innovate in any effective fashion. His own interpretative principle, further set forth in his treatise *Jupiter* (1832), is that laid down with caution but applied without any by Bacon—that myths are symbolical attempts to explain Nature: and to make his treatise broadly scientific it needed that he should have recognized how the principle of so-called fetichism, or the actual primitive personalizing of nature-forces, preceded and conditioned the systems which the writer handled as purposively symbolical, and symbolical only. The anthropological method had been indicated by Heyne, whose system he admitted to be "true at bottom"; but on this side he made no use of it. As it was, he partly rectified the bias towards a single astronomical point of view which narrows the great treatise of Dupuis, *De l'Origine de tous les Cultes* (1795). Concerning that, he rightly admitted that with all its limitations "it still constitutes the most luminous treatise that has been written on mythology";[1]

[1] *Introduction* cited, p. lxv.

and his own contribution may be said to have consisted in adding several wards to Dupuis's key, or new keys to Dupuis's two or three, letting it be seen that the old symbolical interpretation of nature was at once a simpler and a more complicated matter than Dupuis had supposed. At the same time, he made no attempt to carry on the great practical service of Dupuis and his school, the application of the pagan keys to the Christian religion, but confines himself to the Greek.

The same thing falls to be said in some degree of the earlier *Prolegomena* of Karl Ottfried Müller (1828),[1] of which Eméric-David makes no mention, on his principle of not criticising living writers. But none the less had Müller brought to the study of Greek mythology a learning, a genius, and a method which give a really scientific character to his work. Of the school of Dupuis he shows no knowledge. Whether this came of policy or of non-acquaintance we cannot well divine; but it is much to be regretted that he thus failed to come in touch with the most vital problem of his study. On the other hand, he did much to clear up the scientific ground so far as he did go. One of the most intellectual and most alert German scholars of that great period, he brought to bear on all Greek matters an exact and critical knowledge such as had hardly ever before been vigilantly applied to mythology; and though he did not escape the bane of all pioneers—indefiniteness and contradiction—he did not a little to reduce previous confusions. Good samples of his services as a first-hand investigator are his statement[2] of the grounds for holding that the complete myth of Prometheus and Epimetheus is late, and his analysis of the myth of the transformation of Callisto into a bear. In the latter case, by strict scrutiny of all the sources—a thing too seldom thought of before his day—he arrived at the clear demonstration that "Callisto is nothing else than the Goddess and her sacred animal combined in one idea," and that

[1] Translated in English in 1844, under the title *Introduction to a Scientific System of Mythology*, by J. Leitch.

[2] *Introduction*, Eng. tr., p. 58.

"Callisto became a bear, in the original legend, for this reason only, that the animal was sacred to Arcadian Artemis."[1] His deficiency on the concrete side appears in the same connection, when he observes that to Artemis as a Nature-Goddess "the most powerful creatures in nature, *such as the bear*, were sacred." This is unduly vague, and leaves us asking, in the light of later anthropology, whether the bear is not traceable further, and, in the light even of previous explanation, whether the bear was not after all associated with the Goddess because of the verbal resemblance between the names *arktos* (bear) and Artemis.

As regards general principles, Ottfried Müller is perhaps only at two points open to serious criticism. He rightly controverted the view, implicit in Dupuis and explicit in Creuzer (though Creuzer also implied the contrary), that systematic symbolism and allegory were the main and primary sources of myth ; arguing with Schelling that mythi were at the outset essentially spontaneous and unartificial. At the same time, when dealing with the substantially sound thesis of Heyne, that "the mythus [in its early forms] was the infant language of the race," and that "poverty and necessity are its parents,"[2] he is led by his passion for classical antiquity to put an unreasonably flat contradiction,[3] and thus seems to set his face against the fundamental truth that all religion begins in savagery. Thus he inconsistently lays stress[4] on the conscious moral purpose of the myth of Zeus and Lycaon, which he holds to be very early, while disregarding the immorality of others, both earlier and later. The difficulty becomes acute when, making a needless verbal strife over the term "allegory," he insists that, if a certain worship were "allegorical in the *strict* sense, it could be no worship at all."[5] He goes on :—

"Here we have to deal with a mode of contemplating the world which is quite foreign to our notions, and in which it is difficult for us to enter. It is not incumbent on the historical investigation of mythology to

[1] *Id.* pp. 16-17.
[2] Cited by Müller, p. 256. Schelling had said the same thing (*Ueber Mythen*, 1793), cited by Strauss, *Leben Jesu*, Einleit. § 8.
[3] Müller, p. 20. [4] P. 18. [5] P. 61.

ascertain the foundations on which it rests. This must be left to the highest of all historical sciences—one whose internal relations are scarcely yet dreamt of—the history of the human mind."

On which one at once answers, first, that mythology, as distinguished from mere mytho*graphy*, must be of itself a part of the history of the human mind, if it is anything, and that it must in some sort settle its bases as it goes along; and, secondly, that Müller himself, in the next breath, goes on to specify such a foundation when he speaks of a "certain necessity of intuition" as underlying the formation of mythi. But indeed he is thus reasoning out psychological foundations all through his treatise, and we are entitled to say that the deliverance above cited is in plain contradiction of his practice, as well as of his later and really sound decision, given in comment on Creuzer, that "mythology is still an historical science like every other. *For can we call a mere compilation of facts history?* and must we not, in every field of the science of history, *ascend on the ladder of facts to a knowledge of internal being and life?*"[1]

That is the most serious contradiction in the book; and we can but say on the other hand that the reasoner enables us to correct him when he errs. His frequent protests (echoed by Grote) against the attribution of "allegory" to myths in general, do but point to the confessed imperfection of the "history of the human mind"—a consideration which should have made him more circumspect verbally. We are left asking, What *is* allegory? and while we can all agree that early Greeks certainly did not allegorize as did Spenser and Bunyan, and that the Prometheus story in its complete form is clearly late, we are none the less forced to surmise that something of the nature of allegory may enter even into the earliest myths—that at times even the myth-making savage in a dim way necessarily distinguishes *at the outset* between his myth and his other credences, or at least is often in a manner allegorizing when he *makes* his story to explain facts of nature. Where he differs from the scientific man—though not from the religious—is in his power of passing from the half-allegoric conception to the

[1] *Id.* p. 273.

literalist. In any case, it is not historically or psychologically true that, as Müller puts it, "mythus and allegory are ideas lying [necessarily] far apart";[1] and we may, I think, be sure that some of the writers he antagonized were using the word "allegory" in a sense of which the practical fitness is tacitly admitted by his repeated use of the phrase "*strictly* allegorical." All the while he admitted,[2] as does Grote after him,[3] that an allegorical explanation frequently holds good of *parts* even of early myths; which is really a surrender of the essentials in the dispute.

As against these minor confusions, however, we must place to the credit of Ottfried Müller a general lucidity and catholicity of method that make him still a valuable instructor. While he avoided the extravagances of the symbolists, he sensibly recognized and explained many symbols;[4] and while he objected to allegoric systems he gave the sound advice: "Let us therefore, without rejecting anything of that kind, merely hold back, and wait for the development of individual cases."[5] Without laying down the anthropological method, he prepares us for it, especially by his keen attention to the geography of Greek myth; and while disclaiming all-round interpretation he helps us to many. The most helpful of his many luminous thoughts is perhaps his formulation[6] of the principle, implicitly to be gathered from Creuzer,[7] that in many cases "the whole mythus sprang from the worship, and not the worship from the mythus"—a principle accepted from him by Grote[8] and by a number of recent students, including Professor Robertson Smith and Mr. J. G. Frazer, and likely in the future to yield results of the first importance when applied to living as it has been to dead problems.[9] But thereby hangs, as we shall see, a tale to the effect that the course of

[1] *Id.* p. 272. [2] *Id.* pp. 18, 58. [3] *History of Greece*, second par.
[4] *E.g.* that of the Dog-Star, p. 135. [5] P. 18: cp. p. 19.
[6] Pp. 171, 175, 206, and previously in his *Orchomenos* (1820).
[7] Cited by Müller, p. 270, from the introduction to the *Symbolik*.
[8] *History*, end of ch. i.
[9] It must always be kept in mind that the worship which has given rise to a given mythus has itself arisen out of a previous mythus, on a different plane of conception. See below, ch. iii. § 1, *end*, and compare Bergmann, *Le Message de Skirnir et les Dits de Grimnir*, 1871, p. 3.

true mythology does not run smooth. The application of the science to living problems is the weakest point in its present development. Thus far, then, we may round our summary of progress :—

13. Karl Ottfried Müller and Eméric-David, proceeding on earlier studies and laying down general principles for myth interpretation (the former looking narrowly to documentary evidences and the latter putting stress on general symbolic values), alike failed on the one hand to explain the barbarous and primeval element in mythology, and on the other hand to connect mythology with the surviving religions. Each, however, gave sound general guidance, and Müller in particular established some rules of great importance.

§ 3. *The Relation to Christianity.*

So close on the publication of Ottfried Müller's *Prolegomena* as not to be fundamentally affected by it, came Strauss's epoch-marking *Leben Jesu* (1835), after Dupuis the first systematic application of mythological science to the Christian system. For several generations the mythical principle had been partially applied by German scholars to matters of current belief: the stimulus of the English deistical school having borne fruit more continuously among them than elsewhere. Deistical in spirit the movement remained; but it had all the easier a course; and the line of thought entered on by the school of Eichhorn, following on Heyne and Reimarus, was not even blocked, as was the case in England and France, by the reaction against the French Revolution. The Old Testament narratives, of course, were first dealt with; but so fast did criticism go that as early as 1802 there was published by G. L. Bauer a treatise on the Hebrew Mythology of the Old and New Testaments; a work which is noteworthy as already laying down the principle that it is of the highest importance to compare the myths of different races, thereby to learn how parallels may stand not for identity of matter, but for similarity of experience and way of thought among men of a given culture-stage.[1] It also affirms in so many words that "the savage animizes all things (*denkt sich alles belebt*), for only what lives can act, and thus he personifies all."[2] But in his interpretations Bauer follows the early rationalist method of reducing mythic episodes to exaggerations or misconceptions of actual events; and he makes little advance on Semler, who had connected the Samson myth with that of Hercules as early as 1773.[3]

A generation later, whereas Keightley in producing the first edition of his *Mythology of Ancient Greece and Italy* (1831) could say that "in selecting mythology" he "took possession of a field which lay totally unoccupied,"[4] the Germans had a whole library of treatises compared with which even his much improved second edition was but a respectable and prejudiced manual. So far had free scholarship travelled at a time when the teachers of the insular and stipendiary Church of England[5] were declaring that "infidelity" was no longer associated with scholarly names. While English theology and philosophy, under ecclesiastical auspices, were at an absolute standstill, German thought was applying rational tests, strenuously if imperfectly, to nearly every department of traditional knowledge. The progress, of course, was halting and uncertain at best. Strauss has shown[6] how vacillating and inconsistent were most of the innovators in their advance; how they were always trying to limit their concession, attempting first to explain miracles as natural events, then admitting myth to a certain extent, seeking for each myth a historical basis, striving to limit the field of myth to early times, trying later to draw a line between the Old Testament and the New, and next to admit myth as regards only the infancy of Jesus—always compromising in the interests of faith, or of simple peace and quietness. Yet so early as 1799 an anonymous writer on "Revelation and Mythology" had substantially

[1] *Hebräische Mythologie*, 1802, Vorrede, pp. iv. v.
[2] *Id.* i. 17. [3] *Id.* ii. 81. [4] Pref. to 2nd edition, 1838.
[5] "The priest-ridden kingdom of the leopards" was Alexander Humboldt's label for England in the early part of the century.
[6] *Leben Jesu*, Einleitung, § 6, 8–11.

set forth Strauss's own thesis, that "the whole life of Jesus, all that he should and would do, had an ideal existence in the Jewish mind long prior to his birth"; and between this and the more limited treatment of details by intermediate writers the world was partly prepared for Strauss's own massive critical machine.

And yet, though the formidable character and effect of that is the theme of an abundant literature, it was not a decisive force, even for theoretical purposes. On the side of mythological science it was defective in that it overlooked many of the Pagan myth-elements in the Christian cult, above all those bound up with the very central doctrine of theanthropic sacrifice and eucharist; and this by reason of a too exclusive attention to Judaic sources. It dealt with the salient item of the Virgin-birth in the light of general mythology; but it ignored the connecting clue of the numerous ancient ritual cults of a Divine Child. It showed the incredibility and the irreconcilable confusions of the resurrection story; but it did not bring forward the mythic parallels. As regards the process of mythic accretion, it did not properly apply the decisive documentary test that lay to hand in the Pauline epistles. At many points Strauss is Evemeristic even in condemning Evemerism, as when he decides the historic reality of John the Baptist to be certain, and the story of the Sermon on the Mount to be in the main genuine, though manipulated by Matthew in one way and by Luke in another. Dealing with the obviously mythical story of the betrayal by Judas, he never realizes the central preposterousness of the narrative,[1] and treats it as history. On the side of philosophy, again, he strikes a scientific reader dumb by his stupendously naïve assurance that his long investigation of the life of Christ need have no effect on Christian doctrine. "The inner kernel of the Christian faith," he writes in his preface, "the author knows to be entirely independent of his critical researches. Christ's supernatural

[1] Cp. *The Myth of Judas Iscariot*, in the author's *Studies in Religious Fallacy*.

birth, his miracles, his resurrection and ascension, remain eternal truths, however far their reality as historical facts may be put in doubt. Only the certainty of this can give calmness and weight to our criticism, and distinguish it from the naturalistic criticism of previous centuries, which aimed at upsetting the religious truth along with the historical fact, and so necessarily came to conduct itself frivolously. The dogmatic import (*Gehalt*) of the Life of Jesus will be shown by a dissertation at the end of the work to be uninjured." There are different conceptions of what constitutes frivolity; and it would have been pleasant to have Voltaire's estimate of the seriousness of a scholar and theologian who produced an enormously laborious treatise of fifteen hundred pages to disprove every supernatural occurrence connected with the life of Jesus, and at the beginning and end assured everybody that it all made no difference to religion, and that those must be frivolous who thought otherwise. Only in Germany, it may be decided, can such supernatural flimsiness of theory be conceived as solid philosophy; and even in Germany, in the generation of Hegel, there was a good deal of serious[1] if not frivolous comment on Strauss's final advice to the clergy to keep on telling the mythical stories to the people with due attention to the spiritual application, thereby furthering the "endless" progress towards the dissolution of the forms in the consciousness of the community—this in a work in the vernacular. Mr. Arnold gravely if not bitterly complained that Colenso ought to have written in Latin, though Colenso's avowed purpose was to put an end to deception. He might a good deal more relevantly have given the advice to Strauss, whose work he not very ingenuously exalted in comparison.

It was not unnatural that such a teaching should leave the practice of Christendom very much where it found it. If the "rational" critic felt as Strauss did after fifteen hundred pages of destructive argument, there was small call for the priest to alter his course. And what has

[1] *E.g.* Julius Muller *On the Theory of Myths*, tr. in *Voices of the Church against Strauss*, 1845, pp. 176–7.

happened in regard to the mythology of both the Judaic and the Christian systems is roughly this, that after the mythical character of the quasi-supernatural narratives had been broadly demonstrated, specialist criticism, instead of carrying out the demonstration and following it up to its conclusions in all directions, has fallen back on the textual analysis of the documents, leaving the question of truth and reason as much as possible in the background. Later work on Hebrew mythology there has been, but not, as before, on the part of professed theologians; and even that, as we shall see, is to a considerable extent unconvincing, thus failing to counteract the arrest of the study. On the professional Biblicists it seems to have had no practical effect, their lore being at least kept free of any specific acknowledgment. One is inclined to surmise that this process of restriction turns upon one of selection in the personalities of the men concerned. It would seem impossible that after Strauss and Baur and Renan and Colenso the stronger and more original minds could deliberately take up theology as of old; and as a matter of fact no minds of similar energy have appeared in the Churches since that generation completed their work. For Baur we have Harnack; for Bishop Colenso Bishop Barry; the Bishop Creightons meddling with none of these things. The powerful minds of the new generation do not take up orthodox theology at all; the business is for them too factitious, too unreal, too essentially frivolous. So we get a generation of specialists devoutly bent on settling whether a given passage be by P or P^2, by the Yahwist or the Elohist, the Deuteronomist or the Redactor, the Jerusalem Davidian, or the other, or the Saulist or the Samuel-Saulist—an interesting field of inquiry, well worth clearing up, but forming a singular basis on which to re-establish the practice of taking that mosaic of forgery and fiction as the supreme guide to human conduct. Of course this is the only species of rational criticism that can be pursued in theological chairs even in Germany; so that even if a professor recognizes the need for a moral and intellectual criticism of the Judaic literature, he must be fain to confine himself to documentary analysis and platitudes. But the dyer's hand seems to be subdued to what it works in. Even in our own day, men engaged in the analysis tell us that the scribes and interpolators dealt-with really had supernatural qualifications after all.[1] It thus appears that when the higher criticism has done its work, the higher common-sense will have to take up the dropped clues of mythology and conduct us to a scientific sociologico-historical view of religious development. The textual analysis is a great gain; but to end with textual analysis is to leave much of the human significance of the phenomena unnoticed.

So with the mythology of the New Testament and the ritual usages of the Churches. In that regard also we now hear little of the element of myth, but a good deal of the composition of the Gospels; and men supposed to know the results of that analysis are found treating as great spiritual truths, special to Christianity, data and doctrines which entirely appertain to the systems and credences of buried Paganism. The men capable of realizing the seriousness of the fact either remain outside the Church or follow Strauss's counsel inside. The undertaking to frame a psychological presentment of the "real Jesus" is still seriously pursued, albeit the documentary analysis does not leave even a skeleton for the accepted historical figure, wherewith to materialize the silent spectre of Paul's epistles. Thus Evemerism is still the order of the day as regards the Christian mythus; and people who are supposed to have the elements of a sound culture, including the results of mythological science, are often almost entirely ignorant of any bearings of Comparative Mythology on the Gospels, even though they may have learned to disbelieve in miracles. Mythological science has been prudently restricted to other fields, spiritually remote from modern faith and ritual. The principle seems to be that of the legendary preacher who, when arranging with a brother cleric to take his place, warned him against speaking on

[1] See Canon Driver's *Introduction to the Study of the Old Testament*, 1st ed. pref. p. xv.

capital and labour, as the congregation included some large employers, or on temperance, as there were some brewers; but added that "for a perfectly safe subject he might take the conversion of the Jews." Mythology is kept perfectly safe, and made to figure as an academic science, by being kept to the themes of the Dawn, the Tree, the Storm-Cloud, and the heathen Sun-God; to Sanskrit, savagery, totems, fairies, and Folk-Lore.

Chapter II.—Modern Systems.

§ 1.—*The Etymological and Solar Schools.*

While, however, our science has thus faltered and turned back on those of its paths which come the straightest and the nearest to living interests, it has not been idle or altogether ill-employed. Even as the textual analysis of the Jewish and Christian sacred books lays a solid foundation for the mythologist of the future, so the modern schools of mythology, in building up the Comparative Method, with whatever laxities of logic and psychology, have been making the way easier for successors who will not submit to any restriction of their field. While Strauss, Colenso, and Renan were successively disturbing the peace of the Church without much resort to the mass of mythological lore, new and professed mythologists were beginning anew, and with on the whole a scientific bias, the presentment of mythological science so-called, with hardly any avowed recognition of its bearing on current creeds. Unfortunately the new schools are thus far much at issue among themselves, by reason mainly of their differing ways of restricting the application of the Comparative Method. Kuhn, who in Germany began the new investigation on the basis of the Vedas, was an acute or rather ingenious theorist along particular lines of myth-phenomena, his tendency being to reduce all myths to those of the phenomena of storm-cloud, wind, rain, and lightning. To Kuhn, however, belongs the honour of inaugurating the new Comparative Mythology in terms of the affiliation of Greek God-names to Sanskrit;[1] and his brother-in-law Schwartz, who had collaborated with

[1] Steinthal, *The Original Form of the Legend of Prometheus*, Eng. tr. with Goldziher, pp. 363–5; E. H. Meyer, *Indoger. Mythen*, 1883, i. 1.

him in collecting the *Norddeutsche Sagen* (1848), did real service to the science by his analyses and explanations of nature-myths in his *Ursprung der Mythologie* (1860). About the same period in England, Mr. Max Müller founded a separate "Aryan" school, standing mainly on the solar principle as against the storm-system of Kuhn; and inasmuch as this was but a setting of one myth-type in place of another, the scientific advance was not great. On one side, indeed, there was retrogression. At the very outset of his work in 1856, Müller thought fit to insist that

> "As far as we can trace back the footsteps of man.... we see that the divine gift of a sound and sober intellect belonged to him from the very first; and the idea of a humanity emerging slowly from the depths of an animal brutality *can never be maintained again*."[1]

Three years later was published *The Origin of Species*, followed in 1871 by *The Descent of Man*. But Professor Müller's conception of mythology was now fully shaped. Proceeding further mainly on the supposed primordiality of Sanskrit, and preoccupied with the philological problems set up by any comparison of Sanskrit and Greek God-names, he elaborated the theory of Creuzer and Welcker as to verbal confusions, putting it that myths in general originated in a "disease of language,"[2] and that, the disease once developed—like the pearl in the oyster or the wart on the skin—it remained fixed in the languages derived from the given stem. The disease consisted in the primitive tendency to make proper names out of names for phenomena, the embodiment of genders in all names having the effect of setting up the habit of thinking of natural objects as animate and sexual. It is surprising that such a theory should ever be formulated without the theorist's seeing that the problem is shifted further back at once by the bare fact that the genders were attached to the words to begin with. Had Professor Müller merely claimed that in some cases a

[1] *Comparative Mythology*, in *Oxford Essays*, 1856, p. 5; cp. *Chips from a German Workshop*, ed. 1880, ii. 8. The passage ends with the phrase "such unhallowed imputations." In the reprint the adjective becomes "gratuitous."

[2] "Mythology, which was the bane of the ancient world, is in truth a disease of language." *Lectures on the Science of Language*, 3rd ed., p. 11. Cp. p. 240.

myth arose as it were at second-hand by the misunderstanding of a name, he might have made out a reasonable case enough; for certain racial and geographical and other myths can best be so explained. And when he wrote that

> "Nothing is excluded from mythological expression; neither morals nor philosophy, neither history nor religion, have escaped the spell of that ancient sibyl. But mythology is neither philosophy, nor history, nor religion, nor ethics."[1]

he was putting a true conception which transcends the limitary principle of "disease of language." At the same time he declared that "mythology is only a dialect, an ancient form of language." Yet in the previous sentence he had, like his namesake Ottfried, repudiated Heyne's formula, "*ab ingenii humani imbecillitate et a dictionis egestate*"; substituting the anti-evolutionary "*ab ingenii humani sapientia et a dictionis abundantia*"—as if it were *sapientia* to confuse the meanings of words. Thus the false principle overrides the true: sound conceptions passed on by Professor Müller himself have received development at other hands; and for lack of correlation in thinking he has repeatedly assailed his own positions; though, conscious of having held them, he is ready to resume them. Hence his attempts, under stress of controversy, to show that his doctrine was not what opponents represented it, have not only brought upon him some criticisms of much asperity, but have plunged the subject in extreme confusion. At times he has seemed to concede that the philological position is too narrow. After describing comparative mythology as "an integral part of comparative philology,"[2] he protested that he had "never said that the whole of mythology can be explained" as "disease of language," claiming only that "some parts of mythology" are "soluble by means of linguistic tests."[3] Yet he later seems to oscillate between the extreme view and the broader;[4] and he says in so many words that it is a pity that Comparative Mythology has got into any hands save those of Sanskrit scholars.[5] Nor have

[1] Essay on *Comparative Mythology*, end. [2] *Id.* as first cited, p. 86.
[3] *Introd. to Science of Religion*, ed. 1882, p. 252.
[4] *Natural Religion*, 1889, pp. 22, 24. [5] *Id.* p. 484.

his attempts to subsume Schleiermacher's philosophy of religion into his mythology been more fortunate; the philosophy and the psychology are alike inexpert; and not a little of his philological mythology is unsatisfying in detail, apart from all other issues. In particular, certain etymologies which Dr. Müller represented as scientifically certain—*e.g.*, the equations between *gandharra* and *kentauros* (Kuhn), *Erinnys* and *saranyu*, *Daphne* and *Ahana*—have been rejected as unsound by Mannhardt and others, as Mr. Lang is always reminding us.

In all probability this reaction has in turn gone too far; and latterly we find E. H. Meyer, in his *Indogermanische Mythen*, holding to the *gandharra-kentauros* equation against his master, Mannhardt. Pure philology was after all Dr. Müller's specialty; and he will probably stand on that when he has fallen on other issues. Next to his metaphysic and his psychology, it is his confidence of concrete myth-interpretation in terms of names that most weakens his authority. Most careful mythologists will admit that they are apt to put too much faith in their own explanatory theories: that they can hardly help coming at times to conclusions on a very incomplete induction. But Professor Müller has never lost the confidence with which he solved his early problems, while his readers, on the other hand, have in many cases lost the contagion. And this criticism applies in some degree to the brilliant performance of his most powerful English disciple, the Rev. Sir George Cox. That excellent scholar's *Mythology of the Aryan Nations* (1st ed. 1870), the most vivid and eloquent work in mythological science, was constructed on the assumption that the "Aryan" heredity was all decisively made out once for all on the old lines; and that the whole mythology of the races covered by the name is a development from one germ, or at least from a family of germs, found in the "Vedic and Homeric poets." In his second edition he admitted that since he wrote fresh proof had been given of the "influence of Semitic theology on the theology and religion of the Greeks"; but such an admission does not scientifically rectify the theoretic error embodied in his original thesis.

Anthropological as well as mythological research, following on the lines marked out by Fontenelle and De Brosses, had been showing not merely Semitic influences on Greeks, but (1) an interplay of many other influences, and (2) a singular parallelism in the mythology of races not known to have had any intercommunication.[1] These facts supplied reason for a recasting of the mythological scheme, by way of recognizing that there is more than "one story" in hand, and that though "the course of the day and the year" covers a great deal of the matter, there are some other principles also at work. Further, Sir George Cox has quite needlessly grafted Dr. Müller's overbalanced theory of "disease of language" on his exposition. Dr. Müller on his part had classed his disciple as belonging to another school than his own—the Analogical as distinct from the Etymological[2]—and Sir George might profitably have made the same discrimination. For his own part he had rightly represented the primitive "savage" as *necessarily* personifying the things and forces of nature: to him they "were all living beings: could he help thinking that, like himself, they were conscious beings also? His very words would, *by an inevitable necessity*, express this conviction."[3] For this "necessity" Sir George could quote Dr. Müller; but instead of noting that such a proposition dismissed *a fortiori* the theorem of "disease of language," he went on to include the latter, *àpropos* of the principle of Polyonymy (or multiplying of names for the natural elements), which needed no such backing. With his usual candour he proceeded to cite the trenchant comment of M. Baudry, who in his essay *De l'interprétation mythologique*[4] countered Dr. Müller before the "Hottentotic" school did. As M. Baudry pointed out, there was no "disease of language" in the case of secondary myths arising out of polyonymy, but simply failure of memory or loss of knowledge, such as may happen in the

[1] See Schirren's *Die Wandermygen der Neuseeländer und der Mauimythos* 1856, and Tylor's *Researches into the Early History of Mankind*, 1865, p. 326.

[2] *Natural Religion*, pp. 484, 492.

[3] *Mythology of the Aryan Nations*, ed. 1882, p. 21.

[4] Published in the *Revue Germanique*, Fév. 1, 1868.

case of a symbolic sculpture as well as of an epithet. Sir George's solution was that "after all there is no real antagonism" between the two accounts of the matter—a mode of reconciliation rather too often resorted to by Dr. Müller on his own account. There is certainly "no real antagonism" if only Dr. Müller's erroneous formula be dropped, and M. Baudry's substituted; but as it happens Dr. Müller's, instead of undergoing that euthanasia, is still made to cover far more ground than M. Baudry's pretends to touch.

In other countries the linguistic misconception had a hampering effect even on good scholarly research, as in the case of the work of M. Bréal, *Hercule et Cacus: étude de mythologie comparée* (1863). It is there laid down that "Never was the human race in its infancy, however vivacious and poetic may have been the first sallies of its imagination, capable of taking the rain which watered the earth for the milk of the celestial cows, nor the storm......for a monster vomiting flames, nor the sun......for a divine warrior launching arrows on his enemies, nor the roll of the thunder for the noise of the ægis shaken by Jupiter...... Whence came all these images, which are found in the primitive poetry of all the Aryan peoples? From language, which creates them spontaneously without man's taking care *(sans que l'homme y prenne garde)*."[1] If this be true, early man never really personified anything; but his more highly evolved posterity did, merely because he had seemed to do so. In other words, the early man knew the sun to be inanimate though his language made him call it a person; and his descendants consequently regarded it as a person when they were able to describe it as inanimate. Here we have Heyne's old conception of a species of allegorizing which was inevitable and yet not believed in—a theorem more puzzling than the phenomena it explains.

In the circumstances it was natural that there should arise an anthropological reaction against the Sanskritist and "Aryan" school, with its theory of family germs and

[1] Work cited, p. 8.

inherited disease of language; its forcing of philological hypotheses on a psychological science; and its assumption that we can trace nearly every myth with certainty to a definite natural origin. So many myths are inconsistent with themselves; so many are but fumbling explanations of ancient rituals of which the meaning had been lost; so many have been touched up; so many embody flights of imagination that are not mere transcripts from nature;[1] so many are primitively stupid, so many have been combined, that such confidence is visibly excessive; and there are always plenty of cool heads pleased to shatter bubbles. But there is more than mere conservatism arrayed against the confident lore of Professor Müller and the brilliant ingenuity of Sir George Cox: there is the solid opposition of students who, finding myths just like those of the "Aryans" among all manner of savages, proceed to show that what is represented as exquisite fancy among early Aryans is on all fours with the clumsy tales of Dyaks and Hottentots, and that the interpreters are putting more into many Aryan myths than their framers did.

§ 2. *The Movement of Anthropology: Tylor.*

To such criticism a powerful lead was given by Dr. E. B. Tylor's *Researches into the Early History of Mankind* (1865) and *Primitive Culture* (1871), which colligate much of the anthropological science on which alone a sound mythology can be founded. At the outset, indeed, Dr. Tylor ranks himself among the adherents of Kuhn and Max Müller,[2] significantly coupling their names, though Müller had rejected Kuhn's interpretations in terms of cloud and storm and thunder, preferring to stake everything on the sun. But besides bringing into correlation many terms of folk-lore, Dr. Tylor added to the keys already on the mythologist's bunch that of the "Myth of Observation," showing

[1] See Tylor, *Primitive Culture*, 3rd ed. i. 306, as to some of the conditions under which primitive invention is developed.
[2] *Researches into the Early History of Mankind*, 1865, pp. 298, 326.

by many instances how the discovery of peculiar remains had given rise to fabulous interpretation, as in the case, already noted by Darwin, of the savage theory that the large animals whose skeletons are found underground must have been burrowers. By including such ideas under the concept of myth, Dr. Tylor was usefully pointing towards the general truth that all myth is but a form of traditionary error; and in his later work on *Primitive Culture* he further widened the conception, guarding against Müller's limitary view, and pronouncing "material myth to be the primary, and verbal myth to be the secondary formation."[1] Again, while inconsistently separating mythology from religion,[2] he expressly recognized that "the doctrine of miracles became as it were a bridge along which mythology travelled from the lower into the higher culture. Principles of myth formation belonging properly to the mental state of the savage, were by its aid continued in strong action in the civilized world"[3]—restricting his instances, of course, to mediæval Catholicism. Finally, in his summary of "the proof of the force and obstinacy of the mythic faculty," he supplied a very suggestive list of its modes:—

> "In its course there have been examined the processes of animating and personifying Nature, the formation of legend by exaggeration and perversion of fact, the stiffening of metaphor by mistaken realization of words, the conversion of speculative theories and still less substantial fictions into pretended traditional events, the passage of myth into miracle-legend, the definition by name and place given to any floating imagination, the adaptation of mythic incident as moral example, and the incessant crystallization of story into history."[4]

The main logical or scientific flaw in the exposition is one that almost corrects itself—the separation from all this of the study of "Animism," which is separately handled as the basis of Natural Religion. Obviously Animism is involved in the very first of the processes above specified as constituting myth—the animating and personifying of Nature. This is admitted in the earlier announcement, in the first chapter on Mythology (ch. viii.), that the doctrine of Animism "will be considered elsewhere as affecting

[1] *Primitive Culture*, 3rd ed. i. 299.
[2] *Id.* p. 285.
[3] *Id.* p. 371.
[4] *Id.* p. 416.

philosophy and religion, but here we have only to do with its bearing on mythology." But here Animism is one thing or category, Mythology another, and Religion yet another; the two latter ranking as separate departments or processes of intellectual life, and being merely acted on by the third. Such a position marks the limit to the direct service rendered by Dr. Tylor to the science of mythology and of hierology, though his indirect service is unlimited. To make further progress we must recast the psychological concept and statement, recognizing that Animism, Mythology, and Religion are alike but aspects of the general primitive psychosis; and that while we may conveniently make any one of the three names cover the primary phenomena, it is a fallacy to make them stand for three faculties or provinces of intellectual life. Such a conception is only one more unscientific severance of unity, yielding no analytic gain of clearness, but rather obscuring the problem. So much seems to be felt by Dr. Tylor when in his concluding chapter he remarks that

> "Among the reasons which retard the progress of religious history in the modern world, one of the most conspicuous is this, that so many of its approved historians demand from the study of mythology always weapons to destroy their adversaries' structures, but never tools to trim and clear their own."[1]

Unfortunately the schematic fallacy rather than the implications of the comment tends to stand as the author's authoritative teaching; and in one other regard Dr. Tylor regrettably endorses a separatist view of primitive thought. Concluding his exposition of Animism,[2] he writes that

> "Savage animism is almost devoid of that ethical element which to the educated modern mind is the very mainspring of practical religion. Not, as I have said, that morality is absent from the life of the lower races. Without a code of morals, the very existence of the rudest tribe would be impossible; and indeed the moral standards of even savage races are to no small extent well-defined and praiseworthy. But these ethical laws stand on their own ground of tradition and public opinion, comparatively independent of the animistic beliefs and rites which exist around them. The lower animism is not immoral, it is unmoral."

The use of the word "comparatively" shows a half-

[1] *Id.* ii. 447. [2] Ch. xvii. vol. ii. p. 360.

consciousness of the essential error of the proposition. Obviously the animistic beliefs and rites themselves stand on "tradition and public opinion": and the tradition and public opinion in all cases alike subsist in virtue of being those of the same series or congeries of peoples or persons, whose ethic tells of their religion and mythology, and whose religion and mythology are part of the expression of their ethic. As we shall see, a mythologist as separatist as Dr. Tylor himself on the question of religion and mythology is able to controvert him as regards his separation of religion and ethic.

Always the trouble is arbitrary classification and limitation, illusory opposition set up between two aspects of a coherent process; and we seem to be delivered from one obstacle only to collide with another, set up by the deliverer.

§ 3. *A priori Evolutionism: Spencer.*

The fatality is peculiarly striking in the case of the greatest co-ordinating thinker of the time, Mr. Herbert Spencer. Coming in the due course of his great undertaking to the problem of the evolution of religious beliefs, he does indeed necessarily posit unity in the psychological basis of credences, having already well established the psychic unity of the thinking faculty or process from its lowest to its highest stages. But with all the results of Comparative Mythology thus far before him, Mr. Spencer must needs make all religious concepts pass through the single ivory gate of Dreams, reducing all forms of the God-idea to a beginning in the primitive idea of ghosts or souls.[1] Here, indeed, the primitive *Welt-Anschauung* is envisaged as all of a piece; but the manifold of myth and worship is traced to the root of a single mode of error. Thus mythology is poised on a single stem, where inductive research shows it to have had many; and where in particular the study of animal life, which Mr. Spencer was so specially

[1] *Principles of Sociology*, 1876–82, §§ 52–204.

pledged to take into account, reveals a general propensity prior to that special development on which he rests the whole case.

Thus again the science of Mythology, which is the basis of the science of Hierology, is confronted by a principle of schism, as the result of a great thinker's determination to shape the doctrine of evolution in terms of his own specific thought, to the exclusion or subordination of other men's discoveries. Dr. Tylor had fully recognized the play of the ideas of ghost and soul in ancestor-worship, and the bearing of ancestor-worship on other forms; but he had also recognized as a primary fact the spontaneous personification by early man of objects and forces in Nature. Mr. Spencer on his side escapes the false dichotomy between ethics and religion; and he rightly brings myth and religion in organic connection; yet his forcing of all myth-sources back to the one channel of ancestor-worship and the conception of ghosts has given as large an opportunity to reaction as did any of the limitary errors of professed mythologists before him: and specialists with anti-scientific leanings, who set up a false separatism where he does not, are able out of his fallacy to make capital for a fresh version of supernaturalism.

On the constructive side, Mr. Spencer's service is clear and great. He has given new coherence to the conception of the inter-play of subjective and objective consciousness in primitive thought. No one, again, had better established the principle of continuity in the process of intelligence. Where Professor Müller, in the act of insisting on the presence of the "divine gift of a sane and sober intellect" in the lowest men, yet represented them as getting their myths by sheer verbal blundering, Mr. Spencer rightly stipulated that all primitive beliefs are, "under the conditions in which they occur, rational."[1] Where other students had either waived the relation of the higher theology to the lower, or had used the language of

[1] *Id.* § 52. This, it should be noted, is clearly put by Fontenelle two hundred years ago; and from him the principle was accepted by Comte, who esteemed his work.

convention, he consistently traces one process of traditionary error from first to last. Where professed mythologists continue expressly to differentiate Hebrew from all other ancient credences, he decisively asks whether "a small clan of the Semitic race had given to it supernaturally a conception which, though superficially like the rest, was in substance absolutely unlike them?"[1] And yet his limitary treatment of the animistic process has enabled partizans of that other order, who see abnormality in Hebrew lore and who describe the myth-making process as "irrational," to turn his error to the account of theirs—this though the correction of his fallacy had been clearly and conclusively made by a student of his own school, and had been indicated before him by other evolutionists.

§ 4. *The Biological Correction.*

The point at issue is fully indicated by Mr. Spencer himself when he argues[2] that sub-human animals distinguish between the animate and the inanimate, though for them *motion* implies life; that the ability to class apart the animate and the inanimate is inevitably developed by evolution,[3] since failure would mean starvation; and that accordingly primitive man must have had a tolerably definite consciousnesss of the difference,[4] and cannot be supposed to confound the animate and the inanimate "without cause." Hence he must have had a fresh basis for his known Animism; and this came by way of his idea of ghost or soul, reached through his dreams.[5]

But on the face of his own argument, Mr. Spencer has gone astray. If motion be a ground for Animism with animals, and if the instinct be passed on to primitive man with the burden of effecting a closer discrimination among things, many of the phenomena of Nature were thrust upon him without his having the knowledge needed to make such discrimination. For him, the sun, moon, and stars, the

[1] *Id.* § 202. [2] *Id.* § 61. [3] *Id.* § 64.
[4] *Id.* § 65. [5] *Id.* § 73.

clouds, the rain, the winds, the rivers, the sea, the trees and plants, were all instances of more or less unexplained motion. What should he do, then, but personalize them? That problem had been put and the answer given by both Comte and Darwin, who lay to Mr. Spencer's hand; yet he overrides their reasoning as he overrides the crux.

Darwin's clue is given in his story of how his dog, seeing an open parasol suddenly moved by the wind, growled at it as he would at a suddenly appearing strange animal.[1] This clue is systematically developed in the essay of Signor Tito Vignoli on *Myth and Science* (1882), where Mr. Spencer's theory is respectfully but firmly treated as a revival of Evemerism; and where myth is shown to root in the animal tendency in question, on which Signor Vignoli had carefully experimented.[2] And it would not avail for Mr. Spencer to reply that he had already avowed the tendency of the animal to associate life with motion, but that this cannot lead to a fetichism which animises the non-moving. In stating the case as to the animal he had already admitted fetichism in so far as fetichism consists in animizing *inanimate things which are moved.* Thus his statement that fetichism is shown by both induction and deduction to follow instead of preceding other superstitions is already cancelled. It is a self-contradiction for him to argue that the savage, being unable to conceive separate properties, is unable to imagine "a second invisible entity as causing the actions of the visible entity."[3] One answers: Quite so. The savage makes no such detour: he sees or feels motion, to begin with, and takes for granted its quasi-personality: it is only on the ghost-theory, as its author admits, that he assumes "two entities." And having begun to ascribe personality where there is motion without consciousness, he *might* proceed to ascribe personality or consciousness where there is no motion, though on this head we may grant the ghost-theory to have a special footing. But the essential point is that to sun, moon, and stars, to winds

[1] *Descent of Man*, ch. iii. 2nd ed. i. 145. [2] Work cited, ch. ii.
[3] *Principles of Sociology*, § 163.

and waters, to trees and plants, the savage is spontaneously led to ascribe personality, *in so far as he speculates about them.*

Here Mr. Spencer has providently set up another defence, in the proposition[1] that it is an error to conceive the savage as theorizing about surrounding appearances; that in point of fact the need for explanations of them does not occur to him. This is certainly borne out in a measure by much evidence as to *lack* of speculation on the savage's part; but the solution is simple. *He theorizes about the forces that affect or seem to affect him;* else why should he ever reach fetichism at all, with the ghost-idea or without it? The dog, which animizes the suddenly moved stone in his kennel, probably does not animize the wind and the rain, unless they should become violent,[2] or the river, the light, and the darkness; and it may be that many savages could also go through life without doing so on their own account. But the simple noting that the sun rises and sets, if followed by any speculative reflection whatever, must by Mr. Spencer's own admission involve the animizing of the sun by the early savage, who has acquired no knowledge enabling him to explain the sun's motion otherwise; and that is the gist of the dispute. That ghost ideas when formed should affect and develop prior animistic ideas is likely enough: what must be negated is the proposition that they are the beginning of all mythology and superstition.

Thus rectified, Mr. Spencer's teaching, complemented by all the data of anthropology and mythology, gives the true form or standing-ground for mythological science. Taking myth as a form of traditionary error, we note that such error can arise in many ways; and when we have noted all the ways we have barred supernaturalism once for all, be it explicit or implicit. Unfortunately the rectification has been ignored by those mythologists who are concerned to retain either the shadow or the substance of supernaturalism; and until the naturalist position is restated in full, four-square to all the facts, they will doubtless continue to obscure the science.

[1] *Id.* § 46. [2] Cp. Vignoli, pp. 57–67.

The old fatality, indeed, is freshly illustrated in an almost startling fashion by Signor Vignoli, the corrector of the psychology of Mr. Spencer. His thesis includes the perfectly accurate propositions that "the mythical faculty still exists in all men, independently of the survival of old superstitions, to whatever people and class they may belong,"[1] and that it is "in the first instance identical and confounded with the scientific faculty."[2] That is to say, a myth is a wrong hypothesis made to explain a phenomenon, a process, or a practice. And with a fine unconsciousness Signor Vignoli supplies us later on with a sheaf of such hypotheses of his own. Christianity, he tells us, citing his *Dottrina razionale del Progresso*, "was originally based on the divine first Principle, to which one portion of the Semitic race had attained by intellectual evolution, and by the acumen of the great men who brought this idea to perfection"; and again, "*the* Semitic people passed from the primitive ideas of mythology to the conception of the absolute and infinite Being, while other races still adhered to altogether fanciful and anthropomorphic ideas of the Being."[3] Here be old myths: in point of fact the Jewish God *was* anthropomorphic, and was *not* an "absolute idea"; and monotheistic doctrine was current in Egypt long before the Semites had any. Or, if "Semites" had the idea as early as Egyptians, they were certainly not the Hebrews. On the other hand, Signor Vignoli is so oblivious of the facts of comparative mythology as to consider it a specially "Aryan" tendency to desire a Man-God.[4] He has forgotten that Attis and Adonis and Hercules and Dionysos, all of Semitic manufacture, had been as much Man-Gods as Jesus; and he has no suspicion that Samson and half-a-dozen other figures in the Bible had been Man-Gods[5] till they were Evemerized by the Yahwists.

[1] Work cited, p. 3. [2] *Id.* p. 33.
[3] *Id.* p. 175. [4] *Id.* p. 181.

[5] Goldziher indeed writes, *Mythology among the Hebrews*, Eng. tr. (p. 248), that "Samson never got so far as to be admitted, like Herakles, into the society of the Gods." But this view is completely negated by the records of the worship of Samas or Samsu in the Babylonian system. Herakles is late in joining the Greek Gods because he is an imported hero. Samson in the Bible has been Evemerized into a mortal.

But there is an element of new myth in Signor Vignoli's statement over and above these historic errors: he pictures the "Semitic and Chinese races" as having "soon freed themselves from their mental bonds" in virtue of the fact that their "inner symbolism of the mind" was "less tenacious, intense, and productive." All which is simply sociological myth: the reduction of a vast and incoherent complex to an imaginary simplicity and unity of movement. To generalize "the Semite" and "the Aryan" as doing this and that is but to make new myths. Such a phrase as: "*the idea* of Christianity arose in the midst of the Semitic people through him whose name it bears," is merely literary mythology; and "the intellectual constitution of the race" is a psychological myth. Signor Vignoli, in fine, has taken over without scrutiny a group of current historical myths, including the current conception of the Gospel Jesus, and the Renan myth that "the Semites" lacked the faculty for mythology;[1] and he has added to these fresh sociological and psychological and literary myths in the manner of Auguste Comte. He even becomes so conventionally mythological as to rank among the "peculiar characteristics" of "our" [the "Aryan"] race, "a proud self-consciousness, an energy of thought and action, a constant aspiration after grand achievements, and *a haughty contempt for all other nations*."[2] As if the Assyrians, the Egyptians, the Chinese, the Hebrews,[3] and the Fijians lacked the endowment in question. Evidently we must set the mythologist to catch the mythologist.

§ 5.—*Fresh Constructions, Reversions, Omissions, Erasions.*

Happily, gains continue to be made, despite aberrations; and while general principles are being obscured in the attempts to state them, new researches are made from time to time with so much learning and judgment as to give

[1] When Renan committed himself, the Babylonian mythology had not been recovered. Signor Vignoli accepts the myth with the Babylonian mythology before him.

[2] *Id*. p. 180.

[3] Cp. Goldziher, pp. 250–7.

solid help towards clearing up and re-establishing the general principles. Of such a nature, indeed, are most of the first-hand researches of the past generation into the beliefs, rites, and practices of the contemporary lower races. It is safe to say, further, that every systematic survey of Mythology has served to clear up some details as well as to facilitate the recognition of general law by later students. This holds good of J. F. Lauer's posthumous *System der griechischen Mythologie* (1851), though it sets up a superficial classification in defining *Mythos* as a wonderful story dealing with a God, and *Sage* as a story dealing with men. It holds good of the *Griechische Götterlehre* of Welcker; of the admirably comprehensive *Griechische Mythologie* and *Römische Mythologie* of Preller; of the eminently sane and scholarly *Mythologie de la Grèce Antique* of M. Decharme; of the brilliant *Zoological Mythology* of Signor de Gubernatis; of the astronomical and other studies of Mr. Robert Brown, Jr.; of Goldziher's *Hebrew Mythology*, despite the undue confidence of some of its interpretations (as that Joseph is certainly the Rain, Jacob the Night, and Rachel the Cloud); of the theorem of the historical critics that Rachel and Leah and their handmaids may be myths of tribal groups and colonies; and of a multitude of general surveys and monographs, down to the monumental *Ausführliches Lexikon der griechischen und römischen Mythologie*, edited by Dr. Roscher. Yet probably no survey is yet sufficiently comprehensive; and even the most masterly researches are found at times to set up obstacles to the full comprehension of the total mythological process.

No abler or more truly learned monograph has ever been written in mythology than Mr. Frazer's *Golden Bough* (1890). Proceeding partly on the memorable researches of Mannhardt, which as usual were ignored in England till long after they were accepted elsewhere, and partly on those of the late Professor Robertson Smith, it connects Mannhardt's and Smith's data with much cognate lore, and constructs a unitary theory with signal skill and circumspection. In Mr. Frazer's hands a whole province of mythology becomes newly intelligible; and henceforth multitudes of cases fall easily into line in terms of a true insight into primitive psychology. But there accrues in some degree the old drawback of undue limitation of theory. Rightly intent on establishing a hitherto undeveloped principle of mythological interpretation, the cult of the Vegetation Spirit, Mr. Frazer has unduly ignored the conjunction—seen deductively to be inevitable and inductively to be normal—between the concept of the Vegetation-God and that of others, in particular the Sun-God. He becomes for once vigorously polemical in his attack on the thesis that Osiris was a Sun-God, as if that were excluded once for all by proving him to be a Vegetation-God. The answer is that he was both; and that such a synthesis was inevitable.

A few unquestioned facts will put the case in a clear light. Mithra, who, so far as the records go, was primordially associated with the Sun, and was thereby named to the last, is mythically born on December 25th, clearly because of the winter solstice and the rising of the constellation of the Virgin above the horizon. Dionysos and Adonis, Mr. Frazer shows, are Vegetation-Gods. Yet they too are both born on December 25th, as was the Babe-Sun-God Horos, who however was exhibited as rising from a lotos plant.[1] Now, why should the Vegetation-God be born at the winter solstice save as having been identified with the Sun-God?[2] Again, Mr. Frazer very scientifically explains how Dionysos the Vegetation-God could be represented by a bull; animal sacrifices being a link between the Vegetation-Spirit and the human sacrifice which represented him. But then Mithra also was represented by a bull, who is at once the God and his victim; also by a ram, as again was Dionysos. Yet again, Yahweh and Moloch were represented and worshipped as bulls; and it would be hard to show that *they* were primarily Vegetation-Gods, though Yahweh does, like Dionysos, appear "in the bush." Now, the mere identification of different Gods with the

[1] See hereinafter, *Christ and Krishna*, Sec. xii.

[2] It is noteworthy that Apollo had *two* birthdays—at the winter solstice for the Delians, and at the vernal equinox for Delphi. Eméric-David (*Introduction*, p. cvi.) sets down the latter to the jealousy of Delphian priests. It probably stands for another process of syncretism.

same animal, however different might be the original pretexts, would in the ancient world inevitably lead to some identification of the cults; even were it not equally inevitable that the Sun should be recognized as a main factor in the annual revival of vegetation. In the case of Osiris there is the further obvious cause that Isis, his consort, is an Earth-Goddess, this by Mr. Frazer's own admission. The God must needs stand for something else than the Goddess his spouse. For Mr. Frazer, finally, the sun enters the vegetation cult as standing for the fire stored in the sacred fire-sticks.[1] But to assume that only in that roundabout way would primitive man allow for the obvious influence of the Sun on vegetation, is to shut out one of the most obvious of the natural lights on the subject. Once more the expert is unduly narrowing the relations under which he studies his object.

Such questions come to a focus when we bring comparative mythology to bear on surviving religion. The whole line of Mr. Frazer's investigation leads up, though unavowedly, to the recognition of the crucified Jesus as the annually slain Vegetation-God on the Sacred Tree. But Jesus is buried in a rock-tomb, as is Mithra, the rock-born Sun-God[2]; and it is as Sun-God that he is born at the winter solstice; it is as Sun-God (though also as carrying over the administrative machinery of the Jewish Patriarch[3]) that he is surrounded by Twelve Disciples: it is as Sun-God that, like Osiris, he is to judge men after death—a thing not done by Adonis or Attis; it is as Sun-God passing through the zodiac that he is represented successively in art and lore by the Lamb and the Fishes; and it is as Sun-God that he enters Jerusalem before his death on two asses—the ass and foal of the Greek sign of Cancer (the turning-point in the sun's course), on which Dionysos also rides.[4] The Christ cult, in short, was a synthesis of the two most popular Pagan myth-motives, with some Judaic elements as nucleus

[1] *Id.* ii. 369. [2] See hereinafter, *Mithraism*, Sec. 4.

[3] See the author's *Studies in Religious Fallacy*, pp. 164–5, and articles in *National Reformer*, May 8th and 15th, November 20th and 27th, and December 4th, 1887.

[4] Lactantius, *Divine Institutes*, i. 21.

and some explicit ethical teaching superadded. Not till Mr. Frazer had done his work was the whole psychology of the process ascertained.

Such is the nature, indeed, of the religious consciousness that it is possible for some to recognize the exterior fact without any readjustment of religious belief. To the literature of Christian Origins there has been contributed the painstaking work, *Monumental Christianity, or the Art and Symbolism of the Primitive Church as Witnesses and Teachers of the one Catholic Faith and Practice*, by John P. Lundy, "Presbyter" (New York, 1876). Its point of view is thus put by its author in his preface:—"It is a most singular and astonishing fact, sought to be developed in this work, that the Christian faith, as embodied in the Apostles' Creed, finds its parallel, or dimly foreshadowed counterpart, article by article, in the different systems of Paganism here brought under review. No one can be more astonished at this than the author himself. It reveals a unity of religion, and shows that the faith of mankind has been essentially one and the same in all ages. It furthermore points to but one Source and Author. Religion, therefore, is no cunningly devised fable of Priest-craft, but it is rather the abiding conviction of all mankind, as given by man's Maker." On the other hand the author holds by the Incarnation, as being "a more intelligible revelation than Deism, or Pantheism, or all that mere naturalism which goes under the name of Religion."[1] Thus the good presbyter's conscientious reproductions of Pagan emblems serve to enlighten others without deeply enlightening himself, albeit he has really modified at some points his old sectarian conception.

What Mr. Lundy imperfectly indicates—imperfectly, because he has taken no note of many Pagan works of art which are the real originals of episodes in the Gospels—has been set down with great theoretic clearness by M. Clermont-Ganneau in his *L'Imagerie Phénicienne et la mythologie iconologique chez les Grecs* (1880). It is there shown, fully

[1] Work cited, p. 11.

if not for the first time, how a mere object of art with a mythological purport (as in a group or series of figures), passed on from one country to another, may give rise to a new myth of explanation, and may attach to a God of one nation stories which hitherto belonged to another nation. This theory, which M. Clermont-Ganneau ably establishes by some clear instances, has probably occurred independently to many inquirers:[1] in any case it is a principle of the most obvious importance, especially in the investigation of the myths of the Gospels.

As against these important advances, there is to be noted a marked tendency on the part of philologists to revert to etymology as the true and perfect "key to all mythologies." Thus the *Erklärung alles Mythologie* of Herr F. Wendorff (Berlin, 1889) is wholly in terms of the supposed root-meanings of names in ancient myth: and the *Prolegomena zur Mythologie als Wissenschaft, und Lexikon der Mythensprache* of Dr. P. W. Forchhammer (Kiel, 1891) turns on the same conception, with, however, a further insistence on Ottfried Müller's doctrine that it is necessary to study the myth in the light of the topography of its place of origin. Dr. Forchhammer's motto runs: "Only through the knowledge of the local and chronological actualities in myths, and through the knowledge of the myth-language of the Greek poets, is the hidden truth of the mythus to be discovered." The criticism of such claims is (1) that all myths tended more or less to find acceptance in different localities, with or without synthesis of local topographical details—even Semitic myths finding currency and adaptation in Greece; and (2) that the hope to reach certainty about the original values of mythic names all round is vain. Some have an obvious meaning: concerning others philologists are hopelessly at variance. We must seek for broader

[1] The derivations of Christian myths from Pagan works of art hereinafter offered were all made out before I had seen or heard of the work of M. Clermont-Ganneau. See again H. Petersen's *Ueber den Gottesdienst des Nordens während der Heidenzeit* (1876), Ger. trans., 1883, p. 82, for an independent statement of the principle. It is endorsed, again, in Collignon's *Mythologie figurée de la Grèce*, 1884, pp. 113–4.

grounds of comprehension if we are to comprehend the bulk of the phenomena at all.

Finally, account must be taken, in any professedly comprehensive survey, of the play of a principle which in some hands is indeed much overstrained, but which certainly entered largely into ancient religion and symbol, that of phallicism. While some inquirers exaggerate, others evade the issue. But science cannot afford to be prudish; and in this particular connection prudery ends in facilitating nearly every species of general error above dealt with. That the subject can be handled at once scientifically and instructively has been shown by the massive work of General Forlong, entitled *Rivers of Life* (1883), in which the evolution of religious ideas is presented in broad relation with the general movement of the species. It is clear, indeed, that every line of research into human evolution is fitted to elucidate every other; and that there will be no final anthropological science until the intellectual and the material conditions of the process are studied in their connections throughout all history. Every problem of religious growth in a given society raises problems of economics and problems of political psychology. Thus far, however, we are hardly even within sight of such a sociological method as regards mythology. There it is still necessary to strive for the application of ordinary scientific tests as against the pressures of conservatism and reaction.

§ 6. *Mr. Lang and Anthropology.*

The protagonist, if not the main body, of the reactionary school is Mr. Andrew Lang, whose *Custom and Myth* (1884) and *Myth, Ritual, and Religion* (1889, revised ed. 1899) set forth his earlier views of the subject, otherwise condensed in his article on Mythology in the *Encyclopedia Britannica*. Written with a vivacity which somewhat irritates scholars on the other side,[1] and with a limpidity

[1] See Professor Regnaud's *Comment naissent les mythes?* 1878, p. xvii.

which is no small advantage in controversy, Mr. Lang's books perhaps make amends for setting up needless friction, by the fresh impulse they give to mythological study. In large part they stand on the sure ground of evolution and comparative anthropology; and they do unquestionably make out their oft-reiterated main thesis, that myth has its roots in savage lore and savage fancy, and that all bodies of myth preserve traces of their barbarous origin—a proposition specially applied by Mr. Lang to certain of the cruder Greek myths, such as that of Kronos and Saturn, concerning which a variety of "explanations" have been offered by mythologists. This main position no one seems to dispute. If there is any positive counter-theory, it is to be found in Mr. Lang's own later and obscurer argument that a high "religion" arises in the most primitive stage of life, either in or out of connection with a faculty possessed by the very same savages for "supernormal" knowledge[1]—a theory so completely out of relation with his earlier exposition of Mythology that, to understand or expound the latter, we must for the time keep them apart. Taking his earlier mythology by itself, we can credit it with coherence and a general reasonableness. While, however, Mr. Lang may on this score claim to have established all he sought negatively to prove, he in turn is open even there to some criticism, not only for the method of his handling of the point supposed to be in dispute, but for his failure to carry out to its proper conclusions the evolutionary principle by which he professes to abide. It is thus necessary to rectify the course of the science by calling in question some of his doctrine.

To begin with, Mr. Lang has in the opinion of some of us overstated the stress of the difference between his point of view and that of the solar school. He has been over-solicitous to create and continue a state of schism. As a matter of fact, his main tenet is not only perfectly compatible with most of their general doctrine, but implicit in

[1] Cp. in the author's *Studies in Religious Fallacy*, the paper, *Mr. Lang on the Origin of Religion*, and the Appendix.

that. Inasmuch as Sir George Cox and Dr. Müller more or less definitely accept the principle of evolution in human affairs, the former in particular constantly comparing savage myth and folk-lore with the classic mythologies, there is no good ground for saying that they ignore or reject the anthropological method. Sir George expressly points to the primeval savage as the first and typical myth-maker; and he uses phrases similar to Mr. Lang's concerning the "psychological condition" of early man. But Mr. Lang is always charging upon that school a positive rejection of anthropological science. Quoting[1] Fontenelle's phrase,

> "It is not science to fill one's head with the follies of Phœnicians and Greeks, but it is science to understand what led Greeks and Phœnicians to imagine these follies,"

he goes on: "A better and briefer system of mythology could not be devised; but the Mr. Casaubons of this world have neglected it, and even now it is beyond their comprehension." Now, as we shall see, Fontenelle's sentence may really be made an indictment against the method and performance of Mr. Lang himself; but it certainly does not tell against Sir George Cox, who, as the leading English exponent of a system of (implicitly) universal mythology, would naturally figure for Mr. Lang's readers as a typical "Mr. Casaubon" in this connection. The whole purpose of Sir George Cox's work is to "understand what led Greeks and Phœnicians to commit these follies": the only trouble is that, in the opinion of Mr. Lang and some of the rest of us—though we do not all go as far in Pyrrhonism as Mr. Lang—certain of his keys or clues are fanciful. Where Mr. Lang has made of these divergences a ground for challenging the whole body of the work, he was entitled only to call in question given interpretations. Mr. Lang on his own part really seems unable to see the wood for the trees.

There is absolutely nothing in Sir George's works that is incompatible with Fontenelle's doctrine as to the origination

[1] *Myth, Ritual, and Religion*, 1st ed. ii. 324, App. A; 2nd ed. ii. 343.

of mythology among primitive and savage men: on the contrary, that is more or less clearly implied all through them. Indeed, those of us who came to the study of mythology as evolutionists, taking Darwin's theory as substantially proved, found no more difficulty—apart from problems of interpretation—in Sir George Cox's pages than in those of Dr. Tylor, where the mental life of savages is the special theme. In this connection the idea dated back at least a century, to Heyne, with his derivation of the mythus "*ab ingenii humani imbecillitate et a dictionis egestate*," so much objected to by K. O. and Max Müller. We took savage origins as a matter of course, and were puzzled to find Mr. Lang in chapter after chapter insisting on this datum as if it were a struggling heresy, ignored or opposed by all previous mythologists. Nay, we were the more puzzled, because while Sir George Cox, clergyman and theist as he is, leads us definitely through mythology into or up least up to the reigning religion, carrying the principle of evolution further than we could well expect him to do, Mr. Lang not only shows himself more of an *a priori* theist than Sir George, but definitely refuses to apply the evolution principle beyond certain boundaries. Instead of seeking above all things to "understand what led Greeks and Phœnicians to commit these follies," he again and again flouts attempts at explanation, and falls back on the simple iteration that "all this came from savages," which is no explanation at all, but merely a statement of the direction in which explanation is to be sought. Part of his grievance against other schools is that they are too ready with explanations. When he does accept an explanation that goes beyond totemism, he has often the air of saying that it is hardly worth troubling about. Let us take his own definition of his point of view:—

"It would be difficult to overstate the ethical nobility of certain Vedic hymns, which even now affect us with a sense of the 'hunger and thirst after righteousness' so passionately felt by the Hebrew psalmists. But all this aspect of the Vedic deities is essentially the province of *the science of religion rather than of mythology*. Man's consciousness of sin, his sense of being imperfect in the sight of 'larger other eyes than ours,' is a topic of the deepest interest, *but it comes but by accident into*

> *the realm of mythological science.*[1] That science asks, not with what feelings of awe and gratitude the worshipper approaches his gods, but what myths, what stories, are told to or by the worshipper concerning the origin, personal characteristics, and personal adventures of his deities. As a rule, these stories are a mere *chronique scandaleuse*, full of the most absurd and offensive anecdotes, and of the crudest fictions."[2]

It is odd that a writer of Mr. Lang's general tone should thus explicitly maintain that his chosen specialty consists mainly in the mere collection of absurd and offensive anecdotes.[3] He must surely be doing himself an injustice. However that may be, it is clearly on him if on any one that there falls, *pro tanto*, the rebuke of Fontenelle: "It is not science to fill one's head with the follies of Phœnicians and Greeks."

On this head, it cannot be too emphatically said that Mr. Lang's sundering of religion from mythology, his proposition that they come together only "by accident," or that "mythological *science*" has nothing to do with the ethical purport or colouring of myths, is as arbitrary as anything that has been said on the other side of the discussion. Mythology as defined by him is not science at all, but mere mytho*graphy*. Two assertions on this head I shall undertake to support, despite the formidable authority of Dr. Tylor and Mr. Lang, who, as it happens, differ on one issue while concurring on the other:—

1. Primeval myth and primeval ethic are all of a piece: the primitive man's mythology is in terms of his ethic as well as of his science, his logic, his imagination, such as these are.[4]

2. Whatever purification, modification, and sophistication

[1] While retaining this passage in the revised (1899) edition of his earlier work, Mr. Lang complains, in his *Making of Religion* (1898), about "that strangely neglected chapter, that essential chapter, the Higher beliefs of the Lowest savages" (p. 183). Cp. the attack on Huxley's teaching, p. 191.

[2] *Myth, Ritual, and Religion*, 1st ed. ii. 129; 2nd ed. ii. 152.

[3] Sir George Cox, in a note (p. 19) on an early article by Mr. Lang, justly enough protests that "the great body of Vedic, Teutonic, or Hellenic myths is *not* silly, gross, obscene, disgusting, and revolting"; but on this we may let Mr. Lang have his way, if it comforts him.

[4] Save in so far, that is, as savages, like civilized people, vary in mental type. Serious and frivolous savages might well frame myths of a different cast. But as we see in all ages a profession of austere religious belief conjoined with unscrupulous or frivolous practice, we must credit savages with similar inconsequence, explaining it by the human brain structure.

of myth takes place in later ages is largely the outcome of the pressure of a more advanced ethic on the old myth lore, which on the side of form or bare statement is otherwise apt to be blindly reiterated, especially in the absence of authoritative science. Where that is developed, it may cause further inventions and modifications.

A partial if not complete contradiction of these propositions is given in Mr. Lang's later theorem—to be dealt with hereinafter—that the lowest savages are found holding together a high-grade religious theory and a low-grade mythology; and that the former is probably the earlier development. But even on that view, which I hold to be fallacious, it would seem to me clear that to set aside as "accident" the ethical elements or bearings of mythology is to throw away an essential part of the explanation of "what led the Greeks and Phœnicians to commit these follies," and what led them to put a different face on them.

Nor is that all. The spirit of Fontenelle's remark carries us beyond the search for the bare explanation of the groups of pagan myths: it sets us upon tracing the whole connection of mythology with social and intellectual life, with historical religion, with ethics and philosophy as affected by historical religion. In the words of Ottfried Muller, we must "ascend on the ladder of facts to a knowledge of internal being and life." Broadly speaking, there were no "accidents" in these matters save in the strict logical sense that in certain cases there is an intersection of causal connections. It is true that it is not the mythologist's business to discuss the development and variation of reasoned and written religious doctrine, as apart from narrative bases and symbols. That is the work of the hierologist; not that the subjects are separate, but that it is necessary to make a division of labour. But to put aside the mass of written theology, the argumentative side of the later historical systems, is one thing; and to keep out of sight the vital connections and reactions of myth and doctrine is quite another. The one respect in which Mr. Lang's books on Mythology and Religion are consistent is that in each in turn he looks only at one side of the shield—a course so arbitrary and so confusing that it can be explained only in terms of some extra-scientific bias. At the beginning of the historic period, ethics and religion are everywhere inseparably blended with myth; and in so far as religion has remained bound up with myth and with primitive ethic down to our own day, when rational ethic has definitely broken away from the old amalgam, it is supremely important and supremely interesting to trace not merely the earlier forms of myth, ritual, and religion, but their conjunct development into and survival in the latest forms of all. To stop short of that, as Mr. Lang and so many other mythologists do, is wilfully to impoverish and humble the science, keeping it always concerned with "the follies of Phœnicians and Greeks," always among the ancients or the Hottentots, always out of sight or even surmise of the bearings of these matters on the creeds and institutions of the civilized nations of our own day.[1]

After all his iterations about the origination of myths in savagery, it is perplexing, if we cannot call it astonishing, to find Mr. Lang repudiating for religion the fundamental principle of all mental science, on which he has so zealously staked his case in mythology. Modifying the uncompromising dictum above quoted, but still adhering to his arbitrary division of things, he writes in another chapter concerning Greek myths that

> "it must be remembered that, like all myths, they have *far less* concern with religion *in its true guise*—with the yearning after the divine which 'is not far from any one of us,' after the God 'in whom we live, and move, and have our being'—than with the *religio*, which is a tissue of old barbarous fears, misgivings, misapprehensions. The religion which retained most of the myths was that *ancient* superstition which is afraid of 'changing the luck,' and which, therefore, keeps up acts of ritual that have lost their significance in their passage *from a dark and dateless past*."[2]

It would appear from these variations of statement that Mr. Lang has really not thought out his position in the

[1] "Christian conduct *and faith*," writes Mr. Lang, "are no longer affected by the answers" we give to questions about myth origins. *Myth, Ritual, and Religion*, 1st ed. i. 1.

[2] *Myth, Ritual, and Religion*, 1st ed. ii. 65; 2nd ed. ii. 186.

matter; and when we compare them—retained as they are in the lately revised edition of his earlier work—with his recent book on *The Making of Religion*, which inclines to credit primeval savages with a high-grade religion and a "pure" ethic,[1] and to explain their mythology as a later excrescence on these[2]—when we put all the propositions together, the lack of sequence becomes bewildering. In any case, putting aside for the moment the oddly haphazard assertion in the last sentence of the passage before us, we are driven to note that very soon after drawing a line between the science of religion and that of mythology, and claiming to stand only in the latter's province, he here undertakes, in the merest *obiter dictum*, to lay down the law as to what constitutes the "true guise" of religion, just as he repeatedly disparages as "sacerdotage" many phases of the religions of Egypt and India. And we are bound to observe that, whether from his own point of view or from ours, that is none of his affair as a mythologist. From his own standpoint he has no title to speak on it; from ours, inasmuch as he holds that standpoint, he is disqualified to discuss the subject judicially. In this regard, he is doing exactly what he charges on the other mythologists—taking an *a priori* point of departure instead of going to the comparative history of the facts. At the outset he professes to stand on the evolutionist basis now common to the sciences, making no reservation of any department of mental life. But when he has gone a certain distance he asserts not only that "the question of the origin of a belief in Deity does not come within the scope of a strictly historical inquiry," but that "no man can watch the idea of God *in the making* or in the beginning."[3] If this be true, to what purpose is all Mr. Lang's polemic? What is

[1] *Making of Religion*, pp. 175, 185, 206, 208, 211, 235, 273, 289, 309, 334.
[2] *Id.*, pp. 280, 281, 290, 309. This view again is virtually quashed on p. 199.
[3] *Myth, Ritual, and Religion*, 1st ed. i. 307; 2nd ed. i. 305. I do not gather that in the revised edition Mr. Lang abandons this particular sentiment, though he explains (p. 307) that his opinions have become more emphatic as to the remote antiquity of *both* the purer religion and the "puzzling element of myth." Compare *The Making of Religion*, p. 43, as to "beginnings."

the meaning of the title of his last treatise, "The Making of Religion"? If we cannot watch the God-idea in the making, neither can we watch myth in the making. To speak of "the beginning" is neither here nor there, for the proposition must hold equally of myth, since, as Mr. Lang goes on to say, "We are acquainted with no race whose beginning does not lie far back in the unpenetrated past." In other words, the "beginnings" of myth, as we have seen, are pre-human, in terms of the theorem of Darwin and Vignoli, with which Mr. Lang never deals. Then—though Mr. Lang will here dissent—the God-idea must be in similar case; and Mr. Lang indeed proceeds to admit that "the notions of man about the Deity, man's religious sentiments, *and his mythical narratives*, must be taken as we find them." Then is it argued that at no stage do we find myth "in the making"? What else *do* we find when we compare successive stages of the mythology of any one people? And what had Mr. Lang meant when he said previously[1] that "we are enabled to examine mythology as a thing of gradual development and of slow and manifold modifications, corresponding in some degree to the various changes in the general progress of society"?

Such attempts at the separation of growths that are visibly confluent and complementary are necessarily abortive. We not only take myths "as we find them," but we try to understand how they came to be there and to be so: even Mr. Lang tries, albeit fitfully. And as old myths, commonly so called, are either directly or indirectly God-myths, they are among the first data for the history of the God-idea, and their history is part of its history. Even when the God-idea is nominally separated by philosophers from all myth and ritual, it remains none the less a development from the myth-and-ritual stage; and as every one of the historical religions has at *every* stage connected the idea with primitive ritual and what we recognize as myth, it is the merest mutilation of mythology to take the "absurd and offensive anecdotes" of the pagans

[1] *Myth, Ritual, and Religion*, 1st ed. i. 36; 2nd ed. i. 39.

and the heathens *in vacuo*, and then claim to have given us a "mythological science" of them. One of the most laborious of the later German mythologists syncretically decides that "Myth history passes through three main periods: those of belief in Souls, in Ghosts, and in Gods," insisting that "the conception (*Vorstellung*) of the existence of the human soul precedes the animizing of natural objects and phenomena."[1] But while thus drawing a dubious line between the orders of myth-material, he never disputes that all alike belong to "myth-history."

The one way to solve such conflicts of theory is to go to the evidences in anthropology, myth literature, and religious history. And first as regards the mental life of "primeval" man, there is positively no evidence that he passed through successive stages of soul-lore, ghost-lore, and God-lore, adding the second and third one by one to the first. Neither is it possible to show in terms of experimental psychology that a God-idea could come into being only as a fresh superstructure on concepts of soul and ghost: rather the naturalistic surmise is that a God-idea grew up *with* and in terms of the others, and was only by means of reflection or of priestly institutions differentiated from them. If, noting how the process of animism lies deep in animal instinct, we perforce credit the earliest men with a notion of living force behind the phenomena of sun and rain and wind, they had a kind of God-idea at least as early as a ghost-idea or soul-idea. Animals, indeed, seem capable of animizing inanimate things without doing so by rain and wind; but then there is no reason to credit them with a ghost-idea or a soul-idea, though they certainly seem to have dreams; so they give us no reason for putting the germ of the God-idea very late in man. Many of us, in all likelihood, have independently come to the conclusion so decisively put by such a competent student as Professor Giddings:—

"I believe that all interpretations of religion which start from the assumption that fetichism, animal worship, or ancestor worship was a

[1] E. H. Meyer, *Indogermanische Mythen*, 1883, i. p. 211 (*Mythologische Stellung*).

primitive form from which all other forms were derived, are destined to be overthrown. The earliest beliefs were a jumble of ideas, and it was long before the elements of the different kinds of religion were discriminated."[1]

Here we come to the factor of which so many theorists are always tending to get rid, as against those who for the concept "discriminate" and its variants substitute that of deliberate creation. Early man, like later man, albeit much more slowly, proceeded of necessity in his mental life by way of modification and readaptation of his lore; and the work must needs have been done in large part by the few thinking minds for the many. It took relative genius at one stage to create even a myth which to a civilized sense is offensive and absurd;[2] and slow as is all aggregate development, and fatally fixative as is the religious instinct, or the group of emotions so labelled, nothing can hinder that the mass of inherited lore shall be modified from period to period either upwards or downwards, either in terms of increasing knowledge or in terms of deepening ignorance, as the socio-economic conditions may tend; or, it may be, alternately or conflictingly, in terms of a strife of forces and institutions. Thus we have the phenomena of (*a*) the conservation of all manner of primitive thought in systems which yet seek to glose it; and (*b*) the fresh grafting of primitive survivals on systems which have been partly shaped by higher forces. For instance, the Hebrew sacred books crystallize round the most disparate nuclei of older lore; and again the Christian innovation is grafted on by older and lower conceptions of ritual theophagy; and yet again, in the Middle Ages, the Church gradually adds to its stock of myths that of the Immaculate Conception of the Virgin Mother of the God-Man—this in virtue of the same myth-making bias as framed the previous dogma of his Virgin-Birth. Other religions show kindred phenomena.

To say, in view of these long-drawn permutations, that the myth is essentially alien to the religion, or that ethics attaches to either and not to the other, is to override the

[1] *Principles of Sociology*, 3rd ed. 1896, p. 249.
[2] Compare Tylor, *Primitive Culture*, i. 285, 119.

evidence. Yet we shall find one mythologist or anthropologist after another claiming to make such severances; and though the desire to accredit religion is naturally the commonest motive, it is not the only one, since the claim is made in the same fashion by one or two writers on the side of scientific Naturalism. We can but proceed to judge of the different attempts on their merits; and in the same way we must deal with the chronic attempts of writers with an orthodox bias to make out a fundamental difference between Hebrew and Christian myths and those of "Pagans," or, in other words, to deny that Hebrew and Christian religion is mythological.

Chapter III.—The Separatist Fallacy.

§ 1. *The Theistic Presupposition.*

Looking for the grounds of the still common persistence in disjoining the mythical or narrative and the didactic aspects of religion, we find important clues as well as cases in the writings of a mythologist already dealt with. The theorem of Mr. Lang as to a mysterious "purity" and philosophical elevation about the ethic and religion which in certain primitive peoples are found in context with an "absurd and offensive" mythology, furnishes a peculiarly good object-lesson on the fallacy of the separatist method. Here, more definitely than ever, myth is classified as a species of by-product of the primeval mind, something out of touch with the normal psychology of those who produce it, or at least psychologically alien to certain others of their mental processes. Denouncing the doctrines of Dr. Tylor and Mr. Huxley as to there being no connection between the ethics and the religion of the lower savage, Mr. Lang nevertheless insists that there is no real connection between his ethics and his mythology. That primeval men had primordially a "high" conception of a Supreme Being,[1] which they at once "forget"[2] and retain; that the high conception came first, and that animistic degeneration "inevitably" and "necessarily" followed;[3] though all the while both aspects "are found co-existing, in almost all races; and nobody, in our total lack of historical information about the beginnings, *can say which, if either, element, is the earlier*"[4]—such is the motley doctrine with which Mr. Lang has burdened anthropological science.

The puzzle, as Mr. Lang presents it, is of his own

[1] *Making of Religion*, pp. 188, 194, etc.
[2] *Id.* p. 281. [3] *Id.* p. 276. [4] *Id.* p. 199.

making, and does not inhere in his data. We may grant him every one of these, as apart from his glosses—grant him that very primitive tribes may have the notion of a "Supreme Being"; that degeneration may occur at any stage of human evolution; that primitive tribes may be in certain relations much more unselfish in their normal life than highly civilized peoples; that they may be innocent of cruel religious practices found in more advanced civilizations; that they do not discriminate as theologians do between "spiritual" and "material" beings—all this without for a moment concurring either in his arbitrary addenda as to the "purity" of primeval ethics or the actuality of Hebrew narratives, or in the obscure inferences concerning the "supernormal" and the supernatural with which he embroiders the whole.

First in order and importance comes the fallacy as to the "Supreme Being." Because in civilized thought that formula is associated with philosophy, Mr. Lang assumes that any concept which can be described by the words in question must be "high," or "pure," or "deep," or "profoundly philosophic."[1] Now, there appears to be nothing necessarily high or deep about the matter: the bare theory of a Single God is not more but less ethically elevated than the theory of Dualism, which is an effort to find an ethical solution where the former does not even face the problem.[2] The former is perfectly compatible with any measure of barbaric crudity in ethics, and with any degree of "absurdity" in myth. It is itself an "absurd" (that is, fallacious) myth for all of us who have critically rejected it as an explanation of the cosmos.[3] In Mr. Lang's case we have the old fundamentally fallacious presupposition—belief that his own theology is the height of rationality as compared with that of polytheists—turned afresh to the

[1] Work last cited, p. 211.

[2] This is denied by Goldziher, *Mythology among the Hebrews*, Eng. tr. p. 15; but, while arguing implicitly that savages have no ethics at all, he admits a "secondary" ethical element. Here Mr. Lang's view is corrective: savages certainly have ethics, albeit not "high" or "deep."

[3] Mr. Lang notes (*Myth, Ritual, and Religion*, 2nd ed. i. 3) that "it may, of course, be argued that the belief in a Creator is itself a myth." This view he does not attempt to meet, proceeding with a "However that may be."

old account of making out that primeval man was not "left without a witness" as to there being only one God.

In point of fact, Mr. Lang's philosophic savages never do believe in One God. He speaks of their "monotheism" in the act of exhibiting their polytheism,[1] and seems to suppose he solves the contradiction by noting that so-called monotheists as a rule are practically polytheists. Broadly speaking, the savage's High God or Creator is either a God gone out of action or a figure put in to account for the presence of the other Gods, in the fashion of the Indian fable that the earth rests on an elephant, which rests on a tortoise. That primitive men should often account in that fashion for their Gods is not only conceivable but likely. A thoughtful child might readily reason so. On the other hand, a given God may become "supreme" precisely because other Gods are doing the actual work—a development which we shall have occasion to discuss later. Either way, the process of elevation is not primary, but secondary; not early, but late. And one fact to which Mr. Lang constantly adverts without apparently seeing its bearing—the fact that as a rule the savage *pays little heed*[2] to his "Supreme Being"—gives the rationale of the whole matter. That the disregard of the Creator God is not at all *because* he is good, is made clear by the case of the Haidas of North-West America, who have *two* Creator Gods, a good and a bad, and who disregard both alike in comparison with their minor created deities, with whom they are so much more practically concerned.[3]

Mr. Lang's theory appears to be that the Supreme Being in savage theology has been shouldered aside by demons, Ghost-Gods, and what not, in the way of degeneration.[4] But how a God believed to *rule* all things could ever be so shelved by beings *regarded as of a lower grade*, Mr. Lang never explains, though he claims to do so. A just Supreme

[1] *E.g. Myth, Ritual, and Religion*, 2nd ed. ii. 87.

[2] Work last cited, ii., 1–2, etc. We find even the belief "that the Great Spirit that made the world is dead long ago" (Frazer, *Golden Bough*, i. 213).

[3] Max Müller, *Psychological Religion*, 1893, p. 222, citing Rev. C. Harrison.

[4] *Making of Religion*, p. 224.

Being, he argues, would give no such chances to individual egoism as are given by "squarable" lower Gods. He has begged the question. Not once can he point to the existence of a belief that the Supreme Being as such is at once a ruling power and above propitiation:[1] he does not even bethink him to prove that among his primitive savages the conception of inexorable impartiality exists. He has simply given to the phrase "Supreme Being" all its possible connotations, and so burked the real problem. On turning to the known ethic of many savages we find a complete negation of the idea of impartiality. "The African Wakuafi account for their cattle-lifting proclivities by the calm assertion that Engai, that is Heaven, gave all cattle to them......So in South America the fierce Mbayas declare they received from the Caracara a divine command to make war on all other tribes, killing the men and adopting the women and children."[2] "Heaven" would seem to be a sufficiently "high" God; and here are the Wakuafi attaching to him just such an ethic as that of Mr. Lang's Mosaic Hebrews, whom he so strangely represents as returning to an ancient purity of morals. And the God of the Mbayas may have been just as "high."

The right line of inference from the data being thus saved, there is no need to follow Mr. Lang's very assiduous investigation as to the antiquity of any of the savage beliefs on which he rests his case. His anxiety to make out that the First God Ahone was believed in by the redskins before Columbus[3] would seem entirely needless, were it not that Mr. Tylor appears to doubt the aboriginality of all such conceptions. Some of us, however, see no conclusive ground for the doubt. We are ready to make Mr. Lang a donation, at full value—over and above the earlier evidence he cites—of such testimony as that of the missionary

[1] Mr. Lang relies on the apparent *absence* of propitiation in regard to certain primitive deities. *Id.* p. 188. But he never asks whether they regard propitiation as *useless*. On the next page he records a virtual process of propitiation of an "author of all good" among Patagonians.

[2] Tylor, *Primitive Culture*, i. 392, citing Krapf and Southey.

[3] *Myth, Ritual, and Religion*, 2nd ed. preface.

Brainerd, who saw much of the redskins in the second quarter of last century:—

> "I find that in ancient times, before the coming of the white people, some [Indians] supposed there were four invisible powers, who presided over the four corners of the earth. Others imagined the sun to be the only deity, and that all things were made by him; others at the same time having a confused notion of a certain body or fountain of deity, somewhat like the *anima mundi*, so frequently mentioned by the more learned ancient heathens, diffusing itself to various animals, and even to inanimate things, making them the immediate authors of good to certain persons. But after the coming of the white people, they seemed to suppose there were three deities, and three only, because they saw people of three different kinds of complexion—viz., English, Negroes, and themselves."[1]

Brainerd, though an "enthusiast," seems to have inquired without preconceptions, and may pass as a good witness. Here then we have among savages: (1) worship of the Sun by *some* as Sole God;[2] (2) the conception of a Good Supreme Being by Polytheists; and (3) finally general resort to a belief in Three Gods, perhaps an adaptation of Christian Trinitarianism to the needs of the case as seen by the redskin's science. Mr. Lang's theory implies that there has been degeneration in the latter case from a higher to a lower form of faith. In reality there has been no such thing. Social and material degeneration did indeed take place among the redskins after the advent of the white man; but the theory of Three Gods is no more degenerate than the theory of A God, whether apart from others or existing alone. It was a primitively scientific attempt to explain a newly observed phenomenon which the older views did not seem to account for; and the process shows very well how simply and childishly the older theories had been framed. Mr. Lang himself constantly reminds us that the savage does not distinguish as theologians do between "spiritual" and "material" beings;[3] which

[1] Wesley's abridgment of the Life of the Rev. David Brainerd, 4th ed., 1800, p. 179.

[2] This should lead us to modify somewhat Hume's substantially sound thesis that polytheism preceded monotheism. For all *masses* of men it certainly did; but at an early period a monotheist or an atheist might exist among polytheists. Cp. the author's *Short History of Freethought*, ch. ii.

[3] *Making of Religion*, pp. 174, 182, 290; *Myth, Ritual, and Religion*, 2nd ed. ii. 48–50. As Mr. Lang notes, the point was made long ago by Dr. Brinton. But it was made still earlier by Creuzer, as he now notes, *Id.* p. 54.

amounts to saying that they are only at the very first stage of the theistic hypothesis, and have not realized the most elementary objections to its adequacy. So with other aspects of their theism. The notion of a Good Power—as distinct from that of a mere First God to account for the other Gods—would be a simple generalization from the observed cases of propitiousness in Nature, and was neither a higher nor a lower conception than that of a Bad Power or a variety of dangerous powers who did the more abundant harm. If it were the case that the Good Power alone was held not to need propitiation, that would be a specially logical deduction from the datum that his only function was doing good. But there is no reason to suppose any such rigour of logic among savages, any more than among Christians. The question is not one of the character or the hierarchical status of the God, but of his supposed *activity*. To propitiate an Evil Power of any sort would seem to be a most natural course; and we know how simple Christians in all ages have had a sneaking tendency to "speak the Devil fair"; yet, as we have seen, the Haidas are unconcerned about their bad and their good Creator-Gods alike, while they fear and propitiate the nearer Gods of Sun and Sea, who are mixed. The speculative process is visibly from hand to mouth; and the remoter God, even if Creator of Evil, is relatively beneficent simply because he has been relieved of—if he ever had—active administration, not at all because of a primeval loftiness of conception as to his character. That becomes more and more evidently a chimera,[1] and the assertion that the Supreme Being of the lowest savages is "on a higher plane by far than the Gods of Greeks and Semites in their earliest known characters"[2] is absolutely astray. Those very Supreme Beings, by Mr. Lang's own admission, are concurrent with a "low" mythology;[3] and he escapes the force of this admission only by denying that

[1] As I have pointed out elsewhere, sacrifice, which is a form of prayer, is conditioned primarily by scarcity or abundance of food, especially of tame animals—a factor ignored by Mr. Lang in his comments on the absence of sacrifice among ill-fed races. Cp. *A Short History of Freethought*, p. 66.

[2] *Making of Religion*, p. 289.

[3] *Id.* pp. 197, 198; *Myth, Ritual, and Religion*, 2nd. ed. ii. 19, *note*, 33, etc.

the mythology is really "connected" with the religion—a paralogism which might as well be applied to the case of the Greeks and Semites. The savage's ethic, *as* ethic, is superior only where his tribal state is relatively communistic; and he is *never* equally altruistic as regards other tribes.

In another connection, the point as to degeneration is raised by Mr. Lang yet again to fallacious purpose. He having argued that the Australians cannot have got the idea of a Chief-God from a tribe-chief, since they have no chiefs, it is answered that they may once have had them, their present stage being one of social or physiological degeneration. Whereupon Mr. Lang replies that there is no proof of degeneration, inasmuch as no remains of pottery can anywhere be found to show that the Australians were ever higher than at present, when they have no pottery. The degeneration argument, he then triumphantly declares, must be the resort of "despair" on the part of his opponents. This is all pure misconception. It really does not matter, for the confutation of Mr. Lang's apriorism, whether the Australians have degenerated or not, though as regards the question of chiefs, that is possibly the true solution. He himself concedes that Australian Head-Men of tribes are latterly said to count for a good deal.[1] But as we have seen, the idea of a First God who made the others, or of a Good God who does all the favourable things, does not require the concrete fact of chieftainship to suggest it. Mr. Lang's case, then, is not bettered either way.

That the native Australians *have* however undergone degeneration is a proposition incidentally worth clearing up, in the interests of all sides of anthropological science. The case rests on the fact that the Australians are not autochthonous, but must be held to have anciently immigrated, probably by way of New Guinea and Cape York.[2] If, as has been conjectured, they were Dravidians, gradually driven further southwards by invading Papuans,[3] they were

[1] *Making of Religion*, Appendix D.

[2] Peschel, *Races of Mankind*, Eng. tr. 1876, p. 325.

[3] See Nott and Gliddon's *Indigenous Races of the Earth*, 1857, pp. 75–76, for Logan's theory. As put later by Bleek, it is rejected by Peschel, p. 323.

presumably "low" to start with. But inasmuch as races not yet "high" are seen progressing in the environment which the Australians left—the Papuans being their superiors, and actually, in recent times, to some extent their educators[1]—it follows that whether or not they were of the same stock as the Papuans they were in more progressive conditions before than after entering Australia. And that is the gist of the whole matter. Races degenerate not through an inward bias that way, but through their conditions. Now, "nowhere can the retarded development of mankind be more readily accounted for by the unfavourable configuration of the country than in Australia."[2] Only a race bringing to it a high secondary or tertiary civilization, with domestic animals and scientific resources, could there prosper. The mass of the Australians, then, having for ages lived in conditions exceptionally unfavourable to progress, after having lived in much better conditions, must be held to have partly degenerated.[3] It is not a matter of losing pottery but of losing ground in the total struggle with Nature. And that they had chiefs in their "better" days, when they warred with other races, is likely enough, though, as we have seen, the hypothesis is not a necessity for the naturalist explanation of their religion.

It now becomes tolerably obvious that the inference of some "high" and "pure" starting point for savage religion and ethics at what seems to theists their best, is not only arbitrary but obscurantist. Mr. Lang, saddling anthropology with his own theism, tells us that "these high Gods of low savages preserve from dimmest ages of the meanest culture the sketch of a God which our highest religious thought can but fill up to its ideal." On the ordinary definition of "religion" that may be; but if by "highest religious thought" be meant "highest thought" the proposition must here be negated. Mental and other science,

[1] Peschel, p. 325. [2] Peschel, p. 324.

[3] Compare Mr. Lang's own final admissions, *Myth, Ritual, and Religion*, ii. 346–7. The case of the Fuegians, where he admits probable retrogression, is closely similar to that of the Australians. As to the relative richness of the Australian language, see Peschel, p. 333.

happily, can transcend the ancient paralogism of the Good God who made evil; and it will not be permitted to our theists to impose their estimate of primordial theism on sociological science because primitive man anticipated their favourite myth. Those "degenerating"—or, it may be, stationary—Australian tribes have developed among them in a perfectly natural fashion a tribal ethic of altruism, which ethic is very astutely taught to the young by the old in the mysteries. It is extremely important to the old savage that the younger should supply him with food; and the principle naturally takes the shape of a doctrine of "sharing all round," there as in many other primitive communities living mainly by collective hunting. Where other anthropologists see "the tyranny of the old,"[1] Mr. Lang sees a hyper-Christian religion of "selflessness." It is perfectly true that the Australians are much more fraternal and communistic than any Christian community; but it is a bad fallacy to look for the explanation to or through some primordial conception of a "moral Eternal,"[2] a conception aloof from or precedent to "mythology." The true explanation lies in a line of inference from the facts that even among wild animals the male parent will feed the female and the young; that many flocks of birds and beasts live more or less in common; and that even wolves hunt in packs. These are conditions of relative success (= survival) for individual types and for groups of species; and the law holds good for savages just as for lower animals.

If then a savage is found conjoining an "absurd" mythology with an ethic of altruism for his own group, and with the conception of a Creator God, there is nothing incongruous in the matter. If "the whole *crux* and puzzle

[1] Lubbock, *Origin of Civilization*, 5th ed. pp. 451–2.

[2] In the revised edition of *Myth, Ritual, and Religion* (ii. 23) Mr. Lang protests that he "never *hinted* at morals divinely and supernormally revealed," and that he always held the given ethic to be the natural product of the social conditions. One asks the more insistently what he then means by arguing that religion *began* in a *high* ethical conception of deity? His statement that "*all morality* had been *denied* to the Australians" is a complete perversion of the issue.

of mythology," as Mr. Lang now tells us, lies in the colligation of absurd legends with the idea of a Good Creator, the trouble is easily got rid of. Unhappily many real puzzles remain after the false puzzle is put right. The conception of a Creator God is simply a less obvious absurdity than the more *naïf* myths concerning him: it is itself as much myth as they; and it is "irrational" in the sense of being illogical. The ethic of altruism for the group is as perfectly natural as joint hunting, fishing, or fighting; and the mountainous fact that the savage never dreams of a universal altruism—a fact not once envisaged by Mr. Lang—disposes once for all of the theory that he started with a "high" conception of a universal Father. Christians indeed think they have a high conception when they talk of a universal Father without for a moment attempting to practise universal brotherhood. But there is no reason to suppose that the unlettered savage even goes through the process of pretending to himself or to his God that he loves strangers or his enemies. For the rest, there is no vital ethical difference, but only a refinement of manners or *mores*, between the crude practice of sacrifice and the clinging to the theory of a divine sacrifice; and the fact that a given savage, lacking the wherewithal, does not offer sacrifices to his God, does not make him a better man than the slaughterous Hebrew of the days of Jesus. Nor does the latter-day Christian in turn salve his case by substituting for *his* compromising sacrificial idea that of "the sacrifice of a contrite heart"; for his God remains the Cause of Evil, and his ethic is thus incurably unsound. In fine, the ethic that for Mr. Lang is "highest" is intertwined with mythology just as surely as that of the savage who, whether sacrificing or not, imagines a God who punishes wickedness, though according to the same savage (says Mr. Lang) the same God is the Omnipotent Creator of all.[1] In fine, *all* theistic ethic is flagrantly mythological.

If this reasoning holds good, there is nothing left to

[1] Mr. Lang (*Making*, p. 188) assumes to discredit one testimony by the remark: "Why the evil spirit should punish evil deeds is not evident." Yet the evil spirit does so in his own religion.

refute in Mr. Lang's theorem that Animism arose partly if not wholly by way of the "supernormal" powers of savages.[1] After seeming throughout the greater part of his work on *The Making of Religion* to connect such powers with the alleged "high" primeval conception[2] of an "ethical judge," he elects to stand to the position that they rather made for the Animism which *followed* on that theistic conception and corrupted it.[3] By normal powers—such seems to be Mr. Lang's final doctrine—you get "high" conceptions; by supernormal powers you get low—save as regards the belief in a moral future state, which is "priceless."[4] To whom this theory of things gives comfort I am unable to conjecture. But that it is a mere negation of all the data it is very easy to show. It has been established with perfect clearness that the animizing instinct is present in animals; and unless *all* savages are "supernormal," it is in no way dependent on supernormal faculties. Supposing such faculties to exist, they might serve to add certain items to the mass of animistic lore; but there is not a single element in the so-called "corruption" of religion by mythology that is not easily deducible from normal psychic experience. Absurd and gross myths can arise either out of crude fancy or out of gross practice, such as can go on not only among savages, but among primitive rustics in Europe,[5] alongside of formulas about a Supreme or Good God. Low practical ethics can and do subsist alongside of these and of high ethical formulas in civilized countries, independently of "supernormal" corruptions: much more may they do so among savages.

[1] This view, like the more familiar thesis of a primordial monotheism, is found in previous writers. Rougemont (*Le Peuple Primitif*, 3 tom. 1855, liv. i. iii.), supposes the original monotheism to have lapsed into polytheism by way of Pantheism, through a superfluity of religious life, and excess of poetical inspiration.

[2] See in particular pp. 65, 71, 172, 292-3.

[3] *Fortnightly Review*, Nov. 1898.

[4] *Making of Religion*, p. 294.

[5] *E.g.* the unpleasant story of Zeus and Demeter, given by Clemens Alexandrinus (*Protrept.* ii.) and Arnobius (*Adv. Gentes*, v. 21). The symbolic action there described could occur among primitive rustics to-day. It was doubtless a seasonal ceremony, transferred to divine biography in the usual fashion. But if it could latterly be believed in as such an episode, it could be so conceived by the early practisers of the ceremony.

Beliefs in ghosts, souls, resurrection, demons, fairies, and a future state, can and do arise and flourish among savages and more advanced communities independently of any of the "supernormal" processes contended for by Mr. Lang. His whole colligation of these matters with his theory of the making of religion is thus worse than nugatory. We are asked to suppose that primeval man (whom all the while, by natural inference, we must hold to have had animistic habits of mind) *began* with a "high" conception of a righteous or benevolent Supreme Being, as savages conceive righteousness and benevolence: that is, that without a single preliminary animistic concept (though the ape-man had the animistic habit before him) the primal man proceeded straight to a universalist theistic abstraction.[1] Then, having thought out a "righteous" Omnipotent God, a "moral Eternal" who represents only his own morality, the cave man—or whatever else we figure him to have been—developed "supernormal" powers, which revealed to him all manner of forces that do not exist![2]

To insist that "powers" which thus effect in the main mere delusion and corruption, as against the "high" thinking of the earliest men (who in turn might just as well have had such disastrous powers), are rightly to be described as "supernormal," is surely an odd way of classifying things. But the classification is in keeping with Mr. Lang's handling of the phenomena of savage ethics and philosophy; and the total result, I repeat, is doctrinal chaos. The very conceptions of a Supreme Being which he sets over against those of Animism are instances of Animism;[3] and his chronic restriction of the title of

[1] Even this, of course, is strictly Animistic.

[2] This in despite of phrases about "*information* not accessible to the known channels of sense," and about our escaping "at moments from the bonds of Time and the manacles of Space" (Work cited, pp. 71, 292–3).

[3] Mr. Lang argues that *because* the early man did not raise the question of "spirit," "Animism was not *needed* for the earliest idea of a moral Eternal" (*Making*, p. 182). As if the question were ever supposed to be raised in early Animism at all! On *this* view, Animism is indeed not primitive, but late and metaphysical! Mr. Lang has here in effect altered the whole significance of the term. As framed by Mr. Tylor, it applies to exactly the unconscious assumption which Mr. Lang has in view.

"myth" to stories which make Gods figure as animals or as immoral, classifying all stories of "moral" and "creative" Gods as "religion," is not merely a begging of the question, but an ejection of scientific method from the problem. To call one aspect of primitive anthropomorphism "absurd," and another aspect "sacred," when both alike are the best the savage can do to explain his cosmos,[1] is an unscientific inconsequence. And to condemn Huxley and others for making a severance between savage ethic and savage theology,[2] while affirming just such a severance between savage ethic and savage myth, is to give the inconsequence an aggressive emphasis.

In the words of a mythologist with no supernaturalist axe to grind, "to our [savage] predecessors we are indebted for much of what we thought most our own"—a proposition which cuts both ways where Mr. Lang would have it cut only one—"and their errors were not wilful extravagances or the ravings of insanity, but simply hypotheses, justifiable as such at the time when they were propounded, but which a fuller experience has proved to be inadequate."[3] And in the words, again, of a student of a religion as to which there is no special motive to set up arbitrary distinctions, "There is nothing in worship but what existed before in mythology."[4]

[1] In one passage (*Myth, Ritual, and Religion*, 1st ed. ii. 282, 2nd ed. ii. 300) Mr. Lang himself takes up this position. None the less, he elsewhere makes the severance before noted. See above, pp. 43, 46; and cp. work cited, 2nd ed. ii. 141, 147, 156, etc. On p. 147 Mr. Lang expressly posits "a rational and an irrational stream of thought," and confines the "irrational" to "myth and ritual," making "prayers and hymns" on the contrary "rational." As if prayers and hymns were not ritual and myth-narrative!

[2] *Making of Religion*, pp. 191, 195; *Myth, Ritual, and Religion*, 2nd. ed. ii. 5. Mr. Lang is very severe on Huxley's "crude" position, while noting elsewhere that Dr. Tylor had said the same thing.

[3] J. G. Frazer, *The Golden Bough*, i. 211.

[4] Darmesteter, Introd. to trans. of the Zendavesta, 2nd. ed. p. lxxiii. It is to be kept in view, of course, that while ritual thus always presupposes a mythical process, the historic ritual may give rise to new concrete myths. "For myth changes while custom remains constant." Frazer, ii. 62. Cp. Bergmann, as cited above, p. 11.

§ 2. *The Metaphysic of Religion.*

Somewhat similar in form to Mr. Lang's doctrine is that of a learned continental mythologist and Hebraist who preceded him, Dr. Ignaz Goldziher, a professed adherent of the schools of Kuhn and Max Müller, with, however, theoretic formulas of his own, in particular this:—

> "I have given to the conception of the myth a narrower scope than is usually done. I believe it necessary to separate it strictly from the conception of religion, and especially to exclude from the sphere of primitive mythology the questions of Cosmogony and Ethics (the origin of Evil)."[1]

This startling procedure is justified as follows:—

> "The latter point was of especial importance in reference to the Hebrew Myth, since, as I show in the last chapter, the solution of these questions by the Hebrews was produced in the later period of civilization and from a foreign impulse. There is an immense difference between the ancient mythical view of the origin of nature and that later cosmogonic system. So long as mythical ideas are still living in the mind, though under an altered form, when the times are ripe for cosmogonic speculations, a cosmogony appears as a state of development of the ancient myth. But when the myth has utterly vanished from consciousness, then the mind is ready to receive foreign cosmogonic ideas, which can be fitted into the frame of its religious thought and accommodated to its religious views. This was the case with the Hebrews; and hence ....I have not treated as Hebrew mythical matter the Cosmogony of Genesis, which, moreover, is to be regarded rather as a mere literary creation than as a view of the origin of things emanating directly from the mind of the people."

There is here, I think, an obvious confusion, of a kind frequent in mythological discussion, which is so commonly carried on with an unfixed terminology and an irregular logical method. Granted that the Genesaic cosmogony is a literary compilation, made in or after the Exile, mainly from Chaldæo-Babylonian materials, these materials are in the terms of the case myths. Even if the Babylonians got them from the Akkadians, they must at *some* point have rooted in relatively "primitive" fancy. It is immaterial to the question whether at that or any other point in the development they were specially shaped or influenced by men of relatively uncommon genius: the same possibility

[1] *Mythology among the Hebrews*, Eng. tr. 1877, intr. p. xxv.

holds good in every mythological case. What we come to then is this, that the Hebrew Bible contains, besides many remains of primitive Hebrew myth, late adaptations of foreign myths made by way of cosmogonic teaching or quasi-scientific history. It is perfectly fitting, nay, it is incumbent on the mythologist, to mark clearly the distinction between the two orders of mythic matter; but to set aside the second order as non-mythological is simply to renounce one of the most interesting provinces of the study. If the mythologist gives it up, who is to take it in hand? The hierologist may handle the stories of the Fall and the Flood as expressions of the ethical attitude of the adaptors; but the stories about Adam and Eve and Noah remain myths; and the advanced apologist of our own day excitedly protests when they are treated either by believers or by unbelievers as part of "religion." Obviously they come within Mr. Lang's comprehensive species of "absurd and offensive anecdotes."

Nor can we be really sure that these myths are in essentials non-Hebraic. It is quite impossible to grant to Dr. Goldziher that at any point in Hebrew history, in some spontaneous way, "the [old] myth had utterly vanished from consciousness." How could it possibly do so save *after* it had been crowded out by a later myth? Rather we are bound to suppose that the Jews of the Exile, having some simple cosmogonic myths of their own, and finding more elaborate statements current among their more civilized and cultured conquerors, sought to blend all together. As a matter of fact, the redactors have preserved two creation stories, with different God-names, embodying different cosmogonic notions. In any case, the Babylonian myths themselves, though complicated by astronomical knowledge and speculation, clearly retained "primitive" elements in virtue of that tenacious tendency in mythic usage on which Mr. Lang is always insisting.

The attempt to draw a division of species between absolute myth and mythless religion in a visibly composite whole breaks down, on whatever lines it is attempted, leading as it does to the most contradictory results. Such an attempt it is that brings Professor Max Müller to confusion with his Schleiermacher theorem of a perception of the infinite at all stages of thought. That doctrine preceded and presumably inspired the formula of Dr. Goldziher; but it may be well to analyze it afresh in the professedly revised form given to it in Professor Müller's Gifford Lectures of 1888 on what he calls "Natural Religion," as distinguished from the later stages of "Physical," "Anthropological," and "Psychological." It would not be fair to say of Professor Müller that he has never made any progress in his opinions: he has really adopted several new ideas during his polemical career; but it is his tendency all the same to stick faithfully to the old ones; so that his later energies have run a good deal to showing that his different positions are not only reconcilable, but mutually supporting. This comes out notably enough in his fluctuating account of natural religion in the volume under notice. "Religion," he tells us in his fifth lecture,[1] "if it is to hold its place as a legitimate element of our consciousness, must, like all other knowledge, *begin* with sensuous experience." Mark the "begin," which is repeated later on.[2] As the argument proceeds, however, it is insisted that "every perception involves, *whether we are conscious of it or not*, some perception of the infinite";[3] and the conclusion of the lecture is[4] that this perception "*from the very beginning* formed an ingredient, or, if you like, a necessary complement to *all finite knowledge*." Now, it is very plain that if "from the very beginning" men perceive (not conceive) the infinite in perceiving the finite, a dog may do the same: that is to say, he perceives finite objects *whether or not he is conscious that they are finite*. Then a dog might have the beginning of religion. But already[5] the Professor had stipulated that "Real thought......begins when we......combine the percepts of sensation into concepts by discovering something they share in common, and embody that common property in a sign or a name." Then

[1] P. 114. [2] P. 141. [3] P. 125. [4] P. 140. [5] P. 116.

the beginning of religion, on the Professor's showing, is not real thought. Further, we may be conscious of the infinite (which is only a single necessary perception) without really thinking. This is tolerably explicit; but in a little while,[1] after the "whether we are conscious of it or not," the Professor says, "I am told that there are many savage tribes even now who do not possess a word for finite and infinite. Is that an answer?" Of course it is an answer—to him! He has been telling us that there is no "real" thought without words—that thought and language are the same thing—and that thought = reason. His opponents simply meet him on his own ground, and say that a perception of the infinite which is not "real thought" is a chimera.

But that is only one stage of the confusion. Soon it is intimated that "we must restrict the sphere of religion, so far as it is founded on perceptions of the infinite. We must reserve the adjective religious for those *perceptions of the unknown* or the infinite which influence man's actions and his *whole* moral nature";[2] and yet again,[3] we have the definition: "Religion consists in the perception of the infinite under *such manifestations as are able to influence* the moral character of man. I look upon this as a definition of *religion in its origin*" (italics here Dr. Müller's). That is to say, the previously alleged beginning of religion was not a beginning of religion at all, since it did not affect the moral character of man. And yet, after all, we have in the closing lecture[4] the dictum that "anything that lifts a man above the realities of this material life is religion." If that be not explicit enough, we have the story of the old Samoyede woman who saluted the sun at its rising and setting, saying she did what he did; with the lecturer's comment, "It gave her the sense of a Beyond, and *that is the true life of all religion*":—this though there is no moral influence whatever involved. The Professor thus ends in threefold and irreparable

[1] P. 125. [2] P. 168. [3] P. 188. [4] P. 568.

confusion. He explains[1] that his expansion of his definition of religion to include moral influence was made in acknowledgment of the force of the criticisms of Professor Pfleiderer on his previous definition; but he has neither adopted the Pfleiderer position nor adhered to his own. He has simply used the two definitions inconsistently and at random, it being so much his tendency to cleave to any doctrine he has once adopted that he does not logically readjust his thinking even to a change he is disposed to make. His first definition was *a priori*, much as he claims to be historical and anti-theoretic; and the equally *a priori* dogma of Pfleiderer refuses to combine with it. Wundt, who is a good deal more of a psychologist than either of these writers, decides that "all percepts and sentiments become religious as soon as they have reference to some ideal existence which can supply the wishes and requirements of the human heart";[2] and that account covers the great mass of ancient mythology.

Pfleiderer's influence is to be seen in the form given by Israel Sack to the summaries in his meritorious and often luminous work on the transition of Judaism from Bible-dom to Talmudism. It was in the exilic period, he writes, that

> "there came upon the Yahweh religion the pressure of a new element, born of the age, namely the *purely religious* cult, the personal godliness (*Gottesverehrung*) independent of social life. It was the first step towards the releasing of the religion of Israel from Palestinian soil, and generally towards the conceptual (*begrifflichen*) sundering of the religious from the social-ethical."[3]

That is to say, the emergence of the purely religious was only the beginning of a movement *towards* the purely religious. And on the next page Herr Sack notes that it was in the same exilic period, which first really sabbatized the Sabbath, that there was set up the *Zizith* symbol—the "ribbon of blue upon the fringes of the borders of their garments," which is given out in the Mosaic law as a pre-

[1] P. 193.
[2] Cited by Müller, p. 73.
[3] *Die altjüdische Religion im Uebergange vom Bibelthum zum Talmudismus*, 1889, p. 25.

scription by Yahweh to Moses.[1] The second testimony disposes of the first. The conditions of the exile would naturally develop a private as distinguished from a public habit of devotion; but the *Zizith* symbol is precisely the effort to make a substitute for the old nationalistic regimen; and of people in that frame of mind it is idle to assert that they have risen from tribalism, ethical or mythical, to "pure religion." Nor can the claim be any better made out for any later style of Judaism, or any other system that holds by sacred books. Judaism is tribal to this day; and Christianity, instead of progressively denuding itself of myth and symbol and ritual, shows everywhere the tendency to make more of them than ever, the Protestant impulse being on the way to euthanasia in rationalism, while the forces of the myth-mongers and ritualists expand as the restrictive element is removed.

Here, as at other points, we find Sir George Cox avoiding the fallacious extremes to which theological bias has led some lay mythologists. "In one sense," he says, "we may, and in another we may not, draw distinctions between the religion of a people and their mythology."[2] That is to say, we may differentiate aspects, but cannot negate the organic connection. We are hardly even entitled to speak, with Ottfried Müller, of "the history of the worship of the

[1] *Numbers*, xv. 37–41.

[2] *On Greek and Latin Religions*, lecture in *Religious Systems of the World*, 2nd. ed. p. 217. In the *Mythology of the Aryan Nations*, p. 3, Sir George somewhat obscures the point by saying of the Greeks that "we must draw a sharp line of severance between their theology and their religion, if we use religion in the sense attached to it by Locke or Newton, Milton or Butler." But he goes on to insist on the historic unity of the whole system, which is what we are concerned with. In another passage (p. 169) Sir George reverses the difficulty. Speaking of the Romans, he says that in their system "so thin was the disguise [of the natural forces worshipped] that the growth of a Latin *mythology*, strictly so called, became impossible." It is not here meant that the Latins were specially religious, in the elevated sense, but the reverse. Of course the proper statement would be simply that the surviving Latin mythology is bare and commonplace. The phrase cited is an echo of Mommsen (ch. xii. Eng. tr. ed. 1868, i. 184–6); but the idea is one of Mommsen's many self-contradictions. As against it he has twice stated the historic fact: "In Italy, as in Hellas, there lies at the foundation of the popular faith the same common treasure of allegorical and symbolical views of nature" (*History of Rome*, Eng. tr. 1868, i. 28, ch. ii.). "Abstraction and personification lay at the root of the Roman as well as of the Hellenic mythology" (*Id*. i. 183, ch. xii.).

Grecian Gods" as "the auxiliary science of most importance to mythology,"[1] for an auxiliary that is essential is practically a part of one process. In any case, the same sympathetic scholar has well argued that in Homer the conception of Zeus the moral governor and Zeus the cloud-compeller is one twofold thing; and he goes on to cite as essentially and even nobly religious the set of myths in which Zeus has offspring by different females—the "beautiful and sublime fable in the Theogony" wherein Zeus espoused Themis and by her begat the Destinies; and that according to which Eurynome bore to him the Charites. Inasmuch as Zeus here plays as usual the adulterer, the anecdotes become under Mr. Lang's system slightly offensive, if not absurd. But Ottfried Müller, who is reputed to have been a religious man, protests that "He who does not here recognize religion, genuine, true religion, for him have Moses and the prophets written in vain."[2] And Müller would seem to be entitled like another to his view of religion's "true guise." Nay, yet another Müller, Julius to wit, defending Christianity against the mythological interpretation of Strauss, insists that the "inmost and most essential characteristic" of a myth is just "the religious element"[3]—a straining of things the other way in religion's name.

§ 3. *Mr. Grant Allen's Theorem.*

This species of resistance alone would suffice to prove the inexpediency of the latest attempt of all to break up the phenomena of religion into unconnected species—the attempt made, namely, by the late Mr. Grant Allen in the opening chapter of his able and suggestive work on *The Evolution of the Idea of God* (1897). Without noting Mr. Lang's similar undertaking to sunder mythology from religion, Mr. Allen charges upon mythologists in general an erroneous identification of the two, and proceeds in his

[1] *Introduction*, p. 175.
[2] *Id.* p. 186.
[3] Julius Müller, *On the Theory of Myths*, Eng. tr. in *Voices of the Church in Reply to Strauss*, 1845, p. 184.

turn to pass one more verdict of divorce. Devils and Cyclopes and Centaurs, he insists to begin with, are not Gods "or anything like one. They have no more to do with religion, properly so called, than the unicorn of the royal arms has to do with British Christianity. A God, as I understand the word, and as the vast mass of mankind has always understood it, is a supernatural being to be revered and worshipped......Bearing this distinction carefully in mind, let us proceed to consider the essentials of religion."[1]

The reason for this preliminary distinction turns out to be that Mr. Allen, having in view one particular line of descent for the God-idea, desired to have nothing to do with any other. His position is, in brief, that "corpse-worship is the protoplasm of religion," and that "folk-lore is the protoplasm of mythology, and of its more modern and philosophical offshoot, theology."[2] Which recalls the railway guard's decision that "dogs is dogs and cats is dogs, but a tortoise is a hinseck." The decision to connect theology not with religion but with mythology is a course worthy of mythology itself. Arbitrary on any definition, it becomes extravagantly so in view of Mr. Allen's fuller definition of religion, which is that religion properly so called consists in observances, ritual, prayer, ceremonial, sacrifices, and so on.

> "What is not at all essential to religion in its wider aspect—taking the world round, both past and present, Pagan, Buddhist, Mohammedan, Christian, savage and civilized—is the ethical element, properly so called. And what is very little essential indeed is the philosophical element, theology or mythology, the abstract theory of spiritual existences. This theory, to be sure, is in each country or race *closely related* with religion *under certain aspects;* and the stories told about the Gods or God are much mixed up with the cult itself in the minds of worshippers; but they are *no proper part* of religion, *strictly so called*....Religion, as such, is essentially practical: theology or mythology, as such, is essentially theoretical [as if theory and practice were opposite or unconnected]....I also believe....that the two [*i.e.*, the theory and the practice] have to a large extent distinct origins and roots: that the union between them is in great part adventitious: and that, therefore, to account for or explain the one is by no means equivalent to accounting for and explaining the other."[3]

[1] *Evolution of the Idea of God*, p. 21. [2] *Id.* p. 438. [3] *Id.* pp. 22-23.

This differentiation, it will be observed, is in part in almost complete agreement with that of Mr. Lang, whom Mr. Allen supposed himself to be setting aside. Both writers decide that the connection between mythology and religion is "accidental" or "adventitious," but they have very different ideas as to what constitutes religion "strictly so-called." It begins to be pretty clear that these individual decisions as to what religion *is to be* are a mere element of gratuitous confusion, and that in the name of science they must be all disallowed. "Religious" persons protest that religion and theology are different things, but insist that what Mr. Allen calls religion is not religion at all; theologians protest that theology and mythology have nothing to do with each other, and that theology is just religion systematized and explained; Mr. Lang in effect bears them out; Julius Müller protests that religion is of the very essence of myth—as if there were no historical myths; Ottfried Müller finds religion in the higher mythology; Mr. Grant Allen scouts all alike, and declares religion to be simply ritual (which Mr. Lang declares to be mythological and "irrational"); while Dr. Max Müller finds it now in cosmic emotion and now in cosmic apperception, both of which he yet sees in myths; and Sack decides that it only begins after much of mythology and ritual is left behind. In the name of the intellectual commonwealth, we have a right to resist these illicit appropriations on the common domain of terminology.

Scientifically speaking, the term religion covers all the phenomena under notice. Religion in the mass has always been mythological, always ritualistic, always theological, always ethical, always connected with what cosmic emotion or apperception there was. These attributes are in themselves phases of human tendency which make and make-for religion. It is neither here nor there to say that in explaining one we do not explain the other. That is not pretended. But it is very easy to show, as against Mr. Allen, that stories about the God are in hundreds of cases efforts to explain the early ritual, while in other cases particularities of ritual originate in ideas about the God. Mr. Allen's dictum that "the Origin of Tales has *nothing at all to do with* the Origin of Worship"[1] is a mere violence of dogma. To come to the point, how could a ritual of prayer for wind or rain ever originate save in an idea about a God's character and function? Is not the very idea of a God as a protecting Father (insisted on by Mr. Allen as *the* typical God-idea) a matter of telling a story about the God? Is not the idea of a Bad Spirit correlative with that of a Good Spirit, and as such part and parcel of the religion of the believer in the latter? Is Old Harry "nothing like" the Pan from which he came? And above all, how could primitive men so keep their minds in watertight compartments as to make up their religion rigidly in terms of their thought and practice as corpse-worshippers and corpse-eaters, without letting it be affected by their thought and practice as story-tellers and makers of folklore?

The division drawn by Mr. Allen is finally fantastic. Ideas about corpses and ancestors are demonstrably part of folk-lore. Every primitive practice connotes certain ideas, and every primitive idea connotes certain practice. The one force or law of differentiation in the matter is this: that whereas the whole of the ideas and the practices would in the earlier and ruder eras of savagery tend to be coherent or congruous, the elements of ignorance and fear tend to have the effect of maintaining an ancient practice or formula or myth after the ideas turning on it have been greatly modified by changes of life and culture-conditions, either material or social or both; while on the other hand a practice or myth or doctrine that stands for one order of ideas with one set of minds may be imposed on another set with a very different order of ideas. But all alike is "religion." Not only are mythology and theology and ritual and law and ethic originally "connected": they are so of psychological necessity. By all means let us for purposes of elucidation trace their several developments,

[1] P. 29.

and the ever-advancing differentiation of some of them; but let us not plunge anthropology in darkness by denying their perpetual and inevitable inter-reactions.

We return perforce, then, to the anthropological position that primitive man fused instead of discriminating the states of mind which set up his myths and his cosmosophy, his ethic and his ritual. In the words of the supernaturalist Julius Müller—here true to the evidence which his sympathies obscured for him when he came to the concrete problem over his own creed—the historical form and ideal purport of every myth or primitive usage "are inseparable, and penetrate each other; and it is only by the abstraction of a later age, *from which all faith in the myth as such has vanished*, that they are separated."[1] Such a separation is visibly a process of prejudice, and it cannot hold for those who follow scientific methods.

Nor is it merely on grounds of systematic Naturalism that separatist courses are thus to be disallowed. If on the one hand an immature anthropology is found to join with the supernaturalist school in drawing lines of arbitrary severance between the co-operating elements in all historic religion, on the other hand men who still hold by the concept of revelation, but who nevertheless scrutinize religions in general in the spirit of scientific observation, insist that the definition of religion shall be faithful to historic fact. While one of the most eminent historians of religion, Dr. Tiele, persists in classifying all creeds under the two sundering titles of "Nature Religions" and "Ethical Religions"[2]—as if there were nothing ethical in the first, or natural in the second—others, not bent like Mr. Lang on making out the primordiality of "high" conceptions among men, nor yet upon rebutting the special claims of current creeds, recognize the essential continuity and coherence of all the phenomena. It is a Scottish clergyman of missionary experience, capable of elucidating the primitive

[1] Review of Strauss in *Studien und Kritiken*, 1836; Eng. trans. in *Voices of the Church against Dr. Strauss*, 1845, p. 16.

[2] Cp. Chantepie de la Saussaye, *Manual of the Science of Religion*, Eng. tr. 1891, pp. 56–58.

religions he has studied at first hand, who puts the case thus:—

> "Religion in the widest sense may be defined as a man's attitude towards the unseen; and the earliest forms of human thought furnish the clue from which must be traced the development of those great systems of religion that have at different periods been professed by the majority of men. Under the term religion we must include not only beliefs in unseen spiritual agencies, but numerous customs, superstitions, and myths which have usually been regarded, by both travellers and students, as worthless and degrading, till within a comparatively recent period."[1]

This, I cannot but think, is the only scientific attitude towards the phenomena. When a man of moral and reformative genius declares, "my country is the world; and my religion is to do good,"[2] he indeed gives a profoundly necessary stimulus to the moral sense of men hypnotized by tradition and ceremonial; and his conception of a "Religion of Humanity"[3] may be turned to many valuable ends, whether or not we reckon among them a cult which in the name of Positivism imitates anxiously some of the institutions of superstition. But to let such adaptation of old terms to new moral ends set up a hallucination as to the historic reality of religion throughout human evolution would be to effect a confusion which the original adaptor would be the first to repudiate, though he did lay it down that "All religions are in their nature kind and benign, and mixed with principles of morality. They could not have made proselytes at first by professing anything that was vicious, cruel, persecuting, or immoral";[4] and again, "Every religion is good that teaches man to be good; and I know of none that instructs him to be bad."[5] Here we have yet another conception of "the essence of religion." Paine had unhappy cause to unlearn his optimism; though he never flinched in his insistence that what he taught was true religion as against false. Any man is free

[1] Rev. James Macdonald, *Religion and Myth*, 1893 (Nutt), p. 1.

[2] Thomas Paine, *Rights of Man*, part ii. ch. 5, Conway's ed. of Works, ii. 472.

[3] The phrase is used by Paine in his series *The Crisis*, No. 7, dated Nov. 21st, 1778.

[4] *Rights of Man*, part i. ed. cited, ii. 327.

[5] *Id.* p. 504. Written before the *Age of Reason*.

thus to claim a customary name for an uncustomary creed, on the score that honoured names may fitly be given to the systems which best deserve honour. But when we are reducing to scientific form the facts of the mental history of mankind, the only applicable principle is that of the careful comprehension of all facts;[1] and for that purpose we must either reject the word religion altogether, as having no accepted significance, or recognize the plain fact that it is generically extensible to all the credences and practices by which men ever supposed themselves in touch with or aware of what they conceived as Gods, extra-human personalities, intangible lives, and the doings of these. The sum of the matter is that while not all myths are properly to be described as religious, though all are framed under analogous conditions of speculative error, all historic religions are bound up with myth alike in their ethic and their cosmosophy or quasi-science.[2]

In fine, the God-idea = "true guise of religion," chased out of mythology with a fork, returns at every window. And we are led and driven to the solution that this attempt to sunder in the name of God what man primordially joined is an expression of some form of acquired or inherited prejudice—what, it is not necessary to ascertain. In Germany it may be either the ordinary religious heredity or an outcome of the influence of Hegel, who in his simple way classified religions so as to leave Christianity in an order by itself, labelled "Absolute Religion." In England, on the other hand (apart from the case of Mr. Allen), were it not for the line taken by Goldziher and Sack (both, I understand, of Hebrew descent), the attitude in question might be supposed to come of the perception that, the God-idea being common to all mythologies and all religions, it

[1] Compare Arnold: "Some people, indeed, are for calling all high thought and feeling by the name of religion; according to that saying of Goethe: 'He who has art and science, has also religion.' But let us use words as mankind generally use them" (*Literature and Dogma*, 5th ed. p. 21).

[2] My friend Mr. F. J. Gould, in his *Concise History of Religion* (i. 8), gives as an alternative definition of religion "the authority of a moral law" which may be "viewed as a purely human creation"; but I do not find in his interesting and useful volumes any instance of a "religion" which comes under this definition.

must be at least nominally kept out of the discussion, since if we avow this common ground we shall be driven to consider whether the Christian religion is not consanguineous with the rest in myth and ritual as well as in the other thing. And this, of course, must not be considered by a prudent English mythologist, even if he be at the point of view from which the problem can be properly seen. And that is never to be counted on.

Chapter IV.—The Stand for the Bible.

§ 1. *Hebrew Mythology.*

Again our first illustration of the difficulty is furnished by the case of Mr. Lang, who more or less avowedly resists the application of anthropology to the problem of Christianity. He does not want to discuss these things; he dislikes and disparages the view that the Judaic and Christian religions are products of normal evolution; the evolution principle being in his hands valid only for the treatment of anthropology and "absurd and offensive anecdotes." For him, the mythological discussions of the first half of the century, including the argument of Strauss, have been carried on pretty much in vain. On one occasion he has actually glanced at the question of Hebrew mythology; and even on that, considered separately from the New Testament, he stands very much where Eichhorn did, over a hundred years ago. It is àpropos of Renan's *Histoire du Peuple d'Israël* that he writes:—

> "One has a kind of traditional objection to talking about the 'mythical' parts of the Old Testament. It is a way of speaking which must offend many people, perhaps needlessly; and again, it does not convey quite a correct impression. Whatever else the stories in Genesis and Exodus may be, they have moral and intellectual qualities, seriousness, orderliness, sobriety, and, it may even be said, a poetic value, which are lacking in the mass of wild queries and fancies usually called myths. Whence this orderliness, sobriety, and poetry arise, why they are *so solitary, so much confined to the ancient Hebrew literature*, is exactly what we wish to know, and what M. Renan, perhaps, does not tell us."[1]

Save for the absence of fanaticism, this is very much the kind of opposition that was made last century to the earlier suggestions that the Bible contained mythology like the

[1] Art. on "Mythology and the Bible," in *New Review*, vol. i. 1889, p. 279.

sacred books of other religions; and it is significant of the retardative power of orthodox habit among us that it is necessary to-day to examine and answer them at the hands of a professed mythologist.

In the first place, Mr. Lang here implicitly unsays what he has so often said in other connections—that in *Homer*, to say nothing of the Attic tragedians, there are qualities of seriousness, orderliness, sobriety, "and, it may even be said, a poetic value," all imposed upon mythical matter. He has expressly told us, as did others before him, that Homer rejected or ignored "absurd and offensive anecdotes" known to be current in his time; and that Pindar avowedly did the same; and if, after all he has said of Homer, he will not now credit the Iliad with the qualities aforesaid, the rest of us must needs do it as against him. Homer has maintained dominion over men's appreciation all through the Christian period, either in the full understanding that his Gods never existed, or on the assumption that they were "demons"; while the Hebrew Bible has held its place on the express declaration that it was the one divinely-inspired book in the world before the New Testament, and that it contained nothing but the purest truth. In the terms of the case it is impossible that the Greek epics could have held their ground if they had not exhibited seriousness, orderliness, sobriety, in a relatively high degree; and if they had been bound up in one volume with selected works of the tragedians and the philosophers, all of whom use the same God-names, the distinction Mr. Lang seeks to draw could hardly have been ventured on by anybody.

In the second place, if the "absurd and offensive" elements in the best Greek poetry deprive it of title to the qualities ascribed by Mr. Lang to the Pentateuch, there are assuredly absurd and offensive elements enough in that to destroy the credit he so liberally gives it. If Mr. Lang sees nothing but sobriety and orderliness in the two irreconcilable accounts of the creation; in the positing of light before there was sun; in the story of the serpent and the fall; in the talk of Yahweh with Cain; in the cryptogram of the crime of Lamech; in the theory and the procedure of the flood; in the two versions of the tale of the ark; in the anecdotes about the exposure of Noah and the proceedings of Lot's daughters; in the narrative of the command to Abraham to sacrifice his son; in the story of his duplicated dealings with Pharaoh and Abimelech; in the further duplication of the same pleasing anecdote in the case of Isaac; in the allegation that Sara at the age of ninety bore a child to her centenarian husband; in Yahweh's wrangle with her beforehand, and the duplication of the laughing episode; in Yahweh's instructions to Abraham about circumcision; in the tasteful details of the connubial life of Abraham and Jacob; in the massacre of the Sichemites by Simeon and Levi, and the ethical comment of their father; in his allocution to his sons—if in this string of alternately absurd and offensive anecdotes and of obscure rhapsodies, all in the book of Genesis alone, Mr. Lang does not see exactly the characteristics of the "mass" of barbaric myth, one can but say that it is impossible to follow his distinctions. To call such a narrative sober and orderly as a whole in comparison with either Hesiod or Homer is to throw all criticism into confusion.

And the Hebrew compilation, be it observed, represents a relatively late and literary state of Hebrew culture. Even Renan, with all his inconsistencies and laxities of method, sufficiently answers Mr. Lang's question as to how whatever comparative order and sobriety we find in the Pentateuch came to be there. These books represent a prolonged and repeated process of redaction, representing the effects of Assyrian, Egyptian, Babylonian, and Persian culture on the previously semi-civilized Jews—the systematic effort to gloss polytheism into the form of monotheism, and to modify the most glaring crudities of primitive anthropomorphism and pastoral barbarism. It is obvious from the context, for instance, that in the story of Jacob's wrestle with the "man" the antagonist was originally Yahweh—the Yahweh who had familiar conversations with Cain and Abraham and Sarah. And this is but one of a hundred inferrible improvements of the text by the later theologians. Mr. Lang lays special stress on the story of the mutilation of Uranus by Kronos as a sample of the element of savage survival in Greek myth. But if he had perused an easily accessible work on Hebrew mythology he would have learned that in the Rabbinical literature there is preserved the tradition that Cham, "the black" son, *mutilated* his father Noah;[1] and if he had looked further into the matter he would have found that a slight vowel alteration of one word in the present text would give that sense.[2] Now the context makes it practically certain that this was the original form of the story; and we are thus dealing with a Hebrew adaptation on all fours with the oft-cited practice of Pindar, who refused to say that one of the blessed Gods was a mad glutton, and of Homer, who simply left the worst stories out. The difference is that whereas Pindar made a clean breast of the whole matter, and Homer simply set aside the unmanageable, the Hebrew redactors, in their usual way, falsified the text.

This is not the place to attempt even to outline the main features of Hebrew mythology; but it is justifiable to say, first, that a great deal of the heterogeneous narrative of the Biblical books has long been satisfactorily identified as normal primitive mythology—as clearly so as other portions have been shown to be purposive sacerdotal fiction—and that when rational tests are more rigorously and more vigilantly applied, much that still passes as history will probably be resolved into manipulated myth. That Joshua is a purely mythical personage was long ago decided by the historical criticism of the school of Colenso and Kuenen; that he was originally a solar deity can be established at least as satisfactorily as the solar character of Moses, if not as that of Samson. And when we note that in Semitic tradition (which preserves a variety of myths that the Bible-makers for obvious reasons suppressed or transformed) Joshua is the son of the mythical

[1] Goldziher, *Mythology among the Hebrews*, p. 131, citing the *Sanhedrim*, 70a.

[2] The old mythologist Andrew Tooke, in his *Pantheon* (1713), argued that the Greeks had taken their story from Genesis, misreading the word in question as they so easily might.

Miriam[1]—that is to say, that there was probably an ancient Palestinian Saviour-Sun-God, Jesus the son of Mary, we are led to surmise that the elucidation of the Christ myth is not yet complete.

If the religion of Yahweh be compared in its main aspects with those around it, instead of being isolated from them in thought as an "ethical system," it reveals even in its highly sophisticated form the plainest mythical kinships. To say nothing of the various elements of myth dealt with by Dr. Goldziher and other recent mythologists, there are clear connections, some of them noted long ago and since ignored, between the worship of Dionysos and the worship of Yahweh, one of the connecting links being the myth of Moses. In the etymological explanation of the horns[2] of Moses lies a possible clue to the horns of Dionysos. The Hebrew language has but one word, *Keren*, for "horn" and "ray";[3] and as Moses' horns are certainly solar, it may be that there was verbal pressure behind the (Semitic) conception of Dionysos as a bull. In any case, since Yahweh was actually worshipped as a young bull,[4] it appears that Moses is at one point but an aspect of the same myth. Dionysos is among other things the Zeus or Iao of Nysa or Sinai, being the Horned One, dwelling there in the mountain,[5] even as did Yahweh; but for the rest he duplicates mainly with Moses. As the babe Moses is set afloat in the basket of bulrushes, the babe Dionysos is carried in the basket in the sacred procession.[6] Like Moses, Dionysos strikes water from the ground with his rod;[7] like Moses, he crosses the sea with his host;[8] and in the "twofold rocks" of Dionysos[9] lies the probable myth-basis of the two stone tables on

[1] Chronicle of Tabari, ed. Paris, 1867, i. 396. Cited by Baring Gould, *Legends of Old Testament Characters*, 1871, ii. 138. The Jewish books would naturally drop the subject.

[2] Exodus xxxiv. 29, Rev. Vers. marg.

[3] Goldziher, p. 179.

[4] 1 Kings xii. 28; Hosea viii. 4–6. Cp. Judges viii. 27; Hosea viii. 5. Moloch was similarly imaged.

[5] Strabo, xv. 1, § 9.

[6] See hereinafter *Christ and Krishna*, Sec. xii.

[7] Pausanias, iv. 36.

[8] Diodorus Siculus, iii. 65.

[9] Euripides, *Ion*, 1126–7. The statement in the Orphic Hymns that Dionysos wrote his law on two tables of stone—a datum founded on by Voltaire—is now abandoned as a late Jewish forgery. But the passage in Euripides points to the original of all forms of the myth.

which Moses wrote the law on Sinai. On the other hand, it is Yahweh who appears to Moses within a bush;[1] and within a bush Dionysos was frequently represented in ancient art.[2] But the story that the grave of Moses could never be found is evidently a compromise between the Evemerism of the Yahwists and the early myth, in which Moses must needs have gone to heaven like Dionysos, as did Enoch and Elijah.

There are, however, yet other parallels. In the Greek cult of Demeter much was made of the place Petroma, "two large stones fitting into one another." At the annual celebration of the great rites these were detached, and some writings relative to the rites were taken out, read from, and replaced. "By Petroma" was the most sacred oath for the people of Pheneus; and the stones bore a covering, inside which was a mask of Kedarian Demeter. At the annual celebration the priest put on this mask over his robes (even as Moses put on his veil in the presence of the people before and after speaking with the Lord[3]), and in fulfilment of the ancient rite "struck the earth with rods and summoned the Gods of the nether world"[4]—another variant of the acts of Dionysos and Moses. And yet again it was told of the mythic Cretan king and lawgiver Minos—a solar figure of which the traces go clear back to the early Phœnician period—that either once or many times he entered an ancient and holy cave to hold intercourse with his father Zeus, and receive from him laws for the island of Crete.[5]

For the earlier Christian mythologists, the solution of such coincidences was simple: the Pagan stories were of course perversions of the Hebrew history; and our own contemporaries have the encouragement of Mr. Lang to fall back on a similar view—at least to the extent of deciding

[1] *Exodus* iii. 2–4. First it is the "angel of the Lord" who appears in the bush, then it is "God" (*Elohim*), "the Lord" (*Yahweh*) being named in the same sentence—clear traces of the process of redaction. Cp. Deut. xxxiii. 16.

[2] Cp. Frazer, *Golden Bough*, i. 321, and refs.

[3] Exodus xxxiv. 33, 35.

[4] Pausanias, viii. 15.

[5] Preller, *Griech. Myth.* 2nd ed. ii. 119, and refs. Cp. Lactantius, *Div. Inst.* i. 22.

that the Mosaic myth *is* actual history. If anyone with the facts of Comparative Mythology before him can rest in such a faith, he is certainly past argument. If the story of the giving of the law on Sinai be not a myth, the word has no meaning; and nothing but an Irrationalist bias can account for the capacity to accept such a record in the case of men who profess to accept also the principle of evolution in human things. A set of laws which, so far as they are really ethical, represent the alphabet of all social law, and are seen to have been independently attained by all peoples, with or without similar myths of revelation, are alleged to have been communicated by theophany to a tribal leader on a mountain top, and to have been by him there engraved on two tables of stone which he afterwards broke; and we are invited by a professed evolutionist, as we shall see presently, to recognize an abnormal verisimilitude in the tale.

So long, of course, as educated publicists like Professor Max Müller and the late Matthew Arnold talk of Abraham as a historical character, who probably discovered the principle of monotheism;[1] so long as Moses is believed by Positivists[2] to have been a real leader who invented the Ten Commandments; so long as the feats of Elijah and the cheats of Jacob are gravely written about by clerical scholars as natural episodes of Eastern life; so long as authorities like Mr. Gladstone swear by the flood—and, be it added, so long as comparative mythologists can write on the whole matter as does Mr. Lang—it will be difficult to set up in the reading world that state of mind which shall at once encourage and chasten the activity of mythological science in the Biblical direction. But even Mr. Lang seems to perceive, and resent, some such movement of the general intelligence. Complaining of the vagueness of Renan's account of Hebrew religious origins, he speaks somewhat tartly of its being welcomed by "the clever

[1] Müller, *Chips from a German Workshop*, 1868, i. 371–5; *Physical Religion*, 1891, p. 220–1. Arnold, *Literature and Dogma*, 5th ed. p. 32.

[2] See *The New Calendar of Great Men*, edited by Frederic Harrison, 1892, p. 5.

superficial men and women who think that everything has been found out, when next to nothing has been found out at all; who disbelieve in Authority, and do believe in 'authorities.'"[1] The psychic state revealed in this utterance is something to be reckoned with in our inquiry, exhibited as it is further in the previously cited protest against "offending many people" by talking of Old Testament mythology. It is hardly necessary to point out that we are not dealing with a spirit of pure humanitarianism or disinterested benevolence. Mr. Lang has no special scruples about offending a good many sorts of people—"the clever superficial men and women," for instance; and he has never shown any great reluctance to dishearten or to ridicule those persons who, instead of making much of the Paradise and Promised Land of Genesis, try to frame and reach paradises and promised lands for themselves or their posterity. Mr. Lang's mercies are somewhat straitly covenanted. He rather enjoys hinting that those who take a rationalistic view of the reigning religion are at best clever and superficial, and easily gullible by authorities: his protecting sympathies are only for the superficial men and women who are not clever, who think everything that is found out goes to corroborate the Bible, and who believe in both Authority and authorities, holding by the Word of God and taking the word of Dr. Samuel Kinns.

On all which it may suffice to observe, first, that the common run of the men and women in question have themselves never shown the slightest concern for the susceptibilities either of those who cannot accept their creed, or of those who hold other creeds; that on the contrary they have shown a very general disposition to ostracise and ruin those who openly disagree with them, and are thus not entitled to anything more than the normal courtesies of debate on vital issues; and, secondly, that science has nothing to do with susceptibilities beyond taking care to use decent language. Mr. Lang repeatedly applies to non-Christian systems and creeds, some of them contemporary,

[1] Art. cited, p. 284.

such terms as "sacerdotage," "anecdotage," and "foolish faith." Such being his latitude, other mythologists may surely go the length of calling Hebrew mythology Hebrew mythology. And if the good "many people" are hurt by such language, they have always open to them the twofold resort of crying "infidelity" and of turning their backs on the subject. What were they doing in that galley?

Coming back to the sphere of scientific argument, we note that Mr. Lang after all admits some of the most prominent of the Pentateuchal narratives to be as downright myths as any in the world. The stories of the finding of Moses and the passage of the Red Sea, he writes, are "myths found all the world over"—the first being "a variant of 'The Man Born to be King'—Cyrus, Romulus, Oidipous—the exposed Royal child," while variants of the sea-passage are "nearly universal." It is to be feared these concessions will give a good deal of pain to "many people." Mr. Lang, however, adds a demurrer:—

> "But the rest, the wonderful tale of the Plagues, of the death of the first-born, of the pillar and the cloud, the night and the fire? What genius invented these, which are not part of the world's common treasury of myth? This may be a mere literary question, and yet one suspects the presence of some strange historical facts."[1]

It is a little difficult to deal with such very tentative orthodoxy; but we may put the answer in the form of a few questions.

1. Inasmuch as isolated and peculiar myths are found in most systems, is it to be normally assumed that either (*a*) a genius invented them or (*b*) we must surmise "the presence of some strange historical facts"?

2. Is there anything so very staggering to the rationalist position in the view that a Jewish genius may have had a hand in the redaction of the Pentateuch?

3. Is there, after all, anything abnormal in the development of a myth of ten plagues in an intellectual climate in which plagues of drought and flood and vermin and disease and dragons were constantly ascribed to the punitive action of deity? For example, if Apollo had been said to send ten

[1] Art. cited, p. 286.

plagues on the Greeks at Troy instead of one, should we have been any the more entitled to "suspect the presence of some strange historical facts"? Or does a story of ten plagues suggest ten times the amount of genius required to make a story of one plague?

4. Seeing that ten, as the "finishing" and "completing" number,[1] was one of the favourite mythic and regulative numbers in antiquity—*e.g.*, the ten commandments, the ten ages of the Etruscans, the ten spheres of the Pythagoreans, the ten adults needed to make a Jewish synagogue, the ten made by the nine Muses and their head, Apollo; the ten made for Arabs and Persians by the nine heavenly spheres and the earth; the usage of tithes, and so on—is not the particular total of ten plagues rather a reason for inferring pragmatic invention than for suspecting the presence of some strange historical facts?

5. If Mr. Lang had met with a story of ten plagues in any other ancient literature, and all ten of them monstrous miracles, would he have dreamt of raising any question of historical fact? Would he not rather have put the ten tales under his general heading of absurd—if not offensive—anecdotes?

6. Is it exactly wise on the part of a modern Theist, whether writing as a mythologist or as joint author of *The World's Desire*, to suggest that his deity and Heavenly Father, "who is not far from any one of us,"[2] really operated on the intelligence of a stubborn king by decimal affliction and final massacres among that king's subjects?

7. Does "the rest" include the wondrous tales of the performances of the rods of Moses and Aaron; or are these forms of narrative which could be evolved without setting up the impression of "strange historical facts"?

[1] See the references in Bähr, *Symbolik des Mosaischen Cultus*, i. 175–183. So strong was the inclination to apply this principle that in various myths a divine child is said to have been ten months in the womb. *E.g.*, Hermes (Hom. Hymn, l. 11) and the Muses (Hesiod, *Theog.*, 58, where the year = ten months). Cp. Virgil, Ecl. iv. 61; and see Diogenes Laertius (*Pythagoras*, xix.) as to the Pythagorean biology. In the Pythagorean astronomy the "counter-earth" (*Antichthon*) was invented simply to bring up to ten the number of bodies of the central system (sun, moon, earth, five planets, and central fire). Berry, *Short History of Astronomy*, 1898, p. 25.

[2] *Myth, Ritual, and Religion*, 1st ed. i. 340.

Perhaps we have sufficiently considered the wonderful story of the plagues, and may spare ourselves the discussion of the pillars of fire and cloud, remarking that no supernatural genius would seem to be necessary for the adding of these items to a story which all sober Biblical criticism has admitted to be an utterly incredible compilation of fictions.[1] It is hardly worthy of a professed cultivator of a branch of historical and mental science thus to darken counsel for the "superficial men and women" by suggesting that there are some supernatural facts behind a narrative which so many religionists of a rather more earnest sort have definitely given up as unhistorical. But Mr. Lang distorts the problem from first to last. "Manifestly," he writes, "the Chaldæan cosmogonic myth was a medley of early metaphysics and early fable, like other cosmogonies. Why is the Biblical story so different in character?"[2] It is *not* different in character. It *is* a medley of early metaphysics and early fable—early, that is, relatively to known Hebrew history. It ties together two creation stories and two flood stories; it duplicates several sets of mythic personages—as Cain and Abel, Tubal-Cain and Jabal; it grafts the curse of Cham on the curse of Cain, making that finally the curse of Canaan; it tells the same offensive story twice of one patriarch and again of another; it gives an early "metaphysical" theory of the origin of death, life, and evil; it adapts the Egyptian story of the "Two Brothers," or the myth of Adonis, as the history of Joseph; it makes use of various God-names, pretending that they always stood for the same deity; it repeats traditions concerning mythic founders of races—if all this be not a "medley of early fable," what is? Mr. Lang's discrimination is unintelligible unless he be taken merely to mean that the Hebrew redactors, proceeding professionally on collected materials with a sacerdotal purpose, wrought them up in greater

[1] Early in the last century Toland, in his *Hodegus*, undertook to show that the "cloud" was simply the smoke of the night's guiding-fire. We know to-day that the whole story of the life in the wilderness is a myth; but Toland's Evemerism may serve well enough to meet Mr. Lang's supernaturalism.

[2] Art. cited, p. 281.

fulness and elaboration than belonged to the older records. But that is exactly what a dozen Greek mythographers and Hindu poets did with *their* materials: there is no mystery in the matter.

Nor is there anything more than uncritical rhetoric in Mr. Lang's final deliverance that "Behind it all is the mystery of race and of *selection*. It is an ultimate fact in the history and government of the world, the eminent genius of one tiny people for religion." He might here, indeed, cite on his side many sayings of M. Renan's earlier days, the days when he told the world, as Bunsen had done, that the Hebrews were destitute of a mythology—a proposition which has been rejected by nearly every student of mythology, I think, that has discussed it.[1] So incoherent was Renan's thought on the subject that he alternately presented the Semites as marked by a "minimum of religion" and a special genius or instinct for it[2]—the theorem now endorsed by Mr. Lang. But the pre-scientific assumption of an innate genius for anything in an entire people must give way before science, like all other apriorisms. As Mr. Lang indicates, any special development of bias or faculty in any people is a matter of "selection," not in the Darwinian sense that the special development enables the people to survive where others would succumb, but in the sense that special conditions bring the special development about. There is no more mystery in the matter than in any other natural process—much less, indeed, than in those of biology.

This, of course, is a matter of sociology; and sociology among us is kept fully as backward as mythology by religious prejudice; but even in the light of the mere history of Jewry as rationally re-written by modern Hebraists,[3] Mr. Lang's difficulties cease to exist. We have

[1] It is rejected by Kuenen, Goldziher, Steinthal, Robertson Smith, and Max Müller, as well as by Ewald. It is accepted by Nöldeke, Spiegel, Roscher (the economist), Draper, Bluntschli, and Peschel, none of them a mythologist, unless it be Spiegel. See refs. in the author's *Short History of Freethought*, 1899, p. 73.

[2] Cp. Max Müller, *Chips from a German Workshop*, i. 350–1.

[3] *I.e.*, Kuenen, Wellhausen, Sack, Stade, Goldziher, etc.

but to recognize the Hebrews (1) as groups of Palestinian tribes, welded now and then into kingdoms, in one of which, during centuries, the cult of Yahweh, previously special to Judah,[1] is at times officially imposed over all others, setting up at Jerusalem a would-be unique source of sacrificial and other revenue.[2] We are to remember, none the less (2), that in despite of such efforts, which were intermittent (many of the kings being polytheists, or anti-Yahwists), the natural and inveterate polytheism of the people subsists in all directions, so that a Yahwist prophet can describe the inhabitants even of the capital as having as many Baal-altars as streets, and Judah as having no fewer Gods than cities.[3] This polytheistic people (3), after undergoing defeat and depopulation by Assyria, and chronic invasion by other powers, thus going on the whole backward in its civilization and culture, is utterly overthrown, and all save its poorest carried bodily into captivity by the new military power of Babylon, the conqueror of Assyria, where its scholarly and priestly members come into contact with a religion kindred to that of Yahweh, but far more literate, far more fully documented, associated with some development of scientific knowledge, and carried on by an endowed and leisured scholarly class, among whom the monotheistic idea has emerged by way of syncretic philosophy, as it had earlier done in India and Egypt, from either of which directions it may have been carried to Babylonia. This principle (4) is by the Yahweh devotees among the Jews

[1] Saul is described (1 Sam. xiv. 35) as building his first altar to Yahweh after driving out the Philistines with the aid of Judah. Later he massacres the priests of Yahweh (*Id.* xxii. 17–19). That he himself was a worshipper of Baal appears from his son's and grandson's names (1 Chron. viii. 33–34; ix. 39–40), perverted by the Yahwists (2 Sam. ii. 8; iv. 4). Yahweh, on the other hand, was also the God of the Gibeonites, who were Amorites. Cp. 2 Sam. vi. 3 and xxi. 2.

[2] Goldziher (cc. vii. viii.) conceives the special development of Yahwistic monotheism to have occurred in terms of national enthusiasm and patriotic self-consciousness; and no doubt that might assist. But other nations were zealously patriotic without giving up polytheism; and another factor is needed to account for the positive elevation and localization of a cult formerly more widespread, and conjoined with others. The shortcoming of Goldziher's theory lies in the usual tendency to narrow the process of explanation. All the political and psychological conditions must be taken into account.

[3] Jeremiah xi. 13.

imposed on their merely tribal or nationalistic belief, with the result (among the most fanatical) of making out the One God to be the God of the Jews and housed at Jerusalem, the rest of the nations of the world having no real God at all, though haply they might each be allowed a guardian angel whom God punishes with his nation when he goes wrong.[1] Thus far, at most, had its innate genius for religion, in contact with a much wider religious system, carried the "tiny people" by the time of the Captivity.

And now occurred the first main act of a process of "selection" which to this day has sufficed to set on a false scent the amateurs of *a priori* sociology. When Cyrus, having conquered Babylon, gave permission to those Jews who would to return to Jerusalem, it was not "the" Jews who returned, but simply those Jews who, in contact with a higher culture, grew more and not less fanatical in their special tribal cult, albeit they were irresistibly influenced by their surroundings towards putting a higher form on it. That the Return was thus partial and sectarian there is abundant evidence, not only in the new sacerdotal literature, but in the testimony of those much more numerous Jews who remained in Babylon. The account of the latter, apparently endorsed by many of the later Palestinians, is that "they were only the bran, that is, the dregs of the people, that returned to Jerusalem after the end of the Captivity, and that all the fine flour stayed behind at Babylon."[2] Whatever may be the precise value of that estimate, it sufficiently accords with the fact that the Jews of the Return, both under Zerubbabel and under Ezra, were mostly pedantic ceremonialists, who narrowed down the name of Jew to those of the Captivity that had returned and had not intermarried with foreigners. Meantime the natural diversity of thought and faculty which belonged to the Jews as to other nations was merged in the foreign populations, from Media to Egypt, in which they had scattered themselves during century after century of

[1] Dan. x. 13, 20; Isa. xxiv. 21.

[2] Prideaux, *The Old and New Testaments Connected*, part i. bk. iii. (ed. 1815, i. 178), citing Talmud Bab. in Kiddushim.

invasion and oppression, as they did still later after the Roman conquest.

Already, however, the factitious literature even of the fanatical Yahwists had begun to take on the colouring of the Chaldean culture of Babylon, which was actually claimed as a distinction by the men of the Return. Zodiacal ideas, drawn thence, are developed in Jacob's list of his children's characters, and in the story of Joseph's dream; the task of a prophet, formerly exhortation, now becomes prediction, on Chaldean lines; the lore of angels becomes a prominent part of the system; and as time goes on and the Persian cult in turn influences Jewry, the principle of the Adversary, the Evil Power, is woven into the pragmatised history of the past; the idea of a Hades emerges; while the comparatively civilized secular law of the new power, doubtless with modifications, is embodied in the pretended law of Moses, and credited to the theocracy. The very institution of the synagogue dates from the Babylonian sojourn. What is special to the Judaic life is just the systematic writing-up of Yahwism, and the turning of the old local deities into servants of Yahweh, as part of a deliberately-invented though much redacted body of false history. Thus Moses and Joshua, obviously solar personages both, and as such old Saviour-Gods (Mosheh being "the raiser-up," and Joshua or Oshea "the Saviour" or "Conqueror"), are made the leaders of a miraculous theocratic deliverance and conquest in the prehistoric period; while the tribal legends of divine founders become the biographies of patriarchs;[1] and various myths concerning the Gods Shamas and El and David and Saul and Solomon[2] are reduced to biographic details in the lives of Samson, Samuel, Elijah, Elisha, and David. In all this there is doubtless a faculty for cult-building; but it is a kind of faculty on all fours with any other deliberate specialism, such as Brahmanic metaphysic or Roman law;

[1] As to the God-names Jacob and Joseph, see Sayce, Hibbert Lectures on the *Babylonian Religion*, p. 51, and *Records of the Past*, New Series, v. 48.

[2] Sayce, Hibbert Lectures as cited, pp. 52–57, and article on "The Names of the First Three Kings of Israel" in the *Modern Review*, January, 1884.

and it is not very advantageous to religion to describe it as a genius for that.

All that is relatively high in Judaism, in fine, is demonstrably forced or grafted on the primitive cult from without. Renan's phrases about "the clean and sober imagination of Israel," oddly objected to by Mr. Lang, are quite in his own spirit, and belong to the pre-scientific interpretation of history, in which all phenomena are explained in terms of themselves. The most admired Biblical book, that of Job, if written by a Jew at all, is by one who had been in contact with the life and culture of Persia, Arabia, and Egypt, and is certainly post-exilic. The quasi-monotheism and ethical universalism of the later prophets is similarly a product of foreign influences; and to the last it never overcame the indurated tribalism and ceremonialism of the mass of the selected people, for whom its God is the tenant of one temple, so long as that temple lasts; whereafter he figures as the "Chief Rabbi of Heaven." Formerly he had spent three hours a day in "playing with Leviathan"; but after the fall of the holy city the heavenly court is in mourning, and the hours formerly given to recreation are spent in instructing "those who had died in infancy."[1] Such was the "genius for religion" exhibited by the Jewish doctors before they began to acquire new heathen lore from contact with the Saracens. As for their ethic, nowhere does it surpass the measure of altruistic thought which Mr. Lang for another purpose credits to the aborigines of Australia and Africa.[2]

Finally, Christianity is on its theological side an unquestionable adaptation of the Pagan principle of theanthropic sacrifice; and on its ethical side is merely a blending, good and bad, of late Græco-Jewish and Gentile teaching. Its supposed antecedents in Essenism are themselves of late and foreign origination in Jewry. The quality of a genius for religion might just as well be ascribed to the Egyptians, the Chaldeans, the Arabs, the Persians, the Hindus, or the

[1] Edersheim, *History of the Jewish Nation after the Destruction of Jerusalem*, 1856, p. 462, citing the *Aroda Sara*.
[2] *The Making of Religion*, p. 195, etc.

Australians, as to the Jews. The express doctrine of the latter, since the closing of their canon, is a negation of all progress in religion; and their accumulated literature of commentary has less intellectual value than anything of its bulk and kind in the world. The race as a *religious* group in Europe stands collectively for mere mental fixation and separatism, the result first of its own claims and secondarily of the hostile reaction they set up, alike among Pagans and Christians. The fact of the preservation of the bulk of the later heterogeneous Hebrew literature as a mass of sacred books—mutually contradictory as so many of them are—is in itself only another sociological fact, which in its kind is paralleled in different degrees in the cases of Brahmanism, Buddhism, and Mohammedanism, as well as Christianity; and the religious separateness and persistence of the Jews is a phenomenon strictly analogous to that of the Parsees. To call it all a special and peculiar mystery is merely to raise mystification. In medieval and modern times, as in ancient, Jewish faculty like every other is evoked and developed by special conditions and culture-contacts: and the special phenomenon of Jewish religiosity is no more a mystery than Japanese art or Russian fiction.

§ 2. *Christianity and "Degeneration."*

When the mythological basis of Hebrew religion, conceded last century by German theologians, is thus put back in doubt by professedly anthropological mythologists to-day, the problems of Christian mythology are naturally kept far in the background. Excepting Sir George Cox,[1] hardly one of the later professed mythologists, either English or continental, has a word to say on the subject. Only in the last sentence of his valuable book does Mr. Frazer glance at the obvious survival of theanthropic sacrifice and the Tree Cult in the Christian religion. In this connection we find the procedure of the anthropological school completely reversed,

[1] Cp. his lectures in *The Religious Systems of the World*, 3rd ed. pp. 218, 241, 242–3, 245, *end*.

with the tacit consent of such authorities as Mr. Lang. In its treatment of "pagan" myth the aim is always to go back to the earliest forms, to ignore their symbolical development and later ethical connotations: in the treatment of Christianity the principle is to pass over the concrete myth forms altogether and consider only the metaphysic and the ethic that have been grafted on them; or to admit as myths only the Catholic inventions of the Middle Ages.

So rooted is the habit that the most recalcitrant theories are accommodated to it. We have seen Mr. Lang treating the Hebrew religion as disparate and superior to those of other ancient peoples. We have seen him again, in a later work, arguing strenuously for a "pure" primeval monotheism in which the God was not sacrificed to; sacrifice being in his opinion a descent to a lower plane of thought —albeit perhaps by "supernormal" means. Finally, he speaks of the religion of Israel as "probably a revival *and purification* of the old conception of a moral, beneficent creator, whose creed *had been involved in sacrifice* and anthropomorphic myth"[1]—this in the face of the facts that the written Hebrew religion contains a mass of anthropomorphic myths, tempered by interpolated denial, and that the historic Hebrew religion was one of systematic sacrifice, so much so that the temple at Jerusalem had normally the aspect of a shambles. Such are the accommodations granted to the religions that be. Then, when we come to Christianity (a fresh grafting of a pagan sacrificial and propitiatory creed on the old, albeit by way of abolishing animal sacrifice), instead of classifying this on his general principle as a process of "degeneration," Mr. Lang treats it as the consummation of the "pure" theory, with the "priceless" doctrine of immortality added as a gift from Animism. Freely granting that Christianity in the Middle Ages developed a multitude of *märchen*-myths,[2] whereof "the stuff is the same as are nature myths and divine

[1] *Myth, Ritual, and Religion*, 2nd ed. ii. 329.
[2] *Id.* i. 5, 325; ii. 304, etc.

myths,"[1] he does not once recognize that the Gospels themselves contain matter equally mythical. On the contrary, he assumes that Christianity was "given pure," and that only the late popular accretions are mythical.

In this connection, where Mr. Lang sets aside his own doctrine of "degeneration," we may fitly ask what is the true formula. If we suppress most of the facts about Judaism, describing it as a "pure" monotheism, in the misleading fashion of Mr. Lang and Mr. Huxley,[2] we may easily see degeneration in the Christian polytheism grafted upon it. In a certain sense, Mr. Lang's theory of the triumph of the "squarable" God does actually here hold good. As in the Zoroastrian system the cult of Mithra gradually supersedes in a measure that of Ahura-Mazda, so, for the Jews and others who adopted it, the cult of Jesus in a measure superseded that of Yahweh or the "Theos" in general; and this obviously because the humanized and suffering God comes home to "the business and bosoms of men"—and women—so much more easily than does that of the remote Creator. The cults of Attis, Adonis, Dèmètèr and Persephone, Hercules, Dionysos, Isis and Osiris, all flourished for just such reasons in comparison with the cults of Zeus, Ptah, Ra, and the rest of the "high" Gods. And for the same reason, again, the cult of the Virgin Mary in later times overlaid the cult of Jesus, who in turn, as Logos and Judge and part of the Ineffable Trinity, receded into a cloudier majesty in exact proportion as the Mother was obtruded on popular reverence. As Mother and Woman she was, in Mr. Lang's phrase, more easily "squared"; and it was as an intercessor with her more judicial Son that she was generally welcomed. But it is an unscientific use of the term to call this development "degeneration."

That term may indeed be fitly applied to the process whereby a once imageless conception of any God is made fixedly concrete through the use of images; or a multiplication of images and pictures positively destroys in a large population the faculty of thinking reasonably about religion

[1] *Id.* ii. 305. [2] *Collected Essays*, iv. 312, 363.

at all.[1] In some such fashion, indeed, degeneration is always going on alongside of progress. In the higher civilizations, again, degeneration is endemic in so far as bad life-conditions are always creating a larger area of low culture around centres of high culture. In both kinds of case alike, however, there occurs something that Mr. Lang's theory takes no note of—to wit, *a recoil from the vulgar conception towards a higher, not before generally possessed.* Such a law is perhaps not without its comforting side. In any case, it is the fact that (1) a God becomes relatively "high," and positively less unethical, by the very process of introducing another God between him and the worshipper; and (2) that the obtrusion of a crude belief or a crude art on superior intelligences makes for them a stepping-stone to a higher art and a less gross credence. As regards art, we see the process every day. A given convention is contentedly acquiesced in by the majority; but there comes along the man of genius, of finer sensibility, or of more various culture, who revolts from the vulgar model, insists that it does not stand for the truth which he perceives, and proceeds to create something—be it a novel, a picture, a statue, or a poem—which better satisfies his tastes or perceptions. After a time, perhaps after he has been stoned or starved, this better model is accepted by many, till it in turn becomes a convention repellent to a later genius; and again there is innovation.

The process is however complicated at all times by the rule of the environment, which determines whether the majority can or can not rise to the finer presentment, or whether genius itself can evolve to good purpose. And this is the specially important consideration in the case of religion. At all stages, there is reason to think, some minds have risen in some measure above the prevalent ideas, and have sought to correct these; and their success is in the ratio of the total facilities, relatively to the effort made. Thus we find Hebrew prophets (haply, however, interpolated by later hands) rebuking the ethic of their

[1] Cp. the author's *Short History of Freethought*, pp. 63–67.

fellow-monotheists and fellow-prophets; Pindar, as aforesaid, Bowdlerising the current myths; Homer and the Vedas leaving the ugliest out; Egyptian and Brahman priests evolving an esoteric system which turns to symbols the barbarisms of the popular cult. But the socio-political conditions determine the extent to which the higher doctrine is assimilated; and thus far in human history the general law is one of the prevalence of crude and ignorant beliefs, or of their retention alongside of the more refined; the broad reason being that the mass of the people have always been more or less crudely ignorant, either because the majority are always of low mental calibre, or because they are always uncultured, or from both causes concurrently.

All the while, however, there operates the general law above stated, that the simple removal of a God by one or more degrees from direct worship, through the interposition of another God between him and the worshipper, has *pro tanto* an elevating effect on the older God. The process, which Mr. Lang obscures by his polemic, is really very simple. To put it plainly, a God becomes more respectable precisely as he gets less to do. It stands to reason that when he was the near God, meddling in everything, he was so much the more obviously made in the image of his worshippers, more "mythological," so to say, in the sense of having so many more stories told about him. And instead of the adoption of intermediate Spirits or lower Gods being a process of moral declension, as Mr. Lang contends, it may at times be resorted to for the very purpose of refining and exalting the greater God. Thus we know that in the Samaritan Pentateuch later writers deliberately substituted "the Angel of the Lord," for "the Lord,"[1] on the obvious ground that Yahweh's dignity was lowered by making him appear in human guise on parochial errands. But the law has a more general bearing. Zeus in the Greek mythology acquires his relative moral elevation precisely through his hierarchical elevation. To start with, save for the few better minds, he was *not* a "high" God,

[1] Cp. the partial substitution of the angel for the deity in Exod. ii.

even if for some tribes he was the One God. The "low" myths about him, which we are told have no connection with the alleged high primordial religion, are the really old data in the matter. It is when he is put over others in the position of Supreme Judge, overruling the more wayward actions of the younger Olympians, that he begins to lend himself to higher ethical ideals; and the highest of all were those formed when the God-idea became so remote as to elude form, and was pantheistically resolved into the idea of a universal Mind, of which men's minds were portions.

If, on the other hand, a God is made relatively "high" by the simple process of being made to overshadow or *absorb* similar deities—as seems to have happened in the case of Apollo, who is made the father of so many local Sun-Gods, and thus becomes *the* Sun-God for Hellas in general—there is in the terms of the case no proportional ethical elevation, since he has only the more stories told about him, and meddles all the more in human affairs. He *may* be theoretically elevated by a concurrent improvement in general ethical thought; but this is not in virtue of his increased importance; and his continued direct activity will always involve a counter-tendency which in part makes the higher ethic nugatory.

As regards, now, the relation of Christianity to Judaism, it is easy to see that Mr. Lang's theory, supposing it to be applied against his will, would still break down. The One God of the Jews, as generally envisaged, was not "high" at the last any more than at the first. The intervening host of angels and demons, indeed, partly saved his dignity and bore the heavier burdens of the popular superstition; but inasmuch as Yahweh remained, despite the higher ideas of some prophets or their interpolators, a tribal and sacerdotal God, he entailed a tribal and sacerdotal ethic; and though doubtless a few, helped by Greek thought, speculated at a higher level, the Almighty who "plays with Leviathan" and sits as Chief Rabbi in Heaven is not a relatively imposing conception. The first Christists accordingly were but doing what the myth-making and religion-making mind has always done in its innovations—seeking to frame a rather more satisfying ethic. This holds good both of the Judaic Jesuists who demanded "works" and the Pauline party who insisted on faith. The latter did in point of fact adopt a common and ancient Gentile conception—that of a sacrificed Divine Man; but they gradually surrounded this conception, which they could not collectively transcend, with a variety of ethical ideas of which some, the contribution of the saner or finer minds, did transcend the central dogma.

Beginning as a Jewish variation, the cult was developed on a broader ethnic basis, its ethic being *pro tanto* widened. But in the process it became more and more sacerdotal; and when sacerdotalism had come into complete possession the ethic remained fixed in its original crudity, with as many popular myths as might be superadded. Thus it could come about that the spectacle of its crudity and its anthropomorphism could in turn, after ages of social vicissitude, act as a stimulus to the Jewish mind in a new environment, and as a point of repulsion for the new cult of Islam, which movements between them, with the help of recovered Greek thought, thus reached a higher ethic and a higher level of cosmic speculation.

Meanwhile, despite Dupuis and Volney and Strauss and the plain bearings of the latest mythological researches, the European economic system serves to maintain in popular credit the mythology of Christism. Some even who see the untenability of the original ethic seem unable to realize its mythic origin; some who, with Strauss, detect some of the myths, continue to see history in others. Hence the need, in the name at once of mythological science and of social rectitude, to apply to Gospel myths the tests of comparative method, and the cues of accumulated mythological knowledge.

§ 3. *The Psychological Resistance to Evidence.*

Even when the outworks thrown up for Christianity by an imperfect mythology and by economic conditions are removed, however, there will still remain to be met the obstinate resistance offered to every scientific view of religious origins by the forces in the camp—to wit, the enlisted affections, the emotional habit, the acquired code of judgments. So obvious is the play of such bias in every great issue that it should be one of the first duties of every educated man to challenge his own case at every serious encounter with an innovating doctrine. Most men can now see how purely passional, how unjudicial, how prejudiced, has been the resistance offered by orthodoxy to every great scientific advance in succession—to the truths of the roundness and motion of the earth, to the principles of geology, to the principles of Darwin. Yet in every one of these cases, we may be sure, men thought they saw commonsense in the old notion and extravagance in the new; so easy is it to find the rational in the habitual, so hard to consent to see by new light. Hardest of all does it seem to be where the habit has been bound up with worship and chronic religious emotion.

We have seen how Mr. Lang fails to find offence or absurdity in the most offensive and absurd "anecdotes" when they occur in the Pentateuch. He sees at a glance the nonsense and indecency of the myths of savages, even after he has taken to crediting them with "selfless" ethics; and, as he is aware,[1] they can equally see absurdity, if not indecency, in the myths on which he was brought up; whereupon he inadequately observes that "savages and civilized men have different standards of credulity." That is but a superficial explanation. Many civilized men hold with the savages that the Christian myths are preposterous; and some savages can see with civilized men that the savage myths are so. The determining condition of vision is simply freedom, original or acquired, from prepossession in a given direction. But the prepossession, while it lasts, is one of the most blinding of influences. And if any inquirer finds it difficult to understand how modern investigators can make fish of one myth and fowl of another, can

[1] *Myth, Ritual, and Religion*, 1st ed. i. 91.

recognize unreason and fiction in other men's faiths and unconsciously run their heads against them in their own, he should firstly pay heed to the phenomena of inconsistency and self-contradiction which so abound in argumentative literature even where writers are not mastered by the special bias of a creed or prejudice or conservative sentiment, but are merely giving play to the different currents of sentiment set up in them by detached impressions which they do not seek or do not contrive to co-ordinate.

As showing how far such incoherence may go in the case of a writer of repute, and how far it may avail to confuse historical science, it may serve to compare two sets of mutually-annihilative dicta from the second and twelfth chapters of Mommsen's *History of Rome*, with the preliminary assurance that the chapters not only make no attempt at a synthesis of the contradictions, but exhibit no suspicion that they contain any contradictions at all. I quote from the 1868 edition of Dickson's translation:—

"But, on the other hand, the Latin religion sank into a singular insipidity and dulness, and early became shrivelled into an anxious and dreary round of ceremonies. The God of the Italian was, as we have already said, above all things an instrument for helping him to the attainment of very substantial earthly objects" (i. 193; ch. 12).

"At the very core of the Latin religion there lay that profound moral impulse which leads men to bring earthly guilt and earthly punishment into relation with the world of the Gods" (ch. 12; i. 192).

"But....the forms of the Roman faith remained at, or sank to, a singularly low level of conception and of insight" (i. 181).

"Of such notions, the products of outward abstraction—of the homeliest simplicity, sometimes venerable, sometimes ridiculous—Roman theology was in substance made up" (i. 184).

"It [Roman religion] was unable to excite that mysterious awe after which the human heart has always had a longing" (i. 184).

"The Latin religion, like every other, had its origin in the effort to fathom the abyss of thought; it is only to a superficial view, which is deceived as to the depth of the stream because it is clear, that its transparent spirit-world can appear to be shallow" (i. 197).

"This indifference to ideal elements in the Roman religion was accompanied by a practical and utilitarian tendency" (i. 185). "The Latin worship was grounded mainly on man's enjoyment of earthly pleasures...." (i. 191).	"Throughout the whole of nature he [the Roman] adored the spiritual and the universal" (i. 29; ch. 2).
"The language of the Roman Gods was wholly confined to Yea and Nay, or at the most to the making their will known by the method of casting lots....The Romans made efforts, even at an early period, to treasure up such counsels [Greek oracles], and copies of the leaves of the....Cumæan Sibyl were accordingly a highly-valued gift....For the reading and interpretation of the fortune-telling book a special college....was instituted in early times....Romans in search of advice early betook themselves to the Delphic Apollo himself" (i. 198–9).	"Comparatively slight traces are to be found among the Romans of belief in ghosts, fear of enchantments, or dealing in mysteries. Oracles and prophecy never acquired the importance in Italy which they obtained in Greece, and never were able to exercise a serious control over public or private life" (i. 193).

It is given to few, certainly, to dogmatize so chaotically as does Mommsen; but if he can contrive to think thus incoherently on a question on which he has no master-passion to blind him, as in his utterances on the Celtic races and on French civilization; if he can in different moods see spiritual profundity and mere mechanical externality in one and the same set of religious phenomena, it becomes at least much less surprising that men should see in such different lights phenomena which, though cognate and similar, are at least different in particulars and in their circumstances, as well as in degree of familiarity. The believing Christian who for the first time is told, however guardedly, that his creed is historically on all fours with those of its age, and that its prodigies are but myths and false marvels like those of Paganism, is sure to be sincerely scandalized. To him the two sets of phenomena are wholly disparate, because his feelings about them have always been so. And it finally depends on his intellectual qualities, his opportunities, his studies, and his interlocutors, whether he ever gets beyond framing arguments which merely follow the beck of his prejudice.

With the wrecks of such arguments the path of discussion has been more and more thickly strewn for the last two hundred years. But as many still see in the wrecks nothing but good building material, it may be well to scrutinize closely a few arguments which were earnestly or adroitly put together when Strauss fifty years ago gave a new reverberation to the doctrine that Christian supernaturalism is part of the subject-matter of mythology. As had been sought to be done last century in the case of miracles, men strove to show that what were called myths in the Gospels had nothing in common with the admitted myths of Paganism: and that on the other hand, despite its supernaturalism, the life of the Founder was as credible as that of Julius Cæsar.

On the first head the line of argument was very much that of Mr. Lang, only more industriously developed, and with of course more resort to the stock "bluffs" of Christian Evidence. One German inquirer put together a list of the Mohammedan myths about Jesus, and claimed to show that all had an extravagant or frivolous or ill-finished character that was totally absent from the Gospel narrative. In the Gospels, it is claimed, there are no "hyperbolical delineations." "There we find no miracle which is not duly called for by the circumstances—none that serves merely frivolous interests, or that violates the rules of propriety." "Where the supernatural does interpose, it presents itself in a manner so unconstrained, and so suitable to the aim of the whole, that *the only thing that would have created surprise would have been the absence of this element.*"[1]

Place beside these typical assertions, of which even the last is only a delightful development of a common implication, a few of the actual Gospel miracles.

1. The wholesale[2] turning of water into wine at a feast at which a presumable sufficiency of wine had been already consumed.

[1] Part vii. of *Voices of the Church in Reply to Dr. Strauss*, 1845, pp. 35,5–9.

[2] The *quantity* of the wine greatly impressed Strauss, as it did previous German critics. It figures out at over a thousand imperial pints.

2. The miraculous draught of fishes.

3. The catching of the fish with the coin in its mouth to pay the tribute; taken in connection with the statement that Judas normally carried a stock of money for the group.

4. The story that 5,000 persons went into the wilderness with twelve (or more) baskets, containing only five (or seven) loaves and two (or a few) fishes, and that the Founder multiplied that food for the host till there was superfluity enough to fill exactly twelve baskets.

5. The instantaneous cure of a malady of long standing through a touch on the hem of the Messiah's garment.

6. The rebuking of the wind, its instant cessation, and the immediate "great calm" on a tempest-tossed sea.

7. The instantaneous removal of leprosy.

8. The instant restoration of maimed limbs.

9. The walking on the waves.

10. The rebuking and expulsion of the "devil" in epileptic patients.

Nothing save a prepossession approaching to hebetude can obscure the fact that these are just "irrational," that is, ignorant myths of the ordinary Oriental sort, devoid of "propriety," for instructed people, in the completest degree. The so-called Mohammedan myths, which are really flotsam from early Christian lore, set reasonable and even touching thoughts alongside of absurd narratives: the Gospels do the same, yielding a much larger proportion of sane matter simply because they represent the literary travail of several generations and the selected thoughts of many more, all to some extent edited by men bent on making a Christist movement; whereas the Mohammedan myths about Jesus are mere random survivals. Yet if Christians had found in their Gospels the story that when the disciples complained of the smell of the dead dog, Jesus answered "Ah! how beautifully white are the dog's teeth," with the added explanation, they would have been well pleased;[1] and if they could without scandal accept it in

[1] Let the "apocryphal" story be but told in the archaic style of the English versions of the Gospels, and the effect will be tolerable enough. As thus:— "And as Jesus came from that city with his disciples there lay before

exchange for the inept story of the cursing of the fig-tree, many would promptly and gladly make the transaction.

Again, when the apologist claims it to be a specialty of Gospel narrative to contain simple and natural episodes, he does but exclude from his survey one-half of the literature of mythology.

> "That the great Messiah sat down weary at Jacob's well, that he was overcome with sleep in the boat on the lake, that in Gethsemane and on the cross he gave utterance to the deepest feelings of human weakness—all this would as little have appeared in a mytho-poetical picture of his life, as the honest and sober-minded *confessions of their own conduct* which the evangelists so artlessly embody in their narratives."[1]

Such are the devices of "foredeeming." In not a single case does any Gospel attribute any act whatever to its own writer, or indicate who its writer was: the apologist has but adduced myth to defend myth. As for the picture of the God resting by the well, or sleeping in the boat, it can be paralleled on the side of artlessness in a dozen of the most familiar myths of Hellas, and in as many of Buddhism. Can the apologist ever have read of "outworn Dêmêtêr, searching for Persephone"? "By the wayside she sat her down, sore in heart, at the Maiden Well, where the townsfolks drew their water, in the shadow where overhead grew a thicket of olives. In her guise she was like unto an aged woman who is bereft of child-bearing and the gifts of garland-loving Aphrodite......They knew her not: the Gods are hard for men to discern......"[2] This of Great Dêmêtêr, of the many temples and the glorious name.

Met thus at every turn by the challenged parallel, the customary apologist usually ends by insisting that the Gospels stand out from all other sacred histories in respect of their utter aloofness from the instinct of sex—that Jesus alone of the Gods of old is without the passion of the male for the female. But this again is a fallacious plea, for the

them on the way a dead dog. And the disciples were much offended with the smell thereof. And the Lord rebuked them and said, Nay, but see ye not the wondrous whiteness of the dog's teeth? This spake he unto them that they should take heed to see the good in all the works of God, and that they should think not of the faults but of the righteous deeds of their brethren."

[1] Vol. cited, p. 357.

[2] Homeridian Hymn to Dêmêtêr, Edgar's trans. slightly altered.

entire literature of the early Christists is in the same way stamped with the character of an age in which Oriental asceticism has become the standard of sanctity; and the new God is but specialized as Virgin Goddesses had been before him.[1] Apollo himself is acclaimed as *hagnos*, the chaste God; and in Julian we see the now normally sophisticated consciousness of religious men, claiming sexlessness for the old Gods and turning the stories of their appetites to pure allegory. And the principle is dominant in Buddhism no less than in Christism.

Even as the determined believer will not see charm or sobriety in any myth of the heathen, so will he look in the very face of puerility in his own myths and vow that it is surpassingly divine, nay, that prodigy is but a proof of foreknowledge. Thus does no less a teacher than Neander, in an English translation, dispose of the miracle of the fish with the stater in its mouth:—

> "He [Jesus] *wrought no miracle* in order to procure the necessary money, but told Peter to *have recourse to his usual calling*. Providence attached a peculiar blessing to his labours on this occasion; and he found in the *mouth* of the first fish which he caught a coin, which had probably been *swallowed* a short time before.[2] Christ's *foreknowledge of the result* constitutes, as before observed, *the miraculous element* in the transaction."

As if supererogatory absurdity were not enough, the theologian must needs glose the narrative, in which Jesus actually tells Peter in advance that he will find the coin in the mouth of the first fish. The narrative (Mt. xvii. 27) does not even tell further of the fulfilment. If then the miracle here consists simply in the foreknowledge, it does so in every case in which Jesus says anything before a miracle is consummated. The formula is naught.

But the extremity of Neander's bias is best illustrated by his handling of the miracle of Cana. Here he does not

[1] I say nothing of the unpleasant problem raised by the wording of John xiii. 23.

[2] Cp. *Das Leben Jesu Christi*, 4te Aufl. 1845, p. 508. The passage is thus translated in *Voices of the Church*, as before cited, p. 427. The fourth edition of the original says in conclusion only: "Der zuerst gefangene Fisch sollte so viel einbringen, da ein von ihm verschlungener Stater in ihm gefunden wurde."

employ the "foreknowledge" formula, but changes the venue:—

> "If we are to regard the author of that [the fourth] Gospel as a man of Alexandrian culture, whose mind was imbued with the notions of the Gnostics, his selection, for the first miracle of Christ, of a transaction which from his peculiar point of view must have appeared utterly unworthy of the Saviour's dignity, is incomprehensible."[1]

It would be hard to be more arbitrary. The theorem of Strauss[2] and others, that the fourth Gospel suggests Alexandrian or Greek culture and a Gnostic leaning, alleges its Gnosticism only so far forth as the Gospel can be shown to contain Gnostic thought. To reply that *the* Gnostic of Alexandria would have scouted the miracle of Cana is neither here nor there. Gnosticism had many mansions, and no modern is entitled to say that there were not thousands of the earlier Gnostics who would have accepted the miracle with reverence. Clement of Alexandria actually accepted and prized the name of Gnostic; and he never by a single word disparages the miracle. It is true that he never refers to it; while he revels in the doctrine of the Logos; and it might be argued on Neander's premiss that the water-and-wine story was an addition to the original perhaps made after Clement's time. But this view would of course be repudiated by Neander as reducing the miracle to myth once for all. His argument must remain that the story is to be held apostolic *because* it would scandalize an educated Alexandrian. How then came any educated Alexandrian ever to be an orthodox Christian; and how came Clement to let the miracle pass?

The special pathos of the defence lies in the perception it betrays that the story is a scandal to the educated *modern*; that the naïf phrases "manifested his glory," "and his disciples believed on him," reveal a notion of divinity and Messiahship which puts the narrative outside the pale of tolerable testimony for a critical reader. The modern apologist who felt that "in the Gospel miracles the only thing that would have created surprise would have

[1] *Das Leben Jesu Christi*, p. 273, *note*. *Voices of the Church*, pp. 428–9.
[2] *Leben Jesu*, 4te Ausg. i. Kap. vii. § 83, *end*.

been the absence" of the supernatural, was clearly at the true primeval point of view; but even he would have been hard put to it to show that the Christian tale is more dignified or more plausible than the repeatedly "attested" wine-miracle wrought annually in the Dionysian temple of Andros in solemn manifestation of the might of the God over his special element.[1] As for the rest of us, when we collate the two prodigies, what can we say, as reasoning men, but that the Gospel miracle is a parody of the Pagan?

At the next stage of the analysis there arises an issue that is equally set up by other episodes in the Gospels: the question, namely, as to how such a story came *first* to be told. In the Dionysiak miracle, it will probably be allowed, we have a systematic priestly imposture, actually repeated year by year. It may have been done in pursuance of some old tale of the God turning water into wine; or it may have been the priests' reduction to falsehood, *ad captandum vulgus*, of their subtler principle that the Sun-God turned water into wine in ripening the grape;[2] or the story may originally have been told by way of embodying that doctrine in a mythos. In any case, an esoteric idea presumably underlay the annual performance. In the Christian tale there is no such element left above ground; and we are driven to ask whether the first narrator of the Christian version was other than a wilful vendor of fiction. It is hard to see how we can answer favourably: certain as it is that any story once written down in an accepted Gospel was sure to be believed, there must have been a beginning in somebody's deceit. And if on this we are met with the old formula that a wilful fiction is not a myth, we can but answer that the formula will have to be recast. For we really know nothing of the precise manner of origin of, say, the myth of Isis and Osiris. We only know that *it was believed*; and as a belief it was for all practical purposes on all fours with the belief that Alexander was the son of

[1] See the treatise on *The Gospel Myths* in the present volume.

[2] This was actually Augustine's gloss of the Christian miracle, except that in his view the God was miraculous and dramatically repeating what he did annually in the course of nature. *In Joann.* tract. 8, cited by Strauss.

Jupiter Ammon, and the belief that Jesus turned so many firkins of water into wine by divine volition. They were all traditionary forms of error; and the business of mythology is to trace as far as may be how they came to be started and conserved.

§ 4. *The Problem of Non-Miraculous Myth.*

If the foregoing argument be substantially sound, it follows that the conception of "myth" should be allowed broadly to include not only stories of a supernatural cast told of divine personages, but many quasi-historical narratives which fall short of asserting downright miracle; and not only stories of that cast told about non-historical personages, but some told about historical personages. If, for instance, we find related of Julius Cæsar and William the Conqueror and other great captains the tale of a stumble on landing in a new country, and a prompt pretence to lay hold of the land by way of reassuring superstitious soldiers, we are reasonably entitled to say that, though the thing may have happened once, it did not happen repeatedly; just as we decide that the same witticism was not really uttered by Voltaire and Dr. Johnson and Talleyrand and Sidney Smith and Douglas Jerrold, though it has been ascribed to them all; and that there were not four Christian nurses who respectively alleged that they had witnessed the death-beds of Voltaire, Rousseau, Thomas Paine, and Mr. Blank, and would not again see a freethinker die for all the wealth of Indies. Knowing how the human mind manufactures these modern false coincidences, we rather count ourselves to have therein a sidelight on coincidences of a more sacrosanct sort in older times. When all is said, we have hardly any other way of divining how primeval men contrived to tell the same stories with innumerable variations of names and minor details.

But here we must reckon with a logical difficulty of obvious importance, which has been turned to very adroit account by opponents of mythical interpretations of certain religious narratives. This difficulty is that there *are* very odd coincidences in history and literature: and that some perfectly attested modern biographies are found to chime in a queer way with certain myth-cycles of antiquity. The most familiar and the most striking of all such cases is the mock demonstration by Archbishop Whately that Napoleon = Apollo. Many a student must have been for a moment as much bewildered as entertained by the series of data—the birth in a Mediterranean island; the mother-name Laetitia = Leto = Latona; the three sisters = the Graces; the four brothers = the seasons; the surname Bonaparte; the hero's overrunning of Europe; the two wives = Moon and Earth;[1] the apparition in Egypt; the turning-point of the hero's career in the land of winter, which undermines his power; his defeat by the northern hosts; his twelve marshals = the signs of the zodiac; his passing away in the western hemisphere in the midst of the sea. It all seems at first sight uncommonly awkward for the solarists; and a German theologian, in a sufficiently German manner, undertook similarly to confute Strauss by a work supposed to be produced by a Mexican mythologist in the year 2836, *Das Leben Luther's kritisch bearbeitet*, wherein Luther is shown to be a myth.[2] Here the effect is much less striking; and the main hits are made over the mythical appearance of the name Wartburg, and the curious story that Luther was born while his mother was on a journey. In this case it begins to appear that the satire has come home to roost; for the mythical interpretation of the Gospel narrative does *not* rest on a theorem of the unreality of place-names; and the question as to Luther's birth is troublous rather for the Protestant than for the mythologist. The story is very ill vouched: how came it to be told? Is it that an element of myth really *did* get into the biography even of Luther?

Once started, the rebuttal is simple enough. To begin

[1] Or, as a later writer would be apt to put it, Dawn and Twilight.
[2] See it reproduced in *The Voices of the Church in reply to Dr. Strauss*.

with, the clever Archbishop's thesis proves far too much; for Apollo *is* even in his opinion a mythical person; and nine-tenths of the Napoleon data do not apply to Apollo at all; though the Archbishop might have improved his case by noting that the Greek spelling is Apollon, and the modern Greek pronunciation nearly Apoleon = the Apollyon of Bunyan's allegory. Further, Apollo had *not* three sisters and four brothers; and was *not* defeated by northern hosts; and had a great many wives and a great many sons; and never led any hosts, though Dionysos did; and never died, even to rise again. And for the rest, we need but ask the Archbishop and his German emulator, as did the late Professor Baden Powell in the *Essays and Reviews*, whether they mean to suggest that there is nothing more miraculous in the life of Jesus than in the lives of Luther and Napoleon? In fine, was not the Archbishop a little too clever for the safety of the creed?

We have but to restate the mythological argument in this connection to make clear its real strength. As thus: (1) Jesus is said to be born of a Virgin; but not in the original version of the First Gospel; and not in the Second; and not in any writing or by any mouth known to Paul. Here we see how a myth may be superimposed on a cult. As regards (2) the miracles, the Temptation, the Resurrection, the Ascension, they cannot possibly be solved by any record of a real career. (3) We come next to non-miraculous episodes which yet bear the mark of myth in that they are (*a*) duplicates of episodes in previous hero-myths, (*b*) not common to the four Gospels, (*c*) like the miracles, visibly unknown to Paul. Even Mr. Lang admits myth in the story of the exposure of the infant Moses. The Massacre of the Innocents falls by the same tests. (4) Finally comes the category of presumptively-fictitious utterances, of which there is a whole series, reducible to unreality on various grounds, as thus:—

a. All alike are unknown to Paul, and unemployed by the other epistle-writers.

b. The Sermon on the Mount is further demonstrably a

collection of written sayings, and has none of the characteristics of a real discourse.

c. The "Come unto me" formula has no congruity whatever with the main body of the narrative; and is intelligible only as a formula of the mysteries.

d. Many of the parables are similarly impossible as "teachings"; indeed, the Sermon on the Mount, though visibly a written compilation, is almost the only part of the Gospel that has any approach to fitness for popular purposes (cp. Mark iv. 11, 12; Luke viii. 10). The disciples themselves are represented as needing explanations of parables (cp. Matt. xiii. 15–36); and at times Jesus is said to blame them bitterly, at others to be in the habit of explaining to them privately what the multitude cannot understand (Mark ix. 34, etc.).

e. A multitude of absolute contradictions of narrative in the text prove unrestrained invention—*e.g.*, Matt. xiii. 54–58 and Luke iv. 31–44; Matt. x. 5, 6, and xxii. 43; Matt. xii. 30 and Luke ix. 30; Matt. xviii. 3 and xiii. 10–16; Matt. xviii. 17 and verse 22.[1]

f. The decisive difference between the whole cast of the fourth Gospel and that of the Synoptics shows that invention was no less unrestrained as regards doctrine. Any man could set forth anything he would as the teaching of the Messiah.

g. Predictions such as those of the fall of Jerusalem are clearly written after the event. Other teachings were as easy to interpolate.

When any such body of reasons can be given for doubting a pagan narrative, it can to-day find no credence among instructed men. No scholar pretends to believe that all the speeches ostensibly reported in Livy and Thucydides were really delivered; but though it is not recorded that any reports of Jesuine sayings existed in any form in Paul's time we are asked to believe that a multitude of Jesuine

[1] See a number of other instances cited in the author's *Short History of Freethought*, pp. 146–7.

discourses delivered about the year 30 were accurately reproduced, without additions, forty or more years later; and that documents to which during a century anybody might add, in an age of habitual forgery, are valid evidence. Clearly this is the merest fanaticism. All that can rationally be claimed is that a teacher or teachers named Jesus, or several differently named teachers called Messiahs, may have Messianically uttered some of these teachings at various periods, presumably after the writing of the genuine Pauline epistles.[1] To make the whole mass the basis of a conception of a teaching Jesus before Paul, is to ignore all the usual principles of historical judgment.

To put the case broadly, at the end as at the beginning: Primary myth is but one of the primary modes in which men are collectively deceived; the habit of erroneous belief persists thus far in all stages of civilization; and wherever the result is a widespread hallucination, transmitted from age to age through channels of custom and emotional credulity, we are dealing with the same kind of psychological problem, and should apply to it the same kind of tests. The beliefs that Démétér wandered over the wide-wayed earth seeking for Persephone; that Isis searched mourning for the body of Osiris; that Apollo shot arrows of pestilence in punishment among the Greeks; that Athéné miraculously succoured her worshippers; that Perseus and Jesus and a hundred more were supernaturally conceived; that Jesus and Dionysos and Osiris gave men new knowledge and happiness in virtue of Godhood; that Tezcatlipoca and Yahweh were to be appeased by the eating, in reality or in symbol, of human flesh and blood; that Æsculapius and Jesus raised the dead; that Hercules and Dionysos and Jesus went down to Hades, and returned; that Jesus and Mithra were buried in rock tombs and rose again; and that the sacrifice of Jesus brought salvation to mankind as did the annual sacrifice of the God-victim of the Khonds—these beliefs were set up and cherished by the

[1] Cp. essay on "The Jesus Legend and the Myth of the Twelve Apostles," in the author's *Studies in Religious Fallacy*.

same faculties for fiction and fallacy as have conserved the beliefs about the Amazons, Arthur and the Round Table, the primacy of the Pope, witchcraft, fairies, the medicinal value of charms, the *couvade*, the efficacy of prayer for rain, Jenny Geddes and her stool, Bruce's Cave, Wallace's Tree, Julian's saying "Thou hast conquered, O Galilean," the liquefaction of the blood of St. Januarius, the miracles of Lourdes, the miracles of mediums, Boer outrages, the shooting of the apple on the head of his child by William Tell, and the consequent establishment of the Swiss Confederation.

The fortunes of the Tell myth may serve once for all to illustrate the fashion in which a fiction can even in a historical period find general acceptance; and the time and effort required to dispossess such a belief by means even of the plainest evidence. As early as 1598, a Swiss antiquary pronounced the story a fable; and in 1760 another, named Freudenberger, undertook to show its source, the episode being found in the Danish history of Saxo Grammaticus, written centuries before the date assigned to Tell's exploit. It is said that Freudenberger was condemned to be burned alive for his pains; but this looks like yet another myth. Periodically repeated by scholars, however, the exposure was obstinately resisted by learned Swiss historians on various untenable grounds down till the middle of the present century;[1] and when the pressure of criticism at last became irresistible by men of education and capacity, when it was shown past question that the Confederation had been formally established a good many years before the date assigned to Tell, and that no trace of the Gessler episode occurs for generations after the time to which it is ascribed, an accomplished scholar is found in all good faith to contend that, while the apple story is plainly myth and Tell a non-historical person, there is some reason to believe that *some* disturbance occurred about the time in question[2]—as if the reservation

[1] *E.g.*, Vieusseux, *History of Switzerland*, 1840, p. 47, *note*.

[2] Cp. the pamphlet of M. Bordier, *Le Grütli et Guillaume Tell*, Genève et Bâle, 1869.

of such a proposition counted for anything in such a connection.

It would be strange if a set of myths round which centre the popular religious beliefs of Christendom were to be rectified more easily than the Swiss belief in Tell. The great majority of the Swiss people, indeed, probably believe devoutly in the Tell story to this day, so little do the studies and conclusions of scholars represent popular opinion in any age; and those rationalists among ourselves who go about proclaiming that Christian supernaturalism, being detected, is "dead," do but proclaim their own immaturity. Do what we will, myriads of "educated" English people will continue for generations to believe that their deity is present in a consecrated wafer; and the faith of myriads more in their remoter myths will continue proportionally vigorous. It remains for those who do care about reason and critical knowledge to pursue these ends faithfully notwithstanding, leaving popular opinion to develop as social and economic conditions may determine. The science of these conditions is indeed the most vital of all; but such science none the less must be followed up for its own sake; and our general survey may fitly end in a consideration of one of the problems that arise for the mythologist on the borderline of the religious resistance, being broached in the name not of orthodoxy but of historical science.

§ 5. *The Problem of Priority.*

It lies on the face of the foregoing argument that any one religion may influence any other with which it comes in contact; that as Christism borrowed myths of all kinds from Paganism, so it may pass on myths to less developed systems. Hence a possibility of dispute as to whether a given heathen myth discovered in post-Christian times is or is not borrowed from Christianity. Dr. Tylor has shown reason for believing that a deluge-myth was set agoing in Mexico by the early Spanish priests. It may be, then, that in earlier times Christianity was drawn upon here and there in the fashion formerly taken for granted by believers as regards *all* cases of coincidence between Christian and pagan narrative and practice.

Obviously such problems are to be solved, if at all, in terms of *a posteriori* evidence and *a priori* plausibility. If the historical data leave a given case in doubt, we have to ask ourselves which way the psychological probabilities lie. It is easy to see why the Christists adopted the belief in the Virgin Birth and the solar birthday; and, on the other hand, to see how savages could acquire from missionaries a belief in a punitive deluge. But there are less simple cases, in which a variety of tests must be put as to the relative likelihood of a given myth's passing from A to B or from B to A. And so great still is the effect of the so long unchallenged habit of treating Christianity as "absolute religion" that in the name even of scientific mythology there is a persistent tendency to look for imitations of Christianity in myths that had been held by independent scholarship to be prior to Christian propaganda. The theses of Professors Weber and Lorinser and others in regard to Krishnaism (discussed at length hereinafter) are typical. Putting these theses aside for detailed treatment, we may take up for illustration that maintained in recent years by H. Petersen, L. Wimmer, Professor Bugge, E. H. Meyer, and others, as to a Christian derivation of the Scandinavian myth of Balder. It is not necessary to ask here whether or not any one of these writers is influenced by a desire to buttress Christianity: it is quite conceivable that all alike may be indifferent to any such result. The point is that they are apparently influenced by the old habit of treating the Christian system as positively non-mythical, and that their theses are always apt to be turned to the account of orthodox belief.

There is a curious correspondence in the line of argument in the two cases mentioned. As concerning Krishna, so concerning Balder, we are told that "no certain traces are to be found of an actually existing cultus" of the God in early times; the only evidence for the *worship* being late, though there is early evidence for the myth-name.[1] The position is, then, that a little-esteemed Scandinavian deity of old standing could be developed into a highly-esteemed one by grafting on his personality characteristics borrowed from Christism, and this in face of Christist opposition and propaganda. Professor Bugge's general argument is thus summarized[2]:—

> "While the Balder myth includes in itself the most diverse elements ....the main element is Christian. Both in the Elder and the Younger Eddas the elements are Christian or partially Christian....All this fairness and splendour [of Balder's complexion and character] in Professor Bugge's opinion is only a reflection of the Son of God, the White Christ as he has been named....As Balder was depicted by an old Icelandic author as purest white in the colour of his body; so in.... legendary and medieval descriptions Christ is spoken of as fairest of body, and with golden yellow hair....The blind Had [who threw at Balder the fatal mistletoe] is the blind Longinus who drove the spear into our Lord's side....He concludes....that the Balder myth has been influenced by these medieval Christian legends" [of Longinus slaying Christ, etc.]. Further, Professor Bugge suggests that Lucifer is the original of Loki; that the swearing of the trees and plants, excepting the mistletoe, not to injure Balder, is derived from the Jewish anti-Christian Gospel of the Middle Ages, the *Sepher Toldoth Jeschu*, where the trees and bushes swear not to bear Jesus if he be crucified, but where Judas makes a cabbage-stump serve the purpose. And so on.

Now, it is not disputed that Christian and classic ideas probably affected some of the later aspects of Scandinavian paganism. So long ago, indeed, as 1728, the antiquarian Keysler argued for Christian and scholarly influence in the Völuspa Saga;[3] and the thesis was sustained by Von Schlözer in 1773, and by Adelung in 1797 and later. Such views were overborne for a time by the enthusiasm and nationalism aroused by the Brothers Grimm; but E. H. Meyer, an admirer of the latter, declares himself bound to confess that the earlier and less scholarly inquirers were right, and the learned Jacob Grimm wrong. Among recent students some amount of Christian contact before the

[1] H. Petersen, *Ueber den Gottesdienst des Nordens während der Heidenzeit*, Ger. trans. 1882, p. 84; E. H. Meyer, *Germanische Mythologie*, p. 262, cited by W. Nicolson, *Myth and Religion*, Helsingfors, 1892, p. 103.

[2] By Mr. Nicolson, as cited, p. 104.

[3] See E. H. Meyer, *Völuspa: Eine Untersuchung*, 1889, pp. 1–8. Cp. H. Petersen, as cited, p. 114.

composition of the Völuspa and other sagas is generally conceded. Thus Professor Rhys holds that the "prophetic" form in which part of the story is preserved is "due to Christian and Biblical influence."[1] As regards the theological conceptions associated with Odin, again, Professor Müller suggested Christian influence a generation ago;[2] and Dr. Rydberg has shown that certain of the migration myths of the Heimskringla and the Younger Edda belong to the Christian period, and are the work of Latin scholars of the Middle Ages.[3] Dr. Vigfusson, again, sees a marked Christian colouring in the entire myth.[4] But that the main episode in the Balder saga should be an adaptation from an apocryphal Christian legend, and that Balder himself is an adaptation from the White Christ—this is a hypothesis too unplausible to pass without clear evidence. And the more Professor Bugge's theory is examined, the weaker do his evidences seem. Among his incidental conclusions are these: that the funeral pile of Balder is taken from that of Patroklos, in Homer; and that the picture given of the God in Saxo-Grammaticus, which is older than that in the Edda, is derived from Achilles, as regards the item of Balder's consuming passion for Nanna. Thus we are to suppose that Balder was first shaped after a classical model, and later after a Christian; and this on the score of some very remote or very normal parallels.

In the hands of Professor Bugge's adherents, the theory is pushed still further. After being vigorously attacked by the German archæologist Müllenhoff,[5] as by the Anglo-Scandinavian Professor George Stephens,[6] and with less emphasis by Dr. Rydberg, it was embraced by E. H. Meyer, Müllenhoff's most distinguished pupil, who contends in his elaborate treatise on the Völuspa that the Saga is a literary adaptation from some current *Summa* of Christian theology.

[1] Hibbert Lectures on *Celtic Heathendom*, 1888, p. 535.
[2] *Chips from a German Workshop*, 1867, ii. 195–6.
[3] *Teutonic Mythology*, Eng. tr. 1889, i. 39, 65, etc.
[4] *Corpus Poeticum Boreale*, 1883, ii. 466.
[5] *Deutsche Altertumskunde*, Bd. v. 1883.
[6] *Professor Bugge's Studies in Northern Mythology shortly examined*, 1883, pp. 326–345.

Whereas Bugge had argued with comparative diffidence that the Balder and Loki story in the Völuspa Saga, heathen in basis, was worked up by a heathen poet, who had heard Christian and classical legends, gathered by the Vikings, E. H. Meyer decides confidently that the poem is rather the work of a Christian priest of the twelfth century belonging to one of the four theological schools set up in Iceland after its Christianization; and that the whole is a literary mystification,[1] not a genuine reproduction of native myths at all.

It must be said that such a proposition raises acute sociological difficulties. Unless the priest-poet of the twelfth century were a highly-evolved sceptic, he must have been either a Christian or a Pagan. Now, the existence of an impartial artistic scepticism, as distinct from simple unbelief, in such an environment at that period, is a greater improbability than that any of the aspects of the saga should be pagan work. Assume then that he was a believing Christian priest: was ever such a one known to lend new literary attractions to the story of a heathen God, and so to give heathenism the greater glory? The thesis is really exorbitant: Dr. Meyer's conception of such a "mystification," such a "Rätselgedicht," on the part of a medieval Icelandic priest, is but a substitution of a great difficulty for a small. It is one thing to grant that the slain and beloved Balder of the poetic Edda is a marked æsthetic advance on the Balder of Saxo's "history": it is another thing to explain the literary development in the fashion under notice.

And here, once more, there is to be charged on the innovating theorists a lack of comprehensiveness of survey. With all his learning, Dr. Meyer takes no account of the Celtic parallels to the Balder myth. Now, as Professor Rhys has shown, just as there is a plausible mythic equation, Gwydion = Woden = Indra,[2] there is a whole group of

[1] Mr. Nicolson (as cited, p. 130) so summarizes Meyer as to make him seem to hold that the saga-poet had a Christian purpose. Meyer really contends that the poem is not a "tendency" writing at all, being unfitted by its Christian ideas to serve Paganism, and by its pagan terminology to serve Christianity (*Völuspa*, p. 267. Cp. p. 294). Still he speaks of the "entirely Christianized (*ganz verchristlichten*) Balder and Hoder" (p. 220), and finally designates the poem a *Summa Christlicher Theologie* (end).

[2] *Celtic Heathendom*, as cited, pp. 282–304.

parallels between the Celtic Cuchulainn and Balder, besides a number of possible Celtic originals or parallels for the name and character of Loki.[1] In Professor Rhys's opinion such parallels, so far as they may indicate identities, stand for the body of myth common to the Aryan peoples before their divergence. But against this view there stands the difficulty that Balder does not figure at all prominently in the old Scandinavian worship.[2] So far as names of persons and places show, the chief God of Scandinavian paganism was Thor;[3] Odin's supremacy and Balder's prestige being alike apparently late literary developments.[4] Freyr, too, seems to have been the Sun-God alongside of Thor;[5] and, again, Heimdal in the Edda has many of Balder's characteristics;[6] just as, by the common consent of Holtzmann, Bergmann, and Rydberg, the figure of Harbard in the sagas is identical with that of Loki.[7] For Dr. Meyer, the solution in every case is imitation of Christianity: that is to say, the saga-poet or poets created a whole series of new imaginary figures, duplicating one or two figures in the Christian system. Here again we have blank unverisimilitude. As hitherto understood, myths were never made in that fashion. Far less unlikely is the assumption that, to begin with, there were pagan mythical personages with some of the characteristics under notice, and that these were poetically developed.

So far as such a problem can be speculated upon from the outside, the solution seems to lie obviously through the theory of Professors Vigfusson and Powell as to the general development of Icelandic literature.[8] That theory is that the germinal force which wrought the remarkable poetic

[1] *Id.* pp. 538–542.
[2] H. Petersen, as cited, p. 84.
[3] *Id.* pp. 21–71, 76, 83, 87, 90, 94, 111, etc.
[4] As to the original cast of Odin, see a very careful essay *The Cult of Othin*, by H. M. Chadwick (Clay & Sons, 1899).
[5] Petersen, pp. 74–5. Professor Stephens writes: "Even as to Frigg herself, it is certain not only that Frigg and Froya were originally one deity, but also that this Goddess was at first one and the same with the God Froy or Frey, the English Frea" (*Professor Bugge's Studies Examined*, p. 314).
[6] Cp. Rydberg, *Teutonic Mythology*, Eng. tr. pp. 90–97; 402–7.
[7] *Id.* p. 652.
[8] See the article on Icelandic Literature in the *Encyclopædia Britannica*.

evolution in Iceland was contact with the Celtic[1] literary culture of Western Britain and Ireland—a culture resulting from the long-standing Celtic institution of bardism, originally lacking or left rudimentary in Scandinavia. Such a contact could account for many of the mythic parallels noted by Professor Rhys.[2] Not that the negative evidence against the Balder cultus is conclusive. A Balder myth may conceivably have flourished among a stratum of the northern population that had been conquered by the Thor worshippers; for though Balder names are scarce in Scandinavia they appear to survive in Germany.[3] And when such parallels exist as Rydberg has shown between the northern mythology and that of the Vedas, we are not entitled to disallow a single figure in the former as a medieval copy from Christianity. But inasmuch as the æsthetic refinement of the Balder story is one of the main grounds of the latter theory,[4] the play of the Celtic literary influence is an adequate explanation, whereas the theory of a literary mystification, a *Rätselgedicht*, is a flout to all psychological probability.

The Celtic influence, doubtless, might carry with it concrete Christian elements. But against the whole theory of Christian imitation there stands the difficulty that the alleged coincidences are so remote. Dr. Meyer's phrase, "Summa of Christian theology," is a plain misnomer: what his evidence really suggests is an imitation not of the Christian theology but of the mythology. The theology is never once present. There is no sacrifice, as there is no cross. Balder's death is not the salvation of men but a sad catastrophe among the Gods: and the sorrow that prevails until his return connects far more obviously with the mourning cults of the pre-Christian Southern world than with the Christist. Read as a sun-myth, the story is

[1] As to *Slavonic* influence on Scandinavian mythology, see Bergmann, *Le Message de Skirnir et les Dits de Grimnir*, Introd.

[2] A Celtic derivation of the Balder myth is suggested by N. M. Petersen, *Nordisk Mythologi*, pp. 271–282, cited by Nicolson, p. 101.

[3] Grimm, *Teutonic Mythology*, Eng. tr. ch. xi. On the possible significations of the name see also Simrock, *Handbuch der deutschen Mythologie*, 6te Aufl. 1887, § 36, p. 89 ff. Cp. Meyer as cited by Nicolson, pp. 133–4.

[4] Cp. Nicolson, as cited, p. 139.

transparent; as an imitation of Christian theology it is truly a *Rätselgedicht*. As Professor Rhys has pointed out, the detail that Balder cannot return until all nature weeps for his loss is a very close notation of the fact that the sun "returns" in strength only when the winter frosts thaw in the spring, bedewing the whole earth. As regards the "descent into hell," which Professor Bugge thinks must be of Christian derivation, it is part of the normal sun myth,[1] and is obscurely present even in that of Apollo. Now, Professor Bugge thinks that the South-Teutonic God-name Fol, which Dr. Rydberg connects with Falr and Balder, is taken from the name Apollo:[2] why then should not classic sun-myths also have reached the North,[3] supposing them not to have been primary?

Such an item as Balder's funeral pyre, we have seen, Professor Bugge holds to have been suggested by the transmitted story of Patroklos and Achilles, this though the pyre is specifically northern. But what of the pyre of the Sun-God Herakles;[4] and what of the primary phenomenon of sunset, which probably gave the motive? Bugge's theory is that the Christian matter in the myth came through the wandering Vikings. Before even the Vikings, however, Teutons had reached the Græco-Roman world; and thereby hangs the question whether northern myths may not thus at different times have had an entrance into the lore of the south. All the while, Professor Bugge has never asked the obvious questions, Whence came the late cabbage-stalk story in the *Sepher Toldoth Jeschu*? and How came the myth of the blind Longinus into Christian lore? Parts of the *Sepher* are in all probability of late medieval origin. As regards the other myth, the name Longinus may very well be evolved from the spear,

[1] See hereinafter, *Christ and Krishna*, Sec. xvi.; *Mithraism*, § 6.

[2] Citations by Nicolson, pp. 120–1. Cp. Rydberg, p. 464.

[3] In the ancient description of the temple of Upsala by Adam of Bremen the figure of the God Freyr is said to be represented *cum ingenti priapo*. This, like the other statues, suggests an image imported from the south. Cp. H. Petersen, as cited, p. 82, and Grimm, *Teutonic Mythology*, Eng. tr. 1882, i. 104–119.

[4] Robertson Smith, *Religion of the Semites*, p. 353; and O. Müller, as there cited.

longche, of John xix. 34; but the soldier does not become blind in any legend before the ninth century.[1] How did *that* myth originate? It is quite conceivable that the medieval Christians should *adopt* the idea that the soldier who thrust the spear was blind, and had to be guided to the act by others; but on this view the hint had to be given them. Now, though Dr. Rydberg holds that Had or Hoder in the primary form of the Scandinavian myth had not been blind,[2] it is very credible, on mythological grounds, that the Sun-God should be slain by a blind brother = the Darkness or the Winter; and as the northern story turns in the later form upon the magical character of the mistletoe, we are almost driven to conclude that there was a sun-slaying myth of some sort to start with. Why else should the mistletoe have been introduced?[3] It does not follow that the Christians got their idea from the Balder story as we now have it; but the obvious presumption is that a pagan myth preceded theirs; and such a myth may have been current among the Irish Celts, who had contacts alike with northern paganism and southern Christianity. In this way, too, might be explained the entrance of the mistletoe into the northern myth. In its earlier form, the death-dealing weapon is the sword Mistiltein.[4] This would at once suggest the mistletoe; but then the mistletoe is unknown in Iceland and in Sweden.[5] A Celto-Britannic origin would seem to be the only solution.

Again, when Professor Bugge seeks a Christian origin for the weeping of the Mother-Goddess Frigg over the slain Balder, he gives a fair mark for the derision of Professor Stephens.[6] But, common sense apart, it should be noted that in the pre-Christian cults of Attis, Adonis, and Osiris there are similar phenomena, which *do* account for the Christian narrative. So, finally, with the idea that Christ

[1] Cp. Professor G. Stephens, *Bugge's Studies on Northern Mythology*, 1883, as cited, and Nicolson, p. 105.

[2] *Teutonic Mythology*, Eng. tr. i. 653, *note*.

[3] Cp. Rydberg, p. 655, as to the reasoning involved.

[4] Müllenhoff, *Deutsche Altertumskunde*, v. i. 56–7.

[5] Nicolson, as cited, p. 125. But cp. Rydberg, p. 656, as to veneration of the mistletoe among the more southerly Teutons.

[6] Stephens, as cited, p. 339.

was fair-haired. Whence came it? Conceivably from golden-haired Apollo; but then why should not the hyperborean Balder be as fair as the Greek Sun-God Apollo, whose cult was fabled to have come from the hyperboreans?[1] Agni in the Rig-Veda is white, and drives white horses; and Professor Rydberg finds his traits reproduced in Heimdal.[2] Why then seek a later source for the whiteness of Balder? And if *Balder* is an Anglo-Saxon word meaning *Lord*,[3] why are we to assume that it was never applied to a Teutonic God before Jesus, when we know that the title *Lord* was given to many pre-Christian Gods, and that it is the probable original meaning of the Scandinavian God-name Freyr?[4] Above all, why should the consuming love of the Sun-God for Nanna be held to need any literary derivation at a late period from Oenone?

When all is said, the problem of priorities doubtless remains obscure; but enough has been said to show that the confident inference of Christian sources for northern myths which only remotely and in externals compare with the Christian, is thus far a very ill-established and recalcitrant hypothesis. And as the whole Christian legend, in its present terminology, is demonstrably an adaptation of a mass of previous pagan myths, there is in all cases a special ground for doubt as to its being an original for a myth found among a semi-civilized people. The complete justification for such doubt, however, is best to be gathered from a detailed examination of the claim made, as already mentioned, in regard to the myth of Krishna, studied hereinafter.

Meantime, we have seen reason to insist, as regards every species of mythological problem, on a more comprehensive study of relations than is hitherto made by any one school. No single clue will lead us through the maze. Etymology, astronomy, solarism, the vegetation principle,

[1] Pausanias, x. 5. Compare the comments of Hermann Müller, *Das nordische Griechenthum und die urgeschichtliche Bedeutung des nordwestlichen Europas*, 1844, p. 447, ff.; and K. Ottfried Müller, *The Dorians*, bk. ii. c. 4.

[2] *Teutonic Mythology*, pp. 401–6.

[3] Cp. Grimm, i. 220; and Simrock, as cited on p. 123.

[4] Bergmann, *Le Message de Skirnir*, pp. 18–22.

phallicism, symbolism, the influence of art, the pseudo-historical influence of Evemerism, all play their part in elucidating what it concerns us to elucidate—namely, the religious systems of the world in their mythological aspect. It is too much to hope that so vast a growth can be speedily interpreted with scientific certainty; and many a special research must be made before a decisive co-ordination is possible. But at co-ordination we must aim; and the effort towards it must be made *pari passu* with the progress of research, if the latter is not to become unintelligent and sterile.

PART II.

CHRIST AND KRISHNA.

I. The Nature of the Problem.

Some recent English discussion[1] as to the historic relation of the Christ myth and the Krishna myth would seem to make desirable a judicial and yet popular[2] investigation of the subject, from the rationalist point of view. By the rationalist point of view is meant the attitude of disbelief in the supernatural claims of all religions alike—a point of view from which the question of the miraculous origin of Christianity is already disposed of, though of course liable at any time to be reopened. This point of view, however, in no way affects the logic of the following discussion, which lies outside the theological problems, ethical or

[1] The views of Professor Weber, hereinafter discussed, have naturally been welcomed and more or less fully endorsed by many Christian writers, missionary and other. See, for instance, Dr. J. M. Mitchell's *Hinduism, Past and Present*, 1885, pp. 79, 119; Major Jacobs' *Manual of Hindu Pantheism*, 1881, pp. 29–35; article on *Hindu Monism*, by Professor Richard Garbe, in *The Monist*, October, 1892, p. 66; J. Estlin Carpenter, art. on *The Obligations of the New Testament to Buddhism*, in *Nineteenth Century*, December, 1880, pp. 971–2. Mr. Carpenter's acceptance of the pro-Christian view on the historical question typifies the attitude of Christian scholarship. "It is the opinion of the best Indianists," he writes, "that the worship of Krishna did not arise until the fifth or sixth century of our era"; and this confessedly second-hand opinion he immediately erects into a certainty: "Christ can owe nothing to Krishna, because he *preceded him* by four or five centuries." Mr. Carpenter apparently regards Krishna as a historical character.

[2] No pretence is made of indicating the values of Sanskrit consonants, as is done in philological treatises. To the general reader these indications are useless, though vowel accents may not be altogether so. On this head it should be noted that the vowels in Indian names are to be pronounced in the Continental and not in the English manner. That is to say, the names Indra, Krishna, Gita, Veda, Purana, Siva, Rama, are to be pronounced Eendra, Kreeshna, Gheetah, Vehda, Poorahna, Seeva, Rahma. The "a," long or short, is always to be sounded as in "art" or "at," never as in "hate." The long sound is now commonly indicated by a circumflex.

philosophical. What is now in hand is a question of priority of myth forms. Some rationalists have, in my opinion, gone astray over the problem under notice, making errors of assumption and errors of inference in the course of an attempt to settle priority in a particular way; but the detection of these errors does not even settle the point of priority, much less affect the comparative principle.

And here I would point out that, while the Naturalist, like everybody else, is fallible, it is only he, of the two main disputants in this controversy, who can really be impartial, and so do critical service. Inasmuch as he is discussing, not the truth of any religion, but the question as to which religion first developed certain beliefs, he is free to reason justly on the historical data, and so *may* arrive at just conclusions.[1] Rationalists are thus far divided on the historical issue, partly because of the uncertainty of the evidence, partly because of differences or oversights of logical method. But in the case of the disputant who sets out with a belief in the truth of the Christian religion, miracles and all, impartiality is impossible. He holds his own religion to be supernatural and true, and every other to be merely human and false, in so far as it makes supernatural claims. Thus for him every question is as far as possible decided beforehand. He is overwhelmingly biassed to the view that any "myth" which resembles a Christian "record" is borrowed from that; and if, in some instances, he repels that conclusion, it is still for an *a priori* theological reason, as we shall see in the sequel, and not for simple historical reasons. Jesus having been *really* born of a virgin, and the New Testament teaching having been *really* inspired, any other story of a virgin-born demi-god is to be presumed posterior to Pontius Pilate, and any morality which coincides with the Christian is to be presumed an "echo" of that, because otherwise revelation would be cheapened. In the early days of the Church the Christian

[1] "There can be no true objective criticism until a man stands more or less indifferent to the result, and frees himself as far as possible from all subjective relations to the object of criticism." Baur, *Kritische Untersuchung über die kanonischen Evangelien*, 1847, p. 72.

saw, in myths which had confessedly *anticipated* his narratives, devices of the evil Spirit. To-day, the evil Spirit being partly disestablished, this explanation is not officially recognised, and the anticipatory myths of ancient paganism are simply kept out of sight; while as many other myths as possible are sought to be made out post-Christian and therefore borrowed. In this attitude the Christian Church is practically at one. Now, no sound critical result can ever be arrived at on these lines. No conclusion so reached can really strengthen the Christian position, because that position was one of the premises. Christianity remains to be proved all the same. The Naturalist, one says, *may* reason viciously, *may* reach the truth: the believing Christian *must* in such a matter reason viciously, and *can* only add commentary to dogma. But whereas the rationalist inquiry is in this connection logically free of presuppositions, any permanent results it attains are pure gain to human science; and must finally strengthen the Naturalist position if that position be really scientific.

II. The Question of Priority.

We wish to know, then, whether the Krishna myth or legend is in whole or in part borrowed from the Christ myth or Jesus legend, or *vice versâ*. The alternative terms myth or legend,[1] implying respectively the absence and the presence of some personal basis or nucleus for the legends of the Hindu and Christian Incarnations, leave us quite free in our treatment of the historic facts—free, that is, under the restrictions of scientific principle and logical law.

This special question of priority has long been before scholars. In Balfour's *Cyclopædia of India*, in the article "Krishna"—a somewhat rambling and ill-digested compilation—it is stated that "since the middle of the nineteenth century several learned men have formed the opinion that some of the legends relating to Krishna have been taken from the life of Jesus Christ. Major Cunningham

[1] See on this point of terminology Strauss, *Das Leben Jesu*, Einleit. § 10.

believes that the worship of Krishna is only a corrupt mixture of Buddhism and Christianity, and was a sort of compromise intended for the subversion of both religions in India," etc. In point of fact, the theory is much older than the middle of this century, as is pointed out by Professor Albrecht Weber in his exhaustive study of the Krishna Birth-Festival,[1] referred to in the Cyclopædia article. As early as 1762 Father Giorgi, in his *Alphabetum Tibetanum*,[2] discussed the question at length, founding even then on two previous writers, one Father Cassianus Maceratensis, the other the French orientalist, De Guignes (the elder). All three held that the name "Krisna" was only *nomen ipsum corruptum Christi Servatoris*, a corruption of the very name of the Saviour Christ, whose deeds had been impiously debased by inexpressibly wicked impostors. The narratives, Giorgi held, had been got from the *apocryphis libris de rebus Christi Jesu*, especially from the writings of the Manichæans. But his theory did not end there. The Indian epic-names Ayodhya, Yudhishthira, Yadava, he declared to be derived from the scriptural Judah; the geographical name Gomati from Gethsemane; the name Arjuna from John, Durvasas from Peter, and so on.

But long before Giorgi, the English Orientalist Hyde,[3] and long before Hyde, Postel[4] (1552), had declared the name of Brahma to be a corruption of Abraham—a view which appears to have been common among Mohammedans;[5] and Catholic missionaries early expounded this

[1] *Ueber die Krishnajanmâshtami (Krishna's Geburtsfest)* in *Abhandlungen der Königlichen Akademie der Wissenschaften zu Berlin*, 1867. Translated piecemeal in *Indian Antiquary*, vols. iii. vi. (1874–7).

[2] Rome, 1762, pp. 253–263, cited by Weber, p. 311.

[3] *Historia Religionis Veterum Persarum*, 1700, p. 31.

[4] In his commentary on *Abrahami Patriarchæ liber Jesirah*, cited by Maurice, *Indian Antiquities*, 1793, etc. ii. 322 (should be 382—paging twice doubled).

[5] Maurice, as cited, p. 323 (383). It may be, of course, that there is a very remote and secondary connection between the Abraham myth and the religion of India. It has been pointed out (*Bible Folk Lore*, 1884, pp. 25, 110) that Abraham's oak compares with Brahma's tree. The absurdity lies in the assumption that Brahmanism derives from the Hebrew Scriptures. On the problem of the origin and meaning of the name Brahma see Professor Müller's Gifford Lectures on *Psychological Religion*, 1893, p. 240, and citations by him.

discovery among the Hindus, adding that the name of the female deity Saraswati was only a corruption of Sarah.[1] Other propagandists, again, scandalized Sir William Jones by assuring the Hindus that they were "almost Christians, because their Brahma, Vishnu, and Mahesa were no other than the Christian Trinity";[2] and Sir William's shocked protest did not hinder his disciple, the Rev. Thomas Maurice, from speaking of the "almost Christian theology" of Brahmanism;[3] Maurice's general contention being that the Indian and all other Triad systems were vestiges of an original pure revelation.[4] Nor was this all. As early as 1672 the Dutch missionary and trader Balde (Baldæus)[5] maintained a number of the propositions supported in our own generation by Professor Weber (who does not refer to him)—namely, the derivation of parts of the Krishna myth from the Christian stories of the birth of Jesus, the massacre of the innocents,[6] etc.

Following this line of thought, Sir William Jones in 1788 suggested that "the spurious gospels which abounded in the first ages of Christianity had been brought to India, and the wildest part of them repeated to the Hindus, who ingrafted them on the old fable of Cesava, the Apollo of Greece";[7] this after the statement: "That the name of Crishna, and the general outline of his story, were long anterior to the birth of our Saviour, and probably to the time of Homer, we know very certainly."[8] And in the same treatise (*On the Gods of Greece, Italy, and India*) the scholar took occasion to announce that "the adamantine pillars of our Christian faith" could not be "moved by the

[1] Moor's *Hindu Pantheon*, 1810, p. 130. "Writers are found to identify Buddha with the prophet Daniel" (H. H. Wilson, *Works*, ii. 317).

[2] *On the Gods of Greece, Italy, and India*: in *Asiatic Researches*, i. 272.

[3] *Indian Antiquities*, ii. 325.

[4] *Id. ib.* and v. 785, 806, etc. The Rajputs, says the Portuguese historian De Faria y Sousa (17th cent.), "acknowledge one God in three persons, and worship the Blessed Virgin, a doctrine which they have preserved ever since the time of the apostles" (Kerr's *Collection of Voyages*, 1812, vi. 228).

[5] An English translation of his work on Ceylon, etc., was published last century in Churchill's collection of travels, vol. iii.

[6] Cited by Maurice, *History of Hindostan*, 1798, ii. 330, *note*.

[7] *Asiatic Researches*, i. 274.

[8] *Id.* p. 273.

result of any debates on the comparative antiquity of the Hindus and Egyptians, or of any inquiries into the Indian theology."[1] Still later, the French Orientalist, Polier, seeing in the Hebrew Scriptures the earliest of all religious lore, decided that the triumph of Krishna over the serpent Kaliya (whose head he is represented crushing under his foot, and which at times, on the other hand, is seen biting his heel) was "a travesty of the tradition of the serpent-tempter who introduced death into the world, and whose head the saviour of mankind was to crush."[2] These writers had of course taken it for granted that all heathen resemblances to Jewish and Christian stories must be the result of imitation; but on equally *a priori* grounds other Christian writers argued that the "impure" cult of Krishna could never have been derived from Christianity; and the view spread that the Indian myths were of much greater antiquity than had been supposed; the Carmelite monk Paulinus[3] (really Werdin or Wesdin) surmising that the legendary war, with which was connected the story of Vishnu's incarnation in Krishna, was to be dated "a thousand and more years before the birth of Christ."

Thus far both sides had simply proceeded on *a priori* principles, the view that Christianity could not give rise to anything bad being no more scientific than the view that all systems which resembled it must have borrowed from it. A comparatively scientific position was first taken up by the German Kleuker, who, discussing Paulinus' polemic, observed that he "willingly believed that the [Krishna] fable did not first arise out of these [Apocryphal] Gospels," but that nevertheless it might have derived "some matter" from them.[4] According to Weber, the view that the Krishna story was the earlier became for a time the more general one. It is doubtful if this was so; but in 1810 we do find

[1] In the same spirit, Maurice constantly aims at repelling the criticisms of Volney and other sceptics, always begging the question, and resenting its being raised.

[2] *Mythologie des Indous*, i. 445, cited by Weber.

[3] *Systema Brahmanicum*, Rome, 1791, pp. 147, 152; cited by Weber.

[4] *Abhandlungen über die Geschichte und Alterthümer Asiens*, Riga, 1797, iv. 70; cited by Weber. (The work is a translation, by J. F. Fich, of papers from the *Asiatic Researches*, with notes and comments by Kleuker.)

the English Orientalist Moor, following Jones, declaring it to be "very certain" that Krishna's "name and the general outline of his story were long anterior to the birth of our Saviour, and probably to the time of Homer"[1]—this while saying nothing to countenance the theory of borrowing from Christianity, but on the contrary throwing out some new heterodox suggestions. Later the German mythologist Creuzer, in his great work,[2] set aside the supposed Christian parallels, and pointed rather to the Egyptian myth of Osiris. It was impossible, however, that this view should be quietly acquiesced in by Anglo-Indian scholarship, partly bound up as it has been with "missionary enterprise," and subservient as it is to the anti-philosophical spirit which had prevailed in English archæology since the French Revolution. It has been one of the most serious drawbacks to our knowledge of Indian antiquities that not only are the missionaries to such a large extent in possession of the field of research, but the scruples of English pietism, especially during the present century, tend to keep back all data that could in any way disturb orthodoxy at home. Of this tendency we shall find examples as we proceed. How far important evidence has been absolutely suppressed it is of course impossible to say; but observed cases of partial suppression create strong suspicions; and it is certain that the bulk of Christian criticism of the evidences produced has been much biassed by creed.

III. Age of Indian Documents.

On the other hand, however, the case in favour of the assumption of Christian priority has been in a general way strengthened by the precise investigation of Hindu literature, which has gone to show that much of it, as it stands, is of a far later redaction than had once been supposed. It has been truly said by Ritter that "in no literature are so many works to be found to which a remote origin has

[1] *Hindu Pantheon*, p. 200.
[2] *Symbolik*, 3te Aufl. i. 42, cited by Weber.

been assigned on insufficient grounds as in the Indian."[1] The measureless imagination of India, unparalleled in its disregard of fact and its range of exaggeration, has multiplied time in its traditions as wildly as it has multiplied action in its legends, with the result that its history is likely to remain one of the most uncertain of all that are based on documents. It was indeed admitted by the first capable Orientalists that there is, properly speaking, no history in Indian literature at all.[2] All early historical traditions are untrustworthy; but no other people ever approached the flights of fancy of the Hindu mind, which has measured the lives of its mythic heroes by millions of years, and assigned to the Institutes of Menu, certainly not 3,000 years old, an antiquity exceeding 4,320,000 years multiplied by six times seventy-one.[3] Of this delirium of speculation, the true explanation, despite all cavils, is doubtless that of Buckle—the influence of overwhelming manifestations of nature in fostering imagination and stunning the sceptical reason.[4] From even a moderate calculation of Indian antiquity, to say nothing of the fancies of the Brahmans, the step down to documentary facts is startling; and it was not unnatural that scepticism should in turn be carried to extremes.

When the documents are examined, it turns out that the oldest Indian inscriptions yet found are not three centuries earlier than the Christian era.[5] Nor does there seem a probability of much older records being found, there being

[1] *History of Ancient Philosophy*, Eng. tr. 1838, i. 69. Ritter's whole argument, which was one of the first weighty criticisms of the early assumptions of Orientalists, is judicial and reasonable.

[2] See Colebrooke in *Asiatic Researches*, ix. 398–9.

[3] Jones in *Asiatic Researches*, ii. 116. See a number of samples of this disease of imagination cited by Buckle, 3-vol. ed. i. 135–7.

[4] Possibly, too, the partly entranced state of mind cultivated by Hindu sages may involve a repetitive brain process analogous to that seen in dreams, in which objects are multiplied and transformed, and the waking perception of time is superseded.

[5] Those of king Asoka, about 250 B.C. Tiele, *Outlines of the History of Ancient Religions*, Eng. tr. p. 121. See them in *Asiatic Society's Journals*, viii. xii.; in Wheeler's *History of India*, vol iii. Appendix i.; in Rhys Davids' *Buddhism*, pp. 220–8; and in the *Indian Antiquary*, June, 1877, vol. vi. Interesting extracts are given in Professor Müller's *Introduction to the Science of Religion*, ed. 1882, pp. 5, 6, 23.

reason to doubt whether the practice of writing in India dates many centuries earlier. Says Professor Max Müller:—

> "There is no mention of writing materials, whether paper, bark, or skins, at the time when the Indian Diaskeuasts [say, editors] collected the songs of their Rishis [poets or seers]; nor is there any allusion to writing during the whole of the Brahmano period [*i.e.*, according to the Professor's division, down to about 600 or 800 B.C.] . . . . Nay, more than this, even during the Sutra period [600 to 200 B.C.] all the evidence we can get would lead us to suppose that even then, though the art of writing began to be known, the whole literature of India was preserved by oral tradition only."[1]

Professor Müller's division of Indian historical periods is somewhat unscientific; but Professor Teile, who complains of this, accepts his view as to the introduction of the art of writing:—

> "Nearchus (325 B.C.)[2] and Megasthenes[3] (300 B.C.) both state that the Indians did not write their laws; but the latter speaks of inscriptions upon mile-stones, and the former mentions letters written on cotton. From this it is evident that writing, probably of Phœnician origin, was known in India before the third century B.C., but was applied only rarely, if at all, to literature."[4]

But all this, of course, is perfectly consistent with the oral transmission of a great body of very ancient utterance. All early compositions, poetic, religious, and historical, were transmissible in no other way; and the lack of letters did not at all necessarily involve loss. In all probability

[1] *History of Ancient Sanskrit Literature*, pp. 500–1. Cp. p. 244.

[2] One of the generals of Alexander the Great. Only fragments of his account of his voyage on the Indian coast are preserved.

[3] Greek ambassador from Seleucus Nicator to the Indian king Sandracottus (Chandragupta) about 300 B.C. He wrote a work on India, of which, as of that of Nearchus, we have only the fragments preserved by later historians. See them all translated in the *Indian Antiquary*, vols. vi. and vii. (1877–8), from the collection of Schwanbeck.

[4] *Outlines*, as cited. On the general question of the antiquity of writing it was long ago remarked by Jacob Bryant that "The Romans carried their pretensions to letters pretty high, and the Helladian Greeks still higher; yet the former marked their years by a nail driven into a post; and the latter for some ages simply wrote down the names of the Olympic victors from Corœbus, and registered the priestesses of Argos" (Holwell's *Mythological Dictionary*, condensed from Bryant's *Analysis of Ancient Mythology*, 1793, p. 259). The question as regards India, however, cannot be taken as settled. In view of the antiquity of literary habits in other parts of Asia, it may well turn out that the estimates above cited are too low. Tiele's "only rarely, if at all," makes rather too little of the Greek testimony. The Phœnician origin of the Indian alphabets, too, though probable, is only one of many conflicting hypotheses. For a discussion of these see I. Taylor's valuable work on *The Alphabet*, 1883, ii. 304, ff.

ancient unwritten compositions were often as accurately transmitted as early written ones, just because in the former case there was a severe discipline of memory, whereas in the other the facility of transcription permitted of many errors, omissions, and accidental interpolations. And the practice of oral transmission has survived.

"Even at the present day, when MSS. are neither scarce nor expensive, the young Brahmans who learn the songs of the Vedas and the Bráhmanas and the Sutras, invariably learn them from oral tradition, and learn them by heart. They spend year after year under the guidance of their teacher, learning a little day after day, repeating what they have learnt as part of their daily devotion......The ambition to master more than one subject is hardly known in India. ......In the Mahábhárata we read, 'Those who sell the Vedas, and even those who write them, those also who defile them, shall go to hell.' Kumarila [800 C.E.] says: 'That knowledge of the truth is worthless which has been acquired from the Veda, if......it has been learnt from writing or been received from a Súdra.' How then was the Veda learnt? It was learnt by every Brahman during twelve years of his studentship or Bramacharya."[1]

IV. The Special Documents.

In point of fact, no one disputes that the Vedas are in the main of extremely ancient composition (the oldest portions being at least three thousand years old, and possibly much more);[2] and that a large part even of the

[1] Müller, work cited, pp. 501–3. Comp. Tiele, *Outlines*, p. 123. This description corresponds remarkably with Cæsar's account of the educational practices of the Druids. He tells (*De Bello Gallico*, vi. 14) that many entered the Druid discipline, learning orally a great number of verses; some remaining in pupillage as much as twenty years; and this though writing was freely used for secular purposes. Cæsar offers as explanation the wish to keep sacred lore from the many, and the desire to strengthen the faculty of memory. We may add, in regard alike to Druids and Brahmans, the prestige of ancient custom, which in other religions made priests continue to use stone knives long after metal ones were invented. "Brahmanism....has kept to the last to its primitive tools, its penthouses of bamboo, its turf-clods and grass-blades, and a few vessels of wood" (Barth, *The Religions of India*, Eng. tr. p. 129). Modern European parallels will readily suggest themselves.

[2] Barth, p. 6.

literature of commentary upon them, as the Brâhmanas, treatises of ritual and theology, and the Upanishads, religio-philosophical treatises, originated at more or less distant periods before our era. We have seen that Professor Muller makes even the Sutra period—that of the composition of manuals for public and domestic guidance—begin about 600 B.C. But the religious history of India, as of every other country, is that of a process of development: and just as the system of the Vedas was superimposed on simpler forms of nature-worship,[1] so the elaborate system based on the Vedas by the Brahmans was innovated upon from different sides. Thus, four or five centuries before our era, there arose the great movement of Buddhism, in which comparatively new doctrine was bound up with modifications of ancient legends; while on the other hand deities formerly insignificant, or little known, gradually came to be widely popular. Such a development took place in a notable degree in the case of the cult of Krishna, now specially under notice.

At the present moment the worship of Krishna is the most popular of the many faiths of India; and it has unquestionably been so for many centuries. It is equally certain, however, that it is no part of the ancient Vedic system; and that the bulk of the literature in connection with it is not more than a thousand years old, if so much. Mention of Krishna certainly does occur in the earlier literature, but the advent of his worship as a preponderating religion in historic India is late. On the face of the matter, it would seem to have been accepted and endorsed by the Brahmans either because they could not help themselves, or by way of a weapon to resist some other cultus that pressed Brahmanism hard. Hence the peculiar difficulty of the question of origins as regards its details.

The chief documents in which Krishnaism is to be studied are (1) the Mahâbhârata, a great epic poem, of which the events are laid long anterior to our era, and of

[1] In the Veds, says M. Barth, "I recognize a literature that is pre-eminently sacerdotal, and in no sense a popular one" (*Religions of India*, pref. p. xiii.).

which much of the matter is probably pre-Buddhistic;[1] (2) the Bhagavat Gità or "Song of the Most High"; (3) the Puránas, an immense body of legendary and theological literature, including eighteen separate works, of which the earliest written belong to our eighth or ninth century. It is in the latter, especially in the Bhagavat Purána and Vishnu Purána, that the great mass of mythic narrative concerning Krishna is to be found. The tenth book of Bhagavat Purána consists wholly of the Krishna saga. The Gità is a fine poetico-philosophical composition, one of the masterpieces of Indian literature in its kind, in every way superior to the Puránas; and it simply makes Krishna the voucher of its advanced pantheistic teaching, giving no legends as to his life.[2] Of this work the date is uncertain, and will have to be considered later. The Mahâbhárata, again, presents Krishna as a warrior demi-God,[3] performing feats of valour, and so mixed up with quasi-historic events as to leave it an open question whether the story has grown up round the memory of an actual historic personage. But it is impossible to construct for that legendary history any certain chronology; and the obscurity of the subject gives to Christian writers the opportunity to argue that even in the epos Krishna is not an early but a late element —an interpolation arising out of the modern popularity of his cultus. We must then look to analysis and comparative research for light on the subject.

[1] See Professor Goldstücker's essay in the *Westminster Review*, April, 1868; or his *Literary Remains*, ii. 135, 142. The Mahâbhârata, says M. Barth, "which is in the main the most ancient source of our knowledge of these religions, is not even roughly dated; it has been of slow growth, extending through ages, and is besides of an essentially encyclopædic character" (*Religions of India*, p. 187; cp. Goldstücker, ii. 130).

[2] Owing to the Bhagavat Gitâ and the Bhagavat Purâna being alike sometimes referred to as "the Bhagavat," there has occurred the mistake of referring to the Gitâ as containing the legends of Krishna's life.

[3] In one passage "all the heroes of the poem are represented as incarnations of Gods or demons" (Barth, *Religions of India*, p. 172 *n*.).

V. The Krishna Legend.

The outlines of the Krishna saga are well known,[1] but for the convenience of readers I will transcribe the brief analysis given by M. Barth[2]:—

"As a character in the epic....and as accepted by Vishnuism, Krishna is a warlike prince, a hero, equally invincible in war and love, but above all very crafty, and of a singularly doubtful moral character, like all the figures, however, which retain in a marked way the mythic impress. The son of *Vasudeva* and *Devaki*....he was born at Mathurâ, on the Yâmunâ, between Delhi and Agra, among the race of the Yâdavas, a name which we meet with again at a later period in history as that of a powerful Râjput tribe. Like those of many solar heroes, his first appearances were beset with perils and obstructions of every kind. On the very night of his birth his parents had to remove him to a distance beyond the reach of his uncle, King Kamsa, who sought his life because he had been warned by a voice from heaven that the eighth son of Devaki would put him to death, and who consequently had his nephews the princes regularly made away with as soon as they saw the light....Conveyed to the opposite shore of the Yamunâ, and put under the care of the shepherd *Nanda* and his wife *Yaçodâ*, he was brought up as their son in the woods of Vrindâvana, with his brother *Balarâma*, 'Rama the strong,' who had been saved as he was from massacre," and "who has for his mother at one time Devaki herself, at another time another wife of Vasudeva, *Rohini*....The two brothers grew up in the midst of the shepherds, slaying monsters and demons bent on their destruction, and sporting with the Gopîs, the female cowherds of Vrindâvana. These scenes of their birth and infancy, these juvenile exploits, these erotic gambols with the Gopîs, this entire idyll of Vrindâvana....became in course of time the essential portion of the legend of Krishna, just as the places which were the scene of them remain to the present time the most celebrated centres of his worship. Arrived at adolescence, the two brothers put to death Kamsa, their persecutor, and Krishna became king of the Yâdavas. He continued to clear the land of monsters, waged successful wars against impious kings, and took a determined side in the great struggle of the sons of Pându against those of Dhritarâshtra, which forms the subject of the Mahâbhârata. In the interval he had transferred the seat of his dominion to the fabulous city of Dvârakâ, 'the city of gates,' the gates of the West, built on the bosom of the western sea, and the site of which has since been localized in the peninsula of Gujarât. It was there that he was overtaken, himself and his race, by the final catastrophe. After having been present at the death of his brother, and seen the Yâdavas, in fierce struggle, kill one another to the last man, he himself perished, wounded in the heel, like Achilles, by the arrow of a hunter."

[1] See a detailed account in Sir George Cox's *Mythology of the Aryan Nations*, ed. 1882, pp. 367–371.

[2] *Religions of India*, pp. 172–4.

In this mere outline there may be seen several features of the universal legend of a conquering and dying sun-God; and, though the identification of Krishna with the sun is as old as the written legend, it may be well at the outset to indicate the solar meanings that have been attributed to the story by various writers. The name of Krishna means "the black one" (or "blue-black one"),[1] and he thus in the first place comes into line with the black deities of other faiths, notably the Osiris[2] of Egypt, to say nothing of the black manifestations of Greek deities,[3] and of the Christian Jesus.[4] Why then is Krishna, in particular, black? It is, I think, fallacious to assume that any one cause can be fixed as the reason for the attribution of this colour to deities in ancient religions; primary mythological causes might be complicated by the fact that the smoke of sacrifices had from time immemorial blackened[5] statues innumerable, and by the mere fact that, as in Egypt, black stone was very serviceable for purposes of statuary. At Megara there were three ebony statues of Apollo; and the mystic explanation of the choice of material seems to have been purely fanciful.[6] But there are, all the same, primary mythological explanations, which, in view of many of the facts,[7] must be pronounced necessary; and one is offered

[1] See Moor, *Hindu Pantheon*, p. 195, as to the epithet "blue-blooded."

[2] Plutarch, *On Isis and Osiris*, cc. 22, 33.

[3] Pausanias, i. 48; ii. 2; viii. 6, 42; ix. 27.

[4] For a list of black Christian statues of Mary and Jesus (= Isis and Horos) see Higgins's *Anacalypsis*, i. 138. Compare King's *Gnostics*, 2nd ed. p. 173.

[5] Arnobius, *Adv. Gentes*, vi. 16; Baruch, vi. 21. Cp. Pausanias, i. 27, as to the grimy statues of Athênê, said to have been touched by fire when Xerxes took the city.

[6] Pausanias, i. 42. Again, Pausanias asserts (viii. 23) that all River-Gods in Egypt *except* the Nile have white statues, Nilus being figured as black because it flows through Ethiopia!

[7] The Black Demeter may reasonably be assumed to be so as representing the earth; the black-robed Isis is naturally the moon (Plutarch, *I. and O.* 52); and the blue-black robe of Leto (Hesiod, *Theogony*, 406) as Night-Goddess, is obviously significant; but Leto also, like Isis, was further represented as an Earth-Goddess (Macrobius, *Sat.* i. 17), and black in other cases seems to have a more indirect symbolical meaning. The bull Apis and the bull Mnevis, in the Egyptian cults, may be either solar or lunar (Aelian, *De Nat. Animal.*, says Mnevis was sacred to the sun, and Apis to the moon); and we know from Strabo (xvii. 1, § 27) that Mnevis was treated as a God in a temple of the sun at Heliopolis; but both are black. Apis, the "image of the soul of Osiris" (Plutarch, *I. and O.* 20, 29, 39; cp. Macrobius, *Saturnalia*, i. 21), was not only black himself (Strabo, xvii. 1, § 31; Herodotus, iii. 28) but put on black

by Professor Tiele in the present case. Krishna is "the hidden sun-god of the night,"[1] a character attaching more or less to many figures in the Hindu pantheon.

> "That Parasau-Râma, the 'axe-Râma,' is a God of the solar fire, admits of no doubt. He springs from the Brâhman race of the Bhrigus (lightning); his father's name is Jamadagni, 'the burning fire.' Like all Gods of the solar fire, he is the nightly or hidden one, and accordingly he slays Arjuna, the bright God of day....In the myth of Krishna, on the other hand, the two sun-Gods are friendly,[2] the old pair of deities Vishnu and Indra in a new shape."[3]

It should be also noted that Vishnu, of whom Krishna is an Incarnation, is represented as "dark blue,"[4] as is Krishna himself in one statue,[5] and as were at times Kneph[6] and Osiris[7] and Amun[8] in Egypt.

The complications of solar and other mythology, however, are endless; and it is one thing to give a general account such as this, and another to trace with confidence the evolution of such a deity as Krishna from the beginning. Professor de Gubernatis, one of the most acute, if also one of the more speculative of modern mythologists, is convinced of the solar character of Krishna; but points out that in the Rig Veda he is merely a demon[9]—a natural character

robes (Plutarch, *I. and O.* 39, 43.) And Mnevis, said to be the *sire* of Apis, is black to begin with (*I. and O.* 33). Again, the statue of the later God Serapis, like Osiris, was blue or black, as containing many metallic ingredients (Clemens Alexandrinus, *Protrep.* iv.). The alternate ascription of the colour *blue*, as noted below, points to the Night-Sun theory.

[1] *Outlines*, p. 145. Cp. Plutarch, *Isis and Osiris*, c. 9.

[2] In Egypt, Typhon, who was *red* (*Is. and Os.* cc. 22, 30, 31, 33) and was declared to be solar (*Id.* 41), was the enemy of the "good" sun-God Osiris, who was *black*, and who was also declared to represent the *lunar* world (*Id. ib.* Contrast 51, 52). The transpositions are endless—a warning against rigid definitions in less known mythologies.

[3] *Outlines*, p. 145. Arjuna is "himself a name and form of Indra" (Weber in *Indian Antiquary*, iv. 246).

[4] Moor's *Hindu Pantheon*, pp. 26, 27. Goldstücker, *Remains*, i. 309. Compare Pausanias, x. 78, as to a blue-black demon.

[5] Of blue marble, in which he figures as swimming on the water, in the great cistern of Khatmandu (Bähr, *Symbolik des Mosaischen Cultus*, i. 326, and refs.).

[6] Eusebius, *Præparatio Evangelica*, iii. 1.

[7] Cp. Clemens, *Protrept.* iv.; von Bohlen, *Das alte Indien*, i. 228; Kenrick i. 396.

[8] Kenrick, *Ancient Egypt*, i. 370; Tiele, *Egyptian Religion*, Eng. tr. p. 160.

[9] Compare Senart, *Essai sur la Légende du Buddha*, 2e éd. p. 322, *n*. In the early faiths the "dæmon" of mixed characteristics is a constant figure, he being often the deity of outsiders to begin with; while in any case the need to propitiate him would tend to raise his rank. Compare the habit,

of "the black one"; is the enemy of the Vedic God Indra, and only later becomes the God of the cows and cowherds.[1] He remains, however, "the God who is black during the night, but who becomes luminous in the morning among the cows of the dawning, or among the female cowherds."[2] A reasonable presumption is that he was a demon for the Aryan invaders, as being a God of the aborigines; and that for these he was a God of the sky and the rain, hence black, hence God of the night, hence associated with the Night-Sun, hence a Sun-God generally. Again, if Mr. Frazer be right as to the priority of the idea of a Vegetation-God in cults commonly associated with the Sun, Krishna may have been primarily such a God, and as thus associated with the earth may have been black—the explanation of Mr. Frazer for the blackness of Dêmêtêr and Osiris.[3] Or he may have been black merely as a God of the black-skinned natives.[4] In any case he was the rival of Indra,

common in rural Britain till recently, of "speaking the Devil fair," and calling him "the good man." He, being a survival of the genial Pan, exemplifies both of the tendencies to compromise. As to the gradual lowering of the status of dæmons, cp. Grote, *History*, ed. 1888, i. 66. Osiris and Isis, again, were held to be raised "from the rank of good dæmons to that of deities," while Typhon (Set) was discredited, but still propitiated. See Plutarch, l.c. 27, 30. Cp. 25–6, and Pleyte, *La Religion des Pré-Israélites*, Leide, 1865, p. 131. It is thus possible that all three were primarily aboriginal Gods, accepted in different degrees by races of conquerors, though "from the most remote antiquity Set is one of the Osirian circle, and is thus a genuine Egyptian deity" (Tiele, *Egyptian Religion*, Eng. tr. p. 49). The difficulty is to conceive how otherwise Set came to be "in turn revered and hated, invoked and persecuted," till finally his very name was officially proscribed (*Id.* p. 49). Tiele's historical theory is interesting, though not conclusive (pp. 47–51. Cp. E. Meyer, *Geschichte des Alterthums*, i. 69, 71, 112). It is not clear whether Set was not confounded with the alien God Sutech, and thereby discredited (Meyer, p. 135 = § 111. See also his monograph *Set-Typhon*, 1875, pp. 55–62; and cp. Tiele, *Egyptian Religion*, p. 143 and p. 190).

[1] *Zoological Mythology*, 1872, i. 75.

[2] *Id.* p. 51. Cp. Goldziher, *Hebrew Mythology*, Eng. tr. p. 146 ff.

[3] See Note at end of section.

[4] The Greek Hermes, who is surmised (Renan, *Études d'Histoire Religieuse*, pp. 42, 46, following K. O. Müller) to have been a Pelasgic deity, who survived with the ancient race, has many of the characteristics of Krishna, and in particular makes himself black with ashes (Callimachus, *Hymn to Artemis*, 69) in one story. The theory of the commentators (Spanheim, cited in Ernesti's ed. *ad loc.*), that this was not the celestial but a terrestrial Hermes, recalls the formula that the Iliad was written not by Homer but by another poet of the same name. But the old discussions as to the four or five Mercuries, the celestial, the terrestrial, the infernal, and yet others (cp. Cicero, *De Natura Deorum*, iii. 22; Servius on the *Æneid*, iv. 577), point to a number

and so presumably had similar functions. And that original relation to Indra is perfectly borne out by the written legend, in which Krishna is represented as turning away worshippers from Indra,[1] whose cult his probably superseded, and who figures in the account of Krishna's death and ascension as a subordinate God[2] (obviously = the firmament, a character always more or less associated with him in the Vedas, where he is "the pluvial and thundering God"[3]), through whose region of space, Krishna passes on the way to heaven.[4]

But as against all such attempts to explain Krishnaism in terms of the observed mythic tendencies of ancient Aryan religion, there is maintained on the Christian side—not, as we shall see, by any important thinker—the proposition before mentioned, that the entire Krishna legend is a late fabrication, based on the Christian gospels. It is necessary, therefore, to examine that argument in detail before we form any conclusions.

Note on the Black Osiris.

That Osiris was either a Sun-God or the Nile-God in origin is the view most favoured by the evidence in Plutarch (*Isis and Osiris*, cc. 32, 33). Half a century ago, however, Kenrick (*Ancient Egypt*, 1850, i. 400) rejected the solar theory, and identified Osiris with the Earth and the principle of fertility; here anticipating Mr. J. G. Frazer, who in *The Golden Bough* (1890, i. 311, ff.) insists, as against Tiele and others, that Osiris was a God of Vegetation. The solution seems to lie in admitting that the later Osiris combined *all* the characteristics in question. To insist upon any one in particular is to obscure the psychological process of ancient dogmatics.

of syncretic adaptations, of which the result was that Hermes, though not clearly a sun-God to start with, in the end has the solar characteristics (cp. Eméric-David, *Introduction*, end).

[1] *Vishnu Purâna*, b. v. cc. 10, 11. Wilson's trans. 1840, pp. 522–7.

[2] He acknowledges himself vanquished by Krishna (*Id.* c. 30, p. 588) and honours him (*Id.* c. 12, p. 528). Similarly Krishna overthrows Varuna. Muir, *Sanskrit Texts*, iv. ch. ii. § 5.

[3] Gubernatis, i. 403.

[4] Maurice, *History of Hindostan*, ii. 473, professing to follow the Mahâbhârata.

The most obvious grounds for connecting Osiris with Vegetation are his associations with corn and trees (Frazer, i. 303–9). But it is not at all clear that these are the earliest characteristics of the Egyptian God. Rather the strictly historical evidence appears to show that Osiris was originally a Sun-God, whose cultus was latterly modified by foreign elements—that, in fact, the Vegetation-principle, regarded by Mr. Frazer as the root of the cult, was added in imitation of the Adonis cult of Byblos. See Meyer, *Geschichte des Alterthums*, i. 67–69 and refs. The arboreal character of Osiris is shared by him with Dionysos (see above, p. 84), who nevertheless assumed solar characteristics, and was represented as gold-coloured or red (Pausanias, ii. 2); and by Yahweh, who has no other characteristic of the Vegetation-God. If then Yahweh assumed it after having begun as a solar or thundering God, the Osiris cult may have done the same.

The case being thus complicated, it is hardly possible to settle it on the side of one hypothesis by ascribing the blackness of the God to his connection with the earth. As we have seen, there are many grounds on which deities may be represented as black. Osiris was held by some to be black as representing *water* (Plut. 33); while others associated him with sun and moon respectively (*Id.* 43, 51, 52). A similar blending occurs in the case of the Nile-God Sebak (Tiele, *Egyptian Religion*, Eng. tr., pp. 135–137). The water theory may be the most comprehensive solution (cp. Selden, *De Diis Syris*, Syntag. i. cap. 4, ed. 1680, p. 73). Mr. Frazer offers no explanation of Osiris as *blue*, though on his view he can explain him as black or as green (i. 403), which latter colour is said by Wilkinson (*Manners and Customs of Ancient Egyptians*, ed. 1878, iii. 81) to be very common in the Osiris monuments. But we have here to note (1) that Osiris might be green by the mere chance of the medium being green basalt (see Maspero, *Manual of Egyptian Archæology*, Eng. tr. ed. 1895, p. 237); (2) that in the coloured monuments "*the blues have turned somewhat green or grey; but this is only on the surface*" (*Id.* p. 203); and (3) that "*water* is always represented by a flat tint of blue, *or* by blue covered with zig-zag lines in black" (*Id.* p. 204). So in Greece black bulls were sacrificed to Poseidon as representing the colour of the sea (Cornutus, *De nat. Deor.* c. 22). All things considered, it seems likely that in

Egypt, where the soil counted for so little without the Nile overflow, the latter rather than the former would figure as the greater or more worshipful thing.

In any case, Osiris cannot well have been merely an Earth-God or Plant-Spirit. It is not disputed that from the earliest times he is the consort of Isis; and Isis, as Mr. Frazer grants, is an Earth-Goddess and Corn-Goddess; approximating at several points to Dêmêtêr, like whom she is figured as black. But the Earth can hardly have been figured as at once God and Goddess, in a married couple, from time immemorial. If Isis be the Grain or Earth, Osiris might be either the fructifying Nile or the Sun, or both, but hardly Grain or Earth over again. It is true that there was an Earth-God Tellumon (Preller, *Röm. Myth.* p. 402), and that the Earth was described by the later Egyptians as male under the form of rock, and as female under the form of arable land (Seneca, *Quest. nat.* iii. 14; cp. Macrobius, *Saturnalia*, iii. 8, as to the moon). But the rock would not symbolize the fructifying power of Osiris; and the idea was probably drawn late from the cult of Mithra, which rivalled the Osirian. It is true further that Osiris was held lord of all things fiery and spiritual, and Isis ruler of all things dry and moist (Diod. i. 11); and there is some evidence that fruit-bearing trees were called male, and others female; but these are visibly late theories or common fancies, not early God-ideas. Then the blackness of Osiris is not symbolical of the Earth, but of something else. Even the blackness of Isis, however, is not to be ascribed strictly and solely to her as symbolizing the Earth; she unquestionably was associated, whether first or last, with the Moon and the zodiacal Virgin, and would thus be black as Queen of the Night Sky, as was the black Aphrodite. (*Pausanias*, viii. 6; *Orphica*, ii. 1–2; Macrobius, last cit.)

The truth is, there was no means by which any God or Goddess in antiquity, among nations with cognate or competing cults, could be prevented from gradually assimilating to any of the others with similar status. What happened later in the Christ cult, before the period of crystallization under Roman headship, happened perforce in the older cults. As Yahweh grew from the God of a tribe to a God of the nations, so every thriving deity tended to receive wider and wider functions. The process was economic as well as psychic. It was every priest's business to increase the vogue of his temple's divinities, unless he were expressly hindered by the bestowal of a monopoly on a particular God by a particular king; and every worshipper, when smoothly handled, was naturally ready to aggrandize his favourite deity. That this historically took place in the case of Osiris we know from the monuments, which show him to have been assimilated to the Sun-God Ra (Tiele, p. 44. Cp. Diodorus Siculus, i. 25).

But this was only one of many such blendings. We know for instance that Ptah, who was "certainly not originally a Sun-God," is "distinctly called the sun-disc" (Chantepie de la Saussaye, *Manual of the Science of Religion*, Eng. tr. p. 425). Now, Ptah does seem to have been originally an Earth-God or Vegetation-God, and *he* was represented as green (Tiele, *Egyptian Religion*, Eng. tr. p. 160), though he had also "the blue beard and diadem of Amun, whose colour was blue." Amun in turn seems to have been a Nile-God and a Sun-God (Tiele, pp. 146, 148, 149). In short, a unification of *all* the Gods with the Sun-God was one of the most prevalent tendencies in Egyptian religion (noted by Frazer, i. 314), as again in the Mexican. "The Gods of the dead and the elemental Gods were almost all identified with the sun, for the purpose of blending them in a theistic unity" (Maspero, cited by Lang, *M. R. R.* 2nd ed. ii. 134). Compare E. Meyer, *Geschichte des alten Aegyptens*, in Oncken's series, K. iii. p. 249. As to the case of Cham, the Vegetation-God, who was blended with the Sun-God Horos, see Tiele, pp. 122–127. Such combinations may have been deliberately arranged among the priests, who at all times received an enormous revenue (Diodorus Siculus, i. 28, 81).

It is thus doubly unnecessary to resort for explanation of any junction of the solar and vegetal principles to the ingenious theory of Mr. Frazer (ii. 369) that the fire-sticks would be held to contain fire as a kind of sap. Kenrick (i. 403) readily acknowledged that the principle of fertility would involve alike the Sun and the Nile; and the historical data since collected amply bear him out.

VI. The Christian Argument.

Among modern statements of the Christian theory of Krishnaism, one of the most explicit and emphatic is that inserted by an anonymous Sanskritist in a criticism of the first volume of Mr. J. Talboys Wheeler's *History of India*, in the *Athenæum* of August 10th, 1867. The criticism is hostile, pointing out that Mr. Wheeler "is not a Sanskrit scholar, nor has he very carefully examined the translations with which he works," so that "we are never sure, without referring to the original, what particulars [as to Hindu legends] are drawn from the great epic, and what are from the Puránas and other sources." It might have been added that the previous performance of Mr. Wheeler had shown him to be a somewhat biassed historian. He had produced a number of popular abridgments or manuals of Old and New Testament history, in one of which he does not scruple to assert that while "Matthew, who wrote for the Jews, traces the pedigree of Joseph through David to Abraham, Luke, who wrote for the Gentiles, traces the descent of Mary through David to Adam."[1] Such an apologist naturally does not flinch at alleging that Celsus and Porphyry "recognize" the gospels as the "genuine work of the apostles";[2] and for such a reasoner, it is readily intelligible, the "mythic theory" is disposed of by the argument that it would make out the history of Julius Cæsar to be a thorough myth. It will doubtless be comforting to many to learn that this soundly religious writer was made Professor of "Moral and Mental Philosophy and Logic" in the Presidency College of Madras, and that he has written an elaborate history of India with a considerable measure of acceptance.

But the critic of Mr. Wheeler's history in the *Athenæum* is hardly the person to take exception to intellectual tendencies such as these. His own philosophy of history includes the belief that "the history of Krishnah has been borrowed by the Brahmans from the Gospel"; and he proceeds to prove his case by the following account of the legend in the Bhagavat Purána and Mahábhárata—an

[1] *Abridgment of New Testament History*, 1854, p. 35. Cp. *Analysis and Summary of New Testament History*, 1859, by same author (p. 28), where it is explained that Luke went back to Adam because he was "desirous of proving [the Gentiles'] admission into the Gospel covenant"—the descent of David from Adam not being an established hypothesis.

[2] *Analysis*, as cited, p. xxviii.

account which is worth citing at length as indicating a number of the minor myth-resemblances in the Hindu and Christian narratives, and as unintentionally paving the way for a fresh historical investigation of the latter:—

"The recital [in the Purâna] commences with the announcement that to hear the story of Krishnah and believe it is all that is required for salvation; and throughout the narrative the theme of exhortation is faith. Next it is declared that, sin and impiety having spread over the whole world, the Deity resolved to become incarnate in the form of Krishnah. He determined to destroy a tyrant king, whose name signifies Lust, who ruled at Mathurá, and who murdered children. Krishnah is represented as born the nephew of this king, and therefore of royal descent. The name of his tribe is Yadu, which is almost the same as Yahudah in Hebrew. His real mother was Devakí, which signifies the Divine Lady, and his reputed mother Yasoda, or Yashoda. His father's name was Vasudev. In comparing this word with Yúsef, we must remember that Dev in Sanskrit signifies divine, and the *d* appears to have been inserted from that word. The resemblance of the name Krishnah itself to Christ is remarkable enough, but it becomes more so when we consider that the root 'Krish' means 'to tinge,' and *may well be taken to signify also 'anoint.'* Preliminary to the birth of Krishna the four Vedas become incarnate, and the tyrant king is warned by a divine voice that a son is to be born in his house who will destroy him. Upon this he puts to death the infants that are born to the Divine Lady, and makes a great slaughter of the tribe of Yadu. Notwithstanding this, Krishnah is born and placed in a basket for winnowing corn; *in other words, a manger.* His father then carries him off to Gokula (or Goshen, the eastern side of Lower Egypt), which is represented as a country place near Mathurá. On finding that the child has escaped, the tyrant makes a slaughter of infant children. A variety of puerile fables suited to the Hindu taste follow, showing how Krishnah was subject to his reputed mother, and how he reproved her. Being now thought to be the son of a shepherd, Krishnah plays in the wilderness, and is assaulted by the various fiends, and overcomes them all. This temptation winds up with the overthrow of the great serpent, upon whose head, 'assuming the weight of the three worlds, he treads.' Even in the strange recital of Krishnah's sports with the cowherdesses, threads of allusions to the Gospels are not wanting. Krishnah is continually manifesting his divinity, and yet disclaiming it. He goes to an Indian fig-tree and utters a sort of parable, saying, Blessed are those that bear pain themselves and show kindness to others. In another place he says that those who love him shall never suffer death. He proceeds to abolish the worship of Indra, the God of the air, and to invite his followers to worship a mountain. He directs those about him to close their eyes, and issues from the interior of the mountain with a 'face like the moon and wearing a diadem.' In this there seems to be an allusion to the Transfiguration. Then follows a scene suited to Hindu taste. Indra rains down a deluge, and Krishnah defends the inhabitants of Braj by supporting the mountain on his finger, and he is then hailed as the God of Gods. Krishnah now resolves on returning from the country to the city of the tyrant king. He is followed by a multitude of women and by the cowherds. He enters the city in royal apparel. He is met by a deformed woman, who anoints him with sandalwood oil. On this Krishnah makes her straight and beautiful, and promises that his regard for her shall be perpetual; on which her good fortune is celebrated by all the people of the place. In the account of this miracle the narratives in Mark xiv. 3 and Luke xiii. 11 are blended. It may be as well to mention here another miracle, which is mentioned in the Mahá Bhárata. Krishnah is there said to have restored the son of a widow to life: 'And Krishnah laid hold of the dead man's hand and said, Arise, and by the will of the Almighty the dead man immediately arose.'....A great army of barbarians is....assembled by a distant king to destroy the holy city of Mathurá....Krishnah then transports the city and his disciples to Dwarka, which is built in the sea. *This appears to be a distorted account of the siege of Jerusalem and the flight of the Christians.* Krishnah now returns to Mathurá and combats with the barbarians; flies from their chief, and is pursued into a cave of the White mountains, where there is a man sleeping, covered with a silken robe, apparently dead. This man arises from sleep and consumes the pursuer of Krishnah. In this account of the cave there are *evident allusions to the burial and resurrection of Christ;* and in a following chapter there is an account of the descent of Krishnah into Hades and his recovery of certain persons from the dead....At the great sacrifice performed by Yudhishthira.... the task which devolves on Krishnah is that of washing the feet of those present. One person alone is said to have been dissatisfied, and that is Duryodhana, who is generally regarded as an incarnation of the Evil Spirit, and who, like Iscariot, here carries the bag, and acts as treasurer. ....It must be admitted, then, that there are most remarkable coincidences between the history of Krishnah and that of Christ. This being the case, and there being proof positive that Christianity was introduced into Judea at an epoch when there is good reason to suppose the episodes which refer to Krishnah were inserted in the Mahá Bhárata, the obvious inference is that the Brahmans took from the Gospel such things as suited them, and so *added preëminent beauties to their national epic*, which otherwise would in no respect have risen above such poems as the Sháhnámah of the Persians."[1]

As to the authorship of this criticism we can only speculate. In an allusion to the doctrine of the Bhagavat Gitá the writer expresses himself as "willing to admit" that "the Gitá is the most sublime poem that ever came from an uninspired pen"; thus taking up the position of ordinary orthodoxy, which presupposes the supernatural origin of the Christian system, and prejudges every such question as

[1] *Athenæum*, as cited, pp. 168–9.

we are now considering. This is the standing trouble with English scholarship. Even Professor Max Müller, who has produced an *Introduction to the Science of Religion*, is found writing to a correspondent in terms which seemingly imply at once belief in Christian supernaturalism and a fear that the discussion of certain questions in comparative mythology may damage the faith. "Even supposing," he writes, "some or many of the doctrines of Christianity were found in other religions also (and they certainly are), does that make them less true? Does a sailor trust his own compass less because it can be proved that the Chinese had a compass before we had it?" And again: "These questions regarding the similarities between the Christian and any other religions are very difficult to treat, and *unless they are handled carefully much harm may be done*."[1] From scholarship of this kind (though, as it happens, Professor Müller finally opposes the theory of Christian derivation) one turns perforce to that of the continent, where, whatever be the value of the conclusions reached, we can at least as a rule trust the scholar to say candidly what he knows, and to look impartially for the truth.

Thus Professor Weber, who refers to the *Athenæum* critic's argument in his study on the "Geburtsfest," emphatically distinguishes between what he thinks plausible and what seems to him extravagant,[2] though the argument in question goes to support some of his own positions. The identifications of the names Yasoda, Yusef, and Vasudev, Gokula and Goshen, he rightly derides as being "*à la* P. Giorgi"; and he mentions that the stories of the woman's oblation and forgiveness, and also that of the raising of the widow's dead son, are not from the Mahâbhârata at all, but from the Jaimini-Bhârata, a work of the Purâna order[3]—a point which, of course, would not essen-

[1] Letters to C. A. Elflein, printed at end of a pamphlet by the latter entitled *Buddha, Krishna, and Christ*.

[2] He puts a "*sic!*" after the spelling *Yashoda* in quoting this passage, and another after the word "inserted" in the phrase "appears to have been inserted from that word."

[3] *Ueber die Krishnajanmâshtami*, as cited, p. 315, *n*.

tially affect the argument. On the main question he sums up as follows :—

"If we could so construe these words that they should harmonize with the view of Kleuker" [before quoted] "we might contentedly accept them. If, however, they are to be understood as meaning that the history of Krishna in the lump (*überhaupt*) was first taken from the 'Gospel history' (and indeed the author seems not disinclined to that view), then we cannot endorse them."[1]

That is to say, the theory of the Christian origin of the general Krishna legend is rejected by Weber, the most important supporter of the view that *some details* in that legend have so originated. And not only is this rejection overwhelmingly justified, as we shall see, by the whole mass of the evidence, earlier and later, but so far as I am aware no Sanskrit scholar of any eminence has ever put his name to the view maintained by the anonymous writer in the *Athenæum*. Even Mr. Talboys Wheeler, who believes all the Gospels "and more," does not go to these lengths. He is more guarded even where he suggests similar notions.

"The account of Raja Kansa," he observes, "is supposed by many to have been borrowed from the Gospel account of King Herod. Whether this be the case or not, it is certain that most of the details are mythical, and inserted for the purpose of ennobling the birth of Krishna"[2]—

—it being Mr. Wheeler's opinion that the story of Krishna as a whole has a personal and historic basis. He further holds that "the grounds upon which Krishna seems to have forgiven the sins of the tailor" [who made clothes for his companions] "seem to form a travestie of Christianity";[3] and, like the writer in the *Athenæum* and earlier pietists, he thinks that the Gospel stories of the bowed woman and the spikenard "seem to have been thrown together in the legend of Kubja."[4] On the other hand, however, he conceives that the Hindus may have invented some things for themselves :—

"Krishna's triumph over the great serpent Kaliya was at one time supposed to be borrowed from the triumph of Christ over Satan. There

[1] *Id.* p. 316.
[2] *History of India*, i. 464, *note*.
[3] *Id.* p. 471, *n.*
[4] *Id.* p. 470, *n.*

appears, however, to be no allusion whatever to the bruising of the Serpent's head in the sense in which it is understood by Christian commentators."[1]

It may be surmised that Mr. Wheeler, being capable of this amount of prudence, would not be disposed to endorse the more original speculations of his critic in the *Athenæum*, a few of which I have put in italics. It may be noted, too, that he does not think fit to dwell much on the puerility which fits the details of the Krishna legend for the "Hindu taste" and the "Hindu mind," though his earlier writings betray no suspicion of puerility in the tales of the Gospels.

VII. The Central Disproof.

Unsupported as are the Christian theories of the late origin of the Krishna legend, it is necessary to cite the evidence which repels them. The point, indeed, might be held as settled once for all by the evidence of Patanjali's Mahâbhâshya or "Great Commentary," a grammatical work based on previous ones, and dating from the second century B.C., but first made in part accessible to European scholars by the Benares edition of 1872. The evidence of the Mahâbhâshya is thus summed up by the learned Professor Bhandarkar of Bombay, after discussion of the passages on which he founds, as clearly proving :—

"1st. That the stories of the death of Kansa and the subjugation of Bali were popular and current in Patanjali's time.

"2nd. That Krishna or Vasudeva was mentioned in the story as having killed Kansa.

"3rd. That such stories formed the subjects of dramatic representations, as Purânic stories are still popularly represented on the Hindu stage.

"4th. That the event of Kansa's death at the hands of Krishna was in Patanjali's time believed to have occurred at a very remote time."[2]

[1] *Id.* p. 465, *n.*

[2] Art. "Allusions to Krishna in Patanjali's Mahâbhâshya" in the *Indian Antiquary*, Bombay, vol. iii. (1874), p. 16.

Other passages, Professor Bhandarkar thinks, would appear "to be quoted from an existing poem on Krishna"; and, in his opinion, "Not only was the story of Krishna and Kansa current and popular in Patanjali's time, but it appears clearly that the former was worshipped as a God." And the Professor concludes that "If the stories of Krishna and Bali, and others which I shall notice hereafter, were current and popular in the second century B.C., some such works as the Harivansa and the Puranas must have existed then."

Discussing the Mahâbhâshya on its publication (some years after his paper on the Birth-festival), Professor Weber had already[1] conceded that it pointed not only almost beyond doubt to a pre-existing poetic compilation of the Mahâbhârata Sagas, but to the ancient existence of the Kansa myth. Kansa, he pointed out, figured in regard to Bali, in the passages quoted in the Mahâbhâshya, as a *demon*, and his "enmity towards Krishna equally assumed a *mythical* character, into which also the different colours of their followers (the 'black ones' are then also those of Kansa? though Krishna himself signifies 'black'!) would seem to enter. Or," the Professor goes on, speculating at random, "could there be thereby signified some Indian battles between Aryans and the aborigines occupying India before them?" In another place,[2] alluding to the contention of Dr. Burnell[3] that "much in the modern philosophical schools of India comes from some form of Christianity derived from Persia," Professor Weber pointed out that "quite recently, through the publication of the Mahâbhâshya, a much older existence is proved for the Krishna cultus than had previously seemed admissible." Finally, in commenting[4] on the argument of Professor Bhandarkar, Professor Weber allows that the passages cited by the scholar from Patanjali are "quite conclusive and very

[1] *Indische Studien*, xiii. (1873), pp. 354–5, 357.

[2] Notice of vol. iv. of Muir's *Original Sanskrit Texts*, 1873, reprinted in Weber's *Indische Streifen*, iii. 190–1.

[3] *Academy*, June 14th, 1873.

[4] In the *Indian Antiquary*, August, 1875 = iv. 246.

welcome" as to an intermediate form of Krishna-worship; though he disputes the point as to the early existence of literature of the Purâna order—a point with which we are not here specially concerned—and goes on to contend that the passages in question "do not interfere at all with the opinion of those who maintain, on quite reasonable grounds," that the *later* development of Krishnaism "has been *influenced to a certain degree* by an acquaintance with the doctrines, legends, and symbols of the early Christians; or even with the opinion of those who are inclined to find in the Bhagavadgitâ traces of the Bible; for though I for my part am as yet not convinced at all in this respect, the *age* of the Bhagavadgitâ is still so uncertain that these speculations are at least not shackled by any chronological obstacles."

I know of no recent expert opinion which refuses to go at least as far as Weber does here. His persistent contention as to the presence of some Christian elements in the Krishna cult I will discuss later; but in the meantime it is settled that the most conservative Sanskrit scholarship on the continent not only admits but insists on the pre-Christian character of the Krishna mythus, and of such an important quasi-Christian element in it as the story of Kansa, which had so zealously been claimed (and that with Professor Weber's consent in former years) as an adaptation from the Herod story in the Christian Gospel.

VIII. Antiquity of Krishnaism.

The proof of the pre-Christian antiquity of the Krishna cult, however, does not rest merely on the text of the Mahâbhâshya, or the conclusions of scholars in regard to that. The extravagance of the orthodox Christian argument was apparent—it was rejected, we have seen, by Professor Weber—before the passages in the Mahâbhâshya were brought forward. There have long been known at least three inscriptions, in addition to at least one other literary allusion, which prove Krishnaism to have flourished long before the period at which the Christians represent it to have been concocted from the Gospels.

1. The Bhitari pillar inscription, transcribed and translated by Dr. W. H. Mill,[1] and dating from, probably, the second century of our era, proves Krishna to be then an important deity. The Krishna passage runs, in Dr. Mill's translation :—"May he who is like Krishna still obeying his mother Devaki, after his foes are vanquished, he of golden rays, with mercy protect this my design." This translation Lassen[2] corrects, reading thus:—"Like the conqueror of his enemies, Krishna encircled with golden rays, who honours Devaki, may he maintain his purpose"; and explaining that the words are to be attributed to the king named in the inscription (Kumáragupta), and not to the artist who carved it, as Dr. Mill supposed. "As in the time to which this inscription belongs," Lassen further remarks, "human princes were compared with Gods, Krishna is here represented as a divine being, though not as one of the highest Gods." Dr. Mill, on the other hand, holds Krishna to be understood as "the supreme Bhagavat" referred to in other parts of the inscription. However this may be, the cultus is proved to have existed long before the arrival of Christian influences.

2. Two fragmentary inscriptions discovered in 1854 by Mr. E. C. Bayley,[3] of the Indian Civil Service, equally point to the early deification of Krishna. One has the words "Krishnayasasa áráma" in Aryan Pali letters; the other "Krishnayasasya áráma médangisya." The first two words mean "The Garden of Krishnayasas," this name meaning "the glory of Krishna"; and Mr. Bayley thinks that "médangisya," corpulent, is some wag's addition to the original inscription. As to the date, Mr. Bayley writes:—"The form of the Indian letters had already led me to assign them roughly to the first century

[1] In the *Journal of the Asiatic Society of Bengal*, January, 1837, pp. 1–17.

[2] *Indische Alterthumskunde*, ii. (1849), p. 1108, *note*.

[3] *Journal of Asiatic Society*, xxiii. 57.

A.D.[1] On showing them, however, to Major A. Cunningham, he kindly pointed out that the foot strokes of the Aryan letters ally them to those on the coins of 'Pakores'; and he therefore would place them more accurately in the first half of the second century A.D.[1] at the earliest." Major Cunningham, it will be remembered, is one of those who see imitation of Christianity in the Krishna legends, so his dating is not likely to be over early. In any case, Mr. Bayley admits that the inscriptions "would seem to indicate the admission of Krishna into the Hindu Pantheon at the period" when they were cut. "If, however," he adds, "this be eventually established, it by no means follows that the name was applied to the same deity as at present, still less that he was worshipped in the same manner." It is not very clear what Mr. Bayley means by "the same deity"; or whether he would admit the God of the Jews to be the same deity as the Father of Jesus Christ, as worshipped by Archdeacon Farrar. But if he merely means to say that the Hindu conception of Krishna, like his ritual, might be modified after centuries, his proposition may readily be accepted.

3. The Buddal pillar inscription, translated by Wilkins,[2] to which I have observed no allusion in recent writers on Krishnaism, serves equally to prove the early existence of a legend of a divine Krishna born of Devaki and nursed by Yasoda. It contains the passage, alluding to a distinguished lady or princess:—"She, like another Devaki, bore unto him a son of high renown, who resembled the adopted of Yasodha and husband of Lakshmi"—the Goddess Lakshmi being here identified with Krishna's bride. This inscription was dated by Wilkins "shortly B.C.," and by Sir William Jones 67 C.E. I have not ascertained how it is placed by later scholars; but in any case it must long antedate the periods assigned by Professor Weber and the

[1] By "century A.D." Mr. Bayley means "century after Christ." "First century *anno domini*," a form constantly used by academic writers, is nonsense. In this paper I use "C.E." to signify "Christian era," as "B.C." signifies "before Christ." This, or the use of the form "A.C.," is surely the reasonable course.

[2] *Asiatic Researches*, i. 131.

Athenæum critic to the arrival of the Christian influences which are supposed to have affected later Krishnaism.

4. In the Khandogya Upanishad, a document admittedly older than our era, there occurs[1] this passage:—"Ghora Angirasa, after having communicated this (view of the sacrifice) to Krishna, the son of Devaki—and he never thirsted again (after other knowledge)—said," etc. On this passage I transcribe the comment appended by Professor Müller to his translation:—

> "The curious coincidence between Krishna Devakîputra, here mentioned as a pupil of Ghora Angirasa, and the famous Krishna, the son of Devakî, was first pointed out by Colebrooke, *Miscell. Essays*, ii. 177. Whether it is more than a coincidence is difficult to say. Certainly we can build no other conclusions on it than those indicated by Colebrooke, that new fables may have been constructed, elevating this personage to the rank of a God. We know absolutely nothing of the old Krishna Devakîputra except his having been a pupil of Ghora Angirasa, nor does there seem to have been any attempt made by later Brahmans to connect their divine Krishna, the son of Vasudeva, with the Krishna Devakîputra of our Upanishad. This is all the more remarkable because the author of the Sandilya-sutras, for instance, who is very anxious to found a srauta authority for the worship of Krishna Vasudeva as the supreme deity, had to be satisfied with quoting....modern compilations....Professor Weber has treated these questions very fully, but it is not quite clear to me whether he wishes to go beyond Colebrooke, and to admit more than a similarity of name between the pupil of Ghora Angirasa and the friend of the Gopis."

Professor Weber, I may mention in passing, *does* "admit more than a similarity of name"; in his treatise on the Birth Festival[2] he founds on the Upanishad reference as indicating one of the stages in the development of Krishnaism. And as Professor Müller does not dispute in the least the antiquity and authenticity of that reference, but only queries "coincidence," it may be taken as pretty certain that we have here one more trace of the existence of the Krishna legend long before the Christian era. There is nothing in the least remarkable in the fact of the passage not being cited by a writer who wanted texts on the status of Krishna as "the supreme deity," because the passage

[1] iii. 17, 6; Müller's trans., *Sacred Books of the East*, i. 52.
[2] As cited, p. 316.

clearly does not so present Krishna. But it is no part of our case to make out that Krishna was widely worshipped as "the supreme deity" before our era; on the contrary, the evidence mostly goes to show that he attained his eminence, or at least his Brahmanical status, later. The point is that his name and story were current in India long before the Christian legends, as such, were heard of; and the series of mutually supporting testimonies puts this beyond doubt.

IX. Invalid Evidence.

It does not seem likely that the force of the foregoing evidence will be seriously disputed. At the same time, it is necessary to point out that some of the data relied on by some scholars, and in particular by Professor Lassen, to prove the early existence of Krishnaism will not by themselves support that conclusion. Lassen, who identifies Krishna with the Indian Hercules spoken of by Megasthenes, puts his case thus:—

> "Megasthenes, whose account of ancient India is the weightiest because the oldest of all those left to us by foreigners, has.... mentioned [the] connection of Krishna with the Pandavas, and his remarks deserve close attention.... as giving a historical foothold in regard to the vogue of the worship of Krishna. His statement is as follows: He" [*i.e.*, the Indian Hercules] "excelled all men in strength of body and spirit; he had purged the whole earth and the sea of evil, and founded many cities; of his many wives was born only one daughter, Πανδαίη, Pandaia, but many sons, among whom he divided all India, making them kings, whose descendants reigned through many generations and did famous deeds; some of their kingdoms stood even to the time when Alexander invaded India. After his death, divine honours had been paid him. (Diodor. ii. 39. Arrian, *Ind.* 8.) That we are entitled to take this Hercules for Krishna appears from the fact that he was specially honoured by the people of Surasena. (*Ind.* viii. 5.)[1]
>
> "We may from this passage conclude with certainty that in the time of Megasthenes Krishna was honoured as one of the highest of the Gods, and precisely in the character of Vishnu, who incarnated himself when

[1] *Note by Lassen.* Besides Mathura, Megasthenes named another city of the Surasenes, Κλεισόβορα, which Pliny (*Hist. Nat.* vi. 22) calls Carisobara or Cyrisoborea or Chrysobora, and which Von Bohlen (*Altes Indien*, i. 233) with apparent justice reads as *Krishna-Pura*, city of Krishna. Ptolemaios names Mathura the city of the Gods.

the transgressions of the world began to overflow, and wiped them out. When Megasthenes describes him as bearing a club, there becomes apparent that writer's exact acquaintance with Indian matters, for Vishnu also carries a club (hence his name of *Gadâdhara*). That he also, like Hercules, wore a lion's hide, does not correspond to Krishna, and might seem to impute an inclination to make out an identity between the Greek and the Indian hero. Probably Megasthenes was misled by the fact that in Sanskrit the word lion is used to indicate a pre-eminent excellence in men, and specially in warriors.[1] The account of Megasthenes further corresponds with the Indian Saga in respect that there many wives and sons are ascribed to Krishna (16,000 wives and 180,000 sons. See Vishnu Purâna, pp. 440, 591). Of cities founded by him, indeed, we know only Dvârakâ; and Palibothra had another founder. Clearly, however, Pandaia is exactly the name of Pandava, especially when we compare the form Pândavya; and in that connection my previous conclusion seems to be irrefragable, that Megasthenes has signified by the daughter of Krishna the sister, from whom the series of Pandava Kings are descended."[2]

Now, it is sufficiently plain on the face of this exposition that the identification of Krishna with the Indian Hercules of Megasthenes is imperfect. It leaves, says Professor Tiele, "much to be desired."[3] The fashion in which the great Indianist founds on one or two details, and lets go by the board some serious discrepancies, is indeed somewhat characteristic of the scholars of his adopted nation. German scholarship has the defects of its great qualities: with an enormous mass of detail-knowledge it often combines a relatively infirm and erratic judgment. In the whole course of this inquiry the real light will, I think, be found forthcoming rather from France, Holland, India, and Italy, than from Germany: though the mere mass-weight of German scholarship commands attention.

In point of fact, a much more satisfactory identification of the Indian Hercules of Megasthenes lay ready to Lassen's hand in Wilson's introduction to his translation of the Vishnu Purana. "The Hercules of the Greek

[1] Lassen here assumes that Megasthenes knew Sanscrit, which is not at all certain. More probably he needed interpreters, and in talk between these and the Brahmans the poetic epithet "lion" would hardly be used. It would appear from a remark of Arrian (*Exped. Alex.* vi. 30) that only one Macedonian in Alexander's train learned Persian, so little were the Greeks disposed to master foreign languages. In Alexander's expedition communications seem at times to have been filtered through three interpreters.

[2] *Indische Alterthumskunde*, i. (1847), 647–9.

[3] *Outlines*, p. 148.

writers," says that sound scholar, "was indubitably the Bala Râma of the Hindus; and their notices of Mathura on the Jumna, and of the kingdom of the Suraseni and the Pandæan country, evidence the prior currency of the traditions which constitute the argument of the Mahâbhârata, and which are constantly repeated in the Purânas, relating to the Pandava and Yâdava races, to Krishna and his contemporary heroes, and to the dynasties of the solar and lunar heroes."[1] M. Barth, it is true, has tacitly accepted Lassen's view;[2] but does not do so with any emphasis, and points out that it has been contested by Weber,[3] who, regarding Megasthenes' testimony as of uncertain value in any case, declines to accept the reading of Kleisobora as Krishnapura, and considers Wilson's theory of Bala Râma more reasonable. And M. Senart, whose masterly Essay on the Legend of Buddha has put him in the front rank of Indianists and mythologists, very emphatically combats Lassen's position:—

> "In [Megasthenes'] Hercules M. Lassen finds Vishnu; it would be infinitely more *vraisemblable*, even in respect of the association with Krishna, to see in him Bala Râma, for whom his club would constitute, in the eyes of a Greek, an affinity, the more striking because it was exterior, with the son of Alcmena. It is necessary, I think, to accept the same synonymy for the Hercules spoken of by Megasthenes, who seems simply to have confounded under this one name legends appertaining to several of the avatars of Vishnu; it is, in my opinion, an error of over-precision to identify, as M. Lassen has done, that Hercules with Krishna."[4]

When we glance at the description of Bala Râma as he figures in Indian effigies, the view of Wilson and Senart seems sufficiently established:—

> "Bala Râma.... although a warrior, may from his attributes be esteemed a benefactor of mankind; for he bears a plough, and a pestle for beating rice; and he has epithets derived from the names of these implements—viz., Halayudha, meaning *plough-armed*, and Musali, as bearing the *musal*, or rice-beater. His name, Bala, means strength; and the beneficent attributes here noticed are by some called a ploughshare for hooking his enemies, and a club for destroying them; and *being*

[1] Trans. of Vishnu Purâna, 1840, pref. pp. vi. vii.
[2] *Religions of India*, p. 163.
[3] *Indische Studien*, ii. 409 (1853).
[4] *Essai sur la Légende du Buddha*, 2e éd. p. 339, *n*.

sometimes seen with a lion's skin over his shoulders, such statues have been thought to resemble, and allude to, those of the Theban Hercules and their legends." (*Note*. "The pestle is of hard wood, about four feet long, and two inches in diameter, with the ends tipped or ferrelled with iron, to prevent their splitting or wearing.")[1]

We shall have to consider further hereafter the mythological significance of Bala Râma and the other two Râmas. In the meantime, beyond noting how precisely the former corresponds with the Hercules of Megasthenes, it will suffice to say that one of the other Râmas, closely connected with Krishna, corresponds with the Hercules figure so far as to support strongly M. Senart's hypothesis of a combination of various personages in the Greek's conception:—

"It is Rama Chandra, however, who is the favourite subject of heroic and amatory poetics: he is described 'of ample shoulders, brawny arms, extending to the knee; neck, shell-formed; chest, circular and full, with auspicious marks; body, hyacinthine; with eyes and lips of sanguine hue; the lord of the world; a moiety of Vishnu himself; the source of joy to Ikshwaku's race.' He is also called....blue-bodied, an appellation of Krishna, as well as of the prototype of both—Vishnu."[2]

In fine, then, we are not entitled to say with Lassen that Megasthenes clearly shows the worship of Krishna to have attained the highest eminence in India three hundred years before our era; but what is certain is that the whole group of the legends with which Krishna is connected had at that date already a high religious standing; and that an important Krishna cultus, resting on these, existed before and spread through India after that period, but certainly flourished long before the advent of Christian influences.

X. Weber's Theory.

The early vogue of Krishna-worship being thus amply proved, it remains to consider the argument, so long persisted in by Professor Weber, as to the derivation of certain *parts* of Krishnaism from Christianity, keeping in view at

[1] Moor's *Hindu Pantheon*, p. 194. Diodorus tells (ii. 39) that in India Hercules has the club and lion's skin as among the Greeks.

[2] Moor's *Hindu Pantheon*, p. 195.

the same time, of course, the more extensive claims made by the partizans of Christianity. With these Professor Weber is not to be identified: there is no reason to doubt that, even if he be mistaken, he is perfectly disinterested in his whole treatment of the subject. This is not to say, of course, that he has approached it from the first in a perfectly scientific frame of mind. I should rather say that his criticism represents the effects of the *general* European prepossession as regards Christianity on a candid truth-seeker who has not independently investigated Christian origins: that his attitude belongs to the period of criticism in which Christianity was not scientifically studied. It is only fair to mention that besides seeing Christian elements in Krishnaism he finds Homeric elements in the Râmâyana, the next great Hindu epic after the Mahâbhârata. That theory, however, seems to have met very small acceptance among Indianists,[1] and need not be here discussed, any more than his old argument as to the influence of Greek art on India after Alexander, which stands on a different footing. One passage will serve to show his general position, which includes a frank avowal that there is evidence of Hindu influence on Christianity just about the time at which he thinks Christianity influenced Krishnaism:—

> "Still more deep [than the Grecian] has been the influence of Christianity, also chiefly introduced by way of Alexandria, to which is to be attributed the idea of a personal, individual, universal God; and the idea of Faith, which is not to be found in India before this time, but which from this epoch forms a common type of all Hindu sects. In the worship of Krishna, an ancient hero, which now takes an entirely new form, even the name of Christ seems to stand in direct connection with it, and several legends of Christ, as well as of his mother the Divine Virgin, are transferred to him.—In an opposite manner, Hindu philosophy too exercised a decided influence upon the formation of several of the Gnostic sects then rising, more especially in Alexandria. The Manichæan system of religion in Persia is very evidently indebted to Buddhistical conceptions, as the Buddhists in the freshness of their religious zeal, carried on by their principle of universalism, had early sent their missionaries beyond Asia. The great resemblance which the Christian ceremonial and rites (which were forming just at that time) show to the Buddhistic in many respects, can be best explained by the influence of

[1] See it ably criticized in K. T. Telang's *Was the Râmâyana copied from Homer?* Bombay, 1873.

the latter, being often too marked for it to be an independent production of each faith; compare the worship of relics, the architecture of church towers (with the Buddhistic Topes), the monastic system of monks and nuns, celibacy, the tonsure, confession, rosaries, bells, etc."[1]

I do not suppose that, after the banter he has bestowed in *Krishna's Geburtsfest* on the Father Giorgi order of etymology, Professor Weber would now stand to the above suggestion about the name of Christ; or that he would give a moment's countenance to the preposterous argument of the *Athenæum* critic that the name Krishna, = black, might mean "anointed" because the root might mean "to tinge." Apart from that, the argument for a reciprocal action of the two religions is on the face of it plausible enough; and it becomes necessary to go into the details.

In the above extract Professor Weber indicates only two respects in which Krishnaism was in his opinion modified by Christianity—the doctrines, namely, of "a personal, universal God," and of "Faith." In his treatise on the Krishna Birth-Festival he posits a number of concrete details: in particular, the Birth Festival itself; the representation of Krishna as a child suckled by his mother; the curious item that, at the time of Krishna's birth, his foster-father Nanda goes with his wife Yasoda to Mathura "to pay his taxes" (a detail not noted by the *Athenæum* critic); the representation of the babe as laid in a manger; the attempted killing by Kansa; the "massacre of the innocents"; the carrying of the child across the river (as in the Christian "Christophoros" legend); the miraculous doings of the child and the healing virtue of his bath water (as in the Apocryphal Gospels); the raising of the bereaved mother's dead son, the straightening of the crooked woman; her pouring ointment over Krishna; and the sin-removing power of his regard.[2] These concrete details I will first deal with.

§ 1. A most important admission, it will be remembered,

[1] *Modern Investigations of Ancient India.* A Lecture delivered in Berlin, March 4th, 1854, by Professor A. Weber. Translated by Fanny Metcalfe, 1857, pp. 25–6. (*Indische Skizzen*, p. 28.)

[2] Work cited, pp. 328–9.

has already been made by Professor Weber in regard to the story of King Kansa; which he admits to be now proved a pre-Christian myth. So important, indeed, is that withdrawal, that but for the Professor's later restatement I should have surmised him to have lost confidence in his whole position, of which, as it seems to me, the central citadel has fallen. If the story of Kansa be admittedly a pre-Christian myth, and the Christian Herod-story be thus admittedly a redaction of an old Eastern myth; what becomes of the presumption of Indian imitation of other Christian stories which, on the face of them, are just as likely to be mythical as the story of Herod and the massacre of the innocents? Did it ever occur to Professor Weber to consider how the Christian stories in general really originated? It would seem not. His argument simply assumes that the Gospel stories (whether true or not, he does not say) came into circulation at the foundation of Christianity, and so became accessible to the world. But as to the source of these stories—as to how these particular miraculous narratives came to be told in connection with Jesus—he makes (save on one point) no inquiry, and apparently feels no difficulty; though to a scientific eye, one would think, the clearing-up in some way of the *causation* of the Christian legends is as necessary as the explaining how they are duplicated in Krishnaism.

The one exception to which I refer in Professor Weber's investigation is his very straightforward allusion to the likelihood that the representation of the Virgin Mary as either suckling or clasping the infant Jesus may have been borrowed from the Egyptian statues or representations of Isis and Horus. For citing this suggestion from previous writers he has been angrily accused by Mr. Growse, a Roman Catholic Anglo-Indian, of "a wanton desire to give offence";[1] an imputation which the scholar has indignantly and justly resented.[2] Mr. Growse's pretext for his splenetic charge was the claim, cited by Professor Weber himself from De Rossi, that the earliest representations of the

[1] *Indian Antiquary*, iii. 300. [2] *Id.* iv. 251.

Madonna in the Roman catacombs, recently brought to light, follow a classic and not an Egyptian type. Says De Rossi :—

> "The paintings of our subterranean cemeteries offer us the first images of the Holy Virgin with her divine child; and they are much more numerous and more ancient than is indicated by the works hitherto [before 1863] published on the Catacombs of Rome. I have chosen four, which seem to me to be as the models of the different types and of the different periods which one meets from the first centuries to about the time of Constantine." And again (a passage which Weber does not cite): "The frescoes of our illustrations and the monuments cited by me here, demonstrate that in the most ancient works of Christian art the Virgin holding her child is figured *independently of the Magi and of any historic scene.*"[1]

Now, even if it be decided that the earliest "Madonnas" in the Catacombs have a classic rather than an Egyptian cast, nothing would be proved against the Egyptian derivation of the cult of the Virgin and Child. It does not occur to Commendatore De Rossi, of course, to question whether these early Madonnas were really Christian—whether they did not represent the almost universal vogue of the worship of a child-nursing Goddess apart from Christianity. There is no artistic or documentary evidence whatever of Christian Madonna-worship in the first century; and De Rossi's "*premiers siècles,*" and his final claim that his series of images "goes back to the disciples of the apostles," leave matters very much in the vague. The whole question of the antiquities of the Catacombs needs to be overhauled by some investigator as devoted as the Catholics, but as impartial as they are prejudiced. There might indeed be Christian, but there were certainly non-Christian, "Madonnas" of a "classic" cast before the time at which the absolute images of Isis were transferred to Christian churches, and black images of Mary and Jesus were made in imitation of them.[2] The very name Iacchos, one of the special titles of Dionysos,

[1] *Images de la T. S. Vierge, Choisies dans les Catacombes de Rome*, Rome, 1863, pp. 6–7, 21.

[2] See above, p. 142. Cp. Simrock, *Handbuch der deutschen Mythologie*, 6te Aufl. pp. 314, 381; and Maury, *Légendes Pieuses du Moyen Age*, 1843, p. 38.

originally meant a sucking infant;[1] and in the myths he is either suckled by or actually the child of Dêmêtêr,[2] "The Earth Mother," or Ceres *Mammosa*,[3] "the many-breasted," who in turn bore in Greece the name κουροτρόφος,[4] the boy-rearer. In ancient art she is often represented as suckling the Babe-God, especially on Athenian coins.[5] Ino Leucothea, called Mater Matuta by the Romans, mother of Melicerta or Palæmon (= Melkarth and Baal-Ammon),[6] the Roman Portumnus, was represented with her child in her arms,[7] whencè a presumption that among the Semites Melkarth and Baal-Ammon were represented as carried infants. Gaia, again, was sculptured holding the infant Dionysos or Erichthonios.[8]

Nor was the appellation of "The Virgin" any more unfamiliar before than after Christianity in connection with Madonna-worship. In Etruscan and Græco-Roman statuary, Juno (Hèrê), who was fabled to become a virgin anew each year,[9] was represented as suckling a babe—Hercules or Dionysos.[10] On Roman coins, Venus, who also

[1] Bochart, *Geographia Sacra*, ed. 1674, pp. 480–1 (*Chanaan*, l. i. c. 18); Suidas, *s.v.* Ἴακχος. Cp. Preller, *Griech. Myth.* 2nd. ed. i. 614. So the Latin *Liber*.

[2] Diodorus Siculus, iii. 62; Plutarch, *Julius Cæsar*, c. ix.; Strabo, b. iii. c. iii. § 16. Otherwise Dionysos is the child of Persephone—*Korê*, "the Maiden," who, like her mother, was "the Virgin." Diodorus, iii. 64; iv. 4.

[3] Lucretius, iv. 1162.

[4] Pausanias, i. 22; Preller, *Griechische Mythologie*, i. 599. Leto had the same title. *Id.* p. 184, note 3. But it was given to Artemis, the most virginal Goddess of all. Pausanias, iv. 34.

[5] K. O. Müller, *Ancient Art*, Eng. trans. pp. 438–441; Winckelmann, *Monuments Inédits*, i. 28, 68, 71.

[6] Cp. Cox, *Mythology of the Aryan Nations*, p. 326; and Brown, *The Great Dionysiak Myth*, i. 251 sq.; ii. 100.

[7] K. O. Müller, *Ancient Art*, pp. 493, 538.

[8] *Id.* p. 493.

[9] Pausanias, ii. 38. This myth often recurs. Hêrê bears Hephaistos "without having been united in love" (Hesiod, *Theogony*, 927); and in the same way bears Typhon (Homerid. *Hymn to Apollo*). So, in Rome, Juno was identified with the *Virgo Coelestis* (Preller, *Römische Mythologie*, 1865, pp. 377, 752). The idea is ubiquitous. Cybele, the mother of *all* the Gods, was also styled the *Virgo Coelestis* (Augustine, *De Civitate Dei*, ii. 4), and was revered as a virgin, though the mate as well as the mother of Jupiter, and "seized with a love without passion for Attis" (Julian, *In Deorum Matrem*, c. 4). Equally transparent was the mysticism which made Ceres, the earth mother, a virgin too.

[10] Preller's *Griechische Mythologie*, 2nd ed. i. 135; Pausanias, ix. 25; Müller, *Ancient Art*, pp. 430, 554.

was identified with the *Virgo Coelestis*,[1] was represented both as carrying a child and as having one before her, with the sceptre and ball—a form adopted by Christian art.[2] There were abstract Divine Mothers, too, who could be called Virgins without any sense of anomaly, since there was no "male of the species." We know that in Rome in the time of the Republic a special worship was paid by matrons to the image of a nursing mother, Fortune giving suck to the Child Jupiter, and holding at the same time the Child Juno.[3] Similarly the Greeks had statues of the abstract Virgins Peace and Fortune, each carrying Wealth (Plutus) as a child in her arms.[4] For the rest, we know that in old Assyria or Chaldæa there was a popular worship of a child-bearing Goddess. It is agreed that the Goddess Alitta was represented by such images;[5] and there are many specimens of similar ancient Eastern effigies of small size, which were evidently cherished by multitudes. In a case of "Miscellaneous Objects from Assyria and Babylonia," in the Assyrian basement of the British Museum, may be seen[6] old Chaldæan figures of this kind, one of which is described merely as a "female figure holding a child," while another female figure is unhesitatingly labelled "female deity," though the deity of the former is to the full as certain as that of the latter. In another case of "Antiquities from Dali" upstairs, at the outer end of the Egyptian Hall, are a number of similar figures, in the labelling of which officialdom ventures so far as to write "Figure of Female or Aphrodite," "holding smaller figure or child." Beyond question these popular "Madonnas" of the East are much older than Christianity;

[1] K. O. Müller, *Ancient Art*, p. 474; Preller, *Griechische Mythologie*, i. 268; Firmicus, *De Errore Profan. Relig.* iv.

[2] K. O. Müller, as last cited.

[3] "*Is est hodie locus septus religiose propter Jovis pueri, qui lactens cum Junone Fortunæ in gremio sedens, mammam adpetens, castissime colitur a matribus.*" Cicero, *De Divinatione*, ii. 41.

[4] Pausanias, i. 8; ix. 16; Müller, p. 547.

[5] Layard's *Discoveries in the Ruins of Nineveh and Babylon*, 1853, p. 477; Rawlinson's *Herodotus*, i. 257. See the figure reproduced also in Lundy's *Monumental Christianity*, p. 212.

[6] Written in 1889.

and it is even possible that they represent a Chaldæan cultus earlier than the Egyptian worship of Isis.

This being so, the course of surmising a Christian origin for Indian effigies of Devaki nursing Krishna is plainly unscientific, since it passes over an obvious, near, and probable source for a remote and improbable one. To argue that India remained ignorant of or indifferent to all *Asian* presentments of child-nursing Goddesses for many centuries, and at length, when she had a highly-evolved religious system, administered by an exclusive priesthood, suddenly became enamoured of the Christian presentment of Mary and Jesus—this is to set aside all reasonable probability on no better pretext than a guess. Even if there were no old Asian cultus, no multitude of portable Asian images, of a child-bearing Goddess, the idea might obviously have been derived from the Isis-figures of Egypt before Christianity came into existence. Even from the engravings appended to his paper by Professor Weber, it appears that other divine personages than Devaki and Krishna were figured as mother and child in Hindu art and mythology: and the usage might perfectly well have prevailed in India before Krishnaism became anything like universal. In this connection Professor Tiele, one of the sanest of hierologists,[1] passes an unanswerable criticism on Professor Weber's argument in the Dutch *Theologisch Tijdschrift* :—

> "One of the weakest points of his [Weber's] demonstration seems to me to be that in which he compares the delineations of Krishna at the breast of his mother Devaki with Christian pictures of the *Madonna lactans* (the Madonna giving suck), and both with that of Isis and Horos. For in the first place it is not proved that the Indian representations are imitations of Christian models: they might equally well be borrowed from the Egyptian, seeing that India was already in

[1] Let me offer a plea, as well as an excuse, for this most necessary term, which Professor Tiele himself has fathered. It is in the preface to his *Outlines* that he suggests the word "hierology" as a substitute for the cumbrous phrase, "Science of Religions." If this term be adopted, we might when necessary say "Comparative Hierology" instead of "Comparative Mythology," and so satisfy conservatives without having recourse to the question-begging "Comparative Theology," or to the solecism of "Comparative Religion," which is no more justifiable than "Comparative Words" for "Comparative Philology."

communication with Egypt before our era. The Horos sitting on the lotos was certainly borrowed by the Egyptians from Indian pictures; and in return the Isis with the child Horos at her breast may well have been transported to India. Moreover, the Indian illustrations given by Weber, and equally the Christian, are of very late date; and further, it is very doubtful whether they all represent Devakî and Krishna. [*Note.*—Under one of the four is inscribed the name Lakshmi. Another is held to stand for Lakshmi or Maya with Kamadeva. In both the Goddesses have by them a lotos, the emblem of Lakshmi. And a third gives the whole legend, Devakî and Yaçodha each lying on her bed, the first strongly guarded, while the father of Krishna, under the protection of the serpent with seven heads, carries the child through the river, to place it in safety. Hardly one of the four recalls a *Madonna lactans*; but, indeed, Weber acknowledges that that is of very late date.]"[1]

I cannot, with my limited knowledge, speak with Professor Tiele's certainty as to the Horos-on-the-lotos being borrowed from India;[2] but I would suggest that if that were so borrowed, the Isis nursing Horos might be so likewise. We have really no solid ground, that I know of, for assuming that the Indian cult, in some form, was not as old as the Egyptian. We have the decisive testimony of Jerome that in the fourth century the Hindus were known to teach that their Buddha was born of a Virgin[3]—a clear proof that the Virgin myth was current in India long before. Such a dogma could not have gained such vogue in the short time between Jerome and the beginning of Mary-worship. If then Buddha was so early reputed Virgin-born, Krishna, who ranked as an incarnation of Vishnu before him, may reasonably be held to have had the same distinction. In any case, it is clear that, as Professor Tiele urges, the Hindus could perfectly well have borrowed, if they did borrow, from Egypt before Christianity was heard of.

[1] Art. *Christus en Krishna*, in the *Theologisch Tijdschrift*, 1877, p. 65.

[2] In his *History of the Egyptian Religion*, Eng. tr. p. 52, Dr. Tiele puts this view tentatively, as that of Dr. Pleyte.

[3] *Adversus Jovinianum*, i. 42 (Migne, *Patrologiæ Cursus Completus*, xxiii. 273). Professor Rhys Davids, in a letter to Mr. W. S. Lilly (printed in the latter's *Claims of Christianity*, 1894, p. 30), makes a remark as to the Buddha birth-story which sets up some risk of misunderstanding. "The Buddhists," he writes, "did not ascribe to Gotama any divine birth *in the Christian sense*. Before his descent into his mother's womb he was a *deva*...." But Christ also was held to exist from all eternity before his incarnation. The essential point is that the birth was held supernatural. Professor Davids, of course, rejects the notion that Buddhism borrowed from Christianity.

There being thus so little reason for surmising Christian influence in the matter, and so much for discarding any such surmise, there is *a fortiori* a presumption against Professor Weber's final contention as to the precise time of borrowing. There is a Krishnaist custom in India of "name-giving" on the festival day of Krishna's supposed birth; and in answer to criticism the Professor writes[1] that "it is because the custom of the Egyptian Church of celebrating the birth and the baptism of Christ on the *same day* prevailed only from the second half of the fourth century till the year 431, when the celebration of the *birth alone* took its place," that he dates the Krishnaist borrowing of the Birth Festival from Christianity "at the very time during which that custom peculiar to Egypt prevailed." Here we have perhaps the most striking example of Professor Weber's uncritical treatment of Christian origins. Why, one asks, does he not inquire as to how the Egyptian Christians came to adopt that peculiar usage of celebrating the birth and baptism of Christ on one day, for only the short period he speaks of? Was it a mere freak? And if it were, is it reasonable to suggest that this mere temporary provincial ecclesiastical freak in Christendom somehow impressed the remote Brahmans so much that they determined to adopt it, and succeeded in grafting it on the Krishna cultus ever since? Surely it is more reasonable to surmise that the Egyptian Christians were the borrowers, that they borrowed their peculiar usage from some other cult, and that it was rejected by the rest of the Church just because it was so obviously alien in its origin.

To be sure, the usage of the rest of the Church was itself an unquestionable adoption of a current Pagan one. The Western Church, long after the time when the possibility of ascertaining any facts as to the birth of the alleged Founder had ceased, adopted the ancient solar festival of the 25th of December, then specially connected in the Empire with the widespread worship of Mithra.[2] But the Eastern Churches, influenced by the Egyptian and other pre-Christian systems,

[1] *Indian Antiquary*, iv. 249; *Ueber die Krishnaj.* pp. 299, 337.
[2] Julian, *In Regem Solem*, c. 20. Cp. Preller, *Römische Mythologie*, p. 755.

adopted and for some time adhered to another date, equally solar and Pagan in its character. The facts are collected by Bingham, who points out that it is "a very great mistake in learned men" to say that Christ's birthday was always celebrated on 25th December by the churches:—

> "For, not to mention what Clement Alexandrinus (*Stromata*, i.) says of the Basilidian heretics, that they asserted that Christ was born on the 24th or 25th of the month which the Egyptians call Pharmuthi, that is, April; he says a more remarkable thing (*Id.*) of some others, who were more curious about the year and the day of Christ's nativity, which they said was in the twenty-eighth year of Augustus Cæsar, and the 25th day of the month Pachon, which....signifies the month of May, as Mr. Basnage (*Exercit. in Baron. an.* 37, p. 216) has at large demonstrated. But what is more considerable in this matter is that the greatest part of the Eastern Church for three or four of the first ages kept the feast of Christ's nativity on the same day which is now called Epiphany, or the 6th of January, which denotes Christ's manifestation to the world in four several respects which were all commemorated upon this day"—*i.e.* (1) his nativity or incarnation; (2) the appearance of the star, = Epiphany or manifestation to the Gentiles; (3) the "glorious appearance" at Christ's baptism; (4) the manifestation of his divinity at Cana...."And Cassian (*Collat.* x. c. 2) says expressly 'that in his time all the Egyptian provinces under the general name of Epiphany understood as well the nativity of Christ as his baptism.'....But before the time of the Council of Ephesus, anno 431, the Egyptians had altered the day of Christ's nativity....It was not long before this that the Churches of Antioch and Syria came into the Western observation."[1]....

All which is abundantly proved from Epiphanius and Chrysostom. Now, only a supernaturalist criticism can here fail to see that the usages of the Egyptian and Syrian Churches were imitative of pre-existing Eastern astronomico-theological cults; and if we are driven to this conclusion, what right have we left to suppose that India borrowed just such a usage all of a sudden from a short-lived borrowed practice of Eastern Christendom? We have a distinct record that in connection with the ancient solar worship of Hercules among the Sicyonians, who sacrificed lambs to the God, "the first of the days of the Feast which they keep to Hercules they call *Names*, and the second *Hercules' Day*";[2] and there is surely good reason to presume that similar usages prevailed among

[1] *Christian Antiquities*, ed. 1855, vii. 280–2.
[2] Pausanias, ii. 10.

other solar cults long before Christianity. In the old Persian system, in which the festival of the autumn equinox was originally connected with Mithra, after whom the first autumn-month (then current) is named, it was "*auspicious at this season to name children and wean babes.*"[1] Here we have a close correspondence to the Hindu festival, for the month of Mihr is the seventh from the beginning of the Persian year, as the month of Krishna's birth is the seventh in the solar year, counting from the winter solstice. Is it pretended that the Persians borrowed *their* usage from the Christians? If not, why should the Hindu usage not be as old as the Persian and the Greek? The Christian theory is hopeless. If it is good for anything, there is no need to restrict it to the chronological scheme of Professor Weber. As a matter of fact, the usage of *general baptizing on Epiphany* did not disappear from the Christian Church after the Council of Ephesus. It has been preserved down to modern times in the Church of Abyssinia, which has continued to receive its primate from the Church of Alexandria, and which practises general circumcision as well as general baptism on the day in question.[2] Why should not then the Hindu usage have been borrowed from Abyssinia at a much later time than that at which the Alexandrian Church regarded Epiphany as the day of the Nativity? Why indeed should it not have been suggested by the much more general custom in the early Church of reserving all baptisms for Easter-day?[3] And why, finally, should it not have been suggested by the Catholic "Festival of the Name of Jesus," which stands in the Calendar for August 7th, close on the date of the Krishna Birth-Festival? Any one of these hypotheses would be as reasonable as that on which Professor Weber has fastened—as reasonable, and as unreasonable. The whole theory is a mistake.

[1] Wait, *Jewish, Oriental, and Classical Antiquities*, 1823, p. 194, citing the *Berhan-I Katteā*.

[2] Geddes, *Church History of Ethiopia*, 1696, pp. 32–33. Cp. Neale, *History of the Holy Eastern Church: Patriarchate of Alexandria*, 1847, ii. 347.

[3] Bingham, *Christian Antiquities*, as cited, iv. 69–70.

§ 2. A more instructive part of Professor Weber's argument concerning the Krishna Birth-Festival, as now observed in India, consists in showing that no trace of it is to be found even in such late literature as the Purânas. An attempt to find authority for it in the Bhâgavat Purâna, he declares, entirely fails, except as regards quite modern MSS.; and this he considers the more curious because this Purâna, and in particular the tenth book, is the peculiar text-book of the Krishna sect. There is there no suggestion of a Birth-Festival. The time of the God's birth, he mentions, is told in detail in Book x. 3, 1–8, but without a date, save what is implied in the statement that it was under the star Rohinî, and at midnight; and he raises the question whether the Birth-Festival existed at the time of the composition of the Purâna. He decides that it must have done, not on account of internal evidence proving the lateness of the book, but because the grammarian Vopadeva, to whom Colebrooke, Wilson, and Bournouf ascribe the composition of the Purâna as it now stands, was contemporary with Hemâdri, the author in whom we first find specific mention of the Festival. That was about the end of the fourteenth century of our era—about a thousand years after the period at which the Professor thinks the Hindus borrowed their Festival usage from Alexandria. He might thus well decide that the usage existed before Vopadeva; and he offers an explanation of the silence of the Purâna on the subject:—

> "In the Bhâgavat Purâna is presented the modern development of the Krishna cult, which is chiefly concerned with Krishna's love affairs, and in which the Mother of the God passes progressively into the background. In the Birthday Festival, on the other hand....the Mother comes very prominently into the foreground, playing a principal rôle, while of the love affairs of Krishna no notice is or indeed can be taken, for he is here represented as still a suckling at his mother's breast. I do not hesitate here to recognize a quite peculiarly ancient phase of the Festival, the more so because....even in that there appears in time a tendency to suppress this side, and to give the tribute of the Festival to the God alone, without his mother." [1]

That is to say, the Purâna overlooks the Festival because

[1] *Ueber die Krishnajanmâshtami*, pp. 240–2.

it preserves the old practice of honouring the Mother of the God, while at the time the Purâna was written the cult ran to the glorification of the God himself, and the celebration of his exploits. To this explanation I do not think there can be any objection. It is conceived in the historical spirit; and the only perplexity is that Professor Weber, while thus recognizing that the Festival preserves an old *popular rite*, which changed much more slowly than the poetic recitals of the God's exploits, should yet decide that even the popular rite was originally borrowed from the new Western religion of Christism by a people who rated their own religious and historic antiquity high before Christianity was heard of.

I have implied that the Purânas represent the literary development of mythic lore; but this does not mean that even their contents are not mainly made up of matter that in some form long antedates our era. On this subject, it may be well to point out that the absolute preservation of an ancient document in its integrity, unless it be a matter of rote-learned ritual like the Vedas, is not to be looked for in a state of civilization in which manuscripts are not abundant and the knowledge of reading general. There is overwhelming internal evidence of the manipulation of the Christian Gospels: and the reason why, after a certain time, their text became substantially fixed, was just the multiplicity of the copies, and the ecclesiastical habit, derived from old Greek political usage, of meeting in Councils. And even as it was, we know that so late as the fifth century the text of the "three witnesses" was fraudulently inserted in 1 John v., and that this one forgery was ultimately accepted by the entire Western Church from about 1550 down to last century, when earlier copies were authoritatively collated. Now, in India down till recent times, the frame of mind in regard to narratives of the lives of the Gods would be exactly that of the early Christians who manipulated the first and second Gospels, and compiled the third and fourth. There was no such thing as a canon or a received text: there was no "apostolic" tradition; there were no religious councils;

no scholars whose business it was to compare manuscripts. Besides, no manuscript lasted long; Professor Weber has pointed out how unfavourable is the Indian climate to any such preservation.[1] In fine, the *re*-composition of sacred narratives would be a perfectly natural course. But it would be fallacious in the extreme to argue that a late redaction meant late invention; on the contrary, there is good reason to believe that late redactions would often take in floating popular myths of great antiquity, which had merely missed being committed to writing before. For this view, modern research in Folk Lore should have prepared all investigators. Our every-day nursery fables are found to be in substance as old as the art of story-telling, older than literature, as old as religion.

Now, it is a general rule in ancient mythology that the birthdays of Gods were *astrological*;[2] and the simple fact that the Purána gives an astronomical moment for Krishna's birth is a sufficient proof that at the time of writing they *had* a fixed date for it. The star Rohini under which he was born, it will be remembered, has the name given in one variation of the Krishna legend to a wife of Vasudeva who bore to him Ráma, as Devaki (sometimes held to be the mother of Ráma also) bore Krishna. Here we are in the thick of ancient astrological myth. Rohini (our Aldebaran) is "the red," "a mythical name also applied now to Aurora, now to a star."[3] We have seen in the case of Christianity how a universal astrological festival, of immemorial antiquity, came to be specialized for Christians;

[1] *Ind. Ant.* iii. 246; Berlin lecture, p. 30; and *History of Indian Literature*, Eng. tr. pp. 181–2. Cp. Macaulay, Trevelyan's *Life*, 1-vol. ed. p. 323. A friend in Burma, to whom I had sent a book, writes me that it has to be locked up in an air-tight box during the wet season, otherwise it would be destroyed.

[2] This holds good even if we recognize in myths of menaced divine children an idea of the dangers run by the planted seed before it ripens. Some such idea is suggested in the myth that Ino, the second wife of Athamas, sought to destroy the children of the first wife Nephelê (the Cloud), by telling the women of the land to dry the wheat before sowing it. On the failure of the harvest she planned that the messengers sent to consult the oracle should bring the answer that Phrixus, the son of Nephelê, should be sacrificed (Apollodorus, I. ix. 1). But the story of the dried seed-wheat looks like a late fancy framed in elaboration of Ino's plot.

[3] Barth, *Religions of India*, p. 173.

and it is clearly not only possible but likely that every astrological festival of Krishnaism was in vogue in other Indian worships before Krishnaism prevailed. In these matters there is really no invention: there is only readjustment. But that a Hindu festival connected with the star-name Rohini and the birth of Krishna should be borrowed from Christianity, where the birth connects with the rise of the constellation *Virgo*, there is no shadow of reason for supposing. The very fact that no account is given in the older Puranas of the rise of the festival tells in favour of its antiquity. Suppose the festival to be the oldest datum in the case, the omission to date its beginning in the record is just what would happen—just what happened in Christianity. It would have been a simple matter for the early Christians to insert 25th December in their records as the date of their God's birth; but they did *not* do so, just because that was so notoriously a festival of extreme antiquity.[1] And the birthday of Krishna may have been that of another God before him.

But the most singular matter in regard to Professor Weber's argument is the fact that the date of the Krishna Birth-Festival is neither in December nor in January, but in the month of *July*.[2] That is to say, it corresponds not with Christmas but with the Egyptian festival of "the Birthday of the Eyes of Horus, when the Sun and the

[1] It is worth while in this connection to recall the statement of Ovid in his *Fasti* (i. 657) that he went three or four times through the official list of festivals, in vain, looking for the date of the old Sementivæ or Festival of Sowing, which was not written down. See Ovid's explanation and that of Macrobius (*Saturnalia*, i. 16), cited by Keightley in his ed. of the *Fasti*. There were fixed and unfixed festivals, *Stativæ* and *Conceptivæ*, of which the latter were "annually given out, for certain or even uncertain days, by the magistrates or priests." Cp. Frazer, *Golden Bough*, i. 303, *note*.

[2] According to Professor de Gubernatis (*Zool. Myth.* i. 51) it is customary "towards the end of December" to give presents of cows "in celebration of the new solar year, *or the birth of the pastoral God Krishna*"; but this appears to be an error, probably resulting from Professor Weber's omission to lay stress on the date in his standard treatise. But doubtless Gubernatis could explain the midsummer birth of the black Sun-God in terms of solar mythology. It is the white Sun-God who is born at Christmas. But on this head it should be noted that the *death* of the Sun-God Tammuz (Adonis) was celebrated in different climates at different times. See Max Müller, *Natural Religion*, 1889, pp. 529–530; and Frazer, as last cited. And see hereinafter, Sec. xv.

Moon are come into one straight line"[1]—a festival held on the 30th day of the Egyptian month Epap or Epiphi or Emphi = 24th July, which was the last day of the Egyptian year. Yet it never occurs to Weber to connect the Krishnaite Birth-Festival with this purely Pagan and pre-Christian festival. Indeed one may go through Weber's treatise without discovering what the date in question is. As he says in answer to a criticism, "The date itself (December or July, midwinter or midsummer) *plays no part at all in my discussion*, and is only spoken of incidentally" in a parenthesis.[2] So the proposition is that the Hindus celebrated the birthday of Krishna in July by way of imitating the Christian fashion of celebrating Christ's nativity in January. One is at a loss to understand how Professor Weber can thus make so light of such an important item. If the Krishna Birth-Festival were borrowed, why should the borrowers select a midsummer instead of a midwinter date for their importation? Why, indeed, should they not place their God's birthday, if it only occurred to them late in the day to give him a birthday, on one of the other Krishnaist festivals? I have not noticed that Professor Weber theorises on the origin of these; but their probably astronomical origin is surely important to the argument. As the historian Elphinstone has pointed out, "Even Mr. Bentley, the most strenuous opponent of the claims of the Hindus" to an extremely ancient knowledge of astronomy, "pronounces in his latest work that their division of the ecliptic into twenty-seven lunar mansions (which supposes much previous observation) was made 1442 years before our era"[3]—that is, centuries before the first traces of systematic astronomy in Greece. Supposing the division in question to have been derived by the Hindus from the Akkadians, the argument remains the same. Astronomical festivals, in any case, the Hindus must have had from a very remote antiquity;[4] and every argument from analogy

[1] Plutarch, *Isis and Osiris*, c. 52.
[2] *Indian Antiquary*, iv. 249.
[3] *History of India*, ed. 1866, p. 140.
[4] On Vedic festivals see Professor Max Müller's *Natural Religion*, pp. 524–5.

in history goes to support the view that their now popular seasonal festivals are prehistoric, and that some of them may even be derived from Dravidian or pre-Aryan practice. And when we compare a few of their usages with those of Christianity, it becomes plain that we must either suppose them to have borrowed a great deal more than Professor Weber says, or give up his theory altogether and look for, if anything, a reverse historic process. The points of resemblance are numerous and suggestive.

> "The new year of the luni-solar computation now in use [in India] begins with the first of Chaitra, which falls somewhere in the course of March, and in solar reckoning is said to agree with the entrance of the sun into the sign Mesha, or Aries"[1]—

that is, the sign of the Ram or Lamb, which in the Mithraic system was the "new day," the creation day, and the greatest festival,[2] and in Christianity is associated with the sacrifice of the God, symbolized as a Lamb, on a luni-solar and therefore variable date connected with the vernal equinox.

> "There was, however, a period at which a different principle was followed[3]....the new year then commenced on the first of the solar month Màgha, the date of the Makara-Sankrànti, or the sun's entrance into the sign Capricornus, identical with the Uttaráyana, or return of that luminary to the regions of the north, or, in fact, to the winter solstice."[4]

The Indian and European dates do not actually correspond: with us 21st December is the time of the sun's entering Capricorn, the sign of the Goat, while the Hindus put it on the first of their solar month Magha = 12th January. But the astronomical *motive* is explicit; and when we note that this old festival, still in force, lasts three days, and that the day after the sun's entering Capricorn is termed Máttu Pongal, or the feast of cattle, we see a new confirmation of the argument of Dupuis[5] that the myth of a Christian God being born in a stable (which

[1] H. H. Wilson, *Religious Festivals of the Hindus*, Works, ii. 159.
[2] Wait, as cited, p. 189.
[3] *Note by Wilson.* According to Bentley, this was 1181 B.C. *Historical View of Hindu Astronomy*, p. 30.
[4] Wilson, as cited.
[5] *Origine de tous les Cultes*, ed. 1835–6, vii. 104.

corresponds so strikingly with many other myths of Gods—as Krishna, Hermes, Hercules—born or brought up among cattle) is really at bottom or by adaptation astronomical or zodiacal, and is properly to be traced to the relative position of the figures in the fuller zodiac or celestial sphere. Of course the solar element is manifest in the Hindu usage. "The day of the Makara Sankránti, or Perum Pongal, is dedicated to the sun, and the day of the Máttu Pongal to Indra: they are both comprised in the term Pongal, which is an anniversary festival of a week's duration."[1] Now, several of the usages in this and other Hindu festivals are traceable in Europe in non-Christian as well as in Christian times. "The Greeks had a festival in the month Poseidon, or January, in which they worshipped Neptune, or the Sea, in like manner as the Hindus [at the same time] worship the ocean."[2] But there is no more remarkable correspondence than that between the Hindu practice of honouring the cattle at this time and the strange Catholic function of blessing the cattle—cows, horses, goats, asses, etc.—at Rome on St. Anthony's day (January 17th). Let Professor Wilson testify:—

> "The time of the year, the decorating of the cattle, the sprinkling of them with water, and the very purport of the blessing, that they may be exempt from evils, are so decidedly Indian, that could a Dravira Brahman be set down of a sudden in the Piazza, and were he asked what ceremony he witnessed, there can be no doubt of his answer; he would at once declare they were celebrating the Pongal."[3]

Now, no student can well believe that the Roman Catholic usage really originated, as the fable tells, in the fact that St. Anthony tended swine. These are the theories of the Dark Ages. To-day even semi-orthodox scholarship decides that "So far as myths consist of explanations of ritual their value is altogether secondary; and it may be affirmed with confidence that in almost every case *the myth was derived from the ritual, and not the ritual from the myth*; for the ritual was fixed and the myth was variable; the

[1] Wilson, as cited, p. 172.
[2] *Id.* p. 175.
[3] Wilson, as cited, pp. 178–9.

ritual was obligatory, and faith in the myth was at the discretion of the worshipper."[1]

This holds true for every religion; and if we apply the principle in the case of Christianity we shall make an end of more pretences than that as to the borrowing of Christion practices by Krishnaism. It is not argued, of course, that Roman Christianity borrowed its ritual usages direct from India; on the contrary, the presumption is that these usages were even more widespread than the "Aryan race" in pre-historic times. The Roman Catholic celebration of St. Anthony's day probably derives from the ancient Paganalia or Feriæ Sementivæ, agricultural festivities in which the cattle were garlanded at this very season of the year;[2] and it is possible that even the modern name came from that of one of the Antonines. But if Christianity is thus seen deriving its festival days from immemorial custom, what reason is there to surmise that conservative and custom-loving India came to Alexandria for the hint to celebrate the astrological birthday of Krishna? Krishnaism has a number of festivals of which no proper account seems yet to be accessible in England, that given in Balfour's *Indian Cyclopædia* being so inexact that one is at a loss to know whether in some cases different festival-names do not apply to one and the same feast. But it is clear that there is one great Dolu or Dola Yátrá festival, the "swinging festival," which begins about the middle of March (Phalguna) and lasts as a rule fifteen days. In the

[1] Professor Robertson Smith, *The Religion of the Semites*, 1889, p. 19. This maxim of interpretation dates back to Creuzer (*Symbolik*, 1810–12), and to K. O. Müller: *Orchomenos*, 1820, p. 161; *Introduction to a Scientific System of Mythology* (1825), Eng. tr. 1844, pp. 171, 175, 195, 206; *History of Greek Literature* (Eng. tr. pp. 287–8). See it also laid down by Kenrick, *Ancient Egypt*, 1850, i. 411, 413; A. Bertrand, *Etudes de Mythologie et Archæologie grecques*, Rennes, 1858, p. 35; and Grote, end of ch. i. Cp. Miss Harrison, *Mythology and Monuments of Ancient Athens*, 1890, pp. xxvi. xxxiii.; and Mr. Frazer, *The Golden Bough*, passim. "No people ever observed a custom because a mythical being was said to have once acted in a certain way. [An unwarranted negative, by the way.] But, on the contrary, all peoples have invented myths to explain why they observed certain customs." "A myth is never so graphic and precise in its details as when it is a simple transcript of a ceremony which the author of a myth witnessed with his eyes" (Work last cited, ii. 128, 246).

[2] Ovid, *Fasti*, i. 663. Cp. Middleton, *Letter from Rome*, ed. 1741, pp. xv.–xix. and 141–143.

large British towns it is or was restricted to three days on account of the liberties taken; but among the Rajputs it is or was the practice to celebrate it for forty days,[1] with more or less licence. Now this practice has certainly an astronomical or seasonal origin; and is as certainly akin to, or as old as, the ancient celebration of the Dionysia or Liberalia in honour of the Sun- and Wine-God among the Greeks and Romans. There was a "swinging festival" in ancient Greece;[2] and this too has survived to modern times.[3] The 17th of March was the date of the Liberalia in Rome; and licence was the note of the festival. It would be just as reasonable to derive the Indian "swinging festival"[4] of the vernal equinox from the Christian celebration of the rising of Christ from the dead, as to argue that the Krishna Birth-Festival is similarly derived.

XI. The Solar-Child Myth.

The further we collate the main Christian myth-motives with those of Krishnaism, the more clearly does it appear that, instead of the latter being borrowed from the former, they are, not indeed the originals from which Christianity borrowed, but always presumptively the more ancient; and in one or two cases they do appear to be the actual sources of Gospel stories. We have seen how Professor Weber

[1] Rev. W. O. Simpson's ed. of Moor's *Hindu Pantheon*, 1864, pp. 139–144.

[2] Athenæus, xiv. 10.

[3] Miss Harrison, *Mythology and Monuments of Ancient Athens*, pp. xxxix.–xliii.

[4] So called because of the ritual practice of swinging an image in a chair. But this practice, according to Balfour's *Ind. Cyc.* (art. Krishna), would appear to obtain also at another Krishnaite festival of three or five days' duration in the month Shravana = July–August; which I take to be either the Birth Festival proper or the special form of it called *Jayanti*, which depends on a particular conjunction of the star Rohinî (Weber, p. 221; cp. pp. 262–3). On this I can find no exact information. In the month Kartika = October–November, there is yet another festival, celebrating the Gopî revels. In a note to Wilson's *Select Specimens of the Theatre of the Hindus* (1835, ii. 264), citing the Bhavishyottara Purâna, it is explained that many of the Hindu festivals have been displaced. Thus a festival once named the Holikâ is now termed the Dola Yâtrâ (or "swinging of the Gods"); and "the Dola Yâtrâ and Rath Yâtrâ have also been displaced, and in Bengal, at least, transferred to festivals appropriated to Krishna alone, in the months of Jyeshth and Asharh, June–July."

concedes that the story of King Kansa's killing of Devaki's earlier children in the attempt to kill Krishna is not only pre-Christian but of old mythic standing, and that it was the subject of *dramatic representations* before our era. Now, the myth-motive in question is at bottom one that is extremely familiar in ancient legend; and nothing is more unsatisfactory in the modern discussion of Krishnaite origins than the way in which this fact has been overlooked. About a hundred years ago Maurice[1] called attention to the parallel between the story of Krishna's infancy and that of the infancy of Cyrus the Great, as told by Herodotus,[2] four hundred years before our era. The story about Cyrus is briefly as follows. Astyages, king of the Medes, having had a remarkable (and Rabelaisian) dream about his daughter, which portended great things of her progeny, gave her in marriage to a Persian of private station, named Cambyses. A year after her marriage, when she was pregnant, he had a still more alarming if less unmentionable dream, whereupon he sent to Persia for her and put her under a guard, resolving to destroy whatever should be born of her; the Magi having signified that his dream meant that her offspring would reign in his stead. The officer (Harpagus) whom he entrusted with the task, however, shrank from the act, sent for one of the king's cowherds, Mitradates, and ordered him to expose the child on a mountain abounding in wild beasts. All the same, the child was clothed in "gold and a robe of various colours." When the herdsman got home, his wife had just been delivered of a still-born child; and they agreed to give up its body to Harpagus as that of the young prince, dead from exposure, while they actually reared the prince as their own child, giving him another name than Cyrus. When the child grows to boyhood, he of course reveals royal qualities; and while "playing in the village in which the ox stalls were" he is chosen by the other boys as their king, and causes a disobedient playfellow to be scourged. This Astyages discovers, and the

[1] *History of Hindostan*, ii. 478. [2] B. i. 107-130.

story comes out. Astyages punishes Harpagus by causing him unknowingly to eat the flesh of his own child; but is told by the Magi that as his dream has been already fulfilled in the coronation of Cyrus by the village children, he may safely let him go. Later, of course, Harpagus secretly helps Cyrus to make an insurrection; Astyages impales the Magi, but gives the command of his troops to Harpagus, who betrays him; and Cyrus reigns, but without killing his grandfather. Of Cyrus' death, Herodotus tells, there were many accounts; and in one of these[1] he is declared to have been *crucified* by an Amazon queen of Scythians.

Here, then, we have an old myth,[2] in which already, however, certain primeval mythical details are seen modified to suit history. The name Cyrus, in its Persian form, was or stood for that of the sun,[3] and the historic Cyrus simply had fathered on him the popular sun-legend, with modifications. Thus the herdsman's wife's name means "the bitch"; and it is explained that this is how the story arose of Cyrus being suckled by a bitch—a myth which at once recalls the story of Romulus and Remus, suckled by a she-wolf; and of Jupiter, suckled by the she-goat Amalthea.[4] Again, the secret message from Harpagus in Media to Cyrus in Persia is sent enclosed in the body of a hare—an animal which in early mythology repeatedly plays the part of a message-bringer.[5] And the robe "of many colours" is, like Joseph's coat, plainly the many-tinted cloud-drapery of the Sun. Apart from these details, the story of the exposure of the infant hero is plainly cognate with the legends of the exposure of Romulus and Remus, of Æsculapius, of Attis, of Semiramis, of Cybele, of Tēlephos, of Ion, of Iamos, of a dozen other myth-heroes, including Moses, the circumstances of whose exposure are so strikingly recalled by the

[1] Diodorus Siculus, ii. 44.

[2] A similar story appears to have been told of the hero Gilgames in the old Assyrian mythology. See Ælian, *De nat. anim.* xii. 21; and cp. Hartland, *The Legend of Perseus*, i. 6–7.

[3] Plutarch, *Artaxerxes*, beginning.

[4] Callimachus, *Hymn to Zeus*, 49.

[5] Gubernatis, *Zoological Mythology*, ii. 77, 79.

Jesuist story of the massacre of the innocents; and parts of the tale are found closely paralleled in the northern legend of British Arthur, as well as in that of Œdipus.[1] The child Arthur, like Cyrus, is robed in gold, and like him is secretly sent to be suckled by one not his mother.[2] In the older mythology Æsculapius, exposed as a child,[3] is found by Autolaus and nursed by Trygon (= "the turtle-dove"); or, in another myth, suckled by a she-goat and protected by a watch-dog;[4] or, in yet another, reared by the Magnesian centaur. Attis, whom his mother, the river-nymph Nana, bears after impregnation by a miraculous pomegranate, for which her father seeks to starve her to death, is exposed by the father's orders, and is found and nourished by a goatherd,[5] or a goat.[6] Semiramis ("Istar in another guise"[7]) was fabled to have been exposed for a whole year in the desert and nourished by doves, as Elijah is nourished for many days by ravens in the Hebrew myth.[8] Cybele, daughter of Maion and Dindyma, is exposed as an infant by her father on the mountain Cybelus, and is suckled by panthers and other wild beasts.[9] Antiope, bearing the twins Zethos and Amphion to Zeus and Epopeos, leaves them in a grotto in swaddling clothes, and they are found by a shepherd.[10] Télephos, son of Hercules, is born secretly, and his mother Augè hides him in the temple of Athênê, of which she is priestess. Aleus, her father, finding the child, causes him to be exposed on the Parthenian (Virgin) Mount, where he is nourished by a doe, or a goat, or by shepherds; and at the same time Aleus gives Augè to Nauplius to be sold or drowned.[11] In a composite version, Augè and the child, like Danaë and Perseus, Semelé and Dionysos, are put to sea in a chest.[12] Ion is placed by his

[1] Cox, *Mythology of the Aryan Nations*, ed. 1882, pp. 134, 312.
[2] Malory's *Mort d'Arthure*, chap. iii. [3] Pausanius, viii. 25.
[4] *Id.* ii. 26. Pindar, *Pythia*, iii. 64.
[5] Arnobius, v. 6, citing Timotheus. [6] Pausanias, vii. 17.
[7] Sayce, Hibbert Lectures on the Babylonian Religion, p. 271.
[8] 1 Kings xvii. 6.
[9] Diodorus Siculus, iii. 58. [10] Pausanias, i. 38; ii. 6.
[11] Pausanias, viii. 48, 54; Apollodorus, ii. 7, 4; iii. 9, 1; Ælian, *Var. Hist.* xii. 42.
[12] Pausanias, viii. 4.

mother in the rock-cave, a possible prey to beasts and birds.[1] So Phialo, after bearing Aichmagoras to Hercules, is exposed on the mountain Ostracina, with her child, by her father, Alkimedeon, who dwelt there in a cave; and the call of a jay draws to them the attention of Hercules, who saves them.[2] So the prophet-child Iamos, son of Apollo, is left by his mother Evadne, hidden in the rushes, where two azure-eyed dragons feed him with honey.[3] And so Priam's son Alexander was nourished by a she-bear, and Ægisthus, son of Thyestes and Palopea, by a goat.[4] Very rarely is the divine child slain, as happens to the babe borne to Apollo by Psamathe, daughter of Crotopus. Exposed by her for fear (as usual) of her father, it is found by sheep-dogs and killed.[5]

The wish of the bad king to slay the hero-child, again, is the specific subject of many more myths.[6] In an Arab legend of Abraham, his mother hides him at birth because the astrologers and wise men have declared that according to their books a child is to be born who will destroy the worship of idols and overthrow King Nemrod; and the king accordingly gives orders to destroy all the male children who may be born. Hiding him in a cave, she puts a stone at the mouth and there suckles him, without the knowledge even of her husband Azer.[7] The same story is told by the Arabs concerning Daniel,[8] as by the Jews concerning Moses; and it was told at once of John and of Jesus by the early Christists,[9] who were in all likelihood merely freshening up two immemorial forms of

[1] Euripides, *Ion*. 17, 18, 27.

[2] Pausanias, viii. 12.

[3] Pindar, *Olymp*. vi. 60, ff.

[4] Ælian, as cited.

[5] Pausanias, i. 43.

[6] See Mr. Lang's admission in regard to the Moses myth, cited above, p. 87. At times, as in the case of Saturn, the father himself is the would-be slayer. Even Herakles, in frenzy, slays the children borne to him by Megara. Apollodorus, ii. 4, 12.

[7] *Revue de l'Histoire des Religions*, vol. xxii. No. 1, p. 57 (1890. Juil.-Août). As showing the medley of ideas in mythology, it may be noted that in this story the world is ruled at the time by four sovereigns: two unbelievers, Nemrod and Bacht en Naser (Nebuchadnezzar); and two believers, Zoul Qarneïn and the prophet Solomon. Nemrod rules "the seven zones," and dwells at Babylon.

[8] Bochart, pt. i. *Hierozolyma*, l. ii. c. 3.

[9] See the *Protevangelion*, cc. 22, 23.

popular religion in Syria. As the Moses myth is duplicated in the myths of Cyrus[1] and Horus, and unquestionably preceded by the myth of Sargon, it would seem sufficiently idle to suppose later variants to be derived from the New Testament. But with all this parallelism to account for, Professor Weber and the Christian partizans have assumed out-of-hand that the story of Krishna's nativity was just taken from the Gospels, leaving the Gospel story to stand by its own sacrosanctity.

In point of fact there is hardly a leading detail in the Krishna birth legend which is not variously paralleled in other early non-Christian mythology. In the Greek pantheon, God after God, hero after hero, is found to have been reared under difficulties. "Neither in pictures nor in story," says the chorus in the *Ion* of Euripides,[2] "have I heard that the children sprung from the Gods among mortals have a happy life." Ino, mother of Melicerta (Melkarth), leaps into the sea with her child, to save him from his furious father Athamas, who has killed her previous child Learchus; and the two are saved by Nereïds, and changed by Poseidon into sea-deities.[3] Leto, pregnant with Apollo, is driven from place to place by the jealous hate of Hérê.[4] The infant Dionysos, son of Ammon and Amalthea, is sent by his father to a secluded island, and guarded by the virgin Goddess Athênê from the jealous wrath of Rhea, the wife of Ammon.[5] In another version, Semelê, who bears Dionysos to Zeus, is spirited away with her child in a chest by Cadmus: the chest is thrown in the sea and cast ashore; Semelê, found dead, is buried; and the wandering Io (who in the common

[1] There is a further echo of it in the story of the infant Cypselus, concerning whom the oracle warned the oligarchs of Corinth that he would be dangerous to them, and who, they having failed to kill him, finally becomes tyrannos of Corinth (Herodotus, v. 93). As the story further makes the mother hide Cypselus in a chest (κυψέλη), it is pretty clear that his name had pointed the myth-makers to a current myth in which a child so figures.

[2] *Vv.* 506–8.

[3] Pausanias, i. 44; Ovid, *Fasti*, vi. 489–550; *Metam.* iv. 511–541. Apollodorius, I. ix. 2.

[4] Callimachus, *Hymn to Delos*, 55 ff. Homerid. *Hymn to Delian Apollo.*

[5] Diodorus Siculus, iii. 68, 70.

myth is a cow) rears the child in a cave.[1] In another legend, he is excited by Hèrè to go against the Tyrrhenian pirates, who capture him.[2] Similarly, Zeus himself in his infancy is stolen away by the Curetes from fear of his father Kronos (Saturn) and nursed by the nymphs Ithome and Neda;[3] while in the more familiar story Kronos devours his children successively, fearing they will dispossess him, till Rhea his wife gives him a stone wrapped in cloth, which he swallows in place of the new-born Jupiter, whom she brings forth in a distant place and rears in a cave, and who in turn overthrows his father, as Cyrus overthrows Astyages.[4] Yet again, when Arcadian Rhea bears Poseidon, he is "deposited with the flocks and fed with the lambs"; and in this case she gives Kronos a foal to eat.[5] Hèrè in one story exposes the child Hephaistos.[6] In yet another story, Æsculapius narrowly escapes being burned alive with his mother Coronis.[7] Needless to speak of the serpents sent by Hèrè against Apollo and Artemis[8] and the infant Hercules,[9] and the battling of the young Horus against Typhon: the myth is universal. The idea passed, as we have seen, from mythology to regal biography. Ages before Cyrus, it was applied to Sargon, in whose epitaph we have: "My mother the princess conceived: in a secret place she brought me forth. She placed me in a basket of reeds......She gave me to the river which drowned me not......";[10] and again we have it in the myths of Horos and Moses. And yet we are asked to believe that an Indian variant of this myth, closely resembling one current in Persia ages before Christ, is wholly or partly borrowed from the Christian Gospels, canonical and apocryphal.

[1] Pausanias, iii. 24. [2] Euripides, *Cyclops*, 11. [3] Pausanias, iv. 33.

[4] Hesiod, *Theogony*, 477–491; Pausanias, viii. 8.

[5] Last cit. [6] Pausanias, i. 20.

[7] Pausanias, ii. 26. Pindar, *Pythia*, iii. 54–63. Callisto, bearing Arcas to Jupiter, is turned into a she-bear by Artemis; and Hermes has to be sent to save the child. Pausanias, viii. 3–4.

[8] Macrobius, *Saturnalia*, i. 17; Hyginus, fab. 140.

[9] Pindar, *Nem.* i. By M. Clermont-Ganneau this myth is accounted for as a Greek attempt to explain an Egyptian vase-picture of Horus holding the two serpents.

[10] Sayce, Hibbert Lectures, p. 26.

Carrying the comparison further, we note a variety of parallels in regard to which there can be no pretence that Christianity is borrowed from. For instance, Krishna,[1] Apollo,[2] Hermes,[3] and Jesus,[4] all alike speak immediately after birth. Again, the story of the God being born in a cave[5] is anticipated in the case of Hermes and Dionysos, and in the cave-worships of Adonis and Mithra.[6] So thoroughly did this particular notion possess the human intelligence in antiquity that it was grafted on the biography of the philosopher Confucius, of whom it is told that his mother, in obedience to a vision, went to a cave on Mount Ne, where she gave him birth; that genii had announced to her the honour her son would bring her; that the events were heralded by miraculous portents, and that fairies attended at his nativity.[7] In the Greek myth

[1] *Vishnu Purana*, Wilson's trans. p. 502.

[2] Hom. *Hymn to Delian Apollo*, 103–32. Callimachus, *Hymn to Delos*, 86–7, makes Apollo speak *in the womb*.

[3] Hom. *Hymn to Hermes*, 17, 18, 29.

[4] Korân, Sura xix. (lviii.)—"Mary": Arabic *Gospel of the Infancy*, c. i. In Pseudo-Matthew, c. 13, Jesus at birth stands on his feet.

[5] *Protevangelion*, 18, 21 (xii. 14; xv. 9). Arabic *Gospel of the Infancy*, 2, 3, 4, 5 (i. 6, 8, 9, etc.). Pseudo-Matthew, cc. 13, 14.

[6] See the essay on *Mithraism*, hereinafter.

[7] Douglas's *Confucianism*, p. 25. Compare the following native account, given by a Chinese scholar to the "Parliament of Religions":—"I once looked up the derivation of the word 'sing' (surname), which is given by Hsu She, the philologist, to be 'the product of man.' He adds that in ancient times the holy mother conceived a child by heaven, who was called the Son of Heaven; on this account the character 'sing' is made up of two parts—'me' (woman) forming the one part, and 'shang' (born) the other. In the historical sketches of ancient times are recorded many instances of wonderful birth. It was not confined to men of wisdom and virtue. There is an ancient saying that remarkable men have remarkable circumstances attending their births. Tradition has handed down many marvellous circumstances connected with the birth of Confucius. It is said that two dragons wound their bodies round the house where he was born; that five men, venerable with age, representing the five planets, descended unto the open court; that the air was filled with music; that a voice came out of the heavens, saying: 'This is a heaven-born, divine child, hence the sound of melodious music descends'; that a unicorn threw out of its mouth a book of jade, upon which was engraved this inscription: 'Son of the essence of water, who shall succeed to the kingdom of the degenerate house of Chan.' It is also said that the Duke of Chan, who lived five hundred years before Confucius, on coming to the place where Confucius was to be born, said: 'Five hundred years hence, on this sacred spot, shall a divine character be born.' As Confucius appeared at the time predicted, the Duke of Chan is therefore considered to have had a previous knowledge of the coming of Confucius. The fact that Confucius, during his lifetime, often dreamed of the Duke of Chan is also attributed to this circumstance. Tales of this

of Ion, again, the mother Creusa, after bearing the child to Apollo, carries him, swaddled and cradled, "to the same cave where she had been united to the God."[1] Yet further, the account of Jesus as being chosen king by his playfellows,[2] is clearly based on or akin to the Cyrus legend, above recapitulated; and the various accounts of his games with his comrades, which seem to be regarded as having suggested the Gopi revels of Krishna, are similarly indicated in Herodotus; the killing of boys by Jesus[3] being mildly paralleled in the chastising of a boy by Cyrus, as again more completely in the killing of an Egyptian by Moses.[4] What is the precise historic relation between the Krishna and the Cyrus[5] legends is still uncertain, though the connection is undoubtedly close;[6] but on any view the Christian claim is out of the question. The obviously mythical Christian story of the massacre of the innocents

character were scattered broadcast during the Han Dynasty by men who delighted in the mysteries of geomancy, priestcraft, and soothsaying. Though Confucianists do not reject such stories altogether, they do not set much value on them. Marvellous tales have always exerted a sort of fascinating influence over the minds of the Chinese people both in ancient and in modern times." The Hon. Pung Kwang Yu, in paper written for the Parliament of Religions. See Report, 1893, vol. i. p. 426. It should be noted that the "two dragons" occur also in the myths of Ion and Iamos.

[1] Euripides, *Ion*, 16–18. Later (949) she says she bore him in the cave.

[2] Arabic *Gospel of the Infancy*, cc. 41, 42 (xviii. 1, 7).

[3] *Id.* 46, 47 (xix. 21, 24); *Gospel of Thomas* (1st Greek form), 3, 4 (ii. 4, 9).

[4] Exodus ii. 12.

[5] This name, so much altered by our pronouncing the "C" as "S," is in the Greek (Κυρος) and the Persian (Cosroe or Koresh, identified or interchanged, as above noted, with *Khor*, the Sun) sufficiently like Krishna to be at least as capable of connection with that as the name Christ. It may be worth noting that whereas Krishna is a serpent-slayer, in the Persian system the serpent is to be killed "at the end of days" by Keresaspa. M. Müller, *Chips from a German Workshop*, ed. 1880, ii. 172-3.

[6] "As Laios [father of Œdipus] in the Theban myth is the enemy, Dasyu, of the devas or bright Gods, so is Astyages only a Græcised form of Ashdag, the Azidahaka, or biting snake of Hindu legend and the Zohak of the epic of Firdusi." Cox, *Mythology of the Aryan Nations*, p. 324; cp. M. Müller, *Chips*, ed. 1880, ii. 172–4. The view that Astyages = Azidahaka, which appears to have been first advanced by Lenormant, is scouted by Tiele, *Outlines*, p. 179. "Azhi dahâka is a purely Aryan demon, and Astyages has nothing to do with him." This view, however, will have to be tested by the reconstructed theory of Aryan derivation; and in any case it is not clear why Astyages should not rank as "purely Aryan." Cp. Taylor, *Origin of the Aryans*, pp. 190, 319–321; Sayce, *Ancient Empires of the East*, p. 242; and Spiegel, *Erânische Alterthumskunde*, i. 531.

by Herod[1] was doubtless concocted by blending the legend of the child massacre by Pharaoh[2] with the legend of the quasi-Messianic, doom-escaping, and finally crucified Cyrus, who stood high in Jewish esteem as a liberator of the captive race and a believer in their God;[3] and adding the prophecy of Zoroaster.[4]

The item of the God being hastily transported or born on a journey, again, is plainly a phase of the universal and presumably astronomic myth;[5] and though the myth-necessity of taking Jesus to Bethlehem might account for that detail, the flight into Egypt is mythically gratuitous from the purely Messianic point of view; the motive "out of Egypt have I called my Son" being plainly an afterthought. The journey is really made because of invariable mythic precedent. In the old stories, Mandané comes from Persia to be delivered in Media; Rhea goes to bear Zeus in Crete: Latona wanders far to bear Apollo, and Themis[6] nurses him; Cyrênê is carried by Apollo athwart the sea,

[1] It is erroneously stated by the Rev. Mr. Maurice, *Hist. of Hindostan*, ii. 298–9, that the argument of Origen with Celsus shows that the Jews of that day did not dispute the story of the massacre. The fact is that Origen explicitly says (i. 61) that "the Jew of Celsus" denies the story. It may be interesting to note the probable mythological explanation of this story in all its forms, which is, according to the solar school, that the massacred innocents are the stars which disappear as the sun is about to enter, the destroyer being the Power of Darkness. The same idea is turned to very different account in the slaying of Argus by the Day-God Hermes; and yet again in the slaying of Ursula and the eleven thousand virgins. On the other hand, when Krishna steals the milk of the cow-maids, it is the sun who takes away the light of the stars (Cox, p. 369). See below, Section xv. § 2, as to the killing of the six children before the Divine One.

[2] Exod. i. 15–22.

[3] Ezra i.; iii. 7; iv. 3; v. 13; vi. 3; Isaiah xliv. 28; xlv. 1; Daniel vi. 28; etc.

[4] Arab. Gospel, c. 7 (iii. 1).

[5] It could be wished that Mr. Frazer, in his careful and ingenious analysis of the myths of Vegetation Gods, had paid more heed to the differentiating clue of the manner of *birth* of the different species of deity. Dionysos, for instance, is born under difficulties equally with the more strictly solar Apollo and Herakles. It is conceivable that such stories may at times have been understood of the sprouting of a seed in despite of the enmities of cold and of animals. In some cases, too, a wandering mother who bears a child to the God, or is taken by the God over seas, means just the founding of a colony under the God's auspices. But only an astronomic idea can well explain the idea in the case of indisputable Sun-Gods; and in nearly all cases we are led to surmise a customary child-carrying rite, which the myth is framed to explain.

[6] Homerid. *Hymn to Apollo*, 124; Callimachus, as cited.

to Libya, garden of Jove, to bear to him the immortal child Aristæus;[1] Augè (the Shining) in one version flies, in others is sent, from her father's land, after her amour with Herakles, to bear Tèlephos (the Far Light);[2] Evadnè (herself sent afar for nurture by her mother Pitanè, who bore her to Poseidon) goes away secretly to bring forth under dark bushes the inspired son, Iamos, whom she bears to Apollo;[3] Danaë, like Augè, is sent far by her father to bear Perseus, begotten of Zeus; and Zeus conveys the daughter of Opus to Locrus, there to bear Iapetos;[4] Myrrha has to fly far and be transformed into the myrrh-tree before her child Adonis, the Lord, can be born;[5] Rhœo, with child by Apollo, is locked in a chest, thrown into the sea, and cast on Delos, where she bears the child Anios, who is then taken and hidden by his father;[6] and Hèrè goes "far away" from Zeus and men to conceive and bear Typhon—or Mars—or Dionysos.[7] Under all disguises it seems to be the Sun-Child, or Day-God, who is so born; and the purple zone and violet hair of Evadnè, the Dawn or Sunset Goddess, are as significant as the violet colour of her babe. But the motive does duty for all manner of cases. Hagar goes into the wilderness to bear Ishmael; the daughter of Phlegyas follows her roving father far to bear Æsculapius;[8] the mother of the deified Apollonius of Tyana is told in a dream to go into a meadow, and there she is delivered of her child;[9] and in the Buddha legend, Maya (who becomes pregnant at the age of forty-five, a period about as late for India as that of the pregnancy of Sarah would be for Westerns), bears her holy child under a palm-tree (as Latona bears Apollo,[10] and as Mary does

[1] Pindar, *Pythia*, ix. 90 (55); Diodorus Siculus, iv. 81.
[2] Pausanias, viii. 4 and 48.
[3] Pindar, *Olymp.* vi. 49 ff.
[4] *Id. Ol.* ix. 84, ff.
[5] Ovid, *Metam.* xi.
[6] Diodorus Siculus, v. 62.
[7] Hom. *Hymn to Apollo*, 326–331; Ovid, *Fasti*, v. 231–258; Diodorus Siculus, iii. 66.
[8] Pausanias, ii. 26.
[9] Philostratus' *Life of Apollonius*, i. 5. Compare the odd legend of the Epidaurians near the temple of Æsculapius, whose women till the time of Antonine must be delivered in the open air (Pausanias, ii. 27).
[10] Hom. *Hymn to Apollo*, 117; Theognis, l. 5; Callimachus, *Hymn to Delos*, 208; Pliny, *Hist. Nat.* xiv. 44.

Jesus in the Koran)[1] on her way to her father's house.[2] Of course there are variations. Maya dies, as Semelé dies, and Buddha is suckled by her sister, as we have seen so many of the Greek Gods were suckled by nurses; whereas Mary lives and keeps her child; but when Professor Weber assumes that the carrying of Krishna across the river is borrowed from the "Christophoros" legend, he not only overlooks the mythological significance of the river, elsewhere mentioned by himself, but the whole legend of Cyrus, which presents the close parallel of the herdsman's wife being delivered at the same time as Mandané, as Yasoda bears a child simultaneously with Devaki, and Elizabeth simultaneously with Mary. And, as he himself points out twice in his treatise,[3] the river figures in the Krishnaite ritual as the serpent or "serpent-prince," Kaliya, a motive not found in the gospels.[4] On the other hand, however, when the Professor would derive from the third Gospel[5] the item of Nanda's journey to Mathurâ to pay his taxes, we are entitled to meet him with the converse proposition, that here at least it is the Christian Gospel that borrows from the Hindu drama.

The gospel story of Mary and Joseph going to Bethlehem to be taxed under the edict of Augustus is obviously myth: there was no such practice in the Roman world; and in any case Galilee was still independently governed by Herod-Antipas when Quirinius went to tax Judea. Only the late third Gospel tells the story: the narrative in Matthew, added late as it was to the original composition,

[1] Sura xix.—"Mary." Rodwell's trans. 1861, p. 129.

[2] Professor Rhys Davids seems disposed to treat this episode as historic (*Buddhism*, p. 26); and writes that it was "in accordance with custom" that Maya went to be delivered in her father's house. It is evident, however, that the journey is one of the "details" which he admits (p. 27) may be due to the mythopoeic tendency.

[3] *Ueber die Krishnajanmâshtami*, pp. 249, 280. It is further noteworthy that the Yamunâ (*i.e.*, the Jumna) has long had the poetic name of *Kâlindi*, = "daughter of Kalinda," which last is a name of the sun (Wilson, *Theatre of the Hindus*, 1835, i. 302; ii. 90).

[4] Among the Gnostics, however, the serpent-worshippers viewed the serpent as "a moist substance"; and the symbolism of serpent and river is obvious (Hippolytus, *Refutation of all Heresies*, bk. v. c. 4).

[5] The only canonical Gospel, be it observed, which has the story of Elizabeth giving birth to John when Mary bears Jesus.

which obviously began at what is now the third chapter, has no hint of the taxing, but implies that Joseph and Mary lived at Bethlehem; the Gospel of Mary gives the visit without the taxing; and so loosely was the myth credited that in the Protevangelion (c. 17) the statement is that it was decreed "that all should be enrolled, who were in Bethlehem of Judea." In that story, Jesus is born on the journey, in the cave, three miles from Bethlehem (c. 17); and it is after being taken from the cave that he is laid by his mother at Bethlehem "in an ox-stall."[1] Now, if the Krishna legend is clearly bound up with the long pre-Christian legend of Cyrus, why should we here suppose that its taxing-journey motive is borrowed from Christianity, instead of *vice versa?* The latter is plainly the reasonable hypothesis. In the Purana story, Vasudeva, crossing the river Yamunâ, whose waters are stilled and lowered, with the babe Krishna in his arms, sees on the bank "Nanda and the rest, who had come hither to bring tribute due to Kansa."[2] The Bhagavat Purâna version "more consistently makes Vasudeva find Nanda and the rest fast asleep in their houses; and subsequently describes their bringing tribute or tax (*Kara*) to Kansa."[3] Again, in the Vishnu Purâna, the liberated Vasudeva goes "to the waggon of Nanda";[4] and in the Bhâgavat he "does not quit Mathurâ, but goes to the halting ground of Nanda, who has come to that city to pay his taxes." On the exhortation of Vasudeva to go, "Nanda and the other cowherds, their goods being placed in their waggons, and their taxes having been paid to the king, returned to their village." Here is a detailed and circumstantial narrative, which, with its variations, we may with considerable confidence assume to have formed part of those dramatic representations of the birth of Krishna that are established, on the evidence of Patanjali's Commentary, as having flourished before our era. The Hindu story is detailed and dramatic, though

[1] Ch. 22. In the *History of Joseph the Carpenter*, which follows Luke for the enrolment story, Mary brings forth Jesus "*in* Bethlehem, in a cave near the tomb of Rachel" (ch. 7).

[2] *Vishnu Purâna*, Wilson's trans. p. 503.

[3] *Id.* Note by Wilson.

[4] *Id.* p. 506.

of course grounded on a myth motive: the Christian story, given in one only, and that the latest, of the Synoptics, is either a mere myth-echo or is introduced in order to give a basis for the mythical birth of Jesus at Bethlehem, which the second Gospel, the fourth, and the first as it originally stood, do not assert at all. On what explanation can we fall back save that the knowledge of the Indian religious drama, or of some Asian tale of the same mythological origin, had been conveyed to Egypt or Syria, either by travelling Hindus or by Westerns who visited Asia; and that the compilers of the third Gospel got it in that way? How should such a hopeless story have been invented for such a purpose if the hint were not already in circulation?

As for the old attempt of the self-frustrative Maurice[1] to derive the item of Devaki's imprisonment by Kansa within seven gates, from the Christian legend, preserved by the Mohammedans,[2] that Mary during her maidenhood was guarded by Zacharias in the sanctuary within seven doors, the answer here is still more easy. M. Senart,[3] without any thought of Maurice's contention, of which probably he never heard, gives a Hindu antecedent for the story in an utterance of Indra in the Vedas: "Being still in the breast of my mother, I saw the birth of all the devas: a hundred fortresses of brass enveloped me; I escaped with violence in the form of a falcon" (Rig Veda, iv. 27, 1). And we may further point to the close parallel in the Cyrus legend,[4] in which Astyages puts his daughter under a guard, just as Kansa does his sister Devaki; and to the familiar myth of the imprisonment of Danaë in the brazen tower—which in one version becomes an underground chamber.[5] Is it likely that the Hindu imagination would need to come to Christianity for the detail of the seven gates? Is it not much more likely that the Christian-Mohammedan legend and the Hindu drama alike were derived from forms of the ancient myth which makes the

[1] *History of Hindostan*, ii. 314.
[2] Sale's *Koran*, note on chap. iii. (ed. 1734, p. 39 *b*).
[3] *Essai sur la Légende du Buddha*, p. 314.
[4] Herodotus, i. 108.
[5] Pausanias, ii. 23.

Goddess Ishtar pass through the seven gates of Hades,[1] to and fro, to reach and bring back her lover? This, like so many other details of the myth, may well have been pre-Aryan; and it may point mythically either to the notion of the "seven zones," or climates, or seasons, or to the seven planets of ancient astronomy.[2] Alcmenè, who with her husband Amphitryon had come away from her own home,[3] like so many other mothers of Gods, bears Herakles to Zeus and the twin Iphiclus to Amphitryon in seven-gated Thebes;[4] and a similar myth may have been taught in the Dionysiak, the Mithraic, the Osirian, or any other mysteries. Of myth there is no "original," save mankind's immemorial dream.

XII. The Stable and Manger.

After what has been thus far seen of the correspondences between the Christian legends and prior myths, it is unnecessary to lay much stress on the mythical character of the birth in a stable, which corresponds with, and is thought by Christians to have suggested, the legend of the placing of Krishna in a basket, and even, apparently, his upbringing among the Gopis. We have seen that an orthodox English Sanskritist identifies the basket with the Gospel manger; and Professor Weber lays stress[5] on the representation of the birth of Krishna in a cow-shed in the elaborate and dramatic ritual service of the Krishna Birth-Festival, which here departs from the Puranic legend, that making the birth take place in Kansa's fortress. On this head a sufficient answer is given out of hand by M. Senart:—

> "The confusion, in certain sources, of the *sûtikâ-griha* (lying-in room) with a *gokula*, a stable, contrary to the strict details of the recital,

[1] *Records of the Past*, i. 141; Sayce, Hibbert Lectures, pp. 221–227.

[2] In modern Brahmanic ritual occurs the formula:—"Fire! seven are thy fuels; seven thy tongues; seven thy holy sages; seven thy beloved abodes; seven ways do seven sacrificers worship thee. Thy sources are seven" (Colebrooke in *Asiatic Researches*, vii. 273). The number had early become a fixed idea.

[3] Hesiod, *Shield of Hercules*, 1–2.

[4] *Id.* 49.

[5] Treatise cited, p. 269.

seems to him [Weber] one more sign of Christian imitation. But it must be remembered that the sûtikâ-griha must, in the terms of the ritual, contain not only Devakî with her son and Vasudeva, but also, and all together, the images of the shepherds, of the servants of Kansa, the guards of Devakî, of the Apsaras and the armed Dânavas, of Yasoda and Rohinî, without reckoning the representations of all the exploits attributed to the child Krishna [Weber, pp. 268, 280, ff.]. The intention then was not to give a faithful picture of the facts reported in the legend, but to group in a single frame all the personages included in it. How, on that footing, could separation be made of the new-born and the mother, or distinction between the prison and the dwelling of the shepherd? And of what weight is the novelty, illogical if it be, of the arrangement? The idea of representing the young God at the breast of his mother is really too simple to prove anything: there are not wanting examples of it in the religious representations of the Greeks."[1]

But not only is the suckling motive, as we previously saw, pre-Christian; the items of the basket-manger and the stable are equally so. Not only is the Greek *liknon*, or twig basket, used to this day for corn and for cradling children, as in the old Christian pictures, but we know that the infant Dionysos, in the processions of his cult, was represented among the Greeks as being carried in such a basket, which again is represented as being the cradle of Hermes[2] and of Jupiter.[3] In the ancient Greek lexicon of Hesychius (which at this point the Christians certainly did not interpolate, though they did so at others) the word Λικνίτης is defined as ἐπίθετον Διονύσου· ἀπὸ τῶν λίκνων, ἐν οἷς τὰ παιδία κοιμῶνται, "an epithet of Dionysos, from the *liknons* in which children are cradled."[4] Now if, as our Christian apologist argues, a basket is a manger (as it is in the East, and as it is in the well-known picture of the Nativity by Botticelli), it clearly follows on his own reasoning that the Christian story is derived from the

[1] *Essai*, p. 335. Compare our preceding Section X. § 1, and K. O. Müller's *Ancient Art and its Remains*, Eng. tr. p. 493.

[2] ἱερῷ ἐνὶ λίκνῳ, "in the sacred basket." Homerid. *Hymn to Hermes*, 21.

[3] λίκνῳ ἐνὶ χρυσέῳ, "in a golden basket." Callimachus, *Hymn to Zeus*, 48. Cp. *Hymn to Demeter*, 127; and Apuleius, *Metamorphoses*, bk. xi. concerning the *auream vannum congestam ramulis*.

[4] Compare Liddell and Scott, *s. v.* λικνίτης, λίκνον, and λικνοφόρος; and Servius on Virgil, *Georg.* i. 166.

previous Dionysiak cultus.[1] In actual fact we find the God-Child represented, on a sarcophagus in the Catacombs, as cradled in a basket, standing under a shed, as in Botticelli's picture, with an ox and an ass looking on at his feet, in the fashion in which he is to this day represented at Christmas-time, throughout France and Italy.[2] This bas-relief, which includes the father and the mother, and three figures coming with gifts, is claimed as primarily Christian by Christian scholars, who see in it the adoration of the Magi. It has been argued, on the other hand,[3] that the sculpture is originally Mithraic; a view I am much inclined to share: since there is really no other way of explaining the entrance of Magi into the Christian legend. But in any case, Christian or Mithraic, this bas-relief, which probably belongs to the fourth century, proves that a God-Child was early represented as lying swaddled in a basket, with an ox and an ass looking on, or else lying on his mother's knee while the ox and ass eat out of the basket, in circumstances which irresistibly suggest the Gospel legend of the birth of Jesus; and that legend is

[1] Dionysos would be carried in the cradle-basket on Christmas day. The rural or lesser Dionysia, the oldest of all, took place in the Attic month of Posidaon, which would correspond nearly to our December. Again, the great biennial festival, the Trieterika, was celebrated on Parnassus at the time of the shortest day (Müller, *Lit. of Ancient Greece*, Eng. tr. p. 288, following Boeckh). The Bœotians, further, began their year at the winter solstice; and in Bithynia the month beginning on December 24th was known as Dionysos. Under different names, the month began then in the Cretan calendar, which was "the same as that used by most inhabitants of Asia Minor"; while in the Roman period the month Posidaon was in some calendars made to begin on December 25th. Schmitz in Smith's *Dict. of Gr. and Rom. Antiq.* following Clinton, Hermann, and Bergk.

[2] See the reproduction in Northcote and Brownlow's *Roma Sotterranea*, ed. 1879, ii. 258; also in Lundy's *Monumental Christianity*, 1876, Fig. 85, as copied from Nork's reproduction (in Scheible's *Kloster*, vol. vii. pt. i. p. 30); and in an article by Dr. Carus in *The Open Court*, Chicago, December, 1899, p. 723. See also p. 712 for a copy of a less elaborate design on a sarcophagus of the year 343, after Kraus—that given in *Roma Sotterranea*, ii. 235.

[3] First, apparently, by Seel (*Die Mithrageheimnisse*, 1823, pp. 436, 475), cited by Von Bohlen, *Das alte Indien*, i. 258. Von Bohlen lays it down that Mithra's birth was "dramatically represented at the winter solstice; the Sun-Child rests with a nimbus, and surrounded by the sacred animals of Ormuzd." The thesis is urged later by a Dutch rationalist, Dr. H. Hartogh Heijs van Zouteveen, in his *Over den Oorsprong der Godsdienstige Denkbeelden*, p. 56, citing Nork's *Mythen der alten Persen*, which I have not been able to see. But the point is put in Nork's *Die Weihnachts und Osterfeier erklärt aus dem Sonnencultus der Orientalen*, 1838, p. 30.

thus clearly imitative of, for one thing, the old Greek usage of carrying in a basket the infant Dionysos, whose typical animals are the bull and ass. The cradle of Dionysos is a "long basket"[1]—exactly the description of that in the scene in the Catacomb sculpture and the Botticelli picture; as it is of the "basket of bulrushes" in which the sacred child Moses is sent floating on the Nile. A "woven basket-cradle" again figures in the myth of the birth of Ion, whose mother takes him in it to the rock-cave, whence he is carried by Hermes, "cradle, swaddle-clothes, and all," to the temple of his father Apollo.[2] And if it be argued that the stable story is something special to Christianity, the answer is that it is one of the oldest motives in Aryan mythology.

The frequency with which Greek and Indian deities are associated with cows is sufficient to indicate to any student unmesmerized by religion that a nature-myth underlies every case.[3] That the cow is the foremost myth-animal in the Vedas, nobody disputes. The clouds, the firmament, the moon, the earth, all have that aspect in turn; and to the last the idea holds its ground. In the Vishnu Purâna the clouds, the "cattle of Indra," "deluge the earth with milk"; "the cows and the bulls bellow as loud as roaring clouds";[4] and the cow is to the Hindu to-day as sacred as ever, and preserves its cultus. In ancient Egypt and in

[1] Smith's *Dict. of Gr. and Rom. Ant.* ed. 1849, p. 411.—Art. *Dionysia.* That this is the *mystica vannus Iacchi* would seem to be implied by Liddell and Scott, and is asserted by Müller (*Ancient Art*, as cited, p. 494). Cp. Ramage, *Nooks and Byways of Italy*, p. 157. The "mystic winnowing fan" was indeed a basket, but was it not also the *Kaneon* of the Canephoræ? Cp. Spanheim, *Obs. in Hymn. in Cererem Callimachi*, v. 127; and in *Hymn. in Jovem*, v. 48. (Ernesti's ed. ii. 43–4; 822–5.) In Hindu ritual "the winnowing fan, the *mystica vannus Iacchi*, is always used in the rites of Cal, Cali, and Durga; but the Hindus at present affix no other idea of mystery to it than its being an appendage to husbandry. They use it as a tray, on which they place before the image of the Deity the....articles used in the ceremony....On all solemnities the rituals prescribe exclusively the use of this fan, which they call Surp." Patterson, in *Asiatic Researches*, viii. 52.

[2] Euripides, *Ion*, 31–39, 1596.

[3] In Norse cosmogony a cow plays an important part in the creation of man (Grimm's *Teutonic Mythology*, Stallybrass' trans. ii. 559. Cp. p. 665; and Rydberg, *Teutonic Mythology*, pp. 263, 391, 497).

[4] Wilson's trans. pp. 525, 529.

Phœnicia it had the same pre-eminent sacredness.[1] But the myth of cow and stable spread world-wide with the race, so that we find the solar Hercules and Mercury fabled as living with shepherds or dealing with cows; and the thievish "night-awaiting" Mercury, who on the evening of the day of his birth steals the (cloud-) cows of the Day-God Apollo[2] (who himself was a cowherd[3]), was just such a figure as the black Krishna, playing among the cows with the cowherds, untrammelled by commonplace moral principles.[4] So have we seen the solar Cyrus playing among the ox-stalls of his foster-father's home: the sun-child disporting himself in the stable of the sky. In the Homeridian Hymn to Aphrodite, again, the love-sick Goddess comes to Anchises "in the stalls," while the shepherds and the cows and sheep are absent; and he disrobes her; but when these return she breathes sleep into her lover, and herself puts on beautiful garments. Here the myth is that of the Sun-God meeting the Twilight-Goddess in the sky vacant of clouds. Her garments are the returning clouds, coloured by the sun as he sinks to rest—a grace of poetry which tells of a literary civilization that only slightly retains the primitive fancy of cloud-cows and sky-stable. But as we come nearer Christianity the plot thickens. In the worship of Isis, the sacred cow (herself a virgin, supernaturally impregnated by a flash of lightning or by the rays of the moon[5]) was carried seven times round the

[1] Herodotus, ii. 41; Porphyry, *De Abstinentia*, ii. 11.

[2] Homerid. *Hymn to Hermes*, 22 ff. It is noteworthy that in ancient sculpture, as in the Hymn, the child Hermes is represented as lying *in swaddling-clothes*, defending himself from the charge of cattle-stealing, and as "cattle-stealer *in the cradle*" (Müller, *Anc. Art*, as cited, p. 487). Here we have the swaddled and cradled child-God, the Greek *Logos*, figured in connection with cattle.

[3] Iliad, xxi. 446–8.

[4] The antagonism between Hermes and Apollo, as well as that between Indra and Krishna, may be plausibly explained as occurring between a new and an old deity, or the deities of different races. Assuming with Müller that Apollo was the deity of the conquering Dorians, Hermes may be, as above noted, just a solar deity of the native race they conquered; as on the other hand Krishna's superseding of Indra has been above conceived as the final triumph of an aboriginal cult over a Brahmanic. Cp. Renan, as cited above, p. 144.

[5] Herodotus, iii. 28; Plutarch, *Isis and Osiris*, c. 43; Pomponius Mela, i. 9.

temple *upon the eve of the winter solstice*,[1] when the sun-child rose from the lotos;[2] and cow-headed Isis bears the Sun-God Horos, as in Indian legend the sun is born of the cows.[3]

And still closer comes the parallel. We know from Macrobius[4] that the Egyptian priests exhibited a babe to the people on a certain day as being the new-born Sun-God; and from Plutarch we know that the infant Horos was figured on the lotos at the time of the winter solstice. But there is documentary evidence that in the Egyptian system a Babe-Saviour was in pre-Christian times worshipped *in a manger or crib*, in connection with a virgin mother. The proof is furnished by the remarkable record in the Christian *Chronicon Paschale* (formerly but improperly called *Alexandrium*): "The same Jeremiah gave a sign to the Egyptian priests that their idols would be shaken and overthrown by a *child Saviour*, born of a virgin, and laid in a manger (φάτνη). Wherefore they still deify a child-carrying virgin, and adore a child in a manger. And to the inquiry of *King Ptolemy* as to the cause, they answered that they had received this mystery from a holy prophet who gave it to their fathers."[5] The *Chronicon Paschale* dates from the seventh century, and would not by itself suffice to prove the cultus alleged, seeing that a Christian might—though this in the circumstances would be extremely unlikely—invent such a story to support his own faith, that being evidently the purpose with which the chronicler cites it. But read in connection with Macrobius and Plutarch, and the ritual of the birth of Amunoteph, it may be taken as certainly resting on a usage in ancient Egyptian religion. The Virgin and Child must of course have been Isis and Horos, whose worship was much older than Jeremiah. And the expression "Child Saviour" clearly points to a child-worshipping ceremonial, and not to the Christian idea of salvation by the crucified adult. It is needless to remark on the

[1] Plutarch, as cited, c. 52. [2] c. 11.
[3] *Zoological Mythology*, i. 51. [4] *Saturnalia*, i. 18.
[5] Migne, *Patrolog. Curs. Comp., Series Gr.*, T. xcii. col. 385.

possibility that the ox-and-ass myth came from the same quarter, seeing that the temples of the sacred bull, Apis, and of the sacred cow, Isis, were already mystically, and in the former case literally, stables. But for the ox and stable there is yet another precedent. In the worship of Mithra, on the testimony of a Christian writer,[1] the lowing of the sacred heifers was part of a festival ceremony, evidently that of Christmas eve. Now, it has been shown[2] that in a multitude of points the Christian myths are simply based on previous ritual, as myths so often are: shall we then suppose that this primitive myth of the Christian God-born-in-a-stable, which only after a time passed current even with his own worshippers, and which early takes the form of representing him as being born between cow and ass, whose cries, in the popular Catholic fable, hide his,[3] as the cries of the infant Zeus were covered in order to prevent Kronos from hearing them[4] —that this is anything but a variation of the myth-motive of pagan antiquity? The mimic presentment of the scene is one of the immemorial features of the Christmas festival in Southern France and Italy: who can finally doubt that the usage was there before the Christian creed?

That the ox and ass in the Mithraic-Christian birth-scene have a mythic significance is very certain. They are not merely inmates of the "stable"; they are from of old symbolic animals; and they were the two of all the talking beasts who had the widest prophetic reputation.[5] The bull or ox, again, is one of the symbol-animals of the Sun-God; while the ass is not only of phallic repute, but "carries mysteries,"[6] is constantly associated with the Sun-God Dionysos, and is probably at bottom the night-sun,[7] as is

[1] Firmicus, *De Errore*, v. See the treatise on *Mithraism* hereinafter.

[2] *Id.* and in the treatise on *The Gospel Myths*.

[3] *Zoological Mythology*, i. 361.

[4] Callimachus, *Hymn to Zeus*, 53–54.

[5] For ox and cow, see Livy, iii. 10; xxiv. 10; xxvii. 11; xxviii. 11; xxxv. 21; xliii. 13. For the ass, see the legend of Liber in Lactantius, i. 21; also Plutarch's Life of Antony, where the ass's name, *Nikon*, "Victory," predicts to Augustus the triumph of Actium; and the Hebrew legend of Balaam—all widely circulated stories. Cp. Gubernatis, *Zool. Myth.* i. 247, 398. For the talking *horse*, see Grimm, as cited, i. 392.

[6] Aristophanes, *Frogs*, 160; and note in Bohn trans.

[7] Gubernatis, vol. i. ch. 3, *passim*.

Dionysos himself, in contrast to Apollo, the day-sun.[1] In the Jewish ritual[2] the red heifer plays an important part; and the rite, of which the Rabbins seem to have lost the explanation,[3] evidently connects with the similar usage in Egypt, which was associated with the solar cult of Typhon,[4] the Night-God or Winter-God and Principle of Darkness, one of whose symbolic animals was the ass.[5] The latter animal, again, evidently had a special significance for the Jews, since the firstling of the ass was specially redeemable, and on that ground bracketed with humanity.[6] In the sacred processions of Isis, the ox and the ass were the principal if not the only animals, the latter being sometimes adorned with wings.[7] Now, in the Krishna ritual the ox and the ass figure very much as they do in the birth scene of the Catacombs; and Professor Weber decides that this is one of the details borrowed from Christianity. On that view, it would be borrowed from the Apocryphal Gospel of Matthew. The narrative of that document, late in its present form, is doubtless in part based on much older originals, and challenges attention by its peculiarity:—

> "And on the third day after the birth of our Lord Jesus Christ the most blessed Mary went forth out of the cave, and, entering a stable, placed the child in the stall, and the ox and the ass adored him. Then was fulfilled that which was said by Isaiah the prophet, saying: The ox knoweth his owner and the ass his master's crib. The very animals therefore, the ox and the ass, having him in their midst incessantly adored him. Then was fulfilled that which was said by Abakuk the

[1] Macrobius, *Saturnalia*, i. 18. Plutarch, *I. and O.* c. 28. Dionysos, it will be remembered, was pre-eminently the God of the winter months. Preller, *Griech. Myth.* i. 539–541.

[2] Numbers xix.

[3] Spencer, *De Legibus Hebræorum*, l. ii. c. 15, vol. i. p. 340, ed. 1686.

[4] Plutarch, *I. and O.* cc. 31, 41, 52. Cp. Tobit i. 5, as to "the heifer Baal." Red cattle, again, as well as black (*ante*, p. 146), were a special sacrifice to Poseidon (Pindar, *Pythia*, iv. 339). Mr. Frazer plausibly argues (i. 401–2) that the red-haired victim and the red cow were symbols of the Corn-God, and were meant to promote the ripening of the corn.

[5] Plutarch, *I. and O.* 30, 31. The ass in turn was "red" for the Egyptians (*ib.*), and also for the Hebrews. Pleyte, *La religion des Pré-israélites*, 1865, p. 150.

[6] Exodus xxxiv. 20. The legend that the Jews worshipped an ass-headed God doubtless derives from the fact that the Samaritan God Tartak (2 Kings xvii. 31) was so figured. Pleyte, as above, citing the Talmud, *Sanhedrim*, fol. 63. Cp. Pleyte, p. 186, and Pl. ix. x.

[7] Apuleius, *Metamorphoses*, B. xi.

prophet, saying: Between two animals thou art made manifest. In the same place Joseph remained with Mary three days" (c. 14).

Here we have a forced combination of the two myth-motives of cave and stable, both bound up with the worship of the Sun-God, who is cave-born as the offspring of the Earth-Mother, and stable-born for the reasons we are now considering. The reference to Habakkuk (iii. 2) is not to the Hebrew as commonly rendered, but to the Septuagint, in which, by a slight variation in the vocalisation of one Hebrew word and the spelling of another, the words "years" and "make alive" (the marginal reading in the Authorized Version is "preserved alive," the text reading "revive") are made to read as "two living creatures,"[1] so that we have the Greek version ἐν μέσῳ δύο ζώων γνωσθήσῃ, "between two living creatures thou shalt be known." Here then rises the interesting question, Does the Septuagint proceed upon an Egyptian or other version of the ox-and-ass myth? Let us see what the commentators have to say:—

"There is a double reading of these words in the Septuagint version of them, and both very different from the Hebrew text. The one is, *in the midst of two lives thou shalt be known*.... The other, by a change of the accent, is, *in the midst of two animals thou shalt be known*; so the Arabic version. Theodoret makes mention of both, and inclines to the former: 'some (he says) by two animals understand angels and men; some the incorporeal powers near the divine Glory, the cherubim and seraphim; others the Jews and Babylonians; but to me it seems that the prophet does not say animals, but lives, the present and future....' The latter reading is followed by many of the ancients, whose different senses are given by Jerome on the place; some interpreting them of the Son and Spirit, by whom the Father is made known; others of the two cherubim in Exodus, and of the two seraphim in Isaiah; and there were some who understood them of the two Testaments, the Old and New....; and others of Christ's being crucified between two thieves....; but besides these different sentiments many of the ancients concluded from hence that Christ lay in the manger between two animals, the ox and the ass, and to which they refer in their ancient hymns. [*Cognovit bos et asinus Quod puer erat Dominus*]...."[2]

The rest is modern Talmudism—the ancient "demoniacal possession" of verbalism over again. Nothing is to be

[1] Note in the "Ante-Nicene Library" ed. of the Apocryphal Gospels, p. 23.
[2] Gill's *Exposition of the Old Testament*, Doudney's ed. iv. 777.

gathered save that the Septuagint somehow adopted the reading of "two creatures," a formula unintelligible on Biblical grounds, but explicable in all likelihood by the ancient ritual-usage under notice. For the rest, the context in the Septuagint, "thou shalt be acknowledged when the years draw nigh; thou shalt be manifested when the time is come," was well fitted to serve as a Messianic prophecy for the Hellenic Jews. But that a merely accidental reading or misreading of the Hebrew text could be the *origin* of the myth of the stable and the adoring ox and ass, as later found in the apocryphal Gospel, is incredible. The stable, as we have seen, was an established myth, and the ox and ass were at home in the stable. If the translator of Habakkuk in the Septuagint was influenced by an Egyptian or Oriental mystery-doctrine, then we trace to pre-Christian times the entrance of the ox-and-ass myth into Judaic channels; if, on the other hand, the "two animals" was a quite fortuitous reading, we are left to what we otherwise know of the mythological standing of the animals in question. Justin Martyr, who was pretty close to the myth-sources, has a statement that "David predicted that he [Christ] would be born from the womb *before sun and moon*."[1] The reference is to the corrupt passage Ps. cx. 3; and the translators of the Ante-Nicene Library version have this note: "Justin puts 'sun and moon' instead of 'Lucifer.' Maranus says David did predict, not that Christ would be born of Mary before sun and moon, but that it would happen before sun and moon that He would be born of a Virgin." Whatever "David" said, we have here the glyph of the symbolic ox and ass at the Nativity.

And the passage in Pseudo-Matthew is singularly suggestive of just such a process of legend-making from old ritual as has been above contended for. Here, as in the Protevangelion, the laying-in-the-manger is entirely dissociated from the birth, and is therefore the more confidently to be looked upon as a piece of narrative framed to

[1] *Dialogue with Trypho*, c. 76.

meet a purpose; just as the pragmatic account of the lightless cave is evidently intended to have a doctrinal significance. The *need* for such a doctrine lay in the pre-existence of cave-worship, especially in Mithraism, from which Christianity so largely borrowed in other regards, and in the actual practice of a Pagan ritual in which a Child-God (as Ion) was exhibited as born in a cave; and the need for the laying in a manger in presence of ox and ass can be explained only in a similar way. Thus established, the myth would easily reappear in the form of the animation by the child Jesus of figures of oxen and asses,[1] and in the appearance of oxen and asses in the fabulous cortège of the family in Egypt.[2]

Is it then reasonable, is it plausible, to assume that this certainly derivative legend, never accepted as canonical, suddenly captured the Hindus late in our era in its Christianized form? Are we not, on the contrary, driven irresistibly to ask, Is not the Christian ox-and-ass legend one of immemorial antiquity?

And here, at least, the Hindu sacred books and ritual offer something like a decisive answer. To begin with, Agni in the Rig Veda is constantly addressed as a new-born infant, he being primarily the Fire, which is generated afresh every time the *aranis*, the fire-sticks, are rubbed together, a process conserved for religious purposes (as the sacred fire was rekindled in Mexico and elsewhere) for ages after that laborious process had become practically unnecessary. Thus, for one thing, the ever new-born Agni of the Veda is associated with the crossed sticks, which on one theory are the origin of the cross symbol. But not only is Agni repeatedly adored as the new-born by his worshippers, he is held to be similarly adored by the forces of Nature, as is the luminous Christ-child in the Protevangelion,[3] and by the Devas or divinities in general:—

> "Agni, the bright-bodied, as soon as born, fills all dwellings with shining light. When born, thou, O Agni, art the embryo of heaven and

[1] *Arabic Gospel of Infancy*, c. 36. [2] Pseudo-Matthew, c. 19.
[3] c. 19. Cp. *Arabic Gospel of Infancy*, c. 3.

earth,....variegated, infantine, thou dispersest the nocturnal glooms. ....Therefore the genetrices (of all things, the herbs) the cherishers (of all) with food, wait on thee who art the augmenter of food, with the sacrificial viands."[1]

"The Vedic Gods render homage to Agni when he is born, and when he passes resplendent from his parents the *aranis*."[2]

"He [Agni] diffuses happiness in a dwelling like a son newly born."[3]

"He [Agni] it is whom the two sticks have engendered like a new-born babe."[4]

"Thou [Agni] art born unobstructed of two mothers [*i.e.*, either the fire-sticks or the heaven and earth]....they have augmented thee with butter."[5]

So in the western world is Dionysos hailed *ignigenam, satumque iterum, solumque bimatrem*, "fire-born, twice-born, the only one with two mothers."[6] And this transparent infant-myth is curiously interwoven in the Veda with the other primeval myths of cow and cave.

"Agni, as soon as born, blazes brightly, destroying the Dasyus" [demons] "and (dispersing) the darkness by his lustre; he has discovered the cows, the waters, the sun."[7]

"In this world our mortal forefathers departed after instituting the sacred rite, when, calling upon the dawn, they extricated the milk-yielding kine, concealed among the rocks in the darkness (of the cave).

"Rending the rocks they worshipped (Agni) and other (sages) taught everywhere their (acts): unprovided with the means of extricating the cattle, they glorified the author of success, whence they found the light, and were thus enabled (to worship him) with holy ceremonies.

"Devoted (to Agni) those leaders (of sacred rites) with minds intent upon (recovering) the cattle, forced open, by (the power) of divine prayer, the obstructing compact solid mountain, confining the cows, a cow-pen full of kine....

"The scattered darkness was destroyed: the firmament glowed with radiance; then the sun stood above the undecaying mountains, beholding all that was right or wrong among mankind."[8]

This last extra-obscure passage well exemplifies the frequent

[1] Wilson's trans. of *Rig Veda Sanhita*, vi. (1888), pp. 1–2.
[2] Senart, *Essai*, p. 292, citing *Rig Veda*, vi. 7, 4.
[3] Wilson's trans. i. 184. [4] *Id.* iii. 253–4.
[5] *Id.* iii. 256–7. Elsewhere, Agni is *thrice* born—in the air, in the earth, and in the water—the last, doubtless, being on account of the sun's reflection there. Cp. Wilson's tr. iii. 21, 34; vi. 119; and Grassmann's, pp. 45, 73.
[6] Ovid, *Metam.* iv. 11; Diodorus Siculus, iii. 61; iv. 4, 5.
[7] Wilson's trans. iii. 261.
[8] *Id.* iii. 115–6.

difficulty, avowed by the best scholars,[1] of making out what the Vedas mean—a difficulty further deducible from a comparison of the renderings of Wilson and Langlois with those of later German translators, and of these last with each other. But the association of Agni with cattle and cave seems certain from that and the previous extract, and there is no great obscurity in these further passages:—

"Both the auspicious ones (day and night) wait upon him [Agni] like two female attendants, as lowing kine (follow their calves)."[2]

"The night and the day, mutually effacing each other's complexion, give nourishment, combined together, to one infant [Agni] who, radiant, shines between earth and heaven."[3]

Of these two extracts the first is thus rendered from the original in the German metrical version of H. Grassmann:[4] "To thee, Agni, shout for joy (*jauchzen*) Night and the Dawn, as in the stalls cows cry to calves." Is it going too far to surmise that, seeing Agni himself, Fire-God and Sun-God, was in the Veda said to have been, "in the olden time, the bull and the cow,"[5] the symbols of the Night and the Morning, here represented as saluting him, may even then have been the Ox and Ass?

It is idle to seek to force the solution of such a problem; and in so far as the Vedic evidence goes, I leave the matter to the judgment of the reader, merely adding that when we compare the notion of the instantaneous growth of the new-born Agni (who "as soon as born fills heaven and earth with light," and "*fractures, as he advances, the solid*

[1] See Muir, *Original Sanskrit Texts*, ii. 214. It should be noted that Wilson's translation, which is here primarily used, follows the commentary of Sayana, as to the merits of which see Max Müller, pref. to 1st ed. of trans. of Vedic Hymns, *S. B. E.* On comparing the passages here cited with the later renderings of Oldenberg, I find no vital differences. In any case, we want in this connection to have the text *as understood* by the later Brahmans.

[2] *R.V.* I. ii. 2. Wilson's trans. i. 246. Oldenberg translates:—"For thee Nights and Dawns have been lowing, O Agni, as milch-cows in the folds for their calf" (S. B. E. xlvi. 193).

[3] *R.V.* I. xcvi. Wilson's trans. p. 252. Oldenberg's version runs: "Night and Dawn, who constantly destroy each other's appearance, suckle one young calf unitedly. The piece of gold [= Agni] shines between Heaven and Earth" (S. B. E. xlvi. 119).

[4] Leipzig, 1876, p. 8.

[5] Wilson's trans. vi. (1888), p. 11.

cloud";[1] and who is further the "archer" and the "lord of night"[2]), the Vedic address to Indra as having "discovered the cows hidden in the cave,"[3] and the legend that these cows were stolen by the Asuras[4]—when we compare these data with the Greek myth of the night-waiting, cattle-stealing infant Hermes, it is difficult to doubt that the latter fable derives from the Aryan original preserved in the Veda. Whether the "two mothers" were suggested by the common myth of the suckling of the child-God by another than she who bore him, or whether the latter notion grew out of the misunderstood symbol of the two fire-sticks, or the mystic doctrine that the Sun-God was born of both Heaven and Earth,[5] we need not attempt to decide. But as regards the Indian origin of the ox-and-ass myth we get a fresh light when we connect the Vedic myths of the infant Agni (who, by the way, was specially invoked at the vernal equinox[6]) with the Krishnaite ritual of the Birth Festival. In the *Jayanti* form of the festival, *the erecting of a shed*, the watching by it through the night, and *the distribution of images*, are important items.[7] Now, in the Catacomb sarcophagus, the basket containing the child, and the ox and ass, stand *under a sloping shed-roof*, standing on two posts, while none of the other figures do. Here there is neither cave nor inn-stable; there is only a scenic shed, exactly answering to the shed of the Krishnaite ritual; and to the right of that two palm trees, between which the mother sits. Remarkably enough, one of those trees *bends*, as do the palms in the Koran legend of Mary, in the Buddhist legend of Maya, and in the account in Pseudo-Matthew (c. 20) of the wanderings of Mary and Joseph *after* the birth. The trees clearly cannot be reconciled with cave or stable.

How then came this shed to appear in early Christian or semi-Christian sacred art, unauthorized either by the

[1] Wilson's trans. iii. 120. [3] *Id.* i. 186, 188. [3] *Id.* i. 16.
[4] *Id. ib.* Wilson's note.
[5] Oldenberg leaves open both views, citing Bergaigne, *Religion Védique*, i. 28, 238. Elsewhere (S.B.E. xlvi. 51) he notes that "Agni, as is well known, is the son of the two worlds."
[6] *Id.* i. 157, *note*. [7] Weber, p. 223.

generally received cave legend or by the story in the third Gospel? What possible conclusion is open to us save that it represents a usage in the dramatic ritual of some other cultus; and that it was this usage that was in view in the peculiar version of the story in the Apocryphal Gospels? And, apart from the familiar myth of the births of Apollo and Buddha under a palm tree, what ritual usage do we know of that comes so close as that of Krishnaism? Either the scene is Christian or it is Mithraic. If the latter, we have a phase of complete identity between the Persian and the Hindu cult, which need not surprise us; and in that case Mithraism would be the channel through which the myth of ox-and-ass, stable-and-manger, came into Christianity. But if we suppose the bas-relief to be non-Mithraic, then it must be held to be a close imitation of a ritual usage previously existing in India—the usage which survives in our own day. For the ass appears in Indian mythology as early as the Vedas, where already he has two characters, divine and demoniacal, being at one time the symbol of Indra, Krishna's predecessor, and at another his enemy.[1] As the friend of the black and once demonic Krishna, he corresponds, with reversal of colour, to the ass of Egypt, who was the symbol of the evil Typhon.[2] Again, curiously, one of his Vedic epithets is "childlike."[3]

When, therefore, we find in the art of Buddhism, as in the Gandhâra sculptures,[4] a representation of a Nativity scene, in which a woman lays a child in a manger-basket, it is quite out of the question to look for the suggestion to the Gospels. In the scene in question, *horses'* heads appear in the place of those of the familiar ox and ass; and here we are doubtless dealing with another solar symbol; for the horse was in Persia specially associated with the sun. The babe in this case may very well have been Agni, who in the Veda is driver of the white horses of the sun; and though, as we shall see, the Buddha myth has borrowed a

[1] *Zool. Myth.* ii. 370–4.
[2] Plutarch, *Isis and Osiris*, cc. 30, 31.
[3] *Zool. Myth.* ii. 364.
[4] Fergusson and Burgess, *The Cave Temples of India*, 1880, p. 138.

good deal from that of Krishna, it could also draw directly from the Vedic store.

And if Western borrowing there were on the Hindu side —which will hardly now be argued—it could perfectly well have been pre-Christian. The ass might be the ass of Typhon, "who was the chief God of the Semites in Egypt,"[1] though in ill repute with the Christians; and it may have been from this source that the Christians derived it. It is also possible that they made a not uncommon confusion between the ass of Typhon and the *jackal*-headed Anubis, the Egyptian Hermes, "both infernal and celestial," who was held to represent *Time*,[2] and who figured as the attendant of Osisis. And when we are discussing origins, we should not forget the suggestion of Dupuis and Volney,[3] that the birth of the Sun-Child between the ox and the ass is simply a fable based on the fact that in the zodiacal celestial sphere the sun would come, at the winter solstice, between the Bull and the Ursa Major, sometimes represented by the ancients as a Boar, sometimes as the Hippopotamus, sometimes the Ass, of Typhon. But the conception may well be older than the zodiac: the fundamental idea of the stable being, as we have seen, the sky as the home of the cloud-cows. The Sun-God is in this primary sense born of two mothers, Earth and Sky—of the Earth in the cave, of the Sky in the stable.

Another detail comes in to extend the proof that the Christian legend borrows from the East. In the Catacomb fresco representing the (supposed) adoration of the Virgin and child by *two* Magi, as reproduced in large and in colour in De Rossi's *Imagines Selectae Deiparae Virginis*,[4] the dish tendered to the babe or mother by the right-hand man bears a *small human figure*. What is the Christian explanation of that? What hypothesis is more likely than that this is one of the Krishnaite images?

[1] Professor Robertson Smith, *Religion of the Semites*, p. 449. Cp. Tiele, *Hist. of the Egypt. Relig.* Eng. tr. p. 48.

[2] Plutarch, *Isis and Osiris*, c. 44; Sharpe, *Egyptian Mythology*, pp. 8–9.

[3] *Les Ruines*, note on ch. xxii. § 13.

[4] Rome, 1863, pl. v. Cp. *Roma Sotteranea*, as cited, ii. 140, 170.

That, of course, remains a hypothesis. And, indeed, we are bound to keep in view that the manifold Egyptian ritual *may* have included just such a ceremony as that under notice. In the procession of Isis, as described by Apuleius, the ass is accompanied by a feeble old man—exactly the aged Joseph of the Apocryphal Gospels. And we know that the solarized Amunoteph III., who here seems to typify customary royal ceremony, figures in Egyptian sculpture as supernaturally announced, conceived, and born, very much as is Jesus in Christian legend.[1] The messenger-God, Thoth, announces to the maid-mother the coming birth; the Spirit-God Kneph miraculously impregnates her; and the priests kneel and adore the new-born babe, holding up the cross of life. This must have been a matter of ritual. In the Catacomb bas-relief and frescoes, again, the adorers, the "Magi," both in the picture with two and in that with four,[2] wear the Phrygian or Mithraic cap; but, instead of representing the venerable sages of modern Christian fancy, they are all young and beardless. The juvenile angel, again, exactly corresponds to that which figures in the admittedly Mithraic remains in the Catacombs, as reproduced by Father Garucci and accepted by Canons Northcote and Brownlow. On the other hand, in the fragment of the earliest-dated Catacomb sarcophagus[3] held to be Christian, representing the ox and ass, the swaddled child, and two adorers, the men are rather of Western figure; though at the end behind them a hand appears grasping a palm tree or branch. Thus there is the suggestion of the East as well as of Western assimilation. We cannot yet decide with certainty as to the myth's line of travel; we can only decide that all Christian myth *is* an adaptation of previous myth.

The case, I think, is thus far clear. The Krishna birth

[1] See the woodcut and explanation in Sharpe's *Egyptian Mythology*, pp. 18–19.

[2] *Roma Sotterranea*, as cited, ii. 169: *Imag. Sel.* pl. iii.

[3] It bears the names of the consuls of 343 C.E. See the cut in *Roma Sotterranea*, ii. 235, and in *Open Court*, as before cited.

myth is at bottom primeval; and it is highly probable that the Birth-Festival ritual, which Professor Weber supposes to have been based on Christianity, preserves prehistoric practice. At the midnight hour of the God's birth there is a ceremony of a "pouring out of riches"[1] (*ein Guss Reichthums*) which it is a wonder the Professor does not hold to represent the offerings of the Magi. In all probability it *does* point to the *origin* of that myth. The "riches" are symbolic, an offering of melted butter and sugar—surely the "nectar and pleasant ambrosia" with which Themis fed the babe Apollo;[2] and with which the Hours feed the deathless child Aristæus, son of Apollo and Cyrene, and by some called Shepherd, Jove, and chaste Apollo, God of flocks;[3] the milk and honey on which Dionysos and the child Jupiter[4] were nourished; the "butter and honey" that in the Hebrew prophet[5] are named as the food of the child Immanuel to be born of the "virgin" of that time, and that were used in their rites (with milk for butter) by the early Christians, especially in the "Mystery of Infants," till the Council of Trullo (held at Constantinople, in 691) forbad the usage,[6] doubtless because its pagan origin was recognized. And surely the ancient adoration of the ever-new-born Agni was either the origin or the parallel of the offering of butter to the new-born Krishna. Does not the whole mass of data go to suggest that a more or less dramatic ritual has preserved a Babe-Sun-God worship from immemorial antiquity? In pre-Christian India it became actual drama, which the Festival ritual, with its multitude of images, appears to preserve as far as may be; and I am much inclined to suspect that the form of part of the Protevangelion[7] comes of a semi-dramatic ritual, as the adoration of the Magi must have done, and as the legends

[1] Treatise cited, p. 299.
[2] Hom. Hymn, 124.
[3] Pindar, *Pythia*, ix. 97–106; Diodorus Siculus, iv. 81; Athenagoras, *Apol.* xiv.
[4] Callimachus, *Hymn to Zeus*, 49; and note in Bohn trans. p. 123.
[5] Isaiah vii. 14–15.
[6] Bingham's *Christian Antiquities*, xv. 2, § 3 (ed. 1855, vol. v. 242–3).
[7] Chs. xiii. xiv.

of the Lord's Supper and the rock-tomb burial certainly did.[1] Be that how it may, the theory that Krishnaism borrowed either its myths or its rites from Christianity is now evidently enough untenable.

XIII. The Myth of St. Christopher.

The study of a few of the minor myths of Christianity in connection with Krishnaism will be found no less instructive than the comparison of the central myth-motives of the two creeds. Always the lesson is that the mythology of Christianity was derivative; and at times, though there can be no certainty, there is a curiously strong suggestion of direct Christian adoption of Hindu details. I have spoken of the item of the visit of the foster-father of Krishna to the holy city to pay his taxes, which in the Krishna myth is as it were naturally embedded in the narrative, while in the Christ myth it is grafted on loosely and precariously. But the same statement may be made even more emphatically in other regards. Professor Weber[2] has assumed the priority of the "Christophoros" legend, in which St. Christopher under miraculous circumstances carries the rejuvenated Christ, the Christ-child, on his shoulders across a river by night. The Professor does not ask how it was that the idea of regarding Christ *still as a child* came to persist in the Church through so many centuries, and that only gradually did he come to be pictured as a young man, and finally as a man of middle age. We can see what preserves the child image in Krishnaism—the ancient usage of dramatic ritual, which is only partially overruled by the literary presentment of the stories of the God's career. Now,

[1] See hereinafter, *Mithraism*, § 4.

[2] Here adopting a thesis of the pre-scientific Giorgi—cited by Von Bohlen, *Das Alte Indien*, 1830, i. 232. Von Bohlen states that Kleuker held the Christophorus story to be of Indian origin; but I cannot find such a remark in the place cited. Kleuker did, however (*Abhandlungen*, as before cited, ii. 234), argue that it was probably the Christians who borrowed from the Hindus, and that the apocryphal Gospels show distinct traces of Indian influence.

by far the most probable hypothesis of the origin of the Christophoros myth is either that it was framed to explain a Pagan sculpture, or that, like so many others, it was invented late to explain some dramatic or other representation—that there was a ritual in which the Christ-child, like the infant Dionysos in Greece, and the infant Horos in Egypt, was carried on a man's shoulder, long before the legend of the colossal Christ-bearer was framed.

For this hypothesis we have the most convincing evidence in the plural term *Christophoroi*, found applied to martyrs in an alleged letter of the third century quoted by Eusebius.[1] This term every orthodox authority I have seen deduces from the epithet "Theophoros," said to have been applied to Ignatius, Bishop of Antioch; and the usual explanation is that it means "full of Christ," as Theophoros meant "full of God."[2] The Bohn translator, Mr. Crusé, however, insists on the etymological meaning of the word, writing that "the martyrs were called, by a strong figure, Christophori, because they *bore*; and Ignatius was called Theophorus for the same reason." This, I suspect, is nearer the truth than Mr. Crusé was aware of. The name Theophoros would not have been attached to Ignatius had it not been in existence before. It literally meant, in classic usage, one "bearing or carrying a God";[3] and would naturally be applied to those who carried statues of the Gods in ceremonial or procession.[4] There were a score of such names in connection with the Greek rituals. Not to speak of the soldiers and police officers called after the weapons they carried, as the *doryphoroi*, *aichmophoroi*, *mastigophoroi*, *rhabdophoroi*, etc., there were the *liknophoroi*, the women who carried the cradle-basket of Dionysos in his processions; the *kanephoroi*, women who bore sacred baskets of another sort; the *oschophoroi*, noble youths who, in the disguise of women, carried branches of vine in the

[1] *Eccles. Hist.* iii. 10.

[2] So, in effect, Bingham, i. 6; Riddle, *Christian Antiquities*, p. 134; Migne, *ad loc.*; Smith and Cheetham's *Dict. of Christ. Antiq. sub voce*; etc.

[3] Liddell and Scott, *s. v.*, citing Æsch. Fr. 224.

[4] In such cases as those mentioned by Pausanias, ii. 7, 11; vii. 20, 21, etc., or in civic or royal processions.

festival from which came the name; the *deipnophoroi*, women who, as mothers, carried food for the youths; the *arrephoroi* (or *ersephoroi*), maidens who carried the mystic chest with nameless contents in the festival of Panathenaea; the *lampadophoroi*, who carried torches in the torch-races; and so on. Always the meaning is the literal *carrying* of something. Hermes with the ram on his shoulders (the admitted origin of the Christian image of the Good Shepherd[1]) is Hermes *Kriophoros*, the ram-bearer. Only secondarily and indirectly could the word come to have the meaning of "possessed by the God"; and the instance cited by Liddell and Scott,[2] in which the phrase is "pains of *inspiration*," is clearly in close connection with the primary meaning. In all probability the name Theophoros at times became a family one, just as that of Nikephoros, "Victory-bearer,"[3] which continued to subsist long after Pagan times among Christians. The generic name *Christophoroi* must have had some solider basis than an analogy from a metaphor.

That the Christian myth of the Christ-birth is a concoction from previous myths, we have already seen; and that the borrowing was first made by way of "mystery" or ritual, the Catacomb remains go far to prove. We know too that in the Egyptian system, apart from the practice of carrying the new-born Sun-Child to exhibit him to the people,[4] there was a whole order of *Pastophoroi*, bearers of the *pastos*, who according to one theory bore a shawl in the mysteries of Isis and Osiris, but "according to another interpretation"—and a much more tenable one—"were so denominated from carrying, not a shawl, but a shrine

[1] See Smith and Cheetham's Dict. under "Good Shepherd." Cp. Lundy, *Monumental Christianity*, ch. vii.; Didron, *Christian Iconography*. Eng. tr. i. 339, 341, and the figures copied in Dr. Carus's art. in *Open Court*, December, 1899. This type also appears in Buddhist sculpture.

[2] From Æschylus, *Agam.* 1150. [3] See Athenæus, v. 27.

[4] Macrobius, *Saturnalia*, i. 18. It is important to remember that Macrobius says the child is carried *ex adyto*, out of the innermost sanctuary of the temple. The adytum "was almost certainly in its origin a cave; indeed, in Greece it was often wholly or partially subterranean, and is called μέγαρον, which is the Semitic מערה and means a cave" (Smith, *Religion of the Semites*, p. 183; cp. Tiele, *Egyptian Religion*, p. 115). Here once more the Christian myth is led up to.

or small chapel, *containing the image of the God*."[1] These *Pastophoroi* were "a numerous and important body of men," who had allotted to them a part of the Egyptian temples, called the *pastophorion*—a term adopted by the Jews in describing the temple of Jerusalem.[2] And they spread beyond Egypt, having a "college" or brotherhood at Industria, a city of Liguria.[3] Now, it may be argued that the term Christophoroi might be jocularly applied to Christians by analogy from these and other classes with the same name-suffix; but that the Christians should have adopted it without some real reason is hardly supposable. And when we look into the admitted remains of early Christian ritual, we see at least hints of what the reason was. In early frescoes the Christian hierophant bears a *pastos*, or a *kistê*,[4] analogous to the sacred chest of Dionysos. They would hardly carry the serpent, as the *kistê* did; but their shrine or chest carried something.

It might be, then, that this was only the sacred *host*, which to this day is "the good God" in Catholic countries. But whence then came the idea of making the mythic Christophoros, giant as he was, carry the *child* Christ? I can see no explanation save one or all of three: (1) that the persistent Pagan charge against the early Christians of eating a child in their rites[5] rested on a ritual custom of exhibiting or eating the baked *image* of a child,[6] a rite to

[1] Smith's Dict. of Gr. and Rom. Antiq., art. *Pastophorus*. Ed. 1849, p. 871. Compare Apuleius (*Metamorphoses*, bk. 11), who speaks of the Pastophori as carrying "the sacred images" and "breathing effigies" (*simulacra spirantia*). See also last par. of the book.

[2] 1 *Maccabees*, iv. 38.

[3] Smith's Dict. as above, citing Maffei, *Mus. Veron.* p. 230. Apuleius locates a college of them at Cenchreæ.

[4] See *Roma Sotteranea*, ed. 1879, i. 362. Pl. xi.

[5] Justin Martyr, *Apol.* i. 35; ii. 14; Eusebius, *Eccles. Hist.* v. 1; Athenagoras, *Apol.* c. 3; Origen, *Against Celsus*, vi. 27; Min. Felix, cc. 9, 10, 30, 31; Tertullian, *Apolog.* cc. 7, 8, 9.

[6] Note the image on the platter of the "Magus," referred to in Sec. xii. Baked images were known in the sacrifices of the poor in antiquity (Herodotus, ii. 47); and in Mexico dough images of the God were eaten sacramentally. See H. H. Bancroft, *Native Races of the Pacific States*, iii. 297–300, 389; ii. 321. A very extensive list of cases in which either a baked or an unbaked image of a child or adult is ceremonially eaten in ancient and modern times is given by Mr. Frazer, *Golden Bough*, ii. 68, 79–84, and notes. Macrobius (*Saturnalia*, i. 7) gives accounts of the substitution of

which, as being a sacred mystery,[1] the Christians were unwilling to confess;[2] or (2) that in the Christmas celebration a real or dummy child was actually carried in the sacred basket, just as Dionysos was in his, or as Horos was represented in Egypt, and as a child *may* have been in the rites of Mithra; or (3) that the many representations of the carrying of a Divine Child by Hermes or by Hercules in Greek sculpture may have set illiterate Christians, after the

images for human heads as sacrifices to Hades, and again of heads of garlic and poppy for human heads in sacrifice to the Goddess Mania, mother of the Lares. Yet again, Ovid (*Fasti*, v. 621–31) tells of the substitution of rush or straw images for old men formerly sacrificed in the worship of Vesta. Mommsen, whose chapter (xii.) on the religion of Rome is a mosaic of incoherent generalizations, declares in his customary manner that "it is only an unreflecting misconception that can discover in this usage a reminiscence of ancient human sacrifices." He then explains that the Romans acted in the spirit of their merchants, who were legally free to "fulfil their contracts merely in the letter"; that they in all seriousness practised "a pious cunning, which tried to delude and pacify" the deity "by means of a sham satisfaction." Of what then was it a sham?

[1] The existence of secret mysteries among the early Christians after the second century is abundantly shown in Clarkson's *Discourse concerning Liturgies* (*Select Works*, Wycliffe Society's ed. 1846, pp. 266–277). And see Dr. Edwin Hatch's posthumous work, *The Influence of Greek Ideas and Usages upon the Christian Church*, 1890, pp. 292–305, where it is frankly admitted that the Christians imitated Pagan methods. In practising secrecy in particular the Christians only followed the general Pagan usage. Compare Clarkson's citations with Herodotus, *passim*.

[2] See Tertullian, *Apology*, c. 7, where the denial is anything but straightforward. We may rest content with an orthodox explanation: "The method of celebrating baptism, confirmation, and the eucharist; the nature and effect of these ordinances; the sublime doctrine of the Trinity; and the Creed and Lord's Prayer, were only communicated to converts about the time of their baptism. *Christians were absolutely prohibited from revealing this information to catechumens or infidels;* and whenever the early Christian writers speak on such topics (except when controversy compels them to a different course) there is usually some reserve in their manner, some reference to *the peculiar knowledge of the faithful*.... This primitive discipline is sufficient to account for the facts that very few allusions to the liturgy or eucharistic service are found in the writings of the Fathers; and that on the more solemn part of consecration, etc., they are almost entirely silent" (Rev. W. Palmer, *Origines Liturgicæ*, 4th ed. i. 14; cp. p. 33). See also the Rev. W. Trollope's edition of the Greek *Liturgy of St. James*, 1848, p. 15: "The Fathers in general, when speaking of the Eucharist, *enter as little as possible into detail.*" Mr. Trollope's explanation—that they feared to expose the mysteries to ribaldry—is clearly inadequate, and contains but a small part of the probable truth. He comes to the conclusion that no liturgy was published till late in the fourth century, when the Church was no longer in fear of its enemies. The just inference is that, when the popularity of the cult made the old secrecy impossible, its ritual was to a large extent shorn of the grosser usages derived from Paganism. If the eucharist ritual all along was just what was set down in the Gospels, why should the early Fathers have kept up any air of mystery?

fall of Paganism, upon the framing of an explanatory Christian tale. And all three theories are so probable, and so much implicated one with the other, that we are not free to reject any. As to what may seem to many readers the most unlikely of all—the eating of the baked image of a child—there is really most evidence. It is an admitted historic fact that in some of the churches, after the abandonment of the practice of eating an actual lamb in the eucharist at Easter, there arose the practice of eating a baked image of a lamb.[1] Without suggesting a similar process of substitution, we may reasonably surmise that the *infans farre contectus* of the Pagan charge[2] was really a model of a child in dough, after the manner of so many pagan cults in all ages. The more closely we look into Christian myth taken in connection with the distinct records of pre-Christian ritual, the more clear does it become that the accepted notions of the rise of the cult are hopelessly wide of the facts.

First as to the charge of ritual child-eating. On this obscure problem it has to be remembered that others than the Christians were accused of killing children in religious rites. Thus, to say nothing of the Carthaginians and other Semites, Juvenal[3] alleges that the Armenian and Syrian haruspices at Rome would sometimes augur from the entrails of a boy; and, "according to Mohammedan accounts, the Harranians in the Middle Ages annually sacrificed an infant, and, boiling down its flesh, baked it into cakes, of which only freeborn men were allowed to partake."[4] Here, too, of course, there is room for doubt, as there is again in regard to the statement of Procopius[5]

[1] Hatch, as cited, p. 300. [2] Minucius Felix, c. 9.

[3] vi. 548–552. As to the sacrificing of boys, see the passage in Horace, *Epod.* v., which evidently preserves trace of an ancient usage.

[4] Robertson Smith, *Religion of the Semites*, p. 348, citing the *Fihrist*, and Chwolsohn. Cp. the note of Elmenhorstius in Ouzel's ed. of Minucius Felix (1672, p. 87) as to the ancient eucharistic practice of making bread with the blood of a child, which might or might not die. And see in Bury's *History of the Later Roman Empire*, ii. 389, the story of how the people of Pergamos, when besieged by the Arabs in 717, took a pregnant girl, cut up the mother and the fœtus, boiled them, and so made an unguent for the soldiers' gauntlets.

[5] *Gothica*, i. 25. Cp. Mahon, *Life of Belisarius*, 2d. ed. p. 262.

that the Franks in the sixth century sacrificed children to idols. But the important fact remains that the Christians retained for their sacramental food the old name of *hostia*, "the victim," and the Gospels[1] all dwell on the eating and drinking of the God's body and blood with a literalness that is unintelligible on the hypothesis of mere originating allegory. It is true that for the ancients it was a commonplace to call bread "Ceres," and wine "Liber" or "Dionysos";[2] but that was just because in a special and peculiar sense Ceres and Liber stood for the sources of bread and wine, and might with literal fitness be so called in the ritual of their cult; whereas the Christ myth has on the face of it no such pretext. The whole series of the later Fathers anxiously explain that the Gospel phrase is figurative; but no one ever explains why such a revolting figure should have been used. They had need deny the literal meaning, which laid them open to just such reproaches as they were wont to cast at the pagans; but it is clear that in the shadow of the Church there always subsisted a concrete conception, which finally took the doctrinal form of Transubstantiation. And as it is now an admitted principle of comparative mythology that where there is a sacred banquet in connection with a worship, with a specified sacred food, *it is the God that is eaten*, we may take it as nearly certain that just as some Christian groups ate a baked image of a lamb, others would carry the freedom of symbolism further and make a dough image of a child. The lamb itself was the symbol of the God; and the disuse of an actual lamb was doubtless motived by the not uncommon dislike to the eating of flesh. A baked image, after all, would still be a symbol; and when once the symbolism had gone so far, there was no reason why the mystic God should not be represented in the shape of a child, as of old.

When nothing in human or animal form was baked for the old cult-offerings, the mere round cake (often marked

[1] See Matt. xxvi. 26–28; Mark xiv. 22–24; Luke xxii. 19–20; John vi. 48–58.

[2] Cicero, *De Nat. Deor.* iii. 16; Clemens Alexandrinus, *Protrept.* ii. (Trans. in Ante-Nicene Lib. p. 34.)

by a cross, as in the hot-cross-bun still in Christian use) stood for the God or Goddess as Sun or Moon; and this is the explanation of the Catholic wafer, reverently described and worshipped as "Jesus" or "God" in Anglican High Church ritual at the present time. Jesus is there revealed by his devoutest worshippers as a Sun-God. But there is no evidence for an early use of the wafer; which indeed was too close to pagan sun-worship[1] in the pagan period to be readily acceptable by a sect desirous of marking itself off from its leading competitors. It was apparently adopted with other institutions of sun-worship after the Pagan cults were disestablished, when the Church could safely use their symbols and turn their usages to economic account—economic in both senses of the term, since the priestly miracle of the Eucharist was one of the main grounds of ecclesiastical influence and revenue, and the wafer withal was extremely cheap.

Alike then as to the Gospel myth and the charge of child-eating, a baked image seems the probable solution. And that this rite, like the others, was borrowed from previous cults, is proved by a remarkable passage in Pliny as to the praise due to the Roman people for "having put an end to those monstrous rites" in which "to murder a man was to do an act of the greatest devoutness, and to eat his flesh was to secure the highest blessings of health."[2] It is not clear that this refers to the Druids,[3] mentioned in the context; in any case there are many reasons for holding that a sacrament of theophagy was in pre-historic times widely practised;[4] and even if the sacramental and

[1] The usage was to eat round *panicula* after a sacrifice. Pollux, *Onomasticon*, vi. 6. Cp. Suetonius, *in Vitell.* c. 13, and Smith's *Dict. of Ant.*, art. *Canephoros*. See the question of the pagan origin of the wafer discussed in *Roma Antiqua et Recens*, ed. 1889, pp. 44–5.

[2] *Hist. Nat.* xxx. 4.

[3] But see Strabo, bk. iv. c. iv. § 5, where the Druidical sacrifices are specified, with the remark that the victims are said to have been *crucified in the temples*—another noteworthy clue to the Christian myth.

[4] It has been ingeniously argued by Professor Robertson Smith (*Religion of the Semites*, pp. 341–6) that human sacrifices did not ante-date those of animals, but came to be substituted for these at a time when the early way of regarding the animal as a member of the tribe had become psychologically obsolete. The great difficulties in the way of such a theory are (1) that, even

theophagous usages which chronically revived or obscurely persisted among the Jews[1] be held to have died out among them at the beginning of the Christian era, the Christians seem to have had alongside of them, in the cult of Dionysos, an example which they were as likely to follow as that of the Mithraic resurrection-ritual and Lord's Supper. The survival of a symbolical cannibalism—the eating of the baked image of a child—in the Dionysian mysteries,[2] is the most probable explanation of the late myth of the Titans rending the child Dionysos in pieces, and further of the myth of the rending of Orpheus, which was bound up with the Dionysiak. Though the former tale was allegorically understood of the spread of vine-culture,[3] that would hardly account for its invention; nor would the allegory put a stop to the ritual practice.

A connection between the child-carrying and the ritual of child-eating, again, is brought out in the peculiarly parallel case of the ritual of the *arrephoroi* or bearers of "nameless things" in the cult of Erichthonios at Athens.[4] The explanation of the myth of the child in the chest that was not to be opened is probably that given by Miss Harrison,[5] to the effect that the *Kistae* carried by the maidens contained figures of a child and a snake. These figures would hardly

if primitive men sacrificed animals as members of the tribe, they had still a psychic reason for selecting animals rather than men; and (2) that in most cults human sacrifice figured as a far-off thing, while the animal sacrifice survived. Cp. Macrobius, *Saturnalia*, i. 7. Human sacrifices, further, were in many cases avowedly superseded by offerings of *images*, where animal sacrifices went on. In any case, the habit of eating the sacrificed animal would psychologically involve the eating of the sacrificed man, which is the point in hand. As to the deification of the victim, see Smith, as cited, and Frazer's *Golden Bough*, ch. iii.

[1] Compare Robertson Smith, *Religion of the Semites*, pp. 336-340.

[2] Clemens (as cited; trans. pp. 27, 30, 33) distinctly associates the eating of "raw flesh" with the mystery in which the rending of the child Dionysos by the Titans was commemorated; and probably some groups continued to eat one of the God's symbol-animals while others substituted images, as among the Christists. But the Orphic poems, to which we owe this phase of the Dionysiak myth, give the detail that the Titans who surprised the boy had *covered themselves with plaster*, a proceeding of the Dionysiak festivals (Müller, *Lit. Anc. Greece*, c. xvi. § 7); and here we seem to have a derivation from the usage of baked images.

[3] Preller, *Griech. Myth.* i. 554; Diodorus Siculus, iii. 62.

[4] Pausanias, i. 18, 27.

[5] *Mythology and Monuments of Ancient Athens*, 1890, pp. xxvi.-xxxv.

be of marble, which would be impossibly heavy: they are likely enough to have been of baked flour. But the myth of Erichthonios, born of Gaia,[1] the Earth, is only a variant of that of Dionysos, born of Demeter, the Earth Mother, or of Semelé, equally the Earth;[2] and again of that of Agdistis, borne by the Earth to Jupiter.[3] We have seen that the Divine Child figured in the birth-ritual of Dionysos as in that of Horos; and as the images in the other rituals would have a sacrosanct virtue, the eating of them sacramentally would be a natural sequence. In the artistic treatment of the myth of Erichthonios, as Miss Harrison points out, the lid of the chest is of wicker-work. The whole may well have been a basket, like the *liknon* of Dionysos.[4] On that view the carrying of the image was simply a variant of the usage of carrying an actual child—a practice always open to the objection that the child might at any moment take to crying. In ordinary animal sacrifice it was considered fatal to the efficacy of the rite if the victim showed any reluctance;[5] and even if the child were not to be sacrificed, his crying would be apt to pass for a bad omen.[6]

Given, however, the pre-Christian existence of a child-carrying rite, in connection with the Christian festival as observed in the Egyptian and Mithraic cults, or as practised in the Dionysia; and given the adoption of this rite by

[1] Pausanias, i. 2, *end.*

[2] Sir George Cox (*Mythol. of Aryan Nations*, ed. 1882, p. 260, *note*) observes that "no Greek derivation has been attached to this name, which certainly cannot be explained by reference to any Greek word." But it has not been noted that in modern Servia to-day *Semlje* is actually the word for the Earth. And the Servians have many mythic ideas in common with the Greeks. See Ranke, *History of Servia*, Eng. trans. pp. 42–43.

[3] Arnobius, *Adv. Gentes*, v. 5, 10.

[4] But cp. the Eleusinian formula:—"I have received from the box; having done, I put it in the basket, and out of the basket into the chest" (Clemens, as cited, p. 32). This testimony is confused by the different version in the same author:—"I have eaten out of the drum, I have drunk out of the cymbal, I have carried the Cernos [said by the scholiasts to be a fan = *liknon*], I have slipped into the bedroom." Cp. Firmicus, *De Errore*, 19.

[5] As to the same idea in connection with the sacred victim among the Khonds, see Frazer, *Golden Bough*, i. 386–7.

[6] Compare, however, the sinister process of primitive casuistry by which the Mexicans, in sacrificing their children, sought to feel that the inevitable tears were the promise of abundant rain and harvest (Lecture on "The Ancient Religions of America," in *Religious Systems of the World*, p. 360).

Christism, the idea of making the mythic Giant Christophoros separately carry the Christ-child *across a river*, it might be supposed, could be grafted fortuitously on the old ritual-motive. It being necessary to have a story of the child being carried somewhere, a river was a possible enough invention. But here again the hypothesis is upset when we turn to the light which Professor Weber so strangely ignored—that of the mythology of Greece. The carrying of a Divine Child by a Divine Person—a very small child by a very big person—is one of the commonest figures in Greek religious art. In Hindu pictures the babe Krishna is carried by Vasudeva in its swaddling clothes. In Greek sculpture Hermes carries the babe Dionysos "carefully wrapped up" to his nurses. At times he bears it on his shoulder.[1] He also carries the boy to heaven.[2] In the drama of Euripides he carries the swaddled and cradled child Ion to the temple.[3] Similarly he carries the infant Aristæus, the Sun-Child, from his mother to the nourishing Hours:[4] and he carries in turn the child Herakles.[5] Yet again, as Psychopompos, he carries Psyche *over the Styx*;[6] and here, in a myth-motive, we have a marked parallel to the ritual motive of the river-crossing in the Krishna tale. And this recurs, for we have Herakles represented carrying Zeus *over the water*, "a still enigmatical representation," says Müller.[7] Herakles, yet again, carries his own infant Tèlephos in his hand or arm;[8] and Tèlephos is a Divine Child, figuring in a Birth-Ritual in swaddling clothes.[9] On vases, too, we have Peleus holding the child Achilles,[10] and so on—the representations are endless. Dionysos himself, in one myth, carries Hephaistos, drunk, to heaven.[11] How far the motive may have been ritually associated with a passing over

[1] K. O. Müller, *Ancient Art*, pp. 492–4; Apollodorus, bk. iv. c. iii. § 2.
[2] Pausanias, iii. 18.
[3] *Ion*, 31–40, 1597–1600.
[4] Pindar, *Pythia*, ix. 95–97.
[5] Müller, *Ancient Art*, p. 554.
[6] *Id.* p. 486.
[7] *Id.* p. 562. Compare the myth of Typhon carrying the disabled Zeus over the sea on his shoulders. Apollodorus, I. vi. 3.
[8] Müller, p. 558.
[9] *Id.* p. 559.
[10] *Id.* p. 571.
[11] Pausanias, i. 20.

water[1] it is difficult to decide; but when we are asked to believe that the Christophoros legend, in which Pagan myth and art and ritual were eked out with Christian fiction, so impressed the Hindus at an early period in our era that they transferred it bodily to the worship of their God Krishna, it is difficult to take the suggestion seriously. On the contrary, we are again moved to answer that, if either cult borrowed from the other, it must have been the Christians who borrowed from the religious drama or dramatic ritual of the Hindus. Once more, the carrying of the child Krishna across the mythological river by Vasudeva is naturally embedded in the Krishna legend; while in Christian mythology the story is patently alien, arbitrary, and unmotived, save in so far as it rests on the ancient epithet *Christophoros*; on the familiar presentment of Hermes or Herakles carrying a Divine Child, at times over water; and on the inferable usage of carrying a child or an image representing the new-born God in early Christian ritual. And, finally—what I cannot but think a noteworthy coincidence—the festival day of St. Christopher is placed in the Roman Catholic Calendar on the *25th day of July*, precisely at the time of year when, in the Hindu ritual, and almost certainly in the early Hindu drama, Vasudeva would be represented as carrying Krishna across the river.[2] Clearly the Indian *date* cannot be borrowed from the Christian: it depends on the Birth Festival, which is as wide as possible of the Christian

[1] Dionysos, we know, was lord of the whole element of moisture (Plutarch, *I. and O.* 35), and in one myth passes as an adult over the sea (above, p. 83)—a solar item, which might very well be symbolized in the ritual of the Babe-Sun-God. In many Hindu ceremonies, again, water is devotionally employed as being the product of the sun. One suspects the same myth-motive in the story of the kingly child Pyrrhus of Achillean descent being carried across a river, when flying from pursuers, in the arms of a man named *Achilles*. Pyrrhus in the story is put on his father's throne by force at the age of twelve—a very mythical-looking narrative (Plutarch, *Pericles*, cc. 2, 3). Again, the people of Clazomenæ had a grotto called the grotto of Pyrrhus' mother—presumably a Birth Cave—and a tradition about Pyrrhus as a shepherd (Pausanias, vii. 5). Apparently Pyrrhus was mythically handled very much as was Cyrus before him.

[2] This was also, as already noted, the first day of the Egyptian year; and the festival of the "Birthday of the Eyes of Horos" was held on that day or the day preceding.

Nativity. It will need some satisfactory explanation of St. Christopher's date on other lines to destroy the possibility of the surmise that it was determined by the Hindu practice; and in any case we must infer a non-Christian origin.

XIV. Indian and Christian Religious Drama.

In an argument which so often insists on the priority of dramatic ritual to written legend, it may be well to take passing note of the state of opinion as to the origin and history of Indian drama. On that as on so many other points, Professor Weber is found surmising Greek influence, and so putting the great period of the Hindu theatre comparatively late. It is needless here to go into that question fully. The points for us are that in any case Hindu drama was highly developed at a period before the suggested importation of Christian legends; and that, since in all early civilizations religion and drama were closely related because originally one, there must have been an abundance of sacred drama in India before the Christian era, as there has been since. We have seen the concrete proof of this in the admitted existence of an early religious drama in which figured the demonic Kansa as enemy of Krishna. And even if Greek influences did affect Hindu dramatic practice after the invasion of Alexander, even to the extent of bringing Western mystery-ritual into the Indian (a sufficiently unlikely thing), the fact would remain that India had these ritual elements from pre-Christian sources. But inasmuch as Professor Weber's argumentation on Indian matters is in a manner interconnected, and his theory of dramatic imitation tends to prop up his theory of religious imitation, it may be pointed out that his opinion on the dramatic question is widely at variance with that of other distinguished Indianists. Wilson, whom Weber more than once cites in self-support on other questions, is here very emphatically opposed to him. "It is not improbable," says Weber, "that even the rise of the Hindu drama was influenced by the performance of the drama at the courts of Greek kings."[1] Says Wilson, on the other hand :—

> "Whatever may be the merits or defects of the Hindu drama, it may be safely asserted that they....are unmixedly its own. The science of the Hindus may be indebted to modern discoveries in other regions, and their mythology may have derived legends from Paganism or Christianity; but it is impossible that they should have borrowed their dramatic compositions from the people either of ancient or modern times....The Hindus, if they learned the art from others, can have been obliged alone to the Greeks or to the Chinese. A perusal of the Hindu plays will show how little likely it is that they are indebted to either, as, with the exception of a few features in common which could not fail to occur, they present characteristic varieties of conduct and construction, which strongly evidence both original design and national development."[2]

Probably no one who reads Wilson's translations and compares them with the classic drama and, say, the Chinese *Laou-Seng-Urh*[3] will have much hesitation in acceding to Wilson's opinion. Nor is Lassen less emphatic. "In the oldest Buddhist writings," he points out, "a visit of play-actors is spoken of as something customary";[4] and he insists again[5] "that the dramatic art in India is a growth wholly native to the soil, without foreign influence in general or Greek in particular." The origination of Indian drama, he adds, in the former passage, "must certainly be put before the time of the second Asoka; how much earlier it is naturally impossible to say." Any-one who reads Wilson's version of the *Mrichchakati*, "The Toy Cart," dated by him between a century B.C. and the second century C.E., will I think be convinced that the "origination" must be carried a very long way back.[6] That drama really represents in some respects a further evolution—I do not say a higher pitch of achievement—

[1] Berlin lecture cited, p. 25 = *Indische Skizzen*, p. 28.

[2] *Theatre of the Hindus*, pref. pp. xi. xii.

[3] Eng. trans. London, 1817. Cp. the *Brief View of the Chinese Drama* prefixed.

[4] *Indische Alterthumskunde*, ii. 502. See Körösi's analysis of the Tibetan "Dulva," in *Asiatic Researches*, xx. 50, the testimony cited by Lassen. The antiquity of much of the "Dulva" is disputed by Weber, *Hist. of Ind. Lit.* Eng. tr. p. 199. But cp. p. 198, *note* 210.

[5] *Ind. Alt.* ii. 1157.

[6] Lassen (*Ind. Alt.* ii. 1160) dates the play about the end of the first century C.E.; Weber (*Indische Studien*, ii. 148) in the second century. See Muir, *Original Sanskrit Texts*, ii. 11.

than the drama of Greece; and could only have been possible after a very long process of artistic development; hence Kalidasa may well belong, as Weber suggests, to a later period than is commonly supposed.[1] But this still leaves the beginnings of Indian drama very far off. And seeing that the common people in modern times still played the history of Râma on his festival day[2]—apparently following a custom of older date than the Râmâyana poem itself, it is a reasonable conjecture that the literary drama arose in India, as in Greece, out of the representations at the religious festivals. It has certainly small trace of the Greek spirit:[3] it is much more akin to the romantic drama of modern Europe.

For the rest, there is, I suppose, no connection with the theatre in the meaning of the name Devaki, which, it appears, has only loosely and indirectly the significance of "the Divine Lady," and strictly means "the player" or "she-player." Weber translates it *Spielerinn*, and Senart *joueuse*, with no allusion to any theatrical significance.[4] Nor can I find any explanation of the phrases: "I, who am a person of celestial nature, a mortal *Vasudeva*," and "I, a man of rank, a *Vasudeva*," occurring in *The Toy Cart*,[5] save Wilson's note on the former passage that Vasudeva = Krishna. These passages do not seem to have been considered in the discussions on Krishnaism. They serve, however, to repeat, if that be necessary, the refutation of the Christian thesis that the name Vasudeva was

[1] *Hist. of Ind. Lit.* pp. 200–207.

[2] See the *Asiatic Researches*, i. 258; and the *Asiatic Journal*, iv. 130, 185, N. S.

[3] The remark of Donaldson (*Theatre of the Greeks*, 7th ed. p. 7, *note*) that "the Indian stage, even if aboriginal, *may* have derived its most characteristic features from the Greek," is professedly based on the proposition that "there is every reason to believe" that Krishna "*was an imported deity*." K. O. Müller (*Hist. of the Lit. of Anc. Greece*, ch. xxi. § 2) asserts incidentally that "The dramatic poetry of the Indians belongs to a time when there had been much intercourse between Greece and India," but offers no arguments, and presumably follows some earlier Indianist. Weber, while leaning to the view of Greek origins, admits (*Hist.* p. 207) that "no internal connection with the Greek drama exists."

[4] Weber, *Ueber die K.*, pp. 316, 318; Senart, p. 323. Senart points out, however, that in the Mahâbhârata the father of Devakî is a Gandharva—*i.e.*, a "singer of heaven."

[5] *Theatre of the Hindus*, i. 28, 145. Cp. p. 26, *n*.

based on that of Joseph; and Wilson's note indicates sufficiently his conviction of the antiquity of Krishnaism. In Act v. of the same play (p. 90) the epithet *Kesava* ("long-locked," *crinitus*), constantly associated with Krishna, is without hesitation taken by him to apply to the same deity. It is one of the commonest characterizations of the Sun-God in all mythologies.

The question as to the practice of dramatic ritual among the early Christians, of course, needs a fuller investigation than can be thus given to it in a mere comparison of Christism and Krishnaism. Suffice it here to say that already orthodox scholarship is proceeding to trace passages in the apostolic Epistles to surmised ancient liturgies;[1] and that such a passage as opens the third Sermon of St. Proclus[2] (Bishop of Constantinople, 432–446), comparing the pagan and Christian festivals with only a moral differentiation: the repeated exhortations, in his fourth Sermon, to mothers, fathers, and children to "come and see" the Virgin and the swaddled child in the cradle;[3] his long account (Sermon vi.) of the dialogue between Joseph and Mary: and in general all his allusions to festivals and mysteries, point clearly to a close Christian imitation of pagan dramatic practices.[4] It is further a matter not of conjecture, but of history, that the old play on the "Suffering Christ" is to be attributed to Gregory of Nazianzen; and Klein, the German historian of the drama, decides that the sacrament of the Mass or the Communion is "*in itself already a religious drama, and is the original*

[1] See the article of Dr. Jessop in the *Expositor*, June, 1889.

[2] Migne, *Patrologiæ Cursus Completus, Series Græca*, tom. 65.

[3] Serm. iv. 2, Col. 711. The representation as thus described followed the apocryphal Gospels in placing the birth in a cave. But instead of the "ox and ass" of the normal show (which would then be too notoriously Pagan) there are mentioned the "ass and foal" of the entrance into Jerusalem. Col. 713. There appears to have been a whole crowd of New Testament figures, including Paul.

[4] The remark of the Countess Martinengo Cesaresco (art. *Puer Parvulus* in *Contemporary Review*, January, 1900, p. 117), that "there was no actual cult of the infant Saviour till the thirteenth century," is clearly erroneous, though the explicit evidences to the contrary are not abundant. As we have seen, the narratives in the Apocryphal and other Gospels derive from the ancient cult.

Mystery-play":[1] a view accepted and echoed by the orthodox Ulrici,[2] and independently advanced by Renan.[3] Klein has further traced, perhaps fancifully at some points, an interesting series of analogies between the early Christian liturgy and the Greek tragedy, which was essentially a religious service. M. Jubinal, again, in a sketch of the rise of the Mystery-plays, sums up that "the fifth century presents itself with its cortège of religious festivals, during which are simulated (*on mime*) or figured in the church the adoration of the Magi, the marriage of Cana, the death of the Saviour, etc."[4] This statement, made without citations, is repeated by Klein,[5] who quotes as his authority merely the words of M. Jubinal; and by Dr. Ulrici,[6] who, carrying the statement further, merely cites these two writers. Such defect of proof would be suspicious were it not for the above-cited evidence from Saint Proclus; and, though that is so far decisive, there is evident need for a complete research. Milman has made little or none. Admitting that there were pantomimic spectacles at the martyr-festivals, he rejects the view that they represented the deaths of the martyrs, but says nothing as to the early mystery-plays, merely denying that plays such as that by Gregory were written for representation;[7] and in his later work he discusses the Mysteries of the Middle Ages without attempting to trace their origin.[8]

A complete theory would have to deal with (1) the original mystery-plays which preceded and provided the Gospel narrative; (2) the reduction of some of these to pseudo-history and their probable cessation (*e.g.*, in the case of the Last Supper) as complete dramatic representations; and (3) the later establishment of such exhibitions as that of the Nativity, in the teeth of the ascetic objection to all forms of pleasurable art. Here, however, I can

[1] *Geschichte des Dramas*, iv. (= *Gesch. des Ital. Dram.* i.), p. 2.
[2] *Shakespeare's Dramatic Art*, Bohn trans. i. 2.
[3] *Etudes d'Histoire religieuse*, p. 51.
[4] *Mystères Inédits du XVième Siècle*, 1837, pref. p. viii.
[5] iv. 11. [6] i. 4.
[7] *History of Christianity*, bk. iv. ch. 2, ed. Paris, 1840, ii. 320, 326.
[8] *History of Latin Christianity*, bk. xiv. ch. 4.

only posit the fact that such exhibitions did occur, and note that such a conclusion is supported by orthodox clerical statement. Dr. Murdock, discussing the Christian adoption of the Christmas festival, observes that

> "From the *first institution* of this festival, the Western nations seem to have transferred to it many of the follies and censurable practices which prevailed in the pagan festivals of the same season, such as adorning the churches fantastically, *mingling puppet shows and dramas with worship*, universal feasting and merry-making, visits and salutations, revelry and drunkenness."[1]

It is, indeed, one of the commonplaces of Protestant church historians to point out that after the State establishment of Christianity it borrowed many observances from Paganism.[2] What the student has to keep in view is that these usages, especially such a one as that of "puppet shows and dramas," cannot have been suddenly grafted on a religious system wholly devoid of them. The Christians certainly had the practice of celebrating *some* birthday of Christ long before the fourth century; and we have seen some of the reasons for concluding that on that occasion they had a mystery-ritual. It is noteworthy, too, that the subjects first specified as appearing in Christian shows or plays were precisely those which we know to have figured in the cults of Mithra and Dionysos, and in the Egyptian system. Further, it was exactly such subjects that were represented in the earliest medieval Mysteries of which copies remain; and it was especially at Christmas and Easter that these were performed. It is hardly possible to doubt that these representations derive from the

[1] Note on trans. of Mosheim, 4 Cent. pt. ii. ch. 4, § 5.

[2] See, for instance, Mosheim, *Eccles. Hist.* 3 Cent. pt. ii. ch. 4, § 3; 4 Cent. pt. ii. ch. 4, § 1, 2; 5 Cent. pt. i. ch. 3, § 2, etc.; Gieseler, *Compend. of Ec. Hist.* Eng. tr. 1846, ii. 24–26, 32, 51, 61, etc.; Waddington, *Hist. of the Church*, pp. 37, 212–4. Cp. *Roma Antiqua et Recens*, 1665, rep. 1889, *Pagano-Papismus*, 1675, rep. 1844, and Middleton's *Letter from Rome*, 1729, etc., for detailed statements. For later views see Dyer, *History of Rome*, 1877, p. 295; Lord, *The Old Roman World*, 1873, p. 558; Maitland's *Church in the Catacombs*, 1846, p. 306; Seymore's *Evenings with the Romanists*, 1844, p. 221; Merivale's *Four Lectures on some Epochs of Early Church History*; Lechler's *Apostolic and Post-Apostolic Times*, p. 262. See finally some very explicit Catholic admissions by Baronius, *Epitome Annalium*, a Spondano, Lugduni, 1686, p. 79; Polydore Vergil, *De Inventore Rerum*, l. 5, c. 1; Wiseman's *Letters to John Poynder, Esq.*, 1836.

very earliest practices of the Christian sect, established when Paganism was still in full play. The dramatic character of the early Mysteries, which, as we have seen, were almost as inviolably secret as those of the Pagans, pierces through the cautious writings of the Fathers, as read even by clerical eyes :—

"Chrysostom most probably refers to the commemoration of our Saviour's deeds and words at the Last Supper, as used in the liturgy, when he attributes such great importance to the words of institution of our Lord, which he considers as still chiefly efficacious in the consecration of the eucharist. He often speaks of the eucharist under the title of an unbloody sacrifice...."[1]

Other admissions are no less significant :—

"There can be little, if any, doubt that Christian liturgies were not at first committed to writing, but preserved by memory and practice." "When we examine the remains of the Roman, Italian, Gallican, and Spanish liturgies, we find that they all permitted a variety of expression for every particular feast....It appears to me that the practice of the western Churches during the fifth and fourth centuries, in permitting the use of various 'missæ' in the same church, affords room for thinking that something of the same kind had existed from a remote period. For it does not seem that the composition of new 'missæ' for the festivals excited any surprise in these ages, or was viewed as anything novel in *principle*."[2]

That is to say, the first Christians, in their feeble and illiterate way, tried to do what the Greeks had long done in their dramatic mysteries, which must have conformed in some degree to the creative tendency fulfilled on such a splendid scale in their public drama, itself a development of religious ritual.[3]

"The Eleusinian mysteries were, as an ancient writer [Clem. Alex. *Protrept.* p. 12, Potter] expresses it, 'a mystical drama,' in which the history of Demeter and Cora was acted, like a play, by priests and priestesses, though probably only with mimic action, illustrated by a few significant sentences, and by the singing of hymns. There were also similar mimic representations in the worship of Bacchus : thus, at the Anthesteria at Athens, the wife of the second archon, who bore the title

[1] Palmer, *Origines Liturgicæ*, i. 33.

[2] *Id.* pp. 9, 10. Cp. Mosheim, 4 Cent. pt. ii. ch. 4, § 3.

[3] K. O. Müller, *Hist. of the Lit. of Anc. Greece*, ch. xxi. § 2–5; xxvii. § 1. It is true that, as remarked by Fustel de Coulanges in *La Cité Antique* (*8ième. éd.* p. 196), the words and rhythms of the hymns in the ancient domestic and civic rites were preserved unaltered; but this would not apply to the later syncretic mysteries.

of Queen, was betrothed to Dionysus in a secret solemnity, and in public processions even the God himself was represented by a man. [A beautiful slave of Nicias represented Dionysus on an occasion of this kind: Plutarch, *Nic.* 3. Compare the description of the great Bacchic procession under Ptolemy Philadelphus in Athen. v.] At the Bœotian festival of the Agrionia, Dionysus was supposed to have disappeared, and to be sought for among the mountains; there was also a maiden (representing one of the nymphs in the train of Dionysus), who was pursued by a priest, carrying a hatchet, and personating a being hostile to the God. This festival rite, which is frequently mentioned by Plutarch, is the origin of the fable, which occurs in Homer, of the pursuit of Dionysus and his nurses by the furious Lycurgus."[1]

The last proposition is one more application of the principle which has been so often followed in the present essay—that ritual usages are the fountains of myth, and typically the most ancient things in religion. But while the central ritual was immemorial, it may be taken for granted that the secret drama and hymns were innovated upon from time to time. And this frequent or customary change, proceeding from spontaneous devotional or artistic feeling, would seem to have been attempted in some degree, and even in an artistic spirit,[2] by the first Christians, till the religious principle and the church system of centralization petrified everything into dead ritual. And only when we know better than we do at present the details of the process by which they built up alike their liturgy and their legends, their mysteries and their festivals, from the medley of religious systems around them, can we possibly be entitled to say that they did not take something from the ancient drama and ritual of India, to which so many Western eyes were then turned.

Finally, we must remember that in all probability the ancient race of travelling Pagan mummers survived obscurely all through the Dark Ages, as did so much genuine Paganism.[3] It seems to have been their encroachment on the hitherto purely clerical domain of religious

[1] *Id.* xxi. § 3 (Lewis' trans. 1847), pp. 287–8.

[2] Mosheim (1 Cent. pt. ii. ch. 4, § 6) decides that even in the first century the liturgical hymns "were sung not by the whole assembly, but by certain persons during the celebration of the sacred supper and the feasts of charity."

[3] Cp. Warton, *History of English Poetry*, sect. xxxiv.; Symonds, *Shakespeare's Predecessors*, p. 95; Vernon Lee, *Studies of the Eighteenth Century in Italy*, pp. 233–4; Ulrici, as cited, p. 10; *Academy*, April 6th, 1889, p. 231.

play-acting that brought upon things theatrical the curse of the Church, who naturally wanted to destroy the art when she found it slipping from her hands. In any case, we know that, though the early Fathers had often denounced secular drama and actors, doing indiscriminately what Plato had done with discrimination, not till about the thirteenth century did the dramatic art and its devotees begin to come absolutely under the ecclesiastical ban. By that time the Church no longer knew—collectively, indeed, her children had never realised—that primitive drama was the very womb and genesis of the whole faith.

XV.—The Seven Myth.

An examination of two other minor myth-motives of Christianity in connection with Krishnaism will perhaps be found not uninstructive. We have seen that the Catholic Church placed St. Christopher's day at the time when, in the Hindu legend, Vasudeva carries the new-born Krishna across a river. That is not the only detail of the kind. Just a fortnight before, on July 10th, is fixed the Catholic commemoration day of the *Septem Fratres Martyres*, the seven martyred brothers.

§ 1. Here we are at once up to the eyes in universal mythology. On the very face of the Christian martyrology, these Seven Brother Martyrs are mythic: they are duplicated again and again in that martyrology itself. Thus we have the specially so-called *Septem Fratres Martyres*, who are sons of a martyr mother Felicitas, and whose martyrdom is placed in the reign of Antoninus Pius—a safe way off. But on the 18th day of the same month we have the martyred Saint Symphorosa and *her* seven martyred sons, whose date is put under Hadrian, a little earlier still. But yet earlier still we find included in the same martyrology the pre-Christian case of the seven Maccabee brothers[1] and *their* mother, fixed for August 1st. And still the list mounts. On July 27th—we are always

[1] 2 Maccabees, vii.

in or just out of July—is the holy day of the *Septem Dormientes*, our old friends the Seven Sleepers of Ephesus, fabled to have been "walled up in a cave in which they had hid themselves" in the year 250, in the persecution of Decius, and to have waked up—or to have been discovered, as the scrupulous Butler would prefer to put it—in 479.[1] Nor is even this all. There are further the Seven Martyrs of Samosata, whose holy day is somewhat belated, December 9th; and the seven *Virgin* Martyrs of Ancyra, who are placed under Diocletian, so as to help to cover the martyrological ground, and who in the Roman Catholic Calendar are commemorated on May 18th, but in the Armenian Church on June 20th. Doubtless the Seven Virgins, all ladies of about seventy years, have a different mythic origin from the seven brothers or sleepers, who in the four first cases are invariably youths or boys; and the seven of Samosata (whose actual date of martyrdom was June 25th) also divide off from the July group in respect that two of them, the leaders, are old, and that the remaining five in the story are represented as joining these two, who adored the crucifix seven times a day.[2] We are left with four sets of Seven Martyrs, three of them sets of brothers, whose mothers were martyred before or after them, they themselves suffering between July 10th and August 1st.

That the Seven Sleepers are of the same myth stock is clear. In the Musæum Victorium of Rome is, or was, a plaster group of them, in which clubs lie beside two of them; a knotty club near another; axes near two others; and a torch near the seventh. Now the general feature[3] of the other martyrdoms is the variety of the tortures imposed. Of the first seven, one is flogged to death with loaded whips, two with clubs, one thrown over a precipice,

[1] See their story in Gibbon, c. 33, end. This date *should* have been the end of the world, as to which there were even more guesses in the early than in the later Christian times. If the chronology of Julius Africanus were accepted, 469 would be the year of the end of the world, on Tertullian's (Magian) view that it was to last 6,000 years.

[2] For these legends see Butler's or any other *Lives of the Saints*, under the dates given.

[3] Butler, ed. 1812, etc., vii. 359–60.

and three beheaded; and of the sons of Symphorosa each one dies a distinct death. The seven Maccabees are not so much particularised; but of the seven of Samosata, the first, who is old, is flogged with loaded whips like the eldest son of Felicitas; and, though all are crucified, they are finally despatched in three different ways. Again, though the Sleepers are commonly conceived, naturally, in their final Rip Van Winkle aspect; in the plaster group they are beardless, and "in ancient martyrologies and other writings they are frequently called boys." In the Koran again,[1] still youths, and still "testifying" in bad times, they sleep, *with their eyes open*, for 309 years—a longer period than that of the Christian legend, which gives them a sleep of only some 227 years[2]—and they are guarded by a dog: while the Deity "turned them to the right and to the left," and the sun when it arose passed on the right of their cave, and when it set passed them on the left; a sufficiently obvious indication of the solar division of the year. And the mythic dog, Mohammedans believe, is to go with the Seven to heaven. He is, of course, of the breed of the dogs who, in certain old Semitic mysteries, "were solemnly declared to be the brothers of the mystæ";[3] and his connection with the Sleepers doubtless hinges on the ancient belief that he "has the use of his sight both by night and by day."[4]

Seven, as the reader need hardly be reminded, is a "sacred number"[5] that constantly figures in Jewish, Vedic, and other ancient lore; and there is reason to surmise here, as in so many other cases, a Christian connection with Mithraism. Among the admittedly Mithraic remains in the Catacombs is a fresco representing a banquet of seven persons, who are labelled as the *Septem Pii Sacerdotes*, the seven pious priests.[6] Now,

[1] Sura 18, "The Cave." Rodwell's trans. 1st ed. p. 212.
[2] In one version; in others the time is under 200 years.
[3] Robertson Smith. *Religion of the Semites*, p. 273.
[4] Plutarch, *Isis and Osiris*, c. 44. Cp. Diodorus Siculus, i. 87.
[5] "An infinite number of beauties may be extracted from a careful contemplation of it." *Philo Judæus*, Bohn trans. iii. 265.
[6] *Roma Sotterranea*, as cited, Appendix B, vol. ii. p. 355.

the very Catholic authorities who admit the Mithraic character of the picture have put forward an exactly similar one as being Christian, stating that it is common, without a word of misgiving or explanation, beyond an uncalculating suggestion that it represents the meeting of Jesus with *seven* disciples (John xxi. 1–13) after his resurrection. "It is not stated," argue these exegetes, "that He Himself sat down and partook of the meal with them."[1] So that we are to assume the Catacomb artist painted the seven fisher disciples, on the shore of the lake, sitting on a couch, banqueting at an elaborately laid table, in the presence of their Lord and Master, whose figure is considerately left to the imagination. It is plain that the picture is either Mithraic pure and simple or an exact Christian imitation of a Mithraic ceremony; and indeed it is very likely that the story in the fourth Gospel, which is evidently an addition, was one more fiction to explain a ritual usage. The picture could not have been painted for the story; but the story might very well be framed to suit the rite, which existed before the painting. And here at least Mithraism had handed on to Christianity an institution of ancient India, for the seven priests figure repeatedly in the Rig Veda in connection with the worship of Agni.[2] But, again, the rite is probably a widespread one; for in the Dionysiak myth the Child-God is torn by the Titans into seven pieces; and there is reason to surmise that a Banquet of Seven gave rise to that story.[3]

We cannot here, of course, trace such a myth minutely

[1] Plate xvii. vol. ii. and pp. 67–8.

[2] *Rig Veda Sanhita*, Wilson's trans. i. 101, 156; iii. 115, 120, etc. It may have been Mithraic example that led to the creation of seven *epulones*, rulers of the Roman sacrificial feasts, in place of the original three; as later the institution of the seven Christian deacons. The *Septemviri Epulones* appear often in inscriptions. There was, however, a traditional ceremonial banquet of Seven Wise Men at Corinth, the founding of which was attributed to Periander, about 600 B.C. Plutarch, *Banquet of the Seven Wise Men*, ii.

[3] See the bas-relief from the Dionysiak theatre, reproduced in *Mythology and Monuments of Ancient Athens*, by Miss Harrison and Mrs. Verrall, 1890, p. 283. Cp. that on p. 278.

to all its parallels;[1] and there is a risk of oversight in bracketing it with all the Sevens of general mythology. The Rev. Sir George Cox traces these generally to the seven stars of Ursa Major :—

> "The seven stars" [in Sanskrit, first *rikshas*, bears; later *rishis*, shiners, sages] "became the abode of the Seven Poets or sages, who enter the ark with Menu (Minos) and reappear as the Seven Wise Men of Hellas, the Seven Children of Rhodos and Helios (Pind. Ol. vii. 132), and the Seven Champions of Christendom."[2] "Epimenides....while tending sheep, fell asleep one day in a cave, and did not awake until more than fifty years had passed away. But Epimenides was one of the Seven Sages, who reappear in the Seven Manes of Leinster [ref. to Fergusson, *The Irish before the Conquest*] and in the Seven Champions of Christendom; and thus the idea of the Seven Sleepers was at once suggested."[3]

Sir George Cox, however, does not connect these groups with the sets of Seven Martyrs; whereas Christian and Teutonic mythology alike entitle us to do so. In every case the point is that the Seven are to *rise again*, that being the doctrinal lesson in the story of the Maccabees as well as in those of the Christian Martyrs. In the Northern Sagas the Seven Sleepers are the sons of Mimer, "the ward of the middle-root of the world-tree"; they are "put to sleep" in "bad times" after their father's death; and they awake at the blast of the trumpet of Ragnarök. They are in fact the "seven seasons," the seven changes of the weather, the seven "economic months" of Northern lore; and in Germany and Sweden the day of the Seven Sleepers is a popular test-day of the weather, as St. Swithin's day, July 15th—we are always in July—is for us.[4] Now, whereas the names of the Seven Sleepers of Ephesus—Maximian, Malchus, Martinian, Dionysius, John, Serapion, Constantine—have no connection with a weather-myth, the very first name of the *Septem Fratres Martyres* is Januarius, and the list includes the names of Felix, Sylvanus, Vitalis, and

[1] The myth gets into Danish history in the story of the seven young Danes of Jomsburg, who, being captured in Norway, undergo their deaths with unparalleled fortitude, having been trained to despise death and all suffering. Each "testifies" separately. Mallet's *Intr. to Hist. of Denmark*, lib. 4.

[2] *Mythology of the Aryan Nations*, p. 26.

[3] *Id.* p. 225.

[4] Rydberg, *Teutonic Mythology*, pp. 488–494.

Martialis, all of which have a seasonal suggestion. So, too, have the names alike of Felicitas, *Fertility*, and Symphorosa = propitious, useful, profitable. And the source of the legend is put beyond all doubt when we find that *Temporum Felicitas* is actually the inscription on ancient coins or medals representing that Roman Goddess[1] and her children the seasons. On one side she herself is represented with three children, she bearing symbols, but they bearing none; while on the other are four boys, who distinctly stand for the seasons in respect of the symbols they bear.[2] Now, the ancients had two conceptions on the subject—one of *three* Horæ, who were "not seasons, properly speaking, for the winter was never a Hora," and who were often represented without attributes;[3] the other, the more definite notion of the *quatuor anni tempora;* and the medal under notice simply presents both fancies. And the Christian myth-maker in his turn has simply combined them anew, adding the four to the three and making seven sons of *Felicitas*, accounting for the *Temporum* as he thought fit. Thus can myths be made.

It is not to be supposed, of course, that the myth could always keep the same cast; and it may be that it is at bottom the same as that of the seven boy and girl victims of the Minotaur in the legend of Theseus: but there is certainly a close kinship between the Teutonic and Christian forms under notice. In the view of Dr. Rydberg, the myth is originally Teutonic; though he notes that "Gregorius says that he is the first who recorded in the Latin language" the miracle of the Seven Sleepers, "not before known to the Church of Western Europe. As his authority he quotes 'a certain Syrian,' who had interpreted the story for him. There was also need of a man from the Orient as an authority when a hitherto unknown miracle was to be presented—a miracle that had transpired (*sic*

[1] *Felicitas* was separately deified. Augustine, *De Civ. Dei*, iv. 18, 23; Suetonius, *Tiberius*, c. 5.

[2] See the reproduction by Spanheim, *Obs. in Callimachi Hymn. in Cererem* ed. Ernesti, 1761, ii. 815–16.

[3] K. O. Müller, *Ancient Art*, p. 530.

trans.) in a cave near Ephesus." It might be answered to this not only that, as Dr. Rydberg himself candidly notes, the sleeping Endymion was located in a cave in Latmos near Ephesus, but that the seven Pleiades of Greek mythology were rain-givers, and presided over navigation, just as he says the northern Seven Sleepers did. It is doubtless this idea that occurs in the legend of the Seven Virgins of Ancyra, whom the persecutor drowns in a lake, and whose holy day, May 18, is set just about the time the Pleiades rise.[1] Furthermore, the Græco-Syrians had their doctrine of the seven zones or climates into which the earth was divided,[2] just as the northerns had their seven seasons; the zones being doubtless correlative with the "seven bonds of heaven and earth" which in the ancient Babylonian system were developed from the seven planets and their representative spirits.[3] But Gregory's derivation of the Christian myth from the East, where also are located the *Septem Fratres Martyres*, brings us back to our bearings as regards the present inquiry.

§ 2. The occurrence of all these dates of "sevens" in July, or just after July, the seventh month, is a very remarkable coincidence; and it is impossible to miss the surmise that they have a connection with the month's ordinal number. But further surmises are suggested by the fact that in the Krishna legends there is a variation, and an evident confusion, as to the numerical place of the God in the list of his mother's children, of whom he would appear in some versions to have been the seventh, while commonly he is the eighth.[4] Devaki's eight children are

[1] The lake itself, in the Christian legend, is the scene of a local water-worship in connection with Pagan Goddesses. Now, the Semites attached a special sanctity to groups of Seven Wells; and the Arabic name given to (presumably) one such group signifies the Pleiades. See Smith's *Religion of the Semites*, pp. 153, *n.*, 165, 168.

[2] Bardesan, *Fragments*, Eng. tr. Ante-Nicene Lib. vol. xxii. *b.* p. 107.

[3] Sayce, Hibbert Lectures, p. 110. There were seven bad spirits as well as seven good—the number was obligatory. *Id.* pp. 82, 102, 105, 283. Cp. Lenormant, *Chaldean Magic*, Eng. tr. p. 25.

[4] Compare M. Barth's account with that of Maurice (*History of Hindostan*, ii. 330), who follows the Bhâgavat Purâna, but cites Balde, who made Krishna the seventh son.

said to have been seven sons and a daughter; but only the six sons are said to have been killed by Kansa; while in the Bhâgavat Purâna her seventh child is Bala Râma, and, he being "transferred" to the womb of Rohini, her seventh pregnancy is given out as ending in miscarriage. It is hardly possible to doubt that there has been manipulation of an earlier myth-form; and the suspicion is strengthened by the confused fashion in which it is told that after the birth of the divine child the parents' eyes were closed by Vishnu, so that "they again thought that a child was born unto them"—a needless and unintelligible detail.[1] The myth, besides, is certainly pre-Krishnaite. "In the Veda, the sun, in the form of Mârtânda, is the eighth son born of Aditi; and his mother casts him off, just as Devaki, who is at times represented as an incarnation of Aditi, removes Krishna."[2] In other mythologies as in the Hindu the number of the supernatural family varies between seven and eight. "To Kronos [Il or El] were borne by Astarte seven daughters......and again to him were borne by Rhea seven sons, the youngest of whom was consecrated from his birth";[3] but again the divine Eshmun (Asklepios) was the eighth son of Sydyk.[4] The solution is dubious.[5] It is possible that a myth of the birth of seven inferior or ill-fated children, followed by that of one who attains supreme Godhood, may be a primitive cosmogonic explanation of the relation of the "seven planets" to the deity, which is certainly the basis of the familiar myth of the "Seven Spirits" who figure so much in the Mazdean system and in the Christian Apocalypse. Mithra, the chief of the

[1] It is made partly intelligible in the *Prem Sagar* ("Ocean of Love"), a Hindi version at second hand of the tenth book of the Bhâgavat Purâna. The idea there is that the parents are made to forget the preliminary revelation of the divinity. Cp. Cox, p. 368.

[2] Barth, *Religions of India*, p. 173. See Wilson's Rig Veda Sanhita, vi. 199. Aditi "bore Mârtânda for the birth and death of human beings."

[3] Sanchoniathon in Eusebius, *Præp. Evang.*, cited in Cory's *Ancient Fragments*, pp. 13–14.

[4] *Id.* p. 19.

[5] Apollo, reputed born on the seventh day of the month, was probably first known as *seventh-day-born*, ἑβδομαγένης. Scholiasts on Æsch. *Seven against Thebes*, 800, where the epithet is ἑβδομαγέτης. Cp. Plutarch, *Symposium*, viii.

seven Amshaspands or planetary spirits of the Persian system, who are clearly akin to the "Adityas" of the Vedas,[1] rose in his solar character to virtual supremacy; and it is noteworthy that throughout the Avesta the heavenly bodies always appear in the order: Planets, Moon, and Sun, the Sun coming last.[2] In this light, the conception of stars and moon as ghosts or dead divinities in comparison with the sun seems not unlikely. On the other hand, on Mr. Frazer's view of the primitive universality of the worship of a God of Vegetation, whose cult survived in such as those of Dionysos, Osiris, and Adonis, there may have been an association of a myth of the seasons with that of the Life-God, who finally dominates everything. And as there appears to have been a legend of seven slain sons of Devaki,[3] these seven sons of the "celestial man"[4] may be duplicates of the seven sleeping sons of the northern Mimer, whom we have seen identified with "the seven seasons." The Christian legends have shown us how the sleepers (always young) could be transformed into martyrs. It is a curious coincidence, again, that in one version of the myth of the twelve Hebrew patriarchs[5] the undesired Leah bears to the solar Jacob seven children, six sons and a daughter, before the desired Rachel bears the favourite, the solar Joseph; while in the dual legend of Ràma and Krishna the younger brother becomes the greater, as happens in so many Biblical cases of pairs of brothers—Ishmael and Isaac, Esau and Jacob, Reuben and Joseph, Pharez and Zarah, Manasseh and Ephraim.[6]

The suspicion of manipulation is further strengthened by the fact that, while the Birth Festival falls in July, the date

[1] Tiele, *Outlines*, p. 169. [2] Goldziher, *Hebrew Mythology*, p. 61.

[3] M. Pavie, in his translation (*Krishna et sa Doctrine*, 1852) of Lalatch's Hindi version of the tenth book of the Bhâgavat Purâna, heads the first chapter, "King Kansa kills the first seven children of his sister Devakî," though the text is not explicit to that effect.

[4] Barth, as cited, p. 172.

[5] Gen. xxx. 20–24.

[6] Compare the ascendancy of Zeus over his elder brethren. Callimachus, *Hymn to Zeus*, 58–59. In Hesiod (*Theogony*, 453–478) Zeus is the *sixth* and youngest child; but in the Iliad (xv. 182, 204; cp. iv. 60) he is the eldest born.

of the birth in late texts appears to be August. It could be wished that Professor Weber had brought his scholarly knowledge to bear on the problem of the meaning of these dates rather than on the impracticable thesis he has adopted from his supernaturalist predecessors. Sir William Jones gave a clue[1] in noting the fact that in the Brahman almanacs there are two ways of dating Krishna's birthday. One puts it "when the moon is in Rohini, on the eighth of any dark fortnight; the other when the sun is in Sinha." It is a conflict of myths.

As to the "seven seasons" notion in old Aryan mythology, it is impossible to speak. The number in Hindu lore as preserved is six;[2] and though these might be connected with the six slain children of Devaki, they do not square with the eight births of Aditi. But for this last precedent, it might be suspected that Krishna had been made the eighth child of the Divine Lady because he was the eighth Incarnation of Vishnu; but the Aditi myth is a strong reminder that the story of the eight children may be older than the scheme of the Avatars, the genesis of which is so difficult to trace.[3] In Rhodes, Poseidon was held to have six sons and one daughter by Halia; while Helios had seven sons and one daughter by Rhode.[4] And here we are reminded that the number eight figures in the Vedas as well as seven, there being indeed *eight* "planets" in the Indian system.[5] Yet again, in Egyptian mythology there are "eight personified cosmic powers" "from whom the city of Thut, Hermopolis, derived its Egyptian name," and who are "always united with Thut, but nevertheless to be distinguished from his seven assistants."[6] Again, it has been pointed out that the Pythian cycle of eight years was one of ninety-nine lunar months, "at the end of which the revo-

[1] *Asiatic Researches*, iii. 289.
[2] Jones, in *Asiatic Researches*, iii. 258; Patterson, *id.* viii. 66.
[3] For an ingenious if inconclusive attempt to find an astrological solution of the problem, see Salverte's *Essai sur les Noms*, 1824, vol. ii. Note C. Salverte has followed some account which makes Krishna the seventh child of Devaki.
[4] Diodorus Siculus, v. 55, 56.
[5] Barth, as cited, p. 261, *n*.
[6] Tiele, *Outlines*, p. 49. Cp. Herodotus, ii. 43, 46, 145, 156.

lutions of the sun and moon again nearly coincided.[1] Finally, it is not impossible that the old perplexity as to Hesperus and Phosphorus—the question whether it was the same planet, Venus, that was seen now at dawn and now at sunset: a problem which was said to have been settled by Pythagoras[2]—may underlie the alternations of a seven and an eight myth. It would seem as if an eight myth and a seven myth, both of irretrievable antiquity, had been entangled[3] too early to permit of any certainty as to their respective origins.

On that view, of course, the possibility remains that a week-myth may after all be bound up with the legend of Krishna and the six slain children. The names of the days of the week, ancient and modern, remind us that the "seven planets"—that is, the five planets anciently known, and the sun and moon—formed the basis of the seven-day division of time, in which the sun has always the place of honour.[4]

Now, it is a suggestive though imperfect coincidence that among the ancient Semites, who consecrated the

[1] K. O. Müller, *Dorians*, Eng. tr. i. 281. Cp. pp. 263, 270.

[2] Cicero, *De nat. deor.* ii. 2.

[3] Compare Macrobius, *In Somn. Scip.* i. 6. Colebrooke (*Asiatic Researches*, viii. 82–3) notes that "the eight Sactis, or enemies of as many deities, are also called Matris or mothers.... However, some authorities reduce the number to seven." So there are two accounts of the number of children borne by Megara to Herakles, Pherecydes making them seven, and Pindar (*Isth.* iii. 81, 116) eight. (Duncker, *Gesch. des Alterthums*, iii. 98.) Apollodorus in one place (ii. 7, 8) makes the sons four; in another (ii. 4, 11) three. It may very well be that this ancient perplexity is the origin of the odd phrase in *Ecclesiastes* (xi. 2): "Give a portion to Seven, and also to Eight"—a formula which the commentators seem to regard as having no special meaning. The two numbers occur again in Micah, v. 5. See Mr. Gerald Massey's *Natural Genesis*, ii. 80, 104–5, for a surprising number of other instances, one from the Fiji islands! See also the same work, ii. 2, as to the number of the Pleiads.

[4] On this point, in connection with India, see Von Bohlen, *Das Alte Indien*, 1830, ii. 245 ff. The origin of the week appears still to be disputed. Le Clerc long ago urged the planetary basis against Grotius, who accepted the Judaic (*On the Truth of the Chr. Rel.* i. 16); but Professor Whitney (*Life and Growth of Language*, p. 81) writes that "the planetary day-names would have remained to Europe, as to India, a mere astrologers' fancy, but for Christianity and its inheritance of the Jewish seven-day period as a leading measure of time"—a perplexing statement to me. The Day of the Sun or Lord's Day was certainly a popular institution under Paganism. On the general problem cp. Kuenen, *Religion of Israel*, Eng. tr. i. 264; Wellhausen, *Prolegomena*, p. 113; *Indian Antiquary*, March, 1874 (iii. 90); Philostratus, *Life of Apollonius of Tyana*, iii. 41, *end;* Max Müller, *On False Analogies in Comparative Theology*, *Contemporary Review*, 1870.

seventh day (*i.e.*, *Satur*day), to their supreme and sinister deity Saturn, the planet most distant from the sun, the priests on that day, *clothed in black*, ministered to the God in his *black* six-sided temple[1]—he having made the world in six days, the perfect number. This deity, like the black Krishna, bears signs of transformation from bad to good, from inferior to superior, since in ancient Italy he was both a good and a malevolent deity.[2] Of course Ovid's etymology is untenable, but it is none the less significant that for him Saturn, the *Deus Latius*, or God of Latium, is the *Deus Latens*, or "hiding God,"[3] considering that Saturn was commonly opposed to Jupiter, the *Deus Latiaris*, equally God of Latium, the illustrious king of the race.[4] It may be that, as in so many other myths, the name helped the theory as to Saturn's "hidden" character; but in any case the theory was persistent; and Herodian, writing in the third century, tells that the Latins kept the festival of the Saturnalia in December "to commemorate the hidden God,"[5] just before the feast of the New Year in honour of Janus, whose image had two faces, because in him was the end of the old and the beginning of the new year. Thus he was celebrated at the time of the greatest cold, the festival lasting for seven days, from December 17th; but the time was one of universal goodwill, calling up thoughts of the golden age past, and to come.[6] And not the least

[1] Gesenius, *Commentar über d. Jesaia*, 2ter Theil, Beilage, 2, p. 344, citing Nordberg. Lex. p. 76 ff. (Donaldson, *Theatre of the Greeks*, 7th ed. p. 15.)

[2] Cp. Dionysius of Halicarnassus, i. 38; Virgil, *Ecl.* iv. 6; *Georg.* i. 336, ii. 538; Horace, 2 *Carm.* xvii. 23; Augustine, *De Civ. Dei*, vii. 13; Juvenal, vi. 569; Macrobius, *In Somn. Scip.* i. 19. Compare the words "saturnine," signifying gloomy, and "saturnian" as signifying the golden age. See further Lucan, i. 652, on which a curious question arises. Lucan speaks of Saturn as a baleful star with "*black fires*." Bentley proposed to read *Capricorni* for *Saturni*, giving ingenious but doubtful reasons. Mythological confusion was doubtless caused by the meteorological significance of the star, as apart from the deity, who was by many reckoned the chief of the Gods, and identified with the sky and the sun (Macrobius, *Saturnalia*, i. 7, 10, 22). In the Mithraic mysteries Saturn had the "first" gate, the "leaden." Origen, *Against Celsus*, vi. 22.

[3] *Fasti*, i. 238.

[4] Preller, *Röm. Myth.* p. 85.

[5] Bk. i. c. 16. Cp. Tacitus, *Hist.* v. 4; and Preller, p. 413. It is to be noted, too, that Kronos (= Saturn) was represented in art with his head veiled (K. O. Müller, *Ancient Art*, as cited, p. 520).

[6] Preller, p. 414; Macrobius, *Saturnalia*, i. 10.

curious parallel between this and the Krishnaite festival and our own Christmas festival is the old custom of making, at the time of the Saturnalia, little images, which were given as presents, especially to children.[1]

This is away from the week myth. To return to that: we find that in seven-gated Thebes, Apollo the Sun-God is lord of the seventh gate[2] because lord of the number seven, and born on the seventh day of the month;[3] and though in the Hellenic legend of the seven chiefs who die in the attack on the seven-gated city the basal myth is much sophisticated, it can hardly be doubted that there is a dualist nature-myth behind the detail of the mutual slaughter of the two opposed brothers at the gate of Apollo. More obvious is the conception as we have it plausibly explained by Sir George Cox, followed by Mr. Tylor, in the case of Grimm's story of the wolf and the seven little goats. The wolf is the darkness (Kansa was black) who tries to swallow the seven days of the week, and does swallow six, while the seventh *hides*.[4] In the Teutonic story the six days come out again, which they do not in the Hindu; but the myth may be the same at bottom. In any case, here we have six or seven slain "children," whose fate makes part of the story of Krishna, the Hindu God honoured in the seventh month; and these compare strikingly with the Christian sets of Seven Martyrs, who are all either "children" of a mother who dies with them, or simply boys, as in the case of the Sleepers of Ephesus; and who

[1] Preller, last cit.; Macrobius, i. 11.

[2] Æschylus, *Seven against Thebes*, 801. Each gate has its God, and the virgin Athênê presides over all. In the Mithraic mysteries, Mithra, the Sun-God, was lord of the seventh gate, the gates being named from the planets, moon, and sun. Origen, as last cited. The same principle held in Babylon. In ancient Scandinavia, finally, if we can trust the *Grimnismal*, Balder dwells in the seventh celestial house. Bergmann, *Le Message de Skirnir et les dits de Grimnir*, pp. 228, 249, 269. There is no sign of Christian suggestion here. Cp. Donaldson, *Theatre of the Greeks*, 7th ed. p. 14.

[3] Scholiast on Æsch.; Müller, *Dorians*, Eng. tr. i. 348 and refs. In four months, two in each half of the year, the seventh day was sacred to Apollo. Müller, as cited, p. 350. Cp. p. 270. See also Hesiod, *Works and Days*, 770; Diogenes Laertius, *Life of Plato;* and Herodotus (vi. 57), who makes the seventh day of every month as well as the day of each new moon sacred to Apollo in Sparta.

[4] Cox, p. 177, *note*. Cp. Tylor, *Primitive Culture*, i. 302–8.

are so curiously associated with the same month. I am not arguing that the Christian myth must have filtered in the early centuries of our era from India: I have no information as to whether the Hindu ritual includes any allusion to Krishna's martyred brothers. But at the very least the mythological basis of all the stories should be plain enough to help to disabuse all candid minds of the notion that Krishnaism drew its myths from Christianity. Here, again, the myth is embedded in the Hindu story, while it only fortuitously appears in Christian mythology.

§ 3. There is one other possible key to this part of the Krishna myth, which should not be overlooked. It would appear that in old Hebrew usage the *seventh* month was also known as the *first* month, owing to a change which had been made in the reckoning. Wellhausen writes:—

> "The *ecclesiastical* festival of new year in the priestly Code is also autumnal. The *yom teruah* (Lev. xxiii. 24, 25; Num. xxix. 1 seq.) falls on the first new moon of autumn; and it follows from a tradition confirmed by Lev. xxv. 9, 10, that this day was celebrated as new year (ראש השנה). But it is always spoken of as the first of the *seventh* month. That is to say, the civil new year has been separated from the ecclesiastical and been transferred to spring; the ecclesiastical can only be regarded as a relic surviving from an earlier period.... It appears to have first begun to give way under the influence of the Babylonians, who observed the spring era." [*Note.* "In Exod. xii. 2 this change of era is formally commanded by Moses: 'This month (the passover month) shall be the beginning of months unto you; it shall be to you the first of the months of the year.' According to George Smith, the Assyrian year commenced at the vernal equinox; the Assyrian use depends on the Babylonian. (*Assyrian Eponym Canon*, p. 19)."][1]

There seems reason to suppose that a similar change took place earlier in Egypt. "The beginning of the year, or the first of Thoth," says Sir J. Gardner Wilkinson, "was perhaps originally at a very different season."[2] But during the Sothic period, which subsisted from 1322 B.C. onwards, the usage would seem to have been substantially the same as it was in Cæsar's time, when the first of

[1] Wellhausen, *Prolegomena to the History of Israel*, Eng. tr. pp. 108–109.
[2] *Ancient Egyptians*, abridged ed. ii. 254. Cp. *Bible Folk-Lore*, 1884, p. 79, and the *Classical Review*, April, 1900, p. 146.

Thoth, or new year, fell on 29th August.[1] We have to remember, too, that in Krishnaism itself there are different dates for the Birthday Festival, the Våraha Puråna entirely departing from the accepted view. In that Puråna the Krishna Birth-Festival appears to be "only one of a whole series, amounting to twelve, which relate themselves to the ten—or rather eleven !—avatars of Vishnu as Fish, Tortoise, Boar, Man-Lion, Dwarf,[2] Bhårgava (*i.e.*, Parasu Råma), Råma Krishna, Buddha, Kalkin, and Padmanåbha (*sic*)."[3] On which Professor Weber justly observes that the festival calendars of other peoples betray similar discrepancies. A case in point is that of Horus, who had more birthdays than one.[4] But enough, perhaps more than enough, of a mythological problem which on any view is subsidiary to our main inquiry.

XVI. The Descent into Hell.

Finally, a much more important myth-parallel than the last—though I do not even here contend for more than the possibility of direct Christian borrowing—is that between the story of Krishna's "descent into hell" and the Christian dogma and legend of the same purport. In this last case, as in others, Professor Weber would doubtless argue that India borrowed from Alexandria. The known historical fact is that the dogma of the "descent into hell" made its first formal appearance in the Christian Church in the formulary of the church of Aquileia late in the fourth century,[5] having before that time had great popular

[1] Wilkinson, as cited, p. 252.

[2] It is a small matter, but it may be as well to guard the English reader against an error which occurs in the Rev. Mr. Wood's translation of M. Barth's admirable book on *The Religions of India*. On p. 170 there is an allusion to the Avatåra of "the Brahman Nain." This should be "the Brahman Dwarf" or "the Dwarf Bahmun." "Nain" is the French for dwarf, which the translator had misconceived; and "Bahmun," in some versions, was the dwarf's name. It is only fair to say that Mr. Wood has done his work in general very well.

[3] Weber, pp. 260–1.

[4] Plutarch, *Isis and Osiris*, c. 52.

[5] Nicolas, *Le Symbole des Apôtres*, 1867, pp. 221, 364.

vogue, as may be inferred from the non-canonical Gospel of Nicodemus, which gives the legend at much length. Only in the sixth century[1] did it begin to be formally affirmed throughout the Church, Augustine having accepted it without exactly knowing what to make of it.[2] Here clearly was one more assimilation of a Pagan doctrine;[3] for the Pagan vogue of the myth of a God who descended into the underworld was unquestionably very great. Osiris was peculiarly the judge of the dead;[4] and he goes to and comes from the Shades;[5] Hercules went to Hades before he went to heaven, his last labour being to carry away Cerberus, the three-headed dog; and then it was that he took away with him Theseus and Peirithous. Dionysos descends to Hades to bring back his mother Semelė from the dead, and is so represented in art.[6] Hermes, the Psychopompos, is not only the leader of souls to the Shades,[7] but the guide of those who, like Hercules, return:[8] he being the "appointed messenger (angel) to Hades."[9]

[1] *Id.* pp. 217-8.

[2] *Id.* p. 223.

[3] On this compare Dr. Gardiner, *Exploratio Evangelica*, 1899, ch. xxi.

[4] Herodotus, ii. 123. Compare any account of the Egyptian system.

[5] Plutarch, *Isis and Osiris*, c. 19. Professor Tiele, indeed, states that "Osiris, according to the old monuments, comes back to earth no more" (*Hist. of the Egypt. Rel.* Eng. tr. p. 43); but Plutarch's words are explicit as to his return to visit Horus. In any case, the real point is, of course, that the God does not die; and his residence in the other world as Judge of the Dead in the Egyptian system is quite a different thing from residence in the Hades of the Greeks.

[6] Pausanias, ii. 31, 37; Apollodorus, iii. 5, 3; Pindar, *Olymp.* ii. 46–52; *Pyth.* xi. 2; K. O. Müller, *Ancient Art*, pp. 492, 495.

[7] *Odyssey*, xxiv. 1–10.

[8] *Id.* xi. 626.

[9] Hom. Hymn, 572. Long ago, according to the indignant Mosheim (note on Cudworth, Harrison's trans. iii. 298), one Peter a Sarn "dared to compare our blessed Saviour to Mercury, and to advance this as one of the principal arguments by which he attempts to bear out the comparison, that Mercury is said by the poets to discharge the twofold function of dismissing souls to Tartarus and evoking them from thence." Mosheim's own conviction was that "Beyond all doubt a man of that name" [*i.e.* Mercurius, not Hermes] "had lived in ancient Greece and had acquired for himself a high reputation by swiftness of foot, eloquence, and other virtues and vices; and I have scarcely a doubt that he held the office of public runner and messenger to Jupiter, an ancient king of Thessaly." Such was the light of orthodoxy on human history one hundred and fifty years ago. It is noteworthy that Agni, the Child-God, messenger of the Gods, mediator, and "wise one" (the Logos) of the Vedas, was a leader of souls to the Shades (with Pûshan, a form of the sun), just as was Hermes (Barth, p. 23; Tiele, *Outlines*, p. 114). Hermes himself is supposed to be a development of Hermeias, perhaps the Vedic dog

In the myth of Venus and Adonis, the slain Sun-God, or Vegetation-God, passes six months of the year in the upper and six in the under world, as does the Sun itself;[1] Orpheus goes to harp Eurydice out of Hades; and among the Thracian Getæ, who early developed the belief in a happy immortality, the man-God Zamolxis, otherwise Gebeleizis, who had introduced that doctrine, disappeared for three years in a subterraneous habitation he had made for himself, and on his unexpected return the Thracians believed his teaching. So tells the incomparable Herodotus,[2] who "neither disbelieved nor entirely believed" the story in this evidently Evemerized form. But the doctrine is universal, being obviously part of the myth of the death and resurrection of the Sun-God, either in the form of the equinoctial mystery in which he is three days between death and life, or in the general sense that he goes to the lower regions for his winter death before he comes to his strength again. It is bound up with the religion of Mithra, in which, as we gather from later myth-versions, the God originally passed into the "place of torment" at the autumn equinox.[3]

Sârameya, who was once possibly "the child of the dawn," and whose name was given to the two dogs of the Indian Hades (Max Müller, *Nat. Relig.* pp. 453, 483; Tiele, p. 211). This and other identifications of Greek and Indian mythological names have been challenged, along with the whole theory of the derivation of the Aryan race from India. See Mr. Lang's *Myth, Ritual, and Religion*, i. 23, citing Mannhardt; but cp. the remarks above, p. 22. The old race theory may now be said to be exploded (see Dr. Isaac Taylor's work *The Origin of the Aryans*, which gives the results of scholarship on the subject); but the question of the relations between Indian and other myths remains to be worked out on the new lines.

[1] Mr. Frazer (*Golden Bough*, i. 282) will not allow that this myth has any solar significance; asking how the sun in the south can be said to be dead for half or a third of the year. But he is satisfied to say that "vegetation, especially the corn, lies buried in the earth half the year, and reappears above ground the other half," which is surely not accurate. No doubt the Proserpina myth had such a purport; but the explanation given by Macrobius (*Sat.* i. 21) of the Adonis myth is that the sun, passing through the twelve signs of the zodiac, spends six months in the "superior" and six in the "inferior" signs, which last called are the realm of Proserpina, while the others belong to the realm of Venus. For the rest, the fatal boar was held to typify winter, though that part of the myth is certainly not congruous with the rest. But concerning the predominantly solar Apollo it was told that he was present in Delos from the sacred month (January–February) to Hekatombaion (June–July) and absent in Lykia from Metageitnion (July–August) to Lenaion (= Gamelion: December–January). Here is an apparently solar precedent for the Adonisian usage.

[2] B. iv. 93–96.

[3] Wait, as cited, p. 194.

It is even probable that the myth of Apollo's bondage to Admetus (a name of the God of the underworld) originally implied his descent to the infernal regions;[1] a myth rightly connected by Ottfried Müller with the solitary story of Apollo's death. The same conception is fully developed in the Northern myth of the Sun-God Balder, who, wounded in a great battle, in which some of his kindred oppose him, or otherwise by the shaft of magic mistletoe, goes to the underworld of Hel, where he grows strong again by drinking sacred mead, and whence he is to return at the Ragnarök, or Twilight of the Gods, when Gods and men are alike to be regenerated.[2] Common to all races, it appears poetically in our legend of Arthur, the gold-clothed solar child, born as was Hercules of a dissembling father, and like Cyrus secretly reared, who after being stricken in a great battle in the West, in which the British kindred slay each other as do the Yadavas of the Krishna lore, goes to the island valley of Avilion to heal him of his grievous wound, and to return. In pre-Christian Greece, from a very distant period, such a myth was certainly current—witness the visit of the solar Ulysses to the Shades in the Odyssey—and it was doubtless bound up with the doctrine of immortality conveyed in the Mysteries.[3] As the latter belief gained ground, the myth of descent and return, always prominent in the fable of Proserpine, would become more prominent; and in the "Orphic" period this fascinating motive was fully established in religious literature. In one "Orphic" poem, the *Minyas*, which elaborately described the lower regions, we have the exact title-formula of the later Christian doctrine, ἡ ἐς Αΐδου κατάβασις, "the

[1] See K. O. Müller, *Dorians*, Eng. tr. i. 339–340; *Introduction to Mythology*, Eng. tr. pp. 239–246.

[2] See the minute and scholarly examination of this myth in Dr. Rydberg's *Teutonic Mythology*, pp. 249–264, 492, 530–8, 595, 653, 655, etc.; and the account given above, pp. 118–126, of recent discussions. The second part of Dr. Rydberg's great work, which contains a fuller study of the Balder myth, is unfortunately not yet translated into English.

[3] K. O. Müller, *Hist. of Lit. of Anc. Greece*, Lewis's tr. 1847, p. 231. Cp. Professor Nettleship, *Essays in Latin Literature*, pp. 105, 136–140; Dr. Hatch, *Influence of Greek Ideas and Usages upon the Christian Church*, 1890, Lect. ix.; and Mosheim's extracts in note on Cudworth, iii. 296.

Descent into Hades."[1] But there is reason to believe that the "Orphic" system was a result of the influence of Asiatic doctrine;[2] and indeed, of all mythic analogues to the Christian myth of the descent into Hell, I can remember none more exact than the story of the similar descent of Krishna. He too, like Agni and Hermes, is a "conveyer of the souls of the dead," and as such is invoked at funerals by the name of Heri, the cry being "Heri-bol!"[3] Singularly enough, he connects with Hermes further in that he is identified with "Budha," the name given by the Hindus to the planet Mercury;[4] but on the Christian side he exhibits a number of other parallels which do not occur in the Hermes myth as we have it. Take the account of Moor:—

> "It is related in the Padma Purâna, and in the Bhâgavat, that the wife of Kasya, the Guru or spiritual preceptor to Krishna, complained to the incarnate deity that the ocean had swallowed up her children on the coast of Gurjura or Gujerat, and she supplicated Krishna for their restoration. Arriving at the ocean, Varuna, its regent, assured Krishna that not he but the sea-monster Sankesura had stolen the children. Krishna sought and after a violent conflict slew the demon, and tore him from his shell, named Panchajanya, which he bore away in memorial of his victory, and afterwards used in battle by way of a trumpet. Not finding the children in the dominions of Varuna, he descended to the infernal city, Yamapura, and, sounding his tremendous shell, struck such terror into Yama that he ran forth to make his prostrations, and restored the children of Kasya, with whom he returned to their rejoicing mother.
>
> "Sonnerat notices two basso-relievos, placed at the entrance of the choir of Bordeaux Cathedral: one represents the ascension of our Saviour to heaven on an eagle; the other his descent, where he is stopped by Cerberus at the gates of hell, and Pluto is seen at a distance armed with a trident.
>
> "In Hindu pictures Vishnu, who is identified with Krishna, is often seen mounted on the eagle Garuda....And were a Hindu artist to handle the subject of Krishna's descent to hell, which I never saw, he would most likely introduce Cerbura, the infernal three-headed dog[5] of

[1] K. O. Müller, as last cited, p. 233. Cp. Pausanias, ix. 31, as to the poems attributed to Hesiod.

[2] Compare Mr. Lang's *Myth, Ritual, and Religion*, 1st ed., i. 291–3, and Grote and Lobeck as cited by him.

[3] Balfour's *Indian Cyclopædia*, art. NEMI.

[4] Max Müller, art. on "False Analogies" in *Introduction to the Science of Religion*, 1st ed. p. 308.

[5] "Yama, the regent of hell, has two dogs, according to the Purânas, one of them named Cerbura and Sabula, or *varied*; the other Syâma, or *black*;

their legends, and Yama, their Pluto, with the *trisula*, or trident: a further presumption of early intercommunication between the pagans of the eastern and western hemispheres."[1]

For obvious reasons, the whole of this passage is suppressed in the Rev. W. O. Simpson's 1864 edition of Moor's work. But the parallel goes even further than Moor represents; for the descent of Jesus into hell, curiously enough, was anciently figured as involving a forcing open of the jaws of a huge serpent or dragon.[2] Thus, whether or not the Christian adaptation was made directly from Indian communications, it carried on a myth which, appearing in some guise in all faiths, figured in ancient India in a form more closely parallel with the Christian than any other now extant. The appropriation would seem to have been made confusedly, from different sources. Christ in one view went to Hades in his capacity of avenger[3]—an idea evidently derived from the Osirian system, which, however, closely approaches the Indian in the story of Osiris descending to the Shades on the prayer of Queen Garmathone and restoring her son to life.[4] In

the first of whom is also called Trisiras, or *with three heads*, and has the additional epithets of Calmâsha, Chitra, and Cirmira, all signifying *stained* or *spotted*. In Pliny the words Cimmerium and Cerberium seem used as synonymous; but, however that may be, the Cerbura of the Hindus is indubitably the Cerberus of the Greeks" (Wilford, in *Asiatic Researches*, iii. 408). There seems some doubt as to the antiquity of the "three heads" in Indian mythology: M. Barth (p. 23) speaks only of "two dogs" as guarding the road to Yama's realm; but the notion seems sufficiently Hindu. See note above as to the Sârameya, and compare Gubernatis, *Zool. Myth.* i. 49, as to Cerberi. Professor Müller decides (*Nat. Rel.* p. 453) that the name Kerberos is from the Sanskrit *Sarvari*, "the night"—which chimes with Wilford's definitions; but here the assumption of derivation must be discarded. In northern mythology there is sometimes one hell-dog, sometimes more (Rydberg, as cited pp. 276, 280, 362); and there is in the underworld a three-headed *giant* (Rydberg, pp. 295–6; cp. Bergmann, *Le Message de Skirnir*, 1871, pp. 99, 154). In Greek mythology Typhon is hundred-headed (Æschylus, *Prom.* 361; Hesiod. *Theog.* 825; Pindar, *Pyth.* i. 29; viii. 23); while Cerberus is also fifty-headed (*Theog.* 312); and Chimæra, born like Cerberus of the dragon-nymph Echidna, has three heads (*Theog.* 321; Horace, 1 *Carm.* xxvii. 23, 24).

[1] *Hindu Pantheon*, pp. 213–4. Compare the varying account of Maurice (ii. 377), following the Persian version of the Bhâgavat.

[2] See the engraving in Hone's *Ancient Mysteries Described*, and that on p. 385 of Didron's *Christian Iconography*, Bohn trans. In the latter the saved appear *as children*.

[3] Augustine, Letter to Evodius, cited by Nicolas, p. 228, *n*.

[4] Pseudo-Plutarch, *Of the Names of Rivers and Mountains*, *sub tit.* Nile (xvi.).

another view, which prevails in the main legend as given in the Gospel of Nicodemus, the Christ descends to the Shades, where Satan and Death are one, on a mission of liberation, taking all the "saints" of previous history with him to heaven, but further restoring to earth for three days the two sons of the blessed high-priest Simeon, who had taken the babe Jesus in his arms. Now, not only was the Brahman Kasya the Guru of Krishna, but his children were *two sons*.[1] Again, for the more canonical story of Jesus going to preach to "the spirits in prison,"[2] which was adopted by many of the Fathers[3] and became bound up with the Pagan-Christian doctrine of purgatory, there is a parallel in the Purâna myth, in which Krishna, in the earlier part of his search for the lost children, reaches the under-sea or over-sea region of "Cusha-Dweepa," where he "instructed the Cutila-Cesas in the whole system of religious and civil duties."[4] Doubtless we shall be told once more that the Indian legend borrows from the Apocryphal Gospel, without any attempt being made to show how or whence the Christian compiler got his story. To which I once more answer that in the Indian version the myth has all the stamp of the luxuriant and spontaneous Eastern imagination, while in the Christian mythology it is one of the most obviously alien elements, and in the detailed legend it is a confused patchwork. In the Purâna, Krishna's blast on his shell at the gate of the Shades is perfectly Asiatic; as is the Greek legend of Pan's striking terror in the battle of Gods and Titans by his blast on the same instrument;[5] in "Nicodemus" the thunderous voice of Christ at hell-gate may indeed be compared to the shouting

[1] Maurice, as last cited.

[2] 1 Peter iii. 19.

[3] Clemens Alexandrinus, who accepted it, is in that connection, I know not why, stigmatized as heretical. Compare the Abbé Cognat's *Clément d'Alexandrie*, p. 466, and Jortin's *Remarks upon Eccles. Hist.* ed. Trollope, i. 231. These writers speak as if there were no scriptural basis for the doctrine of the preaching in limbo. It is important, however, to remember that Clement drew more systematically on pagan religion than any other Christian before or since. Cp. Mosheim's *Commentaries on Christian Affairs*, Vidal's trans. ii. 115–125, 186–190.

[4] Wilford, in *Asiatic Researches*, iii. 399. Cp. pp. 349, 370.

[5] Eratosthenes, *Catasterismi*, 27; Hyginus, ii. 28.

of Mars in Homer, but is obviously inspired by *some* primitive myth, and may much more easily be conceived as suggested-by than as suggesting the Krishnaite tale. And if we are to choose between (*a*) the proposition that it was through a Christian legend that India became possessed of a myth-motive common to half-a-dozen ancient faiths before Christianity was heard of, and (*b*) the inference that the Christian legend was more or less directly inspired by the Indian legend in something very like the form in which we now have it—there can be little room for hesitation among unprejudiced students. Such an alternative, however, is not really forced on us. There are many reasons for surmising that Hindu and Greek mythology may alike have been influenced by the ancient Asiatic mythology known to us as Akkadian, which on one hand shaped the system of Babylonia, and so wrought on the Greek through Asia Minor, and on the other is likely to have had affinities with the pre-Aryan cults of India. As to this, thus far, we can only speculate, restricting our special reasoning to the problem under notice.

In regard, finally, to some of the myth-parallels dealt with, it might very well be that the Christian appropriation was made through the channel of Buddhism, whence so many elements of the Christian system are now held to have come.[1] That question falls to be considered apart from the present inquiry,[2] but it has an obvious bearing on the problem of the relations between Christianity and Krishnaism. In regard to Buddhism the actual historical *connections* with Christianity are in some measure made out *à posteriori*; and if sometimes points are stretched, the general argument is impressive. But the argument for Buddhist priority over Christianity owes a large part of its strength to the very fact that, as we shall see, the Buddhist legends are to a great extent themselves refashionings of

[1] See Mr. Arthur Lillie's work, *Buddhism in Christendom*, and his smaller work, *The Influence of Buddhism on Christianity*, 1893, for general views and details. As to the general Indian reaction on the West, especially under Asoka, see Professor Mahaffy's *Greek World under Roman Sway*, 1890, ch. ii.

[2] See hereinafter, *The Gospel Myths*, § 10.

Krishna legends. The weakness of the Christian position is that it claims originality for a body of lore which, obviously non-historical, is as obviously myth in a late and literary though unphilosophic stage; and that this claim is made with no attempt at explaining how such myths could so appear without antecedents. For the Buddhist mythology, as M. Senart has shown, many of the antecedents lie in that very Krishnaism which the prejudiced Christist assumes to be borrowed from his own, so to say, virgin-born mythology. For the Krishnaite myths, again, as we have in part seen and shall see further, antecedents lay in part in the simpler Vedic system, and may further be reasonably assumed to have existed in the great mass of popular religion that *must* have flourished outside the sacerdotal system of the Vedas. The scientific grievance against scholars like Professor Weber is that they claim priority on certain points for Christian myth without once asking the question as to whence the Christian myth itself came.

If, then, it be shown that any of the myths before discussed came to Christism through Buddhism, our argument is not impugned, but strengthened, unless (which is unlikely) it be contended that the Buddhist form preceded the Krishnaite. In some cases it is plainly probable that the Buddhist legend was the go-between. Thus the late Christian myth of the synchronous birth of the Christ's cousin, John the Baptist, is reasonably to be traced to the Buddhist myth of the synchronous birth of the Buddha's cousin Ananda,[1] rather than to the Krishnaite motive of Arjuna or Bala Rama; but this course is reasonable chiefly because the Krishnaite system gives an origin for the Buddhist myth. So, too, the motive of the Descent into Hell may have been taken by the Christists from the Buddhist fable of Buddha's expedition to preach "like all former Buddhas" the law to his mother in the upper-world of Tawadeintha, since there not only is the preaching extended to a multitude of others of the unearthly population,

[1] Bigandet's *Life of Gaudama*, Trübner's ed. i. 36.

but there appear also the mythic "two"—in this case "two sons of Nats," who obtain from Buddha "the reward of Thautapan."[1] Certainly Krishna's literal *descent*, and the item of the dragon, are details that come specially close to the Christian myth; and one would have expected the Christian borrower to introduce the Christ's mother if he had before him the Buddha legend as we now have it. But on the other hand he may well have had a different version; or some of the details may have been added to the Christian story at different times, as they must have been in the Buddhist. All I stand upon definitely is that the Krishna stories are almost always the more primitive; and that if they are the basis of the mythology of the Buddhist system—a system which so largely parallels or enters into the Christian—it is exorbitant to presume that Krishnaism would systematically borrow again from Christianity. In the case of the "preaching to the spirits in prison," in particular, the Buddhist myth is on the face of it pre-Buddhistic, yet Indian. Our general argument, then, for the antiquity of Krishnaism as compared with Christianity, holds good through a whole series of myth motives in respect of which Christianity is unquestionably a borrower, and sometimes apparently a borrower from India.

XVII. Spurious and Remote Myth-Parallels.

It remains to consider the minor quasi-coincidences noted by the *Athenæum* critic[2] between the Krishna saga, as given in the Mahâbhârata and elsewhere, and the narrative of the Gospels. These are (1) Krishna's address to the fig-tree; (2) his invitation to his followers to "worship a mountain"; (3) his teaching that those who love the God shall not die; (4) his Transfiguration; (5) his being anointed by a woman; (6) his restoring a widow's dead son to life; (7) his washing of feet; (8) the

[1] *Id.* pp. 219–225.

[2] See above, pp. 150–1.

hostility of the demon-follower who "carries the bag." By this time, perhaps, the reader will be slow to suppose that such items stand for any Hindu adaptation of the Gospels. Raising once more the crucial question, Whence came the Gospel stories? we are rather led to query whether, by way, as before suggested, of Buddhism, the Gospel stories did not come from India.

Some may be put aside as false coincidences. The Krishnaite story of the fig-tree appears to be as edifying as the Christian is otherwise; but there is no sufficient ground even for supposing the latter to be a perversion of the former. So with the "worshipping a mountain," a usage too common in the ancient world to need to be suggested by one race to another within our era. The mystic teaching as to immortality, again, is certainly pre-Christian in Europe and in Egypt, and, in a manner, implicit in Buddhism;[1] and the Transfiguration of Krishna is simply an item in the sun-myth, whence, probably by way of the Neo-Hellenic mysteries, it reached the Christians. The disciplinary washing of feet, again, is one of the established usages of Buddhistic monkery; and there is positively no reason to doubt that it was so before the Christian era. If the Krishna myth borrowed in this instance, it did so at home; but there is every reason to suppose that the religious practice in question was common long before the rise of Buddhism. The miracle of the raising of the widow's son, again, is precedented long before Christianity in the duplicated myth of the Hebrew Elijah and Elisha;[2] and as all Semitic mythology centres round Babylon and points back to the Akkadians, the story presumptively had a common Asiatic currency. In all likelihood it had a solar significance, in common with the myths of the slain Osiris and Adonis and the slain child Dionysos, over the restoration of both of whom there figures a widowed

[1] Cp. Rhys Davids, *Buddhism*, p. 43.

[2] 1 Kings xvii. 21–22; 2 Kings iv. 34–35. In the Elisha story, the mother is not a widow; but the husband is "old"; and it would appear that in the unexpurgated form of the story the solar prophet was the real father.

"mother."[1] On this view the resurrection of the Widow's Son is only an Evemerized form of the resurrection of the Sun-God (himself at his death a widow's son), interpolated in the pseudo-biography of the latter as a miracle wrought by him. To suppose that such an ancient myth-motive was suddenly appreciated for the first time by the miracle-multiplying Hindus only after it had taken Christian form, is a course barred to rational criticism. We are left to the two connected items of the anointing and the hostile attendant with "the bag."

Obviously it matters very little from the rationalist point of view whether or not these items were conveyed to Krishnaism from Christism. But even this scanty measure of debt on the Hindu side is entirely unproved; while there is cause to conclude that on the Christian side we are dealing with just another adaptation. While the story of the raising of the widow's son occurs in only one Gospel,[2] that of the anointing occurs in all; and as it is non-miraculous, the natural tendency is to accept it as historical. Yet a moment's scrutiny shows that its circumstantiality is quite delusive. Both the version of the synoptics and that of John are minutely circumstantial, and each excludes the other, since John tells the story of Mary the sister of Lazarus in her own house, while the synoptics specify another house and a strange woman. John's version might be excluded as false on the face of it, since it represents a pauper household as possessing a peculiarly costly and useless article;[3] but John's myth (itself twice introduced—xi. 2, xii. 3) is only a variant of the other, which in the synoptics is related simply of "a woman," but which later fancy, without Scriptural warrant, attaches to the mythic personality of Mary Magdala, Mary "the

[1] For Lactantius, Isis is the mother of the lost or slain "boy" Osiris (*Divine Institutes*, i. 21); and Dêmêtêr assists at the reanimation of the slain boy Dionysos. Diodorus, iii. 62. So in one view the Goddess who mourned for Adonis was the Earth Mother (Macrobius, *Sat.* i. 21); and in another Adonis is a child (Apollodorus iii. xiv. 4).

[2] Luke, vii. 11.

[3] Evemerism has in private gone so far as the suggestion that Lazarus may have had the ointment given him by "Dives" for his sores! There is really as good ground for believing that as for accepting the story at all.

Nurse" (=Maia=Mylitta), a pseudo-historical variant of Mary the Mother.[1] And on the principle that "a myth is never so graphic and precise in its details as when it is a simple transcript of a ceremony which the author of the myth witnessed with his eyes,"[2] the reasonable presumption is that the anointing was a part of a mystery drama, Christian or pre-Christian, or both;[3] while the ascription of the act to a "Mary" was a normal expedient of the Gospel-makers.

Finally, we have the myth of the discontented Judas carrying "the bag"—a detail unexplained on the Christian side by any dicta as to the source of the money so carried. The story, like that of Lazarus and his household, is found in the fourth Gospel only,[4] and is just another non-miraculous myth added to the primary myth of Judas the Betrayer. On our theory,[5] that "Judas" is simply a fictitious personality made out of "Joudaios," "a Jew," in a Gentile-Christian mystery drama, "the bag" would be to Gentile eyes simply the symbol of the act of betrayal for money, the receptacle for the "thirty pieces of silver," with perhaps a general anti-Semitic suggestion of Jewish usury or avarice. Between this and the remote detail in the Mahabhárata there seems to be only an accidental resemblance. But, if for once there was actually a borrowing by India, the smallness of its significance is in striking contrast with the claim of which it is the last uncancelled item.

XVIII. Explanation of the Krishna Myth.

§ 1. We have seen that the latest claims as to the Christian origin of Krishnaite legends are only repetitions of guesses

[1] See hereinafter, *The Gospel Myths*, § 2.
[2] Frazer, as cited above, p. 182, *note*.
[3] Oil and ointment were alike signified by one Hebrew term (Isa. i. 6. R. V. and marg.); and the usage of anointing was general in the East. Cp. Isa. lvii. 9.
[4] John xii. 6; xiii. 29.
[5] See "The Myth of Judas Iscariot" in the author's *Studies in Religious Fallacy*: and hereinafter, *The Gospel Myths*, § 17.

made by missionaries in the days before comparative mythology, and that there is really no more valid argument behind the later than behind the earlier statements. It is also the fact, however, that sound and satisfying explanations of Krishnaism on the basis of universal mythology were sketched nearly a century ago; though they have been completely ignored by the later adherents of the missionary view, including even the scholarly and open-minded Professor Weber.

Not only was the solar character of Krishna recognized by the first European investigators,[1] being indeed avowed by the Brahmans, but the main elements of the whole myth were soon judiciously analyzed. Take the following early exposition:—

"The Earth is represented as a Cow, the cow of plenty; and, as the planets were considered by the Hindus to be so many habitable Earths, it was natural to describe them by the same hieroglyphic; and as the Sun directs their motions, furnishes them with light, and cherishes them with his genial heat, Krishna, the symbol of the Sun, was portrayed as an herdsman, sportive, amorous, inconstant.[2]

"The twelve signs are represented as twelve beautiful Nymphs: the Sun's apparent passage from one to the other is described as the roving of the inconstant Krishna. This was probably the groundwork of Jayadeva's elegant poem, the Gita Govinda. It is evidently intended by the circular dance exhibited in the Rasijatra. On a moveable circle, twelve Krishnas are placed alternately with twelve Gopis, hand-in-hand, forming a circle; the God is thus multiplied to attach him to each respectively, to denote the Sun's passage through all the signs, and by the rotary

[1] The monk Paulinus (quoted by Kleuker, *Abhandlungen*, as before cited, ii. 236) was satisfied that Krishna "originally (*primigenie*) signified the sun, and indeed the sun in eclipse" [here giving a meaning for the "black"], and that "the fable was accordingly to be referred to astronomy." He had probably met with the myth of Krishna hiding himself in the moon (Jones, *Asiatic Researches*, iii. 290)—a notion found also in the Osiris myth (*I. and O.*, c. 43). He further saw that the mythic wars meant that "the sun in the heavens fought with planets, stars, and clouds," and that the quasi-historic (it is not clear if he thought there was ever a real) Krishna was as it were a "terrestrial sun or" [here anticipating Lassen] "Hercules, as Arrian has it."

[2] It should be added that, as later inquirers have noted, the clouds are cows in the Vedas, as in the myth of Hermes, and that this idea also enters largely into the Krishnaite symbolism.

motion of the machine the revolution of the year is pointed out.

"Krishna obtains a victory on the banks of the Yamuna over the great serpent Caliya Nâga, which had poisoned the air, and destroyed the herds in that region. This allegory may be explained upon the same principle as the exposition given of the destruction of the serpent Python by the arrows of Apollo. It is the Sun, which, by the powerful action of its beams, purifies the air and disperses the noxious vapours of the atmosphere. Both in the Padma and Garuda [Purânas] we find the serpent Caliya, whom Krishna slew in his childhood, amongst the deities 'worshipped on this day, as the Pythian snake, according to Clemens, was adored with Apollo at Delphi.' Perhaps this adventure of Krishna with the Caliya Nâga may be traced on our sphere, for we find there Serpentarius on the banks of the heavenly Yamunâ, the milky way, contending as it were with an enormous serpent, which he grasps with both his hands.

"The identity of Apollo Nomios and Krishna is obvious; both are inventors of the flute; and Krishna is disappointed by Tulasi as Apollo was deluded by Daphne; each nymph being changed to a tree; hence the *tulasi* is sacred to Krishna, as the *laurus* was to Apollo.

"The story of Nâreda visiting the numerous chambers of Krishna's seraglio and finding Krishna everywhere, appears to allude to the universality of the Sun's appearance at the time of the Equinoxes, there being then no part of the earth where he is not visible in the course of the twenty-four hours. The Demons sent to destroy Krishna are perhaps no more than the monsters of the sky, which allegorically may be said to attempt in vain to obstruct his progress through the Heavens. Many of the playful adventures of Krishna's childhood are possibly mere poetical embellishments to complete the picture."[1]

Here is a rational, a scientific explanation of some of the main outlines of the Krishna myth, which holds good independently of the author's further theory that the origin of Krishnaism lay in the separation of the sect of Vaishnavas from the Saivas, and that the legends may

[1] Patterson, in *Asiatic Researches*, viii. (1808), pp. 64–5. As to the astronomic significance of the dance in Greece, see Donaldson, *Theatre of the Greeks*, 7th ed. p. 24.

contain an element of allegory on the persecution of the new sect. The former part of that theory was put forward also by Colebrooke, who held that "the worship of Râma and of Krishna by the Vaishnavas, and that of Mahâdêva and Bhavâni by the Saivas and Sactas, have been introduced since the persecution of the Bauddhas and Jainas."[1] But the same sound scholar declares that he supposes both Ráma and Krishna to have been "known characters in ancient fabulous history," and conjectures "that on the same basis new fables have been constructed, elevating those personages to the rank of Gods."[2] Hence he opposed the surmise that early references to Krishna in the sacred books were interpolations. There can be little doubt, I think, that Colebrooke would have admitted the "new fables" to be in many cases new only in their application, and to be really repetitions of the ancient myths of the race. This proposition, inductively proved, renders impregnable the earlier deductive position.

Every solar hero or deity necessarily repeats certain features in the myths of his predecessors; and this the more surely because on the one hand the popular fancy is so far from being clearly conscious of the identities between God and God, or hero and hero,[3] and because on the other the priest either sees in these, like the Jews, a system of types, or, like the Pagans, sees no harm in mystic correspondences. It is thus that so many dynasties of Gods have been built out of the same fabulous material. Now, though Krishna, figuring as he does as a demon in the Vedas, was presumably an outsiders' God even in the Vedic period, with what qualities we know not, we can find in the Vedas precedent for all his main features. Agni, the Fire-God, always tending to be identified with

[1] *Asiatic Researches*, viii. 474.

[2] *Id.* ix. 293.

[3] "The story of Perseus is essentially the same as the story of his more illustrious descendant [Herakles]; and the profound unconsciousness of the Argives that the two narratives are in their groundwork identical is a singular illustration of the extent to which men can have all their critical faculties lulled to sleep by mere differences of names or of local colouring in legends which are only modifications of a single myth" (Cox, *Mythol. of Aryan Nations*, p. 303).

the Sun, is the prototype of the modern Krishna, not only in respect of being a marvellous child, but of being a lover of maidens: "Agni, as Yama, is all that is born; as Yama, all that will be born: he is the lover of maidens, the husband of wives."[1] That, indeed, is an extremely natural characteristic, whether mystic or anthropomorphic, of all popular deities in primitive times; and M. Senart notes[2] that in a Vedic description of a storm, Soma, the personified God of the libation or eucharist, "plays among the Apas like a man among beautiful young girls." But "it is above all to the atmospheric Agni that we must trace voluptuous legends like those which have received such an important place in the Krishnaite myth";[3] and for the multiplications of Krishna also we find the prototype in the child Agni, who, at his birth, "enters into all houses and disdains no man."[4] And this view is substantially adopted by the leading English mythologists. On the relations of Krishna with the Gopis Sir George Cox writes:—

> "This myth is in strict accordance with the old Vedic phrase addressed to the Sun as the horse: 'After thee is the chariot; after thee, Arvan, the man; after thee the cows; after thee the host of the girls.' Thus, like Agni, Indra, and Yama, he is the husband of the wives, an expression which, in Professor Max Müller's opinion, was probably 'meant originally for the evening sun as surrounded by the splendours of the gloaming, as it were by a more serene repetition of the dawn. The Dawn herself is likewise called the wife; but the expression "husband of the wives" is in another passage clearly applied to the sinking sun, *R. V.* ix. 86, 32: "The husband of the wives approaches the end."' "[5]

The same writer, who makes an independent and able analysis of the Krishna myth, sums up as follows on the general question:—

> "If it be urged that the attribution to Krishna of qualities or powers belonging to other deities is a mere device by which his devotees sought to supersede the more ancient gods, the answer must be that nothing is done in his case which has not been done in the case of almost every other member of the great company of the gods, and that the systematic

[1] Wilson's tr. of Rig Veda Sanhita, i. 181.
[2] *Essai*, p. 321.
[3] *Id.* p. 322.
[4] *Id.* p. 291, citing R. V. x. 91, 2, from Muir's *Original Sanskrit Texts*, v. 204.
[5] Cox, as cited, p. 369, *n*.

adoption of the method is itself conclusive proof of the looseness and flexibility of the materials of which the cumbrous mythology of the Hindu epic poems is composed."[1] And again: "It is true, of course, that these myths have been crystallized round the name of Krishna in ages subsequent to the period during which the earliest Vedic literature came into existence; but the myths themselves are found in this older literature associated with other gods, and not always only in germ. Krishna as slaying the dragon is simply Indra smiting Vritra or Ahi, or Phoibos destroying the Python. There is no more room for inferring foreign influence in the growth of these myths than, as Bunsen rightly insists, there is room for tracing Christian influence in the earlier epical literature of the Teutonic tribes."[2]

The fluidity of the whole of the myth material under notice is yet further illustrated in the following sketch of Krishna's many metamorphoses:—

"He is....also identified with Hari or the dwarf Vishnu, a myth which carries us to that of the child Hermes as well as to the story of the limping Hephaistos. As the son of Nanda, the bull, he is Govinda, a name which gave rise in times later than those of the Mahâbhârata to the stories of his life with the cowherds and his dalliance with their wives; but in the Mahâbhârata he is already the protector of cattle, and like Herakles slays the bull which ravaged the herds [Muir, *Sanskrit Texts*, iv. 206]. His name Krishna, again, is connected with another parentage which makes him the progeny of the black hair of Hari, the dwarf Vishnu [*Ib.* 331]. But he is also Hari himself, and Hari is Narayana, 'the God who transcends all, the minutest of the minute, the vastest of the vast, the greatest of the great.' In short, the interchange or contradiction is undisguised, for he is 'the soul of all, the omniscient, the all, the all-knowing, the producer of all, the God whom the Goddess Devakî bore to Vishnu.'[3]

"The character of Rudra, said to be sprung from Krishna, is not more definite. As so produced, he is Time, and is declared by his father to be the offspring of his anger. But in the character of Mahâdeva, Rudra is worshipped by Krishna, and the necessary explanation is that in so adoring him Krishna was only worshipping himself. Rudra, however, is also Narayana, and Siva the destroyer....It is the same with Râma, who is sometimes produced from the half of Vishnu's virile power, and sometimes addressed by Brahma as 'the source of being and the cause of destruction, Upendra and Mahendra, the younger and the elder Indra.'[4] ....This cumbrous mysticism leads us further and further from the simpler conceptions of the oldest mythology, in which Rudra is scarcely more than an epithet, applied sometimes to Agni, sometimes to Mitra,

[1] *Id.* p. 365. [2] *Id.* p. 371 *n.*

[3] *Sic* in Cox; but Muir, who is cited, has "to Vasudeva," p. 224.

[4] Muir, iv. 146, 250. So cited in Cox; but 250 should apparently be 150, where the passage runs: "Thou art the source of being and cause of destruction, Upendra (the younger Indra), and Madhusûdana. Thou art Mahendra (the older Indra)...."

Varuna, the Asvins, or the Maruts....It was in accordance with the general course of Hindu mythology that the greatness of Rudra, who is sometimes regarded as self-existent, should be obscured by that of his children."[1]

Further illustration could be given, if need were, of this interfluence of myths in the case of the three Râmas, Bala Râma, Parasu[2] Râma, and Râma Chandra, who pass for three different incarnations of Vishnu, but who were early surmised by students to be "three representatives of one person, or three different ways of relating the same history,"[3] and whom M. Senart declares to be indeed mythologically one:—

"In effect, there is really only one Râma. The contrary opinion of Lassen (*Ind. Alt.* ii. 2, 503) rests on an Evemerism which will find, I think, few adherents. But he appears to us under a triple form....the popular Râma, brother of Krishna; the Brahmanic Râma, who destroys the Kshatriyas; the Kshatriya Râma, King's son and happy conqueror. The axe of the second, like the ploughshare of the first, represents the same weapon of thunder, which the hero wields against the demons."[4]

Now, Bala Râma, whom Sir William Jones[5] identified with the Greek and "Indian" Dionysos, but whom we have seen[6] to be probably the Hercules of Megasthenes, "appears to be an ancient agricultural deity that presided over the tillage of the soil and the harvest. He is armed with a ploughshare,[7] whence his surname *Halabhrit*, 'the plough-bearer'; and his distinctive characteristic is an ungovernable passion for bacchanalian revels, inebriation, and sensual love."[8] Like each of his duplicates, he was doubtless contingently a Sun-God (Râma Chandra, who

[1] Cox, pp. 365–7.

[2] According to Moor, "Parasu" means a sword; according to Balfour's *Ind. Cycl.* a club; according to Tiele (before cited), an axe! Here, too, is trinity.

[3] Moor, *Hindu Pantheon*, p. 191.

[4] *Essai*, p. 234, *n.*

[5] *Asiatic Researches*, ii. 132.

[6] Above, pp. 162–3.

[7] See Moor, as cited above, p. 162.

[8] Barth, p. 173. M. Senart writes (p. 325, *n.*): "As to his name of Bala, the analogy of Krishna would suggest that it also had originally a more specially demonic significance, and that the form Bala is only an alteration of Vala, a Vedic personage connected by name and function with Vritra. This is indeed certain as regards the epic Bala, enemy of Indra." In the same note M. Senart draws a connection between Râma and the Persian Râma-gastra, who is an atmospheric genie watching the "pastures" of Mithra, and who figures both as lightning and sun.

represents the moon,[1] being also solar);[2] and it might conceivably have been his fortune to become the supremely popular deity instead of Krishna. He too has a Birth Festival, which Professor Weber supposes to be based on that of Krishna, which it very closely resembles; he too figures then as the Child-God; and he too is associated with the stable-myth in that Jamadagni, the father of Parasu Ráma, was entrusted by Indra with the charge of the boon-granting cow, Kamadenu.[3] His old standing was the cause of his being made Krishna's twin; and at present he ranks next him in popularity.[4] It is even conceivable that he is for historic India the original "Child born in a Stable"; and as a God of Vegetation he may have been carried in the corn-basket by way of an incantation to make the fields fruitful. On the other hand, he has assimilated clearly solar attributes. "Like Krishna, Ráma is a hero, an exterminator of monsters, a victorious warrior. But, idealized by the poetry of a more fastidious age, and one less affected by the myth [*i.e.*, in the Rámáyana], he is at the same time, what we cannot maintain in regard to the enigmatic son of Devaki, the finished type of submission to duty, nobility of moral character, and of chivalric generosity."[5] Krishna in turn, however, has his transfiguration in the Bhagavat Gita. In fine, ancient India, then as now a manifold world of differing peoples and faiths, had a crowd of Sun-Gods apart from those of the priest-made Vedas, but based like those on immemorial myth; and of these Krishna, ancient as the others were ancient, is the one who, by dint of literary and sectarian manipulation, has best been able to "survive."

§ 2. It may be, however, that while the antiquity of the main material of Krishnaism is admitted, it will still be argued, as by Professor Weber, that only in comparatively late times was Krishna a deity at all, and that this alleged lateness of creation permitted of, and partly depended on, the adoption of some of the Christian legends early in our

[1] Barth, p. 177.
[2] See above, p. 143, citing Tiele, and p. 163, citing Moor.
[3] Moor, p. 190. [4] Moor, p. 192. [5] Barth, p. 176.

era. But it will be necessary, I think, only to state Professor Weber's position in contrast with the argument of M. Senart to make clear the soundness of the latter and the untenableness of the former.

Professor Weber seeks to trace the rise of Krishnaism by way of the chronological order of the references in the documents, taking the Vedic allusions as representing the beginnings of the cult, the passage in the Khandogya Upanishad as pointing to a quasi-historic personage, the legends in the Mahâbhârata as a development of his story, and so on.[1] M. Senart, in answer, points first to the admitted fact that the Kansa legend was already old for Patanjali, and contends that the presence in that text of the name of Govinda sufficiently shows that the myth of the sojourn among the shepherds, which was the inseparable preparation for the slaying of the tyrant, was already ancient and popular, and that it was as the companion of shepherds and lover of the Gopis, not as the hero of the epic, that Krishna was first deified.[2] It may be added that the antiquity of the similar myth in connection with Cyrus is a further ground for the same conclusion, as has been shown above. M. Senart then goes on to cite, what is perhaps less important, the testimony of Alexander Polyhistor [fl. 85 B.C.] that in his day the Brahmans worshipped Hercules and Pan. There is, M. Senart argues, no other Hindu deity who could so well suit the latter title as Krishna—a contention which seems to me inconclusive in the circumstances. Might not Alexander's Pan be Siva, whom M. Barth,[3] following Lassen, identifies with the Dionysos of Megasthenes? Certainly the latter is the more plausible conjecture; but is not Dionysos fully as close a parallel to Krishna as Pan would be? In any case, though M. Senart connects his conjecture, as to Krishna being Alexander's Pan, with the rest of his argument, that works itself out independently, and will stand very well on its own merits :—

"This testimony is the more important in that it leads

[1] Treatise cited, p. 316. [2] *Essai*, p. 339. [3] As cited, p. 163.

us to carry further back the date of the legends of this order. M. Lassen, in spite of his opinions on the antiquity of the doctrine of Avataras and the cult of Krishna, seems on this point to go even further than M. Weber. In support of that opinion there is little weight in the negative argument from the silence of the ancient works which have come down to us. What idea should we have had of the date and importance of Buddhism, if we were shut up to the testimony of Brahmanic literature? We can certainly distinguish in Krishna a triple personage; it does not follow, however, that these mean simply three successive aspects of the same type, until it be determined that logically they derive and develop one from the other. Now, the fact is quite the contrary; an abyss separates each one of these stages from the next, if we take them in the supposed order. How could a sacred poet, the obscure disciple of a certain Ghora, suddenly have become the national hero of an important Indian people, the bellicose performer of so many exploits, not merely marvellous, but clearly mythological? And how could this warrior, raised so high, from the epic period, in the admiration and even in the worship of Indians, be subsequently lowered to the position of the adopted child of a shepherd, the companion of shepherds, and mixed up in dubious adventures, which do not fail at times to disquiet and embarrass his devotees? It is clear that the first step at least of such an evolution could be made only under powerful sacerdotal pressure: now there exists in this connection no sign of such a thing in the literature we possess; the cult of Krishna is not a Brahmanic but a popular cult. In fine, there is no doubt that we must reverse the statement. Krishna mnst have been at first the object of a secondary cult, connected especially, as it remained in the sequel, with the legends of his birth, of his infancy, and of his youth. Localized at first among the Sûrasenas and at Mathura, this cult would have sufficed to introduce into the epic legend of the Kshatriyas, fixed in that epoch under Brahmanic influence, the bellicose character in which we know him. On its part, the Brahmanic school, desirous to appropriate him, would put him in the list of its singers and masters, until the ever more powerful spread of his popularity forced it to embrace him, under the title of Avatara of Vishnu, in its new theory and in its modern systems. It must not be forgotten that the organization of castes creates, alongside of the chronological succession, a superposition not only of social classes but of traditions and ideas which could live long side by side in a profound isolation. Thus considered, the history of the cult of Krishna resolves itself into two periods, which I would not, however, represent as necessarily and strictly successive. Krishna was at first a quite popular deity, whose worship, more or less narrowly localized, spread little by little; till at length, identified with Vishnu and admitted to the number of his incarnations, he was *ipso facto* recognized by the superior caste.[1]

"It is possible, indeed, that Christian influences may have developed among the Indians in his connection the monotheistic idea and the doctrine of faith......However that may be, what interests us chiefly at present is the age not so much of his cult, still less of a certain form of his cult, but of the legend of the hero, and more precisely of that part of his legend which embraces his infancy and his youth. Now, this narrative has its roots in the images of a perfectly authentic naturalism; it cannot be isolated from the various kindred mythological series; and if we only apply, without rashness and without prejudice, the customary methods of mythological analysis, it leads us obviously to more ancient conceptions; and the homogeneity which is exhibited by the whole demonstrates the normal and consequent development of all the parts. Several precise testimonies, independent of any argument borrowed from resemblances, attest the existence of essential elements of the legend at an epoch when there can be no question of those influences which have been conjectured; and these influences finally rest on a very limited number of very inconclusive facts, which, besides, only touch entirely secondary details."

This argument has been criticised by Professor Weber in a review of M. Senart's essay, in which, while differing from his conclusions, he speaks in high terms of his French

[1] A passage in the Mahâbhârata shows this evolution clearly enough:—"And thou Krishna, of the Yâdava race, *having become the son of Aditi*, and being called Vishnu, the younger brother of Indra, the all-pervading, becoming a child, O vexer of thy foes, hadst by thy energy traversed the sky, the atmosphere, and the earth, in three strides. Having attained to the sky and the ether, and occupied the abode of the Adityas, thou, O soul of all beings, hast overpassed the sun by thine own force. In these thousands of thy manifestations, O all-pervading Krishna, thou hast slain hundreds of Asuras who delighted in iniquity." Muir, *Original Sanskrit Texts*, iv. 118.

opponent's scholarship and ability. With his invariable candour, the Professor, remarking that the theory of Krishna's herdsmanship being derived from the cloud-cows of the Vedas is new to him,[1] admits that in itself it is very plausible. But he goes on :—

> "Only in the *latest* texts do we find this Gopi idyl: the older records *know nothing of it*, but recognize Krishna only as assiduous pupil or brave hero. Recently, indeed, passages have been made known from the Mahâbhâshya which set forth Krishna's relation to Kansa; even further, from Panini, his being evidently worshipped as Vasudeva: and the existence of his epithet *Kesava*;....but, on the one hand, the herdsman idyl is there awanting:....and on the other hand, in view of the doubts which Burnell and Böhtlingk have expressed in connection with my inquiry, as to the value of the evidence for Patanjali's date given by the words and citations in the Mahâbhâshya, Senart's assumption that that work dates 'from before the Christian era' is very questionable. The testimony of Alexander Polyhistor, that the Brahmans worshipped a Hercules and a Pan, is again too vague to permit of its being founded on in this matter."[2]

The force of the last objection I have admitted; and as to the date of Patanjali, of which Professor Weber had seemed formerly[3] to take Professor Bhandarkar's view (shared by both Senart and Barth), it can only be said that if the "doubts" are ever strengthened, that part of our evidences will have to be reconsidered; though Professor Weber and the doubters will also have to face and explain the fact, which they constantly overlook, of the ancient currency of the Cyrus myth on the Iranian side. In any case Patanjali would have to be dated *very* late to countervail the implied antiquity of the phrases he quotes. But as regards the Professor's objection that the Gopi idyl is not mentioned in the oldest documentary references to Krishna, the reader will at once see that it is no answer to M. Senart, whose argument is that the Gopi idyl is part of an immemorial popular myth, originally current outside the Brahmanic sphere. Nor does the Professor in any way meet M. Senart's refutation of his own development theory, or answer the questions as to how (1) the deity could be

[1] Though, as we have seen, the stealing and herding of cows has such a significance in Greek myths.
[2] *Indische Streifen*, iii. 429. [3] See above, pp. 155–6.

developed out of the student of the Upanishad, and how (2) the warrior hero of the epic could be lowered from that status to the position of the adopted son of a shepherd and companion of shepherds, given to dubious adventures, unless there were an old myth to that effect?[1] These questions, I venture to say, are unanswerable. We are left to the irresistible conclusion that the myths of Krishna's birth and youth are not only pre-Christian but pre-historic.

§ 3. But yet one more reinforcement of the strongest kind is given to the whole argument by M. Senart's demonstration[2] of the derivation of a large part of the Buddha myth from that of Krishna, or from pre-Krishnaite sources. It is needless here to give at length the details, which include such items as the breaking of Siva's bow by Kama, the God of Love, of Kansa's by Krishna, and of various bows by Siddartha (Buddha);[3] the exploit against the elephant, similarly common to the three personages;[4] the parallel between the births of Buddha and Krishna;[5] their early life of pleasure,[6] and their descent from "enemies of the Gods."[7] The prodigy of the divine infant speaking immediately after birth occurs in the Buddha myth as in those of Krishna, Hermes, Apollo, and Jesus;[8] and where Krishna, as Sun-God, takes three miraculous strides, the infant Buddha takes seven marvellous steps.[9] There is, in fine, a "close relationship" between the Buddhist and the Krishnaite legends,[10] as we have partly seen above.

> "In nearly all the variations of this legendary theme one point remains fixed and constant: it is among shepherds that the hero is exiled; and it is impossible to separate from the series either the *vraja* or the herdsmen and herdswomen who surround the youth of Krishna. And this trait is found in the story of Sakya."[11]

[1] There are in the Mahâbhârata allusions which show the herdsman characteristics to have been associated with the hero. See Senart, p. 340, *n.*

[2] *Essai*, p. 297 ff. [3] *Id.* p. 302. [4] *Id.* p. 303.

[5] *Id.* p. 312. [6] *Id.* p. 305. [7] *Id.* p. 315.

[8] See above, p. 190.

[9] Bigandet, *Life of Gaudama*, i. 37; and Beal's trans. of the *Fo-Sho-Hing-Tsan-King*, i. 1 (S. B. E. xix. 3–4).

[10] Senart, *Essai*, p. 326.

[11] *Id.* p. 319.

And while it is impossible to say with certainty how and whence the Buddhist adaptations were made, it is frequently found here, as in the Christian parallels, that the Krishnaite form of a given story is by far the more natural. The exploit against the elephant evidently "belonged to the Krishnaite legend before being introduced into the life of Sakya [Buddha]: it is infinitely better motived in the former than in the latter." Again, the genealogy of Buddha is in large part a variant on that of Râma. If, then, the theory of imitation from Christian legends were sound, we should have to hold either (*a*) that Buddhism, which ostensibly influenced Christianity, did not even borrow from Christianity direct, but did it at second-hand through Krishnaism, or (*b*) that Krishnaism borrowed from Buddhism legends which the Buddhists had already assimilated from the Christians. We have now seen reason enough to decide that such theories are untenable. It remains to investigate the theory of doctrinal as distinct from mythical assimilations.

XIX.—Krishnaite and Christist Doctrine.

§ 1. Professor Weber has more than once advanced the opinion that, in addition to the mythical narratives which we have discussed in the foregoing sections, Krishnaism borrowed from Christianity certain of its leading doctrines, in particular its insistence on the need and value of "faith," and its monotheistic view of its deity. One of his earlier statements of this opinion has been already cited,[1] and he has maintained it to the last. In the "Birth Festival" treatise, after enumerating the alleged myth-imitations, he continues:

> "Their Christian origin is as little to be doubted as the conclusion [*Ind. Studien*, i. 423] that 'in general the later exclusively monotheistic tendency of the Indian sects who worship a particular personal God, pray for his favour, and trust in him (*bhakti* and *sraddhâ*), was influenced by the acquaintance made by the Indians with the corresponding teaching

[1] Above, p. 164.

of Christianity'; or, in the words of Wilson (quoted in Mrs. Speir's *Life in Ancient India*, p. 434: cp. my *Abh. über die Râmâtâp. Up.* pp. 277, 360), 'that the remodelling of the ancient Hindu systems into popular forms, and in particular the vital importance of faith, were directly [*sic*] influenced by the diffusion of the Christian religion.'"[1]

Here, it will be seen, Professor Weber quotes Wilson at secondhand from Mrs. Speir, who cited an Indian magazine. She made the blunder of writing "directly" for "indirectly"; but she states fairly enough that Wilson only "hints" his opinion; and this the Professor overlooks, though doubtless he would have given Wilson's passage fully if he had been able to lay his hands on it. Its effect is so different when quoted in full that I think it well so to transcribe it:—

"It is impossible to avoid noticing in the double doctrine of the Gitâ an analogy to the double doctrine of the early Christian Church; and the same question as to the merits of contemplative and practical religion engendered many differences of opinion and observance in the first ages of Christianity. These discussions, it is true, grew out of the admixture of the Platonic philosophical notions with the lessons of Christianity, *and had long pervaded the East before the commencement of our era;* it would not follow, therefore, that the divisions of the Christian Church originated the doctrine of the Hindus, and there is *no reason to doubt that in all essential respects the Hindu schools are of a much earlier date;* at the same time, it is *not at all unlikely* that the speculations of those schools were reagitated and remodified in the general stimulus which Christianity *seems* to have given to metaphysical inquiry; and it is *not impossible* that the attempts to model the ancient systems into a popular form, by engrafting on them in particular the vital importance of faith, were *indirectly* influenced by the diffusion of the Christian religion. *It is highly desirable that this subject should be further investigated.*"[2]

This, it will be seen, is a very different deliverance from Weber's, and also from what Wilson is made to say in the incomplete and inaccurate quotation of his words.

[1] Treatise cited, p. 339.

[2] H. H. Wilson, in review of Schlegel's trans. of the Bhagavat Gitâ, *Orient. Quart. Rev.* Calcutta, vol. iii.; reprinted in Works, vol. v. pp. 156–7.

Professor Weber, without bringing forward any important new facts, makes a positive assertion where Wilson expressed himself very cautiously and doubtfully, and does not meet (having apparently not seen) Wilson's propositions as to the antiquity in India of the general pantheistic doctrine which prevailed in the East before Christianity.[1]

Before we come to a decision on the point at issue, it may be well to see what it was exactly that Wilson understood by the doctrine of faith, which he thought *might possibly* be *indirectly* influenced by Christianity, and which Weber holds to be without doubt entirely derived thence. In his Oxford lectures Wilson declares that in the Purânas the doctrine of the sufficiency of faith is

> "carried to the very utmost abuse of which it is susceptible. Entire dependency on Krishna, or any other favourite deity, not only obviates the necessity of virtue, but it sanctifies vice. Conduct is wholly immaterial. It matters not how atrocious a sinner a man may be, if he paints his face, his breast, his arms, with certain sectarial marks, or, which is better, if he brands his skin permanently with them with a hot iron stamp; if he is constantly chanting hymns in honour of Vishnu; or, what is equally efficacious, if he spends hours in the simple reiteration of his name or names; if he die with the word Hari or Râma or Krishna on his lips, and the thought of him in his mind, he may have lived a monster of iniquity, he is certain of heaven."[2]

It cannot be denied that all this bears a very close resemblance to the practical applications of the Christian

[1] Professor Weber's misunderstanding as to Wilson's view on *bhakti* seems to have become a fixed idea. In a later letter to Dr. John Muir on the subject, he speaks yet again of "Wilson's theory that the *bhakti* of the later Hindu sects is essentially a Christian doctrine." Wilson, as we have seen, had no such opinion. Dr. Muir might well write: "I am not aware in which, if in any, of his writings Professor Wilson may have expressed the opinion that the Indian tenet of *bhakti* is essentially Christian. I find no express statement to this effect in his *Sketch of the Religious Sects of the Hindus*, though he there says that 'the doctrine of the efficacy of *bhakti* seems to have been an important innovation upon the primitive system of the Hindu religion'" (Art. in *Indian Antiquary*, March, 1875, vol. iv. p. 79).

[2] *Two Lectures on the Religious Practices....of the Hindus*, Oxford, 1840, p. 31, = Works, ii. 75. See also Works, i. 368. It is well to keep in mind that while Krishnaism, like Christism, can be turned to the account of lawlessness, it has similarly been turned to higher ends. Thus the Brahman reformer Chaitanya, who flourished in the sixteenth century, and whose movement still flourishes in Bengal, made "discipline of the intellect and a surrender of all to Krishna" one of his main positions. Max Müller, *Natural Religion*, p. 100.

doctrine of faith in European history, and that that is of all Christian doctrines the one which may with most plausibility be held to have originated, in Europe, with the New Testament. Nor is it incumbent on rationalists to object that such a derivation brings small credit to Christianity. An impartial inquiry, however, reveals that the doctrine of salvation by faith is already fully laid down in the Bhagavat Gità; and the Christian hypothesis involves the conclusion that that famous document is a patchwork of Christian teaching. Now, there are decisive reasons for rejecting such a view.

§ 2. Its most confident and systematic expositor is Dr. F. Lorinser, a German translator of the Gita, whose position is that "the author [of the Gità] knew the New Testament writings, which, so far as he thought fit, he used, and of which he pieced into his work many passages (if not textually, then following the sense, and adapting it to his Indian fashion of composition), though these facts have hitherto not been observed or pointed out by anyone."[1] This startling proposition, which is nominally supported by citation of the general opinions of Professor Weber, rests deductively on early Christian statements as to the introduction of Christianity into "India," and inductively on a number of parallels between the New Testament and the Gità. The statements in question are those of Eusebius as to the mission of Pantænus, and of Chrysostom as to an "Indian" translation of the fourth Gospel, and possibly of the Joannine epistles. The narrative of Eusebius is as follows:—

> "The *tradition* is, that this philosopher was then in great eminence. .... He is said to have displayed such ardour and so zealous a disposition respecting the divine word, that he was constituted a *herald* of the Gospel to the nations of the East, and advanced even as far as India. There were *even there* yet many evangelists of the word, who were ardently striving to employ their inspired zeal after the apostolic example, to increase and build up the divine word. *Of these Pantænus is said to have been one, and to have come as far as the Indies.* And the report is

[1] *Die Bhagavad-Gita, übersetzt und erläutert* von Dr. F. Lorinser, Breslau, 1869, p. 272. (The argumentative appendix has been translated in part in the *Indian Antiquary*, October, 1873, vol. i. pp. 283–296.)

that he there found his own arrival anticipated by some who were acquainted with the Gospel of Matthew, to whom Bartholomew, one of the apostles, had preached, and had left them the Gospel of Matthew in the Hebrew, which was also preserved until this time. Pantænus, after many praiseworthy deeds, was finally at the head of the Alexandrian school."[1]

The statement of Chrysostom, again, is that "the Syrians, and the Egyptians, and the Indians, and the Persians, and the Ethiopians, and innumerable (μυρία) other peoples, were taught, though barbarians, to be philosophers, by his [John's] teachings translated into their own language."[2]

On this latter record Dr. Lorinser comments :—

"It may be argued that the significance of this testimony is weakened by the addition 'and innumerable other peoples.' This apprehension, however, disappears when we consider that all the translations here specified by name, with the single exception of the *Indian*, are both heard of otherwise and still in existence. In any case, Chrysostom would not here have explicitly named the Indians if he had not had positive knowledge of an existing translation in their language. Chrysostom died in the year 407 A.C. The Indian translation of which he had knowledge must have existed *at least* a hundred years earlier, for the knowledge of it to reach him in those days. Apparently, however, Pantænus, the teacher of Clemens Alexandrinus, of whom we know that he had himself been in India, had already brought this knowledge to the West. The origin of this translation may thus possibly go back to the first or second century after Christ."[3]

The most surprising point about this argument is that Dr. Lorinser seems entirely unaware that the names "India" and "Indians" were normally applied by ancient writers to countries and peoples other than India proper. Yet not only is this general fact notorious,[4] but it has

[1] *Eccles. Hist.* v. 10 (Bohn trans.).

[2] Comm. in S. Joann. Hom. ii. (i.) 2, in Cap. i. c. 1. (Migne, *Ser. Gr.* lix. 32).

[3] Work cited, pp. 268–9.

[4] "After the time of Herodotus the name India was applied to all lands in the south-western world, to east Persia and south Arabia, to Ethiopia, Egypt, and Libya; in short, to all dark-skinned peoples, who in Homer's time, as Ethiopians, were allotted the whole horizon (*Lichtrand*) of the South. Virgil and others signify by India just the East; but most commonly it stands for southern Arabia and Ethiopia." (Von Bohlen, *Das alte Indien*, i. 9–10, citing Virg. *Æn.* viii. 705; *Georg.* ii. 116, 172; Diodor. iii. 31; Lucan, ix. 517; Fabric. *Cod. Apoc. N. T.* p. 669; Beausobre, *Hist. du Manichéisme*, i. 23, 40, 404; ii. 129.) Cp. Arnobius, *Adv. Gentes*, ii. 12; and Lucan, x. 29. Von Bohlen states that the name India first appears among the Greeks in Æschylus, *Supplic.* 282. There the reference is clearly not to India proper, the words running: "I hear that the wandering Indians ride on pannier packed camels fleet as steeds, in their land bordering on the Ethiopians."

been made the occasion of much dispute as to what country it was that Pantænus visited, even orthodox opinion finally coming round to the view that it was not India at all. Mosheim wrote that most of the learned had held it to be Eastern India proper—an opinion countenanced by the statement of Jerome that Pantænus was sent *apud Brachmanas*.[1] But the name Brachman was, as he further pointed out, used as loosely by the ancients as that of India; and the evidence of Jerome further varies from that of Eusebius in stating[2] that the "Indians" had sent delegates to Alexandria asking for a Christian instructor, and that Bishop Demetrius sent Pantænus. That Indian Brahmans should have sent such a deputation is simply inconceivable. Vales, Holstein, and others, accordingly surmised that the mission was to Ethiopia or Abyssinia, which was constantly called India by the ancients. Mosheim, rationally arguing that the Hebrew translation of Matthew must have been used by Jews, decided that the delegates came from a Jewish-Christian colony, which he located in Arabia Felix, because he held that to have been the scene of Bartholomew's "Indian" labours.[3] It matters little which view we take here, so long as we recognize the absurdity of the view that the locality was India. Indeed, even if the "Indies" of Eusebius had meant India, the testimony is on the face of it a mere tradition.

The same arguments, it need hardly be said, dispose of the testimony of Chrysostom, who unquestionably alluded to some of the many peoples of Western Asia or Africa commonly dubbed Indians. If further disproof of Dr. Lorinser's initial assumption be needed, it lies in the fact that even Tertullian, in his sufficiently sweeping

[1] *Epist.* 83, quoted by Mosheim.

[2] *Catal. Scriptor. Ecclesiast.* c. 36, cited by Mosheim.

[3] *Commentaries on the Affairs of the Christians*, Vidal's trans. ii. 6–8, *note* (citing Tillemont, *In Vit. Barthol.* in *Mem. Hist. Eccles.* i. 1, 60–1). In the original, pp. 205–7. See also Murdock's note in his trans. of Mosheim's *History*, 2 Cent. part i. c. i. § 3. Compare the admissions of Kirchhofer (*Quellensammlung*, 1840, p. 110); and of Gieseler (*Compendium*, i. 79, 121, *notes*), who thinks Thomas and Bartholomew probably only went to Yemen.

catalogue of the nations that had embraced Christianity—a list which includes Parthians, Medes, Elamites, and the people of "Mesopotamia, Armenia, Phrygia, Cappadocia, Pontus, Asia, and Pamphylia"—the whole Pentecostal series—does not say a word of India;[1] and that Irenæus in his allegation as to the spread of the faith does not do so either.[2] In any case, neither Chrysostom nor Eusebius, nor yet Jerome, pretends that the "Indians" had a complete translation of the books of the New Testament; and nothing less than a complete translation in an Indian tongue is wanted for Dr. Lorinser's argument, as we shall see when we examine his "parallel passages." He admits, in a piquant passage, that it is impossible to say in what dialect the translation was made, whether in one of those spoken by the people or in Sanskrit, then as now only known to the Brahmans. Dr. Lorinser observes that it is all one (*gleichgültig*) to him. No doubt!

§ 3. An argument for the derivation of the teaching in the Bhagavat Gitâ from the New Testament has the advantage, to begin with, involved in the difficulty of fixing the time of the composition of the Gitâ from either internal or external evidence. There can be no doubt that, like so many other Hindu writings, it was formerly dated much too early. Ostensibly an episode in the great epic, the Mahâbhârata, it stands out from the rest of that huge poem as a specifically theological treatise, cast in the form of a dialogue which is represented as taking place between Krishna and the warrior Arjuna on the eve of a great battle. I may say at once that I cannot regard it as having been composed at the same time as the portion of the poem in which it is inserted. Mr. K. T. Telang, the able Hindu scholar who has translated it for the "Sacred Books of the East" series,[3] and who argues persuasively for its antiquity, confessedly holds "not without diffidence"—indeed, very doubtfully—to the view that it is a genuine "portion of the original Mahâbhârata."[4]

[1] *Adversus Judæos*, c. 7. [2] *Adv. Hæreses*, c. 10. [3] Vol. viii. 1882.
[4] Introd. pp. 2, 5, 6. In the introduction to his earlier translation of the Bhagavat Gitâ in blank verse (Bombay, 1875), Mr. Telang took up a stronger

Where he is diffident the rest of us, I fear, must be disbelieving. There is much force in Mr. Telang's contention that the Gitâ belongs to a period before that of the system-makers; indeed, the flat contradiction, to which he alludes,[1] between Krishna's declarations on the one hand that to him "none is hateful, none dear,"[2] and on the other hand that a whole series of doers of good are "dear" to him[3]—this even raises a doubt as to the homogeneity of the document. But it is one thing to reckon the Gitâ ancient, and another to regard it as a portion of the "original Mahâbhârata." It is not easily to be believed that a piece of writing in which Krishna is not only represented as the Supreme Deity, but pantheistically treated, can belong originally to the epic in which he is a heroic demigod. It must surely belong to the period of his Brahmanic supremacy.

Where *that* period begins, however, it is still impossible to say with any approach to precision; and, as Professor Weber remarks, Dr. Lorinser's thesis is thus far unhampered by any effective objections from Hindu chronology. It must, however, stand criticism on its own merits, and we have seen how abjectly it breaks down in respect of the patristic testimony to the existence of an "Indian" mission, and an "Indian" translation of part of the New Testament, in the first Christian centuries. It is morally certain that no such translation existed, even of the Gospels, not to speak of the entire canon, which Dr. Lorinser strangely seems to think is covered by his quotation from Chrysostom. His argument from history being thus annihilated, it remains to be seen whether he succeeds any better in his argument from resemblance. It is not, I think, difficult to show that, even if the Gitâ were composed within the Christian era, it really owes nothing to Christianity.

position; but even there he declared: "I own I find it quite impossible to satisfy myself that there are more than a very few facts in the history of Sanskrit literature which we are entitled to speak of as 'historically certain'" (p. vii.). The earlier essay, however, contains a very able and complete refutation of Dr. Lorinser's arguments, well worthy the attention of those who are disposed for a further investigation of the subject.

[1] P. 12. [2] Gîtâ, ix. 29. [3] *Id.* xii.

The derivation of the Gitá's teaching from the Christian Scriptures Dr. Lorinser claims to prove by about one hundred parallel passages, in which Gitá sentences are matched by texts selected from nearly all the New Testament books. He divides them into three classes: (1) passages in which, with differences of expression, the sense coincides; (2) passages in which a characteristic expression of the New Testament appears with a different application; and (3) passages in which expression and meaning coincide. The nature of these "coincidences" can be best set forth by a simple selection of about a score of them. I have made this quite impartially, taking the majority consecutively as they happen to stand at the heads of the sections, and picking out the remainder because of their comparative importance. It would be easy to make a selection which would put Dr. Lorinser's case in a much worse light:—

BHAGAVAT GITA.[1]	NEW TESTAMENT.
(First Order.)	
The deluded man who, restraining the organs of action, continues to think in his mind about objects of sense, is called a hypocrite. iii. 6.	I say unto you that every one that looketh on a woman to lust after her hath committed adultery with her already in his heart. Matt. v. 28.
But those who carp at my opinion and do not act upon it, know them to be devoid of discrimination, deluded as regards all knowledge, and ruined. iii. 32.	A man that is heretical [after a first and second admonition] refuse; knowing that such a one is perverted, and sinneth, being self-condemned. Titus iii. 10–11.
Every sense has its affections and its aversions towards its objects fixed. One should not become subject to them, for they are one's opponents. iii. 34.	Let not sin therefore reign in your mortal body, that ye should obey the lusts thereof. Romans vi. 12. Because the mind of the flesh is enmity against God, etc. *Id.* viii. 7.
[Arjuna speaks]: Later is your [Krishna's] birth; the birth of the sun is prior. How then shall I understand that you declared (this) first? [Krishna answers]: I have passed through many births, O Arjuna! and you also. I know them all, but you,....O terror of your foes, do not know them. iv. 4.	The Jews therefore said unto him, Thou art not yet fifty years old, and hast thou seen Abraham? John viii. 57. I know whence I came, and whither I go; but ye [*i.e.*, the Jews] know not whence I came, or whither I go. *Id.* 14.

[1] I have followed throughout the prose translation of Mr. Telang; and I have occasionally given in brackets parts of a passage elided by Dr. Lorinser as not bearing on his point. The context clearly ought to be kept in view.

I am born age after age, for the protection of the good, and for the destruction of evil-doers and the establishment of piety. iv. 8.

To this end have I been born, and to this end am I come into the world, that I should bear witness unto the truth. John xviii. 37. The devil sinneth from the beginning. 1 John iii. 8.

He who is ignorant and devoid of faith, and whose self is full of misgivings, is ruined. iv. 40.

He that believeth [and is baptized] shall be saved; but he that disbelieveth shall be condemned. Mark xvi. 16.

To me none is hateful, none dear. ix. 29.

There is no respect of persons with God. Rom. ii. 11.

(Second Order.)

For should I at any time not engage without sloth in action [men would follow in my path from all sides, O son of Pritha!]. *If I did not perform actions*, these worlds would be destroyed. I should be the cause of caste interminglings. I should be ruining these people. iii. 23–4.

My Father *worketh even until now, and I work*. John v. 17. [*As against passage in brackets*]: If any man would come after me, let him deny himself and take up his cross. Matt. xvi. 24.

Even those men who *always act on this opinion of mine* full of faith, *and without carping* [" *die lästern nicht* " in Lorinser] are released from all actions. iii. 31.

If a man *keep my word* [he shall never see death]. John viii. 51.

....that the word of God *be not blasphemed*. Titus ii. 5. [*Compare the preceding sentences of the epistle.*]

....me....*the goal* [" *der Weg* " in Lorinser[1]] than which there is nothing higher. vii. 18.

I am *the way*....No one cometh unto the Father, but by me. John xiv. 6.

(Third Order).

To the man of knowledge I am dear above all things, and he is dear to me. vii. 17.

He [that hath my commandments, and keepeth them, he it is that loveth me....and I will love him. John xiv. 21.

I am not manifest to all. vii. 26.

No man hath seen God at any time. John i. 18.

Whom no man hath seen, nor can see. 1 Tim. vi. 16.

It [*i.e.*, divine knowledge] is to be apprehended directly, and is easy to practise. ix. 2.

My yoke is easy, and my burden light. Matt. xi. 30.

[1] Dr. John Muir, than whom there is no higher authority in this country, rejected Dr. Lorinser's translation of "way" and anticipates Telang's:—"Here, as in many other passages of the Indian writings, [the word] certainly signifies 'the place reached by going,' 'resort,' 'refuge.'" *Indian Antiquary*, March, 1875 (vol. iv.), p. 80. To the same effect, Professor Tiele, in *Theolog. Tijdschr.* 1877, p. 75 *n*.

I am [the father of this universe, the mother, the creator, the grandsire, the thing to be known, the means of sanctification, the syllable Om (= past, present, and future), the *Rik*, Saman, and Yajus also] *the goal* [the sustainer, the lord, the supervisor, the residence, the asylum, the friend], the source and that in which it merges [the support, the receptacle, and the inexhaustible seed]. I cause heat, and I send forth and stop showers. [I am immortality, and also death; and I, O Arjuna! am that which is and that which is not.] ix. 18, 19.	*I am the way* [and the truth, and the life; no one cometh unto the Father but by me]. John xiv. 6. I am the first and the last [and the Living One; and I was dead, and behold I am alive for evermore, and I have the keys of death and of Hades]. Rev. i. 17–18. He maketh his sun to rise [on the evil and the good], and *sendeth rain* [on the just and the unjust]. Matt. v. 45.
[That devotee who worships me abiding in all beings, holding that all is one], lives in me, however he may be living. vi. 30.	[As the living Father sent me, and I live because of the Father; so] he that eateth me, he also shall live because of me. John vi. 57.
But those who worship me with devotion (dwell) in me, and I too in them. ix. 29.[1]	I in them, and they in me [that they may be perfected into one]. John xvii. 23.
I am the origin of all, and all moves on through me. x. 8.	For of him, and through him, and unto him, are all things. Rom. xi. 36.
I am the beginning, and the middle and the end also of all beings. x. 20.	I am the first and the last.[2] Rev. i. 17.

The first comment that must occur to every instructed reader on perusing these and the other "parallels" advanced by Dr. Lorinser is that on the one hand the parallels are very frequently such as could be made by the dozen between bodies of literature which have unquestionably never been brought in contact, so strained and

[1] As to the passage, "They who devoutly worship me are in me, and I in them," Dr. Muir writes: "In the Rig Veda some passages occur which in part convey the same or a similar idea. Thus in ii. 11, 12, it is said: 'O Indra, we sages have been in thee'; and in x. 142, 1: 'This worshipper, O Agni, hath been in thee: O son of strength, he hath no other kinship'; and in viii. 47, 8: 'We, O Gods, are in you as if fighting in coats of mail....And in viii. 81, 32, the worshipper says to Indra, 'thou art ours, and we thine.'" (*Ind. Ant.* as cited, p. 80.)

[2] Dr. Lorinser also brackets the Christian "I am the Alpha and the Omega" with the Gîtâ's "I am A among the letters" (x. 33). But Mr. Telang points out (B. G. trans. in verse, Introd. p. lv.) that the Indian writer merely takes A as the principal letter. Note that the Deity is already "the first and the last" in Isaiah (so-called):—xli. 4; xliii. 10; xlviii. 12. Why should not the Brahmans have studied the prophets?

far-fetched are they; and that on the other they are discounted by quite as striking parallels between New Testament texts and pre-Christian pagan writings. Take a few of the more notable of these latter parallels, in the order in which the New Testament passages occur above:—

He who means to do an injury has already done it. SENECA, *De Irâ*, i. 3.

Though you may take care of her body, the [coerced wife's] mind is adulterous, nor can she be preserved, unless she is willing. OVID, *Amor.* iii. 4, 5.

Not only is he who does evil bad, but also he who thinks to do evil. ÆLIAN, *Var. Hist.* xiv. 28.

In every man there are two parts: the better and superior part, which rules, and the worse and inferior part, which serves, and the ruler is always to be preferred to the servant. PLATO, *Laws*, B. v. (Jowett's tr. v. 298).

[In B. iv. of the *Laws* (Jowett, v. 288–9) is a long sentence declaring that the contemner of right conduct is "deserted by God" and in the end "is utterly destroyed, and his family and city with him."]

The unruly passions of anger and desire are contrary and inimical to the reason. CICERO, *Tusculan Questions*, iv. 5.

I [Cyrus] am persuaded I am born by divine providence to undertake this work. HERODOTUS, i. 126.

The Muses.... whom Mnemosyne.... bare, to be a means of oblivion of ills, and a rest from cares. HESIOD, *Theogony*, 52–5.

The Gods look with just eyes on mortals. OVID, *Metamorph.* xiii. 70.

God is verily the saviour of all, and the producer of things in whatever way they happen in the world. PSEUD-ARISTOTLE, *De Mundo*, 6.

Zeus, cause of all, doer of all.... What can be done by mortals without Zeus? ÆSCHYLUS, *Agam.* 1461–5 (1484–8).

All things are full of Jove: he cherishes the earth; my songs are his care. VIRGIL, *Eclogues*, iii. 60.

The temperate man is the friend of God, for he is like to him. PLATO, *Laws*, B. iv. (Jowett's tr. v. 289).

Not to every one doth Apollo manifest himself, but only to the good. CALLIMACHUS, *Hymn to Apollo*, 9.

It is enough for God that he be worshipped and loved. SENECA, *Epist.* xlvii. 18. Cp. xcv. 50.

God, seeing all things, himself unseen. PHILEMON, *Frag.*

God, holding in his hand the beginning, middle, and end, of all that is. PLATO, *Laws*, B. iv. (Jowett, v. 288.)

Zeus was, Zeus is, Zeus shall be. *Ancient Song*, in PAUSANIAS, x. 12.

God comes to men: nay, what is closer, he comes into them. SENECA, *Epist.* 73.

God is within you. EPICTETUS, *Dissert.* i. 14, 14.

Pythagoras thought that there was a soul mingling with and pervading all things. CICERO, *De Natura Deorum*, i. 11.

Such parallels as these, I repeat, could be multiplied to

any extent from the Greek and Latin classics alone; while the Egyptian "Book of the Dead" furnishes many more. But is it worth while to heap up the disproof of a thesis so manifestly idle? It is difficult to understand how a scholar, knowing the facts, can hope to prove such a proposition by such evidence; much more how he can bring himself to believe in his own case. More than half the resemblances are such as could be manufactured by the dozen between any two books dealing with similar questions. On Dr. Lorinser's principle, Jesus and his followers were indebted to pagans for very much of their ethical teaching—as indeed they were unquestionably indebted for a good many of their theological ideas, not to speak of the narrative myths. But surely a small endowment of common sense, to say nothing of scholarship, suffices to make it clear that certain commonplaces of ethics as well as of theology are equally inevitable conclusions in all religious systems that rise above savagery.[1] Four hundred years before Jesus, Plato[2] declared that it was very difficult for the rich to be good: does anyone believe that Jesus or any other Jew needed Plato's help to reach the same notion? Nay, does anyone even doubt that such a close coincidence as the comparison of the human soul to a team of horses in the Katha Upanishad and Plato's *Phaedrus*, pointed out to Dr. Lorinser by Professor Windisch,[3] might not be quite independent of borrowing?

If all this were not clear enough *a priori*, it is sufficiently

[1] In Dr. John Muir's valuable little pamphlet, *Religious and Moral Sentiments freely translated from Indian Writers* (published in Thomas Scott's series), will be found a number of extracts from the Mahâbhârata and other Sanskrit works, which, on the Christian theory, must have been borrowed from the Gospels. Thus in the epic (v. 1270) we have: "The Gods regard with delight the man who....when struck does not strike again." If this be Christian (it is at least as old as Plato: see the *Gorgias*) whence came this: "The good, when they promote the welfare of others, expect no reciprocity"? (iii. 16796). It is plainly as native to the Indian poet as is the "Golden Rule," thus stated: "Let no man do to another that which would be repugnant to himself; this is the sum of righteousness; the rest is according to inclination." But most Christians are kept carefully in ignorance of the fact that the "Golden Rule" is common to all literatures, and was an ancient saw in China before Jesus was born.

[2] *Laws*, v.

[3] Cited by Dr. Muir in *Ind. Ant.* as last cited, p. 78.

obvious from the context of most of the passages quoted from the Gitâ, as well as from the general drift of its exposition, that the Hindu system is immeasurably removed from the Christian in its whole theosophical inspiration. We are asked to believe that Brahmans expounding a highly developed pantheism went assiduously to the (unattainable) New Testament for the wording of a number of their propositions, pantheistic and other, while assimilating absolutely nothing of distinctively Christian doctrine; choosing to borrow from the Christians their expressions of doctrines which had been in the world for centuries, including some which lay at the root of Buddhism—as that of the religious yoke being easy—though utterly rejecting the Christian doctrine of atonement and blood sacrifice and the Christian claim as a whole. Such a position is possible only to a mesmerised believer.[1] Even were Brahmanic India in doctrinal communication with Christendom at the time in question, which we have seen it was not, it lies on the face of the case that the Brahmanic theosophy was already elaborated out of all comparison with the Christian. It had reached systematic (even if inconsistent) pantheism while Christianity was but vaguely absorbent of the pantheism around it. The law of religious development in this regard is simple. A crude and *naïf* system, like the Christism of the second Gospel and the earlier form of the first, borrows inevitably from the more highly evolved systems with which it comes socially in contact, absorbing myth and mystery and dogma till it becomes as sophisticated as they. It then becomes capable in turn of dominating primitive systems, as Christianity supplanted those of northern Europe. But not even at the height of its influence, much less in the second century, was Christianity capable of dominating Hindu Brahmanism, with its ingrained pantheism, and its mass of myth and ritual, sanctioned

[1] It appears from Dr. Lorinser's notes (p. 82) that he thinks the author of the Gitâ may have profited by a study of the Christian fathers, as Clemens Alexandrinus and Athenagoras. He further implies that the Hindu had read the book of *Wisdom* in the Septuagint!

in whole or in part by rote-learnt lore of the most venerable antiquity. Be the Gitâ pre-Christian or post-Christian, it is unmixedly Hindu.

§ 4. When it is thus seen that all the arguments to prove imitation of the Gospels in the Bhagavat Gitâ are baseless, it is hardly necessary to deal at any length with Professor Weber's favourite general argument as to the necessary derivation of the doctrines of *bhakti* and *sraddha* from Christianity. The very proposition betrays some of the "judicial blindness" laboured under by Dr. Lorinser. It has never occurred to either theorist to ask how the doctrine of salvation by faith came to be developed in Christism, or whether the same religious tendencies could not give rise to the same phenomenon in similar social conditions elsewhere. I cannot burden this already over-lengthy treatise with an examination of the development of the Christian doctrine of faith from the Judaic germs. It must suffice to say that the principle is already clearly indicated in the prophets;[1] that faith in divine protection is expressed in the early documents of other Eastern systems: and that the tendency to believe in the all-sufficiency of devotion, and the needlessness of personal merit, is noted by Plato (to name no other), and is in some degree really an inevitable phase of all systems at some stages. It found special development under Christism in a decaying society, in which the spirit of subjection had eaten away the better part of all self-reliance; and just such a state of things can be seen to have existed in many parts of India from the earliest historic times. It would be small credit to Christianity if it *were* responsible for the introduction into India of a doctrine so profoundly immoral in principle, so demoralizing in practice; but, as it happens, the historic facts discountenance the hypothesis. For though we cannot trace all the stages by which the doctrine of faith reached its full development, we do know that the germs of it lie in the Veda. Take first the testimony of Dr. John Muir:—

[1] Micah iii. 11; Isa. xxvi. 3; l. 7-10; Jer. vii. 14; Nahum i. 7; Zeph. iii. 12; Psalms, *passim*.

"Dr. Lorinser considers (p. 56) that two Sanskrit words denoting faithful and reverential religious devotion (*sraddhâ* and *bhakti*), which often occur in the Bhagavad Gîtâ, do not convey original Indian conceptions, but are borrowed from Christianity. This may or may not be true of *bhakti;* but *sraddhâ* (together with its cognates, participial and verbal) is found even in the hymns of the Rig Veda in the sense of belief in the existence and action of a deity, at least, if not also of devotion to his service. In pp. 103 ff. of the fifth volume of my *Original Sanskrit Texts* a number of passages are cited and translated in which the word occurs, together with a great variety of other expressions in which the worshipper's trust in, and affectionate regard for, the God Indra are indicated. He is called a friend and brother; his friendship and guidance are said to be sweet; he is spoken of as a father and the most fatherly of fathers, and as being both a father and a mother; he is the helper of the poor, and has a love for mortals."[1]

These remarks are endorsed by Mr. Telang, who cites other Vedic passages;[2] and again by Professor Tiele:—

"The opinion that not only did Christian legends find an entry among the Indian sects of later times, but that even peculiarly Christian ideas exercised an influence on their dogmatics or philosophy, that is to say, that the Hindus acquired from the Christians their high veneration for piety or devotion, *bhakti*, and faith, *sraddhâ*—as is contended by Weber (*Indische Studien*, 1850; i. 423), and after him by Nève (*Des Eléments Etrangers du Mythe et du Culte de Krichna*, Paris, 1876, p. 35)—seems to me unjustified. Already in the Rig Veda there is frequent mention of faith (*sraddhâ*) in the same sense as is given to that word later; and although we cannot speak actually of *bhakti*, which there as yet only means 'division' or 'apportionment,' yet this has already in very old sources the sense of 'consecration' (*toewijding*), 'fidelity' (*trouw*), 'love resting on belief' (*op geloof rustende liefde*)."[3]

Take, finally, the verdict of Professor Max Müller—in this connection certainly weighty. Noting that the *principle* of love and intimacy with the Gods is found in the very earliest portions of the Rig-Veda, he cites from the Svetâsoatara Upanishad[4] a pantheistic passage which concludes:—

"If these truths have been told to a high-minded man, who feels the highest devotion (*bhakti*) for God, and as for God so for his Guru, then they will shine forth, then they will shine forth indeed."

[1] *Indian Antiquary*, iv. 81. Also in Dr. Muir's pamphlet *Religious and Moral Sentiments*, as cited, p. vi.
[2] Trans. of B. G. in verse, introd. p. lxxxii.
[3] Art. *Christus en Krishna*, in *Theologische Tijdschrift*, 1877, p. 66.
[4] Müller's trans. in *Sacred Books of the East*, xv. 260.

U

He adds :—

> "Here then we have in the Upanishads the idea of *bhakti* or devotion clearly pronounced; and as no one has yet ventured to put the date of the Svetâsoatara Upanishad later than the beginning of ou era, it is clearly impossible to admit here the idea of an early Christian influence."[1]

Further, the Professor observes that, "even if chronologically Christian influences were possible" at the date of the Gîtâ, "there is no necessity for admitting them." "It is strange that these scholars should not see that what is natural in one country is natural in another also."[2]

For the rest, we have already seen that the idea of the God entering into his worshippers existed in the Veda (as it notoriously did among the ancient Greeks), though that too was held by Dr. Lorinser to be of Christian derivation; and the one rebuttal reinforces the other. We have also seen how completely Professor Weber was mistaken as to the opinion of Wilson. It only remains to say that in the rejection of Weber's own theory we are fully countenanced by M. Barth;[3] and that Dr. Lorinser's special proposition is scouted by M. Senart.[4]

XX. The "White Island."

There is, I think, only one more proposition as to the influence of Christianity on Krishnaism that calls for our attention; and that can be soon disposed of. Among the infirm theses so long cherished by Professor Weber, not the least paternally favoured is his interpretation of a certain mythic tale in the Mahâbhârata,[5] to the effect that once upon a time Nârada, and before him other mythic personages, had visited the Svetadvîpa, or "White Island," beyond the "Sea of Milk"; had there found a race of perfect men, who worshipped the One God; and had there received the knowledge of that God from a supernatural

[1] *Natural Religion*, p. 99. [2] *Id.* p. 97.
[3] *Religions of India*, pp. 218–220, 223. [4] *Essai*, pp. 342–3, *n.*
[5] xii. 12702, ff.

voice. This, the only record that can be pretended to look like a Hindu mention of the importation of Christianity, is fastened upon by Weber and others as a piece of genuine history; and the "White Island" (which might also mean the "island of the white ones") is assumed to be Alexandria, for no other reason than that Alexandria seems the likeliest place whence the knowledge of Christianity could come.[1] Lassen, who followed Weber in assuming that the legend was a historic testimony, surmised on the other hand that Svetadvipa would be Parthia, "because the tradition that the Apostle Thomas preached the gospel in that country is an old one." On the other hand, however, he thought it just possible that there had been an apostolic mission to India, though he admitted that it was not without weighty reasons that many ecclesiastical historians held the "India" of Bartholomew and Pantænus to be Yemen. We are thus left to believe, if we choose, that Christianity was very early imported by Christians into India, and yet that Brahmans went elsewhere to learn it: so loosely can a great scholar speculate. It is worth noting only as a further sample of the same laxity that Lassen thought the hypothesis about Svetadvipa was put on firm ground (*eines festen Grundes*) by citing the fact that in the late Kûrma Purâna there is a legend about Siva appearing in the beginning of the Kali Yuga or Evil Age to teach the "Yoga" system on the Himalayas, and having four scholars, "White," "White horse," "White hair," and "White blood." In the Mahâbhârata legend the Yoga is represented as the source of the true knowledge; hence it follows that both stories refer to the same thing, which is Christianity![2]

It will readily be believed that these assumptions find small favour with later investigators. Telang in India,

[1] Weber, *Ueber die Krishnajanmâshtami*, pp. 318–321; *Indische Studien*, i. 400; *Indische Streifen*, ii. 21. Lorinser, as cited. Weber's view is shared by the French Catholic scholar, Nève, who says "It is even certain, at least highly probable, that the White Island.... is Alexandria" (*Des Eléments Etrangers du Mythe et du Culte de Krichna*, Paris, 1876, p. 24, quoted by Tiele, *Theolog. Tijdschr.* as cited, p. 70). I have not been able to meet with M. Nève's book, which is not in the British Museum. It does not appear, however, to have added anything to the German arguments.

[2] *Indische Alterthumskunde*, ii. (1849), 1099–1101.

Tiele in Holland, Senart and Barth in France, all reject them. Mr. Telang's criticism is especially destructive:—

"I cannot see the flimsiest possible ground for identifying the Svetadvip of the legend with Alexandria, or Asia Minor, or the British Isles [this has been done by Colonel Wilford, *Asiatic Researches*, xi.], or any other country or region in this world. The Dvip is in the first place stated to lie to the north of the Kshirasamudra; and to the north-west of Mount Meru, and above it by thirty-two thousand yojans. I should like to know what geography has any notion of the quarter of this earth where we are to look for the Sea of Milk and the Mount of Gold. Consider next the description of the wonderful people inhabiting this wonderful Dvip. [Sanskrit quoted.] It will be news to the world that there were in Alexandria or elsewhere a whole people without any organs of sense, who ate nothing, and who entered the sun, whatever that may mean! Remember, too, that the instruction which Nàrad receives in this wonderful land is not received from its inhabitants, but from Bhagavàn, from God himself. Nor let it be forgotten that the doctrines which the deity there announces to Nàrad cannot be shown to have any connection with Christianity. On the contrary, I think that it must be at once admitted that the whole of the prelection addressed to Nàrad bears on its face its essentially Indian character, in the reference to the three qualities, to the twenty-five primal principles, to the description of final emancipation as absorption or entrance into the Divinity, and various other matters of the like character. Against all this what have we to consider? Why, nothing more than the description of the inhabitants as white, and as *ekânta*, which, Professor Weber thinks, means monotheists (*Sed quære*). It appears to me that the story is a mere work of the imagination."[1]

The details as to the supernatural character of the inhabitants of the White Island, be it observed, are ignored by both Weber and Lassen, who pursue the Evemeristic method. Professor Tiele emphatically endorses Telang:—

"With all respect for such men as Lassen and Weber, I can hardly conceive of such a species of historical criticism.

[1] *Bhagavat Gita trans. into Eng. blank verse.* Introd. pp. xxxiv.–v.

All the places and persons in the legend are purely mythological: Nárada can as little as his predecessors be reckoned a historical personage." [Quotes Telang.] "We are here in sheer mythology. Svetadvipa is a land of fable, a paradise, a dwelling of the sun, such as we meet with in so many religious systems; and the white inhabitants, exalted above personal needs, are spirits of light. Nárada receives there a monotheistic revelation, not from the inhabitants, but from the supreme deity himself; but one only needs to glance at the words in which it is conveyed to perceive its Indian character. And whencesover the poet may have derived this monotheism, at least the legend says nothing as to its being derived from Alexandria or any other religious centre."[1]

Equally explicit is the decision of M. Senart:—

"It is certain that all the constituent elements of this story are either clearly mythological or, in the speculative parts, of very ancient origin: both belong to India, apart from any Christian influence. It is another matter to inquire if the use made of the materials, the manner of their application (the Katha Upanishad, i. sq. shows us, for instance, Nasiketas going to the world of Yama to seek philosophical instruction) betrays a Western influence, and preserves a vague memory of borrowings made from Christian doctrines. The question cannot be definitively handled save on positive dates, which we do not possess: inductions are extremely perilous. It has been sought to show (Muir, *Sanskrit Texts*, iv., 248, ff.) that the Pandavas were the founders of the cult of Vishnu-Krishna. Who would venture to see in these 'white heroes,' whom Lassen holds on the other hand to be new comers from the West (*Ind. Alt.* i. 800, ff.), the representatives of a Christian influence on the religious ideas of India?"[2]

And M. Barth in turn, even while admitting that Brahmans may have early "visited the Churches of the East," and that there were probably Christian Churches in India "before the redaction of the Mahabhárata was quite finished," regards the Svetadvipa legend as a "purely fanciful relation."[3]

It is needless, for the rest, to go into the question of the

[1] *Theolog. Tijdschr.* art. cited, p. 70. [2] *Essai*, p. 342, *n.* [3] *Relig. of India*, p. 221.

manner of the "introduction" of the monotheistic idea into India, or into the point raised by Professor Weber[1] as to the commemoration of the Milk Sea and the White Island, and the veneration of Nârada, in the Krishnaite ritual. The latter circumstance plainly proves nothing whatever for his case, though he professes to be placed beyond doubt by it; and the idea that Brahmans could derive the idea of monotheism from the Christians of Alexandria, after Athanasius, is on its merits nothing short of grotesque. It is strange that a disinterested scholar can be led by orthodox habit to see an exemplary monotheism in the Christian Trinity; and hardly less strange that he should not recognize how naturally the monotheistic idea tends to be evolved in all religious systems. In other connexions, moreover, Professor Weber assumes the Hindus to have been influenced by Greek thought at and after the conquest of Alexander: why then should they not have had the idea from Greek philosophy—not to speak of Persia or Egypt—before the Christian era? Even Lassen, while holding the Christian theory of Svetadvipa, held that no practical influence on Indian religion could justly be attributed to the Christian missionaries in the early centuries, and rejects the view that the Hindus derived monotheism from Christianity.[2]

XXI. The Crucifixion Myth.

While the Christian claim seems thus to collapse at all points, there incidentally arises, out of an equally mistaken countervailing claim, a problem of which I cannot pretend to offer a solution, but which calls for mention here. A strenuous freethinker of the early part of this century, Godfrey Higgins—a scholar whose energy and learning too often missed their right fruition just because his work was

[1] *Ueber die K.* as last cited.
[2] *Indische Alterthumskunde*, ii. 1102–3–5–9.

a desperate revolt against a whole world of pious obscurantism—unwittingly put rationalists on a false scent by adopting the view that Krishna had in an ancient legend been crucified, and that it was the missionaries who had contrived to withhold the fact from general European knowledge.[1] His assumption rested mainly on an oversight of the archæologist Moor,[2] who in collecting Hindu God-images had a Christian crucifix presented to him as a native "Wittoba"—a late minor Avatar commonly represented as pierced in one foot. Krishna is indeed represented in the Puranic legend as being slain by an arrow[3] which pierced his foot, here comparing curiously with the solar Achilles of Hellenic mythology; but he is not crucified; and Moor later admitted that the figure in question was Christian. It is not at all certain, however, that a crucifixion myth did not anciently flourish in Asia, as we know one did in pre-Christian Mexico. The later missionaries no doubt have suppressed what they conveniently could; and it is far from certain that we yet know all the relevant modern facts. As long ago as 1626, the Portuguese Jesuit Andrade, in his letters from Tibet to the General of his Order, testifies to the existence of a crucifixion myth in that country. They believe, he tells, in the triune God, but give him absurdly wrong names; and

> "They agree with us in saying that Christ" [*i.e.*, their Second Person, known as "the great book"] "died for the saving of the human race; but they do not know the manner of his death, knowing little or nothing of the holy cross, holding only that he died shedding his blood, which flowed from his veins on account of the nails with which he was put to death. It is very true that in their book the cross is represented, with a triangle in the middle, and certain mystic letters which they cannot explain."

Andrade further testifies that there were three or four goldsmiths of the King of Tibet, natives of other countries, to whom he gave money to make a cross; and they told him

[1] *Anacalypsis*, 1836, i. 144–6 (ch. ii.).
[2] *Hindu Pantheon*, pp. 416–20, and pl. 98.
[3] In the Mahâbhârata and the Vishnu Purâna the slayer is the hunter Jara (= "old age," "decay"). In the Bhagavat Purâna the slayer is the forester Bhil. In both cases, the slaying is unintentional but predestined.

that in their country, two months' journey off, there were many such crosses as his, some of wood, others of metals. These were usually in the churches, but on five days in the year they were put on the public roads, when all the people worshipped them, strewing flowers and lighting lamps before them; "which crosses in their language they call Iandar."[1]

This evidence is remarkably corroborated in 1772 by the Jesuit Giorgi, who, in the very act of maintaining that all Krishnaism was a perversion of Christianity, declares on his own knowledge of Tibet that in Nepal it was customary in the month of August to raise in honour of the God Indra *cruces amictas abrotono*, crosses wreathed with abrotonus, and to represent him as crucified, and bearing the sign *Telech* on forehead, hands, and feet. He appends two wood cuts. One is a very singular representation of a crucifix, in which the cross seems wholly covered with leaves, and only the head, hands, and feet of the crucified one appear, the hands and feet as if pierced with nails, the forehead bearing a mark. In the other, only the upper part of the deity's body is seen, with the arms extended, the hands pierced, the forehead marked, but without any cross.[2] Godfrey Higgins reproduced and commented on those pictures, but I find no discussion of the matter in recent writers, though it appears that the Nepalese usage in question still flourishes. Dr. H. A. Oldfield states that in the Indra festival in August-September at the present time "figures of Indra, *with outstretched arms*, are erected all about the city"[3]—*i.e.*, Kathmandu—but he gives no further details. Professor Weber would seem to have entirely overlooked the matter, since he makes no allusion to it. The *prima facie* inference is that we have here a really ancient and extra-Brahmanical development of the Indra cult; since it is hard to conceive how any Christian

[1] *Histoire de ce qui c'est passé av Royavme dv Tibet*, trad. d'Italien en François, Paris, 1629, pp. 45–6, 49–50, 51. Cp. p. 64. Andrade will be found cited by M. V. La Croze, *Hist. du Christ. des Indes*, La Haye, 1724, p. 514. La Croze has a theory of Nestorian influences.

[2] *Alphabetum Thibetanum*, Romae, 1772, p. 208.

[3] *Sketches from Nepal*, 1880, ii. 314.

suggestion should be grafted on that worship in particular, at a time when it had been generally superseded by the cult of Krishna. And there is no suggestion that any Christian doctrine connects with the usage described. When we note that the Persian Sun-God Mithra is imaged in the Zendavesta "with arms stretched out towards immortality,"[1] and that the old Persian symbols seem to explain this by a figure of the sun or the God with outstretched wings, it is seen to be perfectly possible that not merely the cross-symbol, which is universal, but a crucifixion myth, should have flourished in ancient India.

This, however, goes for nothing as regards Krishnaism, though Krishna was the supplanter of Indra. The only suggestions of the cross in Krishnaism apart from its appearance in late sculpture or pictorial art are in the curious legend[2] that the God was buried at the meeting point of three rivers—which would form a cross—and in the story of Yasoda binding the child Krishna to a tree, or to two trees. The trees opened, and there appeared two Brahmans—a tale which the indignant Giorgi held to be a perversion of the crucifixion of Christ between two thieves.[3] The story given by Wilford[4] of the holy Brahman Mandávya, who was crucified among thieves in the Deccan, and afterwards named Sulastha, or "cross-borne," is stated by the narrator to be told at great length in the "Sayadrichandra, a section of the Scanda Purána," and to be given briefly in the Mahábhárata and alluded to in the Bhagavat Purána "and its commentary"; but as the matter is never mentioned by Weber or other later Sanskritists it must be, I presume, one of the frauds practised on Wilford by his pandits.[5] The Christian crucifixion story

[1] *Mihr Yasht*, 31. [2] Balfour's *Ind. Cycl.* art. *Krishna*.

[3] *Alphab. Thib.* p. 253. Giorgi held that the detail of Krishna's commending the care of his 1,600 wives to Arjuna was a fiction based on the records of the multitude of women who followed Christ from Galilee! (p. 259). [4] *Asiatic Researches*, x. 69.

[5] On this see Professor Max Müller's article "On False Analogies in Comparative Theology," in the *Contemporary Review* of April, 1870, reprinted with his *Introduction to the Science of Religion*, 1st ed. 1873. I am not aware that there has been any detailed discrimination of the genuine and the spurious in Wilford's compilations.

falls to be studied in other lights, one of which is indicated above.

It may be that I have in my turn overstrained the possibilities of Christian indebtedness to Krishnaism as regards some minor myth motives: but at least I have in no way staked the argument on such suppositions. I have not even founded on the decision of Wilson (who is so often cited to other purpose by Professor Weber) to the effect that Gnostic Christian doctrines were borrowed from Hinduism in the second century.[1] That there was then "an active communication between India and the Red Sea" is indeed certain; and it is arguable that Christism borrowed from Buddhism: but the testimony of Epiphanius,[2] on which Wilson founds, is clearly worthless, were it only because he uses the term "India" at random, like so many other ancient writers. It is impossible to say what is the force of the reference of Juvenal[3] to the "hired Indian, skilled as to the earth and the stars"; and though there is no great reason to doubt that India was visited by Apollonius of Tyana, and no uncertainty, for instance, as to the embassies sent by Porus to Augustus, and by the king of "Taprobane" to Claudius,[4] it is one thing to be convinced of the communication, and another to know what were the results. I have made no attempt to build on the fact that the Christians made a sacred place of the Egyptian Matarea,[5] which certainly suggests knowledge of Mathura. I simply insist on the proved error of the main Christian assumptions, on the utter illegitimacy of the others, and on the reasonable contrary hypothesis in certain cases.

In so far as I may have gone astray, I know I lay myself open to that kind of criticism which is bestowed on the mistakes of rationalism by writers whose customary frame of mind on religious matters is the negation of

[1] Trans. of *Vishnu Purâna*, Introd. p. viii.

[2] *Adversus Manichæos*, i. (*Hæreses*, xlvi. *sive* lxvi.). [3] *Sat.* vi. 585.

[4] Strabo, xv. 1, 74; Pliny, *Hist. Nat.* vi. 24 (22). It is worth noting that Pliny in this chapter says of the people of Taprobane (doubtless Ceylon) that "Hercules is the deity they worship." This confirms our previous argument as to the antiquity of the hero-God worships.

[5] 1 Infancy, viii.

reason. The believer lives for his own part in a thought-world of lawless credulity; but if the unbeliever should in his research deviate even unimportantly from strict historical or verbal accuracy, he is impeached on the instant as an ignoramus, or worse. And when he errs grossly, like the unfortunate M. Jacolliot, who, ill-fitted for exact study in any case, seems to have fared worse than Wilford at the hands of Hindu Shapiras, his religious critics point to his miscarriage as a sample of rationalist research in general. Jacolliot's *La Bible dans l'Inde*, which has misled freethinkers inexpert in Indian matters, was contemptuously dismissed at the start by such critics as Professor Tiele and M. Senart, who are both "sceptics"; but the Rev. Dr. Ellinwood of New York, who seems to get his whole knowledge on the subject from the review article of Professor Max Müller, discusses Jacolliot's extravagances, with the candour of his profession, in a magazine paper under the heading of "The Credulity of Scepticism."[1] Jacolliot's follies are held to put in countenance the myths of Christianity. Leaving such criticism to play its part, I submit the present research to the good faith of serious readers.

XXII.—Summary.

It may be convenient to sum up concisely the results, positive and negative, of the foregoing investigation. They may be roughly classed under these two heads. On the one hand,

1. The cult of Krishna is proved by documentary evidence to have flourished in India before the Christian era, though it has developed somewhat and gained much ground since.

2. In its pre-Christian form it presumptively, if not certainly, contained some of the myth elements which have been claimed as borrowings from Christianity—such as the

[1] *Missionary Review of the World*, New York, Feb. 1890.

myth of Kansa; and that myth was probably made the subject of dramatic representations.

3. Other leading elements in the myth—such as the upbringing of the God among herdsmen and herdswomen—are found long before Christianity in the solar legend which attached to Cyrus; while this myth and the story of the God's birth are found strikingly paralleled in the pre-Christian mythology of Greece and Egypt. There is thus an overwhelming presumption in favour of the view that these myth elements were Hindu property long before our era.

4. The fact that Krishna is in the Vedas a dæmon is rightly to be taken as a proof of the antiquity of his cult. Its mythology points clearly to an extra-Brahmanic origin, though it includes myth-motives which closely coincide with Vedic myth-motives, notably those connected with Agni. The attribute of blackness in a beloved deity, too, is a mark of ancient derivation, remarkably paralleled in the case of the Egyptian Osiris, to whom also was attributed a dæmonic origin. The same attribute is bound up with the conception of the God as a "hiding one," which is common to the oldest mythologies.

5. Ritual is far more often the basis of myth than the converse; and the Krishnaite Birth-ritual in itself raises a presumption in favour of the antiquity of the cult.

6. The leading elements in the Krishna myth are inexplicable save on the view that the cultus is ancient. If it were of late and Brahmanic origin, it could not conceivably have taken in the legend of the upbringing among herdsmen.

7. The ethical teaching bound up with Krishnaism in the Bhagavat Gitâ is a development on distinctly Hindu lines of Vedic ideas, and is no more derived from the New Testament than it is from the literature of Greece and Rome.

8. The close coincidences in the legends of Krishna and Buddha are to be explained in terms of borrowing by the latter from the former, and not *vice versa*.

In fine, we are led to the constructive position that Krishna is an ancient extra-Brahmanic Indian deity, in his earliest phase apparently non-Aryan, who was worshipped by Aryan-speakers long before our era, and, either before or after his adoption by the Brahmans, or more probably in both stages, was connected with myths which are enshrined in the Vedas. He acquired some of the leading qualities of Agni, and supplanted Indra, whose ancient prestige he acquired. All which positively-ascertained facts and fully-justified conclusions are in violent conflict with the hypothesis that Krishnaism borrowed mythological and theological matter from Christism.

On the other hand,

1. Such phenomena as the Birth-Festival ritual and the pictorial representation of the babe Krishna as suckled by his mother cannot reasonably be held to be borrowed from the Christians, any more than the myths positively proved to be pre-Christian. On the contrary, since the Christian Virgin-myth and Virgin-and-Child worship are certainly of Pagan origin, and of comparatively late Christian acceptance, and since the Virgin-myth was associated with Buddhism even for Westerns in the time of Jerome, the adoration of a Suckling-God is to be presumed pre-Christian in India (which had a Babe-God in Agni in the Veda); and it becomes conceivable that certain parts of the Christian Birth-legend are directly or indirectly derived from Krishnaism. It is an extravagance to suppose the converse.

2. It is equally extravagant to suppose that such a usage as the Krishnaite "name-giving" was borrowed from the short-lived usage of the Church of Alexandria in the matter of combining the Nativity and Epiphany. A similar usage prevailed in the pre-Christian cult of Hercules, and was presumably widespread.

3. Nor can we without defying all probability suppose that such motives as the "ox-and-ass," the "manger," the "tax-paying," and the "Christophoros," were borrowed by the Hindus from Christianity, which itself unquestionably borrowed the first two and the last from Paganism. The fair surmise is rather that the third was borrowed from India: and the necessary assumption, in the present state of our knowledge, is that the others also were ancient in

India, whether or not any of them thence reached Christism in its absorbent stage. It is further possible that the introduction of shepherds into the Christian Birth-legend in the late third Gospel was suggested by knowledge of the Krishna legend. The converse hypothesis has been shown to be preposterous.

4. The myth of the massacre of the innocents is the more to be regarded as pre-Christian in India because it connects naturally with the motive of the attempted slaying of the God-child, and is already found in Semitic mythology in the story of Moses, which is minutely paralleled in one particular in the Egyptian myth of the concealment of Horus in the floating island,[1] and related in others to the universal myth of the attempted slaying of the divine child. The natural presumption is that the Hindu massacre of the innocents is as old as the Kansa myth: the onus of disproof lies with those who allege borrowing from the Gospels.

5. The resemblances between certain Krishnaite and Christian miracles, in the same way, cannot be set down to Hindu borrowing from Christism when so many of the parallel myths[2] are certainly not so borrowed, and so many more presumably in the same case. For the rest, some of the parallels alleged on the Christian side are absurdly far-fetched, and bracketed with etymological arguments which are beneath serious notice.

6. The lateness of the Puránic stories in literary form is no argument against their antiquity. Scholars are agreed that late documents often preserve extremely old myth-material.[3]

Christianity so-called, in short, we know to be wholly manufactured within historic times: Krishnaism we have seen to have had a pre-historic existence. Thus every claim made in this connection by Christians recoils more or less forcibly on their own creed.

[1] Herodotus, ii. 156.

[2] It need hardly be explained that not a tithe of the mythical stories connected with Krishna have been mentioned above. They are extremely numerous, and are all either explicable in terms of the sun-myth or mere poetic adornments of the general legend.

[3] Compare Mr. Lang, *Myth, Ritual, and Religion*, 1st ed. i. 291.

PART III.

THE GOSPEL MYTHS.

Preamble.

If the foregoing pages in any degree effect their purpose, they have shown that a number of data, both miraculous and non-miraculous, in the Christian Gospels, held by Christians to be historical, and held even by some Naturalists to be either historical or at least accretions round the life and doctrine of a remarkable religious teacher and creed-founder, are really mere adaptations from myths of much greater antiquity; and that accordingly the alleged or inferred personality of the Founder is under suspicion of being as mythical as that of the demigods of older lore. It is not here undertaken to offer a complete demonstration of the truth of that surmise; but our survey would be unduly imperfect if the problem were not stated and to some extent dealt with. Broadly, the contention is that when every salient item in the legend of the Gospel Jesus turns out to be more or less clearly mythical, the matter of doctrine equally so with the matter of action, there is simply nothing left which can entitle anyone to a belief in any tangible personality behind the name.

I am well aware that this will still be commonly considered an extravagant position. When in my youth I first heard it put, I so considered it, though I already held the Naturalist view; and my later acquiescence has been the result of the sheer gradual pressure of the argument from analysis—a more thorough analysis, I would fain hope, than that which motived the earlier proposition. I desire to avow, however, that I consider the first recoil from that proposition to have arisen mainly from the mere force of psychological habit even on the plane of innovating criticism. A clear recollection of that psychological state may possibly make the present argument in a measure judicial, if not satisfactory.

The question as to the actuality of the alleged founders of ancient religions may best be approached by the comparative method. It is now agreed that the ancient deities who figure as coming among men to teach creeds, to convey useful knowledge, and to found religious institutions, are purely mythical creations. No student now believes in the historic actuality of Osiris or Dionysos or Krishna, any more than in the existence of Juno or Ashtaroth. The early rationalism of Evemeros, which traced all deities alike to historical personages, is exploded. The so-called Evemerism of Mr. Spencer in no sense reinstates that view: for the theory that primeval man reached his God-idea by way of ancestor-worship gives no shelter to the notion that Hermes and Mithra, for instance, were distinguished personages within the historical period, as was believed last century by Mosheim. Hermes, Mithra, Osiris, Dionysos, Herakles, Attis, Adonis, Horos, are seen to be as certainly mythic as Apollo and Zeus and Brahma and Vishnu.

How then is a line to be scientifically drawn between, on the one hand, the mythic personalities of Dionysos and Osiris and Krishna, and on the other those of Zarathustra and Buddha and Jesus? We all agree that, say, Mohammed is a real historical personage. Significantly enough, the incredibility of the lives of religion-makers is in almost the exact ratio of their historic distance. That circumstance is not, however, in itself decisive against the actuality of any given founder; for though all history becomes more and more clearly mythical the further we go back on any one line of tradition, it is still arguable that if Mohammed founded a religion somewhat in the fashion in which (supernaturalism apart) he is said to have done, a Jewish or an Asiatic prophet in earlier times may have done the same. It will not suffice merely to reply that there are unquestionable myths in the stories of Jesus and Buddha; there are one or two such myths in the story of the life of Confucius, whose historic actuality is not doubted; there is one such myth in the life of Plato, whose historic actuality is no more doubted than that of Aristotle; and there is much myth in the life of Apollonius of Tyana, who appears to be at bottom a real historical personage. And a number of students still believe in the historic actuality of Zarathustra and Buddha, who compare so closely with Jesus as religion-founders, though in their ostensible biographies they are framed in clouds of myth.

Professor Rhys Davids, for instance, agreeing with M. Senart that the Buddha legend is substantially made up of myths from the older lore of Krishna and Râma and Agni, nevertheless cites M. Senart as admitting Buddha's historic actuality. "That the historical basis is *or once was there*, he does not doubt; and he holds that Buddhism, *like every other system*, must have had a human founder, and an historical origin."[1] Like every other system, be it observed: like the cults of Dionysos and Osiris and Herakles; all of which of course had an "historical origin." But what was that origin; and who was their human founder? Clearly there was no one "founder"; there was not even a group or school describable as collective founders: we are dealing with a long process of evolution. If then we reject as we do the pseudo-historical Osiris and Dionysos, why do we accept as historical Buddha and Jesus? Shall we say that behind the mythic figures of Osiris and Dionysos there may have been *some* remote actual man who communicated certain culture and was later worshipped by certain rites? The answer is that such a hypothesis is neither here nor there; it stands for nothing: it makes no impact on our perception. The accredited personalities of Buddha and Jesus, on the other hand, do make a very distinct impression. But is it more forcible than that made *anciently* on men's minds by the stories of Osiris and Attis, or than that made in India to-day by the story and the

[1] *Buddhism*, p. 193.

mystic teaching of Krishna? Is not the difference for us simply one of psychological habit? Is there any more evidence for a real cult-founding Buddha than for a real teaching Krishna?

Carrying the analysis further, we reach some such generalization as this: that where any alleged religion-founder is represented in what appear to be ancient accounts as uttering a coherent and impressive moral doctrine, our tendency is to believe in his actuality, even if he be otherwise quasi-mythical. It is on this account that men cling to the personalities of Moses and Zarathustra and Buddha; and it is because this is lacking in the myths of Dionysos and Osiris that the same men dismiss the notion of *their* actuality. Had the Jesus legend come down to us solely as it stands in the apocryphal Gospels, which give mere miracles without moral teaching, it could not to-day retain any hold among men of education and judgment; though a certain number of such men appear still to believe in the miracle stories of the canonical Gospels. Apart from the sheer force of habit and of partisanship, it is the teaching that to-day upholds any sincere faith in the tale.

Now, it is obvious that in a general way this is no sufficient ground for a critical belief. There are myths of doctrine as well as myths of action. Many fictitious teachings were ascribed to King Solomon, who is at most a historical possibility; and the same thing could easily happen with a pre-Christian Jesus. The story of the promulgation of the Ten Commandments is palpable myth. Even orthodox scholarship admits the late intrusion of doctrinal myth in the New Testament in such a case as the text of the Three Witnesses. Moderately heterodox criticism goes so far as to see a similar process behind the text, "Thou art Peter; and on this rock I will build my Church." Scientific criticism goes a great deal further, and sees, for instance, the same process behind the whole discourses of the Fourth Gospel; though these very discourses only a generation ago set up a special impression of actuality in two such men as the Arnolds, father and son. Where then does the analysis logically stop? Careful comparative study resolves such discourses as the Sermon on the Mount into compilations of the gnomic sayings of many teachers; and the so-called Lord's Prayer is plainly pre-Christian. At what point do we touch biographical bottom?

The strongest way of putting the Christian case, from the rationalist point of view, is one which still passes with many believers for semi-blasphemy: the process, namely, of testing the synoptic Gospels down to an apparent nucleus of primitive narrative. Granting that there has been abundant interpolation, this method proceeds on the axiom that a nucleus there must have been; and argues that its disencumberment amounts to establishing a solid historical basis. Ere long, probably, that will be the position of those Christians who still continue to use the weapons of argument; though the interesting attempt of Mr. A. J. Jolley, in *The Synoptic Problem for English Readers*,[1] to set forth the conclusions reached by Dr. Bernhard Weiss in his works on Mark and Matthew, seems thus far to have attracted hardly any orthodox attention.

Even on the face of it, however, this new position is one of retreat, and is not permanently tenable. Accepting for the argument's sake the "Primitive Gospel" thus educed, we find it to be still a literary patchwork, made up of miracles and unhistorical discourses. The Birth myth and the Crucifixion are not there; but the Temptation Myth and the Transfiguration are. In the forefront stands the compiled Sermon on the Mount; the parables figure as public discourses; the predictions of the fall of Jerusalem, plainly written after the event, are admitted; the mythical Twelve Apostles are already installed; and there is not a single datum of a truly biographical quality. Nor does Mr. Jolley once face the problem, If such Jesuine teachings were actually current, how came it that Paul never cites a single one of them?

I do not here press the point that Dr. Weiss and Mr. Jolley retain obvious patches: for instance, the "except ye

[1] Macmillan & Co. 1893.

repent ye shall all likewise perish," in Luke xiii., where that formula completely stultifies the teaching of the context. Let the text be still further tested down, to the elimination of such evidently heterogeneous tissue, and the invincible difficulty will still face us: the theoretic beginner of the cult has eluded search; we are dealing with myths of doctrine and myths of action. The one tenable hypothesis left to us is still that of a preliminary Jesus "B.C.," a vague cult-founder such as the Jesus ben Pandira of the Talmud, put to death for (probably anti-Judaic) teachings now lost; round whose movement there may have gradually clustered the survivals of an ancient solar worship of a Babe Joshua son of Miriam; and round whose later composite cult, in which "Jesus" *not* of Nazareth figured for Paul as a mere crucified Messiah, a speechless sacrifice, there appear to have coalesced various other doctrinal movements, which perhaps incorporated some actual utterances of several Jesuses of Messianic pretensions, Nazarite and anti-Nazarite, but certainly also gathered up, generation after generation, many documentary compositions and pragmatic and didactic fictions.

The full presentment of this theory, which gradually conducts us from mythology, historically considered, into history, sociologically considered, is necessarily left for another treatise. What is here undertaken is the final step in the preliminary clearing of the mythological ground. In the previous pages we have traced a number of Christian myths to their Pagan origins. There remain a number of Gospel myths of action or narrative, of many of which the Pagan origin is no less clearly demonstrable; and there remain the mythic ascriptions of doctrine with which the other myths coalesced. Without professing to trace all the Gospel myths of either sort, I have attempted a *catalogue raisonné* of a score or more of the former, thus giving a connected and summary view of those already analysed and of a number of others, and I have added some of the proofs that the Gospel teachings, in so far as they purport to be utterances of a wandering and teaching Jesus with twelve disciples, are myths of doctrine.

In the opening treatise I have given reasons for thus bringing into the category of myths such literary fictions as ascribe certain doctrine to a famous personage under conditions which are clearly unhistorical. The myth of Osiris tells that he taught certain things[1] and did certain things; and no one disputes that the entire narrative is myth. It lies on the face of the case that no one man invented agriculture or vine culture or taught men to be civilised. When, however, we come to a legendary personage whose cult survives, or presents a parallel to others which survive, there is an instant recoil from such an admission. Men are fain to believe, even after giving up supernaturalism, that one Moses invented the Ten Commandments, and that one Jesus invented the Golden Rule and ascended a mountain to formulate doctrines of forgiveness and non-resistance. Shown that all of these doctrines were current before the period in question, some men persist in framing formulas about "essential originality," though the personage to whom the originality is ascribed is but an abstraction from the very utterances thus put in his mouth, every detail of the narrative in hand having the stamp of didactic fiction. One must evidently reckon with a certain average incapacity to assimilate more than a modicum of new truth, and look only for gradual psychological adjustments, taking generations to accomplish.

Capacity may be slightly quickened, however, by a survey of the adjustments made in the past. The course of thought, as we have seen, is by way of small concessions. First men seek naturalistic explanations for prodigies in the Old Testament: after a time some consent to see in such prodigies mere myths, based on no one historic episode whatever; the majority, however, still ascribing human personality to many mythical personages. At this stage the prodigies of the New Testament remain unchallenged even for some who see myth in those of the Old; and only gradually is the tentative critical process applied to the later stories also. Here the clinging to personalities

[1] Plutarch, *I. and O.* c. 13.

is strongest, simply because of the closer emotional relation. Much of the delay, however, comes of sheer failure to study the phenomena of comparative mythology. Dean Milman, for instance, was at pains to argue that the Massacre of the Innocents might well pass unnoticed by contemporary historians among the multitude of Herod's barbarities; when a candid glance at earlier forms of the same story might have made it clear to him that he was dealing with a common myth. So, only the other day, we have such a candid and scholarly inquirer as Dr. Percy Gardner repeating[1] once more the fallacious explanation, which has imposed on so many of us, that "an ass and the foal of an ass" represents a Greek misconception of the Hebrew way of saying "an ass"—as if Hebrews even in every-day life lay under a special spell of verbal absurdity—when a glance at the story of Bacchus crossing a marsh on two asses, and at the Greek sign for the constellation Cancer (an ass and its foal), would have shown him that he was dealing with a zodiacal myth.

Broadly speaking, it is by applying *all* the tests of traditionary error, and by recognising that myth formerly so-called is only one form of such error, that we shall reach a just estimate of the historical value of the Gospels. Baur argued, on the whole justly, that Strauss's analysis, able as it was, reached only a negative result because it did not include a comparative criticism of the documents as such.[2] By "negative" he meant, not that the argument was unprofitable because it negated a popular belief—an inept commonplace of which Baur was incapable—but negative in the sense of leaving the question still open: that is to say, that while Strauss offered grounds for rejecting much, he could consistently show no grounds for retaining anything, though he claimed to do so. And the documentary criticism which Baur began or reorganized turns out only to carry Strauss's process further. Strauss clung to the view that while the early Jesuists had little knowledge of

[1] *Exploratio Evangelica*, 1899, p. 156.

[2] *Kritische Untersuchungen über die kanonischen Evangelien*, 1847, pp. 71–73.

the life of the founder they had trustworthy knowledge of many of his teachings. But the effect of the documentary analysis which Strauss failed to make is to leave us no grounds whatever for ascribing any teaching in particular to any one teacher called Jesus; though it is historically possible, and not unlikely, that there were several Jesuses who claimed to be Messiahs. What is certain, *a priori* and *a posteriori*, is that the Gospels are no less absolutely untrustworthy as accounts of any man's teaching than as accounts of any man's deeds, because they gathered up both kinds of statement in the same way. Baur's position was that of an extremely sagacious critic—the acutest of his time, perhaps—who was moving on the true line of scientific inference, but did not live to complete the long journey. "While everything mythic," he tells us, "is unhistorical, not everything unhistorical is mythic."[1] This is the last stage of a pragmatic definition of myth.[2] But the way in which unhistorical statements get to be believed, and unhistorical conclusions to be drawn, is just the way in which myths got to be believed, added to, and pragmatized. The psychology of all such error is substantially the same, and, beyond convenience of descriptive arrangement, nothing is gained by the distinction under notice.

As has already been argued, the mythopœic process is possible to the human mind in all periods, and is actively carried on to-day. Emerson forcibly writes that Christianity "dwells with noxious exaggeration about the person of Jesus. The soul," he protests, "knows no persons"; and he notes that ordinary Christian language "paints a demigod as the Orientals or the Greeks would describe

[1] *Kritische Untersuchungen*, pp. 72–3. Cp. p. 43.

[2] Strauss on this point took up a more scientific position. "Every unhistorical narrative," he writes in reply to Baur in *Das Leben Jesu für das deutsche Volk bearbeitet* (Einleit. iii. § 25, *end*: 3te Aufl. p. 159), "no matter how it arose, in which a religious community see an element of their sacred origins, because of its being an absolute expression of their constitutive feelings and ideas, is a myth." The English translation (i. 214) makes a sad mess of this passage:—"Every *historical* narrative, however it may have arisen, in which a religious community recognizes a component part of their sacred origin as being an absolute expression of *constituent feelings and conceptions*, is a myth." The principle had been put by Strauss in the first *Leben Jesu*, Einleit. § 14, *end*.

Osiris or Apollo."[1] Yet Emerson himself had just been affirming that "Jesus Christ belonged to the true race of prophets. He saw with open eye the mystery of the soul. ......Alone in all history, he estimated the greatness of man......He said in the jubilee of sublime emotion, 'I am divine......'" All of which is absolute myth, as truly myth as the other version.

As against the later literary method of Renan and Arnold, which consists mainly in putting aside the miracles and accepting the narrative that is left, with the arbitrary exception of such teachings as seem unedifying, it may be well to show briefly the effect of the scientific recognition of all the forms of myth in the narrative. Our analysis shows that on the one hand the Twelve Apostles, and on the other hand such prominent teachings as the Sermon on the Mount, are just as mythical as the Virgin Birth, the Temptation, and the Resurrection. At the same time, the documentary analysis shows us that Jesus was at first without cognomen; there was no "of Nazareth" in the legend. In the same way the Johannine discourses fall to the ground. What then is left? What did "Jesus" teach? And who was Jesus? A Nazarite? And if there were no Twelve Apostles, who was there to report his doctrine? Seeing that Paul knew naught of it, how can we consent to suppose that later Christists had any real information? Nay, if these insuperable problems be set aside, how shall we, when delivered from the spell of customary acquiescence, continue to believe that any man ever made a popular movement by enouncing cryptic parables, most of which are proper only to the initiates of a fixed cult, and short strings of maxims some of which represent the last stretch of self-abnegating ethic for brooding men, and are utterly beyond the acceptance of any unselected populace in any age?

One realizes afresh the normal difficulty in even recognizing the problem, when one turns to the notable work of Dr. Percy Gardner, above cited. It marks at some points

[1] *Address to the Senior Class in Divinity College, Cambridge*, 1838.

an advance on even the positions of Dr. Hatch, and it frequently lays down sound caveats. Yet immediately after thus stipulating that "the life of the Master is not, in an objective sense, recoverable beyond a certain point,"[1] it affirms that Francis of Assisi "was like the Founder of Christianity in his gentle spirit, his boundless love for men, his joyful acceptance of poverty and self-denial. He was fond of appealing, like Jesus, to the facts of the visible world, and in hearty sympathy with life in all its forms."[2] Such language implicitly affirms that, however mythical be the Gospel narratives, we can rely on the genuineness of the *logia*. And yet even in the very act of affirming this, Dr. Gardner shows us that he has tacitly eliminated many *logia* for his purpose, since only by a careful selection of passages can we frame the conventional effigy of a Jesus of "gentle spirit," with "boundless love for men." Our explorer even expressly excludes certain Jesuine dicta as obviously mythical. Yet he tacitly founds with absolute confidence on certain others. Dr. Gardner, then, while setting himself the highest standards of historical method, has only repeated with a difference the procedures of Renan and Arnold, and has ignored Baur's reminder to Strauss.

That this is not done in a merely incidental way, or by passing oversight, is made quite clear by a passage in which, again, he pairs with Emerson :—

> "The fact is that the life of Jesus was the occasion and the cause of an enormous development of the spiritual faculties and perceptions of men. He found us children in all that regards the hidden life, and he left us men. The writings of his immediate followers show a fulness and ripeness of spiritual feeling and knowledge, which makes the best of previous religious literature, even the writings of Isaiah and Plato, seem superficial and imperfect. From that time onward (!) men in Christian countries seem to have gained new faculties of spiritual observation. . . ."[3]

For such an affirmation we want, above all things, evidence: we want to know on *which* of the Jesuine sayings the thesis is founded; and why those sayings in particular are held to be genuine. But Dr. Gardner offers no justification, no explanation: he fulminates his

[1] Work cited, p. 172. [2] *Id.* p. 174. [3] Work cited, p. 119.

formula as did Emerson, and there an end. It may well be that even Dr. Gardner's measure of defection from the Myth will take long to win acceptance, and the present indictment of it much longer still; but I cannot conceive that, if men continue to argue the matter at all, criticism can thus sit between the two stools of psychological habit and judicial method. It must in time either surrender unconditionally to the myth or follow reason.

Meantime I can but repeat with insistence and with evidence that the teaching demigod is as essentially a myth as the wonder-working demigod. What Dr. Gardner describes is but an intellectual and psychological miracle: a breach of all evolution. If the apparition of one teacher could thus suddenly bestow subtlety of insight on a whole world before devoid of it, raising to manhood in a generation a humanity which had remained childlike through five thousand years of religious speculation, there need surely be no more hesitation over such trifles as human Parthenogenesis and raising the dead. It ought not to be necessary at this stage of thought to refute such a theory of psychological catastrophism, which really throws back the whole discussion, at this particular point, to a pre-scientific level. Before Dr. Gardner thus apotheosized the mythic Jesus in the name of the historic method, Newman, the foremost of the cultured and reasoning believers of the century, avowed that "There is little in the ethics of Christianity which the human mind may not reach by its natural powers, and which here or there......has not in fact been anticipated."[1]

But it will not suffice merely to counter authority with authority, even where the latter has a special weight. The scientific solution must lie in a fuller presentation of the proof that neither the hypothetic Jesus of the Gospels nor his immediate followers represented any special originality, whether of feeling or of fancy or of thought. A conspectus of that evidence is now submitted, with the claim that no

[1] Letter to Mr. W. S. Lilly, cited in the latter's *Claims of Christianity*, 1894, pp. 30–31.

verdict can be adequate which does not face it. Only, we must dispose effectually of the myths of action before we attempt to estimate the evidence for the doctrine. So little impression has been made on the general intelligence hitherto by the demonstration of mythical elements in the Gospels, that we find even a trained Naturalist, in the very act of applying mythological science to the Christian case, taking for granted the conventional "biographical" data. The late Mr. Grant Allen, in his *Evolution of the Idea of God*, does the excellent practical service of bringing Mr. Frazer's theorem of the Vegetation-Cult in connection with the Christian doctrine of crucifixion and salvation—a step not previously ventured on in any book, though it had been made in Freethought journals. Yet Mr. Allen sets out with the dogmatic decision[1] that the Gospel Jesus was, "at the moment when we first catch a glimpse of him in the writings of his followers, a Man recently deceased, respected, reverenced, and perhaps worshipped by a little group of fellow peasants who had once known him as Jesus the son of the carpenter. On that unassailable Rock of solid historical fact we may well be content to found our argument in this volume. Here, at least, nobody can accuse us of 'crude and gross Euhemerism.' Or rather the crude and gross Euhemerism is here known to represent the solid truth."

It is difficult to understand how solid truth can be crude and gross Euhemerism, which means, and can only mean, the blundering application of a false mythological theory to a given problem of religious origins. I will not call Mr. Allen's Euhemerism (or Evemerism, as the word ought to be written in English) crude and gross; but I do maintain that he has fallen into Evemerism, in the sense of a fallacious theory of the origin of a cult, and that his assumption, instead of serving as a rock foundation for his application of Mr. Frazer's theory to the Christ cult, is really a mine which saps that. So little critical heed has he given to the problem that he actually

[1] Work cited, p. 16.

commits himself to the detail of "the carpenter," which even some supernaturalist critics have admitted to be an unhistorical addition, seeing that for Origen[1] the reading of Mark vi. 3, which makes Jesus himself a carpenter, was not canonical, and that there remains only the phrase in Matt. xiii. 55, for which there is no support in Luke or John. Both alike are excluded from the "Primitive Gospel" even by the school of Weiss; and the rationalistic criticism which dismisses Mary and Joseph as alike mythical must needs dismiss the myth of Joseph's avocation. Naturalism must found itself in a more scientific fashion than this if it is to hold its own against the eternal assault of credulity and organized ecclesiasticism. The following studies, then, are an attempt to clear the ground.

[1] *Against Celsus*, vi. 36, *end*.

FIRST DIVISION.

MYTHS OF ACTION.

§ 1. *The Virgin Birth.*

THOUGH the mystical character of the birth-legend is recognized by all who consent to apply rational tests to the Gospels, it remains important to keep in mind the nature and extent of the documentary proof that the myth is borrowed from Paganism. If that be lost sight of, the conditions of the composition of the Gospels cannot be properly realized. Strauss saw the birth-story to be myth, but failed to note how emphatically it belonged to the surrounding Pagan world, seeing there rather analogies than sources.

Now, the Virgin-Mother myth is universal in Paganism, and certainly has no recognized place in orthodox Judaism before the Jesuist period. The so-called prophecy of Isaiah (vii. 14) could never have been read as an announcement of a long-distant Parthenogenesis by the most insane Talmudism had not the myth of Virgin-birth first obtruded itself from the Pagan side. If, indeed, Judaism was to develop its slowly-formed Saviour-myth at all, it could scarcely avoid the datum that he be born of a Virgin-Mother. All the Saviour-Gods of Paganism were so reputed, either in respect of the mother being a mortal while the father was a God, or in that the mother too was a Goddess, and as such termed a virgin by way of adoring flattery, as all male Gods were termed beneficent, whatever might be the cruelty of their supposed deeds. It was perhaps in the same spirit that those Goddesses who were specially distinguished as virgin, Athênê and Artemis and Persephonė, at times received the title of mother;[1] but the converse was a more familiar usage. Thus, as above noted, Hèrè, wife of Zeus and Queen of Heaven; Cybelė, the "mother of the Gods"; Leto, mother of Apollo and Artemis; Dėmėtėr, the Earth-mother, who, as such, equates with both Ceres and Vesta; and Venus herself, were all "Virgin"[2] as much as Isis, who was at once sister and wife (and in a late version the mother) of Osiris, and was fabled to have been deflowered in the very womb of her own mother.[3] And Dionysos in particular came to figure indifferently as son of Dėmėtėr, the Mother, and of Persephonė, "the Maiden," styled ἁγνης, pure.[4]

All of these Goddesses in turn became associated with the *Virgo Cælestis*, the Virgin of the Zodiacal sphere, who, with her extended branch or ear of corn, was, no doubt, with other ancient figures of fruit-holding Goddesses, the kernel of the myth of Mother Eve and her apple, besides lending herself to the Jewish "prophecy" of the Messianic "branch."[5] Dėmėtėr was καρποφόρος, and ἀμαλλοφόρος, and χλοηφόρος, and ὡρηφόρος, the corn-bearer, the sheaf-bearer, the leaf-bearer, the fruit-bearer. And as regards the special machinery of the Joseph and Mary myth—the warning in a dream and the abstention of the husband—it is a simple duplication of the story of the relations of the father and mother of Plato, the former being warned in a dream by Apollo, so that the child was Virgin-born.[6]

[1] Strabo, x. 3, § 19; 6, § 9; Boeckh, *Corp. Inscr. Græc.* 3993; Aristotle, cited by Clement of Alexandria, *Protrept.* ii.

[2] See refs. above, p. 168, *note* 9. Cp. Firmicus, *De Errore*, iv.; Porphyry, *De Abstinentia*, ii. 32; Lucian, *De Sacrificiis*, c. 6; and the Latin inscription in Wright, *The Celt, the Roman, and the Saxon*, 4th ed. p. 321.

[3] Plutarch, *Isis and Osiris*, c. 12. She is Virgin as identified with Athênê and Persephonê. *Id.* cc. 27, 62.

[4] The association of Dionysos with Dêmêtêr is relatively late, there being no trace of it in the Homeridian hymn; but it is certainly pre-Christian, and is only a transference of the Child-God from one Goddess-Mother to another. Cp. Cicero, *De nat. deor.* ii. 24.

[5] For the figure of this Virgin as represented in the ancient Zodiacs see, for instance, the frontispiece to Volney's *Ruins of Empires*, and the plate in Ernest Bunsen's *Islam, or the True Christianity*, 1889.

[6] Diogenes Laërtius, b. iii. c. i. § 1. It is true that Diogenes wrote in the second or third century after Christ; but for this story he cites (1) Speusippus,

No less significant is the fact that most of the few details given of the Virgin-Mother in the Gospels are in striking correspondence with Pagan myths. Early in January the Egyptians celebrated "the Coming of Isis out of Phœnicia,"[1] from which it appears that Isis was supposed to make a journey either to bring forth Horos or after the birth, as Mary goes into Egypt. But the bringing-forth of the God-child while "on a journey" is an item common to a dozen pre-Christian myths, as those of Hagar and Ishmael, Mandanê and Cyrus, Latona and Apollo, Maya and Buddha, and the stories of Æsculapius and Apollonius of Tyana;[2] and the peculiar motive of the taxpaying is almost certainly derived either from the Hindu legend of Krishna or from a cognate Asiatic myth.[3]

§ 2. *The Mythic Maries.*

The first step of criticism, after recognizing the myth of the Virgin-Birth, is to assume that the mother of the "real" Jesus was nevertheless one Mary (Miriam), the wife of Joseph. For this assumption there is not the slightest justification. The whole birth-story being indisputably late and the whole action mythic, the name is also to be presumed mythical. For this there is the double reason that Mary, or Miriam, was already a mythic name for both Jews and Gentiles. The Miriam of Exodus is no more historical than Moses: like him and Joshua, she is to be reckoned an ancient deity Evemerized; and the Arab tradition that she was the mother of Joshua (=Jesus)[4] raises an irremovable surmise that a Mary the

the nephew of Plato, whose *Funeral Banquet of Plato* was extant; (2) Clearchus' *Panegyric on Plato*, which likewise belongs to Plato's generation; and (3) Anaxilides' *History of Philosophers*. The myth, as regards Plato, is thus evidently pre-Christian. Nor is it confined to Europe even in relation to philosophers, for we find it applied to Confucius, as to Buddha. See above, p. 190.

[1] Plutarch, *I. and O.* c. 50.

[2] See above, *Christ and Krishna*, pp. 190–3.

[3] *Id.* pp. 194–6.

[4] Above, pp. 82–3.

Mother of Jesus may have been worshipped in Syria long before our era.

It is not possible from the existing data to connect historically such a cult with its congeners; but the mere analogy of names and epithets goes far. The mother of Adonis, the slain "Lord" of the great Syrian cult, is Myrrha; and Myrrha in one of her myths is the weeping tree from which the babe Adonis is born. Again, Hermes, the Greek *Logos*, has for mother Maia, whose name has further connections with Mary. In one myth, Maia is the daughter of Atlas,[1] thus doubling with Maira, who has the same father,[2] and who, having "died a virgin,"[3] was seen by Odysseus in Hades. Mythologically, Maira is identified with the Dog-Star, which is the star of Isis.[4] Yet again, the name appears in the East as Maya, the Virgin-Mother of Buddha; and it is remarkable that according to a Jewish legend the name of the Egyptian princess who found the babe Moses was Merris.[5] The plot is still further thickened by the fact that, as we learn from the monuments, one of the daughters of Ramses II. was named Meri.[6]

In the matter of names, it is of some though minor interest to recall that Dêmêtêr is associated in Greek mythology with one Jasius or Jasion—not as mother, but as lover.[7] Jason, we know, actually served as a Greek form of the name Joshua or Jesous;[8] and Jasion, who in one story is the founder of the famous Samothrakian mysteries,[9] is in the ordinary myth slain by Zeus. But the partial parallel of his name is of less importance than the possible parallel of his mythic relation to the Goddess Mother.

In many if not all of the cults in which there figures a

[1] Apollodorus, iii. x. 1, 2. [2] Pausanias viii. 48.

[3] *Id.* x. 30, citing the lost poem, *The Return from Ilium*; see also scholiast on *Odyssey*, xi. 325.

[4] Preller, *Griech. Myth.* i. 359, following Hesychius. Cp. Plutarch, *I. and O.* c. 61.

[5] Eusebius, *Præparatio Evangelica*, ix. 27 (Migne, *Ser. Græc.* xxi. 729), citing Artapanus.

[6] Brugsch, *Egypt under the Pharaohs*, Eng. tr. ii. 117. It is noteworthy that Ramses II. had Semitic blood in him, and introduced into Egypt the Semitic institution of the harem. Rawlinson, *Hist. of Ancient Egypt*, ii. 324.

[7] *Odyssey*, v. 125; Hesiod, *Theogony*, 969.

[8] Josephus, 12 *Ant.* v. 1. [9] Preller, *Griech. Myth.* i. 667.

nursing mother it is found that either her name signifies "the nurse," or that becomes one of her epithets.[1] Thus Maia stands for "the nurse"[2] (τροφός); Mylitta means "the child-bearing one";[3] both Dêmêtêr and Artemis were styled "child-rearers";[4] and Isis was alternately styled "the nurse" and "the mother."[5] Now, one of the most important details of the confused legend in the Talmud concerning the pre-Christian Jesus Ben Pandira, who is conjoined with Ben Stada, is that the mother is in one place named Miriam *Magdala*,[6] Mary "the nurse," or "the hair-dresser."[7] As Isis too plays the part of a hair-dresser,[8] it seems clear that we are dealing here also with myth, not biography. In the Gospels we have Mary *the* Magdalene—that is, of the supposed place Mágdala, which Jesus in one text visits.[9] But Magdala at most simply means a tower or "high place" (the same root yielding the various senses of "nursing"=rearing, and "hair-dressing"); and in the revised text Magdala gives way to Magadan, thus disappearing entirely from the Gospels. There is no documentary trace of it save as a citadel so named by Josephus.[10] Mary the Magdalene, finally, plays in the Gospels a purely mythical part, that of one of the finders of the risen Lord. The interpolated text in Luke (viii. 2), baldly describing her as having had seven devils cast out of her by Jesus, is equally remote from history; but it points towards the probable mythic solution. Maria the Magdalene, who in post-evangelical myth becomes a penitent harlot, is probably cognate with the Evemerized Miriam of the Mosaic myth,

[1] Cp. Hesychius, *s.v.* Ammas, cited by K. O. Müller, *Dorians*, i. 404, note. Selden (*De Diis Syris*, Synt. ii. cap. ii. ed. 1680, p. 182) derives *Ammas* from the Semitic *Aymma* = mother.

[2] Porphyry, *De Abstinentia*, iv. 16.

[3] Bähr, *Symbolik des mosaischen Cultus*, i. 436. [4] Above, p. 168.

[5] Plutarch, *I. and O.* cc. 53, 56.

[6] Cp. Derenbourg, *Essai sur l'histoire et la géographie de la Palestine*, 1e Ptie. 1867, p. 471, *note*.

[7] Jastrow, *Dictionary of the Targumim, Talmud, and the Midrashic Literature*, part iii. 1888, p. 213*a*, citing the *Hagigah*, 4*b*; *Sanh.* 67*a*; *Sabb.* 104*b*—earlier edd. Cp. Reland, *Palestina Illustrata*, lib. iii. *s.v.* Magdala (ed. 1714, p. 884); Lightfoot, *Horæ Hebraicæ: in Luc.* viii. 2 (ed. 1674, p. 101).

[8] Plutarch, *I. and O.* c. 15.

[9] Matt. xv. 39, A.V. [10] *Wars*, xi. 25; *Antiq.* xiii. 23; xviii. 1.

who also is morally possessed by devils, and is expressly punished for her sin before being forgiven. Something else, evidently, has underlain the pseudo-historical tale; and the Talmudic reference, instead of being a fiction based on the scanty data in the Gospels, is presumptively an echo of a mythic tradition, which may be the real source of the Gospel allusions. In Jewry the profession of hair-dressing seems to have been identified with that of *hetaira*—the character ultimately ascribed in Christian legend to Mary the Magdalene.

The Gospels, coming into existence at a time when on all hands asceticism as a religious principle was outfacing phallicism and sexualism, could not admit of any myth representing the God as having sex relations with women; though in the Fourth Gospel, where he is humanly and attractively pictured as the tender friend of the sisters of Lazarus, there is also left open the unpleasant problem before alluded to. Even in this case, however, the friendship with a "Mary" points towards some old myth in which a Palestinian God, perhaps named Joshua, figures in the changing relations of lover and son towards a mythic Mary—a natural fluctuation in early theosophy, and one which occurs with a difference in the myths of Mithra, Adonis, Attis, Osiris, and Dionysos, all of whom are connected with Mother-Goddesses and either a consort or a female double, the mother and the consort being at times identified.[1] And the solution in the case of the Jesus myth becomes pretty clear when we come to the story of the Resurrection.

As at the beginning, so at the end of the story, Mary plays a mythic part. In the Gospels, taken as a whole, she has two typic characters—that of the child-bearer and that of the Mater Dolorosa, mourning for her child slain; and at both of those points we have for the legend those

[1] One mythic source of this double relation lies in the conception of the Sun-God's connection with the Goddesses of Dawn and Twilight. It was equally natural to picture him as *born of* the Dawn, and as the lover who leaves her. Again, he could as easily be figured as born of the Night, and again as the lover of the Night or the Twilight. Cp. Cox, *Mythology of the Aryan Nations*, pp. 33, 241–8; *Manual of Mythology*, pp. 96–97. The story of Œdipus marrying his mother Jocasta was thus mythically originated.

most decisive of all origins, ritual and art. No less general than the figure of the child-suckling Goddess was the conception of a mourning Goddess, or Dolorous Mother. In the myths of Venus and Adonis, Ishtar and Tammuz, Cybelè and Attis, we have at first sight a non-maternal[1] but in another view a maternal mourning;[2] while Dêmêtêr, wailing for Persephonê, was for the Greeks pre-eminently the Mater Dolorosa;[3] and there is a rather remarkable anticipation of the inconsolable "Rachel weeping for her children" in Hesiod's account of Rhea (Cybelè) possessed by "a grief not to be forgotten" because of her children, whom their sire Kronos had devoured.[4] In the cult of Attis the weeping of the Great Mother over the mutilated body of the youth is a ceremonial feature;[5] and in the saga which makes Dêmêtêr the mother of Dionysos it is she who brings together the mangled limbs of the young God (as Isis in one story does with Osiris, and in another with Horos) when he has been dismembered by the Titans, whereafter she bears him again.[6] And most noteworthy of all is the coincidence of the mourning of the two or more Maries with the ritual lamentation of the "divine sisters" Isis and Nephthys for Osiris—a customary funeral service with the Egyptians.[7] That lament was supposed to be made at the spring equinox, the time of the

[1] Diodorus, iii. 59.

[2] In one version of the Aphrodite and Adonis myth Adonis is a child given by Aphrodite in a chest into the charge of Persephone (Apollodorus, b. iii. c. xiv. 4); and Macrobius (*Sat.* i. 21), describing the image of the mourning Goddess at Mount Libanus, goes on to explain that it means the earth (the mother) mourning during winter for the loss of the sun. It is clear from Lucian's account that she combined many Goddess-attributes. (Cp. Ammianus Marcellinus, xix. i. 11.) In the myth of Cybelè and Attis, again, the character of the "mother of the Gods," and her "love without passion for Attis" (so Julian: the popular view was different, according to Arnobius, v. 13; Diodorus, iii. 57; Lucian, *De Sacrificiis*, 7), recall the two Maries of the Christian legend, one the mother, the other the penitent devotee.

[3] Grote and Renan apply the term to her: *History of Greece*, 4th ed. i. 38; *Etudes d'Histoire Religieuse*, p. 53.

[4] Hesiod, *Theog.* 467.

[5] Arnobius, *Adversus Gentes*, v. 7; vii. 343. Cp. Diodorus, as last cited.

[6] Diodorus, iii. 62. In another version the Mother Goddess Rhea performs the function (Cornutus, *De natura deorum*, 30); in yet another Apollo does it by order of Zeus (Clem. Alex. *Protrept.* ii. 18)—a parallel to the function of John in the Christian story.

[7] *Records of the Past*, vol. ii. pp. 113–120.

mythic crucifixion; and it is plain that the Gospel story has been manipulated on some such basis. In Matt. xxvii. 56, we have as mourners "Mary Magdalene and Mary the mother of James and Joses, *and* the mother of the sons of Zebedee." Here the mother of James and Joses is a crux for the orthodox, who dispute as to whether she was simply the whilom Virgin; and the difficulty is not helped by verse 61, where we have "Mary Magdalene *and the other Mary*." Since Mary the mother of Jesus is here not mentioned at all, and nothing whatever has been said as to her dying previously, the inference is that the narratives of the part played by the women at the resurrection were framed *before* the birth-story had become current. The Mary-myth thus grew up from two separate roots.

In Mark, matters are further complicated. "Mary Magdalene and Mary the mother of James the less and Joses" are accompanied by Salome (xv. 40); Mary Magdalene and Mary the (mother ?) of *Joses* see Jesus buried (47); while Mary Magdalene and Mary the (mother?) of *James* with Salome bring the spices (xvi. 1). In Luke, again (xxiv. 10), we have the two latter Maries and *Joanna*, not at the cross, but at the tomb. More complicated still does the matter become in John, where (xix. 25) we have Jesus' mother (not named) and her *sister* Mary the (wife ?) of Clopas, and Mary Magdalene. Of these variations the orthodox explanation is the lapse of memory on the part of the chroniclers—a mere evasion of the problem. In view of all the data, we may turn with some degree of confidence to the solution of an ancient ritual usage, with occasional variations, represented in pictures or sculpture. What we already know of ancient ritual supports the view; and, as we have seen, there are weighty reasons for believing that the Christian legend was first set forth in a dramatic worship.[1] The crowd of women who in all the accounts are represented as following the God from Galilee would on this hypothesis be, equally with the Maries, figures in a ritual lamentation such as belonged to all the

[1] See above, *Christ and Krishna*, pp. 227–235.

pagan worships of a slain Saviour God; as in the usage of the "women weeping for Tammuz," which the Hebrew prophet denounced centuries before.[1] And even as the Goddess wept annually over the image of the beloved Attis or Adonis or Osiris, figuring first as consort or lover and later as mother, so in the early Jesuist mystery-drama, which excluded the lover-motive, would a Maria (a tradition from a similar ancient Goddess-cult) weep over the image of the Crucified One, figuring as his devoted disciple; till the Fourth Gospel, which has no Birth Story, and which, elsewhere as here speaking of Jesus' mother without naming her, introduces her as the first of three Maries who stand by the cross. Thereafter, perhaps against a reluctance of many to give the God an earthly mother at all, the myth-cycle rounded itself for the Christian cultus.

The *finding* of the body by a woman or women, in any case, was equally part of the cults of Osiris and Attis, though there would doubtless be local variations, as in the different Christian versions. And the crowd of women followers is in a general way obviously precedented in the myth of Dionysos, which, as we shall see, Christism copies at several points.

To surmise, in the face of all the mythic data, that there *was* a Mary Magdalene, who with "the other Mary" *thought* she saw either the risen Lord or the angel announcing the Lord's resurrection, is a mere defiance of all critical tests. Renan, accepting the myth for his artistic purposes, notes that Paul says nothing about the women; and he implies a touch of apostolic misogyny. This is but critical caprice. The rational inference is that even the late interpolator who made Paul speak of Jesus as having appeared to five hundred at once, either had not yet met with, or disbelieved, the Magdalene story, though the Gospels were already in existence.

[1] Ezekiel viii. 14.

§ 3. *The Myth of Joseph.*

Alike from the point of view of the mythologist and from that of the believer, there is at first sight something of a crux in the legend which gives the "Virgin" a husband. Had Joseph figured to start with as the father of Jesus, the grafting-on of the myth of the supernatural conception could have happened all the same, that being after all only a new form of the common Hebraic myth of the birth of a sanctified child to aged parents. But the mythical father appears, so far as we know, simultaneously with the mythic mother, albeit only to occasion the assurance that he is not really the father at all. Thus he does not strengthen the claim of the mother's virginity: and there is no ostensible ground for his invention. Apologetics might hereupon argue that the detail is thus obviously genuine biography; and even the naturalist might be so led to surmise that "the" Gospel Jesus had had a known parentage, and that the virgin-birth-myth was merely superimposed on the facts. All the while, however, there is a decisive solution in terms of mythology.

The first preoccupation of the early Judaic myth-makers, evidently, was to present the Messiah as Ben David, "son" of the hero-king, himself clothed about with myth, like Cyrus. For this purpose were framed the two mythic genealogies. But it so happened that the Palestinian tradition demanded a Messias Ben Joseph—a descendant of the mythic patriarch—as well as a Messias Ben David. We are not concerned here with the origin of the former doctrine, which suggests a partial revival of the ancient adoration of the God Joseph as well as that of the God Daoud, though it may have been a tribal matter. "It is not likely," says one scholar,[1] "that the idea of a Messiah the son of Joseph would have its origin anywhere but among the Samaritans, who were always eager to raise the tribe of Joseph at the expense of Judah." The fourth

[1] Nutt, *Fragments of a Samaritan Targum*, 1874, introd. p. 69.

Gospel[1] shows the occurrence of Samaritan contacts with the Jesuist cult; and the book of Acts assumes that it was spread equally through Samaria and Judæa.[2] There were thus sufficient grounds for adopting the favourite Samaritan myth.

But it suffices us that the myth had a general Jewish currency. The Hebraist just cited summarizes the doctrine on the subject as follows: "Messiah the Son of Joseph will come before Messiah the Son of David, will assemble the ten tribes *in Galilee*, and lead them to Jerusalem, but will at last perish in battle against Gog and Magog for the sins of Jeroboam."[3] This, however, overlooks the circumstance that in two Talmudic passages the Messiah Ben David is identified with the Messiah Ben Joseph, or, as he is styled in one case, Ben Ephraim.[4] The obvious motive for this identification would be as natural to Jesuists as to orthodox Judaists. The Messiah being expected under two names, a claimant with either title might be met by denial on the score that he had not the right descent. To make the Son of David a Son of Joseph by the plan of giving him an actual father of the latter name was a device thoroughly on the plane of the popular psychology of that age; since the Davidists[5] could point out to the Josephists that their stipulation was now fulfilled in a manner which showed them to have misunderstood their prophecy.[6]

The myth of Joseph, then, arose as a real accessory to the cult. Once introduced, he would naturally figure as an elderly man, not only in the interest of the Virgin-myth, but in terms of the Hebrew precedent, adopted in the myth

[1] John iv. Cp. Luke xvii. 11. [2] Acts viii. 1, 5, etc.

[3] Nutt, as cited, p. 70. Cp. Leslie, *Short and Easy Method with the Jews*, ed. 1812, pp. 127-130; Lightfoot, *Horæ Hebraicæ: in Matt.* i. 2.

[4] Tract. Succa, fol. 52, 1; Zohar Chadash, fol. 45, 1; and Pesikta, fol. 62, quoted by F. H. Reichardt, *Relation of the Jewish Christians to the Jews*, 1884, pp. 37-38.

[5] The passage duplicated in Matt. xxii. 41-46, Mark xii. 35-36, and Luke xx. 41-44, shows that there was an anti-Davidic group of Jesuists, who interpolated the Gospels for their special purpose.

[6] Renan, who has so many glimpses that come to nothing because of his lawless method, has the note: "Le nom de *Ben Joseph*, qui, dans le Talmud, désigne l'un des Messies, donne à réfléchir" (*Vie de Jésus*, édit 15e. p. 74, *note*). But he goes no further.

of the parentage of John the Baptist. He is accordingly represented in the apocryphal History of Joseph the Carpenter (cc. 4, 7) and in the Gospel of the Birth of Mary (c. 8), though not in those of the canon, as a very old man; and this is the view of Christian tradition. Such a concept might of course very well arise from the simple wish to insist on the point that Joseph was not the real father of Jesus. But here again there is a presumption that the detail, along with that of the leading of the laden ass by Joseph in the journey of the "holy family," was suggested by old religious ceremonial. In the sacred procession of Isis, as described by Apuleius in his *Metamorphoses*, one of the figures is that of a feeble old man leading an ass. It is sufficiently unlikely that the great Isiac cult would adopt such a detail by way of representing an episode originating in a recent system. Grounds for the symbolism in question may be found in Plutarch's statement[1] that in the forecourt of the temple of a Goddess at Sais there were sculptured a child, an old man, and some animal figures, the two former standing simply for the beginning and the ending of life. Further, the Egyptians held that all things came from Saturn[2] (or a similar Egyptian God), who signified at once Time and the Nile,[3] and was always figured as aged. On the other hand, as we have seen and shall see throughout this investigation, the Christian system is a patchwork of a hundred suggestions drawn from pagan art and ritual usage.

§ 4. *The Annunciation.*

This obvious introduction to the supernatural birth is anticipated in several pagan legends; but the most precise parallel is the Egyptian ritual usage or standing myth in regard to the birth of the kings, which is fully set forth in the sculptures on the wall of the temple of Luxor, reproduced and elucidated by Sharpe.[4] There we have first the Annunciation to the maiden queen Mautmes, by the ibis-

[1] *I. and O.* c. 32. [2] *Id.* c. 59. [3] *Id.* c. 32.
[4] *Egyptian Mythology*, pp. 18–19.

headed Thoth, Logos and messenger of the Gods, that she will bear a son. In the next scene the Holy Spirit, Kneph, and the Goddess Athor take the queen's hands and hold to her mouth the *crux ansata*, the cross symbol of life, thus supernaturally impregnating her. In another scene is represented the birth of the babe, and his adoration by deities or priests. This was part of the systematic deification of the Egyptian kings; a process which sometimes included their being raised to the position of the third person in the prevailing Trinity; and it seems to have customarily involved the doctrine that the king's mother was the spouse of the great God Amun-ra, who was therefore the king's father. Thus the post-Pauline creed-makers of Alexandria had well-tried myth material lying ready to their hands in the ancient Egyptian system. A little had to be left out; but there was small need to invent anything new.

§ 5. *The Cave and Stable Birth.*

Forming as it does part of the late fabulous introduction to the third Gospel, the story of the birth of the God-Child in a stable is as obviously unhistorical as the rest of that narrative. And, whether we take the "canonical" story of the inn-stable or the "apocryphal" story of the cave, which has become an accepted Christian tradition, we have clearly an ill-disguised adaptation of a widespread pagan myth.[1] There can be little doubt that the cave shown as the God's birth-place at Bethlehem had been from time immemorial a place of worship in the cult of Tammuz, as it actually was in the time of Jerome;[2] and as the quasi-historic David bore the name of the Sun-God Daoud, or Dodo,[3] who was identical with Tammuz, it was not improbably on that account that Bethlehem was traditionally "the city of David." In view of these variations of God-names, however, and of the close similarities of so many of the ancient cults; and on the hypothesis that the mythical

[1] See above, *Christ and Krishna*, pp. 197–215.
[2] Epist. 58, *ad Paulinum*. [3] Sayce, Hibbert Lectures, pp. 56–57.

Joshua, son of Miriam, was an early Hebrew deity, one form of the Tammuz cult *may* in pre-Christian times have been a worship of a Mother and Child, Mary and Jesus—that in short Maria = Myrrha, and that Jesus was a name of Adonis. Sacred caves were about as common as temples in Greece; and Apollo, Herakles, Hermes, Cybelê, Dêmêtêr, and Poseidon were alike worshipped in them.[1] But above all the great cult of Mithra, the Mediator, made a cave pre-eminently the place for worshipping its God; and it may be taken as certain that he, and similarly Tammuz, being represented to be born on what we now call Christmas Day, would be figured as cave-born. Hermes too, the Logos and Messenger or Mediator, was born of Maia in a cave.[2] The stable motive, again, belongs to an extremely ancient mythology. The stable-shed, which appears in the Catacomb sculptures, was probably pre-historic in the birth-ritual of Krishnaism, and would seem even from these very sculptures to have been borrowed by the Christians from Mithraism.[3] The adoration of the "Magi," which as we have just seen was paralleled in the Egyptian birth-ritual, has every sign of being originally a ritual usage; and the "ox and ass" of Christian legend in all probability had the same origin; as had the legend of the bending palm-tree as given in the Koran—a legend set forth in a Catacomb sculpture, and given with a difference in an apocryphal Gospel, but long anticipated in the myths of the births of Apollo and Buddha.[4] So again with the "child wrapped in swaddling clothes and lying in a manger." That is the exact description of the Babe-God Hermes in Grecian song and sculpture; and equally of the Babe-God Dionysos, who was carried in his manger-basket in ritual-procession, and so represented in art; and of the divine child Ion, who is laid by his mother in his swaddling clothes and basket cradle in the cave of her nuptials, and carried thence, cradled, by Hermes to the temple.[5] In the Catacomb sculpture, the "manger"

[1] Pausanias, ii. 23; iii. 25; vii. 25; viii. 15, 36, 42; x. 32.
[2] Homeridian Hymn to Hermes; Apollodorus, bk. iii. x. 2.
[3] See above, *Christ and Krishna*, pp. 199–213.
[4] *Id.* pp. 193, 210.
[5] *Id.* pp. 198, 199, 200.

is just the long basket or *liknon* of the Greek God-children.[1] A similar ritual, too, is established by Christian evidence[2] as having flourished under the Ptolemies in Egypt. The *Chronicon Paschale* represents that even at that period the customary adoration of a virgin-born child lying in a manger[3] was an ancient mystery; and we know from other sources that the Sun-God Horos, son of the Virgin Isis, was represented annually as born at the winter solstice, at the moment of the appearance of the constellation *Virgo*, in the temple where dwelt the sacred cow and bull, of whom the former, like the Goddess, was held to be supernaturally impregnated.[4] Nothing in hierology is more certain than that the Christian story of the birth of Jesus is a mere adaptation of these ancient pagan materials. The process of myth-manufacturing can be seen going on in the Gospels themselves, Luke adding the shepherds, and the conception of Elizabeth, to the machinery of the other versions, as the Apocryphal Gospels add still more. The shepherds came from the same pre-historic source as the rest. They belong to the myths of Cyrus and Krishna; and they are more or less implied in that of Hermes, who on the day of his birth stole the cloud cows of Apollo, himself a divine shepherd, and God of shepherds.

§ 6. *The Birthday.*

That this must have been placed either on the 25th December, or on some other solar date, soon after the birth

[1] It may be worth noting that so late as the middle of the seventeenth century this symbol survived in Protestant England. "The coffin of our Christmas pies, in shape long," says Selden, "is in imitation of the cratch" (*i.e.*, *crèche*). *Table Talk*, art. CHRISTMAS.

[2] Above, p. 202.

[3] In this case the word is not *liknon* but *phatnē*, the term used in Luke. This was the name given in the ancient astronomy to the nebula of the constellation Cancer (Ass and Foal)—a further connection of the birth-myth with astronomy.

[4] By a ray of light—an idea reproduced in pictorial treatment of the myth of the Virgin Mary. The cow myth was widely spread. See refs. above, p. 201, note 5.

legend took Christian shape, is obvious; and the late recognition of that date by the Church was simply due to the notorious fact of its having been the birthday of the Sun-God in half a dozen other religions—Egyptian, Persian, Phœnician, Grecian, Teutonic. Only when Christism had become as powerful as these could it thus openly outface them. Several sects, indeed, long persisted in fixing the day on the 24th or 25th of April, thus connecting it with the vernal equinox rather than the winter solstice, while others placed it at 25th May; and the greater part of the Eastern Church for centuries made the date 6th January—the day now called Epiphany.[1] All alike were solar, and were chosen on the same principle as had been acted on by the Platonists, who placed the master's birthday on that of Apollo[2]—that is, either at Christmas or at the vernal equinox. As Julian has explained, these dates varied in terms of the different ideas as to when the year began;[3] and the Christian choice would be determined by the prevailing usage near the Christian centres. But even in Palestine the day chosen had long been a sacred one outside the prevailing cult. It was on the 25th of December (Casleu or Chisleu) that Antiochus Epiphanes caused sacrifice to be offered on an "idol altar" placed on the "altar of God";[4] and from what we know of the persistent polytheistic tendencies of the Palestinians at that and earlier stages of their history we may infer that the birthday of the Sun-God was a well-known date for them as for other nations, though after the Maccabean period it would for a time be little heard of in Jewry, save among the country-people.

§ 7. *The Massacre of the Innocents.*

It is hardly necessary to dwell on the unhistorical character of this story, which appears only in the late preface to the first Gospel, being absent even from the

[1] Bingham, *Christian Antiquities*, ed. 1858, vii. 280–2.
[2] Diogenes Laërtius, *Plato*, 2.
[3] *In Regem Solem*, c. 20. See above, *Christ and Krishna*, pp. 177, 179, *notes*.
[4] Macc. i. 54–59.

elaborate narrative of the third, where the element of ritual is so obvious in the first two chapters. It is simply a detail in the universal myth of the attempted slaying of the Child-Sun-God,[1] the disappearance of the stars at morning suggesting a massacre from which the Sun-Child escapes; and we see it already in the legend of Moses, which is either based on or cognate with an Egyptian myth. In the second century Suetonius gives a variant of the myth as accepted history concerning the birth of Augustus.[2] But all the available evidence in regard to the Krishna myth goes to show that the massacre motive already existed in Indian mythology long before the Christian era.

Note on the Moses Myth.

I have been challenged for saying that the story of Moses and the floating basket is a variant of the myth of Horos and the floating island (Herod. ii. 156). But this seems sufficiently proved by the fact that in the reign of Ramses II., according to the monuments, there was a place in Middle Egypt which bore the name I-en-Moshé, "*the island of Moses.*" That is the primary meaning: Brugsch, who proclaims the fact (*Egypt under the Pharaohs*, ii. 117), suggests that it can also mean "the river-bank of Moses." It is very obvious, however, that the Egyptians would not have named a place by a real incident in the life of a successful enemy, as Moses is represented in Exodus. Name and story are alike mythological, and pre-Hebraic, though possibly Semitic. The Assyrian myth of Sargon, which is indeed very close to the Hebrew, may be the oldest form of all; but the very fact that the Hebrews located their story in Egypt shows that they knew it to have a home there in some fashion. The name Moses, whether it mean "the water-child" (so Deutsch) or "the hero" (Sayce, Hib. Lect. p. 46), was in all likelihood an epithet of Horos. The basket, in the later form, was doubtless an adaptation from the ritual of the basket-borne God-Child, as was the birth story of Jesus. In Diodorus Siculus (i. 25) the myth runs that Isis found Horus *dead* "on the water," and brought him to life again; but even in that form

[1] Above, pp. 188–9, 191–2.

[2] *Octavius*, c. 94.

the clue to the Moses birth-myth is obvious. And there are yet other Egyptian connections for the Moses-saga; since the Egyptians had a myth of Thoth (their Logos) having slain Argus (as did Hermes) and having had to fly for it to Egypt, where he gave laws and learning to the Egyptians. Yet, curiously enough, this myth probably means that the Sun-God, who has in the other story escaped the "massacre of the innocents" (the morning stars), now plays the slayer on his own account, since the slaying of many-eyed Argus probably means the extinction of the stars by the morning sun (cp. Eméric-David, *Introduction*, end). Another "Hermes" was son of Nilus, and his name was sacred (Cicero, *De Nat. Deor.* iii. 22; cp. 16). The story of the floating-child, finally, becomes part of the lore of Greece. In the myth of Apollo, the Babe-God and his sister Artemis are secured in floating islands (Arnobius, i. 36), or otherwise Delos floats (Pliny, *Hist. Nat.* ii. 89; iv. 22; Macrob. *Sat.* i. 7; Callimachus, *Hymn to Delos*, 213; Pindar, *Frag.* cited by Müller, *Dorians*, Eng. tr. i. 332; Lucian, *Deor. Dialog.*, *On Delos*).

§ 8. *The Boy Jesus in the Temple.*

Strauss[1] has pointed to the obvious untrustworthiness of the story of the boy Jesus, at the age of twelve, being lost by his parents and then found in the temple, among the doctors, astonishing them by his wisdom. It is found in Luke only. As against those critics who see in the simplicity and non-miraculous character of the story a proof of its genuineness, Strauss points to the extra-Scriptural stories of Moses leaving his father's house at twelve to play the part of an inspired teacher, and of Samuel beginning to prophesy at that age. It was in fact an ordinary Jewish myth-motive. But Strauss as usual has omitted to notice Pagan parallels, one of which supplies the source of the first part of the Gospel story—the losing of the child.

In Strabo's account of Judæa, after the recital of the Greek version of the Moses myth, there is a chapter of reflection on the operation of divine law,[2] where are given

[1] *Das Leben Jesu*, Abs. i. K. v. § 41.
[2] B. xvi. c. 2, § 38 (ed. Casaubon, p. 762).

some quotations telling how among other episodes "parents went to Delphi, 'anxious to learn whether the child which had been exposed was still living,' while the child itself 'had gone to the temple of Apollo, in the hope of discovering its parents.'" The parallel is not exact, but the clue to the Christist myth is obvious enough. Strabo's book on Syria and Judæa was sure to be read by many Greek-speaking Jews, such as constituted the first Jesuist groups; and the myth may very well have been adapted direct from his text, which dates at least a century before the Gospels. The Pagan myth he reproduces may have been reproduced in art; but as a picture could not easily convey by itself the idea that the child had been lost, the written source is in this case the more probable. Jesuists who found Strabo astray in the case of the Moses myth would have no scruple about adapting him in another case.

The detail of the Christ-child prophesying in the *temple*, however, compares further with the Egyptian belief that children playing in the temple courts conveyed prophetic knowledge by their chance cries.[1] And here again we have to reckon with the fact that in one part of the Egyptian ritual Isis figured as wailing for the loss of her *child*, the boy Horos. Lactantius, who gives the detail,[2] names not Horos but Osiris; but is quite explicit as to its being a *boy* who is lost and found again. The ritual occurring in the temple, it was a matter of course that the lost boy should be found there. Thus, then, though the Gospel story of the abnormal wisdom of the child Jesus represents a development alike on Pagan and Jewish lines, the story of the finding in the temple is a specifically Pagan myth.

§ 9. *The Upbringing at Nazareth.*

That the location of the birth of Jesus at Bethlehem is mythical may be taken as granted by all who recognize myth in any part of the Gospel narrative. That the

[1] Plutarch, *I. and O.* c. 14.

[2] *Div. Inst.* i. 21.

Messiah Ben David had to be born in the royal city of Judæa was an obvious pre-requisite. The rationalist criticism of the last generation accordingly proceeded to decide that since Jesus was not born at Bethlehem he was born at Nazareth;[1] Strauss pointing to the number of instances in which he is called "the Nazarene" in the Gospels and the Acts. And, indeed, the fashion in which the first and third Gospels speak of Joseph and Mary as settling in or returning to Nazareth after the birth, while the second makes Jesus come from Nazareth *sans phrase*, points naturally to such a view. But when the texts are investigated and tested down—a method which Strauss never properly applied—the resulting "Primitive Gospel," as thus far educed by inquirers anxious to preserve what they can, presents a Jesus without any cognomen whatever,[2] even as do the Epistles. And any reader who will take the trouble to check down the references to Nazareth in the first Gospel as it stands will find that for the Ebionites, who, as we know, had not the first two chapters,[3] there was there *no mention either of Nazareth or of Jesus the "Nazarite" or Nazarene.* Beginning with the third chapter, we find (*v.* 13) only "from Galilee" where Mark has "from Nazareth of Galilee." In iv. 13, again, we have a plain interpolation in the phrase "leaving Nazareth," since that place is not previously mentioned; while in Luke (iv. 16) the similar introduction of Nazareth is no less clearly spurious, being actually introduced by mistake too early in the chapter, so that it tells of the doings at Capernaum (*v.* 23) before the visit to Capernaum is mentioned, and we go on to read (*v.* 31) of "Capernaum, a city of Galilee," *after* the interpolated mention of it. No more flagrant interpolation exists. There now remains in the first Gospel only one more mention of Nazareth, and that is in the passage (xxi. 11) where, on Jesus entering Jerusalem seated on the ass and the ass's colt, "the multitudes said, This is

[1] So Strauss, First *Leben Jesu*, Abs. i. K. iv. § 39 (4te Aufl. i. 301); Second *Leben Jesu*, B. i. § 31; B. ii. Kap. i. § 35 (3te Aufl. pp. 191, 335); Renan, *Vie de Jésus*, ch. ii.

[2] See, for instance, the work of Mr. Jolley, before cited.

[3] Epiphanius, *Against Heresies*, xxx. 13, 14.

the prophet Jesus, from Nazareth of Galilee"—a myth within a myth. The passage cannot have been in the early Gospel, which, as we have seen, had no previous mention of Nazareth; and it is quite certain that no Galilean prophet could thus have been acclaimed at Jerusalem.

There remains in the first Gospel the solitary passage (xxvi. 71) which, in conformity with the superimposed second chapter, speaks of Jesus the Nazar*ite*.[1] Here, again, to say nothing of the fact that the whole narrative is unhistorical, the passage in question is impugned by the immediately previous occurrence of the same episode, in which the phrase is "Jesus the Galilean." One maid having said that, another must be made to say "Jesus the Nazarite" or Nazarene. The whole passage is either one more late interpolation or a series of such, and we shall see reason to regard the similar passage in Mark as the original.

In the fourth Gospel, again, while Jesus is thrice called "the Nazarite," he is never called "the Nazarene"; and the only passage in which Nazareth is mentioned (i. 45, 46) is plainly interpolated in the same fashion as the early allusions in Matthew and Luke. Philip is made to tell Nathaniel that "we have found him of whom Moses in the law, and the prophets, did write, Jesus of Nazareth, the son of Joseph"; whereupon Nathaniel asks, "Can any good thing come out of Nazareth?" The whole episode, which is nakedly fictitious, is alien to the synoptics; and its spuriousness lies on the face of the text. The narrative runs that "on the morrow," after John has been approached by the priests (*v.* 29), Jesus goes to John; that "again on the morrow" (*v.* 35) John sees Jesus and calls him the Lamb of God; that yet again "on the morrow" Jesus goes into Galilee—meeting Philip; while finally (ii. 1) "*the third day* there was a marriage in Cana of Galilee." *A day*

[1] The Revised Version unjustifiably reads in this place "Nazarene," when the Revisers' own Greek text reads not Ναζαρηνος, but Ναζωραῖος, the standing term for Nazarite in the Old Testament.

has been interposed.[1] At the close of the fourth Gospel, finally, the addition of "the Nazarite" to the inscription on the cross is admittedly the last stroke in the creation of that particular myth, since none of the synoptics have it, though John alleges that "this title therefore read many of the Jews."

Thus, then, "Nazareth," to begin with, disappears from the corrected text of the first and fourth Gospels, and from one passage of the third. There remain in Luke only (1) the mention of Nazareth in the purely mythical prelude, which represents a later stage of Jesuism than even the prelude grafted on Matthew; and (2) the mention in the late myth of the child's visit to the temple—neither of them admissible as an instance of any early biographical datum. We are left facing the occurrence of "Nazareth" and the use of the cognomen "Nazarene" in Mark; the use of both "Nazarene" and "Nazarite" in Luke; and the use of "Nazarite" in the Johannine story of the capture. Mark, in the Greek text agreed upon by the English revisers, has "Nazarene" four times—a significant circumstance, since in two of the instances Matthew, and in the others Luke, fail to correspond, though in one Luke is interpolated in Mark's terms.

In (*a*) Mark i. 24 the demoniac cries "thou Jesus the Nazarene" (not "of Nazareth," as the revisers translate); (*b*) in x. 46 the blind beggar, being told that "Jesus the Nazarene" is passing, cries "Jesus thou son of David"; (*c*) in xiv. 67 the maid says "the Nazarene, Jesus"; and (*d*) in xvi. 6 the angel says "Jesus the Nazarene." In *a*, Luke textually duplicates Mark, and the others have nothing. In *b*, Matthew (xx. 30) has no mention of Nazarene or Nazareth; while Luke (xviii. 37) has "Jesus the Nazar-*ite*." In *c*, where Mark at the outset makes the maid say "Nazarene," and does not repeat the episode or the term, Matthew as above noted makes one maid say "the Galilean," and another "the Nazarene"; while Luke (xxii. 56, ff.) has

[1] That this was later recognized is shown by the fact that in xxi. 2 Nathaniel is suddenly made "of Cana in Galilee," in order to make one day of this episode and that of the marriage miracle.

the maid and a manservant, but no mention of Nazareth or of Jesus with any cognomen, though Peter (*v.* 59) is called a Galilean. John, on the other hand, has two uses of "the Nazar*ite*" in his story of the capture (xviii. 5, 7), where the synoptics have no such passage. Finally, Luke stands absolutely alone with the Emmaus story (xxiv. 18, ff.), in which (*v.* 19) some MSS. have "Nazarite," and some "Nazarene." This being unquestionably a late addendum, the Gospel evidence for "Nazarene" is now narrowed down to Mark.

The peculiar consistency of that Gospel in using the term "Nazarene" may stand *prima facie* either for special biographical knowledge or for a deliberate adjustment, which has been only slightly imitated in the others. And when we note that in *every instance* the cognomen is used in a mythical narrative, leaving only the bare solitary dictum in the first chapter that "Jesus came from Nazareth of Galilee and was baptized of John," how can we hesitate between the alternatives? The fact, shown by Tischendorf, that the form "Nazarene" is supported mainly by the Latin MSS., points to a deliberate control, a reduction to quasi-consistency of the chaos that had been set up by the epithet "Nazarite" and the place-name Nazareth. Even Luke does not conform save in one instance to the redaction; a circumstance which excludes the plea of "special biographical knowledge" for the second Gospel. We come down then to the following facts and inferences :—

1. The earliest texts told only of a Jesus, knowing nothing of Nazareth, and saying nothing of his being a Nazarite. Such is the position of Paul.

2. After Paul, Jesuism appears to have become associated with the old sectarian or ascetic usages of Nazarism. It is doubtful whether, to begin with, the forms Nazarene and Nazarite had the same force, or whether the name Nazarene was set up, on the basis of the "Netzer" or Nazareth myth, to distinguish non-Nazarite Christians from Nazarites.

3. After a time, anti-ascetic groups (see below, *Second Division*, § 1) probably sought to counter-check Nazarism by giving a new quasi-historical basis to the term Nazarene :

that is, they invented the myth of the upbringing of Jesus at Nazareth. This then is probably a later and not an earlier myth than that of the birth of Bethlehem, arising in the order in which the narrative developes in Matthew. It is systematically imposed on Mark by (probably Roman) methodizers, who here ignore the Bethlehem myth, simply because that retains the old confusion by suggesting that Jesus was *Nazoraios* rather than "of Nazareth." If "Nazareth" or "Nazaret," the common form, be the proper spelling, the adjective should have been *Nazaretaios*, or something similar retaining the *t*. The modern name of the village (Nasrah), which drops the *t*, and the occasional reading "Nazara," *may* stand for the mere phonetic decay that is so common in names. But if, as Keim argues, the true Hebrew place-name was *Netzer* or *Nezra*, then the general adoption of the form Nazareth points to a deliberate attempt to make a new basis for "Nazarene" without coming too close to the Hebrew *Nazir* = Nazarite, or *Netzer* = "the branch," forms which would always suggest that the geographical pretence was spurious or mistaken.

This view of the process appears to be confirmed by the phenomena of the text of the book of Acts. There there occur (1) six mentions of "Jesus the Nazarite," and (2) one mention of Nazareth (x. (37) 38):[1] there is no instance of "Nazarene." And the mention of Nazareth is plainly spurious, being thrust into an invertebrate sentence over and above a previously complete characterization of Jesus—all in a mythical (though early) discourse by Peter. The book of Acts, then, throughout calls Jesus the Naza*rite*, as Mark throughout calls him the Nazarene; and the probable solution is that the compilers of the Acts made Jesus a Nazarite because for them his following were now known as Nazarites; while the methodizing redactors of Mark, having decided to ground that term on the place-name Nazareth, took the form Nazarene as being more

[1] The revisers, as usual, obscure the evidence by using the form "of Nazareth" throughout.

easily dissociated from the known historical class of Nazarites.

The problem as to how the Jesuist cult, which for Paul has no connection with Nazaritism, came to be associated with that institution, belongs strictly to the later historical part of our inquiry. It may here be pointed out, however, that while the Jesuists might develop into "Nazarites" by way of using as their symbol the prophetic "Nazar" or Davidic "Branch" of Isaiah, taken in a general Messianic sense, there is a very important special clue to such a departure in the Old Testament legend of Jesus the High Priest, who in Zechariah (iii. 1–8; vi. 11–13) figures as "the Branch" (lit. "the sprout") and plays a quasi-Messianic part, being doubly crowned as priest and king. Here arises a fresh problem. The crucial text, Matt. ii. 23, refers to a prophecy that the Messiah shall be called *Nazoraios* (Heb. *Nazir*); and the only prophetic saying to which it can be attached is that in Isaiah, xi. 1, predicting that "a Branch" (*nazar*, or *netzer*) shall come from the roots of Jesse. In Zechariah the Hebrew word is not *netzer*, but *tsemach*; but it is perfectly possible that the word *netzer* was commonly used in reference to that, and that in the lost Aramaic paraphrase the same word may have been used to render the two passages.[1] That the *tsemach* of Zechariah was held to point to the Messiah equally with the *netzer* of Isaiah is made certain by the Chaldean exegesis of Zechariah, which in ch. iii. 8 gave "a Messiah," and in vi. 12 "a man whose name is Messiah."[2] Here then was an early Messianic Jesus who could specially be described as *Nazir* or Nazarite, in the sense of being the mystic "branch" of Isaiah. It may then have been an express reversion to the symbolism associated with this priestly and Messianic Jesus that Paul denounced as the introduction of "another Jesus whom we did not preach." And the fact that there are signs of tampering with the passage Zech. vi. 11, which would appear to have originally made Zerubbabel wear one

[1] See this argued by Mr. Nicholson, *The Gospel according to the Hebrews*, 1879, p. 33.
[2] Cahen, *in loc.*

of the two crowns,[1] points to some special pre-Christian movement associated with the Jesus of Zechariah. What its nature was we cannot tell;[2] but the fact that the Mazdean item of the "seven eyes" is associated alike with the Jesus of Zechariah (iii. 9) and the Judaic Jesus of the Apocalypse (v. 5–6) suggests some continuous Messianic idea. For the rest, it is arguable that the rise of a special type of "Nazir," professedly named after the *netzer* of Isaiah and Zechariah, may have been the true origin of the form *Nazarene* as distinct from Nazarite.[3]

Whether or not this theory of the line of evolution be sound, there can be no pretence that there remains any tolerable foundation for the belief that the Gospel Jesus was a person born at Nazareth. Even if he had been, it is obviously unlikely that his late followers (his disciples are not so named anywhere, and Paul never uses the term) would be called after the small village of his birth, when practically none of his teaching had been done there. The known historical use of the term "Galilean" to describe certain sectarian or fanatical groups, excludes any such proceeding; and as there were already the numerous Nazarites, the alleged geographical name for the Jesuists would have been a most gratuitous confusion, quite alien to popular habit. But there is positively no reason to believe that any prophetic and cult-founding Jesus was born at Nazareth. To adhere to that view is merely to defy all the critical tests.

[1] Cp. Robertson Smith, *The Old Testament in the Jewish Church*, 2nd ed. p. 446.

[2] It is noteworthy that Josephus names four Jesuses who were high-priests. Of these, one was deprived by Antiochus Epiphanes, and another by Herod.

[3] A special connection between Nazaritism and the Messianic belief, however, is indicated by the fact that vows were made "to be a Nazarite when the son of David will come," and that such vowers appear to have been free to drink wine on Sabbaths, but not on week-days. Tract. *Eiruvin*, fol. 43, col. 2, cited by Hershon, *Genesis with a Talmudical Commentary*, Eng. tr. p. 472.

§ 10. *The Temptation.*

I.

While the birth of the God is seen to be part of the folklore of Europe as well as of Hindostan, the Temptation of the God is a myth of a specifically Oriental stamp, and is not to be found in that form in Hellenistic mythology before the rise of Christism. The latter myth, however, turns out to be at bottom only a variant of the former, different as the stories are; and the proof is reached through certain Hellenic myths of which the origin has not hitherto been traced. There is, however, no more instructive instance of myth-evolution.

In its Christian form, the Temptation story is a fairly close analogue of part of the Temptation of Buddha;[1] and it has a remoter parallel in the Temptation of Zarathustra,[2] both of which myths have been accounted for by M. Darmesteter as originating independently from the nature-myth of the temptation of Saramâ by the Panis in the Rig Veda.[3] As the first part of the Buddhist story has every mark of a nature-myth representing the Sun-God as assailed by the storm-spirits at the outset of his career, this or some other Hindu derivation for that idea seems likely enough: and the Christist myth might fairly be regarded as a later sophistication of the same fancy. There are decisive reasons, however, for concluding that the Christian story was evolved on another line; and in tracing that we may see some reason to surmise a non-Vedic origin for the Zoroastrian form.

The first clue lies in the detail of the "exceeding high mountain" of the first and third Gospels,[4] for which we have a marked parallel in a minor Greek myth. In a story of the young Jupiter given by Ennius in his translation of the *Sacred History* of Evemeros, and preserved for us by

[1] Rhys Davids, *Buddhism*, pp. 36–37; *Buddhist Birth Stories*, i. 84, 96–101, 106–9.

[2] Zendavesta, *Vendidad*, Farg. xix. § 1.

[3] *Ormuzd et Ahriman*, pp. 195–208.

[4] Matt. iv. 8; Luke iv. 5. In the Revised Version the "high mountain" is deleted from the passage in Luke, as not being in the oldest MSS.

the Christian Father Lactantius, "Pan leads him [Jove] to the mountain which is called the pillar of heaven; whereupon he ascended it, and contemplated the lands afar; and there in that mountain he raises an altar to Coelus [or Heaven]. On that altar Jupiter first sacrificed; and in that place he looked up to Heaven as we now call it," etc.[1] This myth itself, as we shall see, is in all likelihood framed to explain a picture or sculpture; but taken as a starting-point it would clearly suffice, when represented either dramatically or in art,[2] to give the Christists the basis for their story.

Pan, being figured with horns and hoofs and tail, represents the Devil as conceived by Christians from time immemorial. As the Terror-Striker, Pan had already even for the Pagans a formidable side, which readily developed itself. Satan showing Jesus all the kingdoms of the world, and asking to be worshipped, is thus merely an ethical adaptation of the Greek story. Any representation of that would show the young God standing by the Demon and the altar on the mountain top; and to a Christian eye this could mean only that the Devil was asking to be worshipped in return for the kingdoms of the earth to which he was pointing; though, for a Pagan, Pan was in his natural place as the God of mountains.[3] The oddest aspect of the Christian story is the naïf recognition of Satan's complete dominion over the earth—another of the many illustrations of the perpetual lapse of Semitic and other ancient monotheism into dualism. But as such an extreme conception of the power of Satan is not normally present in the Gospels, the episode in question is the more likely to have been fortuitously introduced.

It would further connect with the zodiacal astrology of the period; for just as Jesus at the fatal turning-point of

[1] Lactantius, *Divine Institutes*, i. 11.

[2] No monument described by K. O. Müller in his *Ancient Art* is strictly identical with the description just cited; but, as we shall see below, Pan is pictured as the teacher of *Olympus*, the mountain of Zeus, and personified as a youth, and again as beside Apollo on Mount Tmolus. It was all the same myth-cycle; and Pan with Zeus *on* Olympus could easily be conceived as Pan beside the personified Olympus.

[3] Homeridian *Hymn to Pan*.

his career appears on the two asses of the sign of Cancer, so he would be associated at the outset with Capricorn, which "leads the sun from the lower places (*ab infernis partibus*) to the highest," and, in virtue of the goat nature, proceeds always "from low places to the highest rocks."[1] With Capricorn, Pan "the Goat-God" was primarily identified through his goat-legs; but he is further directly associated with the constellation in the myth in which he strikes a Panic terror into the Titans when they fight with Jupiter, and in the other in which Pan expressly takes the form of a goat.[2]

But the symbolic clue leads us further still. In Attica and Arcadia Pan had his special mountains, called by his name; and the rocks in one of their caves were called Pan's goats.[3] And as Pan (originally Paon,[4] the Pasturer) was himself by word-play "the All," Pan's mountain and "the mountain of the world," whence all the kingdoms could be seen, were mythically the same thing. This precise duplication occurs earlier in the Semitic mythology. There the Babylonian God Azága-súga was "the Supreme Goat," his name going back to the Akkadian word for Goat, *Uz*. The Akkadian Sacred Goat was at once a God and the Capricorn of the Zodiac; and on early Chaldean cylinders the goat and the gazelle alike frequently figure as standing beside a deity[5]—the probable artistic origin of the Pan myth preserved by Ennius, as Uz approximated to Pan in being named "the (Great) Spirit," and in being a name for the Sun-God. Now, the Hebrew demon Azazel, who is identified with the goat,[6] is clearly a variant of the Babylonian Goat-God; and concerning Azazel there is an old dispute as to whether the name meant a goat or a mountain.[7]

1 Macrobius, *Saturnalia*, i. 21, *end*.

2 Erastothenes, c. 27; and cp. Diodorus Siculus, i. 88, as to the attributes of the Goat-God in Egypt, which identify him with Pan.

3 Pausanias, i. 32, *end*; viii. 36, 38.

4 Preller, *Griechische Mythologie*, i. 581. So K. O. Müller, Welcker, and others, previously.

5 Sayce, Hibbert Lectures, pp. 284–286.

6 Lev. xvi. 8. A. V., and R. V., marg.

7 Spencer, *De Legibus Hebræorum*, Lib. iii. cap. i. Dissert. 8 (ed. 1686, ii. 451).

Here we seem to have the clue to the whole sequence. In the ancient Akkadian folk-lore the Sun was called "the Goat," *Uz*, because he was *par excellence* the Climber, the High One; and the same name was given in the usual mythological way to the zodiacal constellation which marks the beginning of the sun's upward climb in the heavens. The astronomical idea is curiously clear in the Babylonian sculptures which show the God, clad in a goatskin robe, the sacred dress of the Babylonian priests, "watching the revolution of the solar disk, which is placed upon a table and slowly turned by means of a rope."[1] That the word *uz* was primordially connected with "height" is made probable by the fact that the Semitic Chaldean word *uzzu* meant "glory."[2] But for the Semites in general the word *uz* came to signify a goat; and in Hebrew and Arabic alike *uzaz* meant or could mean a pointed or steep mountain[3]—the root again being evidently one signifying "height." Thus anciently were involved at once the concepts of Goat-God, mountain, "pillar of heaven," and leading up of the sun on high.[4] The whole complex is but a variant of the birth of the new Sun at the winter solstice.

It seems not unlikely that this may be the true solution of several otherwise unintelligible Greek myths, as well as of that of Pan leading Jupiter to the top of the high mountain. For instance, Ovid in the *Metamorphoses* represents Pan as competing in music (like Marsyas) with Apollo on the mountain Tmolus in Lydia, the personalized mountain acting as judge.[5] We have here probably just another variant of the pictorially-based story of Pan taking Jupiter to the mountain-top. Any foreign picture or vase or sculpture which showed a figure like Pan with his syrinx and a figure like Apollo with his lyre—the symbols of identification[6]—standing together on a mountain, would

[1] Sayce, p. 285. [2] *Id. ib.* [3] Spencer, as cited.

[4] Thus at Mendes the Apis bull = the Sun-God was identified with the Goat-God. Plutarch, *I. and O.* c. 73, *end.* [5] *Metam.* xi. 146–169.

[6] That for the Semites to begin with the Sun-God is the bearer of the lyre is made probable by the fact that David, who has so many features of the Sun-God Daoud (Sayce, Hibbert Lectures, pp. 52–57), figures in that light. See Amos vi. 5; and cp. Hitzig, *Die Psalmen*, 1836, ii. 3–4. The Goat-God would bear the syrinx in his capacity of shepherd.

set up a speculation as to what they were doing; and the satisfying Greek guess would be that they were competing as players. In this way even the more developed story of the satyr Marsyas,[1] like the stories of Pan and Jupiter, Jesus and Satan, probably came from the same old Akkado-Semitic astronomical picture of the Goat-God standing beside the Sun-God on the height which was common, as it were, to Goat and Sun. Mount Tmolus, being already personified in Lydian myth, would quite naturally be represented, as in Ovid's verses, as listening and judging; and ass-eared Midas doubtless played an intelligible symbolical part in the original work of art.

Yet again, the old Babylonian symbol-scene may very well be the root of the later Greek stories and pictures of the God Dionysos and his companion Silenus, the latter being, as above noted, a variant of Marsyas, who is a variant of Pan. In late art Silenus has become a comic figure; but in higher forms of the myth he is the young God's worthy teacher and guide, "arousing in him the highest aspirations," and to him it is that Dionysos "owed much of his success and his fame."[2] He is moreover "the first king of [Mount] Nysa, of an ancient line, concerning which nothing is any longer known."[3] From this point of view his tail is respectfully treated as a mysterious peculiarity. In all likelihood this is but another way of explaining the Goat-God who in the symbol stands like a teacher beside the young Sun-God, pointing out to him his course in the heavens; and the subsidiary myth which makes Dionysos, raised to a higher status, give "Olympus" as tutor to the young Zeus when he makes him "king of Egypt,"[4] is another complication of the same primary idea. Silenus the Goat-God is mountain-king and friend of the Sun-God, even as the goat-like Marsyas of Phrygia, in his

[1] Originally, Marsyas was apparently a Phrygian variant of Pan, figuring as Silenus (Herodotus, vii. 26), and the story of his flaying probably grew out of the fact that his symbol was a wineskin. Müller, *Ancient Art*, as cited, p. 450; *Introduction to Mythology*, p. 54; Preller, i. 578.

[2] Diodorus Siculus, iv. 4. Cp. Preller, i. 577, and citations.

[3] Diodorus, iii. 72 (71).

[4] *Id.* iii. 73 (72).

serious and human aspect, was the true friend and companion of the "Mother of the Mount," the Virgin Goddess Cybelé, who took little children in her arms and healed them with magical songs[1]—a blending, for once, of the myths of the Sun in Capricorn and the Sun born of the constellation Virgo at the same astronomical moment. In this myth, too, Silenus teaches men the use of the flute as an improvement on the primitive pastoral syrinx. His later degradation is a sample of the normal play of artistic fancy in religious myth.

It may be, again, that in a symbolic scene of the same order as that under notice lies the clue to the odd myth of Hercules bearing the load of the world for Atlas while Atlas gets for him the Hesperidean apples.[2] Mount Atlas, obviously, was a "pillar of heaven" = "the mountain of the world" (for Atlas bears the pillars of heaven *and* earth);[3] and we have only to suppose a sculpture representing Atlas on his mountain, *holding out the earth-ball to the Sun-God*—another way of showing him all the kingdoms of the earth —in order to get a basis for the otherwise meaningless myth under notice. In one account it is specially affirmed of him that he "first taught men to regard the heaven as a sphere;"[4] and here again the same kind of pictorial representation would suffice to motive the myth. And there are yet other connections between the types of myth before us. Atlas being father of the Pleiades would be apt to have a place in the constellations; and as he figured as a Sea-God[5] he had a further aspect in common with Pan, since the sign of Capricorn ends in a fish's tail,[6] and Pan carries a shell in his hand. Finally, the Hindu mythology preserves record of the mythic Goat "whose office is to support the worlds"[7]—a virtual identification of Pan with Atlas.

[1] *Id.* iii. 88. [2] Apollodorus, ii. 5, § 11. See below, § 24.
[3] Cp. Preller, i. 438.
[4] Diodorus Siculus, iii. 60. [5] *Odyssey*, i. 52.
[6] Eratosthenes and Hyginus, as cited. This detail also goes back to the Babylonian symbol, for the Euphratean sign Capricornus is a "Goat-Fish"—a fish-tailed goat. See R. Brown, jr., in *Proceedings of the Society of Biblical Archæology*, Jan. 1890, pp. 148–151, and March, 1891, pp. 22–23.
[7] Oldenberg, *Die Religion des Veda*, 1894, p. 72.

But these are remoter analogies ; and the myth of Atlas and Hercules brings us back towards our starting-point ; for a representation of half-bent Atlas on a mountain-top, holding out the earth-ball to the Sun-God, might conceivably also serve to an early Christian as a figure of the Evil One offering the kingdoms of the earth to Jesus. In any case, Pan on the mountain pointing to the world below was exactly such a representation. For Judæo-Christians, Pan on the mount was just Azazel the Goat-Demon and Mountain-Demon ;[1] and since Azazel was for Origen simply the Devil,[2] whose typical function in Israel was "temptation,"[3] the early Christians had in their sacred books and glosses every inducement to see their Satan in any figure of the Goat-God.[4] Knowing nothing of the astronomical meaning of the symbols, they turned such a representation into history as they did every other piece of symbolism in their primary documents. We shall see the same process taking place again in the story of the "Sermon on the Mount."

Curiously enough, the goat of the Hebrew ritual-mystery, which has perplexed so many commentators, is really a myth-duplicate of the other ritual-mystery of the red heifer,[5] which in the Egyptian mythology stood for Typhon,[6] the Evil One. In one form or other, the idea of the Evil

[1] The Evil Spirit seems habitually to have been figured by the Jews as goat-like. Cp. J. C. Wolf, *Manichæismus ante Manichæos*, 1707, pp. 36–37; Selden, *De Diis Syris*, Proleg. cap. 3. The word translated *satyr* in Isaiah xxxiv. 14, meaning "hairy one," signifies either *goat* or *dæmon sylvestris*, and evidently has the latter force there (Buxtorf, s.v.). But the Sun too was "the hairy one"—*e.g.*, Samson, and long-haired Apollo. Everywhere the ideas converge.

[2] *Against Celsus*, vi. 43. Cp. Spencer, as cited, ii. 453; and note the development of the myth in the *Book of Enoch*, viii. 1; ix. 6; x. 4; xiii. 1.

[3] See Strauss, *Leben Jesu*, Ab. ii. Kap. ii. § 56, for illustrations. Satan signified at once the "prince of this world" (John xii. 31; xiv. 30; xvi. 11)—that is, the *cosmocrator* or ruler of the heathen kingdoms—the bringer-in of all idolatry, and the inspirer of sexual cults in particular.

[4] By the early Christians the "temptation" was probably understood as sexual, in terms of that side of the Goat-God's character in Egypt and Hellas. The temptation of Eve was so conceived originally. See the argument of J. W. Donaldson, *Jashar*, 1854, p. 46 sqq. And see Bigandet, *Life of Gaudama*, i. 132, as to the secondary temptation of Buddha by a spirit of concupiscence. Cp. Lillie, *Influence of Buddhism on Christianity*, p. 45; *Buddhism in Christendom*, 1889, p. 111.

[5] Numbers xix.

[6] Plutarch, *Isis and Osiris*, c. 30.

Spirit was thus irremovable from the monotheistic systems, though he is ostensibly introduced only to be formally repudiated. But the most instructive aspect of the case is the final mythological lesson, which is, that the Demon, the Tutor, the God, and the Mountain are all mere variants of the one original idea of the Climbing Sun in Capricorn, the High One who rules the world. The same process took place in Egypt, where Osiris and his enemy Typhon are alike forms of the Sun, and where the symbol of the pillar beginning in the lowest and ending in the highest heaven stands for Osiris and his tree.[1] Even so, in the Hebrew ritual, "the Lord" gets his sacrificial goat as well as the Goat-God. All reasoning, a logician tells us, takes place by way of "substitution of similars."[2] The old myth-makers, then, were reasoners, albeit not very deep ones.

If the case be admittedly made out as regards the "exceeding high mountain," thus traced to its mythic origin, it follows that the introductory idea of Jesus going "into the wilderness to be tempted of the devil" has a similar derivation. "The wilderness" was the typical home of the Goat-God, of the Hebrew demons in general,[3] and of mountain-haunting Pan. Dionysos goes with his guide Silenus on a far journey through a waterless land, passing through a waste region where wild beasts dwell, and thereafter he fights with his demon foes the Titans, slaying one and raising "a high hill" over his body.[4] To the neighbouring folk he explains that he is come to punish sin and make men happy. The myth has here become ethical with a difference; but the Christians had a Judaic lead also. It was to the desert that the Hebrew ritual mystery sent Azazel, the scapegoat-God, the sin-bearer; and the desert was the visible home of evil. In the second

[1] Tiele, *Religion of Egypt*, pp. 46, 47, 50. In the Greek form of the Typhon myth he is born of the Earth, half-man half-beast, towering "over all the mountains, his head often touching the stars," and his hands could reach "from the rising of the sun to its setting." "Fire raged from his eyes." He is a Sun-God disestablished and disliked by a new race, or else the hot sun figured as an evil power.

[2] Jevons.

[3] Spencer, as cited, pp. 454, 459, 461. Cp. Isaiah, as cited in note above.

[4] Diodorus, iv. 72 (71).

Gospel, only the desert is mentioned ; there is no mountain or temple-pinnacle ; and it may have been that this was the first form of the Christian story; since Luke also originally lacked the special detail of the mountain, merely making Satan "take him up." But the simplest form of the myth is again traceable to probable art-representations. The myth of Goat, God, and Mountain takes among other forms that of Pan teaching the young Olympus,[1] who elsewhere, as we have seen, is himself the teacher of the young Zeus—an inversion assisted by Zeus's cognomen, the Olympian. In this case the mountain is still mythically present, but Olympus figures as a youth ; and the scene is represented in sculpture, with a circle of mænads and satyrs as spectators.[2] This scene in its turn could give Christists the due suggestion of "temptation"; and the further detail of the demon's simply "taking up" the God might be equally well motived by the sculpture of Heliodorus representing "Pan and Olympus wrestling" (*luctantes*)[3]—itself probably a result of a misconception of some earlier symbolic scene in which the Goat-God carries the Sun-God to the top of the cosmic "mountain." The connection is unfailing ; and we have now good cause to see in such misreadings of ancient symbols the source of myths innumerable.[4]

For the rest, the "pinnacle of the temple" is only a

[1] As does Marsyas. Pausanias, x. 30; K. O. Müller, *Ancient Art*, as cited, p. 502.

[2] Müller, as last cited. [3] Pliny, *Hist. Nat.* xxxvi. iv. 22 (v.).

[4] It may be well to note in conspectus all the myth-forms which we have seen arising more or less clearly from the primary symbol of ancient Chaldæa, the Sun as Goat; (1) A constellation figured as the Goat, because there the Sun begins his climb; (2) the Goat = the Sign Capricornus, separately deified; (3) Goat-God and Sun-God together "on the height"; (4) the Mountain as God; (5) the Mountain (= Goat-God) as companion and leader of the Sun-God; (6) the Goat-God himself as (*a*) tutor of the Sun-God, and (*b*) tutor of the Mountain-God; (7) the Mountain-God as judge between Goat-God and Sun-God; (8) the Goat-God wrestling with or lifting the Sun-God; (9) the Mountain as (*a*) pillar and (*b*) pinnacle of the temple; (10) the Goat-God as Devil, (*a*) tempting the Messiah-Sun-God, and (*b*) carrying him to the Mountain-top; (11) the Sun-God, with the Goat-God, building up the Mountain as grave-mound over the Adversary; and possibly (12) the Goat-God, as showing the Sun-God the earth-ball, figuring as Atlas trying to get rid of his load. Making a table of the names we get out of the primary pair four pairs: Pan and Zeus; Marsyas and Apollo; Silenus and Dionysos; Jesus and Satan.

variant of the mountain or the "pillar of heaven"—another substitution of similars; and the forty days of fasting are a mythic pretext for the (also Pagan-derived) forty days of fasting in Lent, which proceeded also, however, on the sacred precedents of the forty-day fasts of Moses and Elias —Sun-Gods both. It is not impossible that the myth of the "horned" Moses communicating with the God on the mountain-top was in its turn one more derivative from the old Akkadian symbol of the Goat-God and the Sun-God; for Dionysos, who at various points duplicates with Moses,[1] is, as we have seen, often connected with the goat.[2] And here, perchance, we have in Babylonia the true primary derivation for the ritual usage which lies at the root of a great literary evolution; for Greek drama seems to begin with Dionysos and his goat; the word and the thing "tragedy" deriving especially from the "goat song" or "satyr chorus" sung at the Dionysiak festivals.[3] Hebrew religion may possibly owe as much to the Dionysos myth as does Hellene art. But the Moses myth as it stood would not suffice to motive the introduction of Satan into the Jesuist myth; and we are accordingly left finally at our first and last points of comparison—the picture of Pan and the young Jupiter on the mountain-pillar-top; or of Pan and the young Olympus with the nymphs and satyrs around; or of Pan and Olympus apparently wrestling; or of Dionysos with Silenus fighting the Titan in the desert before raising the "high hill" that haunts the whole interfluent dream. From the foursquare parallel there is no escape.

There remains, however, one item of the myth to be accounted for—that of Satan's suggestion that the God shall turn stones into bread. On the face of the matter, it is implied that for the God to break his fast would be a fatal surrender: why? Here there occurs a coincidence

[1] See above, p. 83.

[2] Zeus changes the infant Dionysos into a kid to save him from Hêrê. Apollodorus iv. 3, § 2.

[3] Donaldson, *Theatre of the Greeks*, 7th ed. pp. 40, 68. The old view that *tragos* in this word stood for the goat which at a later period was the prize for the chorus is set aside by Donaldson, who derives the term from the fact that *tragos*, "he-goat," was a name for the satyr-attendant of Dionysos.

of the Jesuist and Buddhist myths so marked that we must either assume one to have copied the other or regard both as copying another cult. The question of priority becomes the more difficult in this case because in both systems the detail under notice is evidently a late addition. In the Gospels we find the first form of the Christian tale in Mark, where there is a bare mention of the forty days' temptation in the wilderness, followed by the ministry of the angels—probably evolved from the pictured Muses or mænads of Apollo or Dionysos. Here there is not even a mention of fasting. In the first and third Gospels we have the elaborated myth—the forty days' fasting, *after* which the God is hungry; the invitation to turn stones into bread, the temptation on the pinnacle, and the duplicated temptation on the mountain-top. The fourth Gospel ignores the whole narrative.

In the Buddhist literature, on the other hand, we have first the simple nature-myth of the demons of the tempest assailing the young Sun-God; and only in the late Lalita Vistara is there interpolated the highly sophisticated account of Siddartha's previous self-mortifications. He practises the severest austerity for six years, till his mother comes down to earth to implore him to spare himself. He consoles her, but does not yield, whereupon the Evil Spirit attempts to persuade him; and the Buddha replies with an elaborate classification of the emotions, regarded as the soldiers of the Demon. They are graded as desires; wearinesses; hunger and thirst; concupiscence; indolence and sleep; fears; doubts; anger and hypocrisy (making eight); and further ambition, flatteries, respects, false renown, self-praise, and blame of others; all which soldiers of the burning demon subjugate the Gods as well as men, but cannot conquer the Buddha. The demon being thus discomfited, the "sons of the Gods" come to suggest that Siddártha shall pretend not to take any food at all, allowing them to instil strength into him by the pores of his skin; but he resists this temptation also. Then follow an attack in force by the armies of the demon, and a fresh temptation by his daughters, the Apsaras; then the mere verbal affirmation by the demon of his power as the spirit of concupiscence;[1] and lastly another vain attack in force.[2] Here we have an obviously late literary development, partly the work of religionists who saw in the demon of the old temptation myth a mere symbol for human passions. In a still later development of the tale, Buddha reclaims and baptises the Evil One and his daughters.[3]

What connects the Buddhist and the Jesuist myths is the idea that the Divine One must not yield to the temptation of hunger, though he can be fed supernaturally if he will. Which, then, copies the other? The true answer is, I think, that both cults here drew from a third. The Gospel myth, as we have seen, is evolved from scenes in Pagan art, themselves developments from an early symbol-scene of which the meaning was lost; and the bare item of the temptation to make bread out of stones would be an unintelligibly slight adaptation from the luxuriant Buddhist myth if the Gospel-interpolators knew it. On the other hand, the Buddhist myth makes no use of the items of the mountain and pillar, and turns the idea of food-temptation to a quite different account. We must look for the common ground outside.

In all likelihood, then, this detail is in both myths an adaptation either from the Mithraic cult or from one on which that was founded. We know that among the trials of the later Mithraic initiation were those of hunger and thirst;[4] and as the Adversary, the Tempter, is a capital figure in all stages of the Mazdean system, it would be almost a matter of course that the initiate should figure as being tempted by him to break down in the probation. The temptation would presumably take the form of a simple offer of food; and in the normal course of myth-making such a ritual episode would be almost inevitably accounted for as a repetition of one in the life of the God.

[1] Given by Bigandet, as cited above.
[2] Saint-Hilaire, *Le Bouddha et sa Religion*, 3e édit. pp. 60–64.
[3] Lillie, *Influence of Buddhism*, p. 45; *Buddhism in Christendom*, p. 112.
[4] See the author's lecture on *Mithraism* in *Religious Systems of the World*, p. 205.

In the so-called Temptation of Zarathustra, the only tempting done is in the offer of Ahriman to the prophet that if he will renounce the good religion of the worshippers of Mazda he shall have a thousand years' dominion; and Zarathustra refuses; predicting the coming of his yet unborn Son, the Saviour Saoshyant, who at the end of time is to destroy Ahriman and raise the dead. Further, though there is no hint of fasting, Zarathustra goes "swinging stones in his hand, stones as big as a house"; and he tells Ahriman that he will repel him by the Word of Mazda, the sacred cups, and the sacramental Haoma or wine. Of these data the first has every appearance of being derived from an old nature-myth[1] of the strife between the Sun-God and the Evil Powers, while the "Word of Mazda" is a later sacerdotal item. Seeing, then, that Mithra in the late cult appears practically to have superseded Zarathustra for most purposes, he is likely to have had transferred to him the temptation-motive and the "stones," which were his own symbol. We may thus reasonably infer that Mithra, in the later growths of his myth, fasted and was tempted of Ahriman; and the God's all-potency would easily suggest the detail that he should be asked to make bread of the stone which typified his own body. Such would be a sufficient ground for the Christists' adaptation of one more Pagan detail in their gradually pieced-out story, when belike they were bent on attracting the Mithraists to their cult.

It does not necessarily follow that the Buddhist myth of the Temptation was borrowed from Mithraism in its later form. When we have once realized what an immense mass of mythology had been accumulated in the cults of ancient Babylon, and how much they influenced later systems in Persia and in Greece, we are forced to admit the likelihood of an early dissemination eastwards of all manner of myths and practices which later appeared in the Mediterranean region. The ethical ideas involved in the Buddhist temptation-myth, however, are beyond doubt relatively

[1] So Darmesteter, *Ormuzd et Ahriman*, as last cited.

late; and if they were not adapted directly from the Persian cult they were presumably, like that, an evolution from an earlier Asiatic system which gave the groundwork. In a Chinese Life of Buddha,[1] the Buddha fasts for forty-nine days; and such fastings were probably features of many Asiatic systems. We are thus finally left questioning whether many of the striking parallels of ritual and emblem and implement between Buddhism and Christism may not have been independently derived from intermediate cults that flourished in Mesopotamia.

In any case, we are entitled to affirm the rise of the Gospel myth of the Temptation as a theological fantasy from the mere misunderstood symbols of the old Babylonian astro-theosophy, poetically modified in a slight degree by Greek art. A process which is often philosophically misconceived as primarily one of ethico-philosophical imagination[2] is thus seen to have been a growth by way of concrete guesses to explain concrete phenomena. The astronomical "allegory" primarily involved had been entirely lost sight of: and only for the later and more educated Christists, apparently, did any new aspect of allegory arise; the immediate framers of the Jesuist myth, presumably, regarding the story as a historical episode, though even here there may have been deliberate trickery at the outset.

§ 11. *The Water-Wine Miracle.*

This, as was long ago pointed out by Dupuis, is certainly an adaptation from the cult of Dionysos. At the nones (the 5th) of January, during the festival of the God, a fountain in the isle of Andros was said to yield wine; and at Elis, at the same festival, there was a custom of publicly placing three empty flagons in a chapel, the door of which was then sealed, with the result that next day, on its being

[1] By Wung Puh, cited by Lillie, *Influence*, p. 44.
[2] Cp. Bruno Bauer, *Kritik der evangelischen Geschichte*, 2te Aufl. 1846, i. 219–244, and his citations, with J. Estlin Carpenter's *The First Three Gospels*, 2nd. ed. pp. 171–6.

reopened, the flagons were found full of wine. This ritual-miracle is certainly very ancient, an account of it being quoted by Athenæus[1] from Theopompus the Chian, who flourished about 350 B.C. The meaning of the ritual is obvious. Dionysos, as Sun-God and Wine-God, was the maker of wine, and was also that force which in Nature actually changes water into wine by transmuting sap into grape-juice. And there is reason to suppose from a passage in Pausanias that some such quasi-miracle was regularly performed in the Eleusinian mysteries. At the end of his long account of the paintings of Polygnotus at Delphi we have this: "There is also a wine-jar in the painting, and an old man, and a boy, and two women, a young woman under a rock, and an old woman near the old man. Some men are bringing water, and the old woman's water-pot appears to be broken, and she is pouring all the water in the pitcher into the wine-jar. *One is inclined to conjecture that they are people making a mock of the Eleusinian mysteries.*"[2] That can hardly have been the intention; but it is clear that the mysteries involved some procedure with water and wine-jars,[3] and the Christian myth is a bold appropriation of the heathen God's prestige. The fact that the Catholic Church places the Cana miracle on 6th January tells its own tale. Twelfth Night in pre-Christian as in Christian times was a date of crowning festivity; and it is to be noted on the mythological side that the "first miracle" is wrought when the Sun-God is twelve days old, even as his appearance in "the temple" is made at twelve years. As we have seen,[4] the one date stood for

[1] B. i. c. 61. Compare Pausanias, vi. 26; and Pliny, *Hist. Nat.* ii. 106 (103), xxxi. 13. Diodorus Siculus, iii. 66 (65), tells also that in Teos at fixed dates a richly odorous well flows with wine, which the people say is proof that Dionysos was born there. Cp. Horace, *Odes*, ii. xix. 10; Euripides, *Bacchæ*, 704 ff. The idea occurs again in the Homeridian Hymn, where wine flows through the ship in which the God is captive.

[2] Pausanias, x. 31.

[3] Mr. Frazer, in his admirable commentary on Pausanias, does not deal with this implication, but very appositely cites Plato (*Gorgias*, 493*b*) as saying that in Hades the uninitiated carry water in a sieve to a broken jar. This does not alter the presumption that Pausanias knew of a procedure of pouring water into *wine*-jars in the mysteries.

[4] Above, p. 173.

four kinds of Epiphany or manifestation of the God—the miracle, the star of the Magi, the baptism with its dove, and the nativity itself, so long held by the Eastern Church to be on 6th January. All four ideas were alike Pagan.

§ 12. *The Scourging of the Money-Changers.*

It has often been shown that this story is wildly improbable as a piece of history. It may be further urged that in all probability it was invented, like so many other narratives, to explain a myth. In the Assyrian and Egyptian systems a scourge-bearing God is a very common figure on the monuments; and though the scourge is an attribute of the Egyptian God Chem,[1] it is specially associated with Osiris, the Saviour, Judge, and Avenger, who also carries the shepherd's crook or crozier.[2] A sculpture of Osiris menacing or chastising thieves, or anybody else, would suffice to motive the Gospel fiction.

§ 13. *The Walking on the Water.*

Here too the concrete basis of the myth is easily found. Poseidon, as God of the Sea, was frequently represented as "draped, and swiftly but softly striding over the surface of the sea, a peaceful ruler of the realm of billows."[3] Even the association of Peter, "the Rock," with the Christian myth might be due to the occasional representation of the Sea-God as resting his foot on a rock.[4] Yet again Dionysos, whose popular cult supplied the Christists with their water-wine miracle, is represented in myth as passing over the sea to return to his followers.[5] This episode too was likely to be represented in religious art. And finally there is the story of Hercules crossing the sea in the cup of the Sun, going to Erythea: "And when he was at sea,

[1] Sharpe's *Egyptian Mythology*, Fig. 5 and 81.
[2] *Id.* Fig. 13, 23, 63, 70, 71, 72.
[3] K. O. Müller's *Ancient Art*, as cited, p. 432. [4] *Id.* pp. 432–3.
[5] Diodorus Siculus, iii. 65.

Oceanus, to tempt him, appeared to him in visible form, tossing his cup about in the waves; and he then was on the point of shooting Oceanus; but Oceanus being frightened desired him to forbear."[1] In the context, more appropriately, it is Hercules who is afraid; and this would be the natural purport of the episode in art. To the child-like imagination of the early Christists, or to the cult-building ingenuity of their leaders, all such representations were so much natural matter for the construction of their own mythology.

§ 14. *The Healing of Two Blind Men.*

It is needless to cite pre-Christian miracles of raising from the dead, since such miracles were recorded not only among the Greeks (chiefly in connection with Æsculapius), but in the sacred books of the Jews. It is more to the purpose to point out that the healing of the two blind men is probably a Jesuist plagiarism from the cult of Æsculapius. There is extant an inscription found in the ruins of a temple of Æsculapius at Rome, which proclaims that that deity had among other cures in the reign of Antoninus restored two blind men to sight.[2] Similar tales must have abounded in Æsculapian temples. This prodigy, thus originated, is related twice over in Matthew, with a curious difference. In one telling (ix. 27–31), Jesus is represented as "sternly threatening" (the translations dilute the force of the Greek words) the healed men, and commanding that they shall let no man know of their cure. In the other version (xx. 30–34) Jesus performs the miracle in the presence of a multitude, and there is no pretence of their being ordered to keep silence. In all probability the latter version, based on some story about

[1] Athenæus, xi. 39, citing Pherecydes.

[2] See the whole inscription in Boeckh, No. 5980; Gruter, *Inscr. Antiq.* ed. 1707, i. p. lxi.; Montfaucon, *Antiq. Expliq.* T. ii. pt. i. p. 247. Four cures are mentioned, those of the blind men being first and last. In the first case the populace are said to have seen the cure performed; in both, the cured men return thanks.

Æsculapius, was adopted first; and the other was interpolated later by way of providing against the cavils of inquirers who could find no local testimony to the miracle. The story of the curing of *one* blind man in the second and third Gospels[1] may easily have had a similar pagan basis; and the name, probably added late to the version of Mark, might even be copied from one of the actual votive tablets which abounded in the pagan temples.[2]

§ 15. *Other Myths of Healing and Resurrection.*

There are obvious reasons for surmising, further, that other miracle stories in the Gospels were adapted in the same way from Pagan originals. The fact that the most remarkable miracles of all, the raisings of dead men, are each found in one Gospel only, points to their late interpolation, and strongly suggests non-Jesuist precedents. The raising of the Widow's Son at Naïn, it has been already urged,[3] is in all probability a variant of the common myth of the raising of the slain young Sun-God, reduced to the status of a private prodigy, as in the myths of Elijah and Elisha. On this view, it will be observed, the gospel-makers are absolved from the charge of fabrication; for had they been bent on invention they could easily have framed many more miracle-tales. The fact that they specify so few raisings from the dead goes to prove that they set down in unreasoning good faith simply the narratives they found current concerning Hebrew and pagan prophets, giving Jesus the glory as a matter of course. The story of Lazarus, indeed, like other parts of the Fourth Gospel, seems to be in part a newly-planned fiction; but the synoptics were compiled on less original lines. It is needless to point out to the rationalist reader that if the compilers of Luke had heard of the story of Jesus raising one Lazarus from the dead, or of Jesus' acquaintance with him (John xi. xii.), they could not conceivably have told

[1] Mark x. 47–8; Luke xviii. 38–9.

[2] Pausanias ii. 28; Strabo viii. 6, § 15.

[3] Above, pp. 259–260.

the parable of Lazarus and the rich man (xvi. 20) or the story of Martha and Mary (x. 38–42) without alluding to the miracle. On the same principle, we may decide that the story of the raising of the widow's son was added late to Luke.

The story of the raising of Jairus' daughter raises a more complex problem. A closely similar story is found in Philostratus' Life of Apollonius of Tyana,[1] the girl in each case being spoken of in such a way as to leave open the question of her having been dead or cataleptic. It is of course impossible to demonstrate that Philostratus, who wrote after the Gospels existed, did not take the story thence; but there are good reasons for thinking that he found it in the earlier Life of Apollonius which he professedly followed, and that it had been connected with Apollonius after having been told of other thaumaturgs in Rome. The girl in that story is a Roman, and is described as being of a consular (ὑπάτους) family. In Matthew,[2] the statement is that there came to Jesus "a ruler" (ἄρχων) or "a certain ruler" (ἄρχων εἷς) who worshipped him and besought him to restore his daughter to life; and that Jesus did so by simply taking the girl's hand. In Mark[3] the father has become "one of the rulers (heads) of the synagogue, Jairus by name"; while in the sequel we have three times over "the ruler of the synagogue" *without* the name Jairus; and now Jesus uses the formula *Talitha coum*. In Luke, again,[4] the father is "a man named Jairus, and he was ruler of the synagogue," though here again the designation is repeated without the name. Now the simple form preserved in Matthew reveals the derivation from the story in Philostratus. The *archon* is just the ancestral ὕπατος of that story brought a stage nearer biographical identification. And seeing that such a story was unsatisfactorily vague for Jerusalem, where there were no archons proper, it was necessary to secure local colour by making the father εἷς τῶν ἀρχισυναγώγων, one of the chiefs of the synagogue. In Luke he is simply

[1] B. iv. c. 45. [2] ix. 18 ff. [3] v. 22. [4] viii. 41.

ἄρχων τῆς συναγωγῆς, "chief of the synagogue," as if there were no others—an evident Gentile blunder, which had to be rectified in Mark. The addition of the name Jairus is evidently the last touch of all. And after all the God is represented as having "charged them that no one should know this," the usual judicious precaution against the cavils of the unbelievers who found that nobody in the district could verify the miracle. Arnobius,[1] reciting a series of Jesuine miracles, some of which are not found in the Gospels, makes no mention of this one: and Lactantius,[2] in a similar list, describes neither the miracle of the widow's son nor that of Lazarus, and has no allusion to any such case as the raising of Jairus' daughter.

§ 16. *The Feeding of the Five Thousand.*

By all save believers in a supernatural Christ, the story of the feeding of the five thousand or four thousand is taken either as pure myth or as a grafting of miracle on a perfectly natural episode. Count Tolstoy and others have pointed out that the detail of the twelve (or seven) baskets plainly implies that food supplies had been carried by the crowd, since they certainly would not have gone into the wilderness with empty baskets. On this view, the original form of the story was something like that of John, vi. 9: "One lad here has five loaves and two fishes"—with the implication, "and so on throughout the crowd." In the same fashion the semi-rationalizing critics would reduce the five thousand men, to whom Matthew (xiv. 21) adds a host of "women and children," to a mere uncounted crowd, besides putting aside the "three days" (Mk. viii. 2) of previous fasting in the story of the four thousand. The stories being, further, so obviously identical in all save the numbers, the two are by such criticism reduced to one. But while this last step is obviously right, the story remains a myth even as regards the bare act of teaching a multitude in the desert.

[1] *Adversus Gentes*, i. 45, 46. [2] *Div. Inst.* iv. 15.

It is notable that, while a discourse is put in the mouth of Jesus on the mount, not a word is given of the "many things" he taught the multitudes fed in the wilderness. So nugatory, on the face of the case, was the machinery for preserving the teacher's utterances. To retain, out of such a self-confuting record, the bare datum that the teacher *did* teach crowds something in the wilderness, would seem a sufficiently idle procedure. There is in reality no reason to regard any part of the story as aught save an attempt to parallel, or an unthinking adaptation of, the stories of Dionysos passing through the desert with *his* followers. As we have seen in tracing the myth of the Temptation, Dionysos in the Libyan lore led his army through a waterless desert against the Titans—a procedure which would involve his supernatural production of liquids—and in this connection it is told[1] that the friendly Libyans gave his army food "in superfluity." But it is part of the Dionysiak myth that the God gave the power of miraculously producing, by touch, corn and wine and oil;[2] and he must needs have been held to have the same power in his own person for the feeding of his host. Pictures of such a distribution of food, with or without a representation of Dionysos in the act, would sufficiently suggest the Christian story, in which, significantly enough, the multitude are described in the second and third Gospels as sitting down "by companies" or "by fifties," in military fashion. In the earlier form of the story, however, as in Matthew, this would not appear: because for the Christist purpose the miracle is not an excrescence but the primary motive. Without it, there is nothing to tell; and the doubling of the story tells of the capital made of such "evidence."

§ 17. *The Anointing.*

As a non-miraculous episode, the story of the anointing of Jesus by a woman has been accepted by some Naturalists as historical, for the sake of its peculiar dramatic and moral

[1] Diodorus Siculus, iii. 72 (71).

[2] Ovid, *Metamorphoses*, xiii. 650–4.

interest. Yet a moment's comparison of the different versions[1] shows that we are dealing with at least a measure of fiction. In Matthew and Mark we have the same story, almost word for word: a woman pours precious nard over the teacher's head: the disciples—or some other bystanders—murmur at the waste; and Jesus commends the woman. He speaks prophetically in his Messianic capacity, not as a human being: the utterance is mythic. In Luke, the woman, described now as "a sinner," kisses his feet, weeps over them, wipes them with her hair, and anoints the feet, not the head. In the fourth Gospel, Mary anoints the feet, and wipes them with her hair, but does not weep. In Matthew and Mark, Jesus says the woman has anointed his body for the burying: in Luke he does not. Which story is to be believed? Shall we say, with some theologians, that there were more anointings than one?

Some such bare incident, though improbable, may certainly have taken place in the life of a popular teacher or mahdi; but we have seen that on every line of investigation thus far tried the Gospel Jesus resolves into a composite of myth; and when yet another story is found to vary extensively in the hands of the different evangel-makers, we are at the very outset debarred from giving it belief as it stands. Not only might the bare story have been true of any teacher, but the comments put in the mouth of Jesus were certainly the composition of a late Jesuist. There is no ground for any specific credence. In the synoptic forms of the story the anointing is simply the act of "a woman"; and John's identification of her with Mary the sister of the mythical Lazarus has no more historical value than the later surmise that she was Mary the Magdalene.

Looking for an origin in the source of so many myths—ritual-mystery[2]—we have first to ask whether such an episode would be likely in such a ritual. And the answer

[1] Matt. xxvi. 6–13; Mark xiv. 3–9; Luke vii. 36–50; John xi. 2; xii. 3–8. See above, p. 260.

[2] See above, *Christ and Krishna*, § xiv.

is, first, that *some* process of anointing is extremely likely to have been thus set forth. Jesus was for his sectaries, as early as Paul, Messiah = Christ = the Anointed One; and even for the later Jews the term was ceremonially significant. Many times over does the term "Messiah" occur in the Old Testament in the sense of "anointed," and it is always so translated. Elisha is thus "Messiah";[1] Isaiah calls himself so;[2] the battle-priest,[3] *sacerdos unctus ad bellum*, was duly anointed with oil.[4] If ever a Messiah were to be nationally accepted by the Jews, he would assuredly have been anointed with priestly oil. But for the earlier Gentile Jesuists, the title of "the Christos" must have had even more concrete meaning than had "Messiah" for the Jews, who may have come to use it in a secondary sense; and for such Gentiles the problem would arise, Why was not the Anointed One really anointed? Here lay the motive for the invention.

As the Gentile Christ was anti-Judaic, he could not be anointed by priestly hands. By whom then should the anointing be done? The hint lay in the myth of the birth and the resurrection ritual; and generally in the great cult of Dionysos, whose special followers are women. Obviously, the story is Gentile, not Jewish: the disciples are disparaged as dull and avaricious: though in the fourth Gospel Judas is made especially to play the unpleasant part. On the other hand, women are repeatedly made to figure in the later interpolations as the teacher's most devoted followers; and to no one more appropriately than to a woman could the anointing be entrusted. Significantly enough, the story in its simplest form is placed as the last item in the "Primitive Gospel" by the school of Weiss. In all probability it is a late addendum, made after the movement had become pronouncedly Gentile. A Jew would have seen nothing edifying in such a performance; whereas a Hellene or Syrian was accustomed to associate women with many rites. It is possible, indeed, that the

[1] 1 Kings xix. 16. [2] Isaiah lxi. 1. Cp. Psalm ii. 2.
[3] Deut. xx. 2.
[4] F. and R. Conder's *Handbook to the Bible*, p. 127, citing Maimonides.

whole circumstances of the anointing, including the detail that it took place in the house of "Simon the Leper," were expressly designed to alienate the Judaic sections of the early Church.[1]

Supposing such an episode, then, to have been introduced in the primitive mystery-drama of the Man-God's life and death and resurrection, it could easily vary, very much as the story does in the Gospels. One group might make the episode curt and ceremonial, a bare anointing; another might make it pathetic and emotional, the thought of the God's approaching death moving the women to the tears which so easily flowed from them in all of the ancient cults of theanthropic sacrifice. Thus would arise the conception that the Lord was being "anointed for his burial"; the attitude of tearful adoration could readily bring about, in communities not used to the other, an anointing of the feet rather than the more sacerdotal anointing of the head; and the surmise that the weeping woman represented a penitent sinner would as easily follow at a later stage.[2] A hundred "pagan" myths and myth-variants arose in such wise; and Christism was only neo-Paganism grafted on Judaism.

§ 18. *The Riding on the Ass and Foal.*

As is remarked above, it has long been an accepted view that the odd detail (Matt. xxi.) of the Messiah riding into Jerusalem on "an ass and a colt the foal of an ass" is a mere verbal blunder, representing an unintelligently literal reading of a Hebrew idiom which merely spoke tautologically of "an ass the foal of an ass." Such is the wording of the "prophecy" in Zechariah (ix. 9); a passage which,

[1] See the noteworthy argument of Mr. Glanville, in *The Web Unwoven*, 1900, p. 44, as to the significance of "Simon a tanner" in Acts xi.

[2] It is not irrelevant to remember how the actress who personated the Goddess of Reason in one of the fêtes of the French Revolution was finally stamped as a courtesan, though there is not the slightest evidence to that effect. In this case the myth was malignant, and the votaries of the creed of the sinners of Jewry considered themselves to have disposed of the Deists by their amiable fiction.

left thus construed, would be as obscure as before. What did *it* signify, either way?

To interpret the passage as an idiomatic tautology when there is no other instance of such a peculiar tautology in the Old Testament, is a sufficiently arbitrary course. On the face of the matter, the Gospel story is a myth, whether we read it of one ass or of two. The teacher is represented as entering Jerusalem for the first time in a triumphal procession, acclaimed as the Son of David, with "a very great multitude" spreading garments and palm branches before him. Not a single item of the story is credible history. In Mark (xi.) and Luke (xix. 30) the two asses become one, the colt never before ridden by man—a detail introduced in a no less mythical fashion, the Messiah exhibiting clairvoyant knowledge, and the owner of the colt showing a mystic obedience to the formula, "The Lord hath need of him." In the fourth Gospel, again, we have simply the colt. Why, when the other three Gospels thus put aside the grotesque detail of the Messiah riding on two asses, was the reading in the first Gospel retained?

The solution lies, not in reducing the passage in Zechariah to an obscure commonplace, but in recognizing that that, to begin with, has a mythic bearing. In all probability it repeats the true reading of the description of Judah in the zodiacal chant put in the mouth of Jacob.[1] In Zechariah the passage occurs in the second of the two parts into which the book divides; but the conservative critics on internal evidence pronounce the passage before us to be very early.[2] However that may be, it proves the currency in Hebrew circles of a Babylonian zodiacal emblem which at a later period we find wrought into the myth of Dionysos. Among the random elements

[1] Genesis xlix. 11. The rendering "foal" follows the Vulgate, which follows the Septuagint. In this case both would readily avoid the zodiacal parallel. But the authoritative version of De Sola, Lindenthal, and Raphall (London, 1844) reads "ass," explaining that the word means a young ass fit for riding, which is not the sense of "foal." Their rendering is also given by Young, by Cahen, and by Martin. Sharpe alone, among the later translators, tries to make the passage mean "a foal, *even* an ass's colt."

[2] Bleek-Wellhausen, *Einleitung in das alte Testament*, § 224, 4te Aufl. p. 440.

of that myth is the story that Dionysos, when made mad by Juno, met in his wanderings two asses, mounted on one of which he passed a vast morass, or river, and so reached the temple of Dodona, where he recovered his senses. In gratitude to the two asses he raised them to the rank of a constellation.[1] Here we have a myth to explain the fact that the Greek sign for Cancer in the Zodiac was two asses (a copy of the Babylonian Ass and Foal sign), and, evidently, to explain some pictorial scene in which Dionysos rides on—or with—two asses.

To this collocation of myths the zodiacal sign gives the clue. Dionysos on the two asses is simply the sun in Cancer, the sign which marks his downward course,[2] as Capricorn marks the beginning of his upward climb. In the Dionysos myth the emblem signifies that the sun in Cancer is passing the period of his raging heat: in that of Jesus it signifies that the Sun-God is at his highest pitch of glory and is coming to his doom, even as the myth of Satan taking him to the mountain-top stands for Pan-Capricorn leading the Sun-God upwards at the outset of his career. The odd phrase in Zechariah and Matthew stood for a gloss of the astronomical symbol, which is at least as old as Babylon,[3] where the emblem of the sun in Capricorn was of necessity complemented with one of the sun in the sign of the summer solstice.

Even the reduction of the two asses to one in the second, third, and fourth Gospels is probably no mere rationalization of the story: it is presumptively another adaptation of a symbol. In the Egyptian symbol-lore we have the record that "they make cakes also at the sacrifice of the month Payni (Paoni) and of Phaophi, and print upon them for device *an ass tied*."[4] Phaophi (the second month of the

[1] Hyginus, ii. 24; Lactantius, *Div. Inst.* i. 21.

[2] Cp. Porphyry, *De antro Nympharum*, c. 22, and Macrobius, *Saturnalia*, i. 22.

[3] See J. Landseer, *Sabean Researches*, 1823, pp. 284, 320. Landseer points out that the Babylonian astronomy followed the precession of the solstices, and placed that of summer in Cancer, represented by the Ass and Foal, and that of winter in Capricorn, while the Hebrews long adhered to the erroneous stations of Leo and Aquarius, the Lion and Man of Ezekiel.

[4] Plutarch, *I. and O.* 30.

Egyptian year) in the time of Julius Cæsar began on 29th September, which brings us to the autumn equinox; while Payni, the tenth month, beginning on May 26th, would end about the summer solstice—both probable occasions of a solar allusion, but the latter in particular coinciding with the entrance of the sun into Cancer. As the reign of the Night-Sun, or Winter-God, begins from that moment, the single ass on the Egyptian cakes would presumably be his symbol.[1]

In Justin Martyr[2] we have a form of the myth which suggests yet another Dionysiak clue, for he speaks of the ass as tied to a vine, citing the mythic description of Judah "binding his foal to the vine," omitting, however, the following clause, "and his ass's colt to the choice vine." But although the new Jesus of the fourth Gospel is made to say "I am the true Vine," the ass tied to the vine was doubtless too obviously Bacchic, as indeed is the old picture of Judah (= Leo) with wine-reddened eyes and milk-white teeth; and three of the four evangels adhered to the simple Egyptian motive, leaving the first to preserve the less obvious or more occult Dionysiak glyph, already diverted from Babylonian to Judaic use in the pre-Christian period. And so well was this form recommended to even the educated Christian world of antiquity that we find Saint Proclus, as above noted,[3] endorsing the "ass and foal" version in his episcopal sermons in the Constantinople of the fifth century. Further, there is preserved a Gnostic gem representing an ass suckling its foal, with the figure of the crab (Cancer) above, and the inscription D.N. IHV. XPS.: *Dominus Noster Jesus Christus*, with the addition, DEI FILIUS.[4] The Gnostics knew the significance of the symbol well enough, as doubtless did St. Proclus. But from the time of the framing of the Hebrew zodiacal myth of the Twelve Patriarchs (in which Judah is just the vinous sun in the sign of Leo, next to the sign of the Ass and Foal) down to

[1] See above, pp. 203–4. [2] *Apol.* i. 32.
[3] Above, p. 280, *note* 3.
[4] I am indebted for a copy of this to Heer J. van der Ende, of *De Dageraad*, Amsterdam.

our own day, the Chaldæan symbol has clung to the two religions which claimed to have put off everything human and heathen.

§ 19. *The Myth of the Twelve Apostles.*

On the face of all the Gospels alike, the choosing of the Twelve Apostles is a fictitious narrative; and in the documents from which all scientific study of Christian origins must proceed—the Epistles of Paul—there is no evidence of the existence of such a body. In only one sentence is it mentioned, and that is demonstrably part of a late interpolation. In two passages of the First Epistle to the Corinthians (xi. 23, ff.; xv. 3, ff.) Paul is made to say that he communicated to his converts that which he "received" concerning the Eucharist and the Resurrection. In the first passage he is made to say that he received his knowledge "of the Lord"; in the second that formula is not used. Both are interpolations;[1] but in the second there is one interpolation on another. The passage runs:—

> "For I delivered unto you first of all that which also I received, how that Christ died for our sins according to the Scriptures; and that he was buried; and that he hath been raised on the third day according to the Scriptures; and that he appeared to Cephas; *then to the twelve;* then he appeared to above five hundred brethren at once, of whom the greater part remain until now, but some are fallen asleep; then he appeared to James; *then to all the apostles;* and last of all, as unto one born out of due time, he appeared to me also."[2]

Seeing that the "five hundred" story is not found in any of the Gospels, we are forced to infer that it was not in Paul's epistle until long after they were composed; for such a testimony, thus made current, would have been too welcome to be neglected. But the further mention of an

[1] See below, § 22. This view, first put by me in 1886, I have since found to be held, as regards the passages singly, by W. Seufert (in *Der Ursprung und die Bedeutung des Apostolates in der christlichen Kirche*, 1887, p. 46), and by Sir G. W. Cox (lecture in *Religious Systems of the World*, 3rd ed. p. 242). It has doubtless been put by others.

[2] It is not unlikely that the whole fifteenth chapter is an interpolation; but I deal here only with the essential portion.

apparition before "all the apostles" is a proof that the previous phrase, "then to the twelve," did not exist in the first interpolation. Had the passage been consecutively penned by one hand, the second phrase would have run "then again to the twelve," or "to the eleven." The mention of "the twelve" is thus the last addition of all; and as this is the one occurrence of the word in the whole Pauline literature, the case is decisively clear.

Paul, then, knew nothing of a "twelve." In the Epistle to the Galatians,, which is probably genuine, though frequently interpolated, he speaks of the "chiefest apostles" and the "pillars," and names Cephas,[1] James, and John, but nothing more. Nowhere, again, does he speak of the other apostles as having been in direct intercourse with Jesus. His references are simply to leaders of an existing sect; and the opening sentence[2] of the Epistle to the Galatians, speaking as it does of apostles sent out by "a man," has presumptive reference to the twelve apostles of the Patriarch, of whom he must have had knowledge. In fine, the word "apostle" for Paul had simply its general meaning of "messenger" or "missionary"; and in all his allusions to the movement of his day he is dealing with Judaizing apostles who preached circumcision—a practice not once enjoined in the Jesuine discourses in the Gospels. To the Gospels then we next turn, only to find palpable myth.

In the Fourth Gospel, supposed to come from "one of the Twelve," Jesus is represented as having collected five disciples, two of them taken from John the Baptist, within three days of his first public appearance (the mythic baptism), and as being there and then "bidden with his disciples to the marriage in Cana of Galilee." Whether or not there was ever a teaching Jesus with twelve disciples, this is fiction. And here it is that we are told how Jesus told Simon on the instant that henceforth his name should

[1] In ii. 7, 8, we have mention of "Peter," though "Cephas" is named immediately after. The former passage is to all appearance a late Gentile interpolation.

[2] This may or may not be spurious: on either view the argument against the early currency of the "twelve" story is the same.

be Cephas, which being interpreted is Petros (= the Rock). Soon after (vi. 60) we find that the disciples are "many"; and yet in that very context Jesus is suddenly made to address "the twelve." There has been no previous hint of the choosing of that number. The twelve are as mythically presented as the five.

In the synoptics the case is no better. In Matthew iv. 18–22, Mark i. 16–20, and Luke v. 1–11, we have one ground-story—nearly identical in the two first, embellished in Luke by a miracle, which in the fourth gospel (xxi. 1–14) figures as an episode after the resurrection—of the election of certain fishermen, who, without a word of instruction, and without the slightest preliminary knowledge of the Messiah, follow him on his bare command, to be made "fishers of men." In Matthew these are four; "Simon called Peter and Andrew his brother," and James and John, sons of Zebedee; in Mark the same, save that Simon is not called Peter, this surname being given him only on his election to the twelve (iii. 16); while in Luke there are only three, Andrew being excluded. From these circumstantial beginnings we advance all along the line by a leap to the appointment of "the twelve"; and even here we have significant variations in the MSS., some reading, in Luke ix. 1, "his twelve disciples," some "the twelve," some "the twelve apostles." Again, Matthew ix. 9 has an isolated story of the call of Matthew the publican; who in Mark ii. 14 becomes Levi the son of Alphæus, and in Luke v. 27 simply Levi; the story being substantially and in large part verbally the same, though the name varies. Between these quasi-circumstantial details, each bringing the others into discredit, and the collective mention of the twelve, there is no pretence of connection. In Matthew x. 1 we have the abrupt and fragmentary intimation: "And when he had called unto him *his twelve disciples*," followed by the list. In Mark iii. 13–19 the hiatus is filled up in a fashion still more suspicious: "And he goeth up *into the mountain*, and calleth unto him whom he himself would. *And he appointed twelve*"; while in Luke vi. 12–13 Jesus prays all night; "And when it was day, he called his disciples: and he chose from them twelve, whom also he named apostles." It is surely plain that, whatever may have been the source of the stories of the fishermen and of Matthew, the introduction of the twelve is arbitrary and unhistorical all over the ground. The slightness of the variations in the lists given in the synoptics only proves community of source to begin with, and therefore collapse of evidence; the variations further proving the degree of freedom with which the texts could be treated if any reason seemed to arise for altering them.[1]

The critical presumption from the documents, then, is that all four Gospels alike, or at least the first, second, and fourth, originally had no mention of twelve disciples. In John the number is thrust in with a suddenness which is conclusive; but the slightly more considerate introduction of it in the synoptics only proves a little more concern to make the statement plausible. Luke, if not interpolated at this point, either proceeds on Mark or upon a mystery-drama which may have been the first Jesuist form of the myth. But for such a mystery, or for a first specification of twelve disciples, the obvious motive lay in the actual Jewish institution of Twelve Apostles of the Patriarch or High Priest, an institution which preceded and survived the Christian myth;[2] and the point at which the myth grows out of the Jewish historical fact is demonstrably the all-important ancient document entitled *The Teaching of the Twelve Apostles*, recovered in 1873 by Monsignor Philotheos Bryennios, Metropolitan of Nicomedia, and published by him in 1883.

As to that document, of the genuineness of which there is no doubt, it is certain that at least the first six paragraphs are purely and unmixedly Judaic,[3] since they have not a

[1] *E.g.*, the tampering with the names Lebbæus and Thaddeus in Matt. x. 3. Such insertions may have been made by way of flattering certain families or dignitaries with a show of apostolic heredity.

[2] Cp. Basnage, *Histoire des Juifs*, ed. 1716, liv. ii. ch. ii. §§ 7, 8, and liv. iii. ch. ii. §§ 10, 11; Milman, *History of the Jews*, 1-vol. ed. p. 453; Mosheim *Commentaries on the Affairs of the Christians*, Vidal's trans. i. 121; Jost, *Geschichte des Judenthums*, 1850, ii. 159–60; Kitto's Cyc. of Bib. Lit. art. *Apostle*.

[3] See the author's articles in *National Reformer*, May 8th and 15th, 1887.

syllable about Jesus, or the Messiah, or the Son of God; and it has been further shown[1] that in all reasonable probability this document represented the teaching carried to the dispersed Jews by the twelve Jewish Apostles aforesaid, who were commissioned by the High Priest to collect tribute from the scattered faithful. No other explanation will square with the remarkable facts of the case. Let the student try to find an escape in any of the following hypotheses, which seem to be the only ones open on the Christian side: (1) That the twelve disciples of the Christian legend drew up a "Teaching" which proceeded for six paragraphs, nearly half its length, in detailed ethical exhortation, without a word about Jesus or the Christ or a Son of God, and then suddenly plunged into a formula of baptism, naming the Father and the Son and the Holy Ghost, without saying who the Son was; (2) That such a document, after being widely circulated, was allowed by the Church to fall into oblivion while believed to be genuine; (3) That post-Apostolic Christists, seeking to forge a "Teaching of (*their*) Twelve Apostles," took the course of making the first six paragraphs absolutely Christless, as aforesaid. All three of those hypotheses being plainly untenable, we are shut up to these conclusions: (1) That at least the first six chapters went to form a document originally entitled The Teaching of the Twelve Apostles, and that the document was non-Christian; (2) That the Twelve Apostles were strictly Judaic, and that this was an official teaching promulgated by them; (3) That the Jesuist sect adopted this teaching in the first or second century, founded on it the Christian myth of the Twelve Apostles of Jesus, and gradually added to it; and (4) that after a time the organized Church decided to drop the document because its purely Judaic origin and drift were plain on the face of it. Only one MS. has come down to us, though there are various references, in Athanasius and elsewhere,

Compare Dr. C. Taylor's lectures on the Teaching (Cambridge, 1886) and the admissions of the Rev. J. Heron, *Church of the sub-Apostolic Age*, p. 57, and Dr. Salmon, cited by Mr. Heron (p. 58).

[1] *National Reformer*, November 20th and 27th, and December 4th, 1887.

showing that in the fourth century the document was still familiar.

We may now, then, trace with some confidence the course of the myth. In the earliest form of the Gospels, by the admission of the school of Weiss, there was no naming of any special disciples, though they assume mention of disciples in general. On this view it is plainly inconsistent to set forth as part of the "primitive" text the phrase, "And when Jesus had called unto him his twelve disciples," with what follows.[1] The message given to the twelve is conspicuously mythical; and the number twelve is demonstrably a late item. The first stage was the mention of the suddenly enlisted fishermen, itself quite unhistorical, but possibly motived by a late memory of the circumstance that men so named were among the leaders of the Jesuist community in its pre-Pauline days. Concerning the story of Simon being mystically surnamed Cephas, there can be no conclusion save that we are in contact with a purposive myth. On this head there is no help from the Talmud, which ascribes to the early Jeschu ben Pandira *five* disciples, named Matthai, Nakai, Netzer, Boni, and Thoda.[2] Here there is reason to suspect a late Rabbinical myth, loosely based, as regards four of the five, on the names Matthew and Mark, and on the sect-names of the Nazarenes and Ebionites. And as John names five primary disciples, Matthew and Mark four, and Luke three, we have no sign even of a tradition as to any ancient group of Jesuist disciples.

That the primary myth sufficed for generations is clear from the fact that even the late Fourth Gospel had not incorporated the myth of the Twelve. That myth, in fact, could not arise until the movement had developed so far in Gentile directions that the solid historical fact of the existence and continued activity of the Jewish Twelve Apostles was practically lost sight of—that is, by the laity; for the heads of the Christian Churches must have known it well enough. To the later Gentile Fathers, of course, it would

[1] Jolley, *The Synoptic Problem*, p. 56.
[2] Cp. Reichardt, as cited, p. 7; Baring-Gould, as cited, p. 61.

seem quite natural that Jesus should name Twelve Apostles by way of superseding the Judaic institution—the view which recommended itself to Mosheim. But the Gospel-makers, as we have seen, could attain no more plausible adjustment than the bald pretence that Jesus suddenly chose twelve disciples out of a larger number, leaving the rest to shift for themselves. So clumsily and arbitrarily was the work done that the list leaves out the Levi mentioned in Mark and Luke.

In the first chapter of the Acts of the Apostles we meet with another crude fiction of the same order in the statement that after the death of Judas the eleven decided to make up their number by lot, the choice falling upon Matthias. It is hardly necessary to dwell on the fictitiousness of the detail. Had there really been twelve Apostles whose number was to be kept up, it ought to have been renewed after the first deaths in the circle; but it is not even pretended that this happened; and most of the Twelve thenceforth pass out of all scriptural notice, to be supplied with martyrdoms, however, by the credulity and the imagination of later ages. The election of Matthias was simply an expedient to meet the difficulty that the Judas story took away from the number of the Twelve Teachers. The "Teaching of the Twelve Apostles" being long an accredited document among Christists, the list had to be ceremonially completed in the fictitious Apostle-history, after Judas's exemplary death. Thus do the "twelve respectable men" of Paley's apologetics finally melt "into thin air"; and the mythic Founder, deprived of his mythic cortège, is once more lost in the mists of antiquity, there being now no documentary foothold left for the theory that his teachings were preserved by followers.

If the reader still scruples to believe that such a myth could be thus imposed on the Gospel history, let him ask himself for an explanation of the story of the mission of "the seventy." That story occurs in the third gospel only (c. x.), and is as certainly mythical as any item in the New Testament; so obviously so that even orthodox scholarship is fain to abandon it; and semi-conservative criticism accounts for it as "an allegory of the preaching to the Gentiles."[1] It visibly connects with the Jewish idea that there were seventy nations in the world, with the myth of the "seventy elders," and with the number of members of the Sanhedrim.[2] More clearly is this the case when we note that many MSS. have the reading "seventy-two," adopted in the Vulgate; for the later Jews varied between seventy and seventy-two in their legendary arithmetic.[3] There is reason to suspect, however, that for the seventy myth, as for that of the twelve, there lay a motive in the actual practice of the Jewish Synagogue before and after the rise of Jesuism. There is evidence that the flow of tribute to Jerusalem from the Jews scattered throughout the Asiatic and Roman empires was great and constant;[4] and to collect such a revenue Twelve Apostles way well have been inadequate. In that case the High Priest—or later the Patriarch—was likely enough to appoint seventy or seventy-two apostles of lower grade, answering to the accepted number of the "nations," to do the primary work of collection;[5] and the later gospel-makers had a motive to exhibit Christ as duplicating or superseding such a Jewish institution as well as that of the Twelve.

But whether the Gospel myth be thus based, or framed merely on the theoretic basis of the seventy or seventy-two nations, myth it certainly is. If, then, such a circumstantial fiction of seventy apostles could be grafted on the narrative, and if yet later fiction could supply a list of the names of the seventy, where is the improbability of an earlier and similar grafting-on of a myth of Twelve Apostles? That it *could* be done is clear; and there

[1] J. E. Carpenter, *The First Three Gospels*, 2nd ed. p. 331.

[2] Strauss, *Leben Jesu*, Abs. ii. K. v. § 75, *end*. Cp. Carpenter, as cited.

[3] Lightfoot, *Horæ Hebraicæ: in Luc.* x. 1.

[4] Josephus, *Antiquities*, b. xiv. c. x. §§ 1, 6, 8, 12, 13, 14, 17, 21, 23, 24, 25; b. xvi. c. vi. §§ 3–7. Cp. Philo, *Legation to Caius (On Ambassadors)* cc. 31, 36, 40.

[5] Philo (as cited, c. 31) expressly speaks of sacred officers (*hieropompoi*) as being sent every year to convey to the temple the gold and silver collected from all the subordinate governments, and he describes the process as being highly laborious.

remains nothing but to accept the clear proof that it was.

§ 20. *The Characteristics of Peter.*

One of the more pressing perplexities of the Gospel narrative, from any point of view, is the peculiar status accorded to Peter, and the striking discordance between some of the Gospel accounts of him and his later standing, as well as between the different parts of the Gospel accounts themselves. He, the leading apostle, said to be chosen by his master as the foundation of his Church, is represented in all the Gospels as having denied that master in a cowardly and discreditable fashion. Early in the Acts, again, we find him not only holding a foremost place in the new movement, but working a miracle-murder on two members whose offence, on any possible view, was much less heinous than his own recent treason. The Acts story is of course clearly unhistorical; but even as a fiction, it raises the difficulty as to how any one who knew the cock-crow story to be current could have written it without a word of misgiving. Still more difficult is it to suppose, however, that if the Gospel Peter were the Cephas of Paul's epistles the latter would not have made some use of the treason story by way of resisting Peter's pretensions. In the Gospels the story is of a most damning kind: why is it never heard of outside these? Paul avows his sins as a persecutor; Peter never once mentions his as a renegade. It is impossible, in all the circumstances, to believe that the treason story was in existence in Paul's time. Once more we find that for Paul there is no trace of any personal connection between the apostles and the Founder.

In seeking to account for the invention of the story, I do not attempt to solve the problem of the historical existence of Peter—a problem still left open after the able demonstration by Baur and his school of the existence of a conflict between a Petrine and a Pauline body in the early Church. The present inquiry has shown reason for rejecting as fictitious many data which Baur accepted as historical; and in particular the legendary conception of the Twelve Apostles has had to be parted with. Further, however, it is impossible to connect the historical Cephas at any point with the legendary Simon Peter of the Gospels and Acts, or to connect either with the writer of the First Epistle of Peter—not to speak of the presumptively forged Second Epistle. Paul's Cephas is simply one of the apostles of a Judaic cult that preaches circumcision, not one of the pupils and companions of the crucified Jesus. Finally, there is found to exist an obvious Pagan basis for the main features of the Petrine myth as developed in the Gospels.

To begin with, there is decisive evidence that one important item in the myth, the appointment of Peter by the Christ as foundation of the Church, was added late to the Gospels as they stand. The use of the word *ecclesia*, which appears nowhere in the Gospels save in this and one other interpolated passage in Matthew (xvi. 18; xviii. 17), is a clear proof of late fabrication; and the passage appears not to have existed in Tatian's Diatessaron. There can be little doubt that this peculiar myth is motived by the doctrine of the divine rock in Mithraism, which system, as we shall see, furnished to Christianity its doctrine of the Lord's Supper and a large part of its resurrection legend. And the mythical bestowal on Peter of the keys of heaven and hell, the power of binding and loosing on earth and heaven, points still more pressingly to the same source, seeing that Mithras in the monuments bears two keys, which clearly connect with the further symbols of raised and lowered torches, standing for life and death. Here in Mithraism, it may be conjectured, lies the point of union between the Christist myth of Peter in its earlier form and the developed forms given to it at Rome.

It is one of the many valuable solutions long ago advanced by Dupuis, that Peter's legend is substantially constructed on the basis of the Roman myth of Janus. Janus, like Peter, bears the keys and the rod; and as opener of the year (hence the name January) he stands at the head of the twelve months, as Peter stands at the head of the Twelve Apostles. The name of Janus doubtless caused him to be reputed the God of doors (*janua*, a door); but he is historically an ancient Italic Sun-God, and he held a very high place in the Roman pantheon, being even paired with Jupiter as the beginning of things, while Jupiter was the highest.[1] He was indeed a "God of Gods,"[2] and in this view was the Cause as well as the Beginning, though his cultus lost ground before that of Jupiter. Originally Dianus,[3] the Sun-God, as Diana was Moon-Goddess, he came to hold a subordinate though always a popular place in the God-group, and was for the later Roman world especially the Key-keeper, the Opener (*Patulcius*) and Closer (*Clusius*).[4] Doubtless these attributes are originally solar, as Preller decides, the sun being the opener and closer of the day;[5] only they become specialised in Janus. He is *Deus Clariger*, the key-bearing God; and as *coelestis janitor aulae*, the gate-keeper of the heavenly palace, he looks *Eoas partes, Hesperiasque simul*, at once on the eastern and the western parts; hence his double head in his images.[6] Not only does he thus control the downward and the upward ways, but it is given to him, as Ovid makes him say, to govern, to bind or loose, open or close, all things in heaven, on earth, on the seas, and throughout the universe:

> "*Quidquid ubique vides, coelum, mare, nubila, terras;*
> *Omnia sunt nostra clausa patentque manu.*
> *Me penes est unum vasti custodia mundi,*
> *Et jus vertendi cardinis omne meum est.*"[7]

It is he who makes peace and lets loose war. Jupiter himself only goes forth and returns by his functioning. To him, therefore, are paid the first offerings, as controlling the means of access to the Gods.[8] There could not be a more exact parallel to the Petrine claims; and the

[1] Varro, quoted by Augustine, *De Civ. Dei*, vii. 9. See all the other ancient data as to Janus in Preller, *Römische Mythologie*, 1865, pp. 57, 148, 164. Cp. Keightley, *Mythology of Ancient Greece and Italy*, 2nd ed. pp. 521–3.

[2] Macrobius, *Saturnalia*, i. 9. [3] *Id. ib.*

[4] Ovid, *Fasti*, i. 129–130; Macrobius, as cited.

[5] Cp. Horace, *Carmen Sæculare*, 9–10.

[6] *Fasti*, i. 228, 139–140; Macrobius, as cited.

[7] *Fasti*, i. 117–120. [8] Macrobius, as cited.

correspondence is extended to minor attributes. As the mythical Peter is a fisherman, so to Janus, on coins, belongs the symbol of a barque,[1] and he is the God of havens. Further, he is the source or deity of wells, rivers, and streams. It is not unlikely, by the way, that a representation of Janus beside Poseidon, in his capacity of sea-regent, may have motived the introduction of Peter into the myth of Jesus walking on the waves, though, as before suggested, the Rock may have given the idea.

Now, if we assume the first elements of the Petrine myth to have come from Mithraism, it becomes easy to understand how, thus started, it should be closely assimilated in Rome to the myth of Janus. Of all the foreign cults of the empire, none seems to have made more headway in official Rome than the Mithraic; and whether before or after the decline of Mithraism, as being the religion of the Persian enemy, the adaptation of the Mithraic features to the strictly Roman cult of Janus would be both natural and easy. Christism, by embracing both, would secure a special hold on the all-important army, since Mithra and Janus were pre-eminently the military deities. Such a combination in the person of the mythic founder of the Church of Rome was an obviously telling stroke of strategy.

These origins of the Christian myth lie on the face of the cults; but it has not been noticed, I believe, that the two-faced image of Janus connects alike with the dual aspect of Mithra, who is two-sexed, and the myth of Peter's repudiation of Jesus. The epithet *bifrons*, two-faced, does not seem to have become for the Romans, as it is for us, a term signifying treachery or duplicity; doubtless because Janus, to whom it belonged, was a benign God. For minds, however, which were about the business of forming myths in explanation of old ritual and old statuary, but doing so in connection with a new cult which rejected the old theosophies, nothing could be more natural than the surmise that the personage with two faces, looking forward and backward, had been guilty of some act of double-dealing.

[1] *Id.* 229–230.

The concoction of such explanations was the life-work of the later Pagan mystics as of the Talmudists; and the rise of the Christian Gnostic sects was only the inevitable extension in the new system of the tendencies which had been at work in the old ones, and which had affected it from the first. It is impossible to overrate either the simple-mindedness or the ignorance of the early Christians; in whose intellectual life the influence of their Pagan surroundings is a constant feature. It is no longer disputed that their early art is wholly a reflex of the Pagan; and their culture was certainly on a lower plane. "Faults of language and of orthography abound in the Christian inscriptions more than in those of Paganism which belong to the same epoch."[1] We have seen how they appropriated to their Saviour-God the ancient miracles of Dionysos and Æsculapius, and the attributes of Poseidon: it was only another step in the same process to identify with the chief of their Twelve Apostles the at once subordinate and pre-eminent Janus of the Roman world, who (himself Winter) led the three seasons of the year as well as the twelve months.

Precisely how the attributes of a Roman deity came to be ascribed to the Jesuist apostle it is of course impossible to show in detail. But the first point of contact may conceivably have been the Greek myth of Proteus, who passed as the Hellenic equivalent of Janus. He, too, singularly enough, bears the keys of things, and, being "first," is entrusted by Nature with the power over all.[2] As Sea-God he walked on the waves, and as the ever-changing one he stood for fickleness—this being doubtless the characteristic which, with his keys, made him for the Romans the parallel of Janus; like whom, further, he knew things past and to come. The very name of Proteus, with its connotation, might serve for a hostile sect as an antithetic name to Petros, the rock.

There are two ways, then, in which the story of Peter's

[1] Raoul Rochette, *Tableau des Catacombes de Rome*, 1853, Introd. p. iii.
[2] See the Orphic hymn to Proteus, the date of which does not affect the point of his attributes.

treachery may conceivably have entered the creed. It might be that his identification with Mithra or Janus, or both, led to the invention of the story as a way of explaining the "two faces"; or, on the other hand, it might be that an early charge of tergiversation against the memory of Peter by a hostile faction in the Church was the cause of his being identified with the two-faced Janus or the fickle Proteus; and that the attributes of key-holding and general vice-gerentship were added later. But there are, as I have shown, insurmountable difficulties in the way of the assumption that the treason story was current in the time of Paul. It is thus certainly a myth; and when we find the other characteristics of Peter obviously borrowed from the attributes of Mithra and Janus and Proteus, it would seem reasonable to suppose that the treason story arose in the same way. As to this, indeed, there can be no certainty. If invented by way of damaging Judaic Christianity, it would still be a myth; and it may have been so invented: though it must have been at a comparatively late period. Had it been floated in the early days of the Church by an anti-Petrine party, the Petrine party must needs have opposed it; but we find it inserted in all the Gospels. Everything points to a late origination, on some basis which raised little or no question of extreme partizanship. That basis, I submit, is found in the two faces of Mithras and the figure of Janus Bifrons, with whom the mythic Peter is otherwise so closely identifiable. On such a basis the story would find easy entrance; and it could well be that an anti-Judaic bias, still surviving in the form it is seen taking in the Acts—that of a sacerdotal tactic of separation from the Judaising Christians—would be gratified by putting a certain blemish on Peter in his pre-Gentile aspect, even while he was retained as head of the Roman Church.

It need only be added that the figure of Janus was one which would meet the Christians of the second and third centuries in many parts of the Empire. The old Janus coins, with the double head on one side and the ship on the other, are said by some writers to have been last struck in Rome by Pompey; but we have evidence that similar coins were in use in Sicily and Greece; and they are found to have been struck by at least one Emperor, Gallienus.[1] They must have been abundant, for Macrobius tells[2] how the boys of Rome in tossing pennies always cried "heads or ships," as we cry "heads or tails."

§ 21. *The Myth of Judas Iscariot.*

While the solution of the myth of Peter is complicated and uncertain, that of the myth of the betrayal by Judas lies on the face of the narrative, studied in the light of the established mythopoeic conditions. No non-miraculous detail in the Gospels is more plainly mythic, though none has been more generally accepted as historical.

Broadly stated, the myth of the betrayal is to the effect that the Lord expected and predicted his execution, knew in advance all the details, and went about openly teaching in Jerusalem while his capture was being decided on; yet, nevertheless, Judas secretly arranged with the high-priests to "betray" his master, whom they could easily have seized by day, or followed up by night, without any such assistance. In the normal way of tentative progress, criticism has put aside the supernaturalist details and ignored the practical incredibility of those which remain.[3] The Gospel narratives, as usual, are full of discrepancies and divergences, from the point as to the degree of premeditation of Judas's act to that of the manner of his death; but still the myth passes for biographical fact.

Looking for outside corroboration, we find in Paul's Epistles only the interpolated passage describing the establishment of the Lord's Supper (1 Cor. xi. 23–27), where

[1] Athenæus, xv. 46; Preller, as cited, p. 164; K. O. Müller, *Ancient Art*, as cited, p. 549.

[2] *Saturnalia*, i. 7.

[3] While many have argued the injustice of blaming Judas for the foreplanned sacrifice in which he is merely a chosen instrument, I have noted only in Derenbourg (*Essai sur l'histoire et la géographie de la Palestine* 1867, Note ix.) any remark on the complete factitiousness of the narrative of events of the betrayal and trial.

there is allusion to a betrayal, but no mention of Judas. In the recently-recovered apocryphal *Gospel of Peter*, the narrator is made to tell how after the crucifixion "we the twelve disciples of the Lord wept and grieved," no hint being given of any defection by any one of the group. At the stage of the composition of this Gospel, then, the Judas myth was not current. It is true that the later Cainites defended Judas; but here there is not even a hint of the action later disputed over. In the "Primitive Gospel," as restored by conservative criticism, the narrative ends before the period of the betrayal and capture is reached. In fine, Judas, like the Twelve of whom he is one, is a late myth; but the Judas myth is the later of the two.

A probable solution, which would dispose of every detail in the problem, lies in the hypothesis of the primitive mystery-play. *There*, where all was poetic and mythic, a "betrayal" of the God would be almost a matter of course, given the primary myth that he died as a sacrifice among the Jews, who would not receive him as their Christ. In the *Gospel of Peter* "the Jews" figure as equivalent factors with Herod and Pilate in the crucifixion; and in a ritual-drama written for an audience so prepared, unnamed Jews would figure as the God's enemies and captors. At a later period, the anti-Jewish animus which led to the presentment of the whole twelve in the Gospel story as deserting their Lord at the supreme moment, would easily develop the idea of the actual treachery of one of the twelve, and to him would be allotted the part of the leading captor, who, to start with, had simply been *Ioudaios*, "a Jew." A bag to hold the reward would be a natural stage-accessory: in this way would arise the further myth that the traitor who "carried the bag" was treasurer of the group, and a miser and thief at that; while out of *Ioudaios* would grow the name Ioudas. Details which, presented as biography, are a mere tissue of incredibilities, could thus arise spontaneously as effective episodes in a mystery-drama. There the God would fitly exhibit foreknowledge of his betrayal, and could yet go through the form of asking the betrayer for what he is come. There he could acceptably say to his captors, in the phraseology of the solar cults, "This is your hour, and the power of darkness." To glose the inconsistencies of the story thus fortuitously framed was left to the compilers: for the uncritical spectators of the primitive mystery-play there was nothing that needed explaining. They believed in the treachery of Judas because they had seen it, and there an end.

§ 22. *The Lord's Supper.*

That the "Lord's Supper" was an imitation of a pre-existing ritual practice lies on the face of Paul's first Epistle to the Corinthians (x. 21) and of the earliest patristic evidence. Father Garucci argues[1] for the priority of the Christian rites on the score that, "instead of recognizing that the Christians had copied the usage of the sectaries of Mithras, the Fathers complained that the latter had imitated the Christians"; and that "it is in this way that they explain their [the Pagans'] austerities, their bathings of regeneration, and their symbols of the resurrection of the body." What the Fathers did say in some of the very passages he himself cites was that "the devil" or "devils" had introduced into the religion of Mithra usages similar to those of the Christians.[2] The very nature of the reproach shows that there could be no pretence of ordinary historical imitation (for in that case there need be no question of the action of devils), but an assumption that the Evil One had conveyed divine secrets to the worshippers of false Gods. Tertullian indeed, in a characteristic passage,[3] tells how, when the Christians preached of judgment and heaven and hell, they were scornfully reminded that these things had been already set forth by the poets and philosophers. "Whence is it, then," asks the Father, "that you have all this, so like us, in the poets and philosophers? The

[1] *Mystères du Syncrétisme Phrygien*, 1854, p. 53.

[2] Justin Martyr, 1 *Apol.* 66 (86). Tertullian, *De praescriptione haereticorum*, 40.

[3] *Apol.* 47.

reason simply is, that they have taken from our religion." And his answer to the Pagan claim of originality is a mere reiteration of that of his own side: "If they maintain their sacred mysteries to have sprung from their own minds, in that case ours will be reflections of what are later than themselves, *which by the nature of things is impossible.*" In other cases, the devout Father avowedly believed things *because* they were impossible. Here, however, he is asserting that the Pagans imitated not Christian but Judaic doctrines; and similarly, long before Tertullian, Justin Martyr[1] accuses the Mithraists of having borrowed their doctrine of the divine rock from Daniel and Isaiah; going on to explain that "the deceiving serpent counterfeited" the story of Perseus being born of a virgin—a legend much older than Isaiah. Above all, after giving the story of the Christian Eucharist as he had found it in the "Memoirs of the Apostles" used by him, he writes: "Which the wicked devils have imitated in the mysteries of Mithras, commanding the same thing to be done." In the same way Tertullian, in the passage before cited, declares that the devil "by the mystic rites of his idols vies with even the most essential things of the sacraments of God." Their pretence of Christian priority is thus discredited by their own language; and when they do allege Pagan imitation they reveal their incapacity to judge. Justin goes about to show that Plato got his ideas concerning the Logos from Moses; and that it was the demons who started the idea of setting images of Korê on fountains, by way of perverting the doctrine of Genesis as to the Spirit of the Lord moving on the waters[2]—a proposition which chances to possess a permanent importance as showing that Justin conceived the Holy Spirit as feminine. It is after a series of philosophic exploits of this description that he sums up[3] that "it is not we who take our opinions from others, but they who take theirs from us."

But even if it were not thus plain from the puerilities of the Fathers that they knew nothing of the history of religious

[1] *Dialogue with Trypho*, 70. [2] 1 *Apol.* 64. [3] *Id.* 60.

ideas, and that they simply swore to whatever seemed necessary in the interests of the faith, we have the decisive evidence of Paul as to the existence of a Pagan Lord's Supper in his day. "Ye cannot drink," he tells his Corinthian flock, "the cup of the Lord and the cup of dæmons: ye cannot partake of the table of the Lord and of the table of dæmons." Here there is no pretence whatever of imitation on the Pagan side, whether by the providence of the devil or otherwise: there is simply an implicit admission that some Jesuists were disposed to eat a Gentile Lord's Supper. It may be left to the defenders of the faith to say whether it is likely that, in the very beginnings of the Church at Corinth, the Gentiles had already set up an institution originated by a poor and despised sect of Jews.

Paul's position on the Lord's supper, however, has been obscured by tamperings with his text. It is evident that the passage in which he is made to state the origin of the rite (1 Cor. xi. 23–27), or at least the first part of it, is an interpolation—in part a late insertion of the words in Luke (xxii. 19–20), which vv. 24–25 closely follow. No one pretends that the third Gospel was in existence in Paul's time; and the only question is whether Luke copied Paul or a late copyist supplemented Paul from Luke. But to the former view the internal evidence is entirely opposed. As the passage in the epistle stands, it is an obvious parenthesis between the 22nd verse, in which, in his most characteristic style, Paul tells his converts he cannot praise them for their scandalous way of eating the Supper, and the 26th or 28th, in which last he goes on, in natural continuation, "But let a man prove himself," etc. The passage has admittedly been tampered with. The Revised Version drops the words "take, eat" (v. 24), which are lacking in all the most ancient manuscripts; and also the word "broken," mentioning that the latter word is found in "many ancient authorities," but saying nothing whatever about the abandonment of the two others. They were clearly taken from Matt. xxvi. 26; probably at the same time that the "eat" was interpolated in Mark xiv. 22, whence also the revisers have now dropped it. We are faced by the old question, If dogmatists or copyists made interpolations even in epistles at a comparatively late date, how can it be doubted that they sometimes interpolated successfully in earlier times? Now, the passage in question has every appearance of being an interpolation. It introduces in a strangely abrupt manner Paul's one written description of the origin of the rite, hurriedly yet minutely summarized in the middle of an exhortation, where it was not needed if, as he is made to say, he had already "delivered" the doctrine; and this is done after he had spoken of the communion of the body and blood (x. 16) without any historic allusion. What is specially remarkable is that he is made to say he "received of the Lord" the doctrine he has "delivered." That, save for the words "of the Lord," is precisely the formula which he is made to use in 1 Cor. xv., where either the whole or a part of the chapter is clearly interpolated. Paul's "gospel" elsewhere does *not* include these details which he there puts forward as specially characteristic; and the double use of the phrase "according to the scriptures," which cannot refer, in the second case at least, to the Old Testament, is eminently significant of intermeddling. According to what "scriptures" save the gospels did Christ rise on the third day; and what scholar now argues that Paul had read the Gospels?

Indeed, all of these closing chapters of First Corinthians, with their abrupt paragraph transitions, their allusions to "the churches" (xiv. 34, 35) at a time when the sect cannot conceivably have had "churches" in Corinth; their oddly obscure direction as to "prophets" (*Ib.* 37); their odd injunction to the Corinthians to do as the Galatians had been ordered to do (xvi. 1–2)—all raise questions of tampering. The two passages which I have above discussed, introduced as they are by the same formula, point to systematic redaction by one hand; and the drift of both is the abnormal specification of details as to Jesus—the preoccupation of a post-Pauline period, and one noticeably absent from the rest of Paul's writings. How could he, just after telling his converts that he had come "determined not to know anything among you, save Jesus Christ, and him crucified," develop such an anxiety to rest his claim on precise details of the founder's teaching, on multiplied testimonies as to the resurrection, and on his having "received" certain of the former details "from the Lord"?

If we could accept as genuine the passage in which Paul says he had "received of the Lord" what he "delivered," the words would give fair ground for the assumption that it was Paul who introduced the Supper into the Jesuist cult, and that his pretence of supernatural tuition was an attempt to outface the plain fact that he had adopted a Mithraic rite. But nowhere does he pretend to have introduced the Christian Supper; and where he claims or is made to claim independence, it is with an implicit admission of concurrence. In the other well-known passage (Gal. i. 11 ff.) in which he claims that he had his Gospel not from man but through revelation, he proceeds to say: "Immediately I conferred not with flesh and blood; neither went I up to Jerusalem to them which were apostles before me: but I went away into Arabia, and again I returned unto Damascus." There are reasons for suspecting the genuineness of this passage also, since it would be somewhat idle, if the Lord's Supper were already established from the first among the Judaic Jesuists, to pretend that he had received supernatural intimation of a particular practice of which he could easily have learned the details even while he was a persecutor. On the other hand, it is quite clear that the Supper was a Mithraic institution, and that Paul recognized its existence outside his sect. As a matter of fact, Tarsus was a Mithraic centre,[1] being the headquarters of the Cilician pirates through whom, in the time of Pompey, Mithraism was introduced into the Roman empire and army.[2] As a native of Tarsus, then, he was doubly unlikely to pretend that the Supper was a rite

[1] Preller, *Römische Mythologie*, p. 758.
[2] Plutarch, *Life of Pompey*, c. 24.

established by Jesus; so that on every ground we may conclude that the narrative of the foundation of the Supper in 1 Cor. xi. is an interpolation made after the Gospels had given the myth currency. The doctrine of the communion over the body and blood (x. 16), which is simply an adaptation of the Pagan symbolism of Sun-worship, could perfectly well be current for a time without any myth-narrative of the God's institution of the practice, though such a myth was bound ultimately to arise.

That that narrative first took Christian shape in a Jesuist mystery-drama seems the most likely view of its origin. The Supper itself was a mystery-drama;[1] and to introduce the God in person was only to do what the Greeks had done long before, as in the *Bacchae* of Euripides, and what the Egyptians did in the rites of Osiris.[2] It is thus probable that the gospel story, interpolated in Paul's Epistle, was just a narrative adaptation of the dramatic ceremony of the Supper. The "take, eat," would merely be an attribution to the God of the words customarily used by the later priest or ministrant. That a Supper on Mithraic lines was established among the earliest Jewish Jesuists may be inferred from the references in the Apocalypse—admittedly Judaic in its origin—to "the Lamb slain for us," a symbol which the description identifies with the lamb of the Mithraists, who are known to have eaten that animal in their Eucharist just as did the early Christians.[3] But they also had the sacrament of bread and water; and we know from Apuleius that in the later rites of Isis an officiating priest bore the name of Mithra[4]—presumably in imitation of a previous combination of the Mithraic cult with that of one of the Mother-Goddesses. That is to say, the ministering priest personified the God. Only at a late period, however, were such usages of the mysteries disclosed in writing. And that the insertion of the story in the Gospels was late indeed is pretty well proved by the absence of the Supper-ritual myth from the

[1] Above, pp. 280–1. [2] Herodotus ii. 171.
[3] See Garucci, *Mystères du Syncrétisme Phrygien*, 1854, § 12.
[4] *Metamorphoses*, b. xi.

fourth Gospel, in which there is no lack of interpolation drawn from the synoptics.

As to the varying usages of wine or water with bread in the Eucharist, it is needless here to inquire, beyond noting that the Christian practice seems to have oscillated between Mithraic and Dionysiak precedent. In the mysteries of Dionysos, God of wine, wine was sure to be drunk, though probably mixed with water, as the God was fabled to have advised;[1] and when his cult was combined with that of Dêmêtèr, the bread and wine were the respective symbols of the Goddess and the God. As regards the later Mithraic sacrament, the actual references tell only of the use of bread and water. But in the older Mazdean system the mystic *haoma*, = the Vedic *soma*, plays an important part; and it seems almost certain that a sacramental wine, following that precedent, would be used in the more important Mithraic ceremonies also. If, as Roscher concludes, Dionysos "is undoubtedly the *haoma*, which in the West would be represented by wine,"[2] Mithra must needs have been no less so. A uniform Christian usage of bread and wine appears to have been finally established only after a long period, in which some groups used water and some ate a lamb at the period of the vernal equinox, or substituted for the lamb a baked image of one. The probability that, further, many groups for a time ate sacramentally a baked image of a child has been discussed at length in the preceding treatise.[3] All the evidence consists with the theory of a final regulation of a long-varying rite; and such regulation could best be accomplished by the insertion of the specific myth in the Gospels.

§ 23. *The Transfiguration and the Passion.*

These mythic episodes, both occurring on a mountain, may be bracketed as being alike, in all probability, derived from a mystery-drama. In the first the white-robed,

[1] Diodorus Siculus, iv. 3. Cp. Athenæus, xv. 17, as to the drinking of watered wine to the name of Zeus the Saviour.

[2] *Ausführliches Lexikon*, col. 3045. [3] See above, pp. 220–3.

shining Sun-God is grouped with Moses and Elias, equally solar figures, known to Jewish religionists—the first as having been similarly transfigured on a mountain, the second as being carried up into heaven. It has been suggested[1] that the actual disciples of an actual Jesus arranged some such performance by way of accrediting him; but this resort to Evemerism is visibly barred by the Gospel narratives themselves, which provide for the denials of opponents by declaring that the disciples were commanded to say nothing of the vision till the Son of Man were risen from the dead.[2] It is idle to seek such a historic basis for a myth unknown to Paul, and declared even by the Gospel-makers to have been kept from the Jews. To carry through a mock-transfiguration on a mountain was a task beyond the powers of the time; but in an indoors mystery-drama it would be managed as such exhibitions were by the pagans, who were wont to introduce a blaze of light at thrilling moments.

And that the Passion in the original mystery-drama may have been connected with the Transfiguration—both being enacted on the scenic mountain—is suggested by the fact that in the third Gospel the accompanying disciples in both cases alike fall asleep, as they do in the story of the Passion in the other synoptics. In the latter case the dramatic origin of the myth is especially suggested by the fact that, the disciples being repeatedly described as unable to keep awake, there is not even a pretence that the words of the Lord, who is at a distance, could be historically reported; whereas the scene, so enacted before the spectators' eyes, would leave them undisturbed by any craving for testimony. The detail of the bloody sweat, given in Luke only (xxii. 44), in what appears to be a late interpolation,[3] may stand for a realistic effort in some particular performance, and was perhaps originally suggested by the effect of the crown of thorns.

The sleep of the disciples during the Passion, finally,

[1] By Mr. Vickers, *The Crucifixion Mystery*, 1895, p. 58.
[2] Matt. xvii. 9; Mark ix. 9. Cp. Luke ix. 36.
[3] It is lacking in the Alexandrian and Vatican codices.

would seem to be one of the items in the Gentile process of disparaging them.[1] In the case of the Passion they figure as failing to give their Lord sympathy and companionship when he most needed it. On the other hand, the introduction of Moses and Elias, the two typic forerunners, in the Transfiguration scene, where also the three apostles answer to Aaron, Nadab, and Abihu, points to a Judaic origin. As Strauss notes, the cloud and the voice are exact repetitions of the Hebrew myth. And the fact that Joshua is there (Ex. xxiv. 13) associated with Moses as his "minister" suggests an indefinite antiquity for the Jesuist myth even as such.

§ 24. *The Crucifixion.*

On a full survey of the data, the crucifixion remains one of the most obscure of the quasi-mythical elements in the Jesuist legend. Here even more than elsewhere the documents are invalid, seeing that in the "Primitive Gospel" as reconstructed by conservative criticism the story of the trial and execution has confessedly no place. Whatever may have been the primary facts, the Gospel story, framed long after the alleged event, and after a Jesus memoir was already current, has no evidential value. And the trial before Pilate, the story of the two thieves, and the sayings on the cross, have all the marks of circumstantial fiction. On the other hand, there are obvious reasons for supposing that this, a datum in Paul's gospel, stands for *some* historical fact. A slain Messiah was so unlikely a basis to be *invented* for a Jewish cult that the historical presumption must be that some teacher of Messianic pretensions had really been put to death, and that his followers had carried on the movement in the faith that he would come again. When, however, we investigate the relation of the Gospels

[1] Compare, however, Strauss's curious parallel of the scene of Socrates outwatching all his companions at the Symposium. *Leben Jesu*, Abs. ii. K. 10, § 107, *note* 19.

to the Epistles, and find not only that Paul's spectral Jesus has no traceable connection with the teaching "Jesus the Nazarite" or "Jesus of Nazareth," but that the Gospels themselves betray plain traces of a factitious connection of these cognomens, and that the original Jesus of the first Gospel had no cognomen at all, we see cause to suspect that the movement really originated with the Talmudic Jesus Ben Pandira,[1] who was stoned to death and hanged on a tree, for blasphemy or heresy, on the eve of a Passover in the reign of Alexander Jannæus (B.C. 106–79). Dr. Löw, an accomplished Hebraist, is satisfied[2] that this Jesus was the founder of the Essene (or Jessean) sect, whose resemblances to the legendary early Christians have so greatly exercised Christian speculation. That, however, must remain a hypothesis, since the Jesus in question is little more than a historic name. His time and place are further obscured through his being identified in the Babylonian Gemara with one Ben Sotada or Stada or Satda, who by one (doubtful) clue is put in the period of Rabbi Akiba in the second century C.E. Of the Talmudic Jesus, as of Ben Stada, it is told that he was stoned and then hanged on a tree on the eve of the Passover; but Jesus is said to have been so executed at Jerusalem, and Ben Stada at Lydda. Rabbinical commentators and later Hebraists generally take the view that two historical personages are thus indicated,[3] and that it was a Rabbinical error to identify them. It seems impossible, however, to trust to the sole chronological clue in the Ben Satda story, which is bound up, as we have seen, with the name of Mary Magdala. We must be content to say that there is a Talmudic trace of *a* Jesus who was put to death on the eve of the Passover a century or more before the time of Pontius Pilate. The question is, then, was this

[1] Cp. Derenbourg, *Essai sur l'histoire et la géographie de la Palestine*, 1867, Note ix.; Lightfoot, *Horæ Hebraicæ: in Matt.* ii. 14; xxvii. 56; *in Luc.* viii. 2; and Baring Gould, *The Lost and Hostile Gospels*, 1874, Pt. i. §§ 3, 4.

[2] Ginsburg's *Essenes*, p. 29.

[3] Cp. Lightfoot *in Matt.* ii. 14; Derenbourg, as cited; and Joel, *Blicke in die religionsgeschichte*, Breslau, 1880, ii. 55.

Jesus literally crucified? It seems certain that the expression "hanging" was frequently used in Greek in the Roman period for crucifixion;[1] and the early Church was content to leave standing the passages in the Acts which described Jesus as "hanged on a tree." The detail, however, remains problematical, since the Talmud expressly talks of hanging on a tree *after* stoning[2]—that is, the hanging up of a dead body, which to crucify would be futile.

If the Jesus of Paul were really a personage put to death under Pontius Pilate, the Epistles would give us the strongest ground for accepting an actual crucifixion. We have seen that certain important passages were interpolated; but the references to a crucified Jesus are constant, and offer no sign of interpolation. But if Paul's Jesus, who has taught nothing, and done nothing but die, be really the Jesus of a hundred years before, it becomes readily intelligible that, even if he had been only hanged after stoning, he should by that time have come to figure mythically as crucified. For, as we shall see, the cross was itself a myth element peculiarly likely to be bound up with the cult of any Saviour God of that period. The historic crucifixion, scourging, and subsequent slaying of Antigonus, the last Asmonean King of the Jews, by Mark Antony,[3] would further supply the motive for the story of Jesus having been crucified with a parade of the kingly title, as Antigonus doubtless would be. And, historically speaking, it is probable enough that a crucified king should have had set on his head, in mockery, a crown of straw and thorns, by way of heightening his degradation. Yet again, Philo tells a singular story of how, during the reign of Caligula, King Agrippa was insulted at Alexandria by the populace, who took a lunatic named (oddly enough) Karabbas, honoured and dressed him as a mock king, and hailed him

[1] Frazer, *Golden Bough*, i. 226, *note*.

[2] Cp. *Soteh*, fol. 23, col. 1, cited by Hershon, *Genesis with a Talmudical Commentary*, Eng. tr. 1883, p. 433.

[3] Dio Cassius, xlix. 23. Josephus does not give the detail of the crucifixion, and most of the Christian historians have ignored it.

"Maris," the Syrian name for king.[1] But here, as in the case of Antigonus, possible history is overlapped by mythology, and it is necessary to take into account the latter factor.

The story of the crown of thorns, the scourging, and the kingly title, is wholly absent, like the rest of the Gospel narratives, from the letters of Paul, and may without hesitation be held to be mythical, whatever we decide to hold concerning the crucifixion. The first explanation that occurs to the student of comparative mythology is that the crown of thorns is simply the ancient nimbus of the Sun-God;[2] and this is in all probability the root-motive. But it happens that in Pagan mythology there is a closer approximation to the crown of thorns than the nimbus; a missing link, so to speak, which would serve to explain the manufacture of this part of the Christist story, as we have seen so many other Christist myths to be framed out of Pagan art and mystery ritual. Two of the leading Saviour figures of Paganism were Prometheus and Herakles, and each of these is mythologically represented as wearing a mock crown. The myth connects the two heroes. According to Athenæus,[3] Jupiter condemned Prometheus, when he released him from captivity, to wear in memory of that a crown of osiers and an iron ring; and the antiquarian further quotes from the lost *Prometheus Unbound* and the *Sphinx* of Æschylus to the effect that worshippers wear a crown in honour of Prometheus, thereby symbolically representing his bondage. The crown was thus a memorial of a sacrifice undergone for the good of mankind.[4] But it is in connection with Prometheus that such a crown is associated with Herakles. According to the old mythologists, when Herakles, seeking the golden apples of the Hesperides, came upon Prometheus and slew the eagle which tortured him, Prometheus in gratitude warned him not to seek the apples himself, but to send Atlas for them; which Herakles did, bearing

[1] Philo Judæus, *Against Flaccus*, c. 6.

[2] Cp. Philo's story of Caius, *Legation to Caius (On Ambassadors)*, c. 13.

[3] B. xv. cc. 13, 16. Pp. 672f, 674d.

[4] On his return to Olympus, Prometheus becomes a prophet and counsellor of the Gods. Preller, *Griechische Mythologie*, 2te Aufl. i. 78.

the burden of the heavens the while in Atlas' place. But when Atlas got the apples he proposed to take them himself to Eurystheus (who had set the finding of them to Herakles as his eleventh labour) and leave Herakles to bear the heavens. Again Prometheus counselled his Saviour to feign acquiescence, and to beg of Atlas a momentary resumption of the load while he (Herakles) made a wisp-pad for his head. Atlas consented, and of course Herakles left him with his load for ever.[1] Thus it is Herakles the Saviour that wears the mock crown. This special detail is probably one of the innumerable stories concocted to explain ancient mystery-ritual; from which we can only conclude that in ritual or mystery Prometheus and Herakles were represented as crowned with osiers or weeds. It may have been that such crowns were actually worn by the initiates; and in a cult like that of Mithra, from which the Christists took their Lord's Supper, an ascetic crown of thorns would be likely enough. A symbolical crown of some sort was certainly used, on the testimony of Tertullian.[2] In the Magian Mithra-worship, too, the sacrificial victim was crowned;[3] and in Pagan cults generally this usage prevailed.[4] We know, too, from Athenæus[5] that in Egypt crowns of thorns had a special religious vogue, there being certain thorn-trees about Abydos whose branches curled into garland form. Any collocation of these garlands with a religious rite could give the hint for the Gospel myth. We have it further from Herodotus[6] that the Greeks had a story that when Herakles landed in Egypt the Egyptians crowned him with a garland and led him in procession, intending to sacrifice him to their supreme

[1] Apollodorus, ii. 5, § 11. Cp. Keightley, *Mythology of Greece*, 2nd ed. p. 362, citing Pherecydes from the Scholiast on Apollonius Rhodius, iv. 1396. See above, § 10, for a theory of the main part of the myth.

[2] *De Præscriptione*, c. 40.

[3] Strabo, xv. 3, § 13. Herodotus, whom Strabo mainly follows, gives the crown to the priest (i. 131); but Strabo seems to have had some other sources. In any case, the crowning of sacrifice-victims was a general usage.

[4] Bähr, *Symbolik*, i. 363, ii. 252 *n.*, and refs.

[5] B. xv. c. 25, citing the lost *History of Egypt* of Hellanicus, and the lost *History of the Things to be seen in Egypt* by Demetrius.

[6] ii. 45.

God; but when he got to the altar the hero fell upon them and slew them. Herodotus warmly repudiates this story, on the score that the Egyptians had no human sacrifices; but it points none the less to an Egyptian ritual in which a Saviour-God was led as a prisoner in procession wearing a crown, probably one of those in use at Abydos. At bottom, as above suggested, the whole ritual might very well be symbolical of the ancient nimbus.

But there is the alternative explanation so ingeniously wrought out by Mr. Frazer in his *Golden Bough*. He has shown that in the ancient Babylonian festival of the Sacaea a prisoner condemned to death was dressed in the king's robes, throned, and allowed to disport himself as the king for five days, whereafter he was stripped, scourged, and crucified.[1] This was a combination of the common practice of sacrificing criminals as scapegoats,[2] and of the special usage of slaying a divine man by way of renewing the youth of vegetation in particular and life in general.[3] In all of these sacrifices, as in that of criminals to Apollo in the festival of Thargelia at Athens,[4] the victim was crowned, like the animal victim in ordinary sacrifices. Here, then, we have a likely source, not only of the tale of the mock crowning of Jesus, but of the proposed substitution of the criminal Barabbas, who in the time of Origen figured in most MSS. as being named *Jesus Barabbas*.[5] And in the care taken by the Greeks in the Thargelia to remove the body of the slain victim to a distance we may have the true clue to the story of the removal of the body of the crucified Christ. Given an ancient Christist ritual mystery, this might well be an integral part of it. The drink of gall, as a matter of fact, figured in the mysteries of Demeter.[6]

Another item in the Gospel story can with still greater probability be traced to Pagan myth and art. One of the

[1] *The Golden Bough*, 1890, i. 226. [2] *Id.* ii. 212. [3] *Id. passim.*
[4] Müller, *Dorians*, tr. i. 260.
[5] See the evidences as to this reading collected by Mr. Nicholson in his work on *The Gospel According to the Hebrews*, 1879, pp. 141–2.
[6] Clem. Alex. *Protrept.* ii.

subsidiary labours of Herakles was the setting up of two pillars at Gades (Cadiz) to mark the boundaries of Europe and Libya.[1] Here the cult of Herakles combines with that of his Phœnician double, the Sun-God Melkarth, worshipped at Gades, of whose mythus the Samson legend in the Hebrew Bible is a variant. The two pillars (represented in the Hebrew as in the Phœnician temples)[2] are simply ancient symbol-limits of the course of the sun in the heavens; and, as usual, we have a variety of legends in the different mythologies to explain them.[3] In the Samson legend they occur twice, figuring in one episode as the gateposts of Gaza[4] which the hero carries off; in another as the two pillars of the Philistine hall, between which the shorn and blinded hero sits in his captivity; Samson here being the winter sun, weak and rayless, at the end of his course, and, therefore, touching at least one pillar. Now, just as Samson in one story carries

[1] Apollodorus, ii. 5, § 10. Cp. Diodorus Siculus, i. 24; Pomponius Mela, i. 5; ii. 6; iii. 6.

[2] Solomon's temple was an imitation of that of Tyre, which we know was dedicated to Herakles, and had two pillars. Herodotus, ii. 44; Lucian, *De Dea Syria*, c. 16. P. 463.

[3] Professor Robertson Smith (*Religion of the Semites*, pp. 190–1, 194, 438) opposes the phallic theory of sacred pillars, though inconclusively, but takes no note of the simple astronomical explanation. Sir George Cox makes the same oversight (as I regard it) in discussing the "pillars" of Herakles, Osiris, Dionysos, and Sesostris, which he makes merely phallic, though assimilating them with the world-tree of Scandinavian mythology or the pillar of Atlas, which supports the heavens (*Mythology of the Aryan Nations*, new ed. pp. 268, 351). Doubtless the "pillars" of Dionysos (Lucian, *De Dea Syria*, last cit.) and Osiris (Diodorus, i. 20) were phallic; and so may have been those of Sesostris (Herodotus, ii. 102, 106), on which see Payne Knight (*Symbol. Lang. of Anc. Art and Mythol.* new ed. p. 94), whom Sir George Cox seems to follow. But still the pillars which mark the course of the Sun-God have an obvious enough non-phallic significance. That an astronomico-geographical meaning was involved is clear from Virgil's reference to the *columnas Protei*, which were in Egypt (Servius on *Æneid*, xi. 262), and from the other notion that Hercules' columns were on the northern coast of Europe (Tacitus, *Germania*, xxxiv.). Pindar repeatedly refers to the Pillars of Herakles as the bounds of possible travel.

[4] Note the correspondence of the names Gaza and Gades. Steinthal (Essay on *Samson*, trans. in vol. with Goldziher's *Hebrew Mythology*, pp. 403–4) connects the Gaza episode only with Herakles' fight at the gate of Hades. I think we may go further. In regard to the pillar-bearing it should be noted that Atlas, whose place Herakles temporarily takes, is bearer of the "pillar of heaven and earth" on his shoulders "in the western regions." Æsch. *Prom. Vinct.* 356–8 (374–6). Cp. Hesiod, *Theogony*, 518, 748; *Odyssey*, i. 53–4—"columns dividing heaven and earth."

the pillars, so did Herakles, as became his strength, carry his pillars to their places; even as, in the Tyrian form of the legend, he dies at the very place where he has set them up.[1] And in ancient art he was actually represented carrying the two pillars in such a way under his arms that they form exactly a cross.[2] Here, probably, we have the origin of the myth of Jesus carrying his own cross to the place of execution.[3] Christian art has always represented him staggering under the load, as even Herakles stoops with the weight of his columns. Singularly enough, the three Synoptics substitute for Jesus as cross-bearer one Simon, a man of Cyrene. Cyrene is in Libya, the legendary scene, as we saw, of the pillar-carrying exploit of Herakles; and Simon (Simeon) is the nearest Greek name-form to Samson—which in Greek might be read as Simson, following the Hebrew.[4] But in Palestine Simon, or Sem, was actually a God-name, representing the ancient Sun-God Semesh, identified with Baal, from whose mythus that of Samson unquestionably arose; and the God Simon was especially worshipped in Samaria.[5] That district, lying between Galilee and Judea, must needs at an early period have tended to affect the Jesuist legend, which in the Fourth Gospel makes the Founder visit the region and make converts in it. What more likely than that a representation of the Sun-Hero Simon (so recognizable by the many Jews settled in Greece), carrying his pillars crosswise, should come to figure as that of a man Simon carrying a cross? The two versions of the cross-bearing satisfy us that the story

[1] Preller, as cited, ii. 209, citing Arnobius i. 36, etc.

[2] See the engraving from Maffei in Montfaucon, *L'Antiquité Expliquée*, T. i. Pt. ii. p. 210, and at the end of Higgins's *Anacalypsis*, vol. ii.

[3] John xix. 17. The myth of Isaac carrying the wood for his sacrifice (Gen. xxii. 6) is a remoter parallel.

[4] The German transliteration of the name is Simson.

[5] Volkmar, *Die Religion Jesu und ihre erste Entwickelung*, 1857, pp. 287, 289. Volkmar traces the legend of Simon Magus (= Simon *Megas*, the Great), "the Great Power of God" (Acts viii. 10), to the Samaritan Sun-God cultus. Cp. Movers, *Die Phönizier*, i. 417, 684, and the Laterculus of Eratosthenes (in Cory's *Ancient Fragments*, pp. 139, 140, 141), where Sem appears in the combinations "Sensaophis" (Saophis = Hermes) and Semphucrates, "who is Hercules Harpocrates."

is a myth: is any hypothesis more probable than that Simon the Cyrenian's task is a variant of that of the Cyrenian Simon-Herakles?

If the cross-bearing and thorn-crown motives in the Jesuist legend be thus reducible, like so many others, to a well-established Pagan type, the greater, clearly, is the likelihood that the idea of crucifixion is a mythic development on the basis of the simple hanging of the original Jesus ben Pandira, a century before the "Christian era." Not only was the cross-symbol, as all scholars now admit, absolutely universal in pre-Christian times, and, as a rule, a recognized symbol of life or immortality, but the actual idea of a mystic or exemplary crucifixion was perfectly familiar in Pagan theology. Obvious myth combined with real and legendary history to crystallize the conception. The crucifixion of Antigonus, King of the Jews, would alone set up an enduring impression in Syria and Egypt; and the story of the crucifixion of Cyrus,[1] who had actually figured as a Messiah, or Christos, for the Jews in their prophetic literature,[2] would go still further to establish the myth-motive of a crucified Messiah wherever the Jews went—that is to say, throughout the Græco-Roman empire. The legend of the prepared sacrifice of Isaac, the Only-begotten Son, in which the Son is bound on wood, and a ram finally takes his place, would further serve the record-worshipping Jews as a forecast; as would the story of the saving of the Israelites by the outstretching of the arms of Moses. But over and above all this, a theological crucifixion-motive pervaded mythology both in the East and the West.

The mystic crucifixion, like the cross-symbol, represents rather the coincidence of a number of symbolic and mystic notions than any one in particular. That the cross is, among other things, a phallic emblem, there can be no reasonable doubt; but it is also highly probable that it was from the earliest times associated with the fire-sticks, which among the Aryans in India retained a theological

[1] Diodorus Siculus, ii. 44. [2] Isaiah xlv. 1. See above, p. 185.

sacredness long after they had ceased to be necessary for household uses. In the Vedas, Agni, the Fire-God, is perpetually figured as a divine child born of the two *aranis;* and to represent the God as being generated by the friction of the crossed sticks would be to figure him on the cross. And this is the probable origin of various symbolic combinations of the cross with the sun: as the figuring of the Deity in the Assyrian system as a cross, of which the upright is a human figure and the transverse beam a conventionalized pair of wings, a type which in Eastern Mithraic remains becomes a crucified figure;[1] that in turn holding out with one hand a wreath or crown, which was doubtless connected with the use of a crown (of thorns?) in the Mithraic mysteries.[2] And in the *Mihr Yasht* ritual, in the Zendavesta, Mithra, the Sun-God, drives in his chariot across the heavens "with his arms lifted up towards immortality."[3] It is a perfectly intelligible variation of the same idea which appears in the myth of Ixion, crucified on his "four-spoked fetter," as Pindar calls it.[4] Ixion was himself, undoubtedly, in some mythology, at some time, the actual Sun-God, and would as such be figured outstretched at once on the fire-cross and on the sun-wheel. But the apparent torture of the mystic position, misunderstood by worshippers of another system, would appear as a punishment, and so we have the myth of the presumptuous guest of Olympus, who dared to aspire to the favours of the Queen of Heaven, and is first baffled by Zeus's substitution of a cloud for Hère, and then bound by Hermes, on Zeus's command, to the fiery wheel which revolves for ever in Hades.[5] How easily any such story found currency is

[1] See Bryant's *Analysis of Ancient Mythology*, 1774, 4to. i. 232–4, 294; also the plates in Lajard's Atlas to his *Introduction à l'Etude du Culte de Mithra*.

[2] Above, p. 398.

[3] Darmesteter's *Zendavesta*, ii. 152 (*Sacred Books of the East*).

[4] Pythians, ii. 74.

[5] Compare Cox, *Mythology*, p. 262:—"The proud Ixion himself is fastened to the four-spoked wheel of noonday, for his presumption in seeking the love of the wife of Zeus. The sun as climbing the heights of heaven, and wooing the bright ether," [Hêrê (Juno) = the Air] "is an arrogant being who must

further shown by the transference of the four-spoked-wheel motive to the bird Iünx[1] (the wryneck) for no better reason, perhaps, than the resemblance of its name to that of Ixion, though here again we may be touching primæval Aryan mythology, for the zig-zagging lightning is in mythology a bird—eagle,[2] hawk, or woodpecker; and certain birds were fabled to be fallen flashes of lightning. At Babylon four Iünxes were figured in gold on the canopy, or roof, of the king's throne-room, "to keep the king in memory of the goddess of vengeance," and the mages called them the "tongues of the Gods."[3] In the Vedic hymns, again, Agni, the fire-God, is a "golden-winged bird,"[4] and his thunderbolts are "well-winged ones"; while Indra, the thunderer, is "the well-winged red one"; and the sun itself and the moon are well-winged birds which fly round the tree of the sky.[5] With all this the winged Sun-God of Assyrian and Egyptian art, and the winged Sun-Angel of Christism, connect easily enough. The step to the Messianic sacrifice is only a stage further.

In this crucifixion of the Sun-God or Fire-God, again, we have one of the clues of the myth of Prometheus. Despite some recent German scepticism, the connection of Prometheus, the fire-bringer or -stealer, with the Sanskrit *Pramantha*, or fire-generating boring-stick, and the variant word *pramâthyus* = Borer,[6] or Robber, seems sufficiently well made out; and the mythical chaining of Prometheus on a rock on the Caucasus, in such wise that he cannot keep the eagle of Zeus from gnawing his liver, implies the posture of crucifixion. Lucian, indeed, expressly describes

be bound to the fiery cross, or whose flaming orb must be made to descend to the west, like the stone of Sisyphus, just when it has reached the zenith, or summit of the hill." It should be added that Ixion may have been originally represented symbolically as the Sun-God on his wheel without any thought of punishment. That is probably a late guess.

[1] Pindar, *Pyth.* iv. 353.

[2] Thus Jupiter's eagle and his thunderbolts are kindred symbols.

[3] Philostratus, *Life of Apollonius*, i. 25.

[4] Steinthal on the Prometheus Legend (trans. in vol. with Goldziher), pp. 366–8, citing Kelly's *Curiosities of Indo-European Tradition and Folk-Lore* on the cognate myths.

[5] Gubernatis, *Zoological Mythology*, ii. 168–9.

[6] In the *Theogony* Prometheus steals the fire in hollow reeds.

him as crucified by Zeus.[1] In one version, however,[2] the chains of Prometheus are passed through the middle of a column; and here we are brought in touch with the form of the suffering-Saviour myth in which the God is fastened to a tree. Phoroneus, son of Inachos the water-God (probably = Noach = Enoch) who in Argos was revered as the fire-bringer,[3] as Prometheus was elsewhere, had for mother the nymph Melia, "the Ash"; and though Steinthal[4] perhaps assumes too readily that he was figured as a bird, from the derivation of his name from the Sanskrit epithet of Agni, *bhuranyus*, "rapid, darting, flying," still the Greek name of his mother connects him with the tree. And the fact that on the one hand Prometheus was said to have made men from clay, and that on the other Phoroneus was fabled by some to be the first man,[5] brings us still further into connection with the Græco-Jewish significance of the God-Christ, who as *Logos* had presided over the creation of the world.

The actual use of the symbolic tree, however, is best known in connection with the widespread ascetic worship of the self-castrated God-man Attis, who was specially honoured in relation to Cybelè, the Virgin Mother, from the 22nd to the 27th March, a date pointing at once to the vernal equinox and the arrival of spring.[6] At that season the Sacred Tree of Attis—a pine—was cut down, and was carried, swathed and crowned with violets, to the temple of the Great Goddess as a symbol of the lost demigod. Then he was sought for in the hills and woods with a ritual of frenzy and lamentation, which after three days[7] was followed by jubilation on his being given out to be

[1] *De Sacrificiis*, c. 6.
[2] Hesiod, *Theogony*, 521.
[3] Pausanias, ii. 19.
[4] As cited, p. 368.
[5] Preller, *Griech. Myth.* ii. 36, citing Clemens Alexandrinus and Plato.
[6] Preller, *Röm. Myth.* p. 736; Macrobius, *Saturnalia*, i. 21.
[7] The confusion of the Gospels as to the time between Jesus' death and resurrection is doubtless due to the fact that other cults varied in this respect. Attis was ritually found on the third or fourth day (cp. Frazer, *Golden Bough*, i. 297; Creuzer, *Symbolik*, 2 Aufl. ii. 38), and Adonis on the second (Lucian, *De Dea Syria*, c. 6). It should always be remembered that Adonis was "the Lord" *par excellence*, and that Attis too would have that title.

found again.[1] Attis was fabled to have been changed into the pine by the Goddess in punishment for his breach of chastity;[2] but the tree seems similarly to have been identified with the nymph he loved;[3] and Julian, telling that the symbolic tree was annually cut down "at the moment when the sun arrives at the extreme point of the equinoctial arc," states that the cutting of the tree "has nothing to do with the rites which it accompanies." These were "holy and not to be divulged," and included "the sacred and ineffable harvest of the God Gallos," *i.e.*, *castratus*. Obviously the cut pine symbolized the cut phallus, the life principle of Nature and humanity. We learn from the Christian Father, Julius Firmicus, who had no scruple about publishing Pagan mysteries, that on the pine tree there was bound the image of a youth;[4] and the same writer reveals that a ritual of tree and image existed also in the worship of Isis and Osiris and in the cult of the Virgin Persephonė.[5] In the Isiac mysteries the coffin[6] of Osiris would seem from this evidence to have been a hollowed pine tree; and in those of Persephonė the "sacred tree," after being cut, was formed into the image of a virgin, over which the worshippers lamented for forty nights, burning it on the fortieth.

Here we have the *arbor crucis*, clearly enough, along with the whole idea of suffering, mourning, resurrection, and rejoicing. Attis, risen, became "Papa," Father and Lord;[7] as Osiris remains the Father-God, Creator and Judge of all flesh, soul of the world, and Saviour of mankind. And Dionysos, on the whole the most popular of the Græco-Roman deities in the period just before Christianity, is in the same way a God of the Sacred Tree, a Saviour, and a

[1] Preller, *Gr. Myth.* i. 509–511; Julian, *In Deorum Matrem*, cc. 3–5; Arnobius, *Adv. Gentes*, v. 16, 17.

[2] Ovid, *Metamorph.* 103–107.

[3] *Fasti*, iv. 231–2.

[4] *De Errore Profanarum Religionum*, xxviii.; cp. Diodorus Siculus, iii. 59.

[5] In the cult of Adonis, animals were hung on tree trunks in the temple, and burned with the trees. Lucian, *De Dea Syria*.

[6] Or coffin-containing tree. See the myth in Plutarch, *Isis and Osiris*, c. xv. Cp. the words of Pompey, "*tectum ligno Osirim*," as cited in Lactantius, i. 21.

[7] Hippolytus, *Refutation of all Heresies*, v. 4; Diod. Sic. iii. 58.

sacrifice. One of his epithets was *Dendrites*,[1] "pertaining to the tree"; he had his sacred pillar; and in Bœotia he was called *endendros*, "in the tree."[2] In his case the divine suffering does not seem to have been undergone in that connection; like Mithra, he *is* the victim sacrificed in his cult;[3] and as Mithra was certainly the divine Bull, and equally the divine Ram or Lamb, so Dionysos was the divine Bull, and doubtless also the divine Ram, which was most commonly sacrificed to him,[4] as being the animal into which, in one legend, he was actually turned by Zeus in his childhood to save him from Hêrê.[5] In his childhood, however, in a common story, he is actually slain by the Titans;[6] and in various legends he suffers persecution. In his case, no doubt, his special association with the vine gave the determining bent to the symbolism of the cult; but his wooden images were made of the phallic fig-tree, and a stump of that sometimes symbolized him.[7] In Egypt, again, all cultivated trees were sacred to Osiris.[8] Whether or not, or in what order, these systems borrowed from one another, it is now very hard to trace; but the presence of the Sacred Tree = Cross in so many cults proves the universality of the idea. Attis, the unsexed youth, though probably in origin a God of Vegetation,[9] finally represents the combination of sun-worship and moon-worship, and the transference to the Moon-God, *Deus Lunus*, of the sex attributes of the Moon-Goddess; while his worship at the vernal equinox in connection with the Mighty Mother identifies him in one aspect with the sun,[10] then supposed to be reunited with the earth, and so to renew vegetation. The cult was to all appearance of Asiatic origin, as was

[1] Preller, i. 555, citing Plutarch, *Symp.* v. 1.
[2] *Id.* p. 562, citing Hesychius. See also above, p. 84.
[3] Compare Frazer, *Golden Bough*, i. 328.
[4] Brown, *The Great Dionysiak Myth*, ii. 65.
[5] Hyginus, cited in Smith's Dict. of Myth. In Apollodorus (iii. 4, 3) he is changed into a kid.
[6] Preller, *Gr. Myth.* ii. 58; Clemens Alexandrinus, *Protrep.* c. 2; Arnobius, i. 40; Justin, 1 *Apol.* 21, 54; Pausanias, viii. 37.
[7] Lang, *Myth, Ritual, and Religion*, ii. 235, citing Maximus Tyrius.
[8] Plutarch, *Isis and Osiris*, c. 35.
[9] Frazer, as cited, i. 298.
[10] Macrobius, *Saturnalia*, i. 21.

certainly that of Mithra, another composite Deity, who, however, represented sun and moon in being twy-sexed, not unsexed, and who is represented in art and symbol with a crescent behind his shoulders, making, as Firmicus vehemently insists, a virtual crucifix.[1] In his cult, too, as we gather from the monuments, there figured the Sacred Tree; and at the foot of this tree, on the sacred anniversary, there was sacrificed a ram, that is, a male lamb,[2] for the sacrifice must be immaculate. Osiris, again, finally represents a great complex of myth, being at once Night Sun and Day Sun, Moon, moisture, Nile, seed, and other principles; and Persephone, yet again, is the buried Germinal One, whom the Mater Dolorosa seeks with lamentations, and who is finally restored to her mother for part of the year, living above as fruit and grain, and beneath as seed: whence the myth of her capture by Pluto and her queenship of Hades.

But the full mythic significance of the Sacred Tree in all these systems cannot here be traced.[3] In the religion of ancient Gaul its cultus seems to have been closely connected with the cannibalistic holy communion, since the victims slain to be eaten were first crucified in the temples.[4] Enough that it seems to have been a world-wide myth; and that in ancient Mexico, strangely enough, there was developed the closest parallel to the Christian cultus. The Sacred Tree was there made into a cross on which was exposed a baked-dough figure of a Saviour God; and this was after a time climbed for, taken down, broken up, and sacramentally eaten.[5] The very name of the Mexican cross meant "tree of our life, or flesh."[6] And there too the cross-figure had a special religious significance, one of the

[1] *De Errore*, xxii. Firmicus quotes Isaiah as to the Son who shall have the "government upon his shoulders," and adds, "these are the horns of the cross," comparing them to Mithra's crescent.

[2] *Id.* xxviii.; Garucci, as cited above, p. 391.

[3] On this wide subject see Mr. J. G. Frazer's masterly research in *The Golden Bough*, and the excellent monograph of Mrs. Philpot, *The Sacred Tree*, 1897. Cp. Cox, p. 351.

[4] Strabo, b. iv. c. iv. § 5; Pliny, *Nat. Hist.* xxx. 4; Plutarch, *Marcellus*.

[5] H. H. Bancroft, *Native Races of the Pacific States of North America*, ii. 386, 509. Cp. Stephens' *Central America*, 1842, ii. 346.

[6] Bancroft, ii. 506.

hideous rites of the system being the standing of the murderous priest in the skin of a newly-slain woman victim, with his hands spread out "like a cross," before the image of the War-God.[1]

That the cross-symbol had already many centuries before the Christian era acquired an abstract or mystical importance in Greek theology is shown by the singular proposition in the *Timæus* of Plato,[2] to the effect that when God had compounded the soul of the universe he divided it lengthways into two parts which he joined together "like the figure of a χ," and so imposed it on the world. Not only does Justin Martyr[3] cite this in support of the doctrine of the crucifixion of the Logos, but we know that the populace of Antioch in the time of Julian, referring to the Christian reign of Constantius as the time of "*Chi* and *Kappa*,"[4] signified their favourite Saviour God's name by the initial letter which itself was one of the names for the cross.[5]

That the phallic significance of the cross should connect with all its other aspects is perfectly intelligible. For primitive peoples—and in that definition we may include the populace of civilized Paganism—such symbolism was in no way monstrous, being perfectly spontaneous and natural; and the raging invective of the Christian Fathers against the Pagan usages proved, not the vice of the Pagans, but the growth of a new sophistication and sense of sin and shame, which, rising in Greece with the ascetic and flesh-mortifying cults as it had done among Jews and Orientals, became specially associated with Christianity, the religion *par excellence* of salvation-buying self-abasement. As Voltaire long ago pointed out, what are to us indecent practices could not have been so to the people who invented them. It was in the nature of religious evolution that symbolism

[1] *Id.* iii. 356.

[2] Jowett's trans. iii. 618.

[3] Plato's doctrine is doubtless a mere theosophizing of the usage of representing the earth as a globe divided in four by crossing bands. See it on a coin of Augustus, in a note of Gronovius on Pomponius Mela, i. 1. This was no doubt the meaning of the cross on the ancient Roman denarius.

[3] 1 *Apol.* 60.

[4] Constantius' name in Greek beginning with K.

[5] Gibbon, note to ch. 24, citing Julian's *Misopogon*.

should crystallize; and long ritualistic association of the Sacred Tree or Cross with the God's suffering and death would give it a special significance of that kind for the devout. Still, the fact remains that the vogue of the symbol was in large measure first secured by its popular emblematic meaning; and inasmuch as the cross was thus already an amulet[1] of life-preserving virtue, Christism profited by its acceptance, and could make that the basis for a new mystico-historical doctrine, of the kind which formed the staple of ancient theology. Wherever Christism went, the cross was before it;[2] and when it was found that the ancient symbolical rosary[3] was tenaciously preserved along with the correlative emblem, Christism simply adopted the rosary as it had done the cross. The vitality of the popular notion has been shown by the retention of phallic ceremonial in parts of Christian France and Italy down to our own time.[4] And in respect of at least one symbol, Christism traded from the outset on Pagan usage. The bishop's crozier, or pastoral staff, had unquestionably an emblematic meaning in the Osirian cult, from which the Christians deliberately appropriated it; and here the symbolism of cross, crozier, and tree of life was, as we saw, specially bound up with the worship of a slain Saviour-God. "The emblem became the *stauros*, or cross of Osiris, and a new source of mythology was thus laid open. To the Egyptian the cross thus became the symbol of immortality, *and the God himself was crucified to the tree which denoted his fructifying power*."[5] The ritual lamentation of the divine sisters, Isis and Nephthys, for Osiris, referred to in a previous section,[6] is found in the temple remains of the island of Philae expressly connected with the representation of Osiris in the form of a crucifix, the God's head standing on the top of a four-barred Nilometer, faced by

[1] It is still so used in Italy. See Payne Knight's *Symbolical Language*, as before cited, p. 30.

[2] See above, *Christ and Krishna*, Sect. xxi.; and for the universal vogue of the symbol see Goblet D'Alviella's *Migration of Symbols*.

[3] *Id.* p. 31. For early Etruscan samples of the cross and rosary see Montfaucon, *Antiq. Expliq. Suppl.* iii. 77.

[4] See Dulaure, *Cultes Differens*.

[5] Cox, *Mythology*, p. 353. [6] Above, p. 323.

the mourning female figures. Here, too, he represents the Trinity, combining the attributes of Phtah-Sokari-Osiris.[1] There need then be no perplexity for rationalist students in regard to the text in Revelation (xi. 8) about "the great city which spiritually is called Sodom and Egypt, where also their [in many Greek versions *our*, as in our A. V.] Lord was crucified."

Yet again, the common representation of the Hermae (figures or emblems of Hermes, God of boundaries, serving as landmarks), in the form of a cross with a head for top,[2] would connect the cross in particular with the doctrine of the Logos or Word, Hermes being the Logos in Greek theosophy long before the Christian era. Yet further, the recognized use of the *crux ansata* as the symbol of Venus, and the worship of it as such in her cult,[3] would connect the emblem just as effectively with a doctrine of Love. In fine, throughout the civilized world, and equally in the uncivilized, the symbol of the cross was found more or less directly associated with deity. It was built into the foundations of Egyptian temples; it is found in mosaic, with a superimposed head of Neptune, making it a crucifix, in the ruins of a Gallo-Roman villa;[4] it was the sign by which Osiris gave eternal life to the spirits of the just; it was the hammer (= lightning) with which northern Thor (Thonr, thunder = Indra) slew the serpent and restored the slain to life.[5] Always it meant salvation, life; often it meant the death of a God.

The instance of Neptune brings us, finally, to another fruitful source of cross-mythology. In his early Etruscan form, as Nethuns, he appears to have been a solar deity, standing for the risen sun.[6] In any case, as a God of the

[1] See the plates in Rossellini's *Monumenti dell' Egitto e della Nubia*, Tom. 3°, Tav. 23; and the description in his *Monumenti del Culto* (Pisa, 1844), p. 157. These wall-pictures appear to have been in a peculiarly sacred and secret chamber. See also Kenrick's *Ancient Egypt under the Pharaohs*, 1850, i. 415.

[2] See the figures in Montfaucon, art. *Mercure*.

[3] Payne Knight, p. 30, citing Proclus, *Paraphr. Ptolem.* iii. p. 97.

[4] Baring-Gould, *Curious Myths of the Middle Ages*, p. 344.

[5] It is worth noting that the serpent itself symbolizes the lightning which slays it. Strabo, xvi. c. ii. § 7.

[6] I. Taylor, *Etruscan Researches*, 1874, p. 139.

underworld, ruling the sea, but meddling with the affairs of the earth,[1] he would figure on a cross as representing his divided or overlapping power. But most clearly does the cosmological significance of the cross appear in the astronomical representation of the Lamb or Ram of the zodiac, which is actually that of a quasi-crucifixion of the animal[2] by the crossing lines of the equinoctial arcs. Astronomically speaking, the back of the zodiacal sign Aries is about ten degrees in length, and the equinoctial colure, or intersecting line, would pass through it at one part or another during seven centuries.[3] Here, then, was the Lamb on the Cross in astronomy, and by consequence in the religious mysteries. Melito of Sardis, arguing that "the Lord was a lamb, like the ram which Abraham saw caught in the bush," explains that the bush "represented the cross."[4] And the killing of the Lamb at the foot of the Sacred Tree, above referred to, was doubtless a symbolic sacrifice of zodiacal bearing, as was the earlier slaying of the Bull by Mithra. The entrance of the sun into Aries, too, was for the ancients the Birthday of the World;[5] and Aries was thus the chief of the signs, all of which were in their turn identified with the Sun-God.[6] The further significance of the Lamb as symbolizing purity is likewise apparent in Pagan cults before Christianity.[7] While Hermes, who as *Kriophoros*, the Ram-bearer, supplied the art-type for the Good Shepherd, had no special repute for purity, Apollo, who also was named *Nomios*, the pastoral, and ἀρνοκόμης, lamb-haired, or lamb-fleeced,[8] is repeatedly specified by Pindar (despite the countervailing legends)

[1] Cp. Catullus, xxxi. 3.
[2] See the figure in Brown's ed. of Aratos.
[3] Whiston's *Confutation of Sir Isaac Newton's Chronology*.
[4] Fragment v.
[5] Macrobius, *In Somnium Scipionis*, i. 21.
[6] *Saturnalia*, i. 21. In the Egyptian slaying of the ram for Ammon, the slain ram was mourned for and laid on the image of the God, and another image of the Sun-God brought to it (Herodotus, ii. 42).
[7] By a process of inversion, the grown ram seems to have signified, when sacrificed, the idea of lust. In Persian mythology, a ram helps to lead the first man and woman into sexuality and sin, and is the first animal they sacrifice (Spiegel, *Erânische Alterthumskunde*, i. 511–2).
[8] *Saturnalia*, i. 17.

as the ἁγνὸς θεός, "the chaste God";[1] and the Greek *hagnos*,[2] chaste, would certainly be coupled with the Latin *agnus*, lamb, throughout the Roman Empire.[3] In Apollo's own temple of Larissa the oracle was given out by a priestess, who once a month tasted by night of the blood of a sacrificed lamb, and became possessed by the God.[4] Here we have one more precedent for the Christian sacrament. But a ritual lament for a slain lamb is further pointed to by the Song of "Linus," a name apparently given by misunderstanding on the part of the Greeks[5] to Adonis or some other Syrian God, who was fabled to have grown up "among the lambs" and been slain by wild dogs, and who probably figured the destruction of the fresh spring by the summer heat.[6] And though the Jewish Passover, with its sacrificed lamb, had a different pretext, that too has clearly an astronomical basis, its date being determined by certain relations of sun and moon. Ancient mythology is a shoreless sea of dreams, of which we can only say that in their strange way they too must represent the working of constant psychological law, if we could but catch and follow the clues.

To sum up, then: the story of the crucifixion, firstly, *may* rest on the remote datum of an actual crucifixion of Jesus Ben Pandira, the probable Jesus of Paul, dead long before, and represented by no preserved biography or teachings whatever. But had this Jesus really been only "hanged on a tree," the factors of a crucifixion myth were strong enough to turn the hanging into a crucifixion.

Secondly, whether or not Jesus Ben Pandira was actually crucified, it was the mythic significance of crucifixion that made the early fortune of the cult, with the aid of the

[1] *Olymp.* vii. 106; *Pyth.* ix. 102; Æschylus, *Suppliants*, 222; Plutarch, *De Ei*, c. 20; *De Exilio*, c. 17. The same adjective was applied to Adonis, Dionysos, Persephonê, and Hephaistos in the Orphic hymns.

[2] In modern Greek the aspirates are not sounded.

[3] Thus the Greek ἄγνος (a tall tree like the willow) is the Latin *agnus castus*. It was with rods of this tree, by the way, that the scapegoat slave was beaten at Chaeronea, as described by Plutarch, who officiated once as chief magistrate (*Convivial Questions*, vi. 8).

[4] Pausanias, ii. 24.

[5] Preller, *Griech. Myth.* i. 360.

[6] K. O. Müller, *Lit. of Anc. Greece*, Lewis' trans. 1847, p. 18.

mythic significance of the name Jesus or Jeschu = Joshua, the ancient Sun-God.

Thirdly, the whole apparatus of the Gospel crucifixion is pure myth. The Last Supper, the Passion, the Betrayal, the Denial, the Trial, the false witnesses, Pilate's wife's dream, Pilate's repudiation of responsibility, the substitution of Barabbas, the crown of thorns, the gall and vinegar, the carrying of the cross, the mocking inscription, the talk of the two thieves, the "My God, my God, why hast thou forsaken me?" (a quotation from Psalm xxii. 1), the "It is finished"—all these details are as truly mythical as the rending of the temple veil, the preternatural darkness, the rising of the saints from their graves, and the rising of the Crucified One from the rock tomb. The non-miraculous items are historically as unfounded as the miraculous. All alike are late accretions, probably dramatic; and to take them as history is no more reasonable than to see history in the *Bacchæ* of Euripides.

§ 25. *The Seamless Tunic.*

The account in the fourth Gospel of the parting of the God's garments among the soldiers is a good instance in little of the process of myth-making. In the synoptics it is simply stated that the soldiers cast lots for the garments, such being doubtless the practice at executions; the "prophecy" in the Psalms (xxii. 18) being as a matter of course kept in mind, though not cited. But in the fourth Gospel a late hand has wrought up the narrative with singular infelicity, describing the Roman soldiers as piously agreeing among themselves to fulfil the Jewish prophecy by abstaining from rending the Lord's *chiton*, or inner garment, which was "without seam, woven from the top throughout," at the same time dividing the other garments into "four parts, to every soldier a part." In order to lay stress on the seamless character of the tunic, resort is had to the absurdity of suggesting that the natural procedure of the soldiers with such a tunic would be to cut it up, thereby making it worthless. Absolute myth is set forth with the circumstantiality of an eye-witness, very likely on the strength of a dramatic representation.

Like the water-wine miracle, equally special to the fourth Gospel, the myth of the seamless robe is specifically Pagan. In Sparta, says Pausanias concerning his own day, "every year the women weave a *chiton* for Apollo at Amyclæ; and they call the place where they weave it *Chiton*."[1] So at Elis every fifth year sixteen matrons wove a *peplos* or shawl for Hère, a special place being appointed for the work in this case also.[2] The function was rated high, and in some cults the robe had a mystic as well as sacred significance. Whether or not this significance was stressed in later Greece, it has entirely disappeared in the Christian myth, where the story of the seamless *chiton* has no point whatever.

The mystic meaning, however, is obvious enough. As Plutarch tells, the robe of the solar Osiris, unlike that of Isis, is one, whole, and indivisible, that robe being the universal light; whereas the light of the moon is variable and chequered, and the robe of Isis is accordingly so made; both robes being actually so represented in the mysteries[3] and in the monuments.[4] But the two symbols blend. The solar child Cyrus, like the young Joseph, is clothed in "a coat of many colours."[5] In the Magian system, again, "Ahura Mazda, together with Mithra, Rashnu, and Spenta Armaita, puts on a garment decked with stars, and made by God in such a way that *nobody can see the ends of its parts*."[6] So in the Orphic and other mysteries the Sun-God's robe is a purple peplos—like that put on Jesus by the mocking soldiery[7]—with a fawnskin added to symbolize the dappled night-sky, and a golden cincture to mark the

[1] B. iii. c. 16. [2] *Id.* v. 16; vi. 24, *end*.
[3] *On Isis and Osiris*, c. 78. Cp. Iamblichus, *De Mysteriis*, i. 9, 19; vii. 3, etc.
[4] Bähr, *Symbolik des mosaischen Cultus*, i. 318.
[5] Herodotus, i. 111.
[6] Haug, *Essays on the Parsis*, p. 207.
[7] Matt. xxvii. 28; Mark xv. 17.

sun's path.[1] Pan, yet again, wears a deerskin of many colours to represent "the all"; and for Clement of Alexandria the robe of the high-priest is "the symbol of the world of sense."[2] Nearly every God has his typic garment. Dionysos, the God of the Night-Sun, wears the dappled deerskin as being "an image of the starlight in which he is clothed";[3] Attis is crowned by Cybelê with a starry cap;[4] and Sosipolis, the guardian God of Elis, is figured as a boy in a many-coloured cloak covered with stars.[5]

It is probable that in the early Christian dramatic mystery most of the details of the symbolic vestures of the other cults were reproduced in the garments divided into "four parts"; and not unlikely that the whole procedure of the "gorgeous apparel" was copied in the first instance from one of the mimic cults already described. But a myth Christianized was a myth materialized; and the seamless tunic has for the Christian world become a meaningless particular, like the many-coloured coat of Joseph.

§ 26. *The Burial and Resurrection.*

Such narratives as those of the rock-burial and resurrection of the Saviour-God in the Gospels are beyond all reasonable doubt simple developments of those mourning rituals which we have seen to be in use in so many ancient systems. The lost Persephonê was mourned for forty nights; the lost Attis and Adonis were sought for with lamentation, followed by rejoicing, when they were ceremonially found; the body of the slain Osiris was searched for with lamentation; and the prepared image, when found, seems to have been further mourned over and then rejoiced over.[6] Whatever may have been the order of the ceremony,

[1] Macrobius, *Sat.* i. 18, *end.* Cp. Clem. Alex. *Stromata*, vi. 2, citing Pherecydes.
[2] Clement, *Stromata*, v. 6. [3] Diodorus Siculus, i. 11.
[4] Julian, *In Matrem Deorum*, cc. 3, 6. [5] Pausanias, vi. 26.
[6] Firmicus, *De Errore*, c. 2; Juvenal, viii. 29. In Plutarch's version of the myth, Isis loses the body after finding it.

it is certain that the burying of an image of the slain God was a regular part of it. And above all in the cult of Mithra is the basis of the Gospel legend apparent. There the stone image of the "God from the rock" was laid on a bier, was mourned for, was placed in his rock tomb in the sacred cave, was withdrawn from that tomb, and was liturgically rejoiced over.[1] The early Christians who adopted the Mithraists' Lord's supper, adopted at the same time their resurrection mystery; and the Church finally made an explanatory legend out of the ritual, just as the Pagans did in myths innumerable. The later authorized myth of the Descent into Hell[2] is only a development or variation of the God's death and burial, and was already especially familiar in the mysteries of Dionysos, who descended to Hades to bring back his mother Semelé and carry her to heaven;[3] and in the worship of Attis, whose "Flight," "Concealment," "Vanishing," and "Descent into the Cave" are all specified by Julian[4] as part of the mysteries of the Vernal Equinox. The only wonder is that, seeing the Athenians celebrated the mysteries of Démétér twice a year, the Lesser mysteries at the vernal equinox and the Greater at the autumnal,[5] the Christist system did not adapt both, as the Attis

[1] Firmicus, *De Errore*, xxiii. (xxii. ed. Halm). Mr. Frazer remarks (*Golden Bough*, i. 297, *n.*, 298, *n.*) that the ceremony here described by Firmicus (*nocte quadam simulacrum in lectica supinum ponitur, et per numeros digestis fletibus plangitur.... Idolum sepelis. Idolum plangitur*, etc.) "may very well be the mourning and funeral rites of Attis, to which he had more briefly referred in c. 3." But he had also referred to the funeral rites of Osiris (again mentioned in c. 27); he had repeatedly referred to Mithraism; and he speaks of the funeral rites of Attis, Mr. Frazer thinks, in c. 27. The details there are different. And in c. 23 (22) there are details which seem to me to point definitely to Mithra and not to Attis. The *idolum* here is of stone (*tu jacentia lapidis membra componis, tu insensibile corrigis saxum*); whereas in the Attis cult the image was wooden (c. 27) like that of Osiris. He describes too a process of anointing, and breaks out, *Habet ergo Diabolus Christos suos*—a phrase more applicable to Mithra than to Attis. Nor is there any reference in the context to the Attisian practice of castration, discussed in c. 4, or to the principle of vegetation, discussed in c. 3. Apart from the special symbolisms, doubtless, the religious comfort given was much the same in the different cults.

[2] See above, *Christ and Krishna*, Sec. xvi.

[3] Pausanias, ii. 31, 37; Apollodorus, iii. 5, 3.

[4] *In Deorum Matrem*, 5, 6. Cp. Macrobius, *Sat.* i. 21.

[5] Julian, last cit. c. 8.

worshippers seem to have done. That it did not do so is doubtless due to the greater vogue (despite the name "Lesser") of the vernal celebration.

That the contradictory Christian details as to the manner of the finding of the slain God's body are to be explained by the natural variations of their special mystery-drama we have already seen. The "Maries" in particular belong to the Judaic environment. Such circumstantialities give an air of reality to the story so long as their discrepancies are ignored. But when all the phenomena are alike taken into account, the solution supplied by comparative mythology is found to meet every aspect of the problem.

§ 27. *The Banquet of Seven.*

In a chapter which is obviously a late appendix to the fourth gospel (xxi.) we have one more addition to the resurrection myth of the synoptics. The risen God appears to seven of his disciples by the sea of Tiberias, and after helping them to a great haul of fish, causes them to partake of a meal of fish and bread, he himself not being represented as eating. In Mark and Luke we have two different stories. Mark gives us a manifestation to the eleven "as they sat at meat"; and Luke gives the story of the "two of them" on the way to Emmaus, to whom the God gives bread, followed by his appearance to "the eleven," on which occasion he himself eats broiled fish. The narrative in Mark is in the admittedly late appendix (xvi. 9–20); and that in Luke also may confidently be pronounced a late compilation, in view of its giving details which the other gospels lack. The unhistorical character of the whole set of stories is too obvious to need enforcement; but it seems possible to throw greater light on their origination than has yet been done. In all, we have stress laid on the act of eating, either by the God or those to whom he ministers; and in a religious ceremonial of eating we may look to find the origin of the various myths.

As regards the party of seven, the cue lies to hand in the Mithraic Catacomb remains. The banquet of the *Septem Pii Sacerdotes,* the seven holy priests, there represented as part of the syncretic cult of Mithras-Sabazios, was in all probability a feature in the cult of Dionysos, who also was identified with Sabazios; and the Christian story is simply one more case of a myth invented to explain a ritual usage. The wide vogue of that is to be inferred from the fact that a set of seven priests figures repeatedly in the Veda; and that a group of seven rulers of sacrificial feasts existed in Pagan Rome.[1] The materials of the banquet in the Catacomb painting are noteworthy. There is a pasty, a hare, a fish, an object which the Abbé Garucci calls a goose, but which is smaller than the hare, and might as well be a lobster; and *eight* cakes or muffins, red in colour, each marked with a cross and four dots or punctures—exactly the cross and "four wounds" of the Christian myth, represented on the solar disc.[2] In the Christian story we have simply bread and fish, as befitted a poor and struggling cultus and the circumstances of the Jesuist legend; but it is significant that in the supposed Christian Catacomb paintings which represent a banquet of seven—and which orthodoxy supposes to represent the episode in the fourth Gospel, without a word of regard to the admittedly Mithraic remains—there are commonly *eight basketsful* of bread. This number is viewed by the Catholics as indicating that the early Christians aimed at a symbolical truth, and to that end deliberately disregarded literal accuracy; not a word being said, again, of the eight cakes or cross-buns on the table of the *Septem Pii Sacerdotes.*[3] It is a curious circumstance that in one of

[1] See above, *Christ and Krishna*, p. 238, and refs. Cp. Garucci, *Mystères du Syncrétisme Phrygien*, 1854. The Persian monarchy, being held theocratic, had seven high officials answering to the seven Amshaspands (Bähr, i. 12); and the same idea would in all probability influence the secret cult.

[2] Thus the "hot-cross-bun" is a Pagan emblem.

[3] Northcote and Brownlow's ed. of *Roma Sotterranea*, 1879, ii. 67–71. I erred in stating, formerly (*Christ and Krishna*, ed. 1889, p. 87), that the figures in the quasi-Christian picture (Pl. xvii.) wore Mithraic caps. They are bareheaded in the sample given; and in Garucci's Mithraic picture only three of the seven wear caps.

these "Christian" catacomb pictures the seven figures are nude. We may surmise that a picture in which one of the seven was clothed would suffice to motive the odd statement (John xxi. 7) that Peter, previously naked, drew a garment about him when he was about to plunge into the sea. The frequency of the subject, as compared with the ostensibly much more important Supper of the Twelve, is a sufficient proof that it rested on some broader and older basis than the solitary narrative of the fourth Gospel.

Whether the story of the meeting with the eleven does not rest on some similar ancient ceremonial, and whether the myth of the meeting on the way to Emmaus is not in turn based on some concrete fact in ancient art or hierology, we cannot at present pretend to decide. Two things only have to be borne in mind in that connection. The story of the treachery of Judas, as we have seen, is as mythical as any of the details we have been considering; and just as the number Twelve is a factitious arrangement, so may the number eleven have been determined by some outside fact, and the betrayal story have been framed in consequence. As our knowledge stands, however, the probable solution seems to be that the banquet of the eleven is a late invention, which sought to supersede or outweigh the Banquet of Seven, of which the Pagan origin and vogue were notorious, by a story more in harmony with the established Christian tradition. On that view, the Banquet of Seven, mythic in itself, is the occasion of the other myth.

§ 28. *The Ascension.*

Of all the Christian miracles, this is perhaps the most obviously a fable born of ignorance. Only in a world living under the primitive delusion of a flat earth and a solid overarching firmament could such a fable have been framed; and it is a standing proof of the moral frailty of the religious intelligence that such a tale is still allowed to perplex and delude the simple. Orthodoxy may however be a little more ready to consent to its disappearance when the mass of Christians realize that it is one more of the standing myths of Paganism. Even as Enoch and Elijah, mythic figures both, ascend to heaven in the Old Testament, so does demigod after demigod ascend to Godhood in the heathen world. Krishna thus mounts through the firmament of Indra.[1] At Byblos, after the annual mourning over the dead Adonis, he was believed to rise on the second day and mount to heaven in the presence of his worshippers.[2] Herakles in turn rises to heaven and immortality from the funeral-pyre which in his case rounds the solar myth,[3] the suggestion coming from the spectacle of the litten clouds of sunset. So Dionysos in one account ascends to heaven with his consort Ariadne,[4] in others with his mother Semelè;[5] which latter myth is supplied, in the Christian system, only after the Gospel-making period, by the doctrine and the festival of the Assumption of the Virgin Mary. Such beliefs were in the ordinary way of opinion in an age in which it was quite worth while to go through the procedure of letting loose an eagle from the funeral pyre of each deceased emperor by way of demonstrating *his* ascent to heaven.

True, there were many scoffers; and it lies on the face of the Gospels, especially of the fourth, that the Gospel-makers relied for credence much more on their elaborated circumstantial stories of the risen God's reappearances than on that of his ascension, which in the synoptics is barely alleged, and which in the fourth Gospel is not asserted at all. But Christianity rose, in an atmosphere of thickening superstition, with the decline of ancient knowledge and civilization; and the ascension myth, once set up for modern Chistendom, is thus far no more expungible by the science of Copernicus and Newton than were the pell-mell of Pagan myths by the better knowledge of antiquity. *Absit omen.*

Be the event what it may, the general truth is such as

[1] Above, p. 145. [2] Lucian, *De Dea Syria*, c. 6. Cp. Frazer, i. 280.
[3] Cp. Robertson Smith, *Religion of the Semites*, pp. 373, 469.
[4] Lactantius, *Div. Inst.* i. 10. [5] Refs. above, p. 250.

he who runs may read. In the fourth century, the exasperated Firmicus, met at every point by Pagan precedent for the legends of his gospels, could only shriek: "*Habet Diabolus Christos suos*[1]—the Devil has *his* Christs." We have now seen in some detail that the Christs, that of Firmicus included, were all man's. The Jesuist system is only one phase in a continuous development of ancient religion, in which God after God, Name after Name, is associated with the same immemorial and dimly comprehended symbols. In all probability there has been no long break for many thousands of years in the celebration of the Sacred Birthday on Christmas Day at the Tammuz-cave at Bethlehem; and only a slight variation in the dramatic ceremonial of the death of the God at Easter, which is still regularly performed at Jerusalem.[2] Long before Biblical Judaism was known, the people of Palestine shared in the universal rituals of the primeval cults of sun and moon, Nature and symbol; and the successive waves of conquest, physical and mystical, have only transformed the primordial hallucination. It might well last two thousand years more after subsisting from the dawn of civilization; and it will disappear only when all hallucination alike is solved in science.

[1] *De Errore*, c. 23 (22).
[2] See the *Church Times*, May 11th, 1888.

SECOND DIVISION.

Myths of Doctrine.

§ 1. *The Jesuine Discourses in General.*

Coming, finally, to the teachings as distinct from the actions attributed to the Gospel Jesus, we shall do well first to recall as closely as may be the tenor and cast of the Jesuine discourses, and to try to imagine their being delivered in antiquity to groups or crowds of Syrian peasants in the fashion the Gospels describe. It is surprising how little misgiving has been shown on this point even by critical students. Dr. Edwin Hatch, the one English ecclesiastic of recent years who has shown any original insight into the problems of Christian origins, remarks concerning the obvious transition from the Sermon on the Mount to the Nicene Creed that "The one belongs to a world of Syrian peasants; the other to a world of Greek philosophers."[1] Is this really a just judgment? Is there any more of the spirit and speech of the peasant in the "Sermon" than in the Creed? Certainly they differ widely enough. The first comes from moralists, the second from pragmatic theologians, combining old theosophy with new. But is the former any more on the plane of Syrian peasants than the other?

With the "Sermon on the Mount" in particular—pronounced by Baur[2] to be undoubtedly, with the parables about the kingdom of God, the most genuine and original

[1] Hibbert Lectures on *The Influence of Greek Ideas and Usages on the Christian Church*, 1890, *beginning*.

[2] *Das Christenthum und die christliche Kirche der drei ersten Jahrhunderte*, 1853, p. 34. Renan, on the other hand, recognizes that the maxims of the Sermon had long been "the current money of the synagogues." *Vie de Jésus*, préf. de la 13e édit. p. xviii. Cp. ch. v. p. 85.

elements of the Jesuine teaching preserved to us—we shall deal in detail below, showing that it was never a Sermon, and that the Mount is just that of the old God-and-Mountain myth over again. But the reader is requested first of all to put to himself in reverie the question whether that cento of crystallized ethical maxims and cryptic sayings was the kind of discourse that would be acclaimed by Syrian or any other illiterate peasants in any age. It is true that a number of the maxims in the Sermon are *as such* much fitter for popular instruction than many of the mystic parables—to say nothing of the impossible discourses of the fourth Gospel. But it is with the total Sermon as a possible discourse delivered extempore to a multitude that we are concerned. The sermons even of educated and thoughtful preachers to educated and comparatively thoughtful audiences in our own day fall far short of the Gospel discourse in brevity and obscurity of phrase and condensation of propositions—as they had need. Contrasting them with the Sermon on the Mount, men in any age might well say that Jesus preached as never man preached. But is not this comment the unwitting confutation of the claim that this unexampled preaching really took place, to the satisfaction of multitudes of Syrian peasants? Will any man to-day undertake to enthral any audience, Syrian or other, to whom the matter is new, by repeating the Gospel compilation of texts as it stands?

The same question forces itself in face of such an utterance as the passage Matt. xi. 25–30, which begins: "At that season Jesus *answered and said*, I thank thee, O Father, Lord of Heaven and earth," and ends, "For my yoke is easy (*chrēstos* = gentle, beneficent) and my burden is light." Such an allocution has not even the semblance of a historical utterance by a teacher. It begins with a prayer to God, and passes without any attempt at juncture into a general address, including the formula, "Come unto me, all ye that are weary and heavy laden, and I will give you rest. Take my yoke upon you......." What was the yoke, and what was the rest? What effect could such an address have upon an audience? There is no preceding explanatory talk, no specification even of a way of life as constituting the "yoke." We are dealing with an utterance put in the mouth of a God, as such, without even an account of circumstances. As history, the statement is simply unintelligible; it can seem otherwise only to those who habitually think of Jesus as a supernatural figure.

Considered as a myth, on the other hand, the passage explains itself at once. It is an utterance of the God in the mystery-drama. In the *Bacchæ* of Euripides the Chorus sings: "Coming from the Asian lands, having left the sacred Tmolus, I dance in honour of Bromius, *a pleasant labour and a toil easily borne*, honouring the God Bacchus."[1] In the mysteries of Mithra, again, the priest recited the formula: "Be of good courage, Mystæ: ye have been instructed of the God: and ye shall have salvation from your sorrows."[2] Similarly, in the mysteries of Isis,[3] the Goddess, first announcing her powers and titles as Jesus announces that "all things have been delivered unto me of my Father," proceeded with phrases of reassurance and comfort: "I come compassionate of your woes: I come, helpful and propitious. Cease from tears and make an end of lamentations; put away despair: now doth my providence cause to shine the salutary day." The believer is told to "fear not that the way is hard"; the priest exhorts him to wear a joyous countenance, in keeping with his white robe, and to bear willingly the "yoke" of his new ministry, enjoying the fruit of his new "liberty"—a liberty dependent on a new strictness of life. By such parallels, the speech of Jesus, inexplicable as it stands in the Gospel, is at once elucidated: it is the dramatic language of the God in the mystery-play, transferred at haphazard to the Gospel as something said by the Messiah in life, àpropos of nothing.

[1] *Bacchæ*, 64–66.

[2] Firmicus, *De Errore*, xxiii. Cp. Damascius, cited by Frazer, i. 298, *note*.

[3] Apuleius (*Metamorphoses*, l. x.) thus makes Isis address the praying Lucius. The language is evidently imitative of that used in the mysteries of initiation, which follow in the tale.

So little concern for verisimilitude had the gospel-makers that in the very next chapter to that in which Jesus is made to declare "I am meek and lowly in heart," he is represented as saying of himself, "a greater than Solomon is here."[1] That utterance, too, is historically irreconcilable with the notion of a sane teacher; it belongs to the process of myth-making. But no less obviously fictitious is the reiterated utterance to the disciples that whatsoever they shall bind on earth shall be bound in heaven.[2] Here we have a figment of church-making priests, who doubly betray themselves by the previous formula, "if he refuse to hear the *ecclesia*, let him be unto thee as the Gentile and the publican"—this at a time when there was for the Jesuists no *ecclesia*. Following on this stands the entirely discordant command that the inveterate offender shall be forgiven "until seventy times seven." Shall we then say that this teaching, which is supported by the parable about forgiving trespasses under fear of future punishment, is the earlier and the genuine one because it is the better, and that the obvious ecclesiastical forgery is necessarily the later? That course is barred, firstly, by the fact that the ecclesiastical forgery belongs still to the Judaic period, while the parable is clearly Gentile; and secondly by the very structure of the higher teaching, for there also Jesus is made to speak Messianically of "*my* heavenly Father," even as he does in the prior teaching about the little ones whose "Angels do always behold the face of *my* father which is in Heaven." These are not the words of an actual teacher: they are formulas put in the God's mouth by his worshippers.

In the case of such teachings, the problem is relatively simple: *a priori* and *a posteriori* the decision must be against the traditional acceptance. But in regard to a number of the Jesuine utterances the grounds for forming an opinion are scantier; and a further process of analysis is necessary before we can say with the same confidence that we have seen a myth constructed. For instance, we

[1] Matt. xii. 42. [2] Matt. xviii. 18–19.

have the story of the warning to the scribe who proposed to become a disciple: "Foxes have holes, and the birds of the air have nests; but the Son of Man hath not where to lay his head."[1] Any wandering Judaic teacher, clearly, might have said this, since any such might call himself "the Son of Man." But that the saying, if traditional, is merely a tradition about "somebody," becomes fairly clear when we note that the episode ends there. The saying is fortuitous: it is flatly opposed to others of "the Gospel Jesus," who immediately afterwards figures as explaining why his disciples do not fast, and as avowing that he has come "eating and drinking": it is, in effect, a pragmatic fiction, framed either to show that the Messiah expected to suffer, or to countervail new doctrines which made him anti-ascetic.[2] In Luke (ix. 59) the utterance is followed by the story of his saying "unto another, Follow me," and of the other asking for leave to bury his father. In Matthew that story is introduced by the phrase, "And *another of his disciples* said unto Him," the scribe in this case being implicitly styled a disciple. But the latter story in both forms is a pragmatic variant on that in the myth of Elijah and Elisha,[3] where Elisha gets the leave which Jesus refuses. We are not dealing with biography at all.[4] In neither case is aught said of the effect of the saying on the "disciple."

Thus the stories of Jesus explaining why his disciples do not fast,[5] and why he comes eating and drinking,[6] are arraigned in advance. If these be biographical, the previous story of professed hardship is not. But since the previous story is myth, may not these be biographical? The second, indeed, might very well be true of a non-ascetic teacher, twitting his censurers. But with what other elements in the Gospels does this story conceivably

[1] Matt. viii. 20.

[2] That there was an anti-ascetic school in Jewry is clear from the number of passages in praise of wine-drinking in the Talmud. See them collected by Hershon, *Genesis with a Talmudic Commentary*, Eng. tr. pp. 229–232.

[3] 1 Kings xix. 20.

[4] "The facility of transfer of a tale from one person to another is a mark of the myth." Dr. Gardner, as cited, p. 112.

[5] Matt. ix. 15.

[6] Matt. xi. 19.

coalesce? With any of the various doctrines of the kingdom of heaven? With the narrow Judaic Messianism which framed one Messianic discourse excluding Gentiles and Samaritans, and another promising that the twelve should sit on twelve thrones judging the twelve tribes? We are not entitled to say that with this last frame of mind it could not consist; but we are entitled to say that a teacher with these for his central doctrines answers only to a fragment of the total tradition, and is not at all the accepted Jesus of modern imagination. And when at least four-fifths of the Gospel teachings collapse into myth on judicial scrutiny, how shall we rationally found on a residuum that merely evades our primary tests? In the lore of Paul there is not even that residuum. That is to say, there was in Paul's time a Jesuism which had a crucified Jesus, but *no* Jesuine teaching; not even that of "the kingdom."

And this elenchus is fatal to the biographical pretensions of even the best Gospel teachings. Some of these are at once proved late by the simple test of comparison of MSS. Dr. Farrar, finding that the saying, "For the Son of Man came not to destroy men's lives, but to save them," is absent from the four earliest codices, exclaims that "this glorious utterance" is "omitted" by the copyists. "There were scribes so ignorant, and so steeped in the Elijah-spirit of persecution, as to regard it as dangerous."[1] Mr. J. Estlin Carpenter justly comments that "this charge seems to be really without foundation. The evidence points to gradual accretion rather than to intentional omission."[2] But the critical process must go further than it has been carried by the school of Mr. Carpenter, who chronically fall back on assumptions as to the genuineness of other Jesuine utterances, and quite unwarrantably salve the fourth Gospel as giving "*interpretations* of the Master's thought."[3]

A scientific criticism must set aside all such obviously

[1] *Expositor*, April, 1889, p. 249.

[2] *The First Three Gospels*, 2nd ed. p. 394.

[3] *Id.* p. 55.

arbitrary compromises; and it must expressly refuse to let the attractiveness of any doctrine in the Gospels certify its genuineness. Jesus at one point is made to insist that every jot and tittle of the Mosaic law must be accomplished, and at another to rebut Sabbatarianism. Paul knows of neither teaching. Shall we then say that the second comes from the Jesus we *wish* to believe in, merely because we like it? Or shall we say this of the humanitarian teaching: "Inasmuch as ye have done it unto the least of these my brethren, ye have done it unto me"? It is impossible: that particular teaching is mythical to the core, being put in the mouth of the God as such, not of any actual teacher. We may, if we are determined to be arbitrary, proceed to say that the man who *wrote* that myth had in him the high quality men used to ascribe to Jesus; and profess to make shift with an idealisation of him. But the teaching in question is a palpable adaptation from the ancient ritual of the Egyptian Book of the Dead, where the soul at the bar of judgment pleads: "I have given bread to him that was hungry, water to him that was thirsty, clothes to the naked, and shelter to the wanderer."[1] Thus are we carried back to the humanism of ancient polytheists, the immemorial rituals of one of the oldest civilisations. And it needed no supernal prophet to frame these any more than the Christian adaptations. King Saneha on his monuments praises himself in the language of the ritual cited; and "that very Saneha who refreshed the thirsty, and protected the oppressed, has no difficulty about punishing his conquered enemy pitilessly. He causes the concubines of this enemy, the innocent victims of his vengeance, to be devoted to the deity. He appropriates all his enemy's goods, plunders his house, and proceeds in all this on the maxim that he ought to do to his enemy as his enemy had meant to do to him."[2] Saneha, alas, is thoroughly historical. Christendom still duly produces its generations

[1] Tiele, *Egyptian Religion*, p. 227. Cp. Kuenen, *The Religion of Israel*, Eng. tr. i. 397.

[2] Tiele, as cited, pp. 129–130.

of moderately modified Sanehas, as regularly as its harvests; and, like him, tells of its religion of love.

If on this it be urged that, even as men are compounds of contradiction—even as a hundred historical teachers, from Plato to Ruskin, give internecine and irreconcilable laws as *their* gospel to men—so may it have been with a Jesus in the days of Pontius Pilate; if this be urged, the answer is that that line of reasoning evades alike the documentary and the psychological problem. The contradictions of the Gospel teaching are not as the incidental self-contradictions of Hegel and Kant and Comte and Arnold and Ruskin: they are as the oppugnant doctrines of these and many more varying men intertwined with each other: they belong to clashing sects, to changing generations, to a hundred hands; they occur in documents which are visibly wrought of shreds and patches; they are inextricably bound up with myths "gross as a mountain, open, palpable"; and all the while they are faced by the eternal veto of the silence of Paul, who knows not a word of Jesuine teaching, and to whom even the later interpolators attribute at most a knowledge of the Dominical ritual of the Eucharist, itself pure myth.

After Paul, there may hypothetically have been, say, three Jesuses who taught and figured as Messiahs—a second Jesus without cognomen, a third who was a Nazarite, a fourth who "came eating and drinking." But to none of these faraway and problematic shadows, passing like changing clouds across the remote horizon of our imagination, can we scientifically ascribe a single saying in the Gospels, any more than we can scientifically credit them with raising the dead. The discourses, like the miracles, reveal their mythic origin to the instructed eye of reason. And when we fully realise what the mythopœic faculty can do, we have positively no reason left for believing that any aspect of the composite Gospel Jesus is projected even remotely by any real person living the life of a wandering teacher. Men who had grafted Gentilism on a neo-Judaic cult of a demi-god Messiah could strike out the conception of a Son of Man "eating and drinking," as they could graft the scattered higher Judaic ethics on a crude cult of salvation by blood sacrifice. Against such liberalism, other and more sectarian adherents could frame the myth that the teaching Jesus was like them a Nazarite, and ascribe to him the teachings they favoured. Against this, in turn, another group or generation could call themselves Nazarenes in the sense of "Netzerenes," members of the Messianic cult of "the Branch"; or they could frame the myth of the sojourn at Nazareth, seeking a neutral etymology which should leave them Jesuists without even a shadow of Nazarite burdens. When we can set formal or pragmatic limits to the generative power of the mythopœic faculty, we may pretend to save some shred of historical fact from the Jesus legend as it stands; but not till then.

Nor can we with any pretence of historical and logical method any longer claim to stamp certain doctrines as framable only by "the" ideal Jesus of tradition. This persistent *petitio principii* is committed by none more arbitrarily than by John Mill, who like Arnold thought to solve the Gospel problem on a mere general survey and inference.[1] "Who among his disciples or among their proselytes," he asks, "was capable of inventing the sayings ascribed to Jesus, or of imagining the life and character revealed in the Gospels? Certainly not the fishermen of Galilee; as certainly not St. Paul......; still less the early Christian writers......About the life and sayings of Jesus there is a stamp of personal originality combined with profundity of insight......"[2] Had Mill known anything about the legend and lore of Buddha; had he paid heed to the evolution of moral ideas in Egypt and China; had he weighed with any comparative care the ethic of Seneca and Marcus Aurelius; and had he taken the trouble to note how often the Jesuine teaching is a mere repetition of teachings in the Old Testament, he could never have penned his headlong endorsement of the average Christian prepossession. His words expressly homologate all the

[1] Cp. Professor Bain's *J. S. Mill*, p. 139.
[2] *Three Essays on Religion*, pp. 253–4.

sayings in the Gospels, though he goes on to contemn the fourth Gospel *en bloc*, on grounds which involve the overthrow of his claim for the synoptics, whose teaching is so often and so profoundly inconsistent. Where the professed rationalist thus outsings the pæans of faith, the devout Newman, as we have seen, deliberately surrenders the claim made as historically false. The sufficient answer to Mill is that if nobody but one in the whole Hellenistic world in the first two centuries of our era was capable of framing the Jesuine teachings, those teachings could not possibly have found any acceptance. His conception is the old historical chimera, a mere survival of supernaturalist concepts. It was certainly not the mythic "fishermen of Galilee" who framed the Gospels, which did not exist in the time at which they are pretended to have lived; and as little was it Paul, whose utter ignorance of any Jesuine teaching might have given Mill pause if he had been doing aught but voice an unreasoning prepossession, acquired from his environment. But in the Judæo-Hellenistic world of the second century there was demonstrably the power to frame each and every doctrine in the New Testament.

The general principles being thus reached and laid out, it remains to trace and anatomise, in series, some of the salient myths of doctrine as we have done with the myths of action. The forms of demonstration vary; but the exhibited processes of fiction, the exposed psychology of error and credence in the two species, are essentially akin.

§ 2. *The Preaching of John the Baptist.*

The menace to the "offspring of vipers"[1] might conceivably be delivered (in a more paraphrased form) in ancient Palestine by any fanatic who expected the speedy coming of a conquering Messiah; it has no relevance whatever to the coming of an ostensibly beneficent and suffering and teaching Messiah. There is therefore some

[1] Matt. iii. 7.

presumption in favour of a real tradition of such preaching by a man named John, and of its having been adapted by Christists to some one of their purposes. But here again arises the normal difficulty: Paul knows nothing of the Forerunner; and again, Why should Christists who represented Jesus as preaching forgiveness and love, desire to make use of such a factor? In the lack of evidence we can only surmise that the Forerunner-motive was introduced (*a*) before the Sermon on the Mount and other passages of a pacific tenor; perhaps (*b*) in the period after the destruction of Jerusalem, when predictions of that event were ascribed to Jesus. The pretended acclaiming of Jesus as Messiah by John is of course absolute myth.

§ 3. *Jesus as a Preacher of Universalism.*

In connection with the miraculous healing of the centurion's servant (Matt. viii. 11) Jesus is represented as declaring that many Gentiles shall enter into the Jewish kingdom of heaven, while "the Children of the Kingdom" shall be cast into perdition. Here, on a quite mythical occasion, we have a teaching possible to a revolutionary mahdist somewhat like John, but in no way congruous with the Judaic doctrine put into the mouth of Jesus in Matt. x. 5–6, where he tells his disciples to go only to the cities of Israel, expressly avoiding the Gentiles and the Samaritans. It is arguable, *prima facie*, that either doctrine may be the earlier, and the other a later interpolation. But on the view that the earlier doctrine was the universalist, we must conclude that a universalist cult was captured by or relapsed into a purely Judaic one—an extremely unlikely development. A narrow cult might be expanded into a broader; but into a cult which began on the broad basis no narrow Judaists would ever have entered. The whole Pauline literature points to the converse process; and on that view the universalist doctrine is a late pro-Gentile fiction; though the story of the sending of the disciples through Israel is also unhistorical, being an item in the myth of the Twelve Apostles. Both of the conflicting teachings are thus alike mythical. The early Jesuist movement *was* anti-Gentile and anti-Samaritan; but the story of the Messiah *preaching* these doctrines is apologetic myth. And the connected conception of a popular teacher avowedly sending forth disciples "as sheep in the midst of wolves," and predicting wholesale massacre for his followers, is myth pure and simple: the creation of the later age in which destructive persecution had actually been suffered; the process being psychologically akin to that which produces myths to explain ritual. After the Master was held to have been put to death, the doctrine that "it is enough for the disciple to be as his master" was an obvious comment when the followers in turn suffered violence; and to put the doctrine into the Master's mouth was in the normal way of mythopoiesis.

§ 4. *Jesus as Messiah.*

Much speculation has been spent on the problem, "In what light did Jesus regard his mission as Messiah?" and no solution has ever been reached which gives any common standing-ground for those who have abandoned the supernaturalist view. On that view the Jewish Messiah's function was to make a tremendous display of miraculous power, to be triumphantly acclaimed at Jerusalem, yet to fail to convert the Jews to belief in his divinity, and thereupon to get put to death by them for the salvation of mankind. Putting such irrationalism aside, men begin to ask whether Jesus had not some humanly-intelligible plan, some scheme of either social or individual reform for his own country, to begin with. He has thus been conceived as predominantly (1) a socialist, (2) an anti-ceremonialist, (3) a mental individualist, in the sense of preaching a care for the higher life as freed from economic concern. But none of these views, nor any other scheme of characterization, serves to explain why, starting as such a teacher, he should call himself the Messiah. For the Jews that word connoted primarily a restorer of the Jewish national fortunes. Later—it matters not to our present problem how long[1] before the reign of Herod—there began to arise, possibly from Mazdean sources,[2] the conception of a spiritual Messiah, who should secure to his followers not an earthly but a heavenly salvation. The question is, How shall we conceive any sane moral teacher as regarding himself in either of these lights?

We have seen that the Gospels swing at the will of their framers and interpolators between a Judaic and a universalist conception of salvation. On either line, wherein was the Messiahship to consist? The sending out of the twelve disciples to Israel is myth: are we then to fall back on the assumption that a real Jesus sought to make a popular movement among the Jews by telling them: "The kingdom of God shall be taken from you and given to a nation bringing forth the fruits thereof"?[3] Are we to be asked to believe that on the strength of such anti-national teaching any man was welcomed by the whole populace of Jerusalem with hosannahs? Or, putting aside both factors of the contradiction as obviously late pragmatic myths, shall we try to conceive of a Jesus who, without the machinery of Twelve Apostles, circulated simply the doctrine of a speedy end of the world, in which he should appear in the clouds as the Son of Man—Son of God? On that view we are dealing with an insane visionary—a possible enough phenomenon in ancient Jewry, but no subject for modern admiration. And here, as always, there faces us the tacit negation of Paul. *Paul's Jesus had given no Messianic teaching. He did but Messianically die.*

There was, in fine, only one sense in which any sane Jew of the period could regard himself as the Messiah, and that was as a national leader against the Roman rule. A series of such Messiahs did actually arise; and as each of them would be called "the Lord" by his followers, it

[1] See Nicolas, *Des Doctrines religieuses des Juifs*, 1860, ch. v., for a concise view of the developments. Cp. Schürer, *Hist. of the Jewish People in the Time of Christ*, Eng. tr. Div. ii. vol. ii. § 29.

[2] Cp. Gustave d'Eichthal, *Les Evangiles*, 1863, i. 38–39, 216–218.

[3] Matt. xxi. 43.

remains a possibility that some of the ethical sayings of one or other of them may have got into circulation and been mistakenly preserved in the Gospels. But the solid fact remains that the Gospels preserve no saying uttered in such Messianic capacity, the position forced on all the Gospel-makers being that the slain and risen Messiah was not a political leader at all. He is represented as being asked what the Jews should do in the matter of tribute, and as returning a juggling answer, the final force of which is that the Roman rule should be submitted to. And the story of the miraculous fish with the coin in its mouth reveals once for all that such teachings are as mythic as the miracle itself.

Thus the whole Messianic teaching of the Gospels exposes itself as pure myth on the most general criticism; and a particular analysis only strengthens the conclusion. A dozen times over Jesus is represented as grounding his Messianic claim on his miracles—myth certifying myth. In one episode, as we have seen, he is made to repudiate the Davidic descent which the genealogies claim for him. Yet again, such a quasi-Messianic utterance as Matt. xviii. 11, "For the Son of Man is come to save that which was lost," is in that connection admittedly spurious, being absent from the oldest codices; and the same passage in Luke (xix. 10) has every mark of fiction. The teacher is represented as saying that *he* has saved Zacchæus, when the sole rational purport of the story is that Zacchæus is saved by his own goodness. For the rest, the teacher's Messianic assumption is again and again connected with teaching that is no less palpably fictitious, as the prediction of the fall of Jerusalem—an utterance discredited on the one hand as implying supernatural knowledge, and on the other hand as unknown to Paul. Always we come back to that dead wall of rebuttal, even if we evade the palpable falsity of the Gospel record.

Any attempt on rational lines, then, to reach a real personality for the Gospel Jesus must at an early stage give up the hypothesis that he claimed to be Messiah in any sense whatever. That is plainly a cult-myth. What sympathetic criticism wants to save is the moral teacher; and the moral teacher is not to be combined with a magistral or theurgic pretence of "saving," either on earth or in heaven. Every such pretence stultifies the function of humanly teaching men how to live aright, though such a pretence could conceivably be foisted by later devotees on a primary moral teaching really given. But the moral teaching in turn must be investigated upon its documentary merits; for when once the presence of superimposed didactic myth is granted, it is obviously illicit to deny the likelihood that the primary moral teaching is itself either in whole or in part mythic.

§ 5. *Jesus as Preparing the Kingdom of God.*

In the lore of "the kingdom of God" we have a position conceivably midway between an impossible profession of spiritual Messiahship by a teacher in his own person, and the simple utterance of moral exhortations or theistic moral philosophy. There at once arises, however, the problem as to what "the kingdom of God" really meant. In the Sermon on the Mount the "kingdom of heaven" is named in the first sentence, and several times afterwards, with no elucidation, but in the ostensible sense simply of "heaven"—a happy and lasting dwelling-place on high. Here, then, and in other passages of the same order, a certain line of conduct is specified simply as securing happiness in a future state; and the meaning attached to the Forerunner's prediction, "the kingdom of heaven [or of God] is at hand," would seem to have been that the earthly order was soon to pass away. Similarly, the "glad tidings of the kingdom of God" would seem to have meant the same doctrine *plus* the assurance of salvation to the poor (or the poor in spirit); to those who keep the law (Matt. v. 17–19); or to those who are peaceable and forgiving, and in general "do the will of my Father which is in heaven." In this aspect the kingdom of God is merely the heaven promised to the good; and any teacher may have thus supported his prescriptions. Such a teaching, too, might later be made a basis for fictitious Messianic claims put in the teacher's mouth. On that view the teachings themselves are a subject for investigation.

In other passages, however, "the kingdom of God" becomes a mystery. "Unto you [the disciples] is given [A. V. "it is given to know"] the mystery of the kingdom of God; but unto them that are without all things are done in parables."[1] Putting aside for the present the still more cryptic context, we have here an entirely different strain from that above noted. About the "kingdom of heaven" in the former teachings there is no alleged or implied mystery; and the delivery of the latter teaching by the same teacher is simply unintelligible. By those who found on the other, this must be set aside as spurious. So with the parables which "liken" the kingdom of heaven to a measure of leaven, a hidden treasure, a fishing net, or a grain of mustard seed that grows into a great tree: the reference is not to the "early heaven," but to the process of the new cult or to the supposed happiness acquired by joining it. Baur's grouping of these with the Sermon on the Mount[2] is his most singular oversight; for the kingdom of heaven in that document is simply the future state of reward, whereas the concept of the parables is, as he himself avows, subjective. It is therefore a secondary doctrinal development.

So, too, with the formula in Matt. xii. 28: "If I by the Spirit of God cast out demons, then is the kingdom of God come upon you"; the purport is supernaturalist, and alien to the simple doctrine of the heavenly reward. Yet again, however, we have in Luke (xvii. 20–21) the remarkable saying, in reply to a question as to the time of the advent, "The kingdom of God cometh not with observation [*i.e.*, "with outward show," "in a visible form"], neither shall they say, Lo, here! or There! for lo, the Kingdom of God is within you." Is *this*, then, the doctrine of the teacher of the Sermon on the Mount and the kindred lore? If so, how is this solitary saying to be explained, as standing

[1] Mark iv. 11; Matt. xiii. 11. [2] As cited above, p. 423.

among a multitude representing an utterly different cast of thought?

The answer is inevitable: this, the one truly remarkable and impressive Gospel saying on the subject of the "kingdom," is a late intellectual development: the "original" thought is an interpolation from or by some unknown thinker. To fasten upon this as a truly Jesuine teaching because it is so striking, is to violate every principle of coherent criticism. If *this* be Jesuine, the whole remaining mass of the Gospels is not only spurious but an immense stultification of a Jesuine doctrine actually current to start with. But this memorable doctrine is not only unknown to Paul: it is the negation of *his* entire cult. Finally, it occurs in the confessedly late third Gospel; and it occurs in context with (1) a passage accrediting the Samaritans and (2) a passage predicting the day of judgment. With neither of these has it any connection. It is one of the most manifest interpolations in the Gospels; and it is in conflict no less with the other "kingdom" passages in Luke than with those in Matthew and Mark. What can criticism do but give it up as a late rationalistic fiction?

As regards the doctrine of the "kingdom of God" then, we must recede for our basis to the simple form of it which pervades the Gospels, and which represents a standing belief in later Judaism. The conception of "the kingdom" as a "mystery" belongs to a Gnostic or priestly influence which repeatedly appears in Mark: the highest form of all is the most impossible as a starting-point. To the primary form there attaches no originality. All the more, of course, it may conceivably have been part of the lore of a non-Messianic moral teacher, part even of the lore of the remote Jesus of Paul, since Paul holds by a heaven and a hell. But no such commonplace of current religion can constitute a significant nucleus for a personality. The significant element must be the moral teaching combined with it—a moral teaching of which, be it noted, Paul shows no knowledge. Let us then waive, for the argument's sake, the veto of Paul's silence and consider whether the moral teachings in turn can have been the genuine utterances of a Jesus broadly answering to the Gospel narratives.

§ 6. *The Sermon on the Mount.*

In the first Gospel (v.–vii.) Jesus is represented as uttering, on a mountain, a short but for the most part highly concentrated ethical discourse, fit for use as a written cult-code, of a primitive sort, but extremely unfit for oral communication to a popular audience, who could not possibly get more than fragments of it by heart. In the third Gospel (vi.), parts of the same document, word for word, with, however, some marked and vital changes of phrase, are represented as being delivered "on the plain." Neither mountain nor plain is named.

The demonstration of the mythical character of both the discourses and the typographical details is to be reached by way of a decomposition of the main document into its component texts, which are nearly all pre-Christian. The *Société Scientifique Littéraire Israélite* a generation ago published a work by its perpetual secretary, M. Hippolyte Rodrigues, entitled *Les Origines du Sermon de la Montagne*,[1] showing that there is hardly an item in it which is not to be found in one form or another in *Jewish* literature, early and late, quite independently of any Christian tradition. A selection of the more important parallels cited by M. Rodrigues (with some others) to the sentences of the Sermon, from Hebrew literature, will suffice to show as much here. Let the passages which follow be compared with the verses in Matt. v., vi., and vii. corresponding to the numbers :—

V. 3. The Lord preserveth the simple: I was brought low and he saved me. Ps. cxvi. 6.

Mysteries are revealed unto the meek.... The Lord.... is honoured of the lowly. Ecclesiasticus iii. 19–20.

He that is of a lowly spirit shall obtain honour ["eternal glory" in the version of M. Rodrigues]. Prov. xxix. 23.

[1] Paris: Michel Lévy Frères, 1868.

Wherever there is any question in the Bible of the greatness of God, his love for the humble is spoken of. Talmud, *Megilla*, p. 31, recto.

I dwell in the high and holy place, with him also that is of a contrite and humble spirit, to revive the spirit of the humble, and to revive the heart of the contrite ones. Isa. lvii. 15.

4. He healeth the broken in heart, and bindeth up their wounds. Ps. cxlvii. 3.

5. The meek shall inherit the land, and shall delight themselves in the abundance of peace. Ps. xxxvii. 11.

He giveth grace unto the lowly. Prov. iii. 34.

6. He that walketh righteously and speaketh uprightly....he shall dwell on high. Isa. xxxiii. 15.

Thou wilt bless the righteous, O Lord. Ps. v. 13. (Cp. xv. 12.)

This is the gate of the Lord; the righteous shall enter into it. Ps. cxviii. 20.

7. He that followeth after righteousness and mercy, findeth life, righteousness, and honour. Prov. xxi. 21.

8. Who shall ascend into the hill of the Lord?....He that hath clean hands and a pure heart. Ps. xxiv. 3, 4.

9. Seek peace and pursue it. Ps. xxxiv. 14.

Love peace and seek it at any price. Talmud, Hillel, *Pirké-Aboth*, i. 12.

10. Remember that it is better to be persecuted than persecutor. Talmud, *Yoma*,—*Derech Eretz*.

Were the persecutor a just man and the persecuted an impious, God would still be on the side of the persecuted. Midrash, *Vayikra-Rabba*, xxvii. 11 and 12.

Verses 13 to 21 are hardly worth comparing, though even their phraseology, and in particular the stress laid on "these least commandments"—a stress which is in flat denial of some of the main dogmas of the Christian religion —is obviously Judaic. At verse 22 we return to specific precepts:—

22. He who causes his brother publicly to blush shall have no part in the future life. Talmud, *Aboth*, iii. 13.

It were better for a man to cast himself in a furnace than to cause his brother to blush in public. Rabbi Simeon, Ben Jochaï, Talmud, *Sota*, fol. 19.

He who causes his neighbour to grow pale in public shall have no part in the world to come. Eléazar of Modein, *Pirké-Aboth*, iii. 15.

Thou shalt not hate thy brother in thine heart. Lev. xix. 17.

The stranger that sojourneth with you....thou shalt love....as thyself. Lev. xix. 34. (Cp. Deut. x. 19.)

24. Bear not hatred to thy neighbour for every wrong, and do nothing at all by injurious practices. Ecclesiasticus x. 6.

Be slow to embroil thyself, and be easy to be reconciled. Talmud, *Pirké-Aboth*, ii. 10.

To whom does God pardon sins? To him who himself forgives injuries. Talmud, *Megilla*, fol. 28.

The friends of God are, he who does not grow wroth, and he who gives the example of humility. Talmud, *Pesachim*, 118.

Whoever is prompt to pardon, his sins also shall be pardoned. Talmud. *Megilla*, fol. 25.

It is [a man's] glory to pass over a transgression. Prov. xix. 11.

[Note in contrast the ethical significance of Matt. v. 26.]

28. Thou shalt not *covet* thy neighbour's wife. Ex. xx. 17. Deut. v. 21.

He who regards a woman with an impure intention has already as it were committed adultery. Talmud, *Kallah*, beginning.

In every act it is above all the thought, the intention, which God inquires into, and which he will judge. Talmud, *Yoma*, fol. 29, *a*.

29. [The doctrine is old in Judaism. *Midrash Jalcout*, Section Wayechi, No. 16, on Gen. v. 48, gives the story of Rabbi Nathia ben Harras, who, tempted by the Devil in the form of a beautiful woman, burned out his eyes with a red-hot nail. The angel Raphael was sent to restore his sight, but he feared fresh temptation. Then God promised that the Evil One should never tempt him again, and he consented to be healed.]

32. A wife must not be sent away save for adultery. Shammai in the Talmud, *Gittin*, p. 90.

The altar itself sheds tears on him who repudiates his wife. Eliezer, *ibid*.

34. Accustom not thy mouth to swearing; neither use thyself to the naming of the Holy One. Ecclus. xxiii. 9.

Let your nay be nay. Let your yea be yea. Talmud, *Baba-Mezia*, fol. 49, verso.

39. Let him give his cheek to him that smiteth him. Lam. iii. 30.

Say not thou, I will recompense evil. Prov. xx. 22.

Say not, I will do so to him as he hath done to me. *Id.* xxiv. 29.

Thou shalt not take vengeance....but thou shalt love thy neighbour as thyself. Lev. xix. 18.

I gave my back to the smiters, and my cheeks to them that plucked off the hair. Isa. l. 6.

Those who undergo injury without returning it, those who hear themselves vilified and do not reply, who have no motive but love, who accept evils with joy, it is of them that the prophet speaks when he says, the friends of God shall shine one day as the sun in all his splendour. Talmud, *Yoma* or *Yom-Kippur*, p. 23, col. 1; *Sabbath*, p. 88; *Gittin*, p. 36.

If thy comrade call thee ass, put on the pack-saddle. Talmud, *Baba-Kama*, 27.

42. The righteous dealeth graciously, and giveth. Ps. xxxvii. 21.

All the day long he dealeth graciously and lendeth. *Id.* 26.

Thou shalt surely give him, and thine heart shall not be grieved when thou givest unto him. Deut. xv. 10.

Stretch thine hand unto the poor, that thy blessing may be perfected. Ecclus. vii. 32.

44. If thine enemy be hungry, give him bread to eat; and if he be thirsty, give him water to drink. Prov. xxv. 21.[1]

45. It is not the wicked we should hate, but wickedness. Talmud, *Berachoth*, p. 10, recto.

There is one event to the righteous and to the wicked. Eccles. ix. 2.

46–7. [See above.]

48. Be like God, compassionate, merciful. Talmud, *Sabbath*, p. 133 verso.

Ch. vi. 1–4. As well not give as give with ostentation in public. Talmud, *Chagiga*, fol. 5 recto.

He who gives alms in secret is greater than Moses himself. Talmud, *Baba-Bathra*, p. 9 verso.

He that hath pity upon the poor lendeth to the Lord. Prov. xix. 17.

Here be the eight degrees of charity:—The first, the highest, is that of the man who *helps the poor before his fall*. The second is that of him who gives without knowing and without being known. The third is that of him who knows to whom he gives, but does not make himself known, etc. Maimonides, *Hilchet-Matanot-Amyim*, x., based on the Talmud.

5–6. Who is it that shall not see the face of God? First, hypocrites; next, liars. Talmud, *Sota*, p. 42.

The doctor who is not within as he is without, does not deserve the name of doctor. Talmud, *Yoma*, fol. 72.

[The "Lord's Prayer" calls for separate treatment, and will be dealt with in the next section, in which we shall offer evidence, which was not available to the compilers of the *Origines du Sermon de la Montagne*, that the entire formula was in Jewish use before the rise of the Jesuist movement.]

Chapter vi. 14 follows up the prayer with a return to a point already put—the necessity of mutual forgiveness; and here again there are close Judaic parallels.

14-15. He that revengeth shall find vengeance from the Lord, and he will surely keep his sins in remembrance. Forgive thy neighbour the hurt that he hath done unto thee, so shall thy sins also be forgiven when thou prayest. One man beareth hatred against another, and doth he seek pardon from the Lord? He showeth no mercy to a man which is like himself, and doth he ask forgiveness of his own sins? If he that is but flesh nourish hatred, who will entreat for pardon of sins? Ecclesiasticus xxviii. 1–5. [See Prov. xix. 11, before cited.]

I have delivered him that without cause was mine adversary. Ps. vii. 4. (Cp. Job xxxi. 29.)

[1] The Gospel statement that of old men were taught, "hate thine enemy," is understood to refer to Deut. xxiii. 6. But even in that context there had been interpolated some higher teachings.

On the question of fasting, the Talmudists have no special parallels to offer; but an important question will arise on this head when we proceed to consider the evidence for a pre-Jesuist use of the "Lord's Prayer." Meantime we take the remaining parallels:—

19. Lay up thy treasure according to the commandments of the Most High [*or, as the Jews translate*, place your treasure where the Most High commands you to place it], and it shall bring thee more profit than gold. Ecclesiasticus xxix. 11.

20–21. I wish to amass inexhaustible treasures, while my fathers have sought perishable gold in this world. Talmud, *Baba-Bathra*, p. 14.

I shall teach my son nothing but the law, for we are nourished by its fruits in this world, and the principal *(le capital)* is secured to us for the life to come. Rabbi Nehoraï, in the Mishna, *Kiduschin*, fol. 82.

Be not as servants who serve their master in view of wages, but be rather as slaves who serve their master without hope of remuneration. Antigone de Socho (2nd c. B.C.), in Talmud, *Pirké-Aboth*, i.

The son of the queen of Abiadena, the king Monabazes, thus answered his brothers, who reproached him with being prodigal in charity: "My ancestors have laid up treasure for earth, I lay up treasure for heaven; my ancestors have laid their wealth in a place where it is in dangers, I have placed mine in an impregnable place; their fortune produced nothing, mine has fruits; they heaped up treasures, I collect treasures of the soul; they saved for others, my savings are for myself; they gathered for this world, I gather for a life to come. Talmud, *Baba-Bathra*, 11a.

Verses 22–23 are obvious commonplaces. Verse 24 has several Judaic equivalents, some of which, like so much of what we have been considering, represent the moral commonplace of all ages. For instance, Prov. xxx. 8–9, which puts the common-sense of the subject rather more persuasively than does the Gospel:—

Give me neither poverty nor riches;....lest I be full and deny thee, and say, Who is the Lord? or lest I be poor and steal, and use profanely the name of my God.

Again we have:—

Many have sinned for a small matter; and he that seeketh for abundance will turn his eyes away [from the law]. Ecclus. xxvii. 1.

As a nail sticketh fast between the joinings of the stones, so doth sin stick close between buying and selling. *Id.* xxvii. 2.

Blessed is the rich that is found without blemish, and hath not gone after gold. xxxi. 8.

Here the note is much less uncompromising than that of

the Gospels, which tell of an anti-plutocratic movement. But the parallels continue :—

24. He that loveth gold shall not be justified, and he that followeth corruption shall have enough thereof. *Ib.* 5.

25–34. Delight thyself also in the Lord, and he shall give thee the desires of thine heart. Ps. xxxvii. 4.

The Lord will not suffer the soul of the righteous to famish. Prov. x. 3.

The *young lions* do lack, and suffer hunger; but they that seek the Lord shall not want any good thing. Ps. xxxiv. 10.

But there is another view :—

Yonder is *the sea*, great and wide, wherein are *creeping things* innumerable.... *These* wait all upon thee, that thou mayest give them their meat in due season....Thou openest thine hand, *they* are satisfied. Ps. civ. 25–28.

27. Watching for riches consumeth the flesh, and the care thereof driveth away sleep. Watching care will not let a man slumber, as a sore disease breaketh sleep....The poor laboureth in his poor estate, and when he leaveth off he is still needy. Ecclus. xxxi. 1–4.

Thou openest thine hand and satisfiest the desire of every living thing. Ps. cxlv. 16.

He giveth food to all flesh, for his mercy endureth for ever. Ps. cxxxvi. 25.

He giveth to the beast his food, and to the young ravens which cry. Ps. cxlvii. 9.

O fear the Lord, ye his saints, for there is no want to them that fear him. Ps. cxxxiv. 9.

He who has only a morsel of bread in his basket, and asks, What shall I eat to-morrow? is a man of little faith. Talmud, *Sota*, p. 586.

Each hour suffices for its trouble. *Id. Barachot*, fol. 9 verso.

VII. 1. Judge not your neighbour when you have not been in his place. *Id. Aboth*, ii. 5.

2. Man is measured by the measure he has meted. *Id. Sota*, p. 8b, and elsewhere.

One should abstain from judging one's friend and one's enemy, for one does not easily see either the faults of one's friend or the merit of one's enemy. *Id. Ketouboth*, 105, col. 2.

He who charitably judges his neighbour shall be charitably judged by God. *Id. Schabbuoth*, i. 27.

3–5. Physician, heal first thine own wound. Midrash Rabba, *Bereschit*, xxiii.

Rabbi Tryphon suggested that the habit of rejoinder hindered men from profiting by remonstrances. "Alas, if you say to someone, Take that straw out of your eye, you get for answer, Take that beam out of your own." Talmud, *Arakhin*, fol. 16.

Rabbi Tryphon seems to have seen a side of the matter which did not strike the Jesuists who compiled the Sermon on the Mount. To the command, "Give not that which is holy unto the dogs," which appears to have signified that the Gospel was not meant for Gentiles and Samaritans, the Jews are naturally not anxious to provide closer parallels than Prov. xxxiii. 9: "Speak not in the hearing of a fool." But the sentiment is in tolerable harmony with many passages of the Old Testament.

7-11. The gates of prayer are never closed. Talmud, *Sota*, p. 49a.

Ye shall seek me and find me when ye shall search for me with all your heart. Jeremiah xxix. 13.

12. Do not unto others that which it would be disagreeable to you to suffer yourself—that is the main part of the law; all the rest is only commentary. Hillel, Talmud, *Sabbath*, 306.

13-14. The way of sinners is made plain with stones, but at the end thereof is the pit of hell. Ecclus. xxi. 10.

15. [Need hardly be paralleled from the writings of the prophets. The Gospel text, be it noted, is plausibly supposed to have been framed by the Judaist Jesuists in denunciation of Paul.]

16. For the work of a man shall be rendered unto him, and cause every man to find according to his ways. Job xxxiv. 11.

17-20. Thou renderest to every man according to his work. Ps. lxii. 12.

I will judge you, O house of Israel, every one according to his ways, saith the Lord God. Ezekiel xviii. 30.

Providence sees all, liberty is given, the world is judged by goodness, and every one is rewarded according to his works. Talmud, *Pirke Aboth*, iii. 19. Rabbi Akiba.

Shall not he render to every man according to his work? Prov. xxiv. 12.

21. Trust ye not in lying words, saying, The temple of the Lord, the temple of the Lord, the temple of the Lord are these....If ye thoroughly amend your ways....then will I cause you to dwell in this place. Jeremiah vii. 4-7.

23. Depart from me, all ye workers of iniquity. Ps. vi. 8.

24-27. As timber girt and bound together in a building cannot be loosened with shaking, so the heart that is stablished by advised council shall fear at no time. A heart settled upon a thought of understanding is as a fair plaistering upon the wall of a gallery. Ecclus. xxii. 16-18.

For the closing verses of the seventh chapter the compilers of the *Origines du Sermon de la Montagne* suggest an emendation to the effect that the people were filled with admiration because Jesus had taught them after the manner of Ben Sirach and Hillel and Shammai, reproducing the brief and incisive maxims in which those teachers abound, and not verbosely after the manner of the scribes. It might be remarked on this, first, that the Oriental mind in general runs to wise commonplaces, and that among the Jews in particular compilations of such were in favour—as the books of Proverbs, Ecclesiastes, Ecclesiasticus, and the Wisdom of Solomon show—because of the lack of imaginative literature. Among the Greeks the maxims of Theognis were not ranked very high, because they had more succulent literary food in Homer and their drama. The Jews had little but proverbs, laws, chronicles, and the declamations of the prophets. But, as we shall see further in dealing with the "Lord's Prayer," there is no reason to believe that the "Sermon" as such was ever delivered by any man.

On the other hand, we now know, from evidence that was not available when the *Origines du Sermon* were compiled, that such fresh stringing together of ethical maxims for didactic purposes was practised in the Jewish community[1] just before the development of Christism. Since the publication of the *Origines* there has been given to the world the most valuable treasure-trove of modern Christian archæology—namely, the *Teaching of the Twelve Apostles*, discovered by M. Bryennios in 1873, published by him in 1883. Of that document, as we have seen, the Judaic origin is incontestable; and no less obvious is the fact that the early document contained matter that has been since embodied in the Sermon on the Mount. The Christian tampering begins, as we have said, in the seventh paragraph. But although there is a clean cleavage between that and the preceding matter, it does not follow that the original document ended with the sixth paragraph. That would have been a very abrupt ending. What is more, the first paragraph contains some of the *ipsissima verba* of the Sermon in Matt. v.; and the eighth section, after the plainly irrelevant plunge into baptism and the Trinity, goes on with more of the words found in the Sermon. The more significant passages in the first paragraph are :—

"Bless them that curse you, and pray for your enemies, and fast for

[1] Cp. Ewald, *Geschichte Christus' und seiner Zeit*, 3te Ausg. 1867, pp. 35–39, as to strings of maxims by Hillel and other Rabbis.

them that persecute you; for what reward have ye if ye love them that love you? Do not the Gentiles also the same? But love ye them that hate you, and ye shall have no enemy. Abstain from the fleshly and worldly lusts. If anyone give thee a blow on the right cheek, turn to him the other also, and thou shalt be perfect; if anyone compel thee to go one mile, go with him twain; if anyone take thy cloak, give him thy coat also; if anyone take from thee what is thine, ask it not back; for indeed thou canst not. To everyone that asketh thee give, and ask not back."

Even in the Christian redaction in which the document has come down to us, it is not in any way suggested that these passages are repetitions from the Gospels. Beyond all candid question, they are parts of the pre-Christian document officially compiled for the moral instruction of Jews living in Pagan communities. That purpose lies on the face of many of the prescriptions; and it was the broad suitability of such instruction to the practical needs of the early Jesuists that caused the *Teaching* so long to pass current among them. There it was, then, that they found the basis for their myth of the Twelve Apostles before the Gospels existed; and there the Gospel makers had a first model for the didactic discourses they attributed to Jesus, and in particular for the Sermon on the Mount. The factitious character of that document is thus established twice over.

If indeed it be dispassionately considered on its *prima facie* claims to credit, it is seen to be factitious. Even had such a string of quotations been delivered as a discourse, who was to report it? Why, again, should the Sermon be so long in the first Gospel and so short in the third if there existed any early documentary basis for the former version? In regard to no unsectarian issue would criticism hesitate to decide that the story of the Sermon was invented to give an air of circumstantiality to the claim made for the compiled teaching. And in the item of "The Mount," finally, we return to a myth of action.

Nothing could be more plainly fictitious than the fashion in which the first and third Gospels at the outset represent Jesus as addressing only his disciples, and finally assert that he had been addressing the multitude.[1] It is clear that either he was originally asserted to have addressed his disciples only, or he was first represented as addressing the multitude, and the preliminary phrase about the disciples and the Mount in Matthew is an interpolation. And this is in every way the probable solution. That the teacher could primarily be described as leading a multitude to a mountain top in order to speak to them for at most ten minutes is not a plausible view. It is the mountain and the twelve that are interposed; and this for clear mythic reasons. It is not merely that Moses gave his law from the Mount, but that the God on the Mount is the Sun-God once more on the "pillar of the world," this time surrounded by his "twelve"—the twelve signs of the Zodiac. It is the same motive that operates in the fiction of the naming of the twelve: "And he goeth into the mountain, and calleth unto him whom he himself would: and they went unto him. And he appointed twelve......"[2] Here we have the language of pure myth. The twelve, as we have seen, are demonstrably unhistorical; and this introduction of them might alone suggest as much. A picture or sculpture of the Sun-God on his Mount, with the zodiac arrayed around him, suggested the repeated Gospel presentments of Jesus choosing and teaching his twelve disciples on "a" or "the" mountain—not any mountain in particular—a narrative which only the spell of tradition and ecclesiasticism enables men to regard as probable. The specification of "the plain" in Luke, finally, is evidently a late device to account for the differences between the two versions of the discourse; the disciples being there also interpolated in imitation of Matthew, perhaps with a view to raising their traditionary status.

[1] Matt. v. 1; vii. 28; Luke vi. 20; vii. 1.
[2] Mark iii. 13–14; cp. Luke vi. 12.

§ 7. *The "Lord's Prayer."*

The so-called Lord's Prayer, placed as it is in the Sermon on the Mount, turns out to derive like that from pre-Christian Jewish lore, and, like parts of the Sermon, from an actually current Jewish document in particular.

First let us take the main parallel passages in the Talmud and the Bible and the Apocrypha, cited by the Jews :—

> On whom do we rest? On our Father who is in Heaven. Talmud *Sotah*, end.
>
> Our God is in the heavens; he hath done whatsoever he pleased. Ps. cxv. 3.
>
> Am I a God at hand, saith the Lord, and not a God afar off?....Do not I fill heaven and earth, saith the Lord? Jeremiah xxiii. 23–4.
>
> Blessed be God every day for the daily bread which he giveth us. Talmud, *Yom-Tob*, p. 16a. Hillel.
>
> Forgive thy neighbour the hurt that he hath done unto thee, so shall thy sins also be forgiven when thou prayest. Ecclus. xxviii. 2.
>
> Whosoever is prompt to forgive, his sins also shall be forgiven him. Talmud, *Megilla*, fol. 28.
>
> Suffer not, O Lord, that we should be led into sin, or into transgression, or into disgrace; put far away from us evil thoughts, in order that we may attach ourselves to those which are good. *Prayer for every day in the Jewish ritual.*
>
> Thine, O Lord, is the greatness, and the power, and the glory, and the victory, and the majesty; for all that is in the heaven and in the earth is thine; thine is the kingdom, O Lord, and thou art exalted as head above all. 1 Chron. xxix. 11.

It is hardly necessary to remark here that the Talmudic parallels to any part of the Sermon on the Mount cannot conceivably have been borrowed by the Rabbis from the Christian Gospels: they would as soon have borrowed from the rituals of the Pagans. This is now tacitly admitted by Christian scholars; and the claim made for the "Lord's" authorship of the prayer ascribed to him takes the following shape :—

> "The prayer is doubtless based upon expressions and sentiments already familiar to the Jews; indeed parallel phrases to nearly all its contents have been discovered in the Talmud. This, however, does not detract from its beauty or *originality, as a whole*."[1]

[1] Art. "Lord's Prayer" in McClintock and Strong's *Biblical Cyclopedia*. Cp. Trollope, *Liturgy of St. James*.

In none save an ecclesiastical cause would such a claim now be made; and it is needless here to deal with it, since it can be shown that the prayer as a whole is pre-Christian. Even the authority cited admits that "The closing doxology is omitted by Luke, and is *probably spurious in Matthew*, as it is not found there in any of the early MSS."

That is to say, even after the Gospels had taken substantially their present shape; even after the third was compiled, Christians did not hesitate to *add to their Lord's Prayer phrases already in Judaic use*. There need then be no difficulty in believing that the other phrases of the prayer were taken even in their present context from a Jewish formula. We have seen in the analysis of the so-called Sermon, as a whole, how much of Judaic ethical commonplace went to make it up; and the habit of borrowing could easily be further illustrated. Take another orthodox testimony.

Of the Talmudic treatise *Sotah*, or "The *Erring Woman*," says Dr. B. Pick, the last sections

> "are very interesting, because they foretell the signs of the approaching Messiah, and wind up with the following remarkable words: 'In the time of the Messiah the people will be impudent and be given to drinking; public-houses will flourish and the vine will be dear;....the wisdom of the scribes will be stinking; fear of God will be despised....The young men will shame the old, the old will rise against the young; the son will despise the father; the daughter will rise against the mother, the daughter-in-law against the mother-in-law, and a man's foes shall be they of his own household. The face of that generation is as the face of a dog; the son shall not reverence the father."[1]

Compare this passage with Matthew x. 35. Here are the very words, first of Micah (vii. 6), and next of a Rabbi, put in the mouth of Jesus as his own; and this in a passage which every rationalist critic must recognize to have been compiled for Christian purposes long after the sect had taken shape, and when it was undergoing persecution. Certainly there has been a process of sifting.

> "In one of the treatises of the Talmud called *Challah* we find, almost verbatim, what our Lord says in Matt. v. 28, and yet that portion of the Talmud is written in language so obscene and immoral that it would be

[1] Art. TALMUD in McClintock and Strong's *Biblical Cyclopædia*, x. 179.

difficult to meet its equal among the most licentious publications of ancient or modern times. We challenge any admirer of the Talmud to translate the treatise and publish it."[1]

Doubtless the believer will decide that it was abnormal good taste that eliminated the objectionable portions; but we shall see that such elimination could very well be made by a mortal and forgotten Jew, whether or not taught by Pagan decorum to rise above the prurient puerilities which occupied so much of the thoughts of the Rabbis.

A much closer and more striking parallel, however, than any cited in the *Origines*, was long ago pointed out by Christian scholars. The Rev. John Gregorie, who wrote over two hundred years ago, presents a compilation from the Jewish "Euchologues" in the following terms:—

"Our Father which art in Heaven, be gracious to us, O Lord our God, hallowed be thy name, and let the remembrance of thee be glorified in heaven above, and upon earth here below. Let thy kingdom reign over us now and for ever. The holy men of old said, remit and forgive unto all men whatsoever they have done against me. And lead us not into temptation, but deliver us from the evil thing. For thine is the kingdom, and thou shalt reign in glory for ever and for evermore."[2]

This is cited by Evan Meredith,[3] who also makes reference to Basnage[4] as saying that the Jews had an ancient prayer called the *Kadish*, "precisely like Jesus's prayer." But these citations are somewhat misleading, alike in Gregorie and in Basnage. The former does not profess to find his compilation as it stands: he takes it piecemeal from the Rabbinical writings.[5] Even in that regard, however, the parallel made out is somewhat closer than that drawn up in the *Origines du Sermon de la Montagne*; and we shall be better able to understand why when we turn to Basnage. Speaking of the regular Jewish worship of his own day (*circa* 1700), that historian says:—

"The minister, supposing that the people have recited their prayers, commences the daily service by a prayer which is called *Kadish*, because

[1] Dr. Pick, as last cited, p. 174.
[2] Gregorie's Works, 4th ed. 1864, p. 168.
[3] *The Prophet of Nazareth*, 1868, p. 426.
[4] *Histoire des Juifs*, liv. vi. chap. xviii. section 7.
[5] Citing *Tephill. Lusitan.* p. 115; *Sepher Hammussar.* xlix. 1; Com. in *Pirké Aboth.* fol. 24; and *Seph. Hammussar.* ix. 12.

it asks of God the *sanctification* of his name: 'O God, be thy name magnified and hallowed in the world which thou hast created according to thy good pleasure; cause thy kingdom to come (*faites regner votre Regne*): let Redemption flourish; and let the Messiah come speedily; let thy name be celebrated,' etc. This prayer is the most ancient of all that the Jews have preserved; and as it is read in the Chaldaic language, there is some ground for supposing that it is one of the prayers which were made at the return from Babylon for the use of the people, who understood Hebrew with difficulty. It is several times repeated in the service as being the most important, and the people are obliged to respond several times, Amen, Amen. Thus it is properly an anthem. If the Germans have cut away what has regard to the Redemption, the coming of the Messiah, and the deliverance of the people, it is not that they believe that this Redeemer is come, but they are persuaded that all these advantages are included in the coming of the Kingdom of God. Jesus Christ seems to have borrowed the first words of this prayer, since he has made us also say 'hallowed be thy name, thy kingdom come'; and this confirms what we have said as to the antiquity of this prayer."

Basnage's version, it will be seen, does not correspond strictly to the Christian formula; but his remarks throw an important light alike on these textual discrepancies and on the absence of all save one or two parallel phrases from the extract given in the modern *Origines du Sermon de la Montagne*. In the first place, the fact that in the time of Basnage the Jewish *Kadish* was read in Chaldean (*i.e.*, Aramaic) is, as he says, a clear proof of its great antiquity. In all probability the proof goes further than he thought; for there is reason to surmise that, as so many of the Jewish legends and myths are originally Babylonian, so the "Lord's" prayer, or Kadish, is *originally a Babylonian prayer*.[1] But Basnage makes the significant intimation that the German Jews had already in his day dropped part of the ancient formula; and he goes on to show incidentally what the forces were that compelled such excisions:—

"After the anthem is usually recited the Decalogue, which is the

[1] This passage was first printed in September, 1891. In the *Journal of the Royal Asiatic Society* for October, 1891, Mr. T. G. Pinches published for the first time a translation of a tablet found at Sippara in 1882, in which there occur, in an invocation of Merodach, the lines:—

"May the abundance of the world descend into thy [the city's] midst;
May thy command be accomplished in time to come....
May [the evil spirit] dwell outside of thee."

Here we have prayer-norms, on the lines of the Lord's Prayer, dating perhaps 4000 B.C.

foundation of the Judaic religion; but the doctors say that they have been *obliged to abolish this usage because of the heretics or Christians*, who insist that God had given only these ten commandments on Sinai. To-day they content themselves with reading some passages of Deuteronomy which they call *Schémah*" (because of the first word).

Here we have the whole solution. The prayer of the Jews has been gradually modified out of fear of persecuting Christians, who would not let them use what passed for a Biblical or Christian formula. The phrase "*Dieu n'avait donné que ces dix commandemens sur la Sinaï*" is not very lucid; but we can easily imagine how Christian fanaticism would argue the case. It is not clear how the French Jews have lost sight of these modifications, or why they do not mention them if they are aware of them; but it is consistent with many known facts that the modifications should have been made. After the revival of Hebrew learning, the Rabbis took precautions[1] to keep out of the published copies of the Talmud those passages referring to the early Jesus who was stoned and hanged on a tree on the eve of the Passover, such allusions being supposed by Christians, and even by some Jews, to refer to the Jesus of the Gospels. They probably *did* so refer, indeed, in a sense which neither side realised, since the chances are that the Gospel biography was originally a collection of mythical matter relating to the early Jesus, and that he was really the Jesus of Paul, who shows no acquaintance with the Gospel narratives. But all we are here concerned with is the fact of the suppression of the passages in the later printed editions of the Talmud. If the Jews had to do that, and had to drop the very decalogue from their ritual, still more likely would be the compulsory abandonment of the gist of a prayer which ran closely parallel to one specially claimed by the Christians as theirs. This was probably not the attitude of the real scholars. Gregorie, who well deserves the latter title, was quite satisfied that Jesus had copied established forms:—

"Note that our Lord gathered up his form of prayer out of the traditions of the elders. It must not seem strange to you: if you know

[1] For some details see Leslie's *Short and Easy Method with the Jews*, ed. 1812, pp. 2–3.

how to consider of it, you will perceive that nothing could be more purposely done."

But it was one thing for a scholar to think thus, and another for the average priest and pietist to tolerate the Jewish use of a form of prayer which seemed a parody of or parallel to their own principal prayer.

We have still to cite, however, one of the main and definitive proofs that the Christian prayer was really in Jewish use before Jesuism began, and that not merely in the form of the *Kadish*, but in the express terms in which we now have it. As we have seen, the Sermon on the Mount absorbs certain typical passages from the early and purely Judaic portion of the *Teaching of the Twelve Apostles*, the Christian additions beginning only with the seventh paragraph, which suddenly prescribes baptism with a Trinitarian formula. But that there remain further portions of the Judaic document is made highly probable by the wording of the eighth paragraph, which would follow quite naturally on the sixth, if we dropped the seventh altogether. The sixth ends :—

"And concerning food, what thou art able, bear; but of that offered to idols, beware exceedingly; for it is a worship of dead Gods."

This is the language of Jews instructing fellow Jews living among polytheists. The eighth paragraph runs :—

"But let not your fastings be in common with the hypocrites; for they fast on the second day of the week and on the fifth; but do ye fast during the fourth and the preparation day. Nor pray ye like the hypocrites, but *as the Lord commanded in his gospel*, thus pray:—Our father who art in heaven, hallowed be thy name, thy kingdom come, thy will be done, as in heaven, so on earth; give us this day our daily bread, and forgive us our debt as we also forgive our debtors, and bring us not into temptation, but deliver us from the evil [one], for thine is the power and the glory for ever. Three times in the day pray ye thus."

Then follows a fresh Jesuist (Ebionitic) paragraph, beginning "Now concerning the Eucharist, thus give thanks." But the words "as the Lord commanded in his gospel" are, be it observed, the very first allusion in the whole document to either the Lord or the Gospel. In the first paragraph we had a quantity of the matter which figures in the Sermon, but not a word of its being taken from the

Lord or "the gospel." It is conceivable, indeed, that the eighth chapter may be wholly a Jesuist addition; but is it not immeasurably more likely that it was in the original Judaic document, and that only the phrase "as the Lord commanded in his gospel" is interpolated?

There is reason to suspect that even the six earlier chapters of the *Teaching*, though still free of Jesuism, do not survive in their earliest form, but had undergone Judaic manipulation before reaching Christian hands; and Christian manipulators would certainly not hesitate to insert a phrase in one of the Judaic chapters, any more than to interpolate Jesuist chapters. Even as it is, the Christian patching shows different stages. The ninth chapter at first introduces only "Jesus thy servant," the formula of the early Ebionites, so that "the Son" of the seventh chapter is a later Trinitarian touch. The eleventh chapter, again, which might easily have followed on the ninth, has no mention of Jesus; and its "the Lord" may be purely Judaic, or may more probably be a Jesuist interpolation, for the sentences in which it occurs are extremely tautological. The name of Jesus does not once occur after the tenth chapter, though "Christ" and "Christian" do in the twelfth, and "the gospel of our Lord" again in the fifteenth. In the sixteenth (the last), notably enough, in the prediction of the end of the world, occur the words: "*then shall appear the world-deceiver as the son of God.*" Is this Judaic or Christian? Critically speaking, it may be either: that is, it may have been first penned by Jesuists protesting against new Messiahs; or it may have been part of a late Jewish edition of the *Teaching* designed to discredit the Jesuists, and may have been copied by Jesuists either wittingly or unwittingly. The former, however, is the more probable solution.

But however that may be, the Jewish origin of the "Lord's Prayer," as of the rest of the Sermon, remains certain. Even the Sermon, as a whole, or much of it, may have been circulated separately by the Jewish Twelve Apostles. Paul knows nothing of it: none of the Epistle-writers cites any part, or speaks of a Lord's Prayer. Is it credible that Paul would have said nothing of the Prayer if it was current in his time? And if it was not, where was the report to come from later? Plainly there was no report, no sermon, no extempore composition of a prayer, in the case. The prayer was an officially promulgated Jewish formula; the Sermon was a documentary compilation, never preached by any man save as such. And it no more came from Paul's Jesus than it did from Paul himself. The orthodox scholar makes an admission which of itself makes an end of the orthodox doctrine:—

> "The earliest reference found to it [the Prayer] as a liturgical formula in actual use, is in the so-called Apostolical Constitutions, which give the form entire, and enjoin its stated use (vii. 44), but solely by baptized persons, a rule which was afterwards strictly observed."[1]

The "Apostolical Constitutions" belong to the third or fourth century; and, as the American editors of the *Teaching* admit, is "largely indebted to the Teaching."[2] The chain of evidence is complete.

§ 8. *The Woman Taken in Adultery.*

No Gospel teaching, probably, has better served to create an idea of Jesus as an original moral teacher (though it does not really warrant such a view) than the story of his rebuke of those who were about to stone the woman taken in adultery. It must therefore have been a shock to many English readers to find that in the Revised Version this story is given up as being absent from the oldest codices, and clearly an interpolation. There is reason to believe, however, that some such story occurred in the lost "Gospel according to the Hebrews";[3] and it is arguable that it may have been there told to the same effect. Is *this*, then, to be taken as biographical?

That such a teaching should have been given by a Jewish moralist is perfectly possible. It is indeed hard to conceive, despite the normal one-sidedness of the morals of sex, that

[1] Art. before cited. [2] Hitchcock and Brown's ed. (Nimmo), p. xlvi.
[3] Nicholson, *The Gospel According to the Hebrews*, pp. 52–58, and App. F.

the Jewish middle class were in general capable of the brutal iniquity of stoning a woman taken in adultery, while the man went scot free. And if we are to understand "the one without sin among you" as meaning "the one innocent of adultery," we are presented in the Gospel story with the picture of a group of men, all themselves adulterers, ready to stone an adulteress to death, if they were not shamed out of their purpose. It is paying no great compliment to Jewish ethics in the first century to grant that a Jewish teacher may have been capable, like an average Greek or Roman, of seeing the atrocity of such a code as this.[1] And the detail of the teacher stooping down and writing on the ground has a distinct air of circumstantial truth.

If, however, the story existed in its present form in the Gospel of the Hebrews *before* the compilation of Matthew. how came it that the latter Gospel, which embodies so many of the other fragments of the lost book, entirely omitted this? Was it that the compiler found the ethic too high for him? This is indeed conceivable, but only on the distinct understanding that the Sermon on the Mount is a late addition. A writer who gave the teaching "Love your enemies," the doctrine of non-resistance, and the precept "Judge not, that ye be not judged," can hardly have blenched before the teaching that sinful men ought not to stone to death their fellow-sinner, man or woman. But the first Gospel chimes with the Hebraic in giving the teaching of forgiveness "until seventy times seven"; and it is unintelligible that a compiler who would accept that would reject the story of the forgiven woman. Recognising the former teaching to be a late addition, we are still left asking why the story of the forgiven woman is not also added. Two hypotheses are framable: (*a*) That the story as it stood in the Hebrew Gospel had not the moral merit of that given in the latter MSS. of the fourth Gospel; or (*b*) that the story was *late in the Hebrew Gospel*. Of these,

[1] Mr. Nicholson writes (p. 57, *note*) that "it is not likely that they had any thought of really stoning this woman. They might not put to death without leave from the Roman Governor, who would hardly give it in such cases as this."

the second alone seems on reflection to be tenable. Whatever the original story was, the later editors of "Matthew" would hardly have set it aside if it had any moral significance whatever. But if we suppose the story to have been added to the Hebrew Gospel some time after the composition of the canonical one, the whole problem is solved.

And to this solution there can be no critical objection.[1] The earliest first-hand allusions to the story as occurring in the Hebrew Gospel belong to the fourth century; and though Eusebius cites Papias as having so mentioned it, even that statement would date the passage no earlier than the middle of the second century, when an early recension of Matthew is known from Papias' own evidence to have existed. Thus, then, there is finally no evidence that the story in question was told of the Gospel Jesus till at least a century after the date given for his death; and we are forced by the silence of the first Gospel to suppose that it really was not. But it does not even follow that the story existed in Papias' time. *His* book, mentioned by Eusebius, was likely to be interpolated like every other Christian writing of the period: indeed more likely than others, seeing that he had no canonical status. The whole story may be a product, then, of the fourth century; and that this was the case is made at least possible by the fact that it is so late to enter a canonical Gospel.

Even if, however, we credit it to the second century, it has no biographical value. It may be true of any teacher; and it presents Jesus as teaching with authority in the temple—an aspect which, by the admission of the school even of Weiss, does not belong to the early portions of the synoptics, and which is in no way countenanced by the Epistles of Paul. It is thus part of the Messianic myth. When all is said, too, it does but represent the teacher as passing a judgment which, by Christian consent, might have been passed in such a case by the Roman governor.

[1] It is noteworthy that the first fragment (Nicholson, pp. 28–30) of the Hebrew Gospel has clear marks of a later stage of growth than we see in the canonicals. Jesus is made to narrate in his own person, and we have the formula, "I will therefore that ye be twelve apostles for a testimony to Israel." Whether we put such writing early or late, it is blankly unhistorical.

It is part of the effect of the sacrosanct connotations of the whole Gospel story to make us overrate on the one hand the moral originality of its better elements, and on the other ignore the faultiness of the worse. On any view of the moral importance of the teaching, however, it is doctrinal myth in so far as it is ascribed to Jesus the Christ.

§ 9. *Gnostic and Cryptic Parables.*

If in the posthumous accounts of any ancient historical personage who had left no written remains we found ascribed to him two sets of teachings so different as those of the Sermon on the Mount and certain sets of sayings and parables ascribed to Jesus, we should without hesitation prounounce the tradition false. A man's teaching may indeed vary with years; but the Gospel Jesus is represented as having taught at the most for two years; the general tradition (which here significantly reverts to a mythological basis) putting the time at one year. It avails nothing, then, to suggest that a moral teacher of exceptional power passed in the course of a few months, or one or two years, from the attitude of a public instructor, laying down principles of universal application, to that of a communicator of occult knowledge. The contrast between the "Come unto me, all ye that are weary" and the "Ask and it shall be given you," on the one hand, and the sinister assurance to the disciples that the mystery of the kingdom of heaven is given unto them alone, the people being judicially blinded—such an antithesis of tone and feeling represents, not any one teacher's vacillations, but the countervailing interpolations of totally different schools or sectaries.

It is not hard to understand how certain sectaries, conscious of the general hostility of Jewry to the Jesuist cult, should retrospectively frame for the teacher a bitter doctrine of exclusiveness. "Unto you it is given to know the mysteries of the kingdom of heaven, but to them it is not given. For whosoever hath not, from him shall be taken away even that which he hath. *Therefore* speak I to them in *parables; because* seeing they see not, and hearing they hear not, neither do they understand. And unto them is fulfilled the prophecy of Isaiah......"[1] This is obviously later doctrine than that which follows in the context, where, after a recital of certain cryptic parables about the kingdom of heaven, it is explained that "without a parable spake he nothing unto them, that it might be fulfilled which was spoken by the prophet, saying, I will open my mouth in parables......"[2] A teacher who speaks invariably in parables either in order to fulfil a prophecy or in order not to be understood, is a doctrinal myth.

But the cryptic parables in themselves, apart from glosses, represent no real teaching. They *are* obscure, and possess no moral value whatever. Nor are they conceivable as popular discourses. Mystic conceptions of the kingdom of heaven under various analogies could but mystify the populace to no purpose, whether the preacher meant it or not. A current phrase is in these parables used in a non-natural sense, standing only for the later mysticism of a sect conscious of possessing an exclusive salvation; and the interpolators reck nothing of the fact that they are stultifying half the Gospel.

All the while, the cancelling of any one of the antithetic teachings counts for nothing in favour of the other. Given that the Sermon on the Mount is myth of doctrine, the cryptic parables do not thereby become more credible as historical utterances. They stand for a totally different kind of factor from the legendary teaching of Jesus. Given, again, that they are myths of doctrine, the Sermon on the Mount is in no way salved. The negative arguments in the two cases are finally independent of the antithesis, though the antithesis is fitly to be made a premiss in the research.

It is no part of the present undertaking to trace the origin of the cryptic parables. But it is historically

[1] Matt. xiii. 11–14. Cp. Mark iv. 11–12; Luke viii. 10.
[2] Matt. xiii. 34–35.

important in passing to take note that here in the Judaist, in the Gospel-making period, we find at work the essential spirit of Gnosticism, that claim to an occult and superior knowledge which Paul denounces or is made to denounce on the Gentile side.

§ 10. *The Late Ethical Parables in Luke.*

A glance at any "Harmony of the Gospels"[1] which exhibits synoptically the distribution of the various elements will show that a whole series of the higher ethical teachings occur only in the Gospel according to Luke. Thus (1) the parable of the Good Samaritan, (2) the story of Martha and Mary, (3) the parable of the covetous rich man, (4) the doctrine that sufferers are not special sinners, (5) the insistence that it is right to heal on the Sabbath, (6) the inculcation of humility, (7) the parable of the angels' joy over one saved sinner, (8) the parable of the prodigal son—these, as well as certain other teachings of less moral or literary value but of a similar individuality, occur in this gospel alone.[2] Since, then, the compiler expressly professes to redact previous narratives, we are faced by this dilemma: Had the compiler of the first Gospel deliberately rejected the teachings under notice, though they were current in written form, or are they additions made to the third Gospel some time after its compilation?

The first alternative seems out of the question; there is nothing in the ethic of these narratives that should have repelled the first editors of "Matthew." What is more, it is unintelligible that the editors of a comparatively late period should not have added these narratives if they were then available in Luke. There is reason to suppose that certain other narratives of good ethical quality which are found both in Luke and Matthew were really added to the first Gospel from the third, and not *vice versa*, belonging as they do to the ethical strain of the better parts of Luke.

[1] *E.g.*, that of the Rev. J. M. Fuller, published by the S.P.C.K.

[2] Luke x. 25–37, 38–42; xii. 13–21; xiii. 1–5; xiv. 1–11; xv. 8–32.

If then additions could thus be made from Luke to Matthew, there is a double presumption that the ethical parables peculiar to Luke are specially late. It is with these as with the formula about the Son of Man coming not to destroy life, but to save it: the doctrine is inserted long after the period assigned to Jesus, and its ascription to him is a myth. The source is still proximately Judaic; but there is no ground for the belief that it originated with a teacher answering to the description of the Gospel Jesus, or that it was orally delivered at all.

To persist in crediting an ideal Jesus with such utterances because they have a more or less high moral quality is to persist in uncritical methods, and in a conception of ethical evolution which is discredited by comparative history. There is positively no reason to doubt that Jews unknown to fame, living in contact with other cultures, were capable of reaching the moderate ethical height of the parable of the Good Samaritan, which is partly precedented in Old Testament teaching.[1] Such teachings, though the best in the Gospels, seem marvellous only in the dim light of the Christian tradition; there is nothing in them which could seem wonderful to a morally-educated Greek, Roman, Egyptian, Chinaman, or Hindu at the beginning of our era.[2] The contrast they present to normal *practice* is only that which always subsists between the higher current ideal and average practice, and which was never more flagrant than to-day.

§ 11. *The Discourses of the Fourth Gospel.*

The first step in the documentary criticism of the Gospel narrative as a whole was the separation of the fourth Gospel from the synoptics as being essentially alien to

[1] Deut. xxiii. 7—an interpolation. Cp. the book of Ruth.

[2] The Cambridge MS. Codex Bezæ or D. inserts in Luke v., after verse 10, a story of Jesus telling a man who worked on the Sabbath that if he knew what he did he was blessed, but if not, cursed. Trollope (*Gospel according to St. Luke*, Rowlandson's ed. 1870, p. 35) notes that "some are inclined to receive this as authentic *on account* of its form and contents." And why should they not, on the usual arbitrary principle?

them in the theology of its preface and in the picture it gives of a mystical teacher. A certain poetic strain in these teachings and the touches of refined pathos in parts of the narrative have won for it all the special liking of many readers of literary tastes, who, however, have more or less consciously put aside the less attractive features of the concretely-wrangling Jesus and fastened on the mystic generalizations. Such minds resist methodical criticism in an unteachable spirit of self-assertion. Thus the late Mr. Arnold, who never made a scientific study of any part of the subject, settled the problem by mere arrogant disparagement of the "insight" of all who opposed his convictions, and praise of the "sure feeling and true insight" of those who agreed with him. In this simple fashion, without a word of relevant argument, Ewald is exalted over Baur, Strauss, and Renan,[1] and the whole complex critical problem is simply burked.

One of the ways in which Mr. Arnold ostensibly satisfied himself that the Johannine discourses must be genuine was to point to the explanatory comment on the saying of Jesus in the passage in John vii. 38–39, and to insist that the teaching is "great and free," and the interpretation "narrow and mechanical"; the teachings of Jesus being thus shown to be "clearly out of the reach" of the writer of the Gospel. This is pure fallacy. Mr. Arnold does not seem ever to have realised the conditions under which the Gospels were compiled and preserved. The "inadequate" comment is, in all probability, a late interpolation; and the original saying may perfectly well have been the invention of the first writer of the Gospel, or even of a later editor.

Taking by itself the saying under notice, we have an illustration of the complete arbitrariness of Mr. Arnold's critical procedure. The Gospel tells that "Jesus stood and cried, saying, If any man thirst, let him come unto me and drink. He that believeth on me as the scripture hath said, out of his belly shall flow fountains of living

[1] *Literature and Dogma*, ch. vi. § 4.

water." It is extremely instructive to realise that a mind like Mr. Arnold's, claiming to work with a delicate tact and the insight of a ripe literary experience, should see in such a deliverance "sweet reasonableness" and intellectual greatness. The meaningless vaunt, the grotesque phraseology, the moral emptiness of the allocution—all are transfigured by the traditionary prepossession, even as every sentence in the Koran is transfigured for the devout Moslem. Professing to apply the test of cultivated intelligence, of the "literary" spirit, the critic turns his back on that spirit, and fanaticises. Had any teacher of an alien cult been represented as thus preposterously crying aloud in the market-place, Mr. Arnold would, like any other educated man, have seen that the story, as such, was a myth, and the pretended utterance a concoction of a narrow and barren fanaticism. It was the moral and intellectual nullity of such utterances that led such a writer as Mill, convinced of the abnormality of the ethics of the synoptics, to protest that "the East was full of men who could have stolen any quantity of this poor stuff, as the multitudinous Oriental sects of Gnostics afterwards did";[1] and such a writer as Renan to defy whoever would to compose a credible life of Jesus, making use of the Johannine discourses—"*ces discours roids et gauches, dont le ton est si souvent faux et inégal.*"[2]

Such deliverances may serve to countervail the mere dogmatism with which Arnold pushed his favourite views. But the decisive critical method is represented by neither of the judgments cited, valid as both are in themselves. The question is not whether the discourses peculiar to the Fourth Gospel have any value, but whether they are (*a*) at all congruous with any of the discourses in the synoptics, or (*b*) whether they are conceivably oral teachings at all. On the first head, hundreds of students have reluctantly answered in the negative. I say reluctantly, for it is from believers in the historic actuality of

[1] *Three Essays on Religion*, p. 254.
[2] *Vie de Jésus*, Introd. éd. 15e. p. lxxvii.

"the Gospel Jesus," and usually from admirers of his supposed teaching, that the admissions have primarily come. It was in order to save what seemed a sound foundation that they withdrew from what they felt to be unsound, because heterogeneous. If the kind of personality broadly presented in the synoptics were real, that presented in the fourth Gospel, they felt, was wholly unreal. The last arguable plea for it was that John might be capable of retaining large portions of the Jesuine utterance which were lost by the other disciples for sheer lack of perception. On that view, the marvellous teacher spent himself in many elaborate discourses to twelve men, of whom only one understood him, or even cared to preserve his words—a conception which stultifies the cause on behalf of which it is framed. And Mr. Arnold stultifies even this plea by contending that the writer of the fourth Gospel was clearly incapable of appreciating most of the discourse he reproduced. Either way, the defence collapses in incoherence. No reasonable and scrupulous critic who holds by "the" synoptic Jesus, or any aspect thereof, can critically hold also by the Johannine.[1]

While, however, critics who see solid ground in the synoptics must discard the mystifying and mysticising Jesus of John, those of us who recognise that the synoptics are but a congeries of myths of action and myths of doctrine are not *thereby* entitled to decide that the Jesus of John is a further congeries of myths. There is always the abstract possibility that a real Jesus may have arisen independently of the line of tradition which evolved the synoptics. The identification of a later real Jesus with the established mythic figure might occur later still. The Johannine Jesus *might* be Paul's "another Jesus whom we

[1] Dr. Gardner (*Exploratio Evangelica*, p. 163), admitting the wide difference between the synoptics and the fourth Gospel, suggests that John had made the difference by his way of reproducing the speeches! As if any mere laxity of reporting could affect the general significance of such formulas as "I am the true vine," "I and the Father are one." So Mr. J. E. Carpenter (*First Three Gospels*, p. 55) makes the compromise that the Johannine discourses are "interpretations" of the Jesuine teaching. For all this there is no judicial justification whatever.

have not preached." But that hypothesis must be properly tested like another; and when the proper tests are applied it vanishes.

Let all the myths of action, some of which we have examined, be stripped away from the fourth Gospel; let it be disencumbered alike of its special miracles and of the mythic narrative which it shares with the synoptics, and we are left merely with palpable myths of doctrine. Its preamble—probably secondary, and visibly interpolated in its second sentence[1]—stands for a new movement of doctrinal myth; and from the outset we have a new presentment of a fictitious Messiah, who claims (iii. 13) to have "descended out of heaven." Instead of a teacher who delivers a discourse of collected maxims, as in Matthew, or one who conveys sane ethical ideas in parables, as in parts of Luke, we have one who trades in mysticity. A would-be disciple, told by him that to enter the kingdom of heaven one must be "born again," answers like a good catechumen with a question as to how a man can re-enter his mother's womb; and the teacher answers with a formula about being "born of water and the Spirit." A modern inquirer can still affirm that "some of the sayings of the discourse [to Nicodemus] are so profound that we cannot easily believe them to come from any but Jesus"[2]—the old *petitio principii*, with even less than the old excuse. It is enough to answer that, even as forgotten men could frame the parable of the good Samaritan and the precept of non-resistance, so many forgotten men were capable of formulas about being born of water and the Spirit, about salvation

[1] Even the first sentence probably ran originally thus: "In the beginning was the Logos, and the Logos was next to God." (That πρὸς is not properly rendered by "with" is recognized by Dr. Paley, who translates it "in relation to." Compare the note of "A Layman" in the translation published by Pickering, 1840. "Next to" is the probable original sense.) The phrase "and the word was God" has every appearance of an addition meant to save the principle of the Son's equality: had the first writer meant to affirm as much, he would not have written the second clause, which is entirely incongruous with the third. But the further phrase, "the same was in the beginning πρὸς τὸν θεόν," is again an attempt to restore the Logos to a subordinate position. Certainly the passage has been tampered with.

[2] Dr. Gardner, *Exploratio Evangelica*, p. 163.

by an only begotten Son, about salvation by eating a God's flesh and blood, and about damnation for non-belief.

Such doctrines—with the possible exception of the last, which suggests a Judaic origin, though it is a natural sequence to the formula of salvation—were part of the stock-in-trade of current paganism. All baptisings stood for the beginning of a new life. The initiate of the *taurobolium* or *criobolium* in the Mithraic and other systems was *in æternum renatus*[1] by the blood of the slain lamb or bull, of which the literal drenching was to wash away his sins. The eating of the flesh and blood of the God was the standing mystery not only of the Dionysiak cult, but, as we have seen, of the typical theophagous cults of all antiquity. The sacrificed only-begotten son is an element in old Semitic myth,[2] of which the story of Abraham and Isaac is an Evemerized survival. And the abstract discourses of the fourth Gospel are as certainly myths of doctrine, put in the God's mouth, as these inculcations of dogma and ritual practice.

Let us attempt for a moment, on the plane of rational judgment, to imagine a teacher delivering the typical discourses of the fourth Gospel, and we are once for all repelled by their blank incredibility. "My Father worketh even until now, and I work"; "The Son can do nothing of himself, but what he seeth the Father do; for what things soever he doeth, these the Son also doeth in like manner"; "For neither doth the Father judge any man, but he hath given all judgment unto the Son"; "I can of myself do nothing: as I hear I judge; and my judgment is righteous"; "I am the living bread which came down out of heaven"; "Except ye believe that I am he, ye shall die in your sins"; "When I am in the world, I am the light of the world"; "All that came before me are thieves and robbers"; "I and the Father are one"; "I am the

[1] See the inscription in Orelli, No. 2352. Cp. Nos, 1899, 1900, 2130, 2199, 2322, 2326, 2330, 2331, 2351, 2353, 2361; also that in Boeckh, 6012, *l.c.* See also Dittenberger, *Inscr. Atticae aetatis Romanae*, Nos. 172, 173.

[2] See the extracts from Sanchoniathon in Eusebius, *Præp. Evang.* i. 6, 10; tr. in *Cory's Ancient Fragments*, ed. Hodges, pp. 16, 22.

true vine, and my Father is the husbandman"—such are the formulas set forth by creed-makers as the spoken words of a teacher, persuading human beings. What historically-trained student, finding them in any cult in which he had not been bred, would hesitate for a moment to class them with the pretended sayings of Krishna in the Bhagavat Gitâ? Such sayings may or may not have been framed for dramatic delivery by the God in a mystery-play: they certainly were never delivered by a teacher in good faith to his disciples.

Discourses which were hopelessly intractable even to the facile undertaking of Renan, making a new pseudo-scientific myth out of the *débris* of the Gospel aggregate, must be recognized as unmitigated myth by any criticism that rises above the wilful assertion of an inherited prejudice. The fourth Gospel is but a fresh Hellenistic adaptation of the Jewish Messianic myth, embodying the Greek and Mazdean idea of the *Logos*,[1] making the God work the standing Dionysiak miracle, and compete with Mithra, "the light of the world," and with Dionysos, "the vine"; making him call himself one with the God-Father, and offer his body and blood as the mystic saving sacrifice, common to half the cults of the period; and giving a new help to the doubted doctrine of immortality by the fresh fable of the resurrection of Lazarus. Whether it be "truly" Gnostic or not, it stands for the fresh process of abstract myth-making of which Gnosticism is the general name. It matters little to what date we assign its composition. The question of the nature of the Gospel narratives is now seen finally to lie outside the question of the dates at which they first entered into circulation as documents. Be they as early as orthodoxy would claim, or as late as scholarly scepticism would argue, they are a

[1] M. Nicolas denied (*Des Doctrines religieuses des Juifs*, ch. ii. § 2) that the Jewish doctrine derived from the others; but his whole argument is that it differs from them in its application. This would only throw back the presumptive origination to the Babylonian system, from which the Mazdean and Egyptian systems alike borrowed. But the fact that for Philo the Logos is, like Mithra, "the Mediator" (*id.* p. 181) suggests a direct Mazdean influence.

baseless fabric of myths of action and myths of doctrine, leaving on scientific analysis "not a wrack behind," save the speechless crucified Messiah of Paul's propaganda, dubiously identifiable with the remote Jesus Ben Pandira of the Talmud, who died for some forgotten heresy a hundred years "before Christ."

EPILOGUE.

It will doubtless be charged upon the foregoing argument, as it has been upon every other process which discredits traditional beliefs, that it is "negative," that it "destroys without building up." But if the main positions be really valid, the charge is even more than usually false. I say more than usually, because it is nearly always false. It is psychologically impossible to destroy a religious belief, commonly so called, without putting in its place other beliefs: for it is only through the establishment of certain affirmations that a contrary affirmation, previously relied on, can be shaken. To prove that the world was not made in six days, it is necessary to show that it grew in another fashion. For the single false and ignorant belief there is thus given a complex of real knowledge, correcting and reacting on one's whole conception of the universe. It may indeed be possible to set up a metaphysic of negation that paralyzes all conviction; but that procedure, in modern times at least, has nearly always been that of men professedly bent on re-establishing the belief in a God on the ruins of belief in what formerly passed for "reality." No more strictly negative and destructive work has ever been done than by religionists of the school and type of Berkeley. And students have been known to declare that the latest development of the theistic argument, the Gospel of "the will to believe," has destroyed in them the very faculty of conviction.

If our analysis of the Gospels as a congeries of myths be broadly accurate, there has been set up not merely a set of more or less sound and tested propositions in place of an aggregate of delusion, not merely a certain body of historic truth in place of much primitive error, but a sustaining and "constructive" conception of human history in place of one profoundly destructive and dispiriting. The champions of the traditional view of the Gospels are the truly negative teachers: they insist to the last that the records represent either a supernatural or a supernormal exhibition of moral greatness; that it needed either a God or a man beyond all compare to give forth such teachings; they imply that only by such moral cataclysms has humanity ever been bettered; and they further imply that there is either no chance or little chance of comparable betterment in the future. It is such teaching as this that peculiarly deserves to be branded as perniciously negative, in that it negates the moral faculty of all mankind. To apply the phraseology of the Christians of past time, it is a blasphemy against Man. It has cast a glamour of mystery round some ancient portions of men's handicraft, and has so taught later men to despair of their own powers. If our "negation" be just, it establishes the momentous affirmation that as Man is the maker of all Gods, so is he the maker of all Christs.

The Christian cult is literally the work of many generations; and though it may be arguable that certain men, as Paul, were specially active in promoting the mere external acceptance of it, it is here maintained that there is no ground for ascribing any of its special doctrines, any section of its Gospels, to any man whose name has been preserved. Alike the best and the worst are the work of men who elude our search; and both alike are clearly within the power of many nameless men of the ancient civilizations.

To say this, however, is to say that the best, on its merits, is no such prodigy of wisdom or insight as has been so commonly asserted. During the Dark Ages, indeed, the Christian world seems to present a relative paralysis of thinking, due largely to the very acceptance of the Gospels as a superhuman product; such acceptance, however, being primarily an outcome of the decay of the intellectual life which followed on a universal despotism.

But though the age of gospel-making was followed by a worse, the Gospels are not thereby vindicated as a great moral code. Had they been the moral marvel they are said to be, they should have prevented the decay which fell upon a world enlightened by them. In plain truth, they are absolutely devoid of the species of light which alone could have arrested that decay. Of political science they show no trace; they implicitly endorse slavery,[1] as does Paul;[2] and their doctrines of a speedy end of the world, and of salvation by blind faith, were the virtual frustration of all the better precepts they contained. If the scrupulous Stoicism of Marcus Aurelius, gravely bent on his public duty, could not arrest Roman dissolution, much less could the Gospels do so.

What is more, the wilder myth-mongering which followed on the gospel-making period is the due sequence of the myth-mongering of the Gospels themselves. Antiquity had slowly risen from a universal mythopoiesis to a measure of rationalism; but the Gospels, which contain some of the moral fruits of the higher thought of Paganism as well as of Judaism, preserve absolutely nothing of Pagan rationalism in the sphere of belief. Thus, passing into the hands of a new world of semi-barbarism, they put no check on mythopoiesis, but rather sanctioned every species of monstrous fiction. As we have seen above, the post-evangelical Christians multiplied their myths on Pagan lines step for step with the building of their Church. The Descent into Hades,[3] the Seven Martyrs,[4] the Trinity, the giant Christopher bearing the Christ-Child,[5] the Assumption of Mary, the Immaculate Conception of Mary by *her* mother Anna, these are all as sequent from pagan practice as the myths of the Gospels, as the machinery of the priesthood. Lactantius[6] makes Jesus

[1] Luke xvii. 7–10; where "servant" should read "slave," as in the Greek.
[2] 1 Cor. vii. 21, where the words meaninglessly rendered "use it rather" certainly mean "remain a slave."
[3] Above, *Christ and Krishna*, § xvi. [4] *Id.* § xv.
[5] Above, *Christ and Krishna*, § xiii. To the pagan types there cited should be added Orion, giant and child-bearer. See K. O. Müller, *Introd. to Mythology*, Eng. trans. App. pp. 336–9.
[6] *Div. Inst.* iv. 7.

"twice-born," like Dionysos; the Pope wears a mitre, like Dionysos,[1] in whose priest's chair he sits, and like Mithra; even as the gospel-makers assimilated Peter to Mithra and to Janus. The machinery of the Apocalypse is simply a manipulation of the symbols of the ancient astronomy, as figured in its celestial sphere.[2] In the Acts of the Apostles, again, the Samaritan God *Semo Megas*, Great Sem or Semo, becomes Simon Magus, an opponent of Paul.[3] The same human faculty for fallacy and fraud works in and after as before the framing of the Gospels.

It is the easier to understand it all when we realize how the same imaginative impulse works in the quasi-scientific historiography of our own time. We have seen an acute analyst of the mythopœic faculty framing myths of ethnology and sociology.[4] In the special sphere of Gospel origins, again, we have Renan dealing with his material very much as an ancient mythographer would, hardly disguising his consciousness that he is building with fables.[5] A man of letters not given to meticulous criticism has pronounced his method "sheer lunacy. You can see him take up the block which he had just rejected and make of it the corner-stone; a maddening way to deal with authorities; and the result so little like history that one almost blames oneself for wasting time. But the time is not wasted, the conspectus is always good, and the blur that remains on the mind is probably just enough."[6] It is true that the time is not wasted: on stepping-stones of Renan we may rise to truer things: but closer students can hardly rest content with the "blur." Dr. Weiss, like Dr. Pusey, has pronounced Renan's work a romance;[7] and such it really is. But Dr. Weiss, who after all his labours over the texts constructs a Life of Christ in which nearly every myth is

[1] Diodorus iv. 4.

[2] See this very clearly shown by Dupuis in his larger and smaller treatises.

[3] See *National Reformer*, Jan. 29th and Feb. 5th, 1893. The theorem of Baur and his school (Baur, *Christenthum*, pp. 79–85; *Paulus*, p. 85, etc. Volkmar, *Die Religion Jesu*, p. 281, ff., Zeller, *On the Origin and Contents of the Acts*, Eng. tr. i. 250, ff.) is not shaken by the orthodox answers.

[4] Above, pp. 33–34.

[5] *Vie de Jésus*, préf. éd. 15e, p. xvi.

[6] R. L. Stevenson, *Vailima Letters*, under date May 20th, 1893.

[7] *Life of Christ*, Eng. tr. i. 205.

rehabilitated as biography to the general satisfaction of ecclesiastics, has only produced a German romance in place of a French one. If we must have romances, many of us would prefer the French to the German variety.

As against the always popular process of romance-making, an attempt has here been made to reach a conception of true causation by the methods of science. It will recommend itself only to the relatively small class with a strong concern for truth as such; and the ingenuity which has been spent on proving the "reality" of confessedly fictitious characters will not here find itself propitiated. What passes for a worship of ideals is too often a mere dogmatism which refuses to recast the ideals of the past, and is psychologically on a par with the worship of idols. Let anyone dispassionately seek to realize for himself the conditions of mind under which savages make fetishes, and civilized men adore images, and he will find that it consists first in a certain process of either wilful or lawless imagination, and secondarily in the contented pursuance of a psychic habit thus set up. Exactly so, on a different plane of culture, do men persist in framing or retaining notions of personalities which they call "ideals," refusing to ask with open minds whether the given ideal satisfies the full-grown moral and intellectual nature, determining to "make believe" that it does, and to disparage those who disparage it. This "ideal," in short, is just an idol, which must be transfigured by the emotions to make it pass muster with the judgment.

How religious minds dispose of the difficulties created for them by veridical methods is well seen in Browning's "Epilogue," where, after making David voice the creed of Israel, and Renan in strangely un-Renanesque phrase express some untranslatable despondency of doubt, the poet proceeds to declare with similar obscurity his own pantheism, according to which

> "That one Face, far from vanish, rather grows,
> Or decomposes but to recompose,
> Become my universe that feels and knows!"

If that were said in the good faith of prose, it might

stand for a practically true solution: the mythic Jesus being indeed but one of a thousand phantoms formed from the breath of universal humanity. But the practical fact is that in such hands the dream-face only too literally "decomposes but to recompose"; the poet's pantheism is but a figure of speech, which does not represent his normal thought; and readers for whom, as for him, truth is that which you like to trow, simply reinstate the myth and call it Master. In the Middle Ages, Christendom had its circumstantial descriptions of the "Face,"[1] all of them as authentic as any portrait of Apollo or of Peter and Paul. In all stages alike we have the same pretension, the pretension to impose fantasy on mankind as fact; and the final Mythology will have to reckon with Browning and Nicephorus Callisti, Renan and Weiss, as so many manipulators of traditionary error to various ends, æsthetic, poetic, and ecclesiastical.

Let it be added that every proved failure, in the process of criticism, to conceive the evidence aright, comes under the same category. Mistaken theories of myth, we say, are but myths with a difference; and such mistakes may well have been made here. Such mistakes, however, are properly to be graded in terms of the degree in which they stand for belatedness of method, for failure to live up to the general light of their age. By such tests, then, let the foregoing reasoning be tried. That it is on the whole loyal to the light reached by prior research is as much as any self-critical investigator will care to claim for his undertaking.

[1] See the *Recherches Historiques sur la personne de Jésus-Christ*, par un ancien Bibliothécaire, Dijon, 1829, pp. 11-29.

INDEX.

Abraham, 81, 132, 187
Achilles, 120, 124, 141, 225, 226, *n.*
Aditi, 242, 244, 271, *n.*
Adityas, the, 243
Adonis, 36, 37, 89, 125, 190, 193, 405, *n.*, 413, 416, 421
Ægisthus, 187
Æsculapius, 186, 189, 193, 242
Agni, 207–211, 238, 250, *n.*, 265, 266, 301, 403, 404, 405
Agrippa, 396
Ahone, 55
Akkadians, the, 65, 179, 256, 259, 345
Alcmene, 197
Alexander, 187
Alexandria, 291–4
Allegory and Myth, 9–11
Allen, Grant, 71–74, 315–316
Alphabet, 137
Amshaspands, the, 243, 419, *n.*
Amun, 143, 148, 188, 412, *n.*
Ananda, 257
Anchises, 201
Andrade, 295
Angels, idea of, 84, *n.*, 99
Animism, 26–28, 31–32, 63
Anios, 193
Annunciation myth, 190–1, 328–9
Anointing, myth of, 260, 363–6
Anthony's Day, 181–2
Antigonus, 396, 402
Antiope, 186
Anthropology and mythology, 3, 7, 11, 40, ff., 52, ff., 72, ff.
Anubis, 212
Aphrodite, 147, 201, 251, *n.*, 318, 323, 411
Apis, 142, *n.*
Apocalypse, 342, 473
Apollo, 36, *n.*, 87, 88, 100, 112–3, 124, 126, 133, 142, 187, 189, 190, 191, 192, 200, 201, 244, 247, 263, 323, *n.*, 346, ff., 412, 415
Apollonius of Tyana, 193, 298, 361
Apostles, the Twelve, 308, 370–8; Jewish, 373, ff., 448
Apostolical Constitutions, 457
Aristaeus, 214, 225
Arjuna, 257
Arnobius, 362
Arnold, M., 15, 77, *n.*, 85, 312, 464, ff.
Art and Mythology, 38–39, 124, *n.*, 127, 199, 344, ff., 358, 401
Artemis, 9, 189, 317, 321
Arthur, 186, 252
Ascension, myth of, 420–2
Ascetic religion, 322, 339, 409, 412–413, 427
Asoka, 136
Ass. See *Myth Motives*
Assimilation in mythology, 36–37, 121, 122, *n.*, 147
Assumption of the Virgin, 421
Astronomy and mythology, 66, 126, 177, 179, 192, 241–5, 262, 344, ff., 367–9, 400, ff., 412, 449
Astyages, 184–5, 191, *n.*, 196
Athênê, 188, 317
Athor, 329
Atlas, 348, 397
Attis, 37, 125, 323, 325, 405, 406, 416, 417
Augê, 186, 193
Augustine, 110, *n.*, 250
Augustus, 333
Australians, aboriginal, 58-60
Authority, 86
Avatars, 244, 249
Azazel, 345, ff.

Babylonian prayers, 453. See *Mythology*
Bacchus. See *Dionysos*
Bacon, 4, 7
Balde, 133
Balder, 118–126, 252
Bali, 154–5
Banier, 5
Barabbas, 399, 414
Barth, 138, *n.*, 139, *n.*, 140, *n.*, 14', 162, 290
Basnage, 5, 452–4
Baudry, 23–24
Bauer, G. L., 12
—— Bruno, xi.–xii.
Baur, ix., xi., 16, 130, *n.*, 310–311, 378, 423, 438
Bayle, 5

Bayley, 157–8
Bergmann, 122
Bethlehem, 329, 336
Bhagavat Gîtâ, 140, 151, 268, 280, ff., 300
—— Purâna, 140, 175, 242, n.
Bhakti, 274, ff., 289, ff.
Bhandarkar, 154
Bible and mythology, 5, 12, 13, 16, 65–66, 79, ff.
Birthday of the world, 412
Birth-myths, 184–197, 209–215, 241–9, 412
Black deities, 142–148, 167
Bochart, 5
Bohlen, von, 215
Brahma, 132.
Brahmanism, 132, 138–9
Brainerd, 56
Bréal, 24
Brinton, 35, 56, n.
Brothers, myths of, 243
Brugsch, 333
Bryant, 137, n.
Bryennios, 373, 447
Buddha, 133, n., 171, 193, 194, 211, 257, 273, 305, 343, ff, 353, ff.
Buddhism in the west, 164, 256, 274
Bugge, 119–121, 124
Bull-gods, 83, 142, n., 212, 266, 407, 412
Bunsen, 90
Burnell, 155
Buttmann, 6

Cæsar, 111, 138, n., 149
Cain, 80, 89
Callisto, myth of, 8
Cannibalism, sacramental, 218–223
Capernaum, 336
Capricorn, 180, 345, ff.
Cancer, 345, ff., 368–9
Carpenter, J. E., 129, n., 428, 466, n.
Catacombs, 167, 237, 419
Cave-worship, 200, 204, 208, 217, n., 330
Celsus, 149
Cerberus, 254, n.
Chaitanya, 276, n.
Cham, 148
Child-god. See *Myth-motives*
Christianity and Hinduism, 164, 274–294
Christians, early, culture of, 382, 421
Christmas-day, 36, 172–3, 178, 199, 331, ff., 422
Christophoros, 165, 194, 215–227
Chrysostom, 279
Clement of Alexandria, 109, 255, n.
Clermont-Ganneau, 38–39
Colenso, 15, 82
Collignon, 39, n.
Colour in mythology, 142–8, 204, 211
Comte, xi., 29, n.
Confucius, 190–1
Constant, B., 3
Cow in mythology, 200, ff., 262, 268
Cox, Sir G., 22–25, 42–43, 44, n., 70, 95, 224, n., 239, 370, n.
Creuzer, 6, 7, 9, 11, 20, 56, n., 135
Criobolium, 468
Cross-buns, 419
Cross, the, 207, 296, 402, 408–412
Crown of thorns, 396–9
Crucifixion myth, 185, 294–7, 394, ff.
Cuchulainn, 122
Cunningham, 131–2, 158
Cybelê, 186, 318, 323, 348, 405
Cyrus, 87, 92, 184–5, 186, 191, 192, 252, 402, 415

Dæmons, 143
Danaë, 186, 193
Daniel, 187
Darmesteter, 64, 343
Darwin, 20, 26
Dates of festivals, 178–180
David and Daoud (Dodo), 93, 326, 329, 346, n.
Davids, Rhys, 171, n., 305
De Brosses, 3, 5
Decharme, 35
Degeneration, 95, ff.
Deluge myth, 117
Dêmêter, 62, n., 84, 107, 142, 144, 224, 318, 320, 321, 399, 417
De Rossi, 166–7
Destinies, the, 71
Devakî, 141, 150, 158, 170–1, 175, 196, 229, 241, 243, 244
Devil, idea of, 57, 72, 74, 93, 143, 144, n., 204, 344, ff.
Dionysos, 36, 83, 84, 146, 186, 188, 193, 198, 203, 208, 219, 223, 224, 225, 226, n., 238, 250, 310, 318, 323, 347, ff., 356–8, 363, 365, 368, 391, 406, 413, n., 416, 417, 421, 425, 469, 473
Dola Yatra, 182
Donaldson, J. W., 229, n.
Drama, religious, 154, 219, 227–235, 323–5, 354–5, 364–6, 385, 422, 425
Dreams, 28, 30, 184–5
Druidism, 138, n., 222
Dupuis, 5, 7, 8, 12, 180, 356, 379

Economic pressures, xii., 101, 147, 148
Egyptian religion, 94, 99, 407, 429

Eichorn, 12, 79
Eight, mythic number, 241–5
Eleusinia, the, 233, 357, 399
Eleven, banquet of, 420
Elijah and Elisha, 84, 85, 93, 259, 394, 427
Elizabeth, 194
Elphinstone, 179
Eméric-David, 3, 7, 8
Endymion, 241
England, mythology in, 13, 20, 135, 331, *n.*
Ennius, 343
Enoch, 84
Epiphany, 172–4
Equinox, myths of, 417
Erichthonius, 223
Eshmun, 242
Essenism, 94
Ethics and mythology, 27, ff., 44, 52, 72, 94
—— Christian and other, 440, ff., 450, ff., 471–2
Etymology and mythology, 19–23, 39, 126
Eucharist, 219, 221, 370, 386–392, 455
Eurynome, 71
Evadné, 193
Eve, 349, *n.*
Evemerus and Evemerism, 4, 5, 6, *n.*, 14, 16, 84, 304, 315, 343–4, 393

Face of Christ, 475
Fall, the, 80
Farrar, Dr., 428
Fasting, myths of, 353, ff.
Fetichism, 5, 30–32
Fire in mythology, 148, 207, ff., 404
Firmicus, 406, 422
Fontenelle, 3, 5, 29, *n.*, 42
Forchhammer, 38
Forgeries, Christian, 176, 456
Forlong, 40
Frazer, J. G., 11, 35–38, 95, 144, 145–8, 192, *n.*, 243, 251, 357, *n.*, 399, 417, *n.*
Freudenberger, 116
Freyr, 122, 124, *n.*, 126
Frigga, 122, *n.*, 125
Fuegians, 59, *n.*

Gardner, vii., ff., xii., 310, 312–314, 466, *n.*, 467
Garucci, 386
Genesis, 65, 81
Ghosts, 29, 30, 31
Giddings, 49–50
Giorgi, 132, 215, *n.*
Gladstone as mythologist, 3, 85
Glanville, 366, *n.*
Gnosticism, 109, 439, 469
Gnostic parables, 460–2
God-eating, 218–223, 468
God idea, 47–49, 52, 98
Goethe, 77, *n.*
Golden Rule, 286, *n.*, 309
Goldziher, 33, *n.*, 35, 65–67, 77, 91, *n.*
Gopis, the, 141, 183, *n.*, 191, 265, 272
Gospels, 307, ff., 322, 331, 336, ff., 360, 371, ff., 375, ff., 423, ff., 471, ff.
—— the Primitive, 307, 336, 385
Gould, F. J., 77, *n.*
Greek influence on India, 164
—— and Hebrew literature, 447
Gregorie, 451, 454–5
Grimm, 119
Grote, 10, 11
Gubernatis, 35, 143
Gwydion, 121

Had (Hoder), 119, 121, *n.*, 125
Hades, Descent into, 249–258
Hagar, 193, 319
Haidas, the, 54, 57
Harbard, 122
Hari, 266, 276
Harrison, Miss, 223–4
Hatch, Rev. E., xii., 219, *n.*, 422
Hegel, 77
Heifer, the red, 349
Heimdal, 122, 126
Hell. See *Hades*
Hephaistos, 189, 225
Herakles, 124, 161, 173, 186, 187, 197, 201, 225, 245, 250, 348, 358–9, 397–9, 400–2, 421
Hêrê, 188, 189, 193, 318, 403, 415
Heri, 253
Hermann, 7
Hermes, 88, *n.*, 144, *n.*, 189, *n.*, 192, *n.*, 198, 201, 217, 225, 250, 334, 403, 412
Herod, 166, 191
Heyne, 6, 7, 9, 21, 24, 43
Hierology, 29, 45
Higgins, 294
Hillel, 446, 447, *n.*
Hindu literature, 135, 176, 227, ff.
—— chronology, 136, 280–1
—— influence on the West, 164
Holtzmann, 122
Holy Ghost, 387
Homer, 6, 71, 80, 82, 99
Horæ, 240
Horos, 36, 148, 170–1, 178, 188, 189, 202, 219, 249, 323, 333, 335
Hostia, 218

Huet, 5
Humboldt, A., 13, *n.*
Hume, 56, *n.*
Huxley, 44, *n.*, 52, 64, 97
Hyde, 132

Iamos, 187
Image-worship, 97
Immanuel, 214
Immaculate Conception, 50
Immortality, idea of, 259, 437, ff.
India, name, 278
Indra, 121, 144–5, 150, 200, 201, *n.*, 210, 266, 411
Ino, 188
Ion, 188, 191, 200, 225
Isaac, 401, *n.*, 402
Ishmael, 193
Isis, 37, 142, *n.*, 144, *n.*, 147, 170–1, 201–4, 318, 319, 321, 323, 328, 406, 410, 415, 425
Islam, 101
Istar, 186, 197
Iunx, the, 404
Ixion, 403

Jacob, 81, 85, 93, 243
Jacolliot, 299
Jairus, 361
Janus, 246, 379–384
Jasius (Jasion), 320
Jerome, 171
Jesus, Strauss on, 14; Emerson on, 311–312; Arnold on, 312; Gardner on, 313; Mill on, 431; Baur on, 423, 438; discourses of, 423, ff., 463; "the real," 17, 130, 303, ff.: the Talmudic, 308, 321, 395, 402, 413; of Zechariah, 341; myths of, 83, 106–116, 172–3, 187, 189, 191, 192, 194, 195, 204–215, 221, 254, 255, 273, 306, 317, ff.; black images of, 142, 167; genealogies of, 149, 326, ff.; face of, 475
Jewish prayers, 450–4
Job, 94
Johannine discourses, 463 ff.
John the Baptist, 14, 257, 432
Jones, Sir W., 133, 244
Jolley, 307
Joseph, 89, 93, 194, 243, 318, 326–8, 415
Joshua, 82–83, 93, 320, 322, 394, 414
Jubinal, 231
Judaism, 65–66, 69–70, 79–95, 100
Judah, 367–9
Judas, 14, 261, 376, 384–6
Juno, 169
Justin Martyr, 286, 387

Kaliya, 153, 194
Kansa, 141, 150, 153, 154, 155, 166, 184, 195, 268
Karabbas, 396
Keightley, 13
Kenrick, 145
Klein, 230
Kingdom of heaven, idea of, 437, ff.
Kleuker, 134, 215, *n.*
Kneph, 143
Korê. See *Persephone*
Krishna, myths of, 131, 133, 139, 141, 150–1, 154, 175, 241, 253, 255, 258, 261–274, 421; Birth-Festival of, 165, 172, 175, 210, 243–4, 249, 301; colour of, 142, 211; cult of, 129, 134, 139, 140, 157–163, 182, 244–9, 253, 276, 297, 300; a demon in the Vedas, 143; a Sun-God, 144
Kronos, 41, 82, 189, 242, 246
Kuenen, 82
Kuhn, 19, 20, 25
Kumarila, 138

Lactantius, 335, 344, 362, 472
Lakshmî, 158, 171
Lamb, sacramental, 220
Lamech, 80
Lang, A., 3, 7, 40–64, 73, 79, ff.
Lassen, 160–2, 291, 294
Latona. See *Leto*
Lauer, 35
Lazarus, 360
Leah, 243
Leto, 142, *n.*, 188, 192, 193, 318
Liturgies, early, 219, *n.*, 233
Logos, the, 97, 387, 409, 411, 469
Loki, 121, 122
Longinus, 124
Lord's prayer, 443, 450, ff.
Lorinser, 277, ff.
Lundy, J. P., 38
Luther, 112

Macdonald, Rev. J., 76
Macrobius, 4, 5
Madonnas, 166, ff., 317, ff.
Magi, 199, 212, 213, 214, 231
Mahâbhârata, 139–140, 280, 293
Mahâbhâshya, 154
Mahâdeva, 266
Maia, 320, 321
Mandanê, 184–5, 192, 194, 319
Manichæism, 164
Mannhardt, 22, 35
Mârtânda, 242
Maries, mythic, 97, 142, *n.*, 194, 210, 260, 319–325
Marsyas, 347, ff.

Mater dolorosa, 125, 322, ff.
Mattu Pongal, 180–1
Maurice, Rev. T., 133, 184, 192, *n.*, 196
Maya, 171, 193, 194, 210, 319
Mazdeism, 97, 242, 354–5, 398, 415, 469
Mbayas, the, 55
Megasthenes, 137, 160
Melito, 412
Melkarth, 400
Mendes, 346, *n.*
Meredith, E., 452
Meri, 320
Merris, 320
Messiah, theories of, 326, 341, 366, 394, 434, ff.
Meyer, E. H., 22, 49, 119, ff.
Mill, J. S., 465
Milman, 231
Mimer, 239, 243
Minos, 84
MIRACLES :—
  Crossing water, 106, 358
  Evoking water, 83, 363
  Feeding, 106, 362–3
  Fish with coin, 106, 108
  Healing, 106, 151, 359–362
  Making wine of water, 105, 108–111, 363, 365–8
  Raising the dead, 250, 252, 255, 259, 360, ff.
Miriam. See *Maries*
Mistletoe, 125
Mithra, cult of, 35, 36, 37, 97, 172, 174, 180, 190, 199, 203, 207, 212–3, 242, 247, 251, 354–5, 379, ff., 386, ff., 398, 403, 408, 412, 417, 425, 468, 469, 473
Mitra, 266
Mitre, 473
Mnevis, 142, *n.*
Mohammed, 304
Moloch, 36
Mommsen, 70, *n.*, 103–4, 219, *n.*
Monotheism, 52, ff., 84, 96, 97, 164
Moon-deities, 142, *n.*, 146, 407, 415
Moor, 253, 293
Moses, 82, 83, 84, 85, 88, 93, 187, 188, 189, 191, 200, 333–4, 402, 449
Mosheim, 15
Mother-Goddesses, 97, 125, 166, 171, 224, 317, ff., 348, 405, ff.
Mountain, myths of, 259, 344, ff., 424, 440, ff., 448, ff.
Muir, Dr. John, 276, 283, *n.*, 286, *n.*, 288
Müllenhoff, 120
Müller, Julius, 71, 73, 75
—— K. O., 4, 8–12, 70–1, 73
Müller, Max, 7, 20–25, 67–69, 73, 85, 137, 152, 289–290, 299
Murdock, 232
Mylitta, 321
Myrrha, 193, 320
Mysteries and mystery-drama, 114, 218–223, 224, 227–235, 237, 252, 323–5, 354–5, 364–6, 385, ff., 422, 425, 469
Mystica vannus Iacchi, 200, *n.*
Myth, essence of, vii.–x., 2, 110, 311; types of, 115–6; theories of, 4, 9–12, 20–32, 43–64, 71, 72–75, 105, 311; normality of, 33, 77, 101; origination of, vii., 10–12, 21, 22–24, 26, 28, 30–32, 64, 181–2, 356; rationality of, 29, 56, 64, 71, 350
Myths of Observation, 25
—— pseudo-scientific, 33–34
—— *märchen*, 96
—— Christian, 105–6, 166, ff., 317, ff.
  See *Mythology* and *Myth-motives*

MYTH-MOTIVES :—
  Ass. See *Ox and Ass*
  Ass and foal, 37, 230, *n.*, 310, 345, 366–9
  Bird, 404
  Boar of winter, 251, *n.*
  Bull, 37, 212, 266, 407, 412
  Cave-birth, 195, 204, 329–331
  Child-God, 14, 193, 197–227, 265, 273, 338
  ——, exposed, 87, 177, *n.*, 184–7
  Cow, 200, 262, 268. See *Ox*
  Descent into Hell, 124, 151, 249, ff., 417
  Dog, 237, 254, *n.*
  Garment of God, 414–416
  Goat, 345, ff.
  Horse, 203, 211
  Keys, 379, ff.
  Lamb. See *Ram*
  Massacre of Innocents, 165, 191, 192, *n.*, 332–3
  Mountain, 344, ff.
  Ox and ass, 199, 203–6, 209
  Ram (Lamb), 37, 180, 220, 407, 412
  Rock, 382, ff., 417
  Serpent, 150, 187, 189, 191, 194, 254, 411
  Stable and manger (= basket), 165, 180, 197, ff., 329–331
  Tree, 37, 95, 147, 193, 210, 211, 405, 406, 408, 410
  Vegetation, 36–37, 251
  Virgin-birth, 14, 50, 113, 118, 133, *n.*, 147, 167, 171, 317, ff.
  See also *Birth*, *Cross*, *Seven*, *Eight*,

Ten, Twelve, Sun, Moon, Seasons, and *Vegetation-Cult*
Mythology, present state of, vi., 2; separatism in, 2, 27, 66; development of, 3, ff., 309; Aryan, 19-25; Babylonian, 65-66, 89, 91, 259, 345, ff., 399; Celtic, 121-3, 125; Comparative, 6, 12, 19-25, 85; Egyptian, 170-1, 178, 201-2, 213, 244, 368-9, 411, 412, 429; Greek (see under deity-names); Hebrew, 12, 16, 30, 65, ff., 79-95, 204-6, 245, 341, 345, ff., 366, ff., 402, 422; Hindu, 135, 139, ff., 238, 241, ff., 403; Mexican, 218, *n.*, 224, *n.*; Persian, 174, 189, 211, 304-6, 343, ff., 412, *n.*, 419; Roman, 103-4, 218-219; Scandinavian, 118-127, 239; Slavonic, 123, *n.*; Tibetan, 295

Nana, 186
Nanda, 141, 165, 194, 195, 266
Nanna, 120, 126
Napoleon, 112-113
Nazareth, ix., 308, 312, 335-342
Nazarites and Nazarenes, x., 308, 336-342, 431
Neander, 108-9
Nemrod, 187
Neptune, 411
Nève, 289, 291, *n.*
Newman, 314, 432
New-year days, 179, 180, 226, *n.*, 246, *n.*, 248
Nicolas, 469, *n.*
Nicolson, 119, 121, *n.*
Nilus, 142, *n.*, 146, 148
Noah, 81, 82
Numbers, sacred, 88-107
Nurse, mythic, 260-1

Oceanus, 359
Odin, 121, 122
Œdipus, 186
Oldfield, 296
Olympus, 347-352
Orpheus, 223, 251
Orphicism, 253, 415
Orthodoxy, 13, 16, 27
Osiris, 36, 37, 125, 135, 142, 143, 144, 145-8, 250, 254, 300, 323, 325, 335, 406, 407, 410, 411, 415, 416

Paine, 76
Palmer, Rev. W., 219, *n.*
Pan, 144, *n.*, 255, 268, 344, ff., 416
Pantænus, 277, ff.
Parables, 460-3
Passion, the, 392-4
Pastophoroi, 217-8
Patanjali, 154-5, 272
Paul, v., 14, 101, 312, 325, 339-342, 370, ff., 378, ff., 388, ff., 428, 429, 430, 435, 456-7
Paulinus, 134
Pausanias, 357, *n.*
Persephone, 251, *n.*, 252, 318, 387, 406, 416
Perseus, 186, 193, 264, *n.*
Peter, 359, 378-384, 420
Petersen, H., 39, *n.*
—— N. M., 123 *n.*
Pfleiderer, 69
Phallicism, 40, 124, *n.*, 127, 400, *n.*, 402, 410
Phialo, 187
Philo, 377, *n.*, 396
Phoroneus, 405
Pick, 451
Pilate, 414
Pillars, myths of, 348, ff., 400, ff., 449
Pindar, 80, 82, 99, 412
Plato, 285, 286, 288, 318
Pleiades, 241, 348
Polier, 134
Porphyry, 149
Poseidon, 146, 181, 189, 244, 358, 381
Positivism, 76, 85
Postel, 132
Preller, discussed, 6, *n.*, 35
Proclus, St., 230, 369
Prometheus, myth of, 8, 10, 397, 404
Prophets, Hebrew, 98
Proserpine. See *Persephone*
Proteus, 382-3
Psamathe, 187
Psyche, 225
Ptah, 148, 411
Pyrrhus, 226, *n.*
Pythagoreanism, 88, *n.*

Race and selection, 90
—— theories of, viii.-ix.
Rachel, 243, 323
Ragnarök, 252
Râma, 141, 143, 162-3, 242, 249, 257, 264, 266, 267
Râmâyana, the, 164
Reimarus, 12
Religion and mythology, 2, 41-64, 65, ff.
Renan, 34, 79, 81, 85, 90, 231, 310, 325, 327, *n.*, 465, 473
Resurrection, the, 405, *n.*, 416, ff.
Rhea, 188, 189, 242
Rhœo, 193
Rhys, 120, 121

Ritter, 135-6
Rodrigues, 440
Robini, 141, 177, 244
Roman religion, 70, *n.*, 103-4, 219, *n.*
Roscher, 35
Rudra, 266
Rydberg, 120, 122, 123, 125, 240

Sack, I., 69, 77
Sacrifice, 57, *n.*, 61, 220-3, 224, *n.*
Salverte, 244, *n.*
Samaritans, 326, 401, 433, 439, 446
Samson, 15, 83, 82, 93, 349, *n.*, 400-2
Samuel, 334
Saneha, 429
Sanskrit drama, 228
Sara, 81, 133
Saracens, 94
Sargon, 188, 189, 333
Saturn, 41, 246
Satyrs, 349, *n.*, 352
Saul, 93
Savages, variation among, 44, *n.*
—— ethics of, 58
Saviour-Gods, 33, 93, 97, 202, 406, 408, 409
Schelling, 9
Schleiermacher, 22, 67
Schwartz, 19
Scourging, myth of, 358
Seasons, myths of, 239-244
Sebak, 146
Selden, 4, 5
Semelê, 186, 188, 224, 421
Semiramis, 186
Semites, 33
Semitic influence on Greece, 22-23, 39
Sem, 401
Semler, 13
Senart, 162, 196, 269, 293, 299, 305
Separatist fallacy, the, 2, 27, 29, 43-44, 52-78
Serapis, 143, *n.*
Sermon on the Mount, 14, 307, 423, 440, ff., 456-7, 458, 460-1
Serpent in mythology, 150, 191, 194, 254, 411
Set, 144, *n.*
Seufert, 370, *n.*
Seven, a mythic number, 197, 235-248
—— martyrs, 235-240
—— sleepers, 236-240
—— priests, 237
—— banquet of, 238, 418-420
—— seasons, 239-240
Seventy, myths of, 376-7
Sex in religion, 107, 322
—— - mythology, 147, 317, 322, ff.
Shammai, 446
Silenus, 347-8, 352
Simon of Cyrene, 401
—— Magus (= Megas), 401, 473
Sirach, ben, 446
Siva, 269
Sleepers, the seven, 236-240
Smith, Robertson, 11, 35, 222, *n.*
Solomon, 93, 306
Soma, the, 265
Sosipolis, 416
Speir, Mrs., 275
Spencer, H., 1, 6, 28-32, 304
—— J., 5
"Spirits," idea of, 53, 56, 63
Stars, myths of, 192, *n.*, 320, 345, ff.
Stephens, G., 120, 125
Stevenson, R. L., on Renan, 473
Strabo, 334
Strauss, xi., 12, ff., 310-311, 334
Sunday, origin of, 245, *n.*
Sun-myth, 4, 24, 37, 119, 122, 124, 126, 143, 144, 145-8, 184-215, 222, 251, 262, 264, 322, *n.*, 345, ff., 357, ff., 400, ff.
Supreme Being, idea of, 52, ff.
Supper. See *Eucharist*
Sutech, 144, *n.*
Swinging festivals, 183
Symbolism, 11, 127, 409

Talmud, ethics of, 440, ff., 451
Tammuz, 329
Tartak, 204, *n.*
Taurobolium, 468
Teaching of the Twelve Apostles, 373, 448, 455
Telang, 280, 292
Têlephos, 186, 225
Tell, 116-7
Tellumon, 147
Temple, Child in, 334-5
Temptations, mythic, ix., 150, 307, 343-356
Ten Commandments, 85, 306, 309, 454
—— Plagues, 87-88
—— a mythic number, 88
Tertullian, 387
Theism, 88
Themis, 71
Thor, 122, 411
Thoth, 329
Tiele, 137, 170-1, 289, 292, 299
Tmolus, 346-7
Toland, 89, *n.*
Tooke, 82, *n.*
Topography and mythology, 39
Tragedy, Greek, 231, 352

Transfiguration, myths of, 258, 259, 392–3
Trinity, 133. *n.*, 329, 447
Trollope, Rev. W., 219, *n.*
Twelfth Night, 357
Twelve Apostles, myth of, v., 308, 370–8, 449
Twilight Goddess, 201
Tylor, E. B., 25–28, 52. 55, 64, *n.*, 117
Typhon, 143, *n.*, 189, 193, 211, 349

Ulrici, 231
Ulysses, 252
Universalism, Jesuist, 433
Uranus, 82
Uz, 345

Varuna, 145, *n.*
Vasudeva, 141, 150, 154, 195, 225, 226, 229
Vedas, 19, 22, 99, 123, 138–9, 288
—— incarnation of, 150
Vegetation-cult, 36–37, 126, 144, 145–8, 192, *n.*, 248, 251
Venus. See *Aphrodite*
Vesta, 219, *n.*
Vico, 5
Vigfusson and Powell, 120, 122
Vignoli, 31, 32–33
Vine, myths of, 368. See *Wine*
Virgo, constellation, 178
Virgin Goddesses, 168–171, 202, 317, ff.
Vishnu, 133, 134, 143, 160–3, 266, 267
—— Purâna, 140
Volney, 5
Voltaire, 111, 409
Völuspa Saga, 119, ff.
Voss, 6
Vossius, 5

Wafer, consecrated, 222
Wakuafi, the, 55
Water in mythology, 146, 225, 226, 358
Weber, 129, *n.*, 132. 152. 155–6, 172. 175, ff., 215, ff., 227, ff., 244, 257. 268, 274, ff., 290
Week, myths of, 245–8
Weiss, x., 307, 365, 473–4
Welcker, 7, 20, 35
Wells, sacred, 241
Wendorff, 39
Whateley, 112–3]
Wheeler, Prof., 149–153
White Island, the, 290–4
Whitney, Prof., 245, *n.*
Widow's Son, raising of, 259, 260, 360–1
Wine, miracles of, 356–8
Wilford, 297
Wilkins, 158
Wilson, H. H., 161, 180–1, 228, ff., 275, 298
Woden, 121, 122
Women taken in adultery, 457, ff.

Yahweh, 36, 80, 81. 88, 91, 93, 97. 99, 100, 146, 147
Yama, 253
Yasoda, 141, 150, 194

Zacchæus, 436
Zarathustra (Zoroaster), 304, 306. 343, ff.
Zechariah, 341–2, 366–7
Zeus, 9, 62, *n.*, 71, 99, 186. 189. 192, 193. 203, 243, *n.*, 343, ff.